French
Pocket Dictionary

French – English
Anglais – Français

Berlitz Publishing

New York · Munich · Singapore

Original edition edited by the
Langenscheidt editorial staff

Compiled by LEXUS

Inset cover photo: © Punchstock/MedioImages

Neither the presence nor the absence of a designation indicating that any entered word constitutes a trademark should be regarded as affecting the legal status thereof.

Printed in Germany
ISBN-13: 978-981-246-869-7
ISBN-10: 981-246-869-2 (vinyl edition)
ISBN-13: 978-981-246-873-4
ISBN-10: 981-246-873-0 (UK paperback edition)

3. 4. 5. 6. 7. 11 10 09 08 07

Contents / Table des matières

Abbreviations / Abréviations

and	&	et
see	→	voir
registered trademark	®	marque déposée
adjective	*adj*	adjectif
adverb	*adv*	adverbe
agriculture	AGR	agriculture
anatomy	ANAT	anatomie
architecture	ARCH	architecture
astronomy	ASTR	astronomie
astrology	ASTROL	astrologie
attributive	*atr*	devant le nom
motoring	AUTO	automobiles
aviation	AVIAT	aviation
biology	BIOL	biologie
botany	BOT	botanique
British English	*Br*	anglais britannique
chemistry	CHIM	chimie
commerce, business	COMM	commerce
computers, IT term	COMPUT	informatique
conjunction	*conj*	conjonction
cooking	CUIS	cuisine
economics	ÉCON	économie
education	EDU	éducation
education	ÉDU	éducation
electricity	ÉL	électricité
electricity	ELEC	électricité
especially	*esp*	surtout
euphemism	*euph*	euphémisme
familiar, colloquial	F	familier
feminine	*f*	féminin
figurative	*fig*	figuré

finance	FIN	finance
formal	*fml*	langage formel
feminine plural	*fpl*	féminin pluriel
geography	GEOG	géographie
geography	GÉOGR	géographie
geology	GÉOL	géologie
geometry	GÉOM	géométrie
grammar	GRAM	grammaire
historical	HIST	historique
IT term	INFORM	informatique
interjection	*int*	interjection
invariable	*inv*	invariable
law	JUR	juridique
law	LAW	juridique
linguistics	LING	linguistique
literary	*litt*	littéraire
masculine	*m*	masculin
nautical	MAR	marine
mathematics	MATH	mathématiques
medicine	MED	médecine
medicine	MÉD	médecine
masculine and feminine	*m/f*	masculin et féminin
military	MIL	militaire
motoring	MOT	automobiles
masculine plural	*mpl*	masculin pluriel
music	MUS	musique
noun	*n*	nom
nautical	NAUT	marine
plural noun	*npl*	nom pluriel
singular noun	*nsg*	nom singulier
oneself	o.s.	se, soi
popular, slang	P	populaire
pejorative	*pej*	péjoratif

pejorative	*péj*	péjoratif
pharmacy	PHARM	pharmacie
photography	PHOT	photographie
physics	PHYS	physique
plural	*pl*	pluriel
politics	POL	politique
preposition	*prep*	préposition
preposition	*prép*	préposition
pronoun	*pron*	pronom
psychology	PSYCH	psychologie
something	*qch*	quelque chose
someone	*qn*	quelqu'un
radio	RAD	radio
railroad	RAIL	chemin de fer
religion	REL	religion
singular	*sg*	singulier
someone	s.o.	quelqu'un
sports	SP	sport
something	*sth*	quelque chose
subjunctive	*subj*	subjonctif
noun	*subst*	substantif
theater	THEA	théâtre
theater	THÉÂT	théâtre
technology	TECH	technique
telecommunications	TÉL	télécommunications
telecommunications	TELEC	télécommunications
typography, typesetting	TYP	typographie
television	TV	télévision
vulgar	V	vulgaire
auxiliary verb	*v/aux*	verbe auxiliaire
intransitive verb	*v/i*	verbe intransitif
transitive verb	*v/t*	verbe transitif
zoology	ZO	zoologie

La Prononciation / Pronunciation

Les consonnes / Consonants

[b]	*bag*	*b*ouche
[d]	*dear*	*dans*
[f]	*fall*	*f*oule
[g]	*give*	*gai*
[h]	*hole*	et *hop*
[j]	*yes*	rad*io*
[k]	*c*ome	*qu*i
[l]	*l*and	*la*
[m]	*mean*	*mon*
[n]	*night*	*nuit*
[p]	*pot*	*pot*
[r]	*r*ight (*la langue vers le haut*)	*r*eine
[s]	*s*un	*s*auf
[t]	*t*ake	*t*able
[v]	*v*ain	*v*ain
[w]	*w*ait	*ou*i
[z]	ro*s*e	ro*s*e
[ŋ]	bri*ng*	feeli*ng*
[ʃ]	*sh*e	*ch*at
[ʧ]	*ch*air	*ch*a-*ch*a-*ch*a
[dʒ]	*j*oin	ad*j*uger
[ʒ]	lei*s*ure	*j*uge
[θ]	*th*ink	langue entres les dents
[ð]	*th*e	langue derrière les dents du haut

Les voyelles anglaises / English vowels

[ɑː]	f*a*r	*â*me
[æ]	m*a*n	s*a*lle
[e]	g*e*t	s*e*c
[ə]	utt*e*r	l*e*
[ɜː]	abs*u*rd	b*eu*rre
[ɪ]	st*i*ck	*i très court*
[iː]	n*ee*d	s*i*
[ɒː]	in-l*aw*s	ph*a*se
[ɔː]	m*o*re	ess*o*r
[ʌ]	m*o*ther	entre *à* et *eux*
[ʊ]	b*oo*k	b*ou*quin (*très court*)
[uː]	h*oo*t	s*ou*s

Les diphtongues anglaises / English diphthongs

[aɪ]	t*i*me	*aïe*
[aʊ]	cl*ou*d	*ciao*
[eɪ]	n*a*me	nez suivi d'un *y* court
[ɔɪ]	p*oi*nt	cow-b*oy*
[oʊ]	s*o*	*eau*

['] indique que la syllabe suivante est accentuée: *ability* [ə'bɪlətɪ]

Some French words starting with h have ' before the h. This ' is not part of the French word. It shows i) that a preceding vowel does not become an apostrophe and ii) that no elision takes place. (This is called an aspirated h).

'hanche **la hanche, les hanches** [no z sound between *les* and *hanches*]

habit **l'habit, les habits** [a z sound between *les* and *habits*]

French – English
Français – Anglais

A

à *lieu* in; *direction* to; ***au bout de la rue*** at/to the end of the street; ***~ 2 heures d'ici*** 2 hours from here; ***~ cinq heures*** at five o'clock; ***~ Noël*** at Christmas; ***~ demain*** until tomorrow; ***c'est ~ moi*** it's mine, it belongs to me; ***aux cheveux blonds*** with blonde hair; ***~ pied*** on foot; ***~ dix euros*** at *ou* for ten euros

abaissement *m* lowering; (*humiliation*) abasement; **abaisser** lower; *fig* (*humilier*) humble; ***s'~*** drop; *fig* demean o.s.

abandonner abandon; *pouvoir* give up; SP withdraw from; ***s'~*** (*se confier*) open up; ***s'~ à*** give way to

abasourdi amazed

abat-jour *m* (lamp)shade

abattre *arbre* fell; AVIAT shoot down; *animal* slaughter; *péj* (*tuer*) kill; *fig* (*épuiser*) exhaust; (*décourager*) dishearten; ***s'~*** collapse

abbaye *f* abbey

abcès *m* abscess

abdomen *m* abdomen

abeille *f* bee

aberrant F absurd

abêtir make stupid

abîmer spoil, ruin; ***s'~*** be ruined; *d'aliments* spoil

aboiement *m* barking

abolir abolish; **abolition** *f* abolition

abominable appalling

abondance *f* abundance

abonné, ~e *m/f* subscriber; **abonnement** *m* subscription; *de transport, de spectacles* season ticket; **abonner**: ***s'~ à*** subscribe to

abord *m*: ***d'~*** first; ***au premier ~*** at first sight; ***~s*** surroundings; **aborder 1** *v/t* (*prendre d'assaut*) board; (*heurter*) collide with; *fig*: *question* tackle; *personne* approach **2** *v/i* land (***à*** at)

aboutir *d'un projet* succeed; ***~ à*** end at; *fig* lead to; **aboutissement** *m* (*résultat*) result

aboyer bark

abréger abridge

abréviation *f* abbreviation

abri *m* shelter; ***être sans ~*** be homeless

abricot *m* apricot; **abricotier** *m* apricot (tree)

abriter (*loger*) take in, shel-

ter; *~ de* (*protéger*) shelter from; *s'~* take shelter
abrupt abrupt; *pente* steep
abruti stupid; **abrutir**: *~ qn* be bad for s.o.'s brain; (*surmener*) exhaust s.o.
absence *f* absence; **absent** absent; *air* absent-minded; **absenter**: *s'~* leave, go away
absolu absolute; **absolument** absolutely
absorber absorb; *nourriture* eat; *boisson* drink; *s'~ dans* be absorbed in
abstenir: *s'~* POL abstain; *s'~ de faire qc* refrain from doing sth; **abstention** *f* POL abstention
abstrait abstract
absurdité *f* absurdity; *~(s)* nonsense
abus *m* abuse; *~ de confiance* breach of trust; **abuser** overstep the mark; *~ de qc* misuse ou abuse sth; *s'~* be mistaken; **abusif, -ive** excessive; *emploi d'un mot* incorrect
académie *f* academy
acajou *m* mahogany
accabler: *être accablé de* be weighed down by; *~ qn de qc* heap sth on s.o.
accalmie *f aussi fig* lull
accaparer ÉCON, *fig* monopolize
accéder: *~ à* reach, get to; INFORM access; *à l'indépendance, au pouvoir* gain; *d'un chemin* lead to
accélérateur *m* AUTO gas pedal, *Br* accelerator; **accélérer** *aussi* AUTO accelerate
accent *m* accent; (*intonation*) stress; *mettre l'~ sur qc fig* put the emphasis on sth; **accentuer** *syllabe* stress, accentuate
acceptable acceptable; **accepter** accept; (*reconnaître*) agree; *~ de faire* agree to do
accès *m aussi* INFORM access; MÉD fit
accessoire 1 *adj* incidental **2** *m* detail; *~s* accessories; THÉÂT props
accident *m* accident; *événement fortuit* mishap; *par ~* by accident, accidentally; **accidentel, ~le** accidental
acclamation *f* acclamation; *~s* cheers, cheering; **acclamer** cheer
acclimater: *s'~* become acclimatized
accolade *f* embrace; *signe* brace, *Br* curly bracket
accommodation *f* adaptation; **accommoder** adapt; CUIS prepare; *s'~ à* adapt to; *s'~ de* make do with
accompagnateur, -trice *m/f* guide; MUS accompanist; **accompagner** accompany
accomplir accomplish; *souhait* realize
accord *m* agreement; MUS chord; *d'~* OK, alright; *être d'~* agree; *tomber d'~* come to an agreement; **accordé**:

(***bien***) ~ in tune
accordéon accordion
accorder *crédit* grant; GRAM make agree; MUS tune; ***s'~*** get on; GRAM agree; ***s'~ qc*** allow o.s. sth
accouchement *m* birth; **accoucher** give birth (***de*** to)
accouder: ***s'~*** lean (one's elbows); **accoudoir** *m* armrest
accoupler connect; ***s'~*** BIOL mate
accourir come running
accoutumance *f* MÉD dependence; **accoutumer**: ***~ qn à qc*** get s.o. used to sth; ***s'~ à qc*** get used to sth
accrocher *manteau* hang up; AUTO collide with; ***s'~ à*** hang on to; *fig* cling to
accroître increase; ***s'~*** grow
accroupir: ***s'~*** crouch, squat
accueil *m* reception, welcome; **accueillir** greet, welcome
accumulation *f* accumulation; **accumuler** accumulate; ***s'~*** accumulate
accusation *f* accusation; JUR prosecution; *plainte* charge; **accusé, ~e** *m/f* **1** JUR: ***l'~*** the accused **2** COMM: ***accusé m de réception*** acknowledgement (of receipt); **accuser** (*incriminer*) accuse (***de*** of); (*faire ressortir*) emphasize
acerbe caustic
acéré sharp
acharnement *m* grim determination; **acharner**: ***s'~ à faire qc*** be bent on doing sth; ***s'~ sur** ou **contre qn*** pick on s.o.
achat *m* purchase; ***faire des ~s*** go shopping
acheter buy
achever finish; ***s'~*** finish
acide 1 *adj* sour; CHIM acidic **2** *m* CHIM acid
acier *m* steel
acné *f* acne
à-coup *m* jerk; ***par ~s*** in fits and starts
acoustique acoustic
acquéreur *m* purchaser; **acquérir** acquire; *droit* win
acquiescer: ***~ à*** agree to
acquis acquired; *résultats* achieved
acquisition *f* acquisition
acquitter *facture* pay; JUR acquit; ***s'~ de*** carry out; *dette* pay
âcre acrid; *goût*, *fig* bitter; **âcreté** *f* bitterness
acrobate *m/f* acrobat; **acrobatie** *f* acrobatics *pl*
acte *m* (*action*) action, deed; (*document officiel*) deed; THÉÂT act; ***~ de mariage*** marriage certificate
acteur, -trice *m/f* actor; actress
actif, -ive 1 *adj* active **2** *m* COMM assets *pl*
action *f* action; COMM share; ***~s*** stock, shares *pl*; **actionnaire** *m/f* shareholder
actionner operate; *alarme etc*

activate
activer (*accélérer*) speed up
activité *f* activity
actualiser update
actualité *f* current events *pl*; **~s** TV news *sg*
actuel, **~le** current, present; (*d'actualité*) topical; **actuellement** currently, at present
adaptation *f* adaptation; **adapter** adapt; ***s'~ à*** adapt to
addition *f* addition; *au restaurant* check, *Br* bill; **additionner** add
adéquat suitable; *montant* adequate
adhérent, **~e** *m/f* member; **adhérer** stick, adhere (***à*** to)
adhésif, **-ive 1** *adj* sticky, adhesive **2** *m* adhesive
adieu *m* goodbye; ***faire ses ~x*** say one's goodbyes (***à qn*** to s.o.)
adjectif *m* GRAM adjective
adjoint, **~e** *m/f & adj* assistant, deputy
admettre (*autoriser*) allow; (*accueillir*) admit, allow in; (*reconnaître*) admit
administrateur, **-trice** *m/f* administrator; **administratif**, **-ive** administrative; **administration** *f* administration; (*direction*) management, running
admirateur, **-trice 1** *adj* admiring **2** *m/f* admirer; **admiration** *f* admiration; **admirer** admire
admissible *candidat* eligible; ***ce n'est pas ~*** that's unacceptable
admission *f* admission
adolescence *f* adolescence; **adolescent**, **~e** *m/f* adolescent, teenager
adopter adopt; **adoption** *f* adoption
adorable adorable; **adorer** REL worship; *fig* (*aimer*) adore
adosser lean; ***s'~ contre*** *ou* ***à*** lean against *ou* on
adoucir soften; ***s'~*** *du temps* become milder
adrénaline *f* adrenalin
adresse *f* address; (*habileté*) skill; ***~ électronique*** email address
adresser *lettre* address (***à*** to); *remarque* direct (***à*** at); ***~ la parole à*** address, speak to; ***s'~ à qn*** apply to s.o.; (*être destiné à*) be aimed at s.o.
adroit skillful, *Br* skilful
adulte 1 *adj* adult; *plante* mature **2** *m/f* adult, grown-up
adultère 1 *adj* adulterous **2** *m* adultery
adverbe *m* GRAM adverb
adversaire *m/f* opponent, adversary
adversité *f* adversity
aération *f* ventilation; **aérer** ventilate; *literie*, *pièce* air
aérien, **~ne** air *atr*; *vue* aerial
aérobic *f* aerobics
aérodynamique aerodynamic

aéronautique aeronautical
aéroport *m* airport
aérosol *m* aerosol
affable affable
affaiblir weaken; **s'~** weaken
affaire *f* (*question*) matter, business; (*entreprise*) business; *marché* deal; (*bonne occasion*) bargain; JUR case; (*scandale*) affair, business; **~s** *biens personnels* things, belongings; ***les ~s étrangères*** foreign affairs; **affairer**: **s'~** busy o.s.
affaisser: **s'~** *du terrain* subside; *d'une personne* collapse
affamé hungry (**de** for)
affectation *f d'une chose* allocation; *d'un employé* assignment; MIL posting; (*pose*) affectation; **affecter** (*destiner*) allocate; *employé* assign; MIL post; (*émouvoir*) affect
affectif, -ive emotional
affection *f* affection; MÉD complaint
affectueux, -euse affectionate
affermir strengthen
affichage *m* billposting; INFORM display; **affiche** *f* poster; **afficher** *affiche* stick up; *attitude*, INFORM display
affilier: **s'~ à** *club* join; ***être affilié à*** be a member of
affiner refine
affinité *f* affinity
affirmatif, -ive affirmative; *personne* assertive; **affirmation** *f* statement; **affirmer** (*prétendre*) maintain; *autorité* assert
affligeant distressing, painful; **affliger** distress
affluence *f*: ***heures*** *fpl* ***d'~*** rush hour *sg*; **affluent** *m* tributary; **affluer** come together
affolement *m* panic; **affoler** (*bouleverser*) madden, drive to distraction; *d'une foule, d'un cheval* panic; **s'~** panic
affranchir free; *lettre* meter, *Br* frank
affreux, -euse horrible; *peur, mal de tête* terrible
affront *m* insult, affront; **affronter** confront, face; SP meet; **s'~** confront ou face each other; SP meet
afin: ***~ de faire*** in order to do, so as to do; ***~ que*** (+ *subj*) so that
africain, ~e African; **Africain, ~e** *m/f* African; **Afrique** *f*: ***l'~*** Africa
agaçant annoying; **agacement** *m* annoyance; **agacer** annoy; (*taquiner*) tease
âge *m* age; ***Moyen-Âge*** Middle Ages *pl*; ***personnes*** *fpl* ***du troisième ~*** senior citizens; ***quel ~ a-t-il?*** how old is he?, what age is he?; **âgé** elderly; ***~ de deux ans*** aged two, two years old
agence *f* agency; *d'une banque* branch; ***~ immobilière***

realtor's, *Br* estate agent's; **~ *matrimoniale*** marriage bureau
agenda *m* diary; **~ *électronique*** (personal) organizer
agenouiller: ***s'~*** kneel (down)
agent *m* agent; **~ *de change*** stockbroker; **~ *immobilier*** realtor, *Br* real estate agent; **~ *de police*** police officer
agglomération *f* built-up area; *concentration de villes* conurbation
aggraver make worse; ***s'~*** worsen
agile agile; **agilité** *f* agility
agios *mpl* ÉCON bank charges
agir act; **~ *sur qn*** affect s.o.; ***il s'agit de*** it's about
agitation *f* hustle and bustle; POL unrest; (*nervosité*) agitation; **agiter** *bouteille* shake; *mouchoir, main* wave; (*préoccuper, énerver*) upset; ***s'~*** *d'un enfant* fidget; (*s'énerver*) get upset
agneau *m* lamb
agonie *f* death throes *pl*
agrafer *vêtements* fasten; *papier* staple; **agrafeuse** *f* stapler
agrandir enlarge; **agrandissement** *m* enlargement; *d'une ville* expansion
agréable pleasant (***à*** to)
agrément *m* approval, consent; ***les ~s*** (*attraits*) the delights
agresser attack; **agresseur** *m* attacker; *pays* aggressor;
agressif, **-ive** aggressive; **agression** *f* attack; PSYCH stress
agriculteur *m* farmer; **agriculture** *f* agriculture, farming
agrumes *mpl* citrus fruit
ahuri astounded; **ahurissant** astounding
aide 1 *f* help, assistance; ***à l'~ de qc*** with the help of sth; ***avec l'~ de qn*** with s.o.'s help **2** *m/f* (*assistant*) assistant; **aider 1** *v/t* help; ***s'~ de qc*** use sth **2** *v/i* help; **~ *à qc*** contribute to sth
aïeul, **~e** *m/f* ancestor; ***aïeux*** ancestors
aigle *m* eagle
aigre sour; *vent* bitter; *critique* sharp; *voix* shrill
aigu, **~ë** sharp; *son* high-pitched; *conflit* bitter; *intelligence* keen; MÉD, GÉOM, GRAM acute
aiguille *f* needle; *d'une montre* hand; *tour* spire
aiguiser sharpen; *fig*: *appétit* whet
ail *m* garlic
aile *f* wing; AUTO fender, *Br* wing
ailier *m* SP wing, winger
ailleurs somewhere else, elsewhere; ***d'~*** besides; ***par ~*** moreover
aimable kind
aimant *m* magnet
aimer like; *parent, enfant, mari etc* love; **~ *mieux*** prefer

aine *f* groin
aîné, ~e 1 *adj* elder; *de trois ou plus* eldest **2** *m/f* elder/eldest; ***il est mon ~ de deux ans*** he is two years older than me
ainsi this way, thus *fml*; ***~ que*** and, as well as
air *m* air; *aspect* look; MUS tune; ***se donner des ~s*** give o.s. airs; **airbag** *m* airbag
aire *f* area; ***~ de jeu*** playground
aisance *f* ease; (*richesse*) wealth
aise *f* ease; ***être à l'~*** be comfortable; ***être mal à l'~*** be uncomfortable; ***prendre ses ~s*** make o.s. at home
aisselle *f* armpit
ajourner postpone (***de*** for); JUR adjourn
ajouter add; ***s'~ à*** be added to
ajuster adjust; *vêtement* alter; (*viser*) aim at; (*joindre*) fit (***à*** to)
alarme *f* alarm; ***donner l'~*** raise the alarm; ***~ antivol*** burglar alarm; **alarmer** alarm; ***s'~ de*** be alarmed by
album *m* album
alcool *m* alcohol; **alcoolique** *adj & m/f* alcoholic; **alcoolisme** alcoholism; **alco(o)test** *m* Breathalyzer®, *Br* Breathalyser®
aléatoire uncertain; INFORM, MATH random
alentour: ***~s*** *mpl* surroundings *pl*; ***aux ~s de*** in the vicinity of; (*autour de*) about
alerte 1 *adj* alert **2** *f* alarm; ***~ à la bombe*** bomb scare; **alerter** alert
algèbre *f* algebra
Algérie *f*: ***l'~*** Algeria; **algérien, ~ne** Algerian; **Algérien, ~ne** *m/f* Algerian
algue *f* BOT seaweed
aligner TECH align (***sur*** with); (*mettre sur une ligne*) line up; ***s'~*** line up; ***s'~ sur qc*** align o.s. with sth
aliment *m* foodstuff; ***~s*** food; **alimentation** *f* food; *en eau, en électricité* supply; ***~ de base*** staple diet; **alimenter** feed; *en eau, en électricité* supply (***en*** with); *conversation* keep going
alinéa *m* paragraph
allaiter breast-feed
allécher tempt
allée *f* (*avenue*) path; ***~s et venues*** comings and goings
allégé *yaourt* low-fat; *confiture* low-sugar; **alléger** lighten; *impôt, tension* reduce
allègre cheerful
Allemagne *f*: ***l'~*** Germany; **allemand, ~e 1** *adj* German **2** *m langue* German; **Allemand, ~e** *m/f* German
aller 1 *v/i* go; ***~ en voiture*** go by car; ***~ chercher*** go for, fetch; ***comment allez-vous?*** how are you?; ***je vais bien*** I'm fine; ***ça va?*** is that OK?; (*comment te portes-tu?*) how are you?; ***ça va***

bien merci fine, thanks; ***~ bien avec*** go well with; ***on y va!*** F let's go!; ***allez!*** go on!; ***allons!*** come on!; ***allons donc!*** come now!; ***s'en ~*** leave; *d'une tâche* disappear; ***cette couleur te va bien*** that color really suits you **2** *v/aux*: ***je vais partir demain*** I'm going to leave tomorrow, I'm leaving tomorrow **3** *m*: ***~ et retour*** round trip, *Br* return trip; *billet* round-trip ticket, *Br* return (ticket); ***~ simple*** one-way ticket, *Br* single; ***match*** *m* **~** away game

allergie *f* allergy; **allergique** allergic (***à*** to)

alliance *f* POL alliance; (*mariage*) marriage; (*anneau*) wedding ring; **allié, ~e 1** *adj* allied; *famille* related by marriage **2** *m/f* ally; *famille* relative by marriage

allô hello

allocation *f* allowance; ***~ chômage*** workers' compensation, *Br* unemployment benefit

allonger lengthen, make longer; *jambes* stretch out; ***s'~*** get longer; (*s'étendre*) lie down

allumage *m* AUTO ignition; **allumer 1** *v/t* light; *chauffage, télévision etc* turn on **2** *v/i* turn the lights on; **allumette** *f* match

allure *f* (*démarche*) walk; (*vitesse*) speed; (*air*) appearance; ***avoir de l'~*** have style

allusion *f* allusion

alors then; (*par conséquence*) so; ***~ que*** *temps* when; *opposition* while

alouette *f* lark

alourdir make heavy

Alpes *fpl*: ***les ~*** the Alps

alphabet *m* alphabet

alpinisme *m* mountaineering; **alpiniste** *m/f* mountaineer

altercation *f* argument

altérer *denrées* spoil; *couleur* fade; *vérité* distort; *texte* alter

alternance *f* alternation; *de cultures* rotation; **alternative** *f* alternative; **alterner** alternate

altitude *f* altitude

alto *m* alto; *à cordes* viola

altruisme *m* altruism

aluminium *m* aluminum, *Br* aluminium

amabilité *f* kindness

amadouer softsoap

amaigri thinner; **amaigrir**: ***~ qn*** cause s.o. to lose weight; ***s'~*** lose weight, get thinner

amalgame *m* mixture, amalgamation

amande *f* almond

amant *m* lover

amarrer MAR moor

amas *m* pile; **amasser** amass

amateur *m* lover; *non professionnel* amateur; ***en ~*** as a hobby

ambassade *f* embassy; **ambassadeur**, **-drice** *m/f* ambassador
ambiance *f* (*atmosphère*) atmosphere
ambigu, **~ë** ambiguous; **ambiguïté** *f* ambiguity
ambitieux, **-euse 1** *adj* ambitious **2** *m/f* ambitious person; **ambition** *f* ambition
ambivalence *f* ambivalence
ambulance *f* ambulance; **ambulancier** *m* paramedic, *Br* ambulance man
ambulant traveling, *Br* travelling
âme *f* soul; ***état*** *m* ***d'~*** state of mind; **~ *charitable*** do-gooder
amélioration *f* improvement; **améliorer** improve; ***s'~*** improve, get better
aménager *appartement* arrange, lay out; *terrain* develop; *vieille maison* convert
amende *f* fine
amender improve; *projet de loi* amend
amener bring; (*causer*) cause; ***s'~*** turn up
amer, **-ère** bitter
américain, **~e 1** *adj* American **2** *m* LING American English; **Américain**, **~e** *m/f* American; **américaniser** Americanize
amérindien, **~ne** Native American; **Amérindien**, **~ne** *m/f* Native American
Amérique *f*: ***l'~*** America; ***l'~ centrale*** Central America; ***l'~ latine*** Latin America; ***l'~ du Nord*** North America; ***l'~ du Sud*** South America
amertume *f* bitterness
ameublement *m* (*meubles*) furniture
ameuter rouse
ami, **~e 1** *m/f* friend; (*amant*) boyfriend; (*maîtresse*) girlfriend; ***devenir ~ avec qn*** make friends with s.o. **2** *adj* friendly; **amiable**: ***à l'~*** amicably; JUR out of court; *arrangement* amicable, friendly; JUR out-of-court
amical, **~e 1** *adj* friendly **2** *f* association
amincir 1 *v/t* make thinner; *d'une robe* make look thinner **2** *v/i* get thinner
amiral *m* admiral
amitié *f* friendship; ***~s*** best wishes
amnésie *f* amnesia
amnistie *f* amnesty
amoindrir diminish, lessen; ***s'~*** diminish
amollir soften
amonceler pile up
amont: ***en ~*** upstream (***de*** from)
amoral amoral
amorcer begin; INFORM boot up
amorphe *sans énergie* listless
amortir *choc* cushion; *bruit* muffle; *douleur* dull; *dettes* pay off; **amortisseur** *m* AUTO shock absorber

amour *m* love; **~s** love life; ***faire l'~*** make love; **amoureux**, **-euse** *regard* loving; *vie* love *atr*; *personne* in love (***de*** with); ***tomber ~*** fall in love; **amour-propre** *m* pride

amphithéâtre *m* amphitheater, *Br* amphitheatre; *d'université* lecture hall

ample *vêtements* loose; *sujet* broad; *ressources* ample; **ampleur** *f d'un désastre etc* scale

amplification *f* TECH amplification; *fig* growth; **amplifier** TECH amplify; *fig*: *problème* magnify; *idée* expand

ampoule *f sur la peau* blister; *de médicament* ampoule; *lampe* bulb

amputer amputate; *fig* cut

amusant funny, amusing

amuse-gueule *m* appetizer

amuser amuse; ***s'~*** have a good time, enjoy o.s.; ***s'~ à faire qc*** have fun doing sth, enjoy doing sth; ***faire qch pour s'~*** do sth for fun

amygdale *f* ANAT tonsil; **amygdalite** *f* tonsillitis

an *m* year; ***le jour*** *ou* ***le premier de l'~*** New Year's Day; ***elle a 15 ~s*** she's 15 (years old)

analogie *f* analogy; **analogique** INFORM analog; **analogue** analogous (***à*** with)

analphabète illiterate; **analphabétisme** *m* illiteracy

analyse *f* analysis; *de sang* test; **analyser** analyze, *Br* analyse; *sang* test; **analytique** analytical

ananas *m* BOT pineapple

anarchie *f* anarchy; **anarchiste** *m* anarchist

anatomie *f* anatomy

ancêtres *mpl* ancestors

anchois *m* anchovy

ancien, **~ne** old; *de l'Antiquité* ancient; **anciennement** formerly

ancre *f* anchor

Andorre *f*: ***l'~*** Andorra

âne *m* donkey; *fig* ass

anéantir annihilate

anecdote *f* anecdote

anémie *f* MÉD anemia, *Br* anaemia

anesthésie *f* MÉD anesthesia, *Br* anaesthesia

ange *m* angel

angine *f* MÉD throat infection; ***~ de poitrine*** angina

anglais, **~e 1** *adj* English **2** *m langue* English; **Anglais**, **~e** *m/f* Englishman; Englishwoman; ***les ~*** the English

angle *m* angle; (*coin*) corner; ***~ mort*** blind spot

Angleterre *f*: ***l'~*** England

anglophone English-speaking

angoisse *f* anguish; **angoisser** distress

anguille *f* eel

anguleux, **-euse** angular

animal 1 *m* animal; ***~ domestique*** pet **2** *adj* animal *atr*

animateur, **-trice** *m/f d'une*

émission host, presenter; *d'une discussion* moderator; *d'activités culturelles, d'une entreprise* leader; *de dessin animé* animator; **animation** *f* (*vivacité*) liveliness; *de mouvements* hustle and bustle; *de dessin animé* animation; **animé** *rue, quartier* busy; *conversation* lively, animated; **animer** *fête* liven up; (*stimuler*) animate; *discussion, émission* host; ***s'~*** come to life; *d'une personne, discussion* become animated

animosité *f* animosity

anneau *m* ring

année *f* year; ***les ~s 90*** the 90s; ***bonne ~!*** happy New Year!

annexe *f d'un bâtiment* annex; *d'un document* appendix; *d'une lettre* enclosure

anniversaire *m* birthday; *d'un événement* anniversary

annonce *f* announcement; *dans journal* ad (vertisement); (*présage*) sign; ***petites ~s*** classified ads; **annoncer** announce; ***s'~ bien/mal*** be off to a good/bad start

annotation *f* annotation

annuaire *m*: ***~ du téléphone*** phone book

annuel, ~le annual, yearly

annulaire *m* ring finger

annulation *f* cancellation; *d'un mariage* annulment; **annuler** cancel; *mariage* annul

anodin harmless; *personne* insignificant; *blessure* slight

anomalie *f* anomaly

anonyme anonymous; ***société f ~*** incorporated *ou Br* limited company

anorak *m* anorak

anorexie *f* anorexia; **anorexique** anorexic

anormal abnormal

anse *f d'un panier etc* handle; GÉOGR cove

antagonisme *m* antagonism

antarctique 1 *adj* Antarctic **2** *m* **l'Antarctique** Antarctica, the Antarctic

antécédents *mpl* history

antenne *f* ZO antenna, feeler; TV, *d'une radio* antenna, *Br* aerial

antérieur (*de devant*) front; (*d'avant*) previous, earlier; ***~ à*** prior to, before

anthropologie *f* anthropology

antibiotique *m* antibiotic

antibrouillard *m* fog lamp

anticipation *f* anticipation; ***payer par ~*** pay in advance; ***d'~*** *roman* science-fiction

anticiper anticipate; ***~ un paiement*** pay in advance

anticonstitutionnel, ~le unconstitutional

antidater backdate

antidérapant *m* AUTO non-skid tire *ou Br* tyre

antidote *m* MÉD antidote

antigel *m* antifreeze

antipathie *f* antipathy
antipelliculaire: ***shampoing*** *m* **~** dandruff shampoo
antiquaire *m* antique dealer; **antique** ancient; *meuble* antique; *péj* antiquated; **antiquités** *fpl* antiques
antisémite 1 *adj* anti-Semitic **2** *m/f* anti-Semite
antiseptique *m & adj* antiseptic
antisocial antisocial
antiterroriste anti-terrorist
antivol *m* anti-theft device
anxiété *f* anxiety; **anxieux, -euse** anxious
août *m* August
apaiser *personne* calm down; *douleur* soothe; *soif, faim* satisfy
apathie *f* apathy
apercevoir see; ***s'~ de qc*** notice sth
apéritif *m* aperitif
à-peu-près *m* approximation
apitoyer: ***~ qn*** move s.o. to pity; ***s'~ sur qn*** feel sorry for s.o.
aplanir flatten, level; *fig*: *différend* smooth over
aplatir flatten; ***s'~*** (*s'écraser*) be flattened; ***s'~ devant*** kowtow to
aplomb *m* self-confidence; (*audace*) nerve; ***d'~*** vertical, plumb; ***je ne suis pas d'~*** *fig* I don't feel a hundred percent
apostrophe *f* (*interpellation*) rude remark; *signe* apostrophe
apparaître appear; ***faire ~*** bring to light
appareil *m* device; AVIAT plane; ***qui est à l'~?*** TÉL who's speaking?; ***~ ménager*** household appliance; ***~ photo*** camera
apparemment apparently
apparence *f* appearance; ***en ~*** on the face of things; ***sauver les ~s*** save face; **apparent** visible; (*illusoire*) apparent
apparenté related (**à** to)
apparition *f* appearance
appartement *m* apartment, *Br* flat
appartenir belong (**à** to); ***il ne m'appartient pas d'en décider*** it's not up to me to decide
appauvrir impoverish; ***s'~*** become impoverished; **appauvrissement** *m* impoverishment
appel *m* call; MIL (*recrutement*) draft, *Br* call-up; JUR appeal; ÉDU roll-call; ***faire ~ à qc*** (*nécessiter*) require; ***faire ~ à qn*** appeal to s.o.; **appeler** call; (*nécessiter*) call for; ***en ~ à qn*** approach s.o.; ***comment t'appelles-tu?*** what's your name?, what are you called?
appendice *m* appendix; **appendicite** *f* MÉD appendicitis
appétissant appetizing; **appétit** *m* appetite; ***bon ~!*** en-

joy (your meal)!
applaudir applaud, clap; **applaudissements** *mpl* applause, clapping
applicateur *m* applicator; **application** *f* application; **appliquer** apply; **s'~** *d'une personne* work hard; **~ *Y sur X*** smear X with Y
apport *m* contribution; **apporter** bring
appréciation *f* estimate; (*jugement*) opinion; COMM appreciation; **apprécier** estimate; *personne*, *musique*, *la bonne cuisine* appreciate
appréhender: **~ *qc*** be apprehensive about sth; **~ *qn*** JUR arrest s.o.; **appréhension** *f* apprehension
apprendre learn; *nouvelle aussi* hear (***par qn*** from s.o.); **~ *qc à qn*** (*enseigner*) teach s.o. sth; (*raconter*) tell s.o. sth
apprenti, **~e** *m/f* apprentice; *fig* beginner; **apprentissage** *m* learning; *d'un métier* apprenticeship
apprivoiser tame
approbateur, **-trice** approving; **approbation** *f* approval
approcher 1 *v/t* bring closer (***de*** to) **2** *v/i* approach; **s'~ *de*** approach
approfondir deepen; (*étudier*) go into in detail
approprié appropriate, suitable (***à*** for); **approprier**: **s'~ *qc*** appropriate sth
approuver *loi* approve; *personne*, *manières* approve of
approvisionnement *m* supply (***en*** of)
approximatif, **-ive** approximate; **approximation** *f* approximation
appui *m* support; *d'une fenêtre* sill; ***prendre ~ sur*** lean on; **appuyer 1** *v/t* lean; (*tenir debout*) support; *fig candidat*, *idée* support, back **2** *v/i*: **~ *sur*** *bouton* press, push; *fig* stress; **s'~ *sur*** lean on; *fig* rely on
après 1 *prép* after; ***d'~ les journaux*** going by what the papers say **2** *adv* afterward **3** *conj*: **~ *que*** after
après-demain the day after tomorrow
après-midi *m ou f* afternoon
apr. J.-C. (= ***après Jésus-Christ***) AD (= anno Domini)
aptitude *f* aptitude
aquarelle *f* watercolor, *Br* watercolour
aquarium *m* aquarium
arabe 1 *adj* Arab **2** *m langue* Arabic; **Arabe** *m/f* Arab; **Arabie** *f*: ***l'~ Saoudite*** Saudi (Arabia)
araignée *f* spider
arbitrage *m* arbitration
arbitre *m* referee; ***libre ~*** *m* free will; **arbitrer** arbitrate
arbre *m* tree; TECH shaft
arbuste *m* shrub
arc *m* ARCH arch; GÉOM arc

arc-en-ciel *m* rainbow
arche *f* arch; *Bible* Ark
archéologie *f* archeology, *Br* archaeology; **archéologue** *m/f* archeologist, *Br* archaeologist
archet *m* archer; MUS bow
archevêque *m* archbishop
architecte *m/f* architect; **architecture** *f* architecture
arctique 1 *adj* Arctic **2** *m* **l'Arctique** the Arctic
ardent *soleil* blazing; *désir* burning; *défenseur* fervent; **ardeur** *f fig* ardor, *Br* ardour
ardoise *f* slate
ardu arduous
arène *f* arena; **~s** arena
arête *f d'un poisson* bone; *d'une montagne* ridge
argent *m* silver; (*monnaie*) money; **~ *liquide* ou *comptant*** cash
argot *m* slang
argument *m* argument; **argumenter** argue
aride arid, dry
aristocrate *m/f* aristocrat; **aristocratie** *f* aristocracy
armateur *m* shipowner
arme *f* weapon (*aussi fig*); **~ *à feu*** firearm; **armée** *f* army; **~ *de l'air*** airforce; **armement** *m* arming; **~s** armaments; **armer** arm (***de*** with); *fig* equip (***de*** with)
armistice *m* armistice
armoire *f* cupboard; *pour les vêtements* closet, *Br* wardrobe
arnaque *f* F rip-off F; **arnaquer** F rip off F
aromate *m* herb; (*épice*) spice; **arome, arôme** *m* flavor, *Br* flavour; (*odeur*) aroma
arracher pull out; *pommes de terre* pull up; **~ *qc à qn*** snatch sth from s.o.; ***s'~ à ou de qc*** free o.s. from sth; ***s'~ qc*** fight over sth
arrangement *m* arrangement; **arranger** arrange; *objet* fix; *différend* settle; ***cela m'arrange*** that suits me; ***s'~ avec qn pour faire qch*** come to an arrangement with s.o. about sth; ***s'~ pour faire qch*** manage to do sth
arrestation *f* arrest; ***en état d'~*** under arrest
arrêt *m* (*interruption*) stopping; *d'autobus* stop; JUR judgment; ***sans ~*** constantly; **arrêter 1** *v/i* stop **2** *v/t* stop; *moteur* turn off; *voleur* arrest; *jour, date* set; **~ *de faire qch*** stop doing sth; ***s'~*** stop
arrière 1 *adv* back; ***en ~*** backward; *regarder* back; (*à une certaine distance*) behind; ***en ~ de*** behind **2** *adj inv* rear **3** *m* AUTO, SP back; ***à l'~*** in back, at the back
arrière-goût *m* aftertaste; **arrière-grand-mère** *f* great-grandmother; **arrière-grand-père** *m* great-grandfather; **arrière-pensée** *f* ul-

terior motive; **arrière-petit-fils** *m* great-grandson

arrivée *f* arrival; SP finish line; **arriver** arrive; *d'un événement* happen; **~ à faire qch** manage to do sth; **~ à qn** happen to s.o.; ***j'arrive!*** (I'm) coming!

arrogance *f* arrogance; **arrogant** arrogant

arrondir *vers le haut* round up; *vers le bas* round down; **arrondissement** *m d'une ville* district

arroser water; **~ qch** *fig* have a drink to celebrate sth; **arrosoir** *m* watering can

art *m* art; ***avoir l'~ de faire qch*** have a knack for doing sth

artère *f* ANAT artery; (*route*) main road

arthrite *f* arthritis

artichaut *m* artichoke

article *m* article, item; JUR article, clause; *de presse*, GRAM article; ***~s de luxe*** luxury goods

articulation *f* ANAT joint; *d'un son* articulation; **articuler** *son* articulate

artificiel, **~le** artificial

artisan *m* craftsman; **artisanal** hand-made; *fromage, pain etc* traditional

artiste 1 *m/f* artist; *comédien, chanteur* performer **2** *adj* artistic

as *m* ace

ascenseur *m* elevator, *Br* lift

ascension *f* ascent; *fig* (*progrès*) rise; ***l'Ascension*** REL Ascension

asiatique Asian; **Asiatique** *m/f* Asian; **Asie** *f*: **l'~** Asia

asile *m* shelter; POL asylum; ***~ de vieillards*** old people's home; ***demandeur*** *m* ***d'~*** asylum seeker

aspect *m* (*vue*) look; (*point de vue*) angle, point of view; *d'un problème* aspect; (*air*) appearance; ***à l'~ de*** at the sight of

asperge *f* BOT stalk of asparagus; ***~s*** asparagus

asperger sprinkle; ***~ qn de qch*** spray s.o. with sth

asphyxier asphyxiate

aspirateur *m* vacuum (cleaner); **aspirer** *de l'air* breathe in, inhale; *liquide* suck up; ***~ à*** (***faire***) ***qch*** aspire to (doing) sth

aspirine *f* aspirin

assagir: ***s'~*** settle down

assaillir *vedette* mob; ***être assailli de*** be assailed by; *de coups de téléphone* be bombarded by

assainir (*nettoyer*) clean up; *eau* purify

assaisonnement *m* seasoning

assassin *m* murderer; *d'un président* assassin; **assassinat** *m* assassination; **assassiner** murder; *un président* assassinate

assemblée *f* gathering; (*réu-

nion) meeting; ~ ***générale*** annual general meeting; **assembler** assemble; ***s'~*** assemble, gather

asseoir: ***s'~*** sit down

assez enough; (*plutôt*) quite; ***~ d'argent*** enough money; ***~ grand*** big enough

assidu *élève* hard-working

assiette *f* plate; ***ne pas être dans son ~*** *fig* be under the weather

assigner assign

assimiler (*comparer*) compare; *connaissances*, *étrangers* assimilate

assis: ***être ~*** be sitting; **assise** *f fig* basis

assistance *f* (*public*) audience; (*aide*) assistance; **assistant**, **~e** *m/f* assistant; ***~e sociale*** social worker; **assister 1** *v/i*: ***~ à qc*** attend sth, be (present) at sth **2** *v/t*: ***~ qn*** assist s.o

association *f* association; **associé**, **~e** *m/f* partner; **associer** associate (***à*** with); ***s'~*** join forces; COMM go into partnership; ***s'~ à*** *douleur* share in

assoiffé thirsty

assombrir: ***s'~*** darken

assommant F deadly boring; **assommer** stun; F bore to death

Assomption *f* REL Assumption

assorti matching; ***~ de*** accompanied by; **assortiment** *m* assortment

assoupir send to sleep; *fig*: *douleur, sens* dull; ***s'~*** doze off; *fig* die down

assourdir deafen; *bruit* muffle

assumer take on, assume

assurance *f* assurance; (*contrat*) insurance

assuré, **~e 1** (*sûr*) confident **2** *m/f* insured party; **assurément** certainly; **assurer** *succès* ensure; *par une assurance* insure; ***s'~*** take out insurance; ***s'~ de qc*** (*vérifier*) make sure of sth, check sth

asthme *m* asthma

astiquer *meuble* polish; *casserole* scour

astre *m* star

astrologie astrology

astronaute *m/f* astronaut

astronomie *f* astronomie; **astronomique** astronomical (*aussi fig*)

astuce *f* (*ingéniosité*) astuteness; (*truc*) trick; **astucieux, -euse** astute

atelier *m* workshop; *d'un artiste* studio

athée *m/f* atheist; **athéisme** *m* atheism

athlète *m/f* athlete; **athlétisme** *m* athletics *sg*

Atlantique *m*: ***l'~*** the Atlantic

atlas *m* atlas

atmosphère *f* atmosphere

atome *m* atom

atout *m fig* asset

atroce dreadful, atrocious;

atrocité *f* atrocity
attachant captivating
attaché-case *m* executive briefcase
attacher 1 *v/t* attach, fasten; *animal* tie up; *prisonnier* secure; *chaussures* do up **2** *v/i* CUIS (*coller*) stick; **s'~ à** become attached to
attaquant, ~e *m/f* SP striker; **attaque** *f* attack; **~ à la bombe** bomb attack; **attaquer** attack; *travail, sujet* tackle; **s'~ à** attack; *problème* tackle
attarder: s'~ linger
atteindre reach; *d'un projectile* strike, hit; *d'une maladie* affect
atteinte *f fig* attack; **porter ~ à qc** undermine sth; **hors d'~** out of reach
attendant: en ~ in the meantime; **en ~ qu'il arrive** (*subj*) while waiting for him to arrive; **attendre** wait; **~ qn** wait for s.o.; **s'~ à qc** expect sth; **~ un enfant** be expecting a baby
attendrir *fig*: *personne* move; *cœur* soften; **s'~** be moved (**sur** by); **attendrissement** *m* tenderness
attentat *m* attack; **~ à la bombe** bombing, bomb attack; **~ à la pudeur** indecent assault
attente *f* wait; (*espoir*) expectation
attentif, -ive attentive (**à** to); **attention** *f* attention; (**fais**) **~!** look out!, (be) careful!; **faire ~ à qc** pay attention to sth
atténuer reduce; *propos, termes* tone down
atterrir AVIAT land; **~ en catastrophe** crash-land
attestation *f* certificate; **attester** certify; (*prouver*) confirm
attirance *f* attraction; **attirer** attract; **s'~ des critiques** come in for criticism
attitude *f* attitude; *d'un corps* pose
attraction *f* attraction
attrait *m* attraction
attraper catch; (*duper*) take in
attrayant attractive
attribuer attribute; *prix* award; *part, rôle* allot; *valeur* attach; **s'~** take; **attribution** *f* allocation; *d'un prix* award; **~s** (*compétence*) competence
attrister sadden
attroupement *m* crowd; **attrouper: s'~** gather
aube *f* dawn; **à l'~** at dawn
auberge *f* inn; **~ de jeunesse** youth hostel
aubergine *f* BOT eggplant, *Br* aubergine
aucun, ~e 1 *adj avec négatif* no, not …any; *avec positif, interrogatif* any **2** *pron avec négatif* none; **~ des deux** neither of the two; *avec positif, interrogatif* anyone, anybody

audace *f* daring, audacity; *péj* audacity; **audacieux, -euse** (*courageux*) daring, audacious; (*insolent*) insolent
au-delà beyond; **~ de** above;
au-dessous: **~** (**de**) below;
au-dessus: **~** (**de**) above;
au-devant: ***aller ~ de*** meet; *désirs* anticipate
audible audible
audience *f d'un tribunal* hearing
audiovisuel, **~le** audiovisual
auditeur, **-trice** *m/f* listener; FIN auditor; **audition** *f* audition; (*ouïe*) hearing; *de témoins* examination
augmentation *f* increase; *de salaire* raise, *Br* rise; **augmenter 1** *v/t* increase; *salarié* give a raise *ou Br* rise to **2** *v/i* increase, rise
aujourd'hui today
auparavant beforehand; ***deux mois ~*** two months earlier
auprès: **~ *de*** beside, near
auquel → ***lequel***
auriculaire *m* little finger
aurore *f* dawn
ausculter MÉD sound
aussi 1 *adv* too, also; ***il est ~ grand que moi*** he's as tall as me **2** *conj* therefore
aussitôt immediately; **~ *que*** as soon as
austère austere
Australie *f*: ***l'~*** Australia; **australien**, **~ne** Australian; **Australien**, **~ne** *m/f* Australian
autant (*tant*) as much (*que* as); *avec pluriel* as many (*que* as); *comparatif*: **~ *de ... que ...*** as much ... as ...; *avec pluriel* as many ... as ...; (***pour***) **~ *que je sache*** (*subj*) as far as I know; ***en faire ~*** do the same
auteur *m/f* author; *d'un crime* perpetrator
authenticité *f* authenticity; **authentique** authentic
autiste autistic
auto *f* car, automobile
autobiographie *f* autobiography
autocollant 1 *adj* adhesive **2** *m* sticker
autodéfense *f* self-defense, *Br* self-defence
autodidacte self-taught
auto-école *f* driving school
autographe *m* autograph
automatique *adj & m* automatic; **automatiquement** automatically; **automatiser** automate
automne *m* fall, *Br* autumn
automobile *f* car, automobile; **automobiliste** *m/f* driver
autonomie *f* independence; POL autonomy
autoradio *m* car radio
autorisation *f* authorization, permission; **autoriser** authorize, allow; **autoritaire** authoritarian; **autorité** *f* authority

autoroute *f* highway, *Br* motorway
auto-stop *m*: ***faire de l'~*** hitchhike
autour: **~ (*de*)** around
autre 1 *adj* other; ***un/une ~ …*** another …; ***nous ~s Américains*** we Americans; ***rien d'~*** nothing else; ***~ part*** somewhere else; ***d'~ part*** on the other hand **2** *pron*: ***un/une ~*** another (one); ***l'~*** the other (one); ***les ~s*** the others; (*autrui*) other people; ***l'un l'~, les uns les ~*** each other, one another
autrefois in the past
autrement (*différemment*) differently; (*sinon*) otherwise
Autriche *f*: ***l'~*** Austria; **autrichien, ~ne** Austrian; **Autrichien, ~ne** *m/f* Austrian
autrui other people *pl*, others *pl*
auxquelles, auxquels → ***lequel***
av. (= ***avenue***) Ave (= avenue)
aval 1 *adv*: ***en ~*** downstream (***de*** from) **2** *m* FIN guarantee
avalanche *f* avalanche
avaler swallow
avance *f* advance; *d'une course* lead; ***d'~*** in advance; ***en ~*** ahead of time; **avancement** *m* progress; (*promotion*) promotion; **avancer 1** *v/t chaise, date* bring forward; *main* put out; *argent* advance; *thèse* put forward **2** *v/i* make progress; MIL advance; *d'une montre* be fast; ***s'~ vers*** come up to
avant 1 *prép* before; ***~ tout*** above all; ***~ de faire qch*** before doing sth **2** *adv temps* before; *espace* in front of; ***en ~*** forward **3** *conj*: ***~ que*** (+ *subj*) before **4** *adj*: ***roue f ~*** front wheel **5** *m* front; *d'un navire* bow; SP forward
avantage *m* advantage; ***~s sociaux*** fringe benefits; **avantager** suit; (*favoriser*) favor, *Br* favour
avant-dernier, -ère last but one
avant-hier the day before yesterday
avant-première *f* preview
avant-propos *m* foreword
avant-veille *f*: ***l'~*** two days before
avare 1 *adj* miserly **2** *m* miser; **avarice** *f* miserliness
avarié *nourriture* bad
avec with
avenir *m* future; ***à l'~*** in future; ***d'~*** promising
Avent *m* Advent
aventure *f* adventure; (*liaison*) affair; **aventurer**: ***s'~*** venture (***dans*** into)
avenue *f* avenue
avérer: ***s'~*** (+ *adj*) prove
averse *f* shower
aversion *f* aversion (***pour** ou **contre*** to); ***prendre qn en ~*** take a dislike to s.o.

avertir inform (***de*** of); (*mettre en garde*) warn (***de*** of); **avertissement** *m* warning; **avertisseur** *m* AUTO horn

aveu *m* confession

aveuglant blinding; **aveugle 1** *adj* blind **2** *m/f* blind man; blind woman; **aveugler** blind

aviateur, **-trice** *m/f* pilot; **aviation** *f* aviation, flying

avide greedy, avid (***de*** for); **avidité** *f* greed

avilissant degrading

avion *m* (air)plane, *Br* (aero-) plane; ***aller en ~*** fly, go by plane; ***par ~*** (by) airmail

aviron *m* oar; SP rowing

avis *m* opinion; (*information*) notice; ***à mon ~*** in my opinion; ***changer d'~*** change one's mind; ***sauf ~ contraire*** unless otherwise stated

aviser: ***~ qn de qc*** advise *ou* inform s.o. of sth; ***s'~ de qc*** notice sth; ***s'~ de faire qch*** take it into one's head to do sth

av. J.-C. (= ***avant Jésus-Christ***) BC (= before Christ)

avocat, **~e 1** *m/f* lawyer; (*défenseur*) advocate **2** *m* BOT avocado

avoir 1 *v/t* (*posséder*) have, have got; (*obtenir*) get; ***j'ai froid/chaud*** I am cold/hot; ***~ 20 ans*** be 20; ***il y a*** there is; *avec pluriel* there are; ***qu'est-ce qu'il y a?*** what's the matter?; ***il y a un an*** a year ago **2** *v/aux* have; ***j'ai déjà parlé*** I have *ou* I've already spoken; ***je lui ai parlé hier*** I spoke to him yesterday **3** *m* COMM credit; (*possessions*) possessions *pl*

avoisiner: ***~ qc*** border on sth

avortement *m* miscarriage; *provoqué* abortion; **avorter 1** *v/t femme* terminate the pregnancy of; ***se faire ~*** have an abortion **2** *v/i* miscarry; *fig* fail

avouer: ~ (***avoir fait qc***) confess (to having done sth)

avril *m* April

axe *m* axle; GÉOM axis; *fig* basis

B

babiller babble

bâbord *m* MAR: ***à ~*** to port

bac[1] *m bateau* ferry; *récipient* container

bac[2] *m* F, **baccalauréat** *m exam that is a prerequisite for university entrance*

bâche *f* tarpaulin

bâcler F botch F

badaud *m* onlooker

badiner joke

baffe *f* F slap

bafouiller 1 *v/t* stammer **2** *v/i* F talk nonsense

bagages *mpl* baggage, luggage; *fig* (*connaissances*) knowledge; ***faire ses ~*** pack
bagarre *f* fight; **bagarrer** F: ***se ~*** fight
bagnole *f* F car
bague *f* ring; ***~ de fiançailles*** engagement ring
baguette *f* stick; MUS baton; *pain* French stick; ***~s*** *pour manger* chopsticks
baie[1] *f* BOT berry
baie[2] *f* (*golfe*) bay; ***Baie d'Hudson*** Hudson Bay
baigner *enfant* bathe, *Br* bath; ***se ~*** go for a swim; **baignoire** *f* (bath) tub
bail *m* lease
bâiller yawn; *d'un trou* gape; *d'une porte* be ajar
bain *m* bath; ***salle f de ~s*** bathroom; ***être dans le ~*** *fig* (*au courant*) be up to speed; ***~ de bouche*** mouthwash; **bain-marie** *m* CUIS double boiler
baiser 1 *m* kiss **2** *v/t* kiss; V screw V
baisse *f* fall; ***être en ~*** be falling; **baisser 1** *v/t* lower; *radio*, *chauffage* turn down **2** *v/i de forces* fail; *de lumière* fade; *d'une température*, *d'un prix* drop, fall; *de vue* deteriorate; ***se ~*** bend down
bal *m* dance; *formel* ball
balade *f* walk, stroll; **balader** walk; ***se ~*** go for a walk *ou* stroll
baladeur *m* Walkman®
balai *m* broom; ***donner un coup de ~ à qch*** give sth a sweep
balance *f* scales *pl*; COMM balance; ASTROL ***Balance*** Libra; **balancer** *jambes* swing; F (*lancer*) chuck F; F (*jeter*) chuck out F; ***se ~*** swing; **balançoire** *f* swing
balayer sweep; *fig*: *gouvernement* sweep from power; *soucis* sweep away
balbutier stammer
balcon *m* balcony
baleine *f* whale
ballade *f* ballad
balle *f* ball; *d'un fusil* bullet; *de marchandises* bale
ballet *m* ballet
ballon *m* ball; *pour enfants*, AVIAT balloon
ballotter 1 *v/t* buffet **2** *v/i* bounce up and down
balnéaire: ***station f ~*** seaside resort
balourd clumsy
balte Baltic; **Baltique**: ***la (mer) ~*** the Baltic (Sea)
balustrade *f* balustrade
bambou *m* bamboo
banal (*mpl* -als) banal; **banalité** *f* banality
banane *f* banana; **bananier** *m* banana tree
banc *m* bench, seat; ***~ de sable*** sandbank
bancaire bank *atr*
bancal (*mpl* -als) *table* wobbly
bandage *m* MÉD bandage

bande *f de terrain, de tissu* strip; MÉD bandage; (*rayure*) stripe; (*groupe*) group; *péj* gang, band; **bander** MÉD bandage; **~ *les yeux à qn*** blindfold s.o.
bandit *m* bandit; (*escroc*) crook
banlieue *f* suburbs *pl*; ***de ~*** suburban
bannière *f* banner
bannir banish
banque *f* bank; ***~ du sang*** blood bank
banquet *m* banquet
banquette *f* seat
banquier *m* banker
baptême *m* baptism; **baptiser** baptize
bar *m* bar; *meuble* cocktail cabinet
baraque *f* shack
barbant F boring
barbare 1 *adj* barbaric **2** *m/f* barbarian
barbe *f* beard; ***~ à papa*** cotton candy, *Br* candy floss
barbecue *m* barbecue
barber F bore rigid F
barbu bearded
barder F: ***ça va ~*** there's going to be trouble
baromètre *m* barometer
barque *f* MAR boat
barrage *m* dam; (*barrière*) barrier
barre *f* bar; MAR helm; (*trait*) line; ***~ des témoins*** JUR witness stand
barreau *m* bar; *d'échelle* rung
barrer (*obstruer*) block, bar; *mot* cross out; ***se ~*** F leave
barrette *f* barrette, *Br* hairslide
barrière *f* barrier; (*clôture*) fence; ***~s douanières*** customs barriers
bar-tabac *m* bar-cum-tobacco store
bas, ~se 1 *adj* low; GÉOGR lower; *instrument* bass; *voix* deep **2** *adv* low; *parler* in a low voice, quietly; ***en ~*** downstairs; ***là-~*** there **3** *m* bottom; (*vêtement*) stocking; ***au ~ de*** at the bottom of
basané weatherbeaten; *naturellement* swarthy
bas-côté *m d'une route* shoulder
basculer topple over
base *f* base; *d'un édifice* foundation; *fig*: *d'une science* basis; ***de ~*** basic; ***à ~ de lait*** milk-based
base *f* **de données** database
base-ball *m* baseball
baser base (***sur*** on); ***se ~ sur*** draw on; *d'une idée* be based on
basilic *m* BOT basil
basket(-ball) *m* basketball; **baskets** *fpl* sneakers, *Br* trainers
basque 1 *adj* Basque **2** *m langue* Basque; **Basque** *m/f* Basque
basse-cour *f* AGR farmyard; *animaux* poultry
bassine *f* bowl

bataille *f* battle; ***livrer ~*** give battle; **batailler** *fig* battle
bâtard *m* bastard; *chien* mongrel
bateau *m* boat; ***faire du ~*** go sailing; ***mener qn en ~*** *fig* put s.o. on, *Br* have s.o. on
bâti 1 *adj* built on; ***bien ~*** well-built **2** *m* frame
bâtiment *m* building; *secteur* construction industry; MAR ship
bâtir build
bâton *m* stick; ***parler à ~s rompus*** make small talk; ***~ de rouge*** lipstick; ***~ de ski*** ski pole *ou* stick
battant 1 *adj pluie* driving **2** *m d'une porte* leaf; *personne* fighter
batte *f de base-ball* bat
battement *m de cœur* beat; *de temps* interval
batterie *f* ÉL battery; MUS drums *pl*; *dans un orchestre* percussion; **batteur** *m* CUIS whisk; *électrique* mixer; MUS drummer; *en base-ball* batter; **battre 1** *v/t* beat; *cartes* shuffle **2** *v/i* beat; *d'un volet* bang; ***se ~*** fight
bavard, **~e 1** *adj* talkative **2** *m/f* chatterbox; **bavarder** chatter; (*divulguer un secret*) talk
baver drool, slobber; **bavure** *f fig* blunder, blooper F; ***sans ~*** impeccable
Bd (= ***boulevard***) Blvd (= Boulevard)
B.D. *f* (= ***bande dessinée***) comic strip
béant gaping
béat *péj*: *sourire* silly
beau, **bel**, **belle** (*mpl* beaux) beautiful, lovely; *homme* handsome; ***il fait beau*** (***temps***) it's lovely weather; ***il a beau dire …*** it's no good him saying …
beaucoup a lot; ***~ de*** lots of, a lot of; ***~ de gens*** lots *ou* a lot of people, many people; ***je n'ai pas ~ d'argent*** I don't have a lot of *ou* much money; ***~ trop cher*** much too expensive
beau-fils *m* son-in-law; *d'un remariage* stepson; **beau-frère** *m* brother-in-law; **beau-père** *m* father-in-law; *d'un remariage* stepfather
beauté *f* beauty
beaux-arts *mpl*: ***les ~*** fine art
beaux-parents *mpl* parents-in-law
bébé *m* baby
bec *m d'un oiseau* beak; *d'un récipient* spout; MUS mouthpiece; F mouth
bedaine *f* (beer) belly
bégayer stutter, stammer
béguin *m fig* F: ***avoir le ~ pour*** have a crush on
beige beige
beignet *m* CUIS fritter
belge Belgian; **Belge** *m/f* Belgian; **Belgique**: ***la ~*** Belgium
bélier *m* ZO ram; ASTROL ***Bé-***

lier Aries
belle → ***beau***
belle-famille *f* in-laws *pl*
belle-fille *f* daughter-in-law; *d'un remariage* stepdaughter; **belle-mère** *f* mother-in-law; *d'un remariage* stepmother; **belle-sœur** *f* sister-in-law
belliqueux, **-euse** warlike
bémol *m* MUS flat
bénédiction *f* blessing
bénéfice *m* benefit; COMM profit; **bénéficier**: ***~ de*** benefit from; **bénéfique** beneficial
Bénélux: ***le ~*** the Benelux countries *pl*
bénévolat voluntary work; **bénévole 1** *adj travail* voluntary **2** *m/f* volunteer
bénin, **-igne** *tumeur* benign; *accident* minor
bénir bless; **bénit** consecrated; ***eau f ~e*** holy water
béquille *f* crutch; *d'une moto* stand
berceau *m* cradle; **bercer** rock; ***se ~ d'illusions*** delude o.s.
béret *m* beret
berger *m* shepherd; *chien* German shepherd, *Br aussi* Alsatian
berline *f* AUTO sedan, *Br* saloon
bermuda(s) *m* (*pl*) Bermuda shorts *pl*
berner fool
besogne *f* job, task
besoin *m* need; ***avoir ~ de*** (***faire***) ***qch*** need (to do) sth; ***au ~*** if need be
bestial bestial
bétail *m* (*sans pl*) livestock
bête 1 *adj* stupid **2** *f* animal; (*insecte*) insect; ***chercher la petite ~*** nitpick; **bêtement** stupidly; **bêtise** *f* stupidity; ***dire des ~s*** talk nonsense; ***une ~*** a stupid thing to do/say
béton *m* concrete
betterave *f* beet, *Br* beetroot
beugler *de bœuf* low; F *d'une personne* shout
beurre *m* butter; ***~ de cacahuètes*** peanut butter
bévue *f* blunder
biais 1 *adv*: ***en ~*** diagonally; ***de ~*** *regarder* sideways **2** *m fig* (*aspect*) angle; ***par le ~ de*** through
biberon *m* (baby's) bottle
Bible *f* bible
bibliothèque *f* library; *meuble* bookcase
bic® *m* ballpoint (pen)
bicentenaire *m* bicentennial, *Br* bicentenary
biceps *m* biceps
biche *f* zo doe
bicyclette *f* bicycle; ***aller en*** *ou* ***à ~*** cycle
bidon *m*: ***~ à essence*** gas *ou Br* petrol can
bidonville *m* shanty town
bidule *m* F gizmo F
bien 1 *m* good; (*possession*) possession; ***le ~*** *ce qui est*

juste good; ***faire le ~*** do good; ***faire du ~ à qn*** do s.o. good; ***~s*** (*possessions*) property; (*produits*) goods **2** *adj* good; (*beau, belle*) good-looking; ***être ~*** feel well; (*à l'aise*) be comfortable; ***ce sera très ~ comme ça*** that will do very nicely; ***se sentir ~*** feel well; ***avoir l'air ~*** look good; ***des gens ~*** respectable people **3** *adv* well; (*très*) very; ***~ des fois*** lots of times; ***eh ~*** well; ***oui, je veux ~*** yes please **4** *conj* ***~ que*** (+ *subj*) although

bien-être *m* welfare; *sensation agréable* well-being

bienfait *m* benefit

bien-fondé *m* legitimacy

bienheureux, **-euse** happy; REL blessed

bienséance *f* propriety

bientôt soon; ***à ~!*** see you (soon)!

bienveillance *f* benevolence

bienvenu, ~e 1 *adj* welcome **2** *m/f* ***être le/la ~(e)*** be welcome **3** *f* ***souhaiter la ~e à*** welcome

bière *f* beer; ***~ blanche*** wheat beer; ***~ brune*** dark beer, *Br* bitter; ***~ pression*** draft (beer), *Br* draught (beer)

bifteck *m* steak

bifurquer: **~ (*vers*)** fork (off onto); *fig* branch out (into)

bigame 1 *adj* bigamous **2** *m/f* bigamist; **bigamie** *f* bigamy

bijou *m* jewel; ***~x*** jewelry, *Br* jewellery; **bijouterie** *f* jewelry store, *Br* jeweller's; **bijoutier, -ère** *m/f* jeweler, *Br* jeweller

bikini *m* bikini

bilan *m* balance sheet; *fig* (*résultat*) outcome; ***faire le ~ de*** take stock of

bilingue bilingual

billard *m* billiards *sg*; *table* billiard table; ***~ américain*** pool

bille *f* marble; *billard* (billiard) ball; ***stylo m (à) ~*** ball-point (pen)

billet *m* ticket; (*petite lettre*) note; **~ (*de banque*)** bill, *Br* (bank)note; **billeterie** *f* ticket office; *automatique* ticket machine; FIN ATM, *Br aussi* cash dispenser

biochimie *f* biochemistry

biodégradable biodegradable

biodiversité *f* biodiversity

biographie *f* biography

biologie *f* biology; **biologique** biological; *aliments* organic

biotechnologie *f* biotechnology

bis 1 *adj*: ***24 ~*** 24A **2** *m* encore

biscornu *fig* weird

biscotte *f* rusk

biscuit *m* cookie, *Br* biscuit

bise *f*: ***faire la ~ à*** kiss

bisexuel, ~le bisexual

bisou *m* F kiss

bissextile: ***année f ~*** leap year

bistro(t) *m* bistro
bit *m* INFORM bit
bitume *m* asphalt
bizarre strange, bizarre
blafard wan
blague *f* joke; ***sans ~!*** no kidding!; **blaguer** joke
blaireau *m* badger; *pour se raser* shaving brush
blâme *m* blame; (*sanction*) reprimand
blanc, **blanche 1** *adj* white; *page* blank; ***nuit f blanche*** sleepless night **2** *m* white; *textile* (household) linen; *par opposé aux couleurs* whites *pl*; *dans un texte* blank **3** *m/f* ***Blanc, Blanche*** white, White
blancheur *f* whiteness; **blanchir 1** *v/t* whiten; *mur* whitewash; *linge* launder, wash; *du soleil* bleach; *fig*: *innocenter* clear **2** *v/i* go white
blasé blasé
blasphème *m* blasphemy; **blasphémer** blaspheme
blé *m* wheat, *Br* corn
blêmir turn pale
blesser hurt (*aussi fig*); *dans un accident* injure; *à la guerre* wound; ***se ~*** injure *ou* hurt o.s.; **blessure** *f d'accident* injury; *d'arme* wound
bleu 1 *adj* blue; *viande* very rare **2** *m* blue; *fromage* blue cheese; *sur la peau* bruise; *fig* (*novice*) rookie F
blindage *m* armor, *Br* armour; **blinder** armor, *Br* armour; *fig* F harden
bloc *m* block; POL bloc; *de papier* pad; ***faire ~*** join forces
bloc-notes *m* notepad
blocus *m* blockade
blond, **~e 1** *adj* blonde; *tabac* Virginian; *sable* golden **2** *m/f* blonde **3** *f bière* beer, *Br aussi* lager
bloquer block; *mécanisme* jam; *roues* lock; *compte* freeze
blouson *m* jacket, blouson
bluff *m* bluff; **bluffer** bluff
bobard *m* F tall tale *ou Br* story
bocal *m* (glass) jar
bock *m*: ***un ~*** a (glass of) beer
bœuf *m* steer; *viande* beef
bohémien, **~ne** *m/f* gipsy
boire drink; (*absorber*) soak up
bois *m matière, forêt* wood; ***en ~*** wooden
boisson *f* drink; ***~s alcoolisées*** alcohol
boîte *f* box; *en tôle* can, *Br aussi* tin; F (*entreprise*) company; ***~ (de nuit)*** nightclub; ***en ~*** canned, *Br aussi* tinned; ***~ à gants*** glove compartment; ***~ aux lettres*** mailbox, *Br* letterbox
boiter limp; *fig*: *de raisonnement* be shaky; **boiteux**, **-euse** *table etc* wobbly; *fig*: *raisonnement* shaky; ***être ~*** *d'une personne* have a limp
boîtier *m* case, housing
bol *m* bowl

bombardement *m* bombing; *avec obus* bombardment; **bombarder** bomb; *avec obus, questions* bombard; **bombe** *f* bomb; (*atomiseur*) spray; *~ à retardement* time bomb; **bombé** bulging

bon, *~ne* **1** *adj* good; *route, moment* right; *de ~ne foi personne* sincere; *être ~ en qch* be good at sth; *à quoi ~?* what's the use?; witticism; *~ anniversaire!* happy birthday!; *~ voyage!* have a good trip!, bon voyage!; *~ne chance!* good luck!; *~ne année!* Happy New Year!; *~ne nuit!* good night!; *ah ~* really **2** *adv*: *sentir ~* smell good; *tenir ~* not give in; *trouver ~ de faire qch* think it right to do sth **3** *m* COMM voucher; *avoir du ~* have its good points; *~ d'achat* gift voucher; *~ du Trésor* Treasury bond

bonbon *m* candy, *Br* sweet; *~s* candy, *Br* sweets

bond *m* leap; *d'une balle* bounce

bondé packed

bondir jump, leap (*de* with)

bonheur *m* happiness; (*chance*) luck; *par ~* luckily; *au petit ~* at random

bonhomme *m* F (*type*) guy F

boniment *m battage* spiel F, sales talk; F (*mensonge*) fairy story

bonjour *m* hello

bonne *f* maid

bonnet *m* hat; *gros ~ fig* F big shot F; *~ de douche* shower cap

bonsoir *m* hello, good evening

bonté *f* goodness

bonus *m* no-claims bonus

bord *m* edge; (*rive*) bank; *d'une route* side; *d'un verre* brim; *au ~ de la mer* at the seaside; *être au ~ des larmes* be on the verge of tears; *monter à ~* go on board

bordel *m* F brothel; (*désordre*) mess F

bordélique F chaotic

border (*garnir*) edge (*de* with); (*être le long de*) border; *enfant* tuck in

bordure *f* border, edging; *en ~ de forêt, ville* on the edge of

borne *f* boundary marker; ÉL terminal; *~s fig* limits; *dépasser les ~s* go too far; **borné** narrow-minded; **borner**: *se ~ à (faire)* restrict o.s. to (doing)

bosse *f* (*enflure*) lump; *d'un bossu, d'un chameau* hump; *du sol* bump

bosser F work hard

bossu, *~e m/f* hunchback

botanique **1** *adj* botanical **2** *f* botany

botte *f chaussure* boot

bouc *m* goat; *~ émissaire fig* scapegoat

bouche *f* mouth; *de métro* entrance; **~ *d'aération*** vent; **~ *d'incendie*** (fire) hydrant
bouché blocked; *temps* overcast
bouche-à-bouche *m* MÉD mouth-to-mouth resuscitation
bouchée *f* mouthful
boucher[1] *v/t* block; *trou* fill (in); ***se ~*** *d'un évier* get blocked; ***se ~ le nez*** hold one's nose
boucher[2], **-ère** *m/f* butcher (*aussi fig*)
boucherie *f magasin* butcher's; *fig* slaughter
bouchon *m* top; *de liège* cork; *fig*: *trafic* hold-up
boucle *f* loop; *de ceinture* buckle; *de cheveux* curl; **~ *d'oreille*** earring; **bouclé** *cheveux* curly; **boucler** *ceinture* fasten; *porte* lock; MIL surround; *en prison* lock away
bouddhisme *m* Buddhism; **bouddhiste** *m* Buddhist
bouder 1 *v/i* sulk **2** *v/t*: **~ *qn/qc*** give s.o./sth the cold shoulder
boudin *m*: **~ (*noir*)** blood sausage, *Br* black pudding
boue *f* mud
bouée *f* MAR buoy
bouffée *f de fumée, vent* puff; *de parfum* whiff
bouffer F eat
bouffi bloated
bouger move; *de prix* change
bougie *f* candle; AUTO spark plug
bouillie *f* baby food
bouillir boil; *fig* be boiling (with rage); ***faire ~*** boil;
bouilloire *f* kettle
bouillon *m* (*bulle*) bubble; CUIS stock; **bouillonner** bubble; *fig*: *d'idées* seethe
bouillotte *f* hot water bottle
boulanger, **-ère** *m/f* baker; **boulangerie** *f* bakery
boule *f* ball; ***jeu m de ~s*** bowls *sg*
bouleau *m* BOT birch (tree)
boulevard *m* boulevard
bouleversement *m* upheaval; **bouleverser** (*mettre en désordre*) turn upside down; *traditions* overturn; *émotionnellement* shatter
boulimie *f* bulimia
boulot *m* F work
bouquet *m* bouquet
bouquin *m* F book; **bouquiner** read
bourde *f* blunder, blooper F
bourdon *m* ZO bumblebee; **bourdonner** *d'insectes* buzz; *de moteur* hum; *d'oreilles* ring
bourgeois, **~e 1** *adj* middle-class **2** *m/f* member of the middle classes
bourgeoisie *f* middle classes *pl*
bourgeon *m* BOT bud
bourrasque *f* gust
bourratif, **-ive** stodgy
bourré crammed (***de*** with); F

(*ivre*) drunk, sozzled F
bourrer *coussin* stuff; *pipe* fill; ***se ~ de qc*** F stuff o.s. with sth
bourru surly
bourse *f d'études* grant; (*porte-monnaie*) coin purse, *Br* purse; ***Bourse*** (***des valeurs***) Stock Exchange
boursouf(f)lé swollen
bousculer (*heurter*) jostle; (*presser*) rush; *fig*: *traditions* overturn
bousiller F *travail* screw up F; (*détruire*) wreck
boussole *f* compass
bout *m* end; (*morceau*) piece; ***au ~ de*** at the end of; ***d'un ~ à l'autre*** right the way through; ***être à ~*** be at an end; ***venir à ~ de*** overcome
bouteille *f* bottle; *de butane* cylinder
boutique *f* store, *Br* shop; *de mode* boutique
bouton *m* button; *de porte* handle; ANAT spot, zit F; BOT bud; **bouton-d'or** *m* BOT buttercup; **boutonner** button; BOT bud; **boutonneux, -euse** spotty
bovin 1 *adj* cattle *atr* **2** *mpl* **~s** cattle *pl*
bowling *m* bowling, *Br* ten-pin bowling; *lieu* bowling alley
boxe *f* boxing; **boxer** box; **boxeur** *m* boxer
boycott *m* boycott; **boycotter** boycott
B.P. (= ***boîte postale***) PO Box (= Post Office Box)
bracelet *m* bracelet
braconnier *m* poacher
braguette *f* fly
brailler bawl
braiser CUIS braise
brancard *m* (*civière*) stretcher
branche *f* branch; *de céleri* stick
brancher connect up (***sur*** to); *à une prise* plug in; ***branché*** F (*informé*) clued up; (*en vogue*) trendy
brandir brandish
braquer 1 *v/t*: **~ *sur*** aim *ou* point at **2** *v/i* AUTO turn the wheel; ***se ~ contre*** *fig* turn against
bras *m* arm; ***avoir le ~ long*** *fig* have influence
brasse *f* stroke
brasser *bière* brew; **brasserie** *f usine* brewery; *établissement* restaurant
brave 1 *adj* brave; (*before the noun*) good **2** *m*: ***un ~*** a brave man; **braver** (*défier*) defy; **bravoure** *f* bravery
break *m* AUTO station wagon, *Br* estate (car)
brebis *f* ewe
bredouiller mumble
bref, -ève 1 *adj* brief, short **2** *adv* briefly, in short
Brésil: ***le ~*** Brazil; **brésilien, ~ne** Brazilian; **Brésilien, ~ne** *m/f* Brazilian
Bretagne: ***la ~*** Britanny
bretelle *f de lingerie* strap;

d'autoroute ramp, *Br* slip road; **~s** *de pantalon* suspenders, *Br* braces
brevet *m* diploma; *pour invention* patent; **breveter** patent
bric-à-brac *m inv* bric-a-brac
bricolage *m* do-it-yourself, DIY; **bricole** *f* little thing; **bricoler** do odd jobs
brièvement briefly; **brièveté** *f* briefness, brevity
brigade *f* MIL brigade; *de police* squad; *d'ouvriers* gang
brillamment brilliantly; **brillant** shiny; *couleur* bright; *fig* brilliant; **briller** shine (*aussi fig*); ***faire ~*** *meuble* polish
brin *m d'herbe* blade; *de corde* strand
brindille *f* twig
brioche *f* CUIS brioche; F (*ventre*) paunch
brique *f* brick
briquet *m* lighter
brise *f* breeze
brisé broken
briser **1** *v/t* break; *vie, bonheur* destroy; (*fatiguer*) wear out **2** *v/i de la mer* break; ***se ~*** *de verre etc* break; *des espoirs* be shattered
britannique British; **Britannique** *m/f* Briton, Britisher, Brit F; ***les ~s*** the British
broc *m* pitcher
brocante *f magasin* second--hand store
broche *f* CUIS spit; *bijou* brooch
brochet *m* pike
brochette *f* CUIS skewer; *plat* shish kebab
brochure *f* brochure
brocolis *mpl* broccoli *sg*
broncher: ***sans ~*** without batting an eyelid
bronches *fpl* ANAT bronchial tubes
bronchite *f* MÉD bronchitis
bronze *m* bronze
bronzé tanned; **bronzer** **1** *v/t peau* tan **2** *v/i* get a tan; ***se ~*** sunbathe
brosse *f* brush; *coiffure* crew-cut; ***~ à dents/cheveux*** toothbrush/hairbrush; **brosser** brush; ***se ~ les dents*** brush one's teeth
brouhaha *m* hubbub
brouillard *m* fog; ***il y a du ~*** it's foggy
brouille *f* quarrel; **brouiller** *œufs* scramble; *cartes* shuffle; *papiers* muddle; *radio* jam; *involontairement* cause interference to; *amis* cause to fall out; ***se ~*** *du ciel* cloud over; *de vitres* mist up; *d'idées* get muddled; *d'amis* fall out
brouillon *m* draft; ***papier m ~*** scratch paper, *Br* scrap paper
broussailles *fpl* undergrowth
broyer grind; ***~ du noir*** *fig* be down

bru *f* daughter-in-law
brugnon *m* BOT nectarine
bruine *f* drizzle
bruit *m* sound; *qui dérange* noise; (*rumeur*) rumor, *Br* rumour; ***faire du ~*** make a noise; *fig* cause a sensation
brûlant burning (*aussi fig*); (*chaud*) burning hot; *liquide* scalding; **brûlé** burnt; **brûler 1** *v/t* burn; *d'eau bouillante* scald; *électricité* use; ***~ un feu rouge*** go through a red light **2** *v/i* burn; ***se ~*** burn o.s.; *d'eau bouillante* scald o.s.; **brûleur** *m* burner; **brûlure** *f sensation* burning; *lésion* burn; ***~s d'estomac*** heartburn
brume *f* mist
brun, ~e 1 *adj* brown; *cheveux, peau* dark **2** *m/f* dark-haired man/woman; ***une ~e*** a brunette **3** *m couleur* brown
brushing® *m* blow-dry
brusque abrupt, brusque; (*soudain*) abrupt, sudden; **brusquement** abruptly, suddenly; **brusquer** rush
brut, ~e 1 *adj* raw; *poids, revenu* gross; *pétrole* crude; *sucre* unrefined; *champagne* very dry **2** *m* crude (petroleum) **3** *f* brute; **brutal** brutal; **brutalement** brutally; **brutaliser** ill-treat; **brutalité** *f* brutality
Bruxelles Brussels
bruyant noisy
buanderie *f* laundry room
bûcher[1] *m* woodpile; (*échafaud*) stake
bûcher[2] *v/i* work hard; ÉDU F hit the books, *Br* swot
budget *m* budget
buée *f* steam, condensation
buffet *m* buffet; *meuble* sideboard
buisson *m* shrub, bush
bulbe *f* BOT bulb
bulgare 1 *adj* Bulgarian **2** *m langue* Bulgarian; **Bulgare** *m/f* Bulgarian; **Bulgarie**: ***la ~*** Bulgaria
bulle *f* bubble
bulletin *m* (*formulaire*) form; (*rapport*) bulletin; *à l'école* report card; ***~ (de vote)*** ballot (paper); ***~ de salaire*** paystub, *Br* payslip
bureau *m* office; *meuble* desk; ***~ de change*** exchange office, *Br* bureau de change; ***~ de poste*** post office; ***~ de tabac*** tobacco store, *Br* tobacconist's
bureaucratie *f* bureaucracy; **bureautique** *f* office automation
bus *m* bus
buste *m* bust
but *m* (*cible*) target; (*objectif*) aim, goal; *d'un voyage* purpose; SP goal; ***sans ~*** aimlessly; **buteur** *m* goalscorer
buté stubborn
buter: ***~ contre qch*** bump into sth; ***~ sur un problème*** hit a problem; ***se ~*** *fig* dig

one's heels in
butin *m* booty; *de voleurs* haul
butte *f* (*colline*) hillock; ***être en ~ à*** be exposed to
buvable drinkable; **buvette** *f* bar; **buveur**, **-euse** *m/f* drinker

C

c' → ***ce***
ça that; ***~ va?*** how are things?; (*d'accord?*) ok?; ***~ y est*** that's it; ***c'est ~!*** that's right
cabale *f* (*intrigue*) plot
cabane *f* (*baraque*) hut
cabaret *m* (*boîte*) night club
cabine *f* cabin; *d'un camion* cab; ***~ téléphonique*** phone booth
cabinet *m petite pièce* small room; *d'avocat* office; *de médecin* office, *Br* surgery; (*clientèle*) practice; POL Cabinet
câble *m* cable
cabosser dent
cabrer: ***se ~*** *d'un animal* rear
cabriolet *m* AUTO convertible
cacah(o)uète *f* BOT peanut
cacao *m* cocoa; BOT cocoa bean
cache-cache *m*: ***jouer à ~*** play hide-and-seek; **cache-nez** *m* scarf; **cacher** hide; ***se ~ de*** hide from
cachet *m* seal; *fig* (*caractère*) style; PHARM tablet; (*rétribution*) fee; ***~ de la poste*** postmark
cachette *f* hiding place; ***en ~*** secretly
cachotterie *f*: ***faire des ~s*** be secretive; **cachottier**, **-ère** secretive
cactus *m* cactus
cadavre *m* (dead) body, corpse; *d'un animal* carcass
caddie® *m* cart, *Br* trolley
cadeau *m* present, gift; ***faire un ~ à qn*** give s.o. a present
cadenas *m* padlock
cadence *f tempo* rhythm; *de travail* rate
cadet, **~te** *m/f* younger; *de plus de deux* youngest; ***il est mon ~ de trois ans*** he's three years younger than me
cadran *m* dial; ***~ solaire*** sundial
cadre *m* frame; *fig* framework; *d'une entreprise* executive; (*environnement*) surroundings *pl*
cafard *m* ZO cockroach; ***avoir le ~*** F be feeling down
café *m* coffee; *établissement* café; ***~ crème*** coffee with milk, *Br* white coffee
cafeteria *f* cafeteria
cafetière *f* coffee pot; ***~ électrique*** coffee maker

cage *f* cage
cagibi *m* F box room
cagneux, -euse knock-kneed
cagoule *f* hood; (*passe-montagne*) balaclava
cahier *m* notebook; ÉDU exercise book
cahoter jolt
cahoteux, -euse bumpy
caille *f* quail
cailler *du lait* curdle; *du sang* clot
caillou *m* pebble, stone
caisse *f* chest; *pour le transport* crate; *de champagne, vin* case; (*argent*) cash; (*guichet*) cashdesk; *dans un supermarché* checkout; **caissier, -ère** *m/f* cashier
cajoler (*câliner*) cuddle
calamité *f* disaster, calamity
calcium *m* calcium
calcul[1] *m* calculation
calcul[2] *m* MÉD stone; **~ *rénal*** kidney stone
calculatrice *f*: **~ (*de poche*)** (pocket) calculator; **calculer** calculate; **calculette** *f* pocket calculator
calé F: ***être ~ en qch*** be good at sth
caleçon *m d'homme* boxer shorts *pl*; *de femme* leggings *pl*
calembour *m* pun
calendrier *m* calendar; *emploi du temps* schedule, *Br* timetable
caler *moteur* stall; TECH wedge
califourchon: ***à ~*** astride
câlin 1 *adj* affectionate **2** *m* (*caresse*) cuddle
calmant 1 *adj* soothing; *contre douleur* painkilling **2** *m* tranquilizer, *Br* tranquillizer; *contre douleur* painkiller
calme 1 *adj* calm; *Bourse, vie* quiet **2** *m* calmness; MAR calm; (*silence*) peace and quiet; **calmement** calmly; **calmer** *personne* calm down; *douleur* relieve; ***se ~*** calm down
calomnie *f* slander; *écrite* libel; **calomnier** insult; *par écrit* libel
calorie *f* calorie
calquer trace
calvitie *f* baldness
camarade *m/f* friend; POL comrade
cambriolage *m* break-in, burglary; **cambrioler** burglarize, *Br* burgle
cambrioleur, -euse *m/f* house-breaker, burglar
camelote *f* F junk
caméra *f* camera
caméscope *m* camcorder
camion *m* truck, *Br aussi* lorry
camionnette *f* van
camomille *f* BOT camomile
camoufler camouflage; *fig*: *intention* hide; *faute* cover up
camp *m* camp (*aussi* MIL, POL); ***ficher le ~*** F get lost F
campagne *f* country, coun-

tryside; MIL, *fig* campaign; ***à la ~*** in the country
camper camp; ***se ~ devant*** plant o.s. in front of; **campeur, -euse** *m/f* camper
camping *m*: (***terrain*** *m* ***de***) ~ campground, campsite; ***faire du ~*** go camping
Canada ***le ~*** Canada; **canadien, ~ne** Canadian; **Canadien, ~ne** *m/f* Canadian
canal *m* channel; (*tuyau*) pipe; (*bras d'eau*) canal
canalisation *f* (*tuyauterie*) pipes *pl*, piping; **canaliser** *fig* channel
canapé *m* sofa; GASTR canapé
canapé-lit *m* sofa-bed
canard *m* duck; F newspaper
canari *m* canary
cancans *mpl* gossip
cancer *m* MÉD cancer; ASTROL ***Cancer*** Cancer
candeur *f* ingenuousness
candidat, ~e *m/f* candidate; **candidature** *f* candidacy; *à un poste* application
candide ingenuous
cane *f* (female) duck; **caneton** *m* duckling
canette *f* (*bouteille*) bottle
caniche *m* poodle
canicule *f* heatwave
canif *m* pocket knife
canin dog *atr*, canine
canine *f* canine
canne *f* cane, stick; ***~ à pêche*** fishing rod
cannelle *f* cinammon
canoë *m* canoe; *activité* canoeing
canon *m* MIL gun; HIST cannon; *de fusil* barrel
canot *m* small boat; ***~ pneumatique*** rubber dinghy; ***~ de sauvetage*** lifeboat
cantine *f* canteen
canular *m* hoax
caoutchouc *m* rubber; (*bande élastique*) rubber band
cap *m* GÉOGR cape; AVIAT, NAUT course
capable capable (***de faire*** of doing)
capacité *f* (*compétence*) ability; (*contenance*) capacity
cape *f* cape
capitaine *m* captain
capital 1 *adj* essential **2** *m* capital; ***capitaux*** capital **3** *f ville* capital (city); *lettre* capital (letter)
capitalisme *m* capitalism
capituler capitulate
capot *m* AUTO hood, *Br* bonnet
capote *f* *vêtement* greatcoat; AUTO top, *Br* hood; ***~ (anglaise)*** F condom
caprice *m* whim; **capricieux, -euse** capricious
Capricorne *m* ASTROL Capricorn
capter *regard* catch; RAD, TV pick up
capteur *m*: ***~ solaire*** solar panel
captif, -ive *m/f & adj* captive; **captivant** *personne* captivating; *lecture* gripping;

captiver *fig* captivate; **captivité** *f* captivity
capture *f* capture; (*proie*) catch; **capturer** capture
capuche *f* hood
car[1] *m* bus, *Br aussi* coach
car[2] *conj* for
carabine *f* rifle
carabiné F: ***un ... carabiné*** one hell of a ... F
caractère *m* character; ***avoir bon ~*** be good-natured; **caractériel** *troubles* emotional; *personne* emotionally disturbed
caractériser be characteristic of; **caractéristique** *f & adj* characteristic
carambolage *m* AUTO pile-up
caramel *m* caramel
caravane *f* AUTO trailer, *Br* caravan
carboniser burn
carburant *m* fuel
carburateur *m* TECH carburet(t)or
cardiaque MÉD **1** *adj* cardiac, heart *atr* **2** *m/f* heart patient
cardinal: ***les quatre points mpl cardinaux*** the four points of the compass
cardiologue *m/f* cardiologist, heart specialist
carême *m* REL Lent
carence *f* (*incompétence*) inadequacy; (*manque*) deficiency
caresse *f* caress; **caresser** caress; *idée* play with; *espoir* cherish
cargaison *f* cargo; *fig* load
caricature caricature
carie *f* MÉD: ***une ~*** a cavity
carié *dent* bad
caritatif, **~ive** charitable
carnage *m* carnage
carnassier, **-ère** carnivorous
carnaval *m* carnival
carnet *m* notebook; *de tickets, timbres* book
carnivore 1 *adj* carnivorous **2** *m* carnivore
carotte *f* carrot; ***poil de ~*** ginger
carpe *f* ZO carp
carpette *f* rug
carré 1 *adj* square; *fig: réponse* straightforward **2** *m* square
carreau *m de fenêtre* pane; *cartes* diamonds; ***à ~x*** checked
carrefour *m* crossroads *sg* (*aussi fig*)
carrelage *m* (*carreaux*) tiles *pl*
carrément bluntly, straight out
carrière *f* quarry; *profession* career; ***militaire m de ~*** professional soldier
carrosserie *f* AUTO bodywork
carrure *f* build
cartable *m* schoolbag; *à bretelles* satchel
carte *f* card; *dans un restaurant* menu; GÉOGR map; NAUT, *du ciel* chart; ***~ bancaire*** debit card, banker's card; ***~ de crédit*** credit card;

~ ***d'embarquement*** boarding pass; ~ ***d'identité*** identity card; ~ ***postale*** postcard; ~ ***téléphonique*** phonecard
carton *m* cardboard; *boîte* cardboard box; ~ ***jaune/rouge*** *en football* yellow/red card
cartouche *f* cartridge; *de cigarettes* carton
cas *m* case; ***en aucun*** ~ under no circumstances; ***dans ce ~-là*** in that case; ***en tout*** ~ in any case; ***en*** ~ ***de*** in the event of
casanier, **-ère** *m/f* stay-at--home
cascade *f* waterfall
case *f* (*hutte*) hut; (*compartiment*) compartiment; *dans formulaire* box; *dans mots--croisés, échiquier* square
caser put; (*loger*) put up; ***se*** ~ (*se marier*) settle down
caserne *f* barracks; ~ ***de pompiers*** fire station
casier *m courrier* pigeonholes *pl*; *bouteilles, livres* rack; ~ ***judiciaire*** criminal record
casino *m* casino
casque *m* helmet; *de radio* headphones *pl*; **casquette** *f* cap
cassable breakable
casse-cou *m inv* daredevil; **casse-croûte** *m* snack; **casse-noisettes** *m* nutcrackers *pl*; **casse-pieds** *m/f inv* F pain in the neck F
casser 1 *v/t* break; *noix* crack; JUR quash; ~ ***les pieds à qn*** F (*embêter*) get on s.o.'s nerves F; ***se*** ~ break **2** *v/i* break
casserole *f* (sauce)pan
casse-tête *m fig*: *problème* headache
cassette *f* cassette; ~ ***vidéo*** video
cassis *m* BOT blackcurrant; (***crème f de***) ~ blackcurrant liqueur
castrer castrate
cataclysme *m* disaster
catalogue *m* catalog, *Br* catalogue; **cataloguer** catalog, *Br* catalogue; F *péj* label
catalytique AUTO: ***pot m*** ~ catalytic converter
cataracte *f* waterfall; MÉD cataract
catastrophe *f* disaster, catastrophe; ***en*** ~ in a rush; **catastrophique** disastrous, catastrophic
catch *m* wrestling
catéchisme *m* catechism
catégorie *f* category; **catégorique** categorical
cathédrale *f* cathedral
catholique 1 *adj* (Roman) Catholic **2** *m/f* Roman Catholic
cauchemar *m* nightmare (*aussi fig*)
cause *f* cause; JUR case; ***à*** ~ ***de*** because of; ***être en*** ~ *d'honnêteté* be in question
causer 1 *v/t* (*provoquer*) cause **2** *v/i* (*s'entretenir*) chat

(***avec qn de*** with s.o. about); **causette** *f* chat; ***faire la ~*** have a chat
caustique CHIM, *fig* caustic
caution *f* security; *pour logement* deposit; JUR bail; *fig* (*appui*) backing; **cautionner** stand surety for; JUR bail; *fig* (*se porter garant de*) vouch for; (*appuyer*) back
cavaler F: ***~ après qn*** chase after s.o.
cavalier, **-ère 1** *m/f pour cheval* rider; *pour bal* partner **2** *m aux échecs* knight **3** *adj* offhand, cavalier
cave *f* cellar; **~ (*à vin*)** wine cellar
caverne *f* cave
caviar *m* caviar
cavité *f* cavity
CD *m* (= ***compact disc***) CD; **CD-Rom** *m* CD-Rom
ce *m* (**cet** *m*, **cette** *f*, **ces** *pl*) **1** *adj* this, *pl* these; ***~ livre-ci*** this book; ***~ livre-là*** that book; ***ces jours-ci*** these days **2** *pron* ***c'est pourquoi*** that is *ou* that's why; ***c'est triste*** it's sad; ***~ sont mes enfants*** these are my children; ***c'est un acteur*** he is *ou* he's an actor; ***c'est que tu as grandi!*** how you've grown!; ***ce que tu fais*** what you're doing; ***ce qui me plaît*** what I like; ***ce qu'il est gentil!*** isn't he nice!; ***sur ~*** with that
ceci this
cécité *f* blindness
céder 1 *v/t* give up; ***cédez le passage*** AUTO yield, *Br* give way **2** *v/i* give in (***à*** to); (*se casser*) give way
cédille *f* cedilla
cèdre *m* BOT cedar
ceinture *f* belt; ANAT waist; ***~ de sécurité*** seatbelt
cela that; ***à ~ près*** apart from that
célèbre famous
célébrer celebrate
célébrité *f* fame; *personne* celebrity
céleri *m* BOT: **~ (*en branche*)** celery; **~(*-rave*)** celeriac
célibat *m* single life; *d'un prêtre* celibacy; **célibataire 1** *adj* single, unmarried **2** *m* bachelor **3** *f* single woman
celle, **celles** → ***celui***
cellophane *f* cellophane
cellule *f* cell
cellulose *f* cellulose
Celsius Celsius
celui *m* (**celle** *f*, **ceux** *mpl*, **celles** *fpl*) the one, *pl* those; ***~ qui ... personne*** he who ...; *chose* the one which; ***celle de Claude*** Claude's; **celui-ci** this one; **celui-là** that one
cendre *f* ash; ***~s de cigarette*** cigarette ash; **cendrier** *m* ashtray
cène *f* REL: ***la ~*** (Holy) Communion; ***la Cène*** *peinture* the Last Supper
censé: ***il est ~ être malade*** he's supposed to be sick

censure *f* censorship; *organe* board of censors; **censurer** censor
cent 1 *adj* hundred **2** *m* a hundred, one hundred; *monnaie* cent; ***pour ~*** per cent; **centaine** *f*: ***une ~ de*** a hundred or so; ***des ~s de*** hundreds of; **centenaire 1** *adj* hundred-year-old **2** *m fête* centennial, *Br* centenary; **centième** hundredth; **centilitre** *m* centiliter, *Br* centilitre; **centimètre** *m* centimeter, *Br* centimetre; *ruban* tape measure
central, ~e 1 *adj* central **2** *m* TÉL telephone exchange **3** *f* power station; **centraliser** centralize
centre *m* center, *Br* centre; ***~ d'accueil*** temporary accommodations *pl*; **centrer** center, *Br* centre
centre-ville *m* downtown area, *Br* town centre
cep *m* vine stock
cèpe *m* BOT cèpe, boletus
cependant yet, however
cercle *m* circle; ***~ vicieux*** vicious circle
cercueil *m* casket, *Br* coffin
céréales *fpl* (breakfast) cereal
cérébral cerebral
cérémonie *f* ceremony; ***sans ~*** *repas etc* informal; *se présenter etc* informally; *mettre à la porte* unceremoniously
cerf *m* deer
cerf-volant *m* kite
cerise *f* cherry; **cerisier** *m* cherry (-tree)
cerne *m*: ***avoir des ~s*** have bags under one's eyes; **cerner** (*encercler*) surround; *fig*: *problème* define
certain 1 *adj* certain; ***être ~ de qc*** be certain of sth; ***d'un ~ âge*** middle-aged **2** *pron*: **certains, -aines** some (people)
certainement certainly; (*sûrement*) probably
certes certainly
certificat *m* certificate; ***~ de mariage*** marriage certificate; **certifier** guarantee; ***~ qc à qn*** assure s.o. of sth
certitude *f* certainty
cerveau *m* brain
cervelle *f* brains *pl*; ***se brûler la ~*** *fig* blow one's brains out
ces → ***ce***
cesser stop; ***~ de faire qch*** stop doing sth; **cessez-le-feu** *m* ceasefire
cession *f* disposal
c'est-à-dire that is, that is to say
cet, cette → ***ce***
ceux → ***celui***
chacun, ~e each (one); ***c'est ~ pour soi*** it's every man for himself
chagrin *m* grief; ***faire du ~ à*** upset
chahut *m* F racket, din; **chahuter** heckle
chaîne *f* chain; *radio*, TV

channel; **~s** AUTO snow chains; **~ hi-fi** hi-fi
chair *f* flesh; ***avoir la ~ de poule*** have goosebumps
chaise *f* chair; ***~ longue*** (*transatlantique*) deck chair
chalet *m* chalet
chaleur *f* heat; *plus modérée* warmth (*aussi fig*); **chaleureusement** warmly
chamailler F: ***se ~*** bicker
chambre *f* (bed)room; JUR, POL chamber; ***~ à air*** *de pneu* inner tube; ***~ à coucher*** bedroom; ***~ à un lit*** single (room); ***~ à deux lits*** twin-bedded room; ***~ d'amis*** spare room
chambré *vin* at room temperature
chameau *m* camel
champ *m* field (*aussi fig*); ***~ de courses*** racecourse
champagne *m* champagne
champêtre country *atr*
champignon *m* fungus; *nourriture* mushroom
champion, **~ne** *m/f* champion; **championnat** *m* championship
chance *f* luck; (*occasion*) chance; ***bonne ~!*** good luck!; ***avoir de la ~*** be lucky; ***c'est une ~ que*** (+ *subj*) it's lucky that
chanceler stagger; *d'un gouvernement* totter
chanceux, **-euse** lucky
chandail *m* sweater
change *m* exchange; ***taux m de ~*** exchange rate; ***donner le ~ à qn*** deceive s.o.; **changeant** changeable; **changement** *m* change; ***~ de vitesse*** AUTO gear shift; **changer** **1** *v/t* change (***en*** into); (*échanger*) exchange (***contre*** for) **2** *v/i* change; ***~ d'avis*** change one's mind; ***se ~*** change
chanson *f* song
chant *m* song; *action de chanter* singing; *d'église* hymn
chantage *m* blackmail
chanter sing; *d'un coq* crow; ***faire ~ qn*** blackmail s.o.
chanteur, **-euse** *m/f* singer
chantier *m* building site; ***~ naval*** shipyard
chaos *m* chaos; **chaotique** chaotic
chaparder F pinch F
chapeau *m* hat; **chapeauter** *fig* head up
chapelet *m* REL rosary
chapelle *f* chapel
chapelure *f* CUIS breadcrumbs *pl*
chapitre *m* chapter; *division de budget* heading; *fig* subject
chaque each
charbon *m* coal; ***~ de bois*** charcoal
charcuterie *f* CUIS cold cuts *pl*, *Br* cold meat; *magasin* pork butcher's; **charcutier** *m* pork butcher
charge *f* load; *fig* burden; ÉL, JUR, MIL charge; (*responsa-*

bilité) responsibility; ***avoir des enfants à ~*** have dependent children; ***~s*** charges; (*impôts*) costs; ***~s fiscales*** taxation
chargement *m* loading; *ce qui est chargé* load; **charger 1** *v/t navire, arme* load; *batterie*, JUR charge; (*exagérer*) exaggerate; ***~ qn de qc*** put s.o. in charge of sth; ***se ~ de*** look after **2** *v/i* charge
chariot *m pour bagages, achats* cart, *Br* trolley; (*charrette*) cart
charisme *m* charisma
charitable charitable; **charité** *f* charity; ***faire la ~ à qn*** give s.o. money
charmant charming, delightful; **charme** *m* charm; **charmer** charm
charnière *f* hinge
charnu fleshy
charognard *m* scavenger
charpente *f* framework; **charpentier** *m* carpenter
charte *f* charter
charter *m* charter
chasse[1] *f* hunting; (*poursuite*) chase; ***prendre en ~*** chase (after); ***~ privée*** private game reserve
chasse[2] *f*: ***~ d'eau*** flush
chasser *gibier* hunt; (*expulser*) drive away; *employé* dismiss; **chasseur** *m* hunter; AVIAT fighter; *dans un hôtel* bellhop, *Br* bellboy
châssis *m* frame; AUTO chassis
chaste chaste
chat[1] *m* cat
chat[2] *m* INFORM chatroom; *conversation* (online) chat
châtaigne *f* chestnut; **châtaignier** *m* chestnut (tree); **châtain** *inv* chestnut
château *m* castle; ***~ fort*** (fortified) castle; ***~ d'eau*** water tower
châtier punish; **châtiment** *m* punishment
chaton *m* kitten
chatouiller tickle
chatte *f* cat
chatter INFORM chat (online)
chaud 1 *adj* hot; *plus modéré* warm; ***il fait ~*** it's hot/warm **2** *m* heat; *plus modéré* warmth; ***j'ai ~*** I'm hot/warm; **chaudière** *f* boiler
chauffage *m* heating; ***~ central*** central heating
chauffard *m* F roadhog
chauffer 1 *v/t* heat (up), warm (up); *maison* heat; ***se ~*** warm o.s.; *d'un sportif* warm up **2** *v/i* warm *ou* heat up; *d'un moteur* overheat
chauffeur *m* driver; *privé aussi* chauffeur; ***~ de taxi*** taxi *ou* cab driver
chaussée *f* pavement, *Br* roadway
chausser *bottes* put on; ***se ~*** put one's shoes on; **chaussette** *f* sock; **chausson** *m* slipper; **chaussure** *f* shoe; ***~s de marche*** hiking boots;

~s de ski ski boots
chauve bald; **chauve-souris** *f* bat
chauvinisme *m* chauvinism
chef *m* (*meneur*), POL leader; (*patron*) boss; *d'une entreprise* head; *d'une tribu* chief; CUIS chef; **au premier ~** first and foremost; **de propre mon ~** on my own initiative
chef-d'œuvre *m* masterpiece
chemin *m* way; (*route*) road; (*allée*) path; **~ de fer** railroad, *Br* railway
cheminée *f* chimney; (*âtre*) fireplace; (*encadrement*) mantelpiece; *de bateau* funnel
cheminot *m* rail worker
chemise *f* shirt; (*dossier*) folder; **~ de nuit** *de femme* nightdress; **chemisier** *m* blouse
chêne *m* BOT oak (tree)
chenil *m* kennels *pl*
chenille *f* ZO caterpillar
chèque *m* COMM check, *Br* cheque; **~ de voyage** traveler's check, *Br* traveller's cheque; **chéquier** *m* checkbook, *Br* chequebook
cher, **-ère 1** *adj* dear (**à qn** to s.o.); *coûteux* dear, expensive **2** *adv*: **payer qch ~** pay a high price for sth **3** *m/f* **mon cher, ma chère** my dear
chercher look for; **~ à faire qch** try to do sth; **aller ~** fetch, go for; **venir ~** collect, come for; **envoyer ~** send for
chéri darling
chétif, **-ive** puny
cheval *m* horse; AUTO horsepower; **aller à ~** ride; **être à ~ sur qch** straddle sth; **chevalier** *m* HIST knight; **chevalière** *f* signet ring
chevelu *personne* long-haired; **chevelure** *f* hair
chevet *m* bedhead; **table** *f* **de ~** nightstand, *Br aussi* bedside table
cheveu *m* hair; **~x** hair; **aux ~x courts** short-haired
cheville *f* ANAT ankle; TECH peg
chèvre *f* goat
chevreau *m* kid
chevreuil *m* deer; CUIS venison
chez: **~ lui** at his place; *direction* to his place; **~ Marcel** at Marcel's; **quand nous sommes ~ nous** when we are at home; **rentrer ~ soi** go home; **aller ~ le coiffeur** go to the hairdresser *ou Br* hairdresser's; **~ Molière** in Molière
chez-soi *m* home
chiant F boring
chic 1 *m* style **2** *adj* chic; (*sympathique*) decent
chicaner quibble (**sur** over)
chicorée *f* BOT chicory
chien *m* dog; **temps de ~** *fig* F filthy weather; **~ d'aveugle** seeing-eye dog, *Br* guide

dog; **chienne** *f* dog; ***le chien et la ~*** the dog and the bitch
chier V shit; ***ça me fait ~*** P it pisses me off P
chiffon *m* rag; **~ (*à poussière*)** duster; **chiffonner** crumple; *fig* F bother
chiffre *m* number; (*code*) cipher
Chili: ***le ~*** Chili; **chilien, ~ne** Chilean; **Chilien, ~ne** *m/f* Chilean
chimie *f* chemistry
chimiothérapie *f* chemotherapy
chimique chemical
Chine: ***la ~*** China; **chinois, ~e 1** *adj* Chinese **2** *m langue* Chinese; **Chinois, ~e** *m/f* Chinese
chiot *m* pup
chips *mpl* chips, *Br* crisps
chirurgie *f* surgery; ***~ esthétique*** plastic surgery; **chirurgien, ~ne** *m/f* surgeon; ***~ dentiste*** dental surgeon
choc *m* shock; *d'opinions, intérêts* clash
chocolat *m* chocolate
chœur *m* choir ***en ~*** in chorus
choisir choose; ***~ de faire*** decide to do; **choix** *m* choice; (*assortiment*) range; ***de*** (***premier***) ***~*** choice
cholestérol *m* cholesterol
chômage *m* unemployment; ***être au ~*** be unemployed; ***~ partiel*** short time; **chômeur, -euse** *m/f* unemployed person; ***les ~s*** the unemployed *pl*
chope *f* beer mug
choquant shocking; **choquer**: ***~ qc*** knock sth; ***~ qn*** shock s.o.
chorale *f* choir
chose *f* thing; ***autre ~*** something else; ***c'est ~ faite*** it's done
chou *m* BOT cabbage; ***~x de Bruxelles*** Brussels sprouts
chouette 1 *f* owl **2** *adj* F great
chou-fleur *m* cauliflower
chrétien, ~ne *adj & m/f* Christian
christianisme *m* Christianity
chrome *m* chrome
chronique 1 *adj* chronic **2** *f d'un journal* column; *reportage* report; **chroniqueur** *m pour un journal* columnist
chronologique chronological
chronométrer time
chuchoter whisper
chut: ***~!*** hush
chute *f* fall; ***~ des cheveux*** hair loss
ci: ***à cette heure-~*** at this time; ***comme ~ comme ça*** F so-so; ***par-~ par-là*** here and there
cible *f* target; **cibler** target
ciboulette *f* BOT chives *pl*
cicatrice *f* scar (*aussi fig*); **cicatriser**: (***se***) **~** heal
ci-contre opposite; **ci-dessous** below; **ci-dessus** above
cidre *m* cider

ciel *m* sky; REL heaven
cigale *f* cicada
cigare *m* cigar
cigarette *f* cigarette
ci-inclus enclosed; **ci-joint** enclosed, attached
cil *m* eyelash
ciment *m* cement
cimetière *m* cemetery
ciné *m* F movie theater, *Br* cinema; **cinéma** *m* movie theater, *Br* cinema; *art* cinema, movies *pl*
cinglé F mad, crazy
cinq five; ***le ~ mai*** May fifth, *Br* the fifth of May; **cinquantaine** *f* about fifty; ***elle approche la ~*** she's getting on for fifty; **cinquante** fifty; **cinquantième** fiftieth **cinquième** fifth
cintre *m* arch; *pour vêtements* coathanger
cirage *m pour parquet* wax, polish; *pour chaussures* polish
circonférence *f* circumference
circonspect circumspect
circonstance *f* circumstance
circuit *m* circuit; *de voyage* tour; SP track
circulaire *adj & f* circular
circulation *f* circulation; *voitures* traffic; **circuler** circulate; ***faire ~*** *nouvelles* spread
cire *f* wax; **cirer** polish; *parquet aussi* wax
cirque *m* circus
cirrhose *f*: ***~ du foie*** cirrhosis of the liver
ciseaux *mpl* scissors *pl*
citadin, ~e 1 *adj* town *atr*, city *atr* **2** *m/f* town-dweller, city-dweller
citation *f* quotation; JUR summons *sg*
cité *f* city; ***~ universitaire*** fraternity house, *Br* hall of residence
citoyen, ~ne *m/f* citizen; **citoyenneté** *f* citizenship
citron *m* lemon; ***~ vert*** lime; **citronnier** *m* lemon (tree)
civière *f* stretcher
civil 1 *adj* civil; *non militaire* civilian; ***état*** *m* ***~*** marital status **2** *m* civilian; ***en ~*** in civilian clothes; *policier* in plain clothes; **civilisation** *f* civilization
civique civic
civisme *m* public-spiritedness
clair 1 *adj* clear; *couleur* light; *chambre* bright **2** *adv voir* clearly; *dire*, *parler* plainly **3** *m*: ***~ de lune*** moonlight
clairière *f* clearing
clairvoyant perceptive
clandestin secret, clandestine; ***passager*** *m* ***~*** stowaway
claque *f* slap; **claquer 1** *v/t porte* slam; *argent* F blow; ***~ des doigts*** snap one's fingers **2** *v/i d'un fouet* crack; *des dents* chatter; *d'un volet* slam
clarifier clarify

clarinette *f* clarinet
clarté *f* (*lumière*) brightness; (*transparence*) clarity
classe *f* class; ***il a de la ~*** he's got class; ***~ économique*** economy class
classement *m* position, place; BOT, ZO classification; *de lettres* filing; **classer** classify; *actes, dossiers* file; ***~ une affaire*** consider a matter closed
classique 1 *adj* classical; (*traditionnel*) classic **2** *m en littérature* classical author; MUS classical music; *film, livre* classic
clause *f* clause; ***~ pénale*** penalty clause
clavicule *f* collarbone
clavier *m* keyboard
clé *f* key; TECH wrench; ***~ de fa*** MUS bass clef; ***fermer à ~*** lock; ***sous ~*** under lock and key
clef *f* → ***clé***
clément merciful
clergé *m* clergy
clic *m bruit*, INFORM click
client, ~e *m/f* (*acheteur*) customer; *d'un médecin* patient; *d'un avocat* client; **clientèle** *f* customers *pl*, clientèle; *d'un médecin* patients *pl*; *d'un avocat* clients *pl*
cligner: ***~ (des yeux)*** blink; ***~ de l'œil à qn*** wink at s.o.
clignotant *m* turn signal, *Br* indicator; **clignoter** *d'une lumière* flicker
climat *m* climate (*aussi fig*)
climatisation *f* air conditioning; **climatisé** air conditioned
clin *m*: ***~ d'œil*** wink; ***en un ~ d'œil*** in a flash
clinique 1 *adj* clinical **2** *f* clinic
cliquer INFORM click (***sur*** on)
clochard, ~e *m/f* hobo, *Br* tramp
cloche *f* bell *f*; F (*idiot*) nitwit F; **clocher 1** *m* steeple **2** *v/i* F: ***ça cloche*** something's not right
cloison *f* partition
cloîtrer *fig*: ***se ~*** shut o.s. away
clonage *m* cloning; **clone** *m* clone; **cloner** clone
clope *m ou f* F cigarette, *Br* F fag; (*mégot*) cigarette end
cloque *f* blister
clôture *f d'un débat* closure; *d'un compte* closing; (*barrière*) fence
clou *m* nail; *fig* main attraction; MÉD boil; **clouer** nail; ***être cloué au lit*** be confined to bed
clown *m* clown
club *m* club; ***~ de gym*** gym
coaguler *du lait* curdle; *du sang* coagulate
cobaye *m* ZO, *fig* guinea pig
coca *m* Coke®
coccinelle *f* ladybug, *Br* ladybird; F AUTO Volkswagen® beetle
cocher *sur une liste* check, *Br*

aussi tick off
cochon 1 *m* zo, *fig* pig **2** *adj* **cochon, ~ne** F dirty; **cochonnerie** *f* F: ***des ~s*** filth; *nourriture* junk food
coco *m*: ***noix f de ~*** coconut
cocotte *f* CUIS casserole; F darling; *péj* tart; ***~ minute*** pressure cooker
code *m* code; ***~ confidentiel*** PIN number; ***~ pénal*** penal code; ***se mettre en ~*** switch to low beams; ***~ postal*** zipcode, *Br* postcode
cœur *m* heart; ***de bon ~*** gladly; ***par ~*** by heart; ***j'ai mal au ~*** I feel nauseous
coffre *m* *meuble* chest; FIN safe; AUTO trunk, *Br* boot; **coffre-fort** *m* safe
cogérer co-manage
cognac *m* brandy, cognac
cogner *d'un moteur* knock; ***~ à ou contre qc*** bang against sth; ***se ~ à ou contre qc*** bump into sth
cohabiter cohabit
cohérent *théorie* consistent, coherent
cohue *f* crowd, rabble
coiffer: ***~ qn*** do s.o.'s hair; ***se ~*** do one's hair; **coiffeur** *m* hairdresser, hair stylist; **coiffeuse** *f* hairdresser, hair stylist; *meuble* dressing table; **coiffure** *f* *de cheveux* hairstyle
coin *m* corner; *cale* wedge
coincer squeeze; *porte, tiroir* jam; ***coincé dans un embouteillage*** stuck in a traffic jam
coïncidence *f* coincidence
col *m* collar; *d'une bouteille, d'un pull* neck; GÉOGR col; ***~ blanc/bleu*** white-collar/ /blue-collar worker
colère *f* anger; ***se mettre en ~*** get angry
colique *f* colic; (*diarrhée*) diarrhea, *Br* diarrhoea
colis *m* parcel, package
collaborateur, -trice *m/f* collaborator ((*aussi* POL *péj*); **collaboration** *f* collaboration, cooperation; POL *péj* collaboration; **collaborer** collaborate, cooperate (***avec*** with; ***à*** on); POL *péj* collaborate
collant 1 *adj* sticky; *vêtement* close-fitting; F *personne* clingy **2** *m* pantyhose *pl*, *Br* tights *pl*
colle *f* glue; *fig* P *question* tough question; (*retenue*) detention
collecte *f* collection; **collectif, -ive** collective; ***voyage m ~*** group tour
collection *f* collection; **collectionner** collect; **collectionneur, -euse** *m/f* collector
collège *m* *école* junior high, *Br* secondary school; **collégien, ~ne** *m/f* junior high student, *Br* secondary school pupil
collègue *m/f* colleague, co-

worker
coller 1 *v/t* stick, glue **2** *v/i* stick (**à** to); ***se ~ contre*** *mur* press o.s against; *personne* cling to
collier *m bijou* necklace; *de chien* collar
colline *f* hill
collision *f* collision; ***entrer en ~ avec*** collide with
colocataire *m/f* roommate, *Br* flatmate
colombe *f* dove (*aussi fig*)
Colombie: ***la ~*** Colombia; **colombien, ~ne** Colombian; **Colombien, ~ne** *m/f* Colombian
colonie *f* colony; ***~ de vacances*** summer camp
colonne *f* column
colorant 1 *adj shampoing* color *atr*, *Br* colour *atr* **2** *m* dye; *dans la nourriture* coloring, *Br* colouring; **colorer** color, *Br* colour
coma *m* coma
combat *m* fight; MIL *aussi* battle; ***mettre hors de ~*** put out of action; **combattant 1** *adj* fighting **2** *m* combatant; **combattre** fight
combien 1 *adv quantité* how much; *avec pl* how many **2** *m*: ***tous les ~*** how often; ***on est le ~ aujourd'hui?*** what date is it today?
combinaison *f* combination; (*astuce*) scheme; *de mécanicien* coveralls *pl*, *Br* boiler suit; *lingerie* (full-length) slip; ***~ de plongée*** wet suit
combiner combine; *voyage, projet* plan
comble 1 *m fig*: *sommet* height; ***~s*** *pl* attic; ***de fond en ~*** from top to bottom **2** *adj* full (to capacity); **combler** *trou* fill in; *déficit* make good; *personne* overwhelm; ***~ qn de qch*** shower s.o. with sth
combustible 1 *adj* combustible **2** *m* fuel
comédie *f* comedy; ***~ musicale*** musical; **comédien, ~ne** *m/f* actor; *qui joue le genre comique* comic actor
comestible 1 *adj* edible **2** *mpl* ***~s*** food
comique 1 *adj* THÉÂT comic; (*drôle*) funny, comical **2** *m* comedian; *acteur* comic (actor); *genre* comedy
comité *m* committee
commande *f* COMM order; TECH control; INFORM command; **commander 1** *v/t* COMM order; (*ordonner*) command, order; MIL be in command of; TECH control **2** *v/i* (*diriger*) be in charge; COMM order
comme 1 *adv* like; ***noir ~ la nuit*** as black as night; ***~ ci ~ ça*** F so-so; ***~ vous voulez*** as you like; ***~ si*** as if; ***il travaillait ~ ...*** he was working as a ...; ***moi, ~ les autres, je ...*** like the others, I ... **2** *conj* as

commencement *m* beginning, start; **commencer** begin, start; **~ *qc par qc*** start sth with sth; **~ *par faire qc*** start by doing sth
comment how; **~?** (*qu'avez--vous dit?*) pardon me?, *Br* sorry?; **~!** *surpris* what!
commentaire *m* comment; RAD, TV commentary; **commenter** comment on; RAD, TV commentate on
commerçant, **~e 1** *adj*: ***rue f ~e*** shopping street **2** *m/f* merchant, trader
commerce *m* trade, commerce; (*magasin*) store, *Br* shop; *fig* (*rapports*) dealings *pl*; **commercial** commercial; **commercialiser** market
commettre commit; *erreur* make
commis *m*: **~ *voyageur*** commercial traveler *ou Br* traveller
commissaire *m* commission member; *de l'UE* Commissioner; SP steward; **commissariat** *m* commissionership; **~ (*de police*)** police station
commission *f* commission; (*message*) message
commode 1 *adj* handy; *arrangement* convenient; ***pas ~*** *personne* awkward **2** *f* chest of drawers; **commodité** *f* convenience
commotion *f* MÉD: **~ *cérébrale*** stroke
commun 1 *adj* common; *œuvre* joint; ***mettre en ~*** *argent* pool **2** *m*: ***hors du ~*** out of the ordinary
communal (*de la commune*) local
communauté *f* community; *de hippies* commune
communication *f* communication; (*message*) message; **~ *téléphonique*** telephone call
communion *f* REL Communion
communiquer 1 *v/t* communicate; *maladie* pass on, give (***à qn*** to s.o.) **2** *v/i* communicate
communisme *m* communism; **communiste** *m/f* & *adj* Communist
commutateur *m* switch
compact compact
compagne *f* companion; *dans couple* wife
compagnie *f* company; **~ *aérienne*** airline
compagnon *m* companion; *dans couple* husband; *employé* journeyman
comparaison *f* comparison; ***par ~ à*** compared with; **comparer** compare (***à*** to, ***avec*** with)
compartiment *m* compartment; *de train* car, *Br* compartment
compas *m* compass
compassion *f* compassion
compatible compatible
compatir: **~ *à*** sympathize

with
compatriote *m/f* compatriot
compenser compensate for
compétence *f* (*connaissances*) ability, competence; JUR jurisdiction; **compétent** competent, skillful, *Br* skilful; JUR competent
compétitif, **-ive** competitive; **compétition** *f* competition
compiler compile
complaire: ***se ~ dans/à faire*** delight in/in doing
complet, **-ète 1** *adj* complete; *hôtel*, *description*, *jeu de cartes* full; *pain* whole wheat, *Br* wholemeal **2** *m* suit; **complètement** completely; **compléter** complete; ***se ~*** complement each other
complexe *adj & m* complex
complication *f* complication
complice 1 *adj* JUR: ***être ~ de*** be an accessory to **2** *m/f* accomplice
compliment *m* compliment; ***mes ~s*** congratulations
compliqué complicated; **compliquer** complicate; ***se ~*** become complicated
comporter (*comprendre*) comprise; (*impliquer*) involve; ***se ~*** behave (o.s)
composer 1 *v/t* (*former*) make up; MUS compose; *livre*, *poème* write; *numéro* dial **2** *v/i transiger* come to terms (***avec*** with); ***se ~ de be*** consist of
compositeur, **-trice** *m/f* composer
composter *billet* punch
compote *f*: ***~ de pommes*** stewed apples
compréhension *f* understanding
comprendre understand; (*inclure*) include; (*comporter*) comprise
compresse *f* MÉD compress
comprimé *m* tablet
compris (*inclus*) included; ***y ~*** including
compromettre compromise
comptabilité *f* accountancy; (*comptes*) accounts *pl*; **comptable** *m/f* accountant
comptant: ***au ~*** cash
compte *m* account; (*calcul*) calculation; ***~s*** accounts; ***en fin de ~*** when all's said and done; ***se rendre ~ de*** realize; ***tenir ~ de qc*** take sth into account; ***~ courant*** checking account, *Br* current account; ***~ rendu*** report; *de réunion* minutes *pl*; **compter 1** *v/t* count; (*prévoir*) allow; (*inclure*) include; ***~ faire*** plan on doing **2** *v/i* count; ***~ sur*** rely on; ***à ~ de*** starting (from); **compteur** *m* meter
comptoir *m d'un café* bar; *d'un magasin* counter
con, **~ne** P **1** *adj* damn stupid F **2** *m/f* damn idiot F
concentration *f* concentration; **concentrer** concentrate; ***se ~*** concentrate

(***sur*** on)
concept *m* concept
conception *f* (*idée*) concept; (*planification*) design; BIOL conception
concernant concerning, about; **concerner** concern
concert *m* MUS concert; ***de ~ avec*** together with
concession *f* concession; AUTO dealership
concevable conceivable; **concevoir** (*comprendre*) understand, conceive; (*inventer*) design; BIOL, *plan, idée* conceive
concierge *m/f* superintendent, *Br* caretaker; *d'école* janitor, *Br aussi* caretaker; *d'un hôtel* concierge
concis concise
concitoyen, **~ne** *m/f* fellow citizen
conclure conclude; ***~ de*** conclude from; **conclusion** *f* conclusion
concombre *m* cucumber
concours *m* competition; (*assistance*) help
concret, **-ète** concrete
concurrence *f* competition; ***faire ~ à*** compete with; **concurrent**, **~e 1** *adj* rival **2** *m/f* competitor
condamnation *f* sentence; *action* sentencing; *fig* condemnation
condamner JUR sentence; *malade* give up; (*réprouver*) condemn; *porte* block up
condescendance *f péj* condescension
condition *f* condition; ***~ préalable*** prerequisite; ***à*** (***la***) ***~ que*** (+ *subj*) on condition that; **conditionner** (*emballer*) package; PSYCH condition
condoléances *fpl* condolences
conducteur, **-trice 1** *m/f* driver **2** *m* PHYS conductor
conduire 1 *v/t* take; (*mener*) lead; *voiture* drive; EL conduct; ***se ~*** behave **2** *v/i* AUTO drive; (*mener*) lead
conduit *m d'eau, de gaz* pipe; ***~ d'aération*** ventilation shaft
conduite *f* (*comportement*) behavior, *Br* behaviour; *direction* management; *d'eau, de gaz* pipe; AUTO driving
cône *m* cone
confection *f* making; *industrie* clothing industry
conférence *f* conference; (*exposé*) lecture; ***être en ~*** be in a meeting
confesser confess; ***~ qn*** REL hear s.o.'s confession; ***se ~*** REL go to confession; **confession** *f* confession; (*croyance*) faith
confiance *f* confidence; ***faire ~ à*** trust; **confiant** confident; (*crédule*) trusting
confidence *f* confidence; ***faire une ~ à*** confide in; **confident**, **~e** *m/f* confidant; con-

fidentiel, ~le confidential
confier: **~ *qc à qn*** (*laisser*) entrust s.o. (with sth); ***se ~ à*** confide in
confirmation *f* confirmation (*aussi* REL); **confirmer** confirm (*aussi* REL)
confiserie *f* confectionery; *magasin* confectioner's; **~*s*** candy, *Br* sweets
confisquer confiscate (***à*** from)
confiture *f* jelly, *Br* jam
conflit *m* conflict; *d'idées* clash
confondre confuse; (*déconcerter*) take aback; ***se ~*** (*se mêler*) merge
conforme: **~ *à*** in accordance with; **conformiste** *m/f* conformist
confort *m* comfort; **confortable** comfortable; *somme* sizeable
confronter confront; (*comparer*) compare
confusion *f* confusion; (*embarras*) embarrassment
congé *m* vacation, *Br* holiday; MIL leave; *avis de départ* notice; ***prendre ~ de*** take one's leave of; ***~ de maladie*** sick leave
congélateur *m* freezer; **congelé** *aliment* frozen; **congeler** freeze
congénital congenital
congestion *f* MÉD congestion; ***~ cérébrale*** stroke; **congestionné** *visage* flushed
congrès *m* convention, conference; ***Congrès*** *aux États-Unis* Congress
conique conical
conjecture *f* conjecture
conjoint, ~e 1 *adj* joint **2** *m/f* spouse
conjonctivite *f* MÉD conjunctivitis
conjugaison *f* GRAM conjugation
conjugal conjugal; *vie* married
conjuguer *efforts* combine; GRAM conjugate
connaissance *f* knowledge; (*conscience*) consciousness; *personne connue* acquaintance; **~*s*** *d'un sujet* knowledge; **connaisseur** *m* connoisseur; **connaître** know; (*rencontrer*) meet; ***s'y ~ en*** be an expert on
connecter TECH connect; ***se ~*** INFORM log on
connerie *f* V: ***une ~*** a damn stupid thing to do/say
connexion *f* connection; ***hors ~*** INFORM off-line
connu well-known
conquérir conquer
conquête *f* conquest
consacrer REL consecrate; (*dédier*) dedicate; *temps*, *argent* spend; ***se ~ à*** dedicate *ou* devote o.s. to
conscience *f* *moral* conscience; *physique*, PSYCH consciousness; ***prendre ~***

de become aware of

consécutif, -ive consecutive; **~ *à*** resulting from

conseil *m* advice; (*conseiller*) adviser; (*assemblée*) council; ***un ~*** a piece of advice; ***~ d'administration*** board of directors

conseiller *personne* advise; ***~ qc à qn*** recommend sth to s.o.

consentir 1 *v/i* consent, agree (***à*** to) **2** *v/t prêt*, *délai* agree

conséquence *f* consequence; ***en ~*** consequently

conservation *f* preservation; *des aliments* preserving

conserve *f* preserve; *en boîte* canned food, *Br aussi* tinned food; **conserver** keep; *aliments* preserve

considérable considerable; **considération** *f* consideration; **considérer** consider

consigne *f* orders *pl*; *d'une gare* baggage checkroom, *Br* left luggage office; *pour bouteilles* deposit; ÉDU detention

consistance *f* consistency; **consistant** *liquide*, *potage* thick; *mets* substantial; **consister**: ***~ en/dans*** consist of; ***~ à faire*** consist in doing

consolation *f* consolation

console *f* console; ***jouer à la ~*** play computer games

consoler console; ***se ~ de*** get over

consolider consolidate

consommateur, -trice *m/f* consumer; *dans un café* customer; **consommation** *f* consumption; *dans un café* drink; **consommer 1** *v/t* consume, use **2** *v/i dans un café* drink

consonne *f* consonant

conspiration *f* conspiracy; **conspirer** conspire

constamment constantly

constance *f* (*persévérance*) perseverance; *en amour* constancy

constant constant; *ami* staunch; *efforts* persistent

constater observe

consternation *f* consternation; **consterner** fill with consternation, dismay

constipation *f* MÉD constipation

constituer constitute; *comité*, *société* form; *rente* settle (***à*** on); ***se ~*** *fortune* build up

constitution *f* (*composition*) composition; ANAT, POL constitution; *d'un comité*, *d'une société* formation

construction *f* construction, building; **construire** construct, build; *théorie*, *roman* construct

consul *m* consul; **consulat** *m* consulate

consultation *f* consultation; **consulter 1** *v/t* consult **2** *v/i* be available for consultation

contact *m* contact; ***se mettre***

en ~ avec contact; ***mettre/ couper le ~*** AUTO switch the engine on/off
contagieux, **-euse** contagious; *rire* infectious
contaminer contaminate; MÉD *personne* infect
conte *m* story, tale
contempler contemplate
contemporain *m & adj* contemporary
contenir contain; *foule* control; *larmes* hold back; *peine* suppress; ***se ~*** contain o.s.
content pleased, content (***de*** with)
contenu *m* content
contestation *f* discussion; (*opposition*) protest; **contester** challenge
contexte *m* context
continent *m* continent
contingent *m* (*part*) quota
continu continous; ÉL *courant* direct; **continuer 1** *v/t* continue; *rue*, *ligne* extend **2** *v/i* continue, go on; *de route* extend; ***~ à ou de faire*** continue to do, go on doing; **continuité** *f* continuity; *d'une tradition* continuation
contorsion *f* contorsion
contour *m* contour; *d'une fenêtre*, *d'un visage* outline; ***~s*** (*courbes*) twists and turns
contourner get around
contraceptif, **-ive** contraceptive; **contraception** *f* contraception
contracter *dette* incur; *maladie aussi* contract; *obligation*, *engagement* enter into; *assurance* take out; *habitude* acquire
contradiction *f* contradiction
contraindre: ***~ qn à faire qc*** force s.o. to do sth; **contrainte** *f* constraint; ***sans ~*** freely, without restraint
contraire 1 *adj sens* opposite; *principes* conflicting; *vent* contrary **2** *m*: ***le ~ de*** the opposite *ou* contrary of; ***au ~*** on the contrary
contrarier *personne* annoy; *projet* thwart
contraster contrast
contrat *m* contract
contravention *f* infringement; (*procès-verbal*) ticket
contre 1 *prép* against; (*en échange*) (in exchange) for; ***tout ~ qch*** right next to sth; ***par ~*** on the contrary; ***quelque chose ~ la diarrhée*** something for diarrhea **2** *m*: ***le pour et le ~*** the pros and the cons *pl*
contrebande *f* smuggling; *marchandises* contraband; **contrebandier** *m* smuggler
contrebasse *f* double bass
contrecœur: ***à ~*** reluctantly
contrecoup *m* after-effect
contredire contradict
contrée *f* country
contrefaire counterfeit; *signature* forge; *personne*, *gestes* imitate; *voix* disguise
contre-nature unnatural

contrepartie *f* compensation; ***en ~*** in return
contre-plaqué *m* plywood
contrer counter
contresens *m* misinterpretation; ***prendre une route à ~*** go down a road the wrong way
contretemps *m* hitch
contribuable *m* taxpayer; **contribuer** contribute (***à*** to); ***~ à faire*** help to do
contrôle *m* (*vérification*) check; (*domination*) control; (*maîtrise de soi*) self-control; ***~ douanier*** customs inspection; ***~ radar*** radar speed check; **contrôler** *identité, billets etc* check; (*maîtriser, dominer*) control; ***se ~*** control o.s.
controversé controversial
contusion *f* MÉD bruise
convaincre (*persuader*) convince; ***~ qn de faire qch*** persuade s.o. to do sth
convalescent, **~e** *m/f* convalescent
convenable suitable; (*correct*) *personne* respectable; *salaire* adequate; **convenance** *f*: ***les ~s*** the proprieties
convenir: ***~ à qn*** suit s.o.; ***~à qc*** be suitable for sth; ***~ de qc*** (*décider*) agree on sth; ***~ que*** (*reconnaître que*) admit that; ***comme convenu*** as agreed
convention *f* convention
converger converge
conversation *f* conversation; ***~ téléphonique*** telephone conversation, phonecall
conversion *f* conversion
convertir convert
conviction *f* conviction
convive *m/f* guest; **convivialité** *f* conviviality, friendliness; INFORM user-friendliness
convocation *f d'une assemblée* convening; JUR summons *sg*
convoi *m* convoy
convoquer *assemblée* convene; JUR summons; *candidat* notify; *employé, écolier* call in
convoyer MIL escort
convulsion *f* convulsion
coopération *f* cooperation; **coopérer** cooperate (***à*** in)
coordination *f* coordination
coordonnées *fpl* MATH coordinates *pl*; *de personne* contact details
copain *m* F pal
copie *f* copy; ÉDU paper; **copier** copy (***sur qn*** from s.o.)
copieux, **-euse** copious
copine *f* F pal
copropriétaire *m/f* co-owner, part owner
coq *m* rooster
coquelicot *m* BOT poppy
coquetier *m* eggcup
coquetterie *f* flirtatiousness; (*élégance*) stylishness
coquillage *m* shell; ***des ~s***

shellfish
coquille *f* shell; *erreur* misprint, typo
coquin, **~e** **1** *adj enfant* naughty **2** *m/f* rascal
corbeau *m* ZO crow
corbeille *f* basket; *au théâtre* circle
corbillard *m* hearse
corde *f* rope; MUS, *de tennis* string
cordialité *f* cordiality
cordon *m* cord; ***~ littoral*** offshore sand bar
cordonnier *m* shoe repairer
Corée: ***la ~*** Korea; **coréen**, **~ne** **1** *adj* Korean **2** *m langue* Korean; **Coréen**, **~ne** *m/f* Korean
corne *f* horn
cornée *f* cornea
corneille *f* crow
corner *m en football* corner
cornet *m sachet* (paper) cone; MUS cornet
cornichon *m* gherkin
corporation *f* body; HIST guild
corporel, **~le** *hygiène* personal; *châtiment* corporal; *art* body *atr*
corps *m* body; *mort aussi* corpse; MIL corps; ***prendre ~*** take shape
corpulence *f* stoutness, corpulence
correct correct; *tenue* suitable; F (*convenable*) acceptable, ok F
correcteur *m*: ***~ orthographique*** spellchecker
correction *f qualité* correctness; (*modification*) correction; (*punition*) beating
correspondance *f* correspondence; *de train etc* connection; **correspondre** correspond; *de salles* communicate; **~ à** *réalité* correspond with; *preuves* tally with; *idées* fit in with
corridor *m* corridor
corriger correct; *épreuve* proof-read; (*battre*) beat
corrompre corrupt; (*soudoyer*) bribe
corrosion *f* corrosion
corruption *f* corruption; (*pot-de-vin*) bribery
corsage *m* blouse
corse Corsican; **Corse** **1** *m/f* Corsican **2** *f* **la Corse** Corsica
corsé *vin* full-bodied; *sauce* spicy; *café* strong; *facture* stiff; *problème* tough
cortège *m* cortège; (*défilé*) procession
cortisone *f* cortisone
corvée *f* chore; MIL fatigue
cosmétique *m & adj* cosmetic
cosmopolite *m & adj* cosmopolitan
costaud F sturdy
costume *m* costume; *pour homme* suit
cote *f en Bourse* quotation; *d'un document* identification code

côte *f* ANAT rib; (*pente*) slope; *à la mer* coast; *viande* chop; **~ à ~** side by side
côté *m* side; ***à ~*** (*près*) nearby; ***à ~ de*** next to; ***de ~*** aside; ***de l'autre ~ de*** on the other side of; ***du ~ de*** in the direction of; ***sur le ~*** on one's/its side; ***mettre de ~*** put aside
côtelette *f* CUIS cutlet
cotisation *f* contribution; *à une organisation* subscription
coton *m* coton
côtoyer rub shoulders with; ***~ qc*** border sth
cottage *m* cottage
cou *m* neck
couchant 1 *m* west **2** *adj*: ***soleil m ~*** setting sun
couche *f* layer; *de peinture aussi* coat; *de bébé* diaper, *Br* nappy
coucher 1 *v/t* (*mettre au lit*) put to bed; (*héberger*) put up; (*étendre*) put *ou* lay down **2** *v/i* sleep; ***se ~*** go to bed; (*s'étendre*) lie down; *du soleil* set, go down **3** *m*: ***~ du soleil*** sunset
coucou *m* cuckoo; (*pendule*) cuckoo clock
coude *m* ANAT elbow; *d'une route* turn
coudre sew; *bouton* sew on; *plaie* sew up
couette *f* comforter, *Br* quilt
couler 1 *v/i* flow, run; *d'eau de bain* run; *d'un bateau* sink **2** *v/t liquide* pour; (*mouler*) cast; *bateau* sink
couleur *f* color, *Br* colour
coulisse *f*: ***~s*** THÉÂT wings; ***dans les ~s*** *fig* behind the scenes
couloir *m* passage, corridor; *d'un bus, avion* aisle
coup *m* blow; *dans jeu* move; ***boire un ~*** F have a drink; ***du ~*** and so; ***après ~*** after the event; ***tout d'un ~, tout à ~*** suddenly, all at once; **coup de couteau** stab; **coup de foudre**: ***ce fut le ~*** it was love at first sight; **coup de main**: ***donner un ~ à qn*** give s.o. a hand; **coup d'œil**: ***au premier ~*** at first glance; **coup de pied** kick; **coup de poing** punch; ***donner un ~ à*** punch; **coup de téléphone** (phone) call; **coup de soleil**: ***avoir un ~*** have sun stroke
coupable 1 *adj* guilty **2** *m/f* culprit, guilty party
coupe[1] *f de cheveux, d'une robe* cut
coupe[2] *f* (*verre*) glass; SP cup; *de fruits, glace* dish
coupe-ongles *m inv* nail clippers *pl*
couper 1 *v/t* cut; *morceau, eau* cut off; *robe, chemise* cut out; *vin* dilute; *animal* castrate **2** *v/i* cut; ***se ~*** cut o.s.; (*se trahir*) give o.s. away
couple *m* couple
coupon *m de tissu* remnant; COMM coupon; (*ticket*) ticket

coupure *f* cut; *de journal* cutting; (*billet de banque*) bill, *Br* note; **~ de courant** power outage, *Br* power cut
cour *f* court; ARCH courtyard; ***Cour internationale de justice*** International Court of Justice
courage *m* courage, bravery; **courageux, -euse** brave, courageous
couramment fluently
courant 1 *adj* current; *eau* running; *langage* everyday **2** *m* current (*aussi* ÉL); ***~ d'air*** draft, *Br* draught; ***être au ~ de qch*** know about sth
courbature *f* stiffness; ***avoir des ~s*** be stiff
courbe 1 *adj* curved **2** *f* curve; **courber** bend; ***se ~*** (*se baisser*) stoop, bend down
coureur *m* runner; *péj* skirt-chaser
courge *f* BOT squash, *Br* marrow
courgette *f* BOT zucchini, *Br* courgette
courir 1 *v/i* run (*aussi d'eau*); *d'un bruit* go around **2** *v/t* *risque, danger* run; ***~ les magasins*** go around the stores
couronne *f* crown; *de fleurs* wreath; **couronnement** *m* coronation
courrier *m* mail, *Br aussi* post; (*messager*) courier; ***~ électronique*** electronic mail, e-mail
courroie *f* belt
cours *m* course; ÉCON price; *de devises* rate; (*leçon*) lesson; *à l'université* class, *Br aussi* lecture; ***donner libre ~ à*** give free rein to; ***en ~ de route*** on the way
course *f à pied* running; SP race; *en taxi* ride; (*commission*) errand; ***~s*** (*achats*) shopping; ***faire des ~s*** go shopping
court[1] *m* (*aussi **~ de tennis***) (tennis) court
court[2] *adj* short; ***à ~ de*** short of
court-circuit *m* ÉL short circuit
courtier *m* broker
courtiser *femme* court
courtoisie *f* courtesy
cousin, ~e *m/f* cousin
coussin *m* cushion
coût *m* cost; **coûter 1** *v/t* cost; ***combien ça coûte?*** how much is it?, how much does it cost? **2** *v/i* cost; ***~ cher*** be expensive
couteau *m* knife
coûteux, -euse expensive, costly
coutume *f* custom; ***avoir ~ de faire*** be in the habit of doing
couture *f* sewing; *d'un vêtement, bas etc* seam
couvée clutch; *fig* brood
couvent *m* convent
couver 1 *v/t* hatch; *personne* pamper **2** *v/i d'un feu* smolder, *Br* smoulder; *d'une révolution* be brewing

couvercle *m* cover
couvert 1 *adj ciel* overcast; **~ de** covered with *ou* in **2** *m à table* place setting; **~s** flatware, *Br* cutlery; ***mettre le ~*** set the table; **couverture** *f* cover; *sur un lit* blanket
couvrir cover (**de** with *ou* in); **~ *qn*** *fig* (*protéger*) cover (up) for s.o.; ***se ~*** (*s'habiller*) cover o.s. up; *du ciel* cloud over
covoiturage *m* carpooling; ***faire du ~*** carpool
crabe *m* crab
cracher spit
crachin *m* drizzle
craie *f* chalk
craindre fear, be frightened of; ***~ de faire*** be afraid of doing; **~ *que* (*ne*)** (+ *subj*) be afraid that
crainte *f* fear; ***de ~ de*** for fear of
craintif, -ive timid
cramoisi crimson
crampe *f* MÉD cramp
crampon *m* crampon
cran *m* notch; ***il a du ~*** F he's got guts F
crâne *m* skull
crâner F (*pavaner*) show off
crapaud *m* zo toad
crapule *f* villain
craquelé cracked
craquement *m* crackle; **craquer** crack; *d'un parquet* creak; *de feuilles* crackle; *d'une couture* split; *d'une personne* (*s'effondrer*) crack up
crasse 1 *adj ignorance* crass **2** *f* dirt
cravate *f* necktie, *Br* tie
crayon *m* pencil; ***~ à bille*** ballpoint pen; ***~ de couleur*** crayon
créance *f* COMM debt; **créancier, -ère** *m/f* creditor
création *f* creation; *de mode, design* design; **créativité** *f* creativity
créature *f* creature
crèche *f* day nursery; *de Noël* crèche, *Br* crib
crédibilité *f* credibility; **crédit** *m* credit; (*prêt*) loan; (*influence*) influence; ***acheter à ~*** buy on credit; ***faire ~ à qn*** give s.o. credit
créditeur, -trice 1 *m/f* creditor **2** *adj solde* credit *atr*; ***être ~*** be in credit
crédule credulous
créer create; *institution* set up; COMM *produit* design
crématorium *m* crematorium
crème 1 *f* cream; ***~ anglaise*** custard; ***~ dépilatoire*** hair remover; ***~ solaire*** suntan cream **2** *m* coffee with milk, *Br* white coffee **3** *adj inv* cream
créneau *m* AUTO space; COMM niche
crêpe *f* CUIS pancake
crépiter crackle
crépu frizzy
crépuscule *m* twilight

crétin, **~e** *m/f* idiot, cretin
creuser hollow out; *trou* dig; *fig* look into
creux, **-euse 1** *adj* hollow; ***assiette** f **creuse*** soup plate **2** *adv*: ***sonner ~*** ring hollow **3** *m* hollow
crevaison *f* flat, *Br* puncture
crevant F (*épuisant*) exhausting; (*drôle*) hilarious
crevasser crack; ***se ~*** crack
crever 1 *v/t ballon* burst; *pneu* puncture **2** *v/i* burst; F (*mourir*) kick the bucket F; F AUTO have a flat *ou Br* puncture
crevette *f* shrimp
cri *m* shout, cry; ***c'est le dernier ~*** *fig* it's all the rage
cribler sieve; ***criblé de*** *fig* riddled with
cric *m* jack
crier 1 *v/i* shout; ***~ au scandale*** protest **2** *v/t* shout
crime *m* crime; (*assassinat*) murder; **criminel**, **~le 1** *adj* criminal **2** *m/f* criminal; (*assassin*) murderer
crinière *f* mane
criquet *m* zo cricket
crise *f* crisis; MÉD attack; ***~ cardiaque*** heart attack
crisper *muscles* tense; *visage* contort; *fig* F irritate; ***se ~*** tense up
crisser squeak
cristal *m* crystal
critère *m* criterion
critique 1 *adj* critical **2** *m* critic **3** *f* criticism; *d'un film etc* review; **critiquer** criticize; (*analyser*) look at critically
croc *m* (*dent*) fang; *de boucherie* hook
crochet *m* hook; *ouvrage* crochet; *d'une route* sharp turn; ***~s*** *en typographie* square brackets
crochu *nez* hooked
crocodile *m* crocodile
croire 1 *v/t* believe; (*penser*) think; ***~ qc de qn*** believe sth about s.o. **2** *v/i*: ***~ à qc*** believe in sth; ***~ en Dieu*** believe in God **3**: ***il se croit intelligent*** he thinks he's intelligent
croisade *f* crusade
croisement *m* crossing (*aussi* BIOL); *animal* cross; **croiser 1** *v/t* cross (*aussi* BIOL); ***~ qn dans la rue*** pass s.o. in the street **2** *v/i* MAR cruise; ***se ~*** *de routes* cross; *de personnes* meet
croisière *f* MAR cruise
croissance *f* growth
croissant *m de lune* crescent; CUIS croissant
croître grow
croix *f* cross; ***mettre une ~ sur qc*** *fig* give sth up
croquer 1 *v/t* crunch; (*dessiner*) sketch **2** *v/i* be crunchy
croquis *m* sketch
crotte *f* droppings *pl*
crouler collapse (*aussi fig*)
croupir stagnate (*aussi fig*)
croustillant crusty
croûte *f de pain* crust; *de fromage* rind; MÉD scab

croûton *m* crouton
croyance *f* belief; **croyant**, **~e** *m/f* REL believer
cru 1 *adj* raw; *lumière*, *verité* harsh; *paroles* blunt **2** *m* (*domaine*) vineyard; *de vin* wine
cruauté *f* cruelty
cruche *f* pitcher
crucial crucial
crucifier crucify; **crucifix** *m* crucifix
crudité *f* crudeness; *de paroles* bluntness; *de lumière* harshness; *de couleur* garishness; **~s** CUIS raw vegetables
cruel, **~le** cruel
crustacés *mpl* shellfish *pl*
Cuba *f* Cuba; **cubain**, **~e** Cuban; **Cubain**, **~e** *m/f* Cuban
cube MATH **1** *m* cube **2** *adj* cubic; **cubisme** *m* ART cubism
cueillir pick
cuiller, cuillère *f* spoon; **cuillerée** *f* spoonful
cuir *m* leather; **~ *chevelu*** scalp
cuirasse *f* armor, *Br* armour
cuire cook; *au four* bake; *rôti* roast
cuisine *f* cooking; *pièce* kitchen; ***la ~ italienne*** Italian cooking *ou* cuisine; **cuisiner** cook; **cuisinière** *f* cook; (*fourneau*) stove
cuisse *f* ANAT thigh; CUIS *de poulet* leg
cuisson *f* cooking; *du pain* baking; *d'un rôti* roasting
cuit cooked, done; *rôti*, *pain* done
cuivre *m* copper; **~ *jaune*** brass; **~s** brasses
cul *m* V ass P, *Br* arse P
cul-de-sac *m* blind alley; *fig* dead end
culminer *fig* peak
culotte *f* short pants *pl*, *Br* short trousers *pl*; *de femme* panties *pl*
culpabilité *f* guilt, culpability
culte *m* worship; (*religion*) religion; (*service*) church service; *fig* cult
cultivateur, **-trice** *m/f* farmer; **cultiver** cultivate (*aussi fig*); *légumes*, *tabac* grow; ***se ~*** improve one's mind
culture *f* culture; AGR cultivation; *de légumes*, *fruits etc* growing
culturel, **~le** cultural
cumuler: **~ *des fonctions*** have more than one position
cupidité *f* greed, cupidity
cure *f* MÉD course of treatment; **~ *de repos*** rest cure
curé *m* curate
cure-dent *m* tooth pick
curiosité *f* curiosity; *objet rare* curio
curry *m* curry
curseur *m* INFORM cursor
cuvée *f de vin* vatful; *vin* wine, vintage; **cuver 1** *v/i* mature **2** *v/t*: **~ *son vin*** *fig* sleep it off
cuvette *f* (*bac*) basin; *de cabinet* bowl
CV *m* (= ***curriculum vitae***) ré-

sumé, *Br* CV (= curriculum vitae)
cybercafé *m* Internet café
cycle *m* cycle; **cyclisme** *m* cycling; **cycliste** *m/f* cyclist
cyclone *m* cyclone
cygne *m* swan
cylindre *m* cylinder
cynique 1 *adj* cynical **2** *m/f* cynic
cystite *f* MÉD cystitis

D

dactylo *f* typing; *personne* typist
daigner: ***~ faire qch*** deign to do sth
daim *m* zo deer; *peau* suede
dalle *f* flagstone
daltonien, **~ne** colorblind, *Br* colourblind
dame *f* lady; *aux échecs*, *cartes* queen; ***jeu m de ~s*** checkers *sg*, *Br* draughts *sg*
damner damn
Danemark: ***le ~*** Denmark
danger *m* danger; ***courir un ~*** be in danger
dangereux, **-euse** dangerous
danois, **~e 1** *adj* Danish **2** *m langue* Danish; **Danois**, **~e** *m/f* Dane
dans in; ***boire ~ un verre*** drink from a glass
danse *f* dance; *action* dancing; ***~ folklorique*** folk dance; **danser** dance; **danseur**, **-euse** *m/f* dancer
dard *m d'une abeille* sting
date *f* date; ***de longue ~*** *amitié* long-standing; ***~ limite*** deadline; ***~ limite de conservation*** use-by date; **dater 1** *v/t* date **2** *v/i* ***~ de*** date from; ***à ~ de ce jour*** from today
datte *f* date
davantage more
de 1 *prép origine* from; *possession* of; ***il vient ~ Paris*** he comes from Paris ***la maison ~ mon père*** my father's house; ***un film ~ Godard*** a movie by Godard; ***~ jour*** by day; ***trembler ~ peur*** shake with fear; ***cesser ~ travailler*** stop working **2** *partitif*: ***du pain*** (some) bread; ***des petits pains*** (some) rolls; ***je n'ai pas d'argent*** I don't have any money, I have no money; ***est-ce qu'il y a des disquettes?*** are there any diskettes?
dé *m jeu* dice; ***~ (à coudre)*** thimble
dealer *m* dealer
déambuler stroll
débâcle *f de troupes* rout; *d'une entreprise* collapse
déballer unpack
débandade *f* stampede
débarbouiller: ***~ un enfant***

wash a child's face
débardeur *m vêtement* tank top
débarquement *m de marchandises* unloading; *de passagers* landing, disembarkation; **débarquer 1** *v/t marchandises* unload; *passagers* land, disembark **2** *v/i* land, disembark; ~ ***chez qn*** *fig* F turn up at s.o.'s place
débarrasser *table etc* clear; ~ ***qn de qc*** take sth off s.o.; ***se ~ de*** get rid of
débat *m* debate; (*polémique*) argument
débattre: ~ ***qc*** discuss *ou* debate sth; ***se ~*** struggle
débauche *f* debauchery; **débaucher** (*licencier*) lay off; F lead astray
débile 1 *adj* weak; F idiotic **2** *m*: ~ ***mental*** mental defective
débit *m* (*vente*) sale; *d'un stock* turnover; *d'une usine* output; (*élocution*) delivery; FIN debit; **débiter** *marchandises* sell (retail); *péj*: *fadaises* talk; *texte étudié* deliver, *péj* recite; *d'une pompe* deliver; *d'une usine, de produits* output; *bois, viande* cut up; FIN debit (***de*** with); **débiteur, -trice 1** *m/f* debtor **2** *adj compte* overdrawn; *solde* debit
déblayer *endroit* clear; *débris* clear (away)
débloquer 1 *v/t* TECH release; *prix, compte* unfreeze; *fonds* release **2** *v/i* F be crazy; ***se ~*** *d'une situation* get sorted out
déboguer debug
déboires *mpl* disappointments
déboisement *m* deforestation
déboîter 1 *v/t* MÉD dislocate **2** *v/i* AUTO pull out; ***se ~ l'épaule*** dislocate one's shoulder
débonnaire kindly
débordé snowed under (***de*** with); ~ ***par les événements*** overwhelmed by events; **déborder** *d'une rivière* overflow its banks; *du lait, de l'eau* overflow
débouché *m d'une vallée* entrance; COMM outlet; **~*s*** *d'une profession* prospects; **déboucher 1** *v/t tuyau* unblock; *bouteille* uncork **2** *v/i*: ~ ***de*** emerge from; ~ ***sur*** lead to (*aussi fig*)
débourser (*dépenser*) spend
debout standing; *objet* upright, on end; ***être ~*** stand; (*levé*) be up, be out of bed; ***se mettre ~*** stand up, get up
déboutonner unbutton
débraillé untidy
débrancher ÉL unplug
débrayer AUTO declutch; *fig* down tools
débris *mpl* debris *sg*; *fig* remains

débrouillard resourceful; **débrouiller** disentangle; *fig*: *affaire* clear up; ***se ~*** cope
début *m* beginning, start; **~s** THÉÂT, POL debut; **débutant, ~e** *m/f* beginner
décacheter *lettre* open
décadent decadent
décaféiné: ***café*** *m* **~** decaffeinated coffee, decaff F
décalage *m dans l'espace* moving; (*différence*) difference; *fig* gap; **décaler** *rendez-vous* change the time of; *dans l'espace* move
décamper F clear out
décaper *surface* clean; *meuble vernis* strip
décapiter decapitate
décapotable *f* (***voiture*** *f*) **~** convertible
décapsuleur *m* bottle opener
décarcasser: ***se ~*** F bust a gut F
décéder die
déceler (*découvrir*) detect; (*montrer*) point to
décembre *m* December
décemment decently; (*raisonnablement*) reasonably
décennie *f* decade
décent decent,
décentralisation *f* decentralization
déception *f* disappointment
décerner *prix* award
décès *m* death
décevoir disappoint
déchaîner *fig* provoke; ***se ~*** *d'une tempête* break; *d'une personne* fly into a rage
décharge *f* JUR acquittal; *dans fusillade* discharge; **~ *électrique*** electric shock; **décharger** unload; *batterie* discharge; *arme* fire; *accusé* acquit; *colère* vent (***contre*** on); **~ *qn de qch*** relieve s.o. of sth
décharné skeletal
déchausser: ***se ~*** take one's shoes off
déchéance *f* decline; JUR forfeiture
déchets *mpl* waste
déchiffrer decipher
déchiqueté *côte* jagged; **déchiqueter** *corps*, *papier* tear to pieces
déchirant heart-breaking; **déchirer** *tissu* tear; *papier* tear up; *fig*: *silence* pierce; ***se ~*** *d'une robe* tear; ***se ~ un muscle*** tear a muscle
décidé (*résolu*) determined (***à faire qc*** to do sth); **décidément** really; **décider 1** *v/t* decide on; *question* settle, decide; **~ *qn à faire qc*** convince s.o. to do sth; **~ *de faire qch*** decide to do sth **2** *v/i* decide; ***se ~*** make one's mind up, decide (***à faire qch*** to do sth)
décimal decimal
décimer decimate
décimètre *m*: ***double ~*** ruler
décisif, -ive decisive; **décision** *f* decision; (*fermeté*)

determination
déclaration *f* declaration, statement; *d'une naissance* registration; *de vol, perte* report; **déclarer** declare; *naissance* register; **se ~** declare o.s.; *en amour* declare one's love; *d'un feu, d'une épidémie* break out
déclencher trigger; **se ~** be triggered
déclic *m bruit* click
déclin *m* decline
décliner 1 *v/i du soleil* go down; *du jour, des forces, du prestige* wane; *de la santé* decline **2** *v/t offre* decline
décoder decode; **décodeur** *m* decoder
décoiffer *cheveux* ruffle
décollage *m* AVIAT take-off; **décoller 1** *v/t* peel off **2** *v/i* AVIAT take off; **se ~** peel off
décolleté 1 *adj robe* low-cut **2** *m* neckline
décolorer *tissu, cheveux* bleach; **se ~** fade
décombres *mpl* rubble
décommander cancel; **se ~** cancel
décomposer *produit* break down (**en** into); CHIM decompose; **se ~** *d'un cadavre* decompose; *d'un visage* become contorted
décompresser F unwind, chill out F
décompte *m* deduction; *d'une facture* breakdown
déconcentrer: **~ qn** make it hard for s.o. to concentrate
déconcertant disconcerting
déconfit disheartened
déconfiture *f* collapse
décongeler *aliment* thaw out
décongestionner *route* decongest; *nez* clear
déconnecter unplug, disconnect; **se ~** INFORM log off, log out
déconner P *actions* fool around; *paroles* talk crap P
déconseiller advise against
décontenancer disconcert
décontracter relax; **se ~** relax
décor *m* decor; *fig* (*cadre*) setting; **~s** *de théâtre* sets, scenery; **décorateur, -trice** *m/f* decorator; THÉÂT set designer; **décorer** decorate (**de** with)
découler: **~ de** arise from
découper cut up; *photo* cut out (**dans** from); **se ~ sur** *fig* stand out against
décourager discourage (**de faire qc** from doing sth); **se ~** lose heart, become discouraged
découvert, **~e 1** *adj tête, épaules* bare, uncovered; **à ~** FIN overdrawn **2** *m* overdraft **3** *f* discovery; **découvrir** uncover; (*trouver*) discover; *ses intentions* reveal; (*comprendre*) find (**que** that); **se ~** *d'une personne* take off a couple of layers; (*enlever son chapeau*) take

off one's hat; *du ciel* clear
décret *m* decree
décrire describe; **~ *une orbite autour de*** orbit
décrocher *tableau* take down; *fig* F *prix, bonne situation* land F; **~ *le téléphone*** pick up the receiver; *pour ne pas être dérangé* take the phone off the hook
décroître decrease, decline
déçu disappointed
décupler increase tenfold
dédaigner 1 *v/t* scorn; *personne* treat with scorn **2** *v/i*: **~ *de faire qch*** disdain to do sth; **dédaigneux, -euse** disdainful; **dédain** *m* disdain
dedans inside
dédicace *f* dedication; **dédier** dedicate
dédommager compensate (***de*** for)
dédouanement *m* customs clearance; **dédouaner**: **~ *qch*** clear sth through customs; **~ *qn*** *fig* clear s.o.
dédoublement *m*: **~ *de personnalité*** split personality; **dédoubler** split in two; ***se* ~** split
dédramatiser play down, downplay
déduction *f* deduction; **déduire** COMM deduct; (*conclure*) deduce (***de*** from)
déesse *f* goddess
défaillance *f* weakness; *fig* shortcoming; *technique* failure; **défaillir** weaken; (*se trouver mal*) feel faint
défaire undo; (*démonter*) take down, dismantle; *valise* unpack; ***se* ~** come undone; ***se* ~ *de qn/qc*** get rid of s.o./sth; **défait** *visage* drawn; *chemise, valise* undone; *armée, personne* defeated; **défaite** *f* defeat; **défaitisme** *m* defeatism
défaut *m* (*imperfection*) defect; *morale* shortcoming, failing; (*manque*) lack; JUR default; ***faire* ~** be lacking; ***par* ~** INFORM default *atr*
défavorable unfavorable, *Br* unfavourable; **défavorisé** disadvantaged; ***les milieux* ~*s*** the underprivileged classes
défectueux, -euse defective
défendre defend; **~ *à qn de faire qc*** forbid s.o. to do sth
défense *f* defense, *Br* defence *f*; *d'un éléphant* tusk; **~ *de fumer*** no smoking; **défenseur** *m* defender; *d'une cause* supporter; JUR defense attorney, *Br* counsel for the defence; **défensif, -ive** *adj & f* defensive
déférent deferential; **déférer**: **~ *qn à la justice*** prosecute s.o.
défi *m* challenge; (*bravade*) defiance
défiance *f* distrust, mistrust
déficience *f* deficiency; **~ *immunitaire*** immune deficien-

cy

déficit *m* deficit; **déficitaire** *balance* showing a deficit; *compte* in debit

défier (*provoquer*) challenge; (*braver*) defy; **~ qn de faire qch** dare s.o. to do sth

défigurer disfigure; *fig*: *réalité* misrepresent

défilé *m* parade; GÉOGR pass; **~ de mode** fashion show; **défiler** parade, march

défini definite; **bien ~** well defined; **définir** define; **définitif, -ive** definitive; **en définitive** in the end; **définition** definition; **définitivement** definitely; (*pour de bon*) for good

déflagration *f* explosion

défoncer *voiture* smash up, total; *porte* break down; *terrain* break up

déformer deform; *chaussures* stretch (out of shape); *visage, fait* distort; *idée* misrepresent; **se ~** *de chaussures* lose their shape

défouler: **se ~** give vent to one's feelings

défroisser *vêtement* crumple

défunt, ~e 1 *adj* late **2** *m/f*: **le ~** the deceased

dégagement *m d'une route* clearing; *de chaleur* release; **dégager** (*délivrer*) free; *route* clear; *odeur, chaleur* give off; **se ~** free o.s.; *d'une route, du ciel* clear

dégât *m* damage; **~s** damage

dégel *m* thaw (*aussi* POL)

dégeler 1 *v/t frigidaire* defrost; *crédits* unfreeze **2** *v/i d'un lac* thaw

dégénérer degenerate (**en** into)

dégivrer defrost; TECH de-ice

déglutir swallow

dégonfler let the air out of, deflate; **se ~** deflate; *fig* F lose one's nerve

dégourdi resourceful; **dégourdir** *membres* loosen up; **se ~ les jambes** stretch one's legs

dégoût *m* disgust; **dégoûtant** disgusting; **dégoûter** disgust; **~ qn de qc** put s.o. off sth; **se ~ de qc** take a dislike to sth

dégrader MIL demote; *édifice* damage; (*avilir*) degrade; **se ~** deteriorate; *d'un édifice* fall into disrepair

degré *m* degree; (*échelon*) level

dégressif, -ive *tarif* tapering

dégringoler fall

dégriser sober up

déguerpir clear off

dégueulasse P disgusting; **dégueuler** F vomit

déguisement *m* disguise; *pour bal masqué etc* costume; **déguiser** disguise; *enfant* dress up (**en** as); **se ~** disguise o.s.; *pour bal masqué etc* dress up

dégustation *f* tasting; **déguster** taste

dehors 1 *adv* outside 2 *prép*: ***en ~ de*** outside 3 *m* exterior
déjà already; ***c'est qui déjà?*** F who's he again?
déjeuner 1 *v/i midi* (have) lunch; *matin* (have) breakfast 2 *m* lunch; ***petit ~*** breakfast
déjouer thwart
DEL *f* (= ***diode électroluminescente***) LED (= light-emitting diode)
délabré dilapidated
délacer loosen, unlace
délai *m* (*temps imparti*) time allowed; (*date limite*) deadline; (*prolongation*) extension; ***sans ~*** without delay
délaisser (*abandonner*) leave; (*négliger*) neglect
délassement *m* relaxation; **délasser** relax; ***se ~*** relax
délateur, -trice *m/f* informer; **délation** *f* denunciation
délayer dilute, water down; *fig*: *discours* pad out
délecter: ***se ~ de*** take delight in
délégué, ~e *m/f* delegate; **déléguer** delegate
délibération *f* deliberation; (*décision*) resolution; **délibéré** deliberate; **délibérer** deliberate
délicat delicate; *problème* tricky; (*plein de tact*) tactful; **délicatesse** *f* delicacy; (*tact*) tact; **délicatement** delicately
délicieux, -euse delicious
délier loosen, untie; ***~ la langue à qn*** loosen s.o.'s tongue
délimiter define
délinquance *f* crime, delinquency
délire *m* delirium; *enthousiasme* frenzy; ***foule en ~*** ecstatic crowd; **délirer** be delirious; F *être fou* be stark raving mad
délit *m* offense, *Br* offence; ***commettre un ~ de fuite*** leave the scene of an accident
délivrance *f* release; (*soulagement*) relief; (*livraison*) delivery; *certificat* issue
délivrer release; (*livrer*) deliver; *certificat* issue
délocaliser relocate
déloyal disloyal; ***concurrence f ~e*** unfair competition
deltaplane *m* hang-glider; ***faire du ~*** go hang-gliding
déluge *m* flood
demain tomorrow; ***à ~!*** see you tomorrow!
demande *f* (*requête*) request; *écrite* application; ÉCON demand; ***sur** ou **à la ~ de*** at the request of; **demandé** popular, in demand; **demander** ask for; *somme d'argent* ask; (*nécessiter*) call for; ***~ qch à qn*** ask s.o. for sth; (*vouloir savoir*) ask s.o. sth; ***~ à qn de faire qc*** ask s.o. to do sth; ***se ~ si*** wonder if

démanger: ***le dos me démange*** my back itches; ***ça me démange depuis longtemps*** I've been itching to do it for ages
démanteler dismantle
démaquillant *m* cleanser; ***lait*** *m* **~** cleansing milk; **démaquiller**: **se ~** take off one's make-up
démarcation *f* demarcation
démarchage *m* selling
démarche *f* step (*aussi fig*); ***faire des ~s*** take steps
démarquer: **se ~** stand out (**de** from)
démarrage *m* start; **démarrer** start (up)
démasquer unmask
démêlé *m* argument; ***avoir des ~s avec la justice*** have problems with the law; **démêler** disentangle; *fig* clear up
déménager move; **déménageurs** *mpl* movers, removal men
démence *f* dementia; **dément** demented; ***c'est ~*** *fig* F it's unbelievable
démener: **se ~** struggle; (*s'efforcer*) make an effort
démenti *m* denial
démentir (*nier*) deny; (*infirmer*) belie
démerder: **se ~** F manage, sort things out
démesuré enormous; *orgueil* excessive
démettre *poignet* dislocate; ***se ~ de ses fonctions*** resign one's office
demeure *f* residence; **demeurer** (*habiter*) live; (*rester*) stay, remain; **demeuré** retarded
demi 1 *adj* half; ***une heure et ~e*** an hour and a half; ***il est quatre heures et ~e*** it's four thirty, it's half past four **2** *adv* half; **à ~** half **3** *m* half; *bière* half a pint; *en football, rugby* halfback
demi-cercle *m* semi-circle
demi-finale *f* semi-final
demi-frère *m* half-brother
demi-heure *f* half-hour
démilitariser demilitarize
demi-litre *m* half liter *ou Br* litre
demi-mot: ***il nous l'a dit à ~*** he hinted at it to us
demi-pension *f* American plan, *Br* half board
demi-pression *f* half-pint of draft *ou Br* draught beer
demi-sel *m* slightly salted butter
demi-sœur *f* half-sister
démission *f* resignation; *fig* renunciation; **démissionner 1** *v/i* resign; *fig* give up **2** *v/t* sack
demi-tarif *m* half price
demi-tour *m* AUTO U-turn; ***faire ~*** *fig* turn back
démocrate democrat; **démocratie** *f* democracy
démodé old-fashioned
démographique demo-

graphic; ***poussée*** *f* ~ population growth
demoiselle *f* (*jeune fille*) young lady; ~ ***d'honneur*** bridesmaid
démolir demolish (*aussi fig*); **démolition** *f* demolition
démon *m* demon
démonstration *f* demonstration
démonter dismantle; *fig* disconcert
démontrer demonstrate, prove; (*faire ressortir*) show
démoraliser demoralize
démordre: ***il n'en démordra pas*** he won't change his mind
démotiver demotivate
démuni penniless
dénaturer distort
dénicher find
dénier deny
dénigrer denigrate
dénivellation *f* difference in height
dénombrer count
dénomination *f* name
dénoncer denounce; *à la police* report; *contrat* terminate; ***se ~ à la police*** give o.s. up to the police; **dénonciateur, -trice** *m/f* informer; **dénonciation** *f* denunciation
dénoter indicate, denote
dénouement *m* ending; **dénouer** loosen; ***se*** ~ *fig d'une scène* end; *d'un mystère* be cleared up
denrée *f*: ***~s*** (***alimentaires***) foodstuffs
dense dense; **densité** *f* density; *du brouillard, d'une forêt* denseness
dent *f* tooth; ***j'ai mal aux ~s*** I've got toothache; ***avoir une ~ contre qn*** have a grudge against s.o.; **dentaire** dental
dentelle *f* lace
dentier *m* false teeth *pl*; **dentifrice** *m* toothpaste; **dentiste** *m/f* dentist
dénuder strip
denué: ***~ de qc*** devoid of sth; ***~ de tout*** deprived of everything; **denuement** *m* destitution
déodorant *m* deodorant
dépannage *m* AUTO *etc* repairs *pl*; (*remorquage*) recovery; **dépanner** repair; (*remorquer*) recover; ***~ qn*** *fig* F help s.o. out; **dépanneur** *m* repairman; *pour voitures* mechanic; **dépanneuse** *f* wrecker, *Br* tow truck
départ *m* departure; SP, *fig* start; ***au ~*** at first
départager decide between
départemental departmental; ***route ~e*** secondary road
dépassé out of date, old-fashioned; **dépasser** *personne* pass; AUTO pass, *Br* overtake; *but etc* overshoot; *fig* exceed; ***se ~*** surpass o.s.
dépaysement *m* disorienta-

tion; *changement agréable* change of scene

dépêcher dispatch; ***se ~ de faire qch*** hurry to do sth; ***dépêche-toi!*** hurry up!

dépendance *f* dependence; ***~s*** *bâtiments* outbuildings; ***entraîner une (forte) ~*** be (highly) addictive; **dépendre**: ***~ de*** depend on; *moralement* be dependent on

dépens *mpl*: ***aux ~ de*** at the expense of

dépense *f* expenditure; *d'essence, d'électricité* consumption, use; **dépenser** spend; *son énergie, ses forces* use up; *essence* consume, use; ***se ~*** exert o.s., be physically active; **dépensier, -ère 1** *adj* extravagant **2** *m/f* spendthrift

dépérir waste away; *fig d'une entreprise* go downhill

dépeuplement *m* depopulation

dépilatoire: ***crème f ~*** hair remover, depilatory cream

dépistage *m d'un criminel* tracking down; MÉD screening

dépit *m* spite; ***en ~ de*** in spite of

dépité crestfallen

déplacé out of place; (*inconvenant*) uncalled for; POL displaced; **déplacer** move; *personnel* transfer; *problème* shift the focus of; ***se ~*** move; (*voyager*) travel

déplaire: ***~ à qn*** (*fâcher*) offend s.o.; ***cela lui déplaît de faire ...*** he dislikes doing ...

déplaisant unpleasant

dépliant *m* leaflet; **déplier** unfold

déploiement *m* MIL deployment; *de forces, courage* display

déplorable deplorable

déporter POL deport; ***se ~*** *d'un véhicule* swing

déposer 1 *v/t* put down; *armes* lay down; *passager* drop; *roi* depose; *argent, boue* deposit; *projet de loi* table; *ordures* dump; *plainte* lodge **2** *v/i d'un liquide* settle; JUR testify; ***se ~*** *de la boue* settle; **dépôt** *m* deposit; *chez le notaire* lodging; *d'un projet de loi* tabling; *des ordures* dumping; (*entrepôt*) depot

dépouiller *animal* skin; (*voler*) rob (**de** of); (*examiner*) go through; ***~ le scrutin*** *ou* ***les votes*** count the votes

dépourvu: ***~ de*** devoid of; ***prendre qn au ~*** take s.o. by surprise

dépoussiérer dust; *fig* modernize

dépraver deprave

déprécier *chose* decrease the value of; *personne* belittle; ***se ~*** depreciate, lose value; *d'une personne* belittle o.s.

dépression *f* depression; ***fai-***

re une ~ be depressed
déprime *f* depression; **déprimer** depress
dépuceler deflower
depuis 1 *prép* since; *espace* from; ***j'attends ~ une heure*** I have been waiting for an hour; ***~ quand permettent-ils que ...?*** since when do they allow ...? **2** *adv* since **3** *conj*: ***~ que*** since
député *m* POL MP, Member of Parliament; ***~ européen*** *m* Euro MP
déraciner uproot; (*extirper*) root out, eradicate
dérailler go off the rails; *fig* F: *d'un mécanisme* go on the blink; (*déraisonner*) talk nonsense; **dérailleur** *m d'un vélo* derailleur
déraisonnable unreasonable
dérangement *m* disturbance; **déranger** disturb
déraper AUTO skid
déréglé *vie* wild
déréglementer deregulate
dérégler *mécanisme* upset
dérision *f* derision; ***tourner en ~*** deride
dérisoire derisory, laughable
dérivatif *m* diversion; **dériver 1** *v/t* MATH derive; *cours d'eau* divert **2** *v/i* MAR, AVIAT drift; ***~ de*** *d'un mot* be derived from
dermatologue *m/f* dermatologist
dernier, -ère last; (*le plus récent*) *mode, roman etc* latest; *extrême* utmost; ***ce ~*** the latter; **dernièrement** recently, lately
dérobée: ***à la ~*** furtively; **dérober** steal; ***~ qch à qn*** rob s.o. of sth, steal sth from s.o.; ***se ~ à*** *discussion* shy away from; *obligations* shirk
déroger JUR: ***~ à*** make an exception to, depart from
déroulement *m* unfolding; ***le ~ du projet*** the running of the project; **dérouler** unroll; *bobine, câble* unwind; ***se ~*** take place; *d'une cérémonie* go (off)
dérouter (*déconcerter*) disconcert
derrière 1 *adv* behind **2** *prép* behind **3** *m* back; ANAT bottom; ***de ~*** *patte etc* back *atr*
dès from, since; ***~ lors*** from then on; (*par conséquent*) consequently; ***~ lundi*** as of Monday; ***~ que*** as soon as
désabuser disillusion
désaccord *m* disagreement
désaffecté disused; *église* deconsecrated
désagréable unpleasant, disagreeable
désappointement *m* disappointment
désapprobateur, -trice disapproving
désapprouver disapprove of
désarmement *m* MIL disarmament; **désarmer** disarm (*aussi fig*)
désarroi *m* disarray

désastre *m* disaster
désavantage *m* disadvantage; **désavantager** put at a disadvantage
désaveu *m* disowning; *d'un propos* retraction; **désavouer** disown; *propos* retract
descendance *f* descendants *pl*; **descendant**, **~e** *m/f* descendant
descendre 1 *v/i* go/come down; *d'un bus* get off; *d'une voiture* get out; *de température*, *prix* go down; *d'un chemin* drop; AVIAT descend; **~ chez qn** stay with s.o.; **~ de qn** be descended from s.o. **2** *v/t* (*porter vers le bas*) bring down; (*emporter*) take down; *passager* drop off; F (*abattre*) shoot down; *vallée*, *rivière* descend; **~ les escaliers** come/go downstairs; **descente** *f* descent; (*pente*) slope; *en parachute* jump; **~ de lit** bedside rug
description *f* description
désemparé at a loss
déséquilibré PSYCH unbalanced
désert 1 *adj* deserted; **une île ~e** a desert island **2** *m* desert; **déserter** desert; **déserteur** *m* MIL deserter
désertification *f* desertification
désertion *f* desertion
désespérant depressing
désespérer 1 *v/t* drive to despair **2** *v/i* despair
désespoir *m* despair; **en ~ de cause** in desperation
déshabillé *m* negligee; **déshabiller** undress; **se ~** get undressed
déshériter disinherit
déshonorer disgrace, bring dishonor *ou Br* dishonour on
déshydraté *aliments* dessicated; *personne* dehydrated; **déshydrater**: **se ~** become dehydrated
design *m*: **~ d'intérieurs** interior design
désigner (*montrer*) point to, point out; (*appeler*) call; (*nommer*) appoint (**pour** to), designate
désillusion *f* disillusionment
désinfectant *m* disinfectant
désintéressé disinterested, impartial; (*altruiste*) selfless; **désintéresser**: **se ~ de** lose interest in
désintoxication *f*: **faire une cure de ~** go into detox
désinvolture *f* casualness
désir *m* desire; (*souhait*) wish
désirer want; *sexuellement* desire; **~ faire qch** want to do sth; **désireux**, **-euse** eager (**de faire** to do)
désister POL: **se ~** withdraw, stand down
désobéir disobey; **~ à** disobey; **désobéissant** disobedient

désobligeant disagreeable
désodorisant *m* deodorant
désolé upset (**de** about, over); ***je suis ~*** I am so sorry
désopilant hilarious
désordre *m* untidiness; ***en ~*** untidy
désorganisé disorganized
désormais now; *à partir de maintenant* from now on
désosser remove the bones from
despote *m* despot; **despotique** despotic
dessécher dry out; *de fruits* dry
dessein *m* intention; ***à ~*** intentionally; ***dans le ~ de faire qc*** with the intention of doing sth
desserrer loosen
dessert *m* dessert
desservir *des transport publics* serve; (*s'arrêter à*) stop at; *table* clear; ***~ qn*** do s.o. a disservice
dessin *m* drawing; (*motif*) design; **dessiner** draw
dessoûler F sober up
dessous 1 *adv* underneath; ***en ~*** underneath **2** *m* underside; ***ci-~*** below; ***les voisins du ~*** the downstairs neighbors
dessous-de-plat m inv table mat
dessus 1 *adv* on top; ***sens ~ dessous*** upside down; ***en ~*** on top; ***par-~*** over; ***ci-~*** above **2** *m* top; ***les voisins du ~*** the upstairs neighbors; ***avoir le ~*** *fig* have the upper hand; **dessus-de-lit** *m inv* bedspread
déstabilisant unnerving; **déstabiliser** destabilize
destin *m* destiny, fate
destinataire *m* addressee; **destination** *f* destination; **destinée** *f* destiny; **destiner** mean, intend (**à** for)
destituer dismiss; MIL discharge
destructeur, **-trice** destructive; **destruction** *f* destruction
désuet, **-ète** obsolete; *mode* out of date
détachable detachable; **détacher** detach; *ceinture* undo; *chien* release; *employé* second; (*nettoyer*) clean; ***se ~ sur*** stand out against
détail *m* detail; COMM retail trade; ***vendre au ~*** sell retail; ***prix m de ~*** retail price; ***en ~*** detailed
détaillant *m* retailer
détartrage *m* descaling
détecteur *m* sensor
détective *m* detective
déteindre fade; ***~ sur*** come off on; *fig* rub off on
détendre slacken; ***se ~*** *d'une corde* slacken; *fig* relax
détenir hold; JUR detain, hold
détente *f d'une arme* trigger; *fig* relaxation; POL détente
détention *f* holding; JUR detention

détenu, **~e** *m/f* inmate
détergent *m* detergent
détériorer damage; **se ~** deteriorate
déterminant decisive; **déterminer** establish, determine
déterrer dig up
détester detest, hate
détonation *f* detonation
détour *m* detour; *d'un chemin, fleuve* bend; ***sans ~*** *fig: dire qch* straight out
détourné *fig* indirect; **détourner** *trafic* divert; *avion* hijack; *tête, yeux* turn away; *de l'argent* embezzle; ***se ~*** turn away
détresse *f* distress
détriment *m*: ***au ~ de*** to the detriment of
détritus *m* garbage, *Br* rubbish
détroit *m* strait
détromper put right
détruire destroy; (*tuer*) kill
dette *f* debt
deuil *m* mourning; ***il y a eu un ~ dans sa famille*** there's been a bereavement in his family
deux 1 *adj* two; ***les ~*** both; ***nous ~*** the two of us, both of us; ***~ fois*** twice **2** *m* two; ***en ~*** in two, in half; ***~ à*** *ou* ***par ~*** in twos, two by two;
deuxième second; *étage* third, *Br* second; **deux-pièces** *m inv bikini* two-piece swimsuit; *appartement* two-room apartment; **deux-points** *m inv* colon
dévaliser *banque* rob, raid; *maison* burglarize, *Br* burgle; *personne* rob; *fig: frigo* raid
dévalorisant demeaning; **dévalorisation** *f* drop in value; *fig* belittlement; **dévaloriser** devalue; *fig* belittle
dévaluation *f* devaluation; **dévaluer** devalue
devancer be ahead of; *désir, objection* anticipate
devant 1 *adv* in front; ***droit ~*** straight ahead **2** *prép* in front of; ***passer ~ l'église*** go past the church; ***~ Dieu*** before God **3** *m* front
devanture *f* shop window
dévaster devastate
développement *m* development; **développer** develop; ***se ~*** develop
devenir become; ***il devient vieux*** he's getting old; ***que va-t-il ~?*** what's going to become of him?
dévergondé *sexuellement* promiscuous
déverser *ordures* dump; *passagers* disgorge
dévêtir undress
déviation *f d'une route* detour; (*écart*) deviation
dévier 1 *v/t* divert, reroute **2** *v/i* deviate (**de** from)
deviner guess
devis *m* estimate
dévisager stare at
devise *f* FIN currency; (*moto,*

règle de vie) motto; ***~s étrangères*** foreign currency
dévisser unscrew
dévoiler unveil; *secret* reveal, disclose
devoir 1 *v/t de l'argent* owe **2** *v/aux*: ***il doit le faire*** he has to do it, he must do it; ***il aurait dû me le dire*** he should have told me; ***tu devrais l'acheter*** you should buy it; ***ça doit être cuit*** it should be done **3** *m* duty; *pour l'école* homework
dévorer devour
dévouement *m* devotion; **dévouer**: ***se ~ pour*** dedicate one's life to
dextérité *f* dexterity, skill
diabète *m* diabetes *sg*
diable *m* devil; **diabolique** diabolical
diagnostic *m* MÉD diagnosis; **diagnostiquer** MÉD diagnose
diagonal, ~e 1 *adj* diagonal **2** *f* diagonal (line); ***en ~e*** diagonally
diagramme *m* diagram
dialogue *m* dialog, *Br* dialogue
diamant *m* diamond
diamètre *m* diameter
diapositive *f* slide
diarrhée *f* diarrhea, *Br* diarrhoea
dictateur *m* dictator; **dictature** *f* dictatorship
dictée *f* dictation
dictionnaire *m* dictionary
diesel *m* diesel
diète *f* diet
Dieu *m* God; ***~ merci!*** thank God!
diffamer slander
différence *f* difference; **différencier** differentiate
différend *m* dispute
difficile difficult; (*exigeant*) hard to please; **difficulté** *f* difficulty
difformité *f* deformity
diffusion *f* spread; RAD, TV broadcast; *de chaleur etc* diffusion
digérer digest
digestion *f* digestion
digital digital; ***empreinte f ~e*** fingerprint
digne (*plein de dignité*) dignified; ***~ de*** worthy of; **dignité** *f* dignity; (*charge*) office
digue *f* dyke
dilapider squander
dilater expand; *pupille* dilate
dilemme *m* dilemma
diluer dilute
dimanche *m* Sunday
dimension *f* dimension; (*taille*) size; *d'une faute* magnitude
diminuer 1 *v/t nombre, prix* reduce; *joie, forces* diminish; *mérites* detract from; *souffrances* lessen, decrease **2** *v/i* decrease
diminutif *m* diminutive; **diminution** *f* decrease, decline; *d'un nombre, prix* reduction

dinde *f* turkey; **dindon** *m* turkey
dîner 1 *v/i* dine **2** *m* dinner
dingue F crazy, nuts F
diplomate *m* diplomat; **diplomatie** *f* diplomacy
diplôme *m* diploma; *universitaire* degree; **diplômé** diploma holder; *de l'université* graduate
dire say; (*informer, réveler, ordonner*) tell; ***~ à qn de faire qch*** tell s.o. to do sth; ***à vrai ~*** to tell the truth; ***cela va sans ~*** that goes without saying
direct direct; ***en ~*** *émission* live; **directement** directly; **directeur, -trice 1** *adj comité* management **2** *m/f* manager; *plus haut dans la hiérarchie* director; ÉDU principal, *Br* head teacher; **direction** *f* (*sens*) direction; (*gestion, directeurs*) management; AUTO steering; ***~ assistée*** power steering; **directive** *f* instruction; *de l'UE* directive
dirigeant *m* leader; **diriger** manage, run; *pays* lead; *orchestre* conduct; *voiture* steer; *arme, critique* aim (***contre*** at); *regard, yeux* turn (***vers*** to); *personne* direct; ***se ~ vers*** head for
discerner make out; ***~ le bon du mauvais*** tell good from bad
discipline *f* discipline
disc-jockey *m* disc jockey, DJ
discontinu *ligne* broken; *effort* intermittent
discorde *f* discord
discothèque *f* (*boîte*) discotheque, disco; *collection* record library
discours *m* speech
discréditer discredit
discret, -ète (*qui n'attire pas l'attention*) unobtrusive; *couleur* quiet; *robe* simple; (*qui garde le secret*) discreet; **discrétion** *f* discretion
discrimination *f* discrimination
disculper clear, exonerate; ***se ~*** clear o.s.
discussion *f* discussion; (*altercation*) argument; **discuter** discuss; (*contester*) question
disjoncter 1 *v/t* ÉL break **2** *v/i* F be crazy; **disjoncteur** *m* circuit breaker
disparaître disappear; (*mourir*) die; *d'une espèce* die out; ***faire ~*** get rid of
disparition *f* disappearance; (*mort*) death; ***espèce en voie de ~*** endangered species
dispenser: ***~ qn de*** (***faire***) ***qc*** excuse s.o. from (doing) sth
disperser disperse; ***se ~*** (*faire trop de choses*) spread o.s. too thin
disponibilité *f* availability; **disponible** available
disposer (*arranger*) arrange;

~ *de qn/qc* have s.o./sth at one's disposal; ***se ~ à faire qc*** get ready to do sth
dispositif *m* device
disposition *f* (*arrangement*) arrangement; *d'une loi* provision; (*humeur*) mood; (*tendance*) tendency; ***être à la ~ de qn*** be at s.o.'s disposal; ***avoir des ~s pour qch*** have an aptitude for sth
disputer *match* play; ***~ qc à qn*** compete with s.o for sth.; ***se ~*** quarrel, fight
disqualifier disqualify
disque *m* disk; SP discus; ***~ compact*** compact disc; **disquette** *f* diskette, disk; ***~ de sauvegarde*** backup disk
dissertation *f* ÉDU essay
dissimuler conceal, hide (***à*** from)
dissiper dispel; *brouillard* disperse; *fortune* squander; ***se ~*** *du brouillard* clear
dissoudre dissolve
dissuader: ***~ qn de faire qc*** dissuade s.o. from doing sth, persuade s.o. not to do sth; **dissuasion** *f* dissuasion
distance *f* distance; ***prendre ses ~s avec qn*** distance o.s. from s.o.; **distancer** outdistance
distiller distill; **distillerie** *f* distillery
distinct distinct; ***~ de*** different from; **distinctif, -ive** distinctive; **distinguer** (*percevoir*) make out; (*différencier*) distinguish (***de*** from); ***se ~*** (*être différent*) stand out (***de*** from)
distraction *f* (*passe-temps*) amusement; (*inattention*) distraction
distraire *du travail, des soucis* distract (***de*** from); (*divertir*) amuse, entertain; ***se ~*** amuse o.s.; **distrait** absent-minded
distribuer distribute; *courrier* deliver; **distributeur** *m* distributor; ***~ automatique*** vending machine
dit (*surnommé*) referred to as; (*fixé*) appointed
divaguer talk nonsense
divan *m* couch
diverger diverge; *d'opinions* differ
divers (*différent*) different, varied; *au pl* (*plusieurs*) various
diversifier diversify
diversion *f* diversion
diversité *f* diversity
divertir amuse, entertain; **divertissement** *m* amusement, entertainment
divin divine; **divinité** *f* divinity
diviser divide; ***se ~*** be divided (***en*** into); **division** *f* division
divorce *m* divorce; ***demander le ~*** ask for a divorce; **divorcé, ~e** *m/f* divorcee; **divorcer** get a divorce (***d'avec*** from)

dix ten; **dix-huit** eighteen; **dixième** tenth; **dix-neuf** nineteen; **dix-sept** seventeen; **dizaine** *f*: ***une ~ de*** about ten, ten or so
D.J. *m/f* (= ***disc-jockey***) DJ, deejay (= disc jockey)
docile docile
docteur *m* doctor; **doctorat** *m* doctorate, PhD
doctrine *f* doctrine
document *m* document; **documentation** *f* documentation; **documenter**: ***se ~*** collect information
dodu chubby
dogmatique dogmatic
doigt *m* finger; ***~ de pied*** toe; ***croiser les ~s*** keep one's fingers crossed
dollar *m* dollar
domaine *m* estate; *fig* domain
dôme *m* dome
domestique 1 *adj* domestic **2** *m* servant
domicile *m* place of residence; **domicilié**: ***~ à*** resident at
domination *f* domination; **dominer 1** *v/t* dominate **2** *v/i* (*prédominer*) be predominant; ***se ~*** control o.s.
dommage *m*: (***quel***) ***~!*** what a pity!; ***c'est ~ que*** (+ *subj*) it's a pity (that); ***~s et intérêts*** JUR damages
dompter *animal* tame; *rebelle* subdue; **dompteur** *m* trainer
DOM-TOM *mpl* (= ***départements et territoires d'outre-mer***) overseas departments and territories of France
don *m* donation; (*cadeau, aptitude*) gift; ***~ du ciel*** godsend; **donation** *f* donation
donc *conclusion* so; ***écoutez ~!*** do listen!; ***comment ~?*** how (so)?; ***allons ~!*** come on!
données *fpl* data *sg* (*aussi* INFORM), information; **donner 1** *v/t* give **2** *v/i*: ***~ sur la mer*** look onto the sea
dont whose; ***le film ~ elle parlait*** the movie she was talking about; ***la manière ~ elle me regardait*** the way (in which) she was looking at me
doré *bijou* gilded; *couleur* golden
dorénavant from now on
dorer gild
dormeur, -euse *m/f* sleeper; **dormir** sleep
dortoir *m* dormitory
dos *m* back; ***~ d'âne*** *m* speed bump; *pont* hump-backed bridge
dose *f* MÉD dose; PHARM proportion; **doser** measure out
dossier *m d'une chaise* back *f*; *de documents* file, dossier; ***~ médical*** medical record(s)
douane *f* customs *pl*; **douanier, -ère 1** *adj* customs *atr* **2** *m/f* customs officer
double 1 *adj* double **2** *m*

deuxième exemplaire duplicate; *au tennis* doubles (match); ***le ~*** double, twice as much; **doubler 1** *v/t* double; AUTO pass, *Br* overtake; *film* dub; *vêtement* line **2** *v/i* double; **doublure** *f d'un vêtement* lining
doucement gently; (*bas*) softly; (*lentement*) slowly; **douceur** *f d'une personne* gentleness; ***~s*** (*jouissance*) pleasures; (*sucreries*) sweet things
douche *f* shower; ***prendre une ~*** shower, take a shower
doué gifted; ***~ de qc*** endowed with sth
douleur *f* pain
douloureux, -euse painful
doute *m* doubt; ***sans ~*** without doubt; ***sans aucun ~*** undoubtedly; **douter**: ***~ de qn/qch*** doubt s.o./sth; ***se ~ de qc*** suspect sth; ***se ~ que*** suspect that; **douteux, -euse** doubtful
doux, douce sweet; *temps* mild; *personne* gentle; *au toucher* soft
douzaine *f* dozen; **douze** twelve; **douzième** twelfth
dragée *f* sugared almond
draguer *rivière* dredge; F *femmes* try to pick up; **dragueur** *m* F ladies' man
dramatique dramatic; **dramatiser** dramatize; **drame** *m* drama
drap *m de lit* sheet
drapeau *m* flag
drap-housse *m* fitted sheet
dresser put up; *contrat* draw up; *animal* train; ***~ qn contre qn*** set s.o. against s.o.; ***se ~*** straighten up; *d'une tour* rise up; *d'un obstacle* arise
drogue *f* drug; ***~ douce*** soft drug; ***~ récréative*** recreational drug; **drogué, ~e** *m/f* drug addict; **droguer** drug; MÉD (*traiter*) give medication to; ***se ~*** take drugs; MÉD *péj* pop pills; **droguerie** *f* hardware store
droit 1 *adj côté* right; *ligne* straight; (*debout*) erect; (*honnête*) upright **2** *adv* ***tout ~*** straight ahead **3** *m* right; (*taxe*) fee; JUR law; ***être en ~ de faire qch*** be entitled to do sth; ***~s d'auteur*** royalties
droite *f* right; *côté* right-hand side; ***à ~*** on the right(-hand side)
drôle funny; ***une ~ d'idée*** a funny idea
dubitatif, -ive doubtful
duc *m* duke
duchesse *f* duchess
duel *m* duel
dûment duly
dune *f* (sand) dune
Dunkerque Dunkirk
duper dupe
duplex *m* duplex
duquel → ***lequel***
dur 1 *adj* hard; *climat* harsh;

viande tough **2** *adv travailler, frapper* hard
durable durable, lasting; *croissance, utilisation de matières premières* sustainable
durant during; ***des années ~*** for years
durcir 1 *v/t* harden **2** *v/i*: ***se ~*** harden
durée *f* duration; ***~ de vie*** life; *d'une personne* life expectancy
durement harshly; ***être frappé ~ par*** be hard hit by
durer last
duvet *m* down; (*sac de couchage*) sleeping bag
DVD *m* DVD (= digitally versatile disk)
dynamique 1 *adj* dynamic **2** *f* dynamics
dynamo *f* dynamo
dyslexique dyslexic

E

eau *f* water; ***tomber à l'~*** fall in the water; *fig* fall through; ***~ courante*** running water; ***~ gazeuse*** carbonated water, *Br* fizzy water; ***~ de Javel*** bleach
eau-de-vie *f* brandy
ébahi dumbfounded
ébaucher *tableau, roman* rough out; *texte* draft; ***~ un sourire*** smile faintly
ébéniste *m* cabinetmaker
éblouir dazzle (*aussi fig*)
éboueur *m* garbageman, *Br* dustman
éboulement *m* landslide
ébouriffé tousled; **ébouriffer** *cheveux* ruffle
ébranler shake; ***s'~*** move off
ébriété *f* inebriation
ébruiter *nouvelle* spread
ébullition *f* boiling point; ***être en ~*** be boiling
écaille *f de coquillage, tortue* shell; *de poisson* scale; *de peinture, plâtre* flake; *matière* tortoiseshell; **écailler** *poisson* scale; *huître* open; ***s'~*** *de peinture* flake (off); *de vernis à ongles* chip
écart *m* (*intervalle*) gap; (*différence*) difference; *moral* indiscretion; ***à l'~*** at a distance (***de*** from)
écarter *jambes* spread; *fig*: *idée* reject; *danger* avert; ***s'~ de*** (*s'éloigner*) stray from
écervelé scatterbrained
échafaudage *m* scaffolding
échancré low-cut
échange *m* exchange; ***~s extérieurs*** foreign trade; ***en ~*** in exchange (***de*** for); **échanger** exchange (***contre*** for);
échangeur *m* interchange
échantillon *m* COMM sample
échappement *m* AUTO exhaust; ***tuyau m d'~*** tail pipe;

échapper *d'une personne* **~ à qn** escape from s.o.; **~ à qc** escape sth; **l'~ belle** have a narrow escape; **s'~** escape
écharde *f* splinter
écharpe *f* scarf; *de maire* sash; **en ~** MÉD in a sling
échauffer heat; **s'~** SP warm up; **~ les esprits** get people excited
échéance *f d'un contrat* expiration date, *Br* expiry date; *de police* maturity
échec *m* failure; **essuyer un ~** meet with failure
échecs *mpl* chess; **jouer aux ~** play chess
échelle *f* ladder; *d'une carte, des salaires* scale; **à l'~ mondiale** on a global scale
échelonner space out; *paiements* spread, stagger (**sur un an** over a year)
échevelé disheveled, *Br* dishevelled
échiner F: **s'~ à faire qch** go to great lengths to do sth
échiquier *m* chessboard
écho *m* echo
échotier, -ère *m/f* gossip columnist
échouer fail; **(s')~** *d'un bateau* run aground
éclabousser spatter
éclair *m* flash of lightning; CUIS eclair; **comme un ~** in a flash; **éclairage** *m* lighting
éclaircie *f* clear spell; **éclaircir** lighten; *fig: mystère* clear up; **s'~** *du ciel* clear
éclairer light; **~ qn** light the way for s.o.; *fig* enlighten s.o.
éclat *m de verre* splinter; *de métal* gleam; *des yeux* sparkle; *de couleurs, fleurs* vividness; **~ de rire** peal of laughter; **un ~ d'obus** a piece of shrapnel; **éclatant** dazzling; *couleur* vivid; *rire* loud; **éclater** *d'une bombe* blow up, explode; *d'un ballon, pneu* burst; *d'un coup de feu* ring out; *d'une guerre, d'un incendie* break out; *fig: d'un groupe, parti* break up; **~ en sanglots** burst into tears
éclipser eclipse (*aussi fig*); **s'~** F vanish, disappear
éclore *d'un oiseau* hatch out; *de fleurs* open
écluse *f* lock
écœurement *m* disgust; (*découragement*) discouragement; **écœurer** disgust, sicken; (*décourager*) dishearten; **~ qn** *d'un aliment* make s.o. feel nauseous
école *f* school; **~ maternelle** nursery school; **~ primaire** elementary school, *Br* primary school **~ publique** state school; **écolier** *m* schoolboy; **écolière** *f* schoolgirl
écologie *f* ecology; **écologique** ecological
économe economical, thrifty
économie *f* economy; *science*

economics *sg*; ~ ***souterraine*** black economy; **~s** savings; **économiser** save; ~ ***sur qc*** save on sth; **économiseur** *m* **d'écran** INFORM screen saver
écorce *f d'un arbre* bark; *d'un fruit* rind
écorcher *animal* skin; (*égratigner*) scrape; *fig*: *nom*, *mot* murder
écossais, **~e** Scottish; **Écossais**, **~e** *m/f* Scot; **Écosse** *f*: **l'~** Scotland
écoulement *m* flow; COMM sale; **écouler** COMM sell; **s'~** flow; *du temps* pass; COMM sell
écourter shorten; *vacances* cut short
écoute *f*: ***être à l'~*** be always listening out; ***aux heures de grande ~*** RAD at peak listening times; TV at peak viewing times; **écouter 1** *v/t* listen to **2** *v/i* listen; **écouteur** *m* TÉL receiver; **~s** RAD headphones
écran *m* screen; ***porter à l'~*** TV adapt for television; ~ ***tactile*** touch screen; ~ ***total*** sunblock
écrasant overwhelming; **écraser** crush; *cigarette* stub out; (*renverser*) run over; ***s'~ au sol*** *d'un avion* crash
écrémé: ***lait*** *m* ~ skimmed milk
écrevisse *f* crayfish
écrier: **s'~** cry out
écrire write; ***comment est-ce que ça s'écrit?*** how do you spell it?; **écrit** *m* document; ***l'~*** *examen* the written exam; ***par ~*** in writing; **écriteau** *m* notice; **écriture** *f* writing; COMM entry; ***les*** (***Saintes***) ***Écritures*** Holy Scripture
écrivain *m* writer
écrou *m* nut
écrouler: **s'~** collapse
écru *couleur* natural
écueil *m* reef; *fig* pitfall
éculé *chaussure* worn-out; *fig* hackneyed
écume *f* foam
écureuil *m* squirrel
écurie *f* stable
édenté toothless
édifice *m* building; **édifier** erect; *fig* build up
éditer *livre* publish; *texte* edit; **éditeur**, **-trice** *m/f* publisher; (*commentateur*) editor; **édition** *f* publishing; *action de commenter* editing; (*tirage*) edition; ***maison*** *f* ***d'~*** publishing house; **éditorial** *m* editorial
édredon *m* eiderdown
éducatif, **-ive** educational; **education** *f* education; (*culture*) upbringing
éduquer educate; (*élever*) bring up
effacer erase; **s'~** *d'une inscription* wear away; *d'une personne* fade into the background
effarement *m* fear; **effarer**

frighten
effectif, **-ive 1** *adj* effective **2** *m* manpower, personnel; **effectivement** true enough
effectuer carry out
efféminé *péj* effeminate
effervescent effervescent; *fig*: *foule* excited
effet *m* effect; COMM bill; ***en ~*** sure enough; ***faire de l'~*** have an effect; ***~s*** (personal) effects
efficace *remède* effective; *personne* efficient; **efficacité** *f* effectiveness; *d'une personne* efficiency
effleurer brush against; (*aborder*) touch on
effondrement *m* collapse; **effondrer**: ***s'~*** collapse
efforcer: ***s'~ de faire qch*** try very hard to do sth
effort *m* effort; ***faire un ~*** make an effort, try a bit harder
effraction *f* JUR breaking and entering
effrayant frightening; **effrayer** frighten; ***s'~*** be frightened (***de*** at)
effroi *m* fear
effronterie *f* impertinence, effrontery
effroyable terrible, dreadful
égal 1 *adj* equal; *surface* even; *vitesse* steady; ***ça lui est ~*** it's all the same to him **2** *m* equal; ***sans ~*** unequaled, *Br* unequalled; **également** (*pareillement*) equally; (*aussi*) as well, too; **égaler** equal;
égaliser 1 *v/t haies, cheveux* even up; *sol* level **2** *v/i* SP tie the game, *Br* equalize; **égalité** *f* equality; *en tennis* deuce; ***être à ~*** be level; *en tennis* be at deuce
égard *m*: ***à cet ~*** in that respect; ***à l'~ de qn*** to(ward) s.o.; ***par ~ pour*** out of consideration for; ***~s*** respect
égarer *personne* lead astray; *chose* lose; ***s'~*** get lost; *du sujet* stray from the point
égayer cheer up
église *f* church
égocentrique egocentric
égoïsme *m* selfishness, egoism; **égoïste 1** *adj* selfish **2** *m/f* egoist
égorger: ***~ qn*** cut s.o.'s throat
égout *m* sewer
égoutter drain
égratignure *f* scratch
Égypte *f*: ***l'~*** Egypt; **égyptien**, **~ne** Egyptian; **Égyptien**, **~ne** *m/f* Egyptian
éjecter eject; F *personne* kick out
élaborer *projet* draw up
élan *m* momentum; SP run-up; *de tendresse* upsurge; *de générosité* fit; (*vivacité*) enthusiasm
élancer *v/i*: ***ma jambe m'élance*** I've got shooting pains in my leg; ***s'~*** dash; SP take a run-up
élargir widen, broaden; *vêtement* let out; *débat* widen

élastique **1** *adj* elastic **2** *m* elastic; *de bureau* rubber band

électeur, **-trice** *m/f* voter; **élection** *f* election; **électorat** *m droit* franchise; *personnes* electorate

électricien, **~ne** *m/f* electrician; **électricité** *f* electricity; **~ *statique*** static (electricity); **électrique** electric; **électriser** electrify

électrocuter electrocute

électroménager: ***appareils*** *mpl* **~*s*** household applicances

électronique **1** *adj* electronic; ***livre*** **~** e-book, electronic book **2** *f* electronics

élégance *f* elegance; **élégant** elegant

élément *m* element; (*composante*) component; *d'un puzzle* piece; **~*s*** (*rudiments*) rudiments; **élémentaire** elementary

éléphant *m* elephant

élevage *m* breeding; **~** (***du bétail***) cattle farming

élève *m/f* pupil

élevé high; *esprit* noble; *style* elevated; ***bien/mal*** **~** well/badly brought up; **élever** raise; *prix, température* raise, increase; *statue* put up, erect; *enfants* bring up, raise; *animaux* breed; ***s'*~** rise; *d'une tour* rise up; *d'un cri* go up; ***s'~ contre*** rise up against; ***s'~ à*** amount to; **éleveur**, **-euse** *m/f* breeder

élimination *f* elimination; *des déchets* disposal; **éliminatoire** *f* qualifying round; **éliminer** eliminate; *difficultés* get rid of

élire elect

elle *f* she; *après prép* her; *chose* it

elle-même herself; *chose* itself

elles *fpl* they; *après prép* them

elles-mêmes themselves

éloigné remote

éloigner move away; *soupçon* remove; ***s'~*** move away (***de*** from); ***s'~ de qn*** distance o.s. from s.o.

éloquence *f* eloquence; **éloquent** eloquent

élu, **~e** **1** *adj*: ***le président*** **~** the President elect **2** *m/f* POL (elected) representative

élucider *mystère* clear up; *question* clarify

émacié emaciated

e-mail *m* e-mail

émanciper emancipate; ***s'~*** become emancipated

emballage *m* packaging; **emballer** package; *fig* F thrill; ***s'~*** *d'un moteur* race; *fig* F get excited; ***emballé sous vide*** vacuum packed

embargo *m* embargo

embarquer **1** *v/t* load **2** *v/i ou* ***s'~*** embark; ***s'~ dans*** F get involved in

embarras *m* difficulty; (*gêne*) embarrassment; ***être dans l'~*** be in an embarrassing position; *sans argent* be short of money; **embarrassant** embarrassing; (*encombrant*) cumbersome; **embarrasser** embarrass; (*encombrer*) *escaliers* clutter up
embaucher take on, hire
embellir 1 *v/t* make more attractive; *fig* embellish **2** *v/i* become more attractive
embêtant F annoying; **embêter** F (*ennuyer*) bore; (*contrarier*) annoy; ***s'~*** be bored
emblème *m* emblem
emboîter insert; ***~ le pas à qn*** fall into step with s.o. (*aussi fig*); ***s'~*** fit together
embolie *f* embolism
embonpoint *m* stoutness
embouchure *f* GÉOGR mouth; MUS mouthpiece
embouteillage *m* traffic jam
emboutir crash into
embranchement *m* branch; (*carrefour*) intersection, *Br* junction
embrasser kiss; *période, thème* take in, embrace; *métier* take up; ***~ du regard*** take in at a glance
embrayage *m* AUTO clutch; *action* letting in the clutch
embrouiller muddle; ***s'~*** get muddled
embryon *m* embryo
éméché F tipsy
émeraude *f & adj* emerald
émerger emerge
émerveiller amaze; ***s'~*** be amazed (***de*** by)
émetteur *m* RAD, TV transmitter
émettre *radiations etc* give off, emit; RAD, TV broadcast, transmit; *opinion* voice; *action, nouveau billet* issue; *emprunt* float
émeute *f* riot
émietter crumble
émigration *f* emigration; **émigré, ~e** *m/f* emigré; **émigrer** emigrate
émincer cut into thin slices
éminent eminent
émission *f* emission; RAD, TV program, *Br* programme; COMM, FIN issue
emmagasiner store
emmêler *fils* tangle; *fig* muddle
emménager: ***~ dans*** move into
emmener take
emmerder F: ***~ qn*** get on s.o.'s nerves; ***s'~*** be bored rigid
emmitoufler wrap up; ***s'~*** wrap up
émotion *f* emotion; F (*frayeur*) fright
émouvant moving; **émouvoir** (*toucher*) move; ***s'~*** be moved
emparer: ***s'~ de*** seize; *clés, héritage* grab; *des doutes, de la peur* overcome
empâter: ***s'~*** thicken

empêchement *m*: ***j'ai eu un ~*** something has come up; **empêcher** prevent; ***~ qn de faire qc*** prevent *ou* stop s.o. doing sth; ***(il) n'empêche que*** nevertheless
empereur *m* emperor
empiéter: ***~ sur*** encroach on
empiffrer F: ***s'~*** stuff o.s.
empiler pile (up)
empire *m* empire; *fig (maîtrise)* control
empirer get worse, deteriorate
emplacement *m* site
emplette *f* purchase; ***faire des ~s*** go shopping
emplir fill; ***s'~*** fill (***de*** with)
emploi *m* (*utilisation*) use; ÉCON employment; ***~ du temps*** schedule, *Br* timetable; ***chercher un ~*** be looking for work *ou* for a job
employé, **~e** *m/f* employee; **employer** use; *personnel* employ; ***s'~ à faire qc*** strive to do sth; **employeur**, **-euse** *m/f* employer
empocher pocket
empoigner grab, seize
empoisonner poison
emporter take; *prisonnier* take away; (*entraîner, arracher*) carry away; *du courant* sweep away; *d'une maladie* carry off; ***l'~ sur qn/qc*** get the better of s.o./sth; ***s'~*** fly into a rage
empreinte *f* impression; *fig* stamp; ***~ génétique*** genetic fingerprint
empresser: ***s'~ de faire qc*** rush to do sth; ***s'~ auprès de qn*** be attentive to s.o.
emprise *f* hold
emprisonnement *m* imprisonment; **emprisonner** imprison
emprunt *m* loan; **emprunter** borrow (***à*** from); *chemin, escalier* take
ému moved, touched
en[1] *prép* in; *direction* to; ***agir ~ ami*** act as a friend; ***~ voiture*** by car; ***~ or*** of gold; *en même temps* while, when; *mode* by
en[2] *pron*: ***qu'~ pensez-vous?*** what do you think about it?; ***il y ~ a deux*** there are two (of them); ***j'~ ai*** I have some; ***j'~ ai cinq*** I have five; ***je n'~ ai pas*** I don't have any; ***il ~ est mort*** he died of it
encadrer *tableau* frame; ***encadré de deux gendarmes*** *fig* flanked by gendarmes
encaisser COMM take; *chèque* cash; *fig* take
en-cas *m* CUIS snack
encastrer build in
enceinte[1] *adj* pregnant
enceinte[2] *f* enclosure; ***~ (acoustique)*** speaker
encens *m* incense
encercler encircle
enchaîner chain up; *fig*: *pensées, faits* link (up)
enchanté enchanted; ***~!*** how do you do?; **enchanter** (*ra-*

vir) delight; (*ensorceler*) enchant
enchère *f* bid; ***vente f aux ~s*** auction
enchevêtrer tangle; *fig*: *situation* confuse; ***s'~ de fils*** get tangled up; *d'une situation* get muddled
enclin: ***être ~ à faire qch*** be inclined to do sth
encoche *f* notch
encolure *f* neck; *tour de cou* neck (size)
encombrant cumbersome; ***être ~*** *d'une personne* be in the way; **encombrer** *maison* clutter up; *rue*, *passage* block; ***s'~ de*** load o.s. down with
encore *de nouveau* again; (*toujours*) still; ***pas ~*** not yet; ***~ une bière?*** another beer?; ***~ plus rapide*** even faster
encourageant encouraging; **encourager** encourage; *projet*, *entreprise* foster
encrasser dirty; ***s'~*** get dirty
encre *f* ink
encyclopédie *f* encyclopedia
endetter: ***s'~*** get into debt
endeuillé bereaved
endive *f* chicory
endolori painful
endommager damage
endormi asleep; *fig* sleepy; **endormir** send to sleep; *douleur* dull; ***s'~*** fall asleep
endosser *vêtement* put on; *responsabilité* shoulder; *chèque* endorse
endroit *m* (*lieu*) place; *d'une étoffe* right side
enduire: ***~ de*** cover with; **enduit** *m de peinture* coat
endurance *f* endurance
endurcir harden
endurer endure
énergie *f* energy; **énergique** energetic; *protestation* strenuous
énervant irritating; **énerver**: ***~ qn*** (*agacer*) get on s.o.'s nerves; (*agiter*) make s.o. edgy; ***s'~*** get excited
enfance *f* childhood
enfant *m ou f* child
enfer *m* hell (*aussi fig*)
enfermer shut *ou* lock up; *champ* enclose; ***s'~*** shut o.s. up
enfiler *aiguille* thread; *perles* string; *vêtement* slip on; *rue* turn into
enfin (*finalement*) at last; (*en dernier lieu*) lastly, last; (*bref*) in a word
enflammer set light to; *allumette* strike; MÉD inflame; *fig*: *imagination* fire; ***s'~*** catch; MÉD become inflamed; *fig*: *de l'imagination* take flight
enfler swell; **enflure** *f* swelling
enfoncer 1 *v/t clou*, *pieu* drive in; *couteau* thrust, plunge (**dans** into); *porte* break down **2** *v/i dans sable etc* sink (**dans** into); ***s'~*** sink

enfreindre infringe
enfuir: **s'~** run away
engagement *m* (*obligation*) commitment; *personnel* recruitment; THÉÂT booking; (*mise en gage*) pawning
engager (*lier*) commit (**à** to); *personnel* hire; TECH (*faire entrer*) insert; *discussion* begin; (*entraîner*) involve (**dans** in); THÉÂT book; (*mettre en gage*) pawn; **s'~** (*se lier*) commit o.s. (**à faire qc** to doing sth); (*commencer*) begin; MIL enlist
engelure *f* chillblain
engendrer *fig* engender
engin *m* machine; MIL missile; F *péj* thing
englober include
engloutir (*dévorer*) devour, wolf down; *fig* engulf
engouffrer devour, wolf down; **s'~ dans** *de l'eau* pour in; *fig*: *dans un bâtiment* rush into; *dans une foule* be swallowed up by
engourdir numb; **s'~** go numb
engraisser fatten
engrenage *m* gear
engueuler F bawl out; **s'~** have an argument
énigme *f* enigma; (*devinette*) riddle
enivrer intoxicate; *fig* exhilarate
enjamber step across; *d'un pont* span
enjeu *m* stake
enjoliveur *m* AUTO wheel trim, hub cap
enjoué cheerful, good humored, *Br* good-humoured
enlèvement *m* (*rapt*) abduction, kidnap; **enlever** take away, remove; *vêtement* take off, remove; (*kidnapper*) abduct, kidnap; **~ qc à qn** take sth away from s.o.
enneigé *route* blocked by snow; *sommet* snow-capped
ennemi, **~e 1** *m/f* enemy **2** *adj* enemy *atr*
ennui *m* boredom; **~s** problems; **ennuyer** (*contrarier*, *agacer*) annoy; (*lasser*) bore; **s'~** be bored; **ennuyeux**, **-euse** (*contrariant*) annoying; (*lassant*) boring
énoncé *m* statement; *d'une question* wording; **énoncer** state; **~ des vérités** state the obvious
énorme enormous; **énormément** enormously; **~ de** F an enormous amount of
énormité *f* enormity
enquête *f* inquiry; *policière aussi* investigation; (*sondage d'opinion*) survey; **enquêter**: **~ sur** investigate
enraciné deep-rooted
enregistrement *m* registration; *de disques* recording; AVIAT check-in; **enregistrer** register; *disques* record; *bagages* check in
enrhumer: **s'~** catch (a) cold
enrichir enrich; **s'~** get richer

enrouer: **s'~** get hoarse
enrouler *tapis* roll up; **~ *qc autour de qch*** wind sth around sth
enseignant, **~e** *m/f* teacher
enseignement *m* education; *d'un sujet* teaching; **enseigner** teach (***qc à qn*** s.o. sth)
ensemble 1 *adv* (*simultanément*) together **2** *m* (*totalité*) whole; (*groupe*) group, set; MUS, *vêtement* ensemble; MATH set; ***dans l'~*** on the whole
ensevelir bury
ensoleillé sunny
ensommeillé sleepy
ensuite then; (*plus tard*) after
entacher smear
entaille *f* cut; (*encoche*) notch; **entailler** notch; ***s'~ la main*** cut one's hand
entamer start; *économies* make
entasser *choses* pile up; *personnes* cram
entendre hear; (*comprendre*) understand; (*vouloir dire*) mean; ***~ faire qc*** intend to do sth; ***~ dire que*** hear that; ***s'~*** (***avec qn***) get on (with s.o.); (*se mettre d'accord*) come to an agreement (with s.o.); **entendu** *regard* knowing; ***bien ~*** of course; **entente** *f* agreement
enterrement *m* burial; *cérémonie* funeral; **enterrer** bury
en-tête *m* heading; INFORM header; COMM letterhead; *d'un journal* headline
entêtement *m* stubbornness; **entêter**: **s'~** persist (***dans*** in; ***à faire qc*** in doing sth)
enthousiasme *m* enthusiasm; **enthousiasmer**: ***s'~ pour*** be enthusiastic about
enticher: ***s'~ de*** *personne* become infatuated with; *activité* develop a craze for
entier, **-ère** whole, entire; (*intégral*) intact; *confiance*, *satisfaction* full
entonnoir *m* funnel
entorse *f* MÉD sprain
entortiller (*envelopper*) wrap
entourage *m* entourage; (*bordure*) surround; **entourer**: ***~ de*** surround with; ***s'~ de*** surround o.s. with
entraide *f* mutual assistance; **entraider**: **s'~** help each other
entrailles *fpl* intestines
entrain *m* liveliness; **entraînement** *m* SP training; TECH drive; **entraîner** (*charrier*, *emporter*) sweep along; SP train; *fig* result in; *frais* entail; *personne* drag; TECH drive; **s'~** train
entrave *f fig* hindrance; **entraver** hinder
entre between; ***le meilleur d'~ nous*** the best of us; ***~ autres*** among other things
entrebâiller half open
entrechoquer: **s'~** knock against one another

entrecôte *f* rib steak
entrée *f* entrance, way in; *accès au théâtre, cinéma* admission; (*billet*) ticket; (*vestibule*) entry(way); CUIS starter; INFORM *touche* enter (key); *de données* input; **~ *interdite*** no admittance
entrejambe *m* crotch
entrelacer interlace
entremets *m* CUIS dessert
entremise *f*: ***par l'~ de*** through (the good offices of)
entreposer store; **entrepôt** *m* warehouse
entreprenant enterprising; **entreprendre** undertake; **entrepreneur, -euse** *m/f* entrepreneur; **entreprise** *f* enterprise; (*firme*) company, business
entrer 1 *v/i* come/go in, enter; **~ *dans*** come/go into, enter; *voiture* get into; *pays* enter; *catégorie* fall into; *l'armée, le parti etc* join **2** *v/t* bring in; INFORM input, enter
entre-temps in the meantime
entretenir *maison, machine etc* maintain; *famille* keep, support; *amitié* keep up; ***s'~ de qc*** talk to each other about sth
entretien *m* maintenance, upkeep; (*conversation*) conversation
entrevoir glimpse; *fig* foresee
entrevue *f* interview
entrouvrir half open
énumérer list, enumerate
envahir invade; *d'un sentiment* overwhelm; **envahissant** *personne* intrusive; *sentiments* overwhelming
enveloppe *f d'une lettre* envelope; **envelopper** wrap; ***enveloppé de*** *brume, mystère* enveloped in
envenimer poison (*aussi fig*)
envergure *f d'un oiseau, avion* wingspan; *fig* scope; *d'une personne* caliber, *Br* calibre
envers 1 *prép* toward, *Br* towards **2** *m d'une feuille* reverse; *d'une étoffe*: wrong side; ***à l'~*** *pull* inside out; (*en désordre*) upside down
envie *f* (*convoitise*) envy; (*désir*) desire (**de** for); ***avoir ~ de*** (***faire***) ***qc*** want (to do) sth; **envier** envy; ***~ qc à qn*** envy s.o. sth
environ 1 *adv* about **2** *mpl*: ***~s*** surrounding area; ***dans les ~s*** in the vicinity
environnement *m* environment
envisager (*considérer*) think about; (*imaginer*) envisage
envoi *m* shipment; *d'un fax* sending
envoler: ***s'~*** fly away; *d'un avion* take off; *fig*: *du temps* fly
envoyé *m* envoy; *d'un journal* correspondent; **envoyer** send; *gifle* give

éolienne *f* wind turbine
épais, **~se** thick; *foule* dense; **épaisseur** *f* thickness; **épaissir** thicken
épancher: ***s'~*** pour out one's heart (***auprès de*** to)
épanouir: ***s'~*** blossom
épargne *f* saving; ***~s*** (*économies*) savings; **épargner 1** *v/t* save; *personne* spare; ***~ qc à qn*** spare s.o. sth **2** *v/i* save
éparpiller scatter
épars sparse
épatant F great, terrific; **épater** astonish
épaule *f* shoulder
épave *f* wreck (*aussi fig*)
épée *f* sword
épeler spell
éperdu *besoin* desperate; ***~ de*** beside o.s. with
épi *m* ear
épice *f* spice; **épicer** spice; **épicerie** *f* grocery store, *Br* grocer's; **épicier**, **-ère** *m/f* grocer
épidémie *f* epidemic
épier spy on; *occasion* watch for
épilepsie *f* epilepsy; ***crise*** *f* ***d'~*** epileptic fit
épiler remove the hair from
épinards *mpl* spinach
épine *f d'une rose* thorn; *d'un hérisson* spine, prickle; **épineux**, **-euse** *problème* thorny
épingle *f* pin; ***~ de sûreté*** safety pin; ***tiré à quatre ~s*** *fig* well turned-out
Épiphanie *f* Epiphany
épisode *m* episode
éploré tearful
éplucher peel; *fig* scrutinize; **épluchures** *fpl* peelings
éponge *f* sponge; **éponger** sponge down; *flaque* sponge up; *déficit* mop up
époque *f* age, epoch; ***meubles*** *mpl* ***d'~*** period *ou* antique furniture
époumoner: ***s'~*** F shout o.s. hoarse
épouse *f* wife; **épouser** marry; *principe etc* espouse
épousseter dust
époustouflant F breathtaking
épouvantable dreadful
épouvantail *m* scarecrow
épouvanter horrify; *fig* terrify
époux *m* husband; ***les ~*** the married couple
éprendre: ***s'~ de*** fall in love with
épreuve *f* trial; SP event; *imprimerie* proof; *photographie* print; ***à toute ~*** *confiance etc* never-failing; ***à l'~ du feu*** fireproof
éprouver test, try out; (*ressentir*) experience
épuisé exhausted; *livre* out of print; **épuiser** exhaust; ***~ les ressources*** be a drain on resources; ***s'~*** tire o.s. out (***à faire qch*** doing sth); *d'une source* dry up

épurer purify
équateur *m* equator
équilibre *m* balance, equilibrium; **équilibrer** balance
équipage *m* crew
équipe *f* team; *d'ouvriers* gang; **~ de nuit** night shift; **~ de secours** rescue party; **équipement** *m* equipment; **équiper** equip (**de** with)
équitable just, equitable
équitation *f* riding
équivalent 1 *adj* equivalent (**à** to) **2** *m* equivalent
équivoque 1 *adj* equivocal, ambiguous **2** *f* ambiguity; (*malentendu*) misunderstanding
érable *m* BOT maple
érafler scratch; **éraflure** *f* scratch
ère *f* era
érection *f* erection
éreinter exhaust; **s'~** exhaust o.s. (**à faire qch** doing sth)
ériger erect; **s'~ en** set o.s. up as
érosion *f* erosion
érotisme *m* eroticism
errer roam; *des pensées* stray
erreur *f* mistake, error; **~ de calcul** miscalculation
érudit erudite; **érudition** *f* erudition
éruption *f* eruption; MÉD rash
escabeau *m* (*tabouret*) stool; (*marchepied*) stepladder
escalade *f* climbing; **~ de** *violence etc* escalation in; **escalader** climb
escalator *m* escalator
escale *f* stopover; **faire ~ à** MAR call at; AVIAT stop over in
escalier *m* stairs *pl*, staircase; **dans l'~** on the stairs; **~ de secours** fire escape
escalope *f* escalope
escamoter (*dérober*) make disappear; *antenne* retract; *fig*: *difficulté* get around
escapade *f*: **faire une ~** get away from it all
escargot *m* snail
escarpement *m* slope
esclaffer: **s'~** guffaw, laugh out loud
esclavage *m* slavery; **esclave** *m/f* slave
escompte *m* discount; **escompter** discount; *fig* expect
escorter escort
escrime *f* fencing; **escrimer**: **s'~** fight, struggle (**à** to)
escroc *m* crook
espace *m* space; **espacer** space out; **s'~** become more and more infrequent
Espagne *f* Spain; **espagnol**, **~e 1** *adj* Spanish **2** *m langue* Spanish; **Espagnol**, **~e** *m/f* Spaniard
espèce *f* kind, sort (**de** of); BIOL species; **~ d'abruti!** *péj* idiot!; **en ~s** COMM cash
espérer 1 *v/t* hope for; **~ que** hope that; **~ faire qc** hope to do sth **2** *v/i* hope; **~ en** trust in
espiègle mischievous

espion, **~ne** *m/f* spy; **espionnage** *m* espionage, spying; **espionner** spy on
espoir *m* hope
esprit *m* spirit; (*intellect*) mind; (*humour*) wit
esquisse *f* sketch; *fig*: *d'un roman* outline; **esquisser** sketch; *fig*: *projet* outline
esquiver dodge; ***s'~*** slip away
essai *m* (*test*) test, trial; (*tentative*) attempt, try; *en rugby* try; *en littérature* essay; ***à l'~*** on trial
essaim *m* swarm
essayage *m*: ***cabine f d'~*** changing cubicle; **essayer** try; (*mettre à l'épreuve, évaluer*) test; *vêtement* try on; ***~ de faire qc*** try to do sth; ***s'~ à qc*** try one's hand at sth
essence *f* essence; *carburant* gas, *Br* petrol; BOT species *sg*
essentiel, **~le 1** *adj* essential **2** *m*: ***l'~*** the main thing; *de sa vie* the main part
essieu *m* axle
essor *m fig* expansion
essorer wring out; *d'une machine à laver* spin
essoufflé out of breath
essuie-glace *m* (windshield) wiper, *Br* (windscreen) wiper; **essuie-mains** *m* hand-towel; **essuyer** wipe; *fig* suffer
est 1 *m* east ***à l'~ de*** (to the) east of **2** *adj* east, eastern
est-ce que: ***~ c'est vrai?*** is it true?; ***est-ce qu'ils se portent bien?*** are they well?
esthéticienne *f* beautician
esthétique esthetic, *Br* aesthetic
estimatif, **-ive** estimated; ***devis m ~*** estimate; **estimation** *f* estimation; *des coûts* estimate
estime *f* esteem; **estimer** *valeur* estimate; (*respecter*) have esteem for; (*croire*) feel, think; ***s'~ heureux*** consider o.s. lucky
estival summer *atr*
estomac *m* stomach
Estonie *f* Estonia
estrade *f* podium
estropier cripple
estuaire *m* estuary
et and; ***~ … ~ …*** both … and …
étable *f* cowshed
établi *m* workbench
établir *entreprise* establish, set up; , *contact*, *ordre* establish; *salaires*, *prix* set, fix; *facture*, *liste* draw up; *record* set; *culpabilité* establish, prove; *raisonnement*, *réputation* base (***sur*** on); ***s'~*** (*s'installer*) settle; **établissement** *m* establishment; *de salaires*, *prix* setting; *d'une facture*, *liste* drawing up; *d'un record* setting; *d'une loi*, *d'un impôt* introduction
étage *m* floor, story, *Br* storey; *d'une fusée* stage
étagère *f meuble* bookcase,

shelves *pl*; *planche* shelf
étain *m* pewter
étalage *m* display; ***faire ~ de qch*** show sth off; **étaler** *carte* spread out; *peinture*, *paiements* spread (***sur*** over); *vacances* stagger; *marchandises* display; *fig* (*exhiber*) show off; ***s'~*** *de peinture* spread; *de paiements* be spread out (***sur*** over); (*se vautrer*) sprawl; *par terre* fall flat
étanche watertight; **étancher** make watertight
étang *m* pond
étape *f lieu* stopover, stopping place; *d'un parcours* stage, leg; *fig* stage
état *m* state; (*liste*) statement, list; ***en tout ~ de cause*** in any case, anyway; ***hors d'~*** out of order
États-Unis *mpl*: ***les ~*** the United States
été *m* summer
éteindre *incendie*, *cigarette* put out; *électricité*, *radio*, *chauffage* turn off; ***s'~*** *de feu*, *lumière* go out; *de télé etc* go off; *euph* (*mourir*) pass away
étendre *malade*, *enfant* lay (down); *beurre*, *enduit* spread; *peinture* apply; *bras* stretch out; *linge* hang up; *vin* dilute; *sauce* thin; *influence* extend; ***s'~*** extend, stretch (***jusqu'à*** as far as, to); *d'une personne* lie down; *d'un incendie*, *d'une maladie* spread; *d'un tissu* stretch; **étendue** *f* extent; *d'eau* expanse; *de connaissances*, *d'une catastrophe* extent
éternel, **~le** eternal; **éternité** *f* eternity
éternuer sneeze
éthique 1 *adj* ethical **2** *f* ethics
étinceler sparkle; **étincelle** *f* spark
étiqueter label (*aussi fig*)
étiquette *f* label; (*protocole*) etiquette
étirer: ***s'~*** stretch
étoffe *f* material; **étoffer** *fig* flesh out
étoile *f* star (*aussi fig*); ***~ filante*** falling star, *Br* shooting star; ***~ de mer*** starfish
étonnement *m* astonishment, surprise; **étonner** astonish, surprise; ***s'~ de*** be astonished *ou* surprised at; ***s'~ que*** (+ *subj*) be suprised that
étouffant stifling, suffocating; **étouffée** CUIS: ***à l'~*** braised; **étouffer** suffocate; *avec un oreiller* smother, suffocate; *fig*: *bruit* quash; *révolte* put down, suppress; *cri* smother; *scandale* hush up
étourderie *f* foolishness; *action* foolish thing to do
étourdi foolish, thoughtless; **étourdir** daze; ***~ qn*** *d'alcool*, *de succès* go to s.o.'s head;

étourdissement *m* (*vertige*) dizziness, giddiness
étrange strange
étranger, **-ère 1** *adj* strange; *de l'étranger* foreign **2** *m/f* stranger; *de l'étranger* foreigner **3** *m*: **à l'~** abroad; *investissement* foreign, outward
étrangler strangle; *fig*: *critique*, *liberté* stifle
être 1 *v/i* be; ***nous sommes lundi*** it's Monday; ***nous avons été éliminé*** we were eliminated; **~ *à qn*** *appartenir à* belong to s.o. **2** *v/aux* have; ***elle n'est pas encore arrivée*** she hasn't arrived yet; ***elle est arrivée hier*** she arrived yesterday **3** *m* being; *personne* person
étreindre grasp; *ami* embrace, hug; *de sentiments* grip; **étreinte** *f* hug, embrace; *de la main* grip
étrenner use for the first time
étrennes *fpl* New Year's gift
étroit narrow; *tricot* tight, small; *amitié* close; ***être ~ d'esprit*** be narrow-minded
étroitesse *f* narrowness
étude *f* study; *salle à l'école* study room; *de notaire* office; *activité* practice; ***faire des ~s*** study; ***~ de marché*** market research; **étudiant**, **~e** *m/f* student; **étudier** study
étui *m* case
étuvée CUIS: ***à l'~*** braised
euphorique euphoric
euro *m* euro
Europe *f*: ***l'~*** Europe; **européen**, **~ne** European; **Européen**, **~ne** *m/f* European
eux *mpl* they; *après prép* them
eux-mêmes *mpl* themselves
évacuation *f* evacuation
évadé *m* escaped prisoner, escapee; **évader**: ***s'~*** escape
évaluer (*estimer*) evaluate; *tableau*, *meuble* value; *coût*, *nombre* estimate
évanouir: ***s'~*** faint; *fig* vanish, disappear
évaporer: ***s'~*** evaporate
évasif, **-ive** evasive; **évasion** *f* escape
éveil *m* awakening; ***en ~*** alert; **éveiller** wake up; *fig* arouse; ***s'~*** wake up; *fig* be aroused
événement *m* event
éventail *m* fan; *fig*: *de marchandises* range
éventé *boisson* flat; **éventer** fan; *fig*: *secret* reveal
éventualité *f* eventuality, possibility; **éventuel**, **~le** possible
évêque *m* bishop
évertuer: ***s'~ à faire qc*** try one's hardest to do sth
évident obvious
évier *m* sink
éviter avoid; ***~ qc à qn*** spare s.o. sth; ***~ de faire qc*** avoid doing sth
évoluer develop, evolve; **évolution** *f* development; BIOL

evolution
évoquer *esprits* conjure up; **~ un problème** bring up a problem
exact *nombre*, *poids* exact, precise; *reportage* accurate; *calcul*, *date*, *solution* right, correct; *personne* punctual; **exactitude** *f* accuracy; (*ponctualité*) punctuality
ex æquo: **être ~** tie, draw
exagération *f* exaggeration; **exagérer** exaggerate
exalter excite; (*vanter*) exalt
examen *m* exam; MÉD examination; **passer un ~** take an exam; **être reçu à un ~** pass an exam; **examiner** examine
exaspérer exasperate
excédent *m* excess; *budgétaire*, *de trésorerie* surplus; **~ de bagages** excess baggage; **excéder** exceed; (*énerver*) irritate
excellence *f* excellence; **Excellence** Excellency; **excellent** excellent; **exceller** excel (**dans** in; **en** in, at; **à faire qch** at doing sth)
excepté 1 *adj*: **la Chine ~e** except for China **2** *prép* except; **~ que** except for the fact that; **~ si** unless, except if; **excepter** exclude, except; **exception** *f* exception; **à l'~ de** with the exception of; **exceptionnel, ~le** exceptional
excès *m* excess; **à l'~** to excess, excessively; **~ de vitesse** speeding; **excessif, -ive** excessive
excitation *f* excitement; (*provocation*) incitement (**à** to); *sexuelle* arousal; **exciter** excite; (*provoquer*) incite (**à** to); *sexuellement* arouse; *appétit* whet; *imagination* stir
exclamation *f* exclamation; **exclamer**: **s'~** exclaim
exclure exclude
exclusion *f* expulsion; **à l'~ de** to the exclusion of; (*à l'exception de*) with the exception of
exclusivité *f* COMM exclusivity, sole rights *pl*; **en ~** exclusively
excursion *f* trip, excursion
excuse *f* excuse; **~s** apology; **excuser** excuse; **s'~** apologize (**de** for); **excusez-moi** excuse me
exécuter *ordre*, *projet* carry out; MUS perform; *loi*, *jugement* enforce; *condamné* execute; **exécution** *f d'un ordre*, *projet* carrying out; MUS performance; *d'une loi*, *un jugement* enforcement; *d'un condamné* execution
exemplaire 1 *adj* exemplary **2** *m* copy; (*échantillon*) sample; **en deux ~s** in duplicate
exemple *m* example; **par ~** for example; **donner l'~** set a good example
exempt exempt (**de** from); *souci* free (**de** from); **exempter** exempt (**de** from);

exemption *f* exemption
exercer *corps* exercise; *influence* exert, use; *pouvoir* use; *profession* practice, *Br* practise; *mémoire* train; MIL drill; **s'~** (*s'entraîner*) practice, *Br* practise; **exercice** *m* exercise (*aussi* ÉDU); *d'une profession* practice; COMM fiscal year, *Br* financial year; MIL drill
exhiber exhibit; *document* produce; **s'~** make an exhibition of o.s.; **exhibitionniste** *m* exhibitionist
exigeant demanding; **exigence** *f* demand; **exiger** demand
exigu, ~ë tiny
exil *m* exile; **exilé, ~e** *m/f* exile; **exiler** exile; **s'~** go into exile
existence *f* existence; **exister** exist
exonérer exempt
exorbitant exorbitant
exotique exotic
expansion *f* expansion
expatrier *argent* move abroad *ou* out of the country; **s'~** settle abroad
expédier send; COMM ship, send; *travail* do quickly
expéditeur, -trice *m/f* sender; COMM shipper, sender; **expédition** *f* sending; COMM shipment; (*voyage*) expedition
expérience *f* experience; *scientifique* experiment
expérimenté experienced; **expérimenter** (*tester*) test
expert, ~e *adj & m/f* expert; **expertise** *f* (*estimation*) valuation; JUR expert testimony
expier expiate
expiration *f d'un délai* expiration, *Br* expiry; *de souffle* exhalation; **expirer** *d'un contrat, délai* expire; (*respirer*) exhale; (*mourir*) die, expire *fml*
explication *f* explanation; **expliquer** explain; **s'~** explain o.s.; ***s'~ avec qn*** talk things over with s.o.
exploit *m sportif, médical* feat; *amoureux* exploit
exploitant, ~e *m/f agricole* farmer
exploitation *f d'une ferme, ligne aérienne* running; *du sol* farming; *de richesses naturelles péj*: *des ouvriers* exploitation; (*entreprise*) operation
exploiter *ferme, ligne aérienne* run; *sol* farm; *richesses naturelles* exploit (*aussi péj*)
explorateur, -trice *m/f* explorer; **explorer** explore
exploser explode (*aussi fig*); ***~ de rire*** F crack up F; **explosif, -ive** *adj & m* explosive; **explosion** *f* explosion (*aussi fig*)
exportateur, -trice 1 *adj* exporting **2** *m* exporter; **exportation** *f* export; **exporter** export

exposé *m* account, report; ÉDU presentation; **exposer** *art, marchandise* exhibit, show; *problème, programme* explain; *à l'air, à la chaleur* expose (*aussi* PHOT); **exposition** *f d'art, de marchandise* exhibition; *d'un problème* explanation; *au soleil* exposure (*aussi* PHOT)
exprès[1] *adv* (*intentionnellement*) deliberately, on purpose; (*spécialement*) expressly
exprès[2], **-esse 1** *adj* express **2** *adj inv* ***lettre*** *f* ***exprès*** express letter
express 1 *adj inv* express **2** *m train* express; *café* espresso
expressément expressly
expression *f* expression
exprimer express; ***s'~*** express o.s.
expulser expel; *d'un pays* deport; **expulsion** *f* expulsion; *d'un pays* deportation
exquis exquisite
extase *f* ecstasy
extension *f des bras, jambes* stretching; (*prolongement*) extension; *d'une épidémie* spread; INFORM expansion
exténuer exhaust
extérieur 1 *adj* external; *mur aussi* outside **2** *m* (*partie externe*) outside, exterior; ***à l'~ de*** outside; **extérioriser** express, let out; ***s'~*** *d'un sentiment* find expression; *d'une personne* express one's emotions
exterminer exterminate
externaliser COM outsource
externe external
extincteur *m* extinguisher
extinction *f* extinction (*aussi fig*)
extirper *mauvaise herbe* pull up; MÉD remove; *fig renseignement* drag out
extorquer extort
extorsion *f* extortion
extraction *f* extraction
extrader extradite
extraire extract
extrait *m* extract
extraordinaire extraordinary
extraterrestre *m/f* extraterrestrial, alien
extravagance *f* extravagance; *d'une personne, d'une idée* eccentricity
extraverti extrovert
extrême 1 *adj* extreme **2** *m* extreme; ***à l'~*** to extremes
Extrême-Orient *m*: ***l'~*** the Far East
extrémiste *m/f* POL extremist;
extrémité *f d'une rue* (very) end; *d'un doigt* tip; (*situation désespérée*) extremity; ***~s*** ANAT extremities
exubérant exuberant
exulter exult
eye-liner *m* eyeliner

F

fable *f* fable

fabricant, ~e *m/f* manufacturer, maker; **fabrication** *f* making; *industrielle* manufacture; **fabriquer** make; *industriellement aussi* manufacture; *histoire* fabricate

fabuleux, -euse fabulous

fac *f* (= ***faculté***) uni, university

façade *f* façade

face *f* face; *d'une pièce* head; ***en ~ (de)*** opposite; ***faire ~ à*** face up to; **face-à-face** *m inv* face-to-face (debate)

fâché annoyed; **fâcher** annoy; ***se ~*** get annoyed; ***se ~ avec qn*** fall out with s.o.; **fâcheux, -euse** annoying; (*déplorable*) unfortunate

facile easy; *personne* easy-going; **facilement** easily; **facilité** *f* easiness; *à faire qch* ease; ***~s de paiement*** easy terms; **faciliter** make easier, facilitate

façon *f* (*manière*) way, method; ***de ~ (à ce) que*** (*+subj*) so that; ***de toute ~*** anyway, anyhow; ***de cette ~*** (in) that way; ***à la ~ de*** like, in the style of

facteur *m* mailman, *Br* postman; MATH, *fig* factor

factrice *f* mailwoman, *Br* postwoman

facture *f* bill; COMM invoice; **facturer** invoice

facultatif, -ive optional

faculté *f* faculty

fade insipid

faible 1 *adj* weak; *bruit, lumière, espoir* faint; *avantage* slight **2** *m pour personne* soft spot; *pour chocolat etc* weakness; **faiblesse** *f* weakness; **faiblir** weaken

faille *f* GÉOL fault; *dans théorie* flaw

faillible fallible; **faillir**: ***il a failli gagner*** he almost won

faim *f* hunger; ***avoir ~*** be hungry; ***mourir de ~*** starve (*aussi fig*)

fainéant, ~e 1 *adj* idle, lazy **2** *m/f* idler

faire 1 *v/t* do; *robe, meuble, repas, liste* make; ***~ de la natation/du ski*** swim/ski, go swimming/skiing; ***cinq plus cinq font dix*** five and five are *ou* make ten; ***ça ne fait rien*** it doesn't matter; ***~ rire qn*** make s.o. laugh; ***~ peindre la salle de bain*** have the bathroom painted **2** *v/i*: ***~ vite*** hurry up, be quick **3** *impersonnel*: ***il fait chaud/froid*** it is *ou* it's warm/cold **4**: ***ça ne se fait pas*** it's not done; ***se ~ rare*** become

rarer; ***se ~ à qc*** get used to sth; ***je ne m'en fais pas*** I'm not worrried
faisable feasible
faisan *m* pheasant
faisceau *m* bundle; *de lumière* beam
fait[1] *m* fact; (*action*) act; (*événement*) development; ***au ~*** by the way; ***de ce ~*** consequently; ***en ~*** in fact; ***tout à ~*** absolutely; ***un ~ divers*** a brief news item
fait[2] *adj*: ***être ~ pour qn/qch*** be made for s.o./sth; ***c'est bien ~ pour lui*** serves him right!
falaise *f* cliff
falloir: ***il faut un visa*** you need a visa, you must have a visa; ***il faut l'avertir*** we have to warn him; ***il me faut sortir, il faut que je sorte*** (*subj*) I have to go out, I must go out; ***s'il le faut*** if necessary; ***il aurait fallu prendre le train*** we should have taken the train; ***comme il faut*** respectable; ***il ne faut pas que je sorte*** (*subj*) I mustn't go out
falsifier *argent* forge; *document* falsify; *vérité* misrepresent
famélique starving
fameux, **-euse** (*célèbre*) famous; (*excellent*) wonderful
familiariser familiarize; **familiarité** *f* familiarity; **familier**, **-ère** familiar
famille *f* family
famine *f* famine
fanatique **1** *adj* fanatical **2** *m/f* fanatic; **fanatisme** *m* fanaticism
faner: ***se ~*** fade
fanfare *f* (*orchestre*) brass band; (*musique*) fanfare; **fanfaron**, **~ne** **1** *adj* boastful **2** *m* boaster
fantaisie *f* imagination; (*caprice*) whim
fantasme *m* fantasy; **fantasmer** fantasize
fantasque strange, weird
fantastique **1** *adj* fantastic; (*imaginaire*) imaginary **2** *m*: ***le ~*** fantasy
fantôme *m* ghost
farce *f au théâtre* farce; (*tour*) joke; CUIS stuffing; **farceur**, **-euse** *m/f* joker; **farcir** CUIS stuff; *fig* cram
fard *m* make-up; ***~ à paupières*** eye shadow
fardeau *m* burden (*aussi fig*)
farder: ***se ~*** make up
farine *f* flour; ***~ de maïs*** corn starch, *Br* cornflour
farouche (*timide*) shy; *volonté, haine* fierce
fascination *f* fascination; **fasciner** fascinate
faste *m* pomp
fast-food *m* fast food restaurant
fastidieux, **-euse** tedious
fastueux, **-euse** lavish
fatal fatal; (*inévitable*) inevitable; **fatalisme** *m* fatalism;

fataliste 1 *adj* fatalistic **2** *m/f* fatalist; **fatalité** *f* fate
fatigant tiring; (*agaçant*) tiresome; **fatigue** *f* tiredness; **fatiguer** tire; (*importuner*) annoy; ***se ~*** get tired
faubourg *m* (working-class) suburb
fauché F broke F; **faucher** *fig* mow down; F (*voler*) pinch F
faufiler: ***se ~ dans une pièce*** slip into a room
faune *f* wildlife, fauna
faussaire *m* forger; **fausser** *calcul, vérité* distort; *clef* bend
faute *f* mistake; (*responsabilité*) fault; ***par sa ~*** because of him; ***~ de*** for lack of; ***sans ~*** without fail
fauteuil *m* armchair; ***~ roulant*** wheelchair
fauve 1 *adj* tawny **2** *m félin* big cat
faux, fausse 1 *adj* false; *incorrect aussi* wrong; *bijoux* imitation, fake; ***fausse couche*** *f* miscarriage; ***~ témoignage*** perjury **2** *adv*: ***chanter ~*** sing out of tune **3** *m copie* forgery, fake
faux-filet *m* CUIS sirloin
faux-monnayeur *m* counterfeiter, forger
faux-semblant *m* pretense, *Br* pretence
faveur *f* favor, *Br* favour; ***de ~*** *traitement* preferential; *prix* special; ***en ~ de*** in favor of
favorable favorable, *Br* favourable; **favori, ~te** *m/f & adj* favorite, *Br* favourite; **favoriser** favor, *Br* favour; *faciliter, avantager* promote; **favoritisme** *m* favoritism, *Br* favouritism
fax *m* fax; **faxer** fax
féconder fertilize; **fécondité** *f* fertility
fécule *f* starch
fédéral federal; **fédération** *f* federation
fée *f* fairy
feeling *m* feeling; ***avoir un bon ~ pour qc*** have a good feeling about sth
feindre: ***~ l'étonnement*** pretend to be astonished, feign astonishment; ***~ de faire qch*** pretend to do sth; **feinte** *f* feint
fêler: ***se ~*** crack
félicitations *fpl* congratulations; **féliciter** congratulate (***de*** on)
fêlure *f* crack
femelle *f & adj* female
féminin 1 *adj* feminine; *sexe* female; *problèmes, magazines, mode* women's **2** *m* GRAM feminine; **féministe** *m/f & adj* feminist; **féminité** *f* femininity
femme *f* woman; (*épouse*) wife; ***~ battue*** battered wife; ***~ au foyer*** homemaker, *Br* housewife
fendre split; (*fissurer*) crack; *cœur* break; ***se ~*** split; (*se fissurer*) crack

fenêtre *f* window
fenouil *m* BOT fennel
fente *f* crack; *d'une boîte à lettres, jupe* slit; *pour pièces de monnaie* slot
fer *m* iron; **~ à cheval** horseshoe; **~ à repasser** iron
férié: **jour** *m* **~** (public) holiday
ferme[1] **1** *adj* firm; **terre** *f* **~** dry land, terra firma **2** *adv travailler* hard; **s'ennuyer ~** be bored stiff
ferme[2] *f* farm
fermé closed, shut; *robinet* off; *club* exclusive
fermenter ferment
fermer 1 *v/t* close, shut; *eau, gaz, robinet* turn off; *manteau* fasten; **ferme-la!** shut up! **2** *v/i* close, shut; *d'un manteau* fasten; **se ~** close, shut
fermeté *f* firmness
fermeture *f* closing; *définitive* closure; *mécanisme* fastener; **~ éclair** zipper, *Br* zip (fastener)
fermier 1 *adj œufs, poulet* free-range **2** *m* farmer
féroce fierce, ferocious; **férocité** *f* fierceness, ferocity
ferré, ~e: **voie** *f* **~e** (railroad *ou Br* railway) track
ferroviaire railroad *atr*, *Br* railway *atr*
fertile fertile; **~ en** full of; **fertilité** *f* fertility
fervent fervent
fesse *f* buttock; **~s** butt, *Br* bottom; **fessée** *f* spanking
festin *m* feast
festival *m* festival
festivités *fpl* festivities
fêtard *m* F reveler, *Br* reveller; **fête** *f* festival; (*soirée*) party; *publique* holiday; REL feast (day), festival; *jour d'un saint* name day; **les ~s (de fin d'année)** the holidays, Christmas and New Year; **faire la ~** party; **~ foraine** fun fair; **Fête des mères** Mother's Day; **Fête nationale** Bastille Day; **fêter** celebrate; (*accueillir*) fête
feu *m* fire; AUTO, MAR light; *de circulation* (traffic) light, *Br* (traffic) lights *pl*; *d'une cuisinière* burner; *fig* (*enthousiasme*) passion; **coup** *m* **de ~** shot; **prendre ~** catch fire; **vous avez du ~?** got a light?; **~ arrière** AUTO taillight
feuillage *m* foliage; **feuille** *f* leaf; *de papier* sheet; **~ d'impôt** tax return; **~ de paie** payslip; **feuilleter** *livre etc* leaf through
feuilleton *m* serial; TV soap opera
feutre *m* felt; *stylo* felt-tipped pen; *chapeau* fedora
février *m* February
fiable reliable
fiançailles *fpl* engagement; **fiancé, ~e** *m/f* fiancé; **fiancer**: **se ~ avec** get engaged to

fibre *f* fiber, *Br* fibre; ***avoir la ~ paternelle*** *fig* be a born father; ***la ~ patriotique*** patriotic feelings
ficeler tie up; **ficelle** *f* string; *pain* thin French stick
fiche *f pour classement* index card; *formulaire* form; ÉL plug
ficher F (*faire*) do; (*donner*) give; (*mettre*) stick; ***fiche-moi la paix!*** leave me alone!; ***je m'en fiche*** I don't give a damn
fichier *m* INFORM file; ***~ joint*** attachment
fichu F (*inutilisable*) kaput F; (*sale*) filthy; ***être mal ~*** *santé* be feeling rotten
fictif, **-ive** fictitious; **fiction** *f* fiction
fidèle 1 *adj* faithful **2** *m/f* REL, *fig*: ***les fidèles*** the faithful *pl*; **fidélité** *f* faithfulness
fier[1]: ***se ~ à*** trust
fier[2], **-ère** *adj* proud (***de*** of); **fierté** *f* pride
fièvre *f* fever; ***avoir de la ~*** have a fever; **fiévreux**, **-euse** feverish
figer congeal; ***se ~*** *fig*: *d'un sourire* become fixed
figue *f* fig; **figuier** *m* fig tree
figurant, **~e** *m/f de théâtre* walk-on; *de cinéma* extra; **figure** *f* figure; (*visage*) face; **figuré** figurative; **figurer** figure; ***se ~ qc*** imagine sth
fil *m* thread; *de métal*, ÉL, TÉL wire; ***coup m de ~*** TÉL (phone) call
filature *f* spinning; *usine* mill; ***prendre qn en ~*** *fig* tail s.o.
file *f* line; *d'une route* lane; ***~ (d'attente)*** line, *Br* queue
filer 1 *v/t* spin; F (*donner*) give; (*épier*) tail F **2** *v/i* F (*partir vite*) race off; *du temps* fly past
filet *m d'eau* trickle; *de pêche*, *tennis* net; CUIS fillet
filial, **~e 1** *adj* filial **2** *f* COMM subsidiary
fille *f* girl; *parenté* daughter; ***vieille ~*** old maid; **fillette** *f* little girl
filleul *m* godson; **filleule** *f* goddaughter
film *m* movie, *Br aussi* film; *couche* film; ***~ policier*** detective movie *ou Br aussi* film; **filmer** film
fils *m* son; ***~ à papa*** (spoilt) rich kid
filtre *m* filter; **filtrer 1** *v/t* filter; *fig* screen **2** *v/i* filter through; *fig* leak
fin[1] *f* end; ***à la ~*** in the end; ***mettre ~ à qc*** put an end to sth; ***sans ~*** endless; *parler* endlessly
fin[2] **1** *adj* fine; (*mince*) thin; *taille*, *cheville* slender; *esprit* refined; (*rusé*, *malin*) sharp **2** *adv* fine(ly)
final, **~e 1** *adj* final **2** *m*: **~e** MUS finale **3** *f* SP final; **finale 1** *m* MUS finale **2** *f* SP final; **finaliser** finalize; **finaliste** *m/f* finalist

finance *f* finance; **financer** fund, finance; **financier, -ère 1** *adj* financial **2** *m* financier
finesse *f* (*délicatesse*) fineness
fini 1 *adj* finished **2** *m* finish; **finir 1** *v/t* finish **2** *v/i* finish; **~ *de faire qc*** finish doing sth; **~ *par faire qc*** finish up doing sth
finlandais, ~e 1 *adj* Finnish **2** *m langue* Finnish; **Finlandais, ~e** *m/f* Finn; **Finlande** *f*: ***la ~*** Finland
firme *f* firm
fisc *m* tax authorities *pl*
fissure *f* crack
fixe 1 *adj* fixed; *adresse, personnel* permanent **2** *m* basic salary; **fixer** fasten; (*déterminer*) fix, set; PHOT fix; (*regarder*) stare at; ***se ~*** (*s'établir*) settle down
flageolet *m* flageolet bean
flagrant flagrant; ***en ~ délit*** red-handed
flair *m* sense of smell; *fig* intuition; **flairer** smell (*aussi fig*)
flambant: ***~ neuf*** brand new; **flamber 1** *v/i* blaze **2** *v/t* CUIS flambé
flamme *f* flame; *fig* fervor, *Br* fervour
flan *m* flan
flancher quail
flâner stroll
flanquer flank; F (*jeter*) fling; *coup* give
flaque *f* puddle
flasque flabby
flatter flatter; ***se ~ de qc*** congratulate o.s. on sth; **flatterie** *f* flattery; **flatteur, -euse 1** *adj* flattering **2** *m/f* flatterer
flèche *f* arrow; *d'un clocher* spire; ***monter en ~*** *de prix* skyrocket
fléchir 1 *v/t* bend; (*faire céder*) sway **2** *v/i d'une poutre* bend; *fig* (*céder*) give in; (*faiblir*) weaken; *d'un prix, de ventes* fall
flegmatique phlegmatic
flemme *f* F laziness; ***j'ai la ~ de le faire*** I can't be bothered
flétrir: ***se ~*** wither
fleur *f* flower; *d'un arbre* blossom; **fleurir** flower, bloom; *fig* flourish; **fleuriste** *m/f* florist
fleuve *m* river
flexibilité *f* flexibility; **flexible** flexible
flic *m* F cop F
flinguer F gun down
flipper 1 *m* pinball machine; *jeu* pinball **2** *v/i* F freak out F
flirter flirt
flocon *m* flake; ***~ de neige*** snowflake
Floride *f* Florida
florissant *fig* flourishing
flot *m* flood (*aussi fig*); **~s** waves; ***remettre à ~*** refloat (*aussi fig*)
flottant floating; *vêtements* baggy

flotte *f* fleet; F (*eau*) water; F (*pluie*) rain; **flotter** *d'un bateau* float; *d'un drapeau* flutter; *d'un sourire, air* hover; *fig* waver
flou blurred, fuzzy; *robe* loose-fitting
fluctuation *f* fluctuation; **fluctuer** COMM fluctuate
fluide 1 *adj* fluid; *circulation* moving freely **2** *m* PHYS fluid; **fluidité** *f* fluidity
fluorescent fluorescent
flûte *f* MUS, *verre* flute; *pain* thin French stick
fluvial river *atr*
flux *m* MAR flow
fœtus *m* fetus, *Br* foetus
foi *f* faith; ***être de bonne/mauvaise ~*** be sincere/insincere
foie *m* liver; ***une crise de ~*** a stomach upset
foire *f* fair
fois *f* time; ***une ~*** once; ***deux ~*** twice; ***trois ~*** three times; ***il était une ~ …*** once upon a time there was …; ***quatre ~ six*** four times six; ***à la ~*** at the same time
foisonner be abundant
folie *f* madness; ***faire des ~s*** *achats* go on a spending spree
folk *m* folk (music)
folklore folklore
follement madly
fomenter foment
foncé *couleur* dark; **foncer** *de couleurs* darken; AUTO speed along; ***~ sur*** rush at
foncier, -ère COMM land
foncièrement fundamentally
fonction *f* function; (*poste*) office; ***faire ~ de*** act as; ***en ~ de*** according to; ***prendre ses ~s*** take up office
fonctionnaire *m/f* public servant
fonctionnement *m* functioning; **fonctionner** work; *du système* function
fond *m* bottom; *d'une salle, armoire* back; *d'une peinture* background; (*contenu*) content; *d'un problème* heart; *d'un pantalon* seat; ***à ~*** thoroughly; ***au ~, dans le ~*** basically
fondamental fundamental
fondateur, -trice *m/f* founder; **fondation** *f* foundation;
fondé 1 *adj* well-founded **2** *m*: ***~ de pouvoir*** authorized representative; **fondement** *m fig* basis; ***sans ~*** groundless; **fonder** found; ***~ qch sur*** base sth on; ***se ~ sur*** *d'une personne* base o.s. on; *d'une idée* be based on
fondre 1 *v/t neige* melt; *dans l'eau* dissolve; *métal* melt down **2** *v/i de la neige* melt; *dans l'eau* dissolve; ***~ sur*** *proie* pounce on
fonds *m* **1** *sg* fund; *d'une bibliothèque* collection; ***~ de commerce*** business **2** *pl* (*argent*) funds
fondu melted

fondue *f* CUIS fondue; **~ bourguignonne** beef fondue
fontaine *f* fountain; (*source*) spring
fonte *f métal* cast iron; **~ des neiges** spring thaw
football *m* soccer, *Br aussi* football; **~ américain** football, *Br* American football; **footballeur, -euse** *m/f* soccer player, *Br aussi* footballer
footing *m* jogging; **faire du ~** jog, go jogging
force *f* strength; (*violence*) force; **à ~ de travailler** by working; **de ~** by force; **~s armées** armed forces
forcené, ~e *m/f* maniac
forcer force; **se ~** force o.s.
forestier, -ère 1 *adj* forest *atr* **2** *m* ranger, *Br* forest warden
forêt *f* forest
forfait *m* COMM package; (*prix*) all-in price; **déclarer ~** withdraw
formaliser: **se ~ de** take offense *ou Br* offence at; **formalité** *f* formality
format *m* format; **formater** format
formation *f* formation; (*éducation*) training; **~ continue** continuing education
forme *f* form; **en ~ de** in the shape of; **être en ~** be in form, be in good shape; **formel, ~le** formal; (*explicite*) categorical; **formellement** *adv*: **~ interdit** strictly forbidden; **former** form; (*instruire*) train; **se ~** form
formidable enormous; F great F
formulaire *m* form
formulation *f* wording
formule *f* formula; **formuler** formulate; *vœux, jugement* express
fort 1 *adj* strong; (*gros*) stout; *coup, pluie* heavy; *somme* big; **être ~ en qch** be good at sth **2** *adv parler* loudly; *pousser, frapper* hard; (*très*) extremely; (*beaucoup*) a lot **3** *m* strong point; MIL fort; **fortement** *pousser* hard; (*beaucoup*) greatly
fortifier strengthen
fortuit chance
fortune *f* luck; **de ~** makeshift
fosse *f* pit; (*tombe*) grave; **fossé** *m* ditch; *fig* gulf; **fossette** *f* dimple
fossile *m & adj* fossil
fou, folle 1 *adj* mad; (*incroyable*) incredible; **être ~ de qn/qc** be mad *ou* crazy about s.o./sth; **~ de** *joie etc* beside o.s. with **2** *m/f* madman; madwoman
foudre *f* lightning; **coup** *m* **de ~** *fig* love at first sight
foudroyer strike down; **~ qn du regard** give s.o. a withering look
fouet *m* whip; CUIS whisk
fougueux, -euse fiery
fouiller 1 *v/i* dig; (*chercher*) search **2** *v/t de police* search;

en archéologie excavate
fouiner nose around
foulard *m* scarf
foule *f* crowd; ***une ~ de*** masses of
fouler trample; *sol* set foot on; ***se ~ la cheville*** twist one's ankle; **foulure** *f* sprain
four *m* oven; TECH kiln; *fig* F (*insuccès*) flop F
fourchette *f* fork; (*éventail*) bracket; **fourchu** forked; ***cheveux*** *mpl* ***~s*** split ends
fourgon *m* baggage car, *Br* luggage van; *camion* van; **fourgonnette** *f* small van
fourmi *f* ant
fourmillements *mpl* pins and needles; **fourmiller** swarm (***de*** with)
fournaise *f fig* oven; **fourneau** *m* furnace; CUIS stove
fourni: ***bien ~*** well stocked; **fournir** supply (***de***, ***en*** with); *occasion* provide; *effort* make; ***~ qc à qn*** provide s.o. with sth; **fournisseur** *m* supplier; ***~ d'accès (Internet)*** Internet service provider, ISP; **fourniture** *f* supply; ***~s scolaires*** school stationery and books
fourré¹ *m* thicket
fourré² *adj* CUIS filled; *vêtement* lined
fourrer stick, shove; (*remplir*) fill; ***se ~ dans*** get into
fourrière *f* pound
fourrure *f* fur
fourvoyer: ***se ~*** go astray
foutre F do; (*mettre*) stick; *coup* give; ***se ~ de qn*** make fun of s.o.; *indifférence* not give a damn about s.o.; ***je m'en fous!*** I don't give a damn!
foyer *m* fireplace; *d'une famille* home; *de jeunes* club; (*pension*) hostel; *d'un théâtre* foyer; *d'un incendie* seat; *d'une infection* source
fracas *m* crash; **fracasser** shatter
fractionner divide (up) (***en*** into)
fracture *f* MÉD *m* fracture; **fracturer** *coffre* break open; *jambe* fracture
fragile fragile; *santé* frail; *cœur* weak; **fragiliser** weaken; **fragilité** *f* fragility
fragment *m* fragment
fraîcheur *f* freshness; (*froideur*) coolness (*aussi fig*); **fraîchir** *du vent* freshen; *du temps* get cooler
frais¹, **fraîche 1** *adj* fresh; (*froid*) cool; *peinture* wet; *nouvelles* recent; ***servir ~*** serve chilled; ***il fait ~*** it's cool **2** *adv* freshly, newly **3** *m*: ***prendre le ~*** get a breath of fresh air
frais² *mpl* expenses *pl*; COMM costs *pl*; ***faire des ~*** incur costs; ***à mes ~*** at my (own) expense; ***~ bancaires*** bank charges; ***~ généraux*** overhead, *Br* overheads
fraise *f* strawberry

framboise *f* raspberry
franc[1], **franche** *adj* frank; *regard* open; COMM free
franc[2] *m* franc
français, ~e 1 *adj* French **2** *m langue* French; **Français, ~e** *m/f* Frenchman; Frenchwoman; ***les ~*** the French *pl*; **France** *f*: ***la ~*** France
franchir cross; *obstacle* negotiate
franchise *f caractère* frankness; (*exemption*) exemption; COMM franchise; *d'une assurance* deductible, *Br* excess
franco *adv*: **~ (*de port*)** carriage free; ***y aller ~*** *fig* F go right ahead
francophone 1 *adj* French-speaking **2** *m/f* French speaker
franc-parler *m* outspokenness
frange *f* bangs *pl*, *Br* fringe
frappant striking; **frappe** *f* INFORM keying; ***faute*** *f* ***de ~*** typo, typing error; **frapper 1** *v/t* hit, strike; (*impressionner*) strike **2** *v/i* (*agir*) strike; *à la porte* knock (***à*** at); ***~ dans ses mains*** clap (one's hands)
fraternel, ~le brotherly, fraternal; **fraternité** *f* brotherhood
fraude *f* fraud; ÉDU cheating; ***passer en ~*** smuggle; **frauduleux, -euse** fraudulent
frayer: ***se ~*** *chemin* clear
frayeur *f* fright
fredonner hum
frein *m* brake; ***sans ~*** *fig* unbridled; ***~ à main*** parking brake, *Br* hand brake; **freiner 1** *v/i* brake **2** *v/t fig* curb, check
frêle frail
frelon *m* hornet
frémir shake; *de feuilles* quiver; *de l'eau* simmer; **frémissement** *m* shiver; *de feuilles* quivering
frénésie *f* frenzy; ***avec ~*** frenetically
fréquemment frequently; **fréquence** *f* frequency; ***quelle est la ~ des bus?*** how often do the buses go?; **fréquent** frequent; *situation* common
fréquentation *f d'un théâtre etc* attendance; ***tes ~s*** (*amis*) the company you keep; **fréquenter** *endroit* go to regularly, frequent; *personne* see; *groupe* go around with
frère *m* brother
fret *m* freight
frétiller wriggle
friable crumbly
friand: ***être ~ de qc*** be fond of sth; **friandises** *fpl* sweet things
fric *m* F money, dosh F
friche *f* AGR: ***en ~*** (lying) fallow
friction *f* friction; *de la tête* scalp massage; **frictionner** massage

frigidaire *m* refrigerator
frigide frigid
frigo *m* F icebox, fridge; **frigorifier** refrigerate
frileux, -euse: ***être ~*** feel the cold
frimer show off; **frimeur, -euse** show-off
fringues *fpl* F clothes, gear F
frire 1 *v/i* fry **2** *v/t*: ***faire ~*** fry
frisé curly; **friser** *cheveux* curl; *fig*: *le ridicule* verge on
frissonner shiver
frit fried; **(*pommes*) *frites*** *fpl* (French) fries, *Br aussi* chips; **friteuse** *f* deep fryer; **friture** *f poissons Br* whitebait, *small fried fish*; *huile* oil; *à la radio*, TÉL interference
frivole frivolous; **frivolité** *f* frivolity
froid 1 *adj* cold (*aussi fig*); ***j'ai ~*** I'm cold; ***prendre ~*** catch (a) cold **2** *m* cold; ***humour m à ~*** dry humor; **froidement** *fig* coldly; (*calmement*) coolly; *tuer* in cold blood; **froideur** *f* coldness
froissement *m bruit* rustle; **froisser** crumple; *fig* offend; ***se ~*** crumple; *fig* take offense *ou Br* offence
fromage *m* cheese; ***~ blanc*** fromage frais; ***~ à tartiner*** cheese spread
froncer gather; ***~ les sourcils*** frown
front *m* front; ANAT forehead; ***de ~*** from the front; *fig* head-on; ***marcher de ~*** walk side by side
frontière *f* frontier, border
frotter 1 *v/i* rub **2** *v/t* rub (***de*** with); *meuble* polish; *sol* scrub; *allumette* strike
frousse *f* F fear; ***avoir la ~*** be scared
fructifier BOT bear fruit; *d'un placement* yield a profit
fructueux, -euse fruitful
fruit *m* fruit; ***~s*** fruit; ***~s de mer*** seafood
frustrant frustrating; **frustration** *f* frustration
fugitif, -ive 1 *adj* runaway; *fig* fleeting **2** *m/f* fugitive
fugue *f d'un enfant* escapade; MUS fugue; ***faire une ~*** run away
fuir 1 *v/i* flee; *du temps* fly; *d'un tuyau* leak; *d'un robinet* drip; *d'un liquide* leak out **2** *v/t* shun; *question* avoid; **fuite** *f* flight (***devant*** from); *d'un tuyau etc* leak; ***prendre la ~*** take flight
fulgurant dazzling; *vitesse* lightning
fumé smoked; *verre* tinted
fumée *f* smoke; **fumer** smoke; **fumeur, -euse** *m/f* smoker
funèbre funeral *atr*; (*lugubre*) gloomy
funérailles *fpl* funeral
funeste fatal
fur: ***au ~ et à mesure*** as I/you *etc* go along; ***au ~ et à mesure que*** as

fureter ferret around
fureur *f* fury; ***faire ~*** be all the rage
furie (*colère*) fury; *femme* shrew; **furieux**, **-euse** furious (***contre qn*** with s.o.; ***de qch*** with *ou* at sth)
furtif, **-ive** furtive, stealthy
fuseau *m*: ***~ horaire*** time zone
fusée *f* rocket
fusible *m* ÉL fuse
fusil *m* rifle; ***~ de chasse*** shotgun; **fusiller** execute by firing squad
fusion *f* COMM merger; PHYS fusion; **fusionner** COMM merge
futé cunning, clever
futile futile; *personne* frivolous
futur *m & adj* future
fuyant *menton* receding; *regard* evasive

G

gabarit *m* size; TECH template
gâcher *fig* spoil; *travail* bungle; *temps*, *argent* waste
gâchis *m* (*désordre*) mess; (*gaspillage*) waste
gadget *m* gadget
gaffe *f* F blooper F, blunder; ***faire ~ à*** F be careful of
gaffer F make a gaffe *ou* blooper F
gage *fig* forfeit; (*preuve*) token; ***tueur m à ~s*** hitman; ***mettre en ~*** pawn
gagnant, **~e** **1** *adj* winning **2** *m/f* winner
gagne-pain *m* livelihood
gagner win; *salaire*, *amitié etc* earn; *place*, *temps* gain; *endroit* reach; *de peur etc* overcome; ***~ sa vie*** earn one's living
gai cheerful; *un peu ivre* tipsy; **gaieté** *f* cheerfulness
gain *m* gain; (*avantage*) benefit; ***~s*** profits; *d'un employé* earnings
gaine *f* sheath
galant galant; ***homme ~*** gentleman
galaxie *f* galaxy
galère *f*: ***il est dans la ~*** *fig* F he's in a mess; **galérer** F sweat
galerie *f* gallery; AUTO roof-rack; ***~ d'art*** art gallery; ***~ marchande*** mall
galet *m* pebble
Galles *fpl*: ***le pays m de ~*** Wales; **gallois**, **~e** **1** *adj* Welsh **2** *m langue* Welsh; **Gallois**, **~e** *m/f* Welshman; Welsh woman
galop *m* gallop; **galoper** gallop
galopin *m* urchin
galvaniser galvanize
gambader gambol, leap
gamin, **~e** **1** *m/f* kid **2** *adj*

childlike
gamme *f* MUS scale; *fig* range; ***bas de ~*** downscale, *Br* downmarket
gang *m* gang
gangster *m* gangster
gant *m* glove; ***~ de toilette*** washcloth, *Br* facecloth
garage *m* garage; **garagiste** *m* auto mechanic; *propriétaire* garage owner
garant, ~e *m/f* guarantor; **garantie** *f* guarantee; **garantir** guarantee
garce *f* F bitch
garçon *m* boy; (*serveur*) waiter; ***~ d'honneur*** best man; ***~ manqué*** tomboy; **garçonnière** *f* bachelor apartment *ou Br* flat
garde[1] *f* care (***de*** of); MIL guard; ***prendre ~*** be careful; ***être de ~*** be on duty; ***mettre qn en ~*** put s.o. on their guard; ***~ à vue*** police custody
garde[2] *m* guard; ***~ forestier*** (forest) ranger
garde-boue *m* AUTO fender, *Br* wing
garde-fou *m* railing
garde-malade *m/f* nurse
garder *objet* keep; *vêtement* keep on; (*surveiller*) guard; *malade, enfant* look after; ***se ~ de faire qch*** be careful not to do sth
garderie *f* daycare center, *Br* daycare centre
gardien, ~ne *m/f de prison* guard, *Br* warder; *d'un musée* attendant; *d'immeuble, d'école* janitor; *fig* guardian; **~ (*de but*)** goalkeeper **~ *de la paix*** police officer
gare[1] *f* station; ***~ routière*** bus station
gare[2]: ***~ à toi!*** watch out!; *ça va mal se passer* you'll be for it!
garer park; ***se ~*** park; *pour laisser passer* move aside
gargariser: ***se ~*** gargle
gargouiller gurgle; *de l'estomac* rumble
garnement *m* rascal
garnir (*fournir*) fit (***de*** with); (*orner*) trim (***de*** with); **garniture** *f légumes* vegetables *pl*
gars *m* F guy F
gasoil *m* gas oil, *Br* diesel
gaspillage *m* waste; **gaspiller** waste; **gaspilleur, -euse 1** *adj* wasteful **2** *m/f* waster
gastroentérite *f* gastroenteritis
gastronome *m/f* gourmet; **gastronomie** *f* gastronomy
gâteau *m* cake; ***~ sec*** cookie, *Br* biscuit
gâter spoil; ***se ~*** *d'un aliment* spoil; *du temps* deteriorate
gauche 1 *adj* left; *manières* gauche **2** *f* left; ***à ~*** on the left (***de*** of); **gaucher, -ère 1** *adj* left-handed **2** *m/f* left-hander
gaufre *f* waffle; **gaufrette** *f* wafer

gaver *oie* force-feed; ***~ qn de qch*** *fig* stuff s.o. full of sth
gaz *m* gas; ***mettre les ~*** step on the gas; ***~ à effet de serre*** greenhouse gas
gaze *f* gauze
gazeux, -euse *boisson* carbonated, *Br* fizzy
gazinière *f* gas cooker
gazole *m* gas oil, *Br* diesel
gazon *m* grass
gazouiller twitter
géant, ~e 1 *adj* gigantic, giant *atr* **2** *m/f* giant
geindre groan
gel *m* frost; *fig*: *des prix* freeze; *cosmétique* gel
gélatine *f* gelatine
gelée *f* frost; CUIS aspic; *confiture* jelly, *Br* jam; **geler 1** *v/t* freeze **2** *v/i d'une personne* freeze; ***il gèle*** there's a frost
Gémeaux *mpl* ASTROL Gemini
gémir groan; **gémissement** *m* groan
gênant (*embarrassant*) embarrassing
gencive *f* gum
gendarme *m* policeman; **gendarmerie** *f* police force; *lieu* police station
gendre *m* son-in-law
gêne *f* (*embarras*) embarrassment; (*dérangement*) inconvenience; *physique* difficulty; ***sans ~*** shameless; **gêner** bother; (*embarrasser*) embarrass; (*encombrer*) be in the way
général, ~e 1 *adj* general; ***en ~*** generally **2** *m* MIL general **3** *f* THÉÂT dress rehearsal; **généraliser** generalize; ***se ~*** spread; **généraliste** *m* MÉD generalist; **généralités** *fpl* generalities
générateur *m* generator; **générer** generate
généreux, -euse generous; **générosité** *f* generosity
génétique genetic; **génétiquement** genetically; ***~ modifié*** genetically modified, GM
génétiquement genetically; ***~ modifié*** genetically modified, GM
Genève Geneva
génial of genius; (*formidable*) terrific; **génie** *m* genius; TECH engineering; ***avoir du ~*** be a genius; ***~ civil*** civil engineering
genou *m* knee; ***à ~x*** on one's knees
genre *m* kind, sort; GRAM gender; ***bon chic, bon ~*** preppie *atr*
gens *mpl* people *pl*
gentil, ~le nice; *enfant* good; **gentillesse** *f* (*amabilité*) kindness
géographie *f* geography
géologie *f* geology; **géologue** *m/f* geologist
géomètre *m/f* geometrician; **géométrie** *f* geometry
gérance *f* management; **gé-**

rant, ~e *m/f* manager
gerbe *f de blé* sheaf
gercé *lèvres* chapped
gérer manage
gériatrie *f* geriatrics
germain: ***cousin*** *m* **~**, ***cousine*** *f* ***~e*** (first) cousin
germe *m* germ (*aussi fig*); **germer** germinate
gestation *f* gestation
geste *m* gesture; **gesticuler** gesticulate
gestion *f* management; **gestionnaire** *m/f* manager
ghetto *m* ghetto
gibier *m* game
giboulée *f* wintry shower
gicler spurt
gifle *f* slap (in the face); **gifler** slap (in the face)
gigantesque gigantic
gigaoctet *m* gigabyte
gigot *m d'agneau* leg
gigoter F fidget
gilet *m* vest, *Br* waistcoat; (*chandail*) cardigan; **~ *de sauvetage*** lifejacket
gin *m* gin; **~ *tonic*** gin and tonic
gingembre *m* BOT ginger
girafe *f* giraffe
giratoire: ***sens*** *m* **~** traffic circle, *Br* roundabout
gisement *m* GÉOL deposit; **~ *pétrolifère*** *ou* ***de pétrole*** oilfield
gitan, ~e *m/f* gypsy
gîte *m* holiday home
givre *m* frost; **givré** covered with frost; *avec du sucre* frosted; F (*fou*) crazy
glace *f* ice; (*miroir*) mirror; AUTO window; (*crème glacée*) ice cream; *d'un gâteau* frosting, *Br* icing; *d'une tarte* glaze; **glacer** freeze; (*intimider*) petrify; *gâteau* frost, *Br* ice; *tarte* glaze; ***se*** **~** freeze; *du sang* run cold; **glacial** icy (*aussi fig*); **glacière** *f* cool bag; *fig* icebox; **glaçon** *m* icicle; *artificiel* icecube
glaise *f* (*aussi* ***terre*** *f* **~**) clay
gland *m* acorn
glande *f* gland
glander F hang around F
glaner *fig* glean
glapir shriek
glauque *eau* murky; *couleur* blue-green
glissade *f* slide; *accidentelle* slip; **glissant** slippery; **glissement** *m* **~ *de terrain*** landslide; **glisser 1** *v/t* slip (***dans*** into) **2** *v/i* slide; *sur l'eau* glide (***sur*** over); (*déraper*) slip; *être glissant* be slippery; ***se*** **~ *dans*** slip into
global global; *prix, somme* total, overall; **globalisation** *f* globalization; **globe** *m* globe; **~ *oculaire*** eyeball
gloire *f* glory; **glorieux, -euse** glorious; **glorifier** glorify
glousser cluck; *rire* giggle
gluant sticky
glycine *f* wisteria
gnangnan F *film, livre* sloppy F
goal *m* goalkeeper

gobelet *m* tumbler; *en carton, plastique* cup
gober gobble; F *mensonge* swallow
godet *m récipient* pot; *de vêtements* flare
gogo F: ***à ~*** galore
goinfrer: ***se ~*** *péj* stuff o.s.
golf *m* SP golf; *terrain* golf course
golfe *m* GÉOGR gulf
gomme *f* gum; *pour effacer* eraser; **gommer** (*effacer*) erase
gond *m* hinge; ***sortir de ses ~s*** fly off the handle
gondole *f* gondola
gonflable inflatable; **gonfler** **1** *v/i* swell **2** *v/t* blow up; (*exagérer*) exaggerate
gonzesse *f* F *péj* chick F
gorge *f* throat; (*poitrine*) bosom; GÉOGR gorge; ***avoir mal à la ~*** have a sore throat; **gorgée** *f* mouthful; **gorger**: ***se ~*** gorge o.s. (***de*** with)
gosier *m* throat
gosse *m/f* F kid F
goudron *m* tar
gouffre *m* abyss; *fig* depths *pl*
goujat *m* boor
goulot *m* neck; ***boire au ~*** drink from the bottle
goulu greedy
gourd numb (with the cold)
gourde *f récipient* water bottle; *fig* F moron F
gourer F: ***se ~*** goof F, *Br* boob
gourmand, **~e** **1** *adj* greedy **2** *m/f* gourmand; **gourmandise** *f* greediness; **~s** *mets* delicacies; **gourmet** *m* gourmet
gourmette *f* chain
gourou *m* guru
gousse *f* pod; ***~ d'ail*** clove of garlic
goût *m* taste; ***de bon ~*** tasteful, in good taste; ***de mauvais ~*** tasteless, in bad taste; ***avoir du ~*** have taste; **goûter** **1** *v/t* taste; *fig* enjoy **2** *v/i prendre un goûter* have an afternoon snack **3** *m* afternoon snack
goutte *f* drop; ***~ de pluie*** raindrop; **goutte-à-goutte** *m* MÉD drip; **goutter** drip; **gouttière** *f* gutter
gouvernement *m* government; **gouverner** *pays* govern; *passions* master, control; MAR steer; **gouverneur** *m* governor
grâce *f* grace; (*bienveillance*) favor, *Br* favour; JUR pardon; ***faire ~ à qn de qc*** spare s.o. sth; ***~ à*** thanks to; **gracier** reprieve; **gracieux**, **-euse** graceful; ***à titre ~*** free
grade *m* rank; **gradé** *m* MIL noncommissioned officer
gradins *mpl* SP bleachers, *Br* terraces
graduellement gradually
graduer (*augmenter*) gradually increase; *instrument* graduate
graffitis *mpl* graffiti *sg ou pl*
grain *m* grain; MAR squall; ***~ de***

beauté mole, beauty spot; ***~ de raisin*** grape
graine *f* seed
graissage *m* lubrication, greasing; **graisse** *f* fat; TECH grease; **graisser** grease, lubricate; (*salir*) get grease on; **graisseux**, **-euse** greasy
grammaire *f* grammar; **grammatical** grammatical
gramme *m* gram
grand 1 *adj* big; (*haut*) tall; (*adulte*) grown-up; (*long*) long; (*important, glorieux*) great; ***il est ~ temps*** it's high time; ***~e surface*** *f* supermarket; ***les ~es vacances*** *fpl* the summer vacation, *Br* the summer holidays; ***~ ensemble*** new development, *Br* (housing) estate **2** *adv ouvrir* wide **3** *m* giant, great man
grand-chose: ***pas ~*** not much
Grande-Bretagne: ***la ~*** Great Britain
grandeur *f* (*taille*) size; ***~ nature*** lifesize
grandiose magnificent
grandir 1 *v/i* grow **2** *v/t*: ***~ qn*** make s.o. look taller; *de l'expérience* strengthen s.o.
grand-mère *f* grandmother
grand-père *m* grandfather
grands-parents *mpl* grandparents *pl*
granit(e) *m* granite
granuleux, **-euse** granular
graphique 1 *adj* graphic **2** *m* chart; MATH graph; INFORM graphic
grappe *f* cluster; ***~ de raisin*** bunch of grapes
grappin *m*: ***mettre le ~ sur qn*** get one's hands on s.o.
gras, **~se 1** *adj* fatty, fat; *personne* fat; *cheveux, peau* greasy; ***faire la ~se matinée*** sleep late **2** *m* CUIS fat
gratification *f* (*prime*) bonus; PSYCH gratification; **gratifier**: ***~ qn de qc*** present s.o. with sth
gratiné CUIS with a sprinkling of cheese; *fig* F *addition* colossal
gratitude *f* gratitude
gratte-ciel *m* skyscraper; **gratter** scrape; (*griffer, piquer*) scratch; (*enlever*) scrape off; *mot* scratch out; ***se ~*** scratch; **grattoir** *m* scraper
gratuit free; *fig* gratuitous
gravats *mpl* rubble
grave serious; *son* deep; ***ce n'est pas ~*** it's not a problem
graver engrave; *disque* cut
gravier *m* gravel
gravillon *m* grit; ***~s*** gravel, *Br* loose chippings *pl*
gravir climb
gravité *f* seriousness; PHYS gravity
gravure *f* ART engraving; (*reproduction*) print
gré *m*: ***bon ~, mal ~*** like it or not; ***contre mon ~*** against

my will; ***de bon ~*** willingly; ***de son plein ~*** of one's own free will
grec, ~que 1 *adj* Greek **2** *m langue* Greek; **Grec, ~que** *m/f* Greek; **Grèce**: ***la ~*** Greece
greffe graft; ***~ du cœur*** MÉD heart transplant; **greffer** graft; *cœur, poumon* transplant
greffier *m* clerk of the court
grêle[1] *adj jambes* skinny; *voix* shrill
grêle[2] *f* hail; **grêler**: ***il grêle*** it's hailing; **grêlon** *m* hailstone
grelotter shiver
grenade *f* BOT pomegranate; MIL grenade
grenadine *f* grenadine, pomegranate syrup
grenier *m* attic
grenouille *f* frog
grès *m* sandstone; *poterie* stoneware
grésiller sizzle; RAD crackle
grève[1] *f* strike; ***être en ~, faire ~*** be on strike; ***se mettre en ~*** go on strike; ***~ de la faim*** hunger strike
grève[2] *f* (*plage*) shore
gréviste *m/f* striker
gribouillage *m* scribble; (*dessin*) doodle; **gribouiller** scribble; (*dessiner*) doodle
grief *m* grievance
grièvement *blessé* seriously
griffe *f* claw; COMM label; *fig* (*empreinte*) stamp; **griffer** scratch
griffonner scribble
grignoter 1 *v/t* nibble on; *économies* nibble away at **2** *v/i* nibble
grill *m* broiler, *Br* grill; **grillade** *f* broil, *Br* grill
grillage *m* wire mesh; (*clôture*) fence
grille *f d'une fenêtre* grille; (*clôture*) railings *pl*; *d'un four* rack; (*tableau*) grid; **grille-pain** *m inv* toaster; **griller 1** *v/t viande* broil, *Br* grill; *pain* toast; *café, marrons* roast **2** *v/i d'une ampoule* burn out; ***~ un feu rouge*** go through a red light
grillon *m* cricket
grimace *f* grimace; ***faire des ~s*** pull faces
grimper climb
grincement *m de porte* squeaking; **grincer** *d'une porte* squeak; ***~ des dents*** grind one's teeth
grincheux, -euse grouchy
grippe *f* MÉD flu; ***prendre qn en ~*** take a dislike to s.o.; **grippé** MÉD: ***être ~*** have flu
gris gray, *Br* grey; *temps, vie* dull; (*ivre*) tipsy
grisant exhilarating
grisâtre grayish, *Br* greyish
griser: ***~ qn*** go to s.o.'s head; ***se laisser ~ par*** get carried away by
grisonner go gray *ou Br* grey
grognement *m* (*plainte*)

grumbling; *d'un cochon etc* grunt; **grogner** (*se plaindre*) grumble; *d'un cochon* grunt; **grognon, ~ne**: **être ~** be grumpy

grommeler mutter

gronder 1 *v/i* growl; *du tonnerre* rumble; *d'une révolte* brew **2** *v/t* scold

gros, ~se 1 *adj* big; (*corpulent*) fat; *lèvres* thick; *rhume*, *souliers* heavy; *chaussettes* thick; *plaisanterie* coarse; *vin* rough; **~ mots** *mpl* bad language **2** *adv*: **gagner ~** win a lot; **en ~** (*globalement*) on the whole; COMM wholesale **3** *m personne* fat man; COMM wholesale trade

groseille *f* BOT currant; **~ à maquereau** gooseberry

grossesse *f* pregnancy

grosseur *f* (*corpulence*) fatness; (*volume*) size; (*tumeur*) growth

grossier, -ère (*rudimentaire*) crude; (*indélicat*) coarse; (*impoli*) rude; *erreur* big

grossir 1 *v/t au microscope* magnify; *nombre*, *rivière* swell; (*exagérer*) exaggerate; **~ qn** *d'une robe etc* make s.o. look fatter **2** *v/i d'une personne* put on weight

grotesque grotesque

grotte *f* cave

grouiller: **~ de** be swarming with; **se ~** F get a move on

groupe *m* group; **~ sanguin** blood group; **grouper** group; **se ~ autour de qn** gather around s.o.

grue *f* ZO, TECH crane

grumeleux, -euse lumpy

gué *m* ford

guenilles *fpl* rags

guêpe *f* wasp

guère: **ne … ~** hardly

guéridon *m* round table

guérir 1 *v/t* cure (**de** of) **2** *v/i* heal; *d'un malade* get better; **guérison** *f* (*rétablissement*) recovery

guerre *f* war; **en ~** at war; **faire la ~** be at war (**à** with); **~ civile** civil war; **~ des gangs** gang warfare; **guerrier, -ère 1** *adj* warlike **2** *m* warrior

guet *m*: **faire le ~** keep watch; **guet-apens** *m* ambush; **guetter** keep an eye open for; (*épier*) watch

gueule *f* F mouth; (*visage*) face; **ta ~!** F shut it! F; **~ de bois** hangover; **gueuler** F yell

gueuleton *m* F enormous meal

guichet *m de banque*, *poste* wicket, *Br* window; *de théâtre* box office; **~ automatique** ATM, *Br aussi* cash dispenser

guide 1 *m* guide **2** *f* girl scout, *Br* guide **3**: **~s** *fpl* guiding reins; **guider** guide

guidon *m de vélo* handlebars *pl*

guillemets *mpl* quote marks

guindé stiff

guirlande *f* garland; **~s de Noël** tinsel
guise *f*: **agir à sa ~** do as one likes; **en ~ de** as, by way of
guitare *f* guitar; **guitariste** *m/f* guitarist
guttural guttural
Guyane: **la ~** Guyana
gym *f* gym; **gymnase** *m* SP gym; **gymnaste** *m/f* gymnast; **gymnastique** *f* gymnastics *sg*; *corrective, matinale* exercises *pl*
gynécologue *m/f* MÉD gynecologist, *Br* gynaecologist
gyrophare *m* flashing light

H

habile skillful, *Br* skilful; **habileté** *f* skill; **habilité** JUR authorized
habillé (*élégant*) dressy; **habiller** dress; **s'~** get dressed, dress; *élégamment* get dressed up
habit *m*: **~s** clothes
habitable inhabitable; **habitant, ~e** *m/f* inhabitant; **habitation** *f* living; (*domicile*) residence; **habiter 1** *v/t* live in **2** *v/i* live
habitude *f* habit, custom; **d'~** usually; **par ~** out of habit; **habitué, ~e** *m/f* regular; **habituel, ~le** usual; **habituer**: **~ qn à qch** get s.o. used to sth; **s'~ à** get used to
'hache *f* ax, *Br* axe; **'hacher** chop; **viande** *f* **hachée** ground beef, *Br* mince
'hachisch *m* hashish
'hachoir *m* *appareil* meat grinder, *Br* mincer; *couteau* cleaver; *planche* chopping board
haddock *m* smoked haddock
'haie *f* hedge; SP hurdle; *pour chevaux* fence, jump; **une ~ de policiers** *fig* a line of police
'haillons *mpl* rags
'haine *f* hatred; **'haineux, -euse** full of hatred
'haïr hate
'hâle *m* (sun)tan
haleine *f* breath; **hors d'~** out of breath
'haleter pant
'hall *m d'hôtel, immeuble* foyer; *de gare* concourse
'halle *f* market
halloween *f* Halloween
hallucination *f* hallucination
halogène *m*: (**lampe** *f*) **~** halogen light
'halte *f* stop; **faire ~** halt, make a stop
haltère *m* dumbbell; **faire des ~s** do weightlifting
haltérophilie *f* weightlifting
'hamac *m* hammock
'hameau *m* hamlet
hameçon *m* hook
'hamster *m* hamster

'hanche *f* hip
'handicap *m* handicap; **'handicapé, ~e 1** *adj* disabled, handicapped **2** *m/f* disabled *ou* handicapped person
'hangar *m* shed; AVIAT hangar
'hanter haunt
'hantise *f* fear, dread
'happer catch; *fig*: *de train, bus* hit
'haras *m* stud farm
'harassant *travail* exhausting
'harceler harass
'hard *m* hardcore; MUS hard rock
'hardi bold
'hareng *m* herring
'hargne *f* bad temper; **'hargneux, -euse** venomous; *chien* vicious
'haricot *m* BOT bean; ***c'est la fin des ~s*** F that's the end
harmonie *f* harmony; **harmoniser** match (up); MUS harmonize; ***s'~ de couleurs*** go together; ***s'~ avec*** go with
'harpe *f* MUS harp
'harpon *m* harpoon
'hasard *m* chance; ***au ~*** at random; ***par ~*** by chance; **'hasarder** hazard; ***se ~ à faire qc*** venture to do sth
'hâte *f* hurry, haste; ***en ~*** in haste; ***avoir ~ de faire qc*** be eager to do sth; **'hâter** hasten; ***se ~*** hurry
'hausse *f* increase, rise; **'hausser** increase; ***~ les épaules*** shrug (one's shoulders)
'haut 1 *adj* high; *immeuble* tall, high; *cri, voix* loud; *fonctionnaire* high-level **2** *adv* high; ***de ~*** from above; ***de ~ en bas*** from top to bottom; *regarder qn* up and down; ***en ~*** above; ***en ~ de*** at the top of **3** *m* top; ***du ~ de*** from the top of; ***des ~s et des bas*** ups and downs
'hautain haughty
'hauteur *f* height; *fig* haughtiness; ***être à la ~ de qc*** be up to sth
hebdomadaire *m* & *adj* weekly
hébergement *m* accommodations *pl*, *Br* accommodation; **héberger**: ***~ qn*** put s.o. up; *fig* take s.o. in
hébreu *m*: ***l'~*** Hebrew
hectare *m* hectare (approx 2.5 acres)
'hein F eh?; ***c'est joli, ~?*** it's pretty, isn't it?
'hélas alas
'héler hail
hélice *f* MAR, AVIAT propeller; ***escalier*** *m* ***en ~*** spiral staircase
hélicoptère *m* helicopter
hémisphère *m* hemisphere
hémorragie *f* hemorrhage, *Br* haemorrhage
'hennir neigh
hépatite *f* hepatitis
herbe *f* grass; CUIS herb; ***mauvaise ~*** weed; ***fines ~s*** herbs
héréditaire hereditary; **hérédité** *f* heredity

hérésie *f* heresy; **hérétique 1** *adj* heretical **2** *m/f* heretic
'hérissé ruffled
'hérisson *m* hedgehog
héritage *m* inheritance; **hériter 1** *v/t* inherit **2** *v/i*: **~ *de qc*** inherit sth; **~ *de qn*** receive an inheritance from s.o.; **héritier, -ère** *m/f* heir
'hernie *f* MÉD hernia; **~ *discale*** slipped disc
héroïne[1] *f drogue* heroin
héroïne[2] *f* heroine
héroïque heroic
héroïsme *m* heroism
'héron *m* heron
'héros *m* hero
herpès *m* herpes
hésitation *f* hesitation; **hésiter** hesitate
hétérogène heterogeneous
hétérosexuel, ~le heterosexual
heure *f* hour; ***arriver à l'~*** arrive on time; ***de bonne ~*** early; ***à tout à l'~!*** see you soon!; ***quelle ~ est-il?*** what time is it?; ***il est six ~s*** it's six (o'clock); **~ *locale*** local time; ***~s d'ouverture*** opening hours
heureusement luckily, fortunately; **heureux, -euse** happy; (*chanceux*) fortunate
'heurt *m de deux véhicules* collision; *fig* (*friction*) clash; **'heurter** collide with; *fig* offend; ***se ~*** collide (***à*** with); *fig* (*s'affronter*) clash (***sur*** over)
hiberner hibernate
'hibou *m* owl
'hideux, -euse hideous
hier yesterday
'hiérarchie *f* hierarchy
high-tech *inv* high tech, hi-tech
hilare grinning
hippique SP equestrian; ***concours m ~*** horse show; **hippodrome** *m* race course
hirondelle *f* swallow
hirsute hairy
hispanique Hispanic
'hisser *drapeau, voile* hoist; (*monter*) lift, raise; ***se ~*** pull o.s. up
histoire *f* history; (*récit, conte*) story; ***faire des ~s*** make a fuss
historique 1 *adj* historic **2** *m* chronicle
hiver *m* winter
H.L.M. *m ou f* (= ***habitation à loyer modéré***) low cost housing
'hocher: ***~ la tête*** *approbation* nod (one's head); *désapprobation* shake one's head
'hockey *m sur gazon* field hockey, *Br* hockey; *sur glace* hockey, *Br* ice hockey
'holding *m* holding company
'hold-up *m* holdup
'hollandais, ~e 1 *adj* Dutch **2** *m langue* Dutch; **'Hollandais, ~e** *m/f* Dutchman; Dutchwoman; **'Hollande**: ***la ~*** Holland
'homard *m* lobster

homéopathie *f* homeopathy
homicide *m* homicide; **~ *involontaire*** manslaughter; **~ *volontaire*** murder
hommage *m* homage; ***rendre ~ à*** pay homage to
homme *m* man; **~ *d'affaires*** businessman; **~ *d'État*** statesman
homologue *m* counterpart, opposite number; **homologuer** *record* ratify; *tarif* authorize
homophobe homophobic
homosexuel, **~le** *m/f & adj* homosexual
'Hongrie *f*: ***la ~*** Hungary; **'hongrois**, **~e** **1** *adj* Hungarian **2** *m langue* Hungarian; **Hongrois**, **~e** *m/f* Hungarian
honnête honest; (*convenable*) decent; (*passable*) reasonable; **honnêteté** honesty
honneur *m* honor, *Br* honour; ***en l'~ de*** in honor of; ***faire ~ à qc*** honor sth; **honorable** honorable, *Br* honourable; **honoraire** **1** *adj* honorary **2** ***~s*** *mpl* fees; **honorer** honor, *Br* honour; **honorifique** honorific
'honte *f* shame; ***avoir ~ de*** be ashamed of; **'honteux**, **-euse** (*déshonorant*) shameful; (*déconfit*) ashamed
'hooligan *m* hooligan
hôpital *m* hospital; ***à l'~*** in the hospital, *Br* in hospital
'hoquet *m* hiccup; ***avoir le ~*** have (the) hiccups
horaire **1** *adj* hourly **2** *m emploi du temps* timetable, schedule; *des avions, trains etc* schedule, *Br* timetable
horizon *m* horizon
horizontal horizontal
horloge *f* clock
'hormis but
hormonal hormonal; **hormone** *f* hormone
horodateur *m dans parking* pay and display machine
horoscope *m* horoscope
horreur *f* horror; (*monstruosité*) monstrosity; ***avoir ~ de qc*** detest sth; (***quelle***) ***~!*** how awful!
horrible horrible
horrifiant horrifying
'hors: ***~ de*** (*à l'extérieur de*) outside; ***~ de danger*** out of danger; ***~ sujet*** beside the point; ***être ~ de soi*** be beside o.s.
'hors-bord *m* outboard
'hors-d'œuvre *m* CUIS appetizer, starter
'hors-jeu offside
horticulture *f* horticulture
hospice *m* REL hospice; (*asile*) home
hospitalier, **-ère** hospitable; MÉD hospital *atr*
hospitaliser hospitalize
hospitalité *f* hospitality
hostile hostile; **hostilité** *f* hostility
'hot-dog *m* hot dog
hôte *m* host; (*invité*) guest

hôtel *m* hotel; ~ ***de ville*** town hall
hôtellerie *f*: ***l'~*** the hotel business
hôtesse *f* hostess; ~ ***de l'air*** air hostess
'houblon *m* BOT hop
'houille *f* coal
'houle *f* MAR swell; **'houleux, -euse** *fig* stormy
'housse *f* protective cover
'houx *m* BOT holly
'hublot *m* NAUT porthole; AVIAT window
'huer boo, jeer
huile *f* oil; ~ ***solaire*** suntan oil; **huiler** oil
'huis *m*: ***à ~ clos*** behind closed doors; JUR in camera; **huissier** *m* JUR bailiff
'huit eight; ~ ***jours*** a week; ***demain en ~*** a week tomorrow; **'huitaine** *f*: ***une ~ de*** about eight, eight or so; ***une ~ (de jours)*** a week; **'huitième** eighth
huître *f* oyster
humain human; *traitement* humane; **humaniser** humanize; **humanitaire** humanitarian; **humanité** *f* humanity
humble humble
humecter moisten
'humer breathe in
humeur *f* mood; (*tempérament*) temperament; ***être de bonne/mauvaise ~*** be in a good/bad mood
humide damp; (*chaud et ~*) humid; **humidifier** moisten; *atmosphère* humidify; **humidité** *f* dampness; humidity
humiliation *f* humiliation; **humiliant** humiliating; **humilier** humiliate
humour *m* humor, *Br* humour; ***avoir de l'~*** have a (good) sense of humor
'huppé exclusive
'hurlement *m d'un loup* howl; *d'une personne* scream; **'hurler** *d'un loup* howl; *d'une personne* scream; ~ ***de rire*** roar with laughter
hydratant *cosmétique* moisturizing
hydraulique hydraulic
hydroélectrique hydroelectric
hydrogène *m* CHIM hydrogen
hydroglisseur *m* jetfoil
hygiène *f* hygiene; ***avoir une bonne ~ de vie*** have a healthy lifestyle; **hygiénique** hygienic; ***papier ~*** toilet paper; ***serviette ~*** sanitary napkin, *Br* sanitary towel
hymne *m* hymn; ~ ***national*** national anthem
hyperactif, -ive hyperactive
hypersensible hypersensitive
hypertension *f* MÉD high blood pressure
hypertexte: ***lien m ~*** hypertext link
hypnotiser hypnotize
hypocrisie *f* hypocrisy; **hy-**

pocrite 1 *adj* hypocritical **2** *m/f* hypocrite
hypothèque *f* COMM mortgage
hypothèse *f* hypothesis; **hypothétique** hypothetical
hystérie *f* hysteria; **hystérique** hysterical

I

ici here; ***jusqu'~*** to here; (*jusqu'à maintenant*) so far; ***par ~*** this way; (*dans le coin*) around about here; ***d'~ là*** by then, by that time
icône *f* icon
idéal *m & adj* ideal; **idéaliser** idealize; **idéalisme** *m* idealism; **idéaliste 1** *adj* idealistic **2** *m/f* idealist
idée *f* idea; (*opinion*) view; ***avoir dans l'~ de faire qch*** be thinking of doing sth; ***tu te fais des ~s*** (*tu te trompes*) you're imagining things; ***~ fixe*** obsession
identifier identify (***avec, à*** with); ***s'~ avec** ou **à*** identify with
identique identical (***à*** to)
identité *f* identity; ***pièce f d'~*** identity, ID
idéologie *f* ideology
idiomatique idiomatic
idiot, ~e 1 *adj* idiotic **2** *m/f* idiot; **idiotie** *f* idiocy; ***dire des ~s*** talk nonsense
idole *f* idol
idylle *f* romance
ignare *péj* **1** *adj* ignorant **2** *m/f* ignoramus
ignoble vile
ignorance *f* ignorance; **ignorant** ignorant; **ignorer** not know; *personne, talent* ignore
il he; *chose* it; *impersonnel* it; ***~ va pleuvoir*** it is *ou* it's going to rain
île *f* island; ***les ~s britanniques*** the British Isles
illégal illegal
illégitime *enfant* illegitimate
illettré illiterate
illicite illicit
illimité unlimited
illisible illegible; *mauvaise littérature* unreadable
illogique illogical
illuminer light up, illuminate; *par projecteur* floodlight
illusion *f* illusion; ***se faire des ~s*** delude o.s.; **illusoire** illusory
illustration *f* illustration; **illustrer** illustrate; ***s'~*** distinguish o.s. (***par*** by)
îlot *m* (small) island; *de maisons* block
ils *mpl* they
image *f* picture; *dans un miroir* reflection, image; (*ressemblance*) image
imaginaire imaginary; **ima-**

gination *f* imagination; **imaginer** imagine; (*inventer*) devise; ***s'~ que*** imagine that
imbattable unbeatable
imbécile 1 *adj* idiotic **2** *m/f* idiot, imbecile
imbiber soak (***de*** with)
imbu: ***~ de*** *fig* full of
imitation *f* imitation; THÉÂT impersonation; **imiter** imitate; THÉÂT impersonate
immaculé immaculate
immangeable inedible
immatriculation *f* registration; ***plaque f d'~*** AUTO license plate, *Br* number plate; **immatriculer** register
immature immature
immédiat 1 *adj* immediate **2** *m*: ***dans l'~*** for the moment; **immédiatement** immediately
immense immense
immerger immerse; ***s'~*** *d'un sous-marin* submerge
immeuble *m* building
immigrant, **~e** *m/f* immigrant; **immigration** *f* immigration; **immigrer** immigrate
imminent imminent
immiscer: ***s'~ dans qc*** interfere in sth
immobile immobile
immobilier, **-ère 1** *adj*: ***biens mpl ~s*** real estate **2** *m* property
immobiliser immobilize; *train, circulation* bring to a standstill; *capital* tie up; ***s'~*** (*s'arrêter*) come to a standstill
immonde foul
immoral immoral; **immoralité** *f* immorality
immortaliser immortalize; **immortalité** *f* immortality; **immortel**, **~le** immortal
immuniser immunize; ***immunisé contre*** *fig* immune to; **immunité** *f* JUR, MÉD immunity
impact *m* impact
impair 1 *adj* odd **2** *m* blunder
impardonnable unforgiveable
imparfait imperfect
impartial impartial
impasse *f* dead end; *fig* deadlock, impasse
impassible impassive
impatience *f* impatience; **impatient** impatient; **impatienter**: ***s'~*** get impatient
impayé unpaid
impeccable impeccable
impénétrable impenetrable
impératif, **-ive 1** *adj* imperative **2** *m* (*exigence*) requirement; GRAM imperative
impératrice *f* empress
imperceptible imperceptible
imperfection *f* imperfection
impérieux, **-euse** *personne* imperious; *besoin* urgent
impérissable immortal; *souvenir* unforgettable
imperméabiliser waterproof; **imperméable 1** *adj tissu* waterproof **2** *m* rain-

coat
impersonnel, **~le** impersonal
impertinence *f* impertinence; **impertinent** impertinent
imperturbable imperturbable
impétueux, **-euse** impetuous
impitoyable pitiless
implacable implacable
implanter *fig* introduce; *usine* set up; ***s'~*** become established; *d'une industrie* set up
implicite implicit
impliquer *personne* implicate; (*entraîner*) mean, involve; (*supposer*) imply
implorer *aide* beg for; ***~ qn de faire qch*** implore *ou* beg s.o. to do sth
impoli rude, impolite
impopulaire unpopular
importance *f* importance; *d'une ville* size; *d'une somme, catastrophe* magnitude;
important **1** *adj* important; *ville, somme* large, sizeable **2** *m*: ***l'~, c'est que …*** the important thing is that …
importateur, **-trice** **1** *adj* importing **2** *m* importer; **importation** *f* import; **importer** **1** *v/t* import; *mode, musique* introduce **2** *v/i* matter, be important (***à*** to); ***n'importe quand*** any time; ***n'importe quoi!*** nonsense!
importun troublesome; **importuner** bother
imposable taxable
imposant imposing; **imposer** impose; *marchandise* tax; ***s'~*** (*être nécessaire*) be essential; (*se faire admettre*) gain recognition
impossible **1** *adj* impossible **2** *m*: ***faire l'~ pour faire qch*** do one's utmost to do sth
imposteur *m* imposter
impôt *m* tax; ***déclaration f d'~s*** tax return
impotent crippled
impraticable *projet* impractical; *rue* impassable
imprécis vague, imprecise
imprégner impregnate (***de*** with); ***imprégné de*** *fig* full of
impression *f* impression; *imprimerie* printing; **impressionnant** impressive; (*troublant*) upsetting; **impressionner** impress; (*troubler*) upset; **impressionniste** *m/f & adj* impressionist
imprévisible unpredictable
imprévu **1** *adj* unexpected **2** *m*: ***sauf ~*** all being well
imprimante *f* INFORM printer; ***~ laser*** laser printer; ***~ à jet d'encre*** ink-jet (printer); **imprimé** *m* (*formulaire*) form; *tissu* print; *poste* ***~s*** printed matter; **imprimer** print; INFORM print out; *édition* publish
improbable unlikely, improbable
improductif, **-ive** unproduc-

tive
impropre *mot, outil* inappropriate; **~ *à la consommation*** unfit for human consumption
improviste: ***à l'~*** unexpectedly
imprudence *f* imprudence; **imprudent** imprudent
impudence *f* impudence; **impudent** impudent
impudique shameless
impuissance *f* powerlessness; MÉD impotence; **impuissant** powerless; MÉD impotent
impulsif, **-ive** impulsive; **impulsion** *f* impulse; *à l'économie* boost
impuni unpunished
impur *eau* dirty, polluted; (*impudique*) impure
imputer attribute (***à*** to); FIN charge (***sur*** to)
inabordable *prix* unaffordable
inacceptable unacceptable
inaccessible inaccessible; *personne* unapproachable; *objectif* unattainable
inachevé unfinished
inactif, **-ive** idle; *population* non-working; *remède, méthode* ineffective; *marché* slack
inadéquat inadequate; *méthode* unsuitable
inadmissible unacceptable
inadvertance *f*: ***par ~*** inadvertently
inanimé inanimate; (*mort*) lifeless; (*inconscient*) unconscious
inaperçu: ***passer ~*** pass unnoticed
inapproprié inappropriate
inapte: **~ *à*** unsuited to; MÉD, MIL unfit for
inattendu unexpected
inattention *f* inattentiveness; ***erreur d'~*** careless mistake
inaudible inaudible
inaugurer inaugurate
inavouable shameful
incapable incapable (***de faire*** of doing)
incapacité *f* (*inaptitude*) incompetence; *de faire qch* inability
incarcérer imprison
incassable unbreakable
incendiaire incendiary; *discours* inflammatory; **incendie** *m* fire; **~ *criminel*** arson; **incendier** set fire to
incertain uncertain; *temps* unsettled; (*hésitant*) indecisive; **incertitude** *f* uncertainty
incessamment any minute now
inchangé unchanged
incident *m* incident; **~ *de parcours*** mishap
incinérer incinerate; *cadavre* cremate
incisif, **-ive** incisive; **incision** *f* incision
inciter encourage (***à faire qch*** to do sth); *péj* egg on, incite

inclinable tilting; **inclinaison** *f* slope
inclination *f fig* inclination (**pour** for); **~ de tête** (*salut*) nod; **incliner** tilt; **s'~** bend; *pour saluer* bow; **s'~ devant qc** (*céder*) yield to sth; **s'~ devant qn** *aussi fig* bow to s.o.
inclure include; *dans une lettre* enclose; **inclus**: **ci-inclus** enclosed; **jusqu'au 30 juin ~** to 30th June inclusive
incohérence *f de comportement* inconsistency; *de discours* incoherence
incolore colorless, *Br* colourless
incomber: **il vous incombe de le lui dire** it is your duty to tell him
incommoder bother
incomparable incomparable
incompatibilité *f* incompatibility; **incompatible** incompatible
incompétence *f* incompetence; **incompétent** incompetent
incomplet, -ète incomplete
incompréhensible incomprehensible; **incompréhension** *f* lack of understanding
incompris misunderstood (**de** by)
inconcevable inconceivable
inconditionnel, ~le 1 *adj* unconditional **2** *m/f* fan, fanatic
inconfortable uncomfortable
inconnu, ~e 1 *adj* (*ignoré*) unknown; (*étranger*) strange **2** *m/f* stranger
inconscient unconscious; (*irréfléchi*) irresponsible
inconsidéré rash, thoughtless
inconsistant inconsistent; *fig*: *raisonnement* flimsy
inconsolable inconsolable
incontestable indisputable
incontesté outright
incontournable: **être ~** be a must
inconvénient *m* disadvantage *m*; **si vous n'y voyez aucun ~** if you have no objection
incorporer incorporate (**à** with, into); MIL draft
incorrect wrong, incorrect; *tenue, langage* improper
incorrigible incorrigible
incrédule (*sceptique*) incredulous; **incrédulité** *f* incredulity
incriminer *personne* blame; JUR accuse; *paroles, actions* condemn
incroyable incredible, unbelievable
inculpé, ~e *m/f*: **l'~** the accused, the defendant; **inculper** JUR charge, indict (**de, pour** with)
inculquer: **~ qc à qn** instill *ou Br* instil sth into s.o.
inculte *terre* waste *atr*, uncultivated; (*ignorant*) unedu-

cated
incurable incurable
incursion *f* MIL raid, incursion; *fig*: *dans la politique etc* venture (***dans*** into)
Inde *f*: ***l'~*** India
indécent indecent; (*incorrect*) inappropriate, improper
indécis undecided; *personne, caractère* indecisive
indéfini indefinite; (*imprécis*) undefined
indéfinissable indefinable
indélicat *personne, action* tactless
indemne unhurt; **indemniser** compensate (***de*** for); **indemnité** *f* (*dédommagement*) compensation; (*allocation*) allowance
indéniable undeniable
indépendance *f* independence; **indépendant** independent (***de*** of); *travailleur* freelance; **indépendantiste** (pro-)independence *atr*
indescriptible indescribable
indésirable undesirable
indéterminé unspecified
index *m* index; *doigt* index finger
indicateur, **-trice** *m* (*espion*) informer; TECH gauge, indicator
indicatif *m* TÉL code
indication *f* indication; (*information*) piece of information; ***~s*** instructions
indice *m* (*signe*) sign, indication; JUR clue
indien, **~ne** Indian; *d'Amérique aussi* native American; **Indien** *m/f* Indian; *d'Amérique aussi* native American
indifférence *f* indifference; **indifférent** indifferent
indigène *adj & m/f* native
indigeste indigestible; **indigestion** *f* MÉD indigestion
indignation *f* indignation
indigne unworthy; *parents* unfit
indigner make indignant; ***s'~ de qc/contre qn*** be indignant about sth/with s.o.
indiqué appropriate; ***ce n'est pas ~*** it's not advisable; **indiquer** indicate, show; *d'une pendule* show; (*recommander*) recommend
indirect indirect
indiscipline *f* indiscipline; **indiscipliné** undisciplined; *cheveux* unmanageable
indiscret, **-ète** indiscreet; **indiscrétion** indiscretion
indispensable indispensable
indistinct indistinct
individu *m* individual; **individualisme** *m* individualism; **individuel**, **~le** individual; *secrétaire* private, personal; *liberté* personal; *chambre* single; *maison* detached
indivisible indivisible
indolent lazy, indolent
indolore painless
indomptable *fig* indomitable
indu: ***à une heure ~e*** at some

ungodly hour
indubitable indisputable
induire: ~ ***qn en erreur*** mislead s.o.
indulgence *f* indulgence; *d'un juge* leniency; **indulgent** indulgent; *juge* lenient
industrialisé industrialized; **industrialiser** industrialize; **industrie** *f* industry; **industriel, ~le 1** *adj* industrial **2** *m* industrialist
inébranlable solid (as a rock)
inédit (*pas édité*) unpublished; (*nouveau*) original, unique
inégal unequal; *surface* uneven; *rythme* irregular; **inégalité** *f* inequality; *d'une surface* unevenness
inepte inept; **ineptie** *f* ineptitude; **~s** nonsense
inépuisable inexhaustible
inerte *corps* lifeless, inert; PHYS inert; **inertie** *f* inertia
inespéré unexpected, unhoped-for
inestimable *tableau* priceless; *aide* invaluable
inévitable inevitable; *accident* unavoidable
inexact inaccurate
inexcusable inexcusable, unforgiveable
inexistant non-existent
inexplicable inexplicable
inexprimable inexpressible
infaillible infallible
infantile *mortalité* infant *atr*; *péj* infantile; *maladie* children's
infarctus *m* MÉD: ~ ***du myocarde*** coronary (thrombosis)
infatigable tireless, indefatigable
infect disgusting; *temps* foul; **infecter** infect; *air, eau* pollute; **s'~** become infected; **infectieux, -euse** infectious; **infection** *f* MÉD infection
inférieur, ~e 1 *adj* lower; *qualité* inferior **2** *m/f* inferior; **infériorité** *f* inferiority
infernal infernal
infidèle unfaithful; REL pagan *atr*; **infidélité** *f* infidelity
infiltrer: ***s'~ dans*** get into; *fig* infiltrate
infime tiny, infinitesimal
infini 1 *adj* infinite **2** *m* infinity
infirme 1 *adj* disabled **2** *m/f* disabled person; **infirmerie** *f* infirmary; ÉDU sickbay; **infirmier, -ère** *m/f* nurse; **infirmité** *f* disability
inflammation *f* MÉD inflammation
inflation *f* inflation
inflexible inflexible
infliger *peine* inflict (**à** on); *défaite* impose
influence *f* influence; **influencer** influence; **influent** influential
influer: ~ ***sur*** affect
info *f* F RAD, TV news item; ***les ~s*** the news *sg*
informaticien, ~ne *m/f* com-

puter scientist
information *f* information; JUR inquiry; ***une ~*** a piece of information; ***les ~s*** RAD, TV the news *sg*; ***traitement m de l'~*** data processing
informatique 1 *adj* computer *atr* **2** *f* information technology, IT; **informatiser** computerize
informe shapeless
informer inform; ***s'~*** find out (***de qc auprès de qn*** about sth from s.o.)
infraction *f* infringement (***à*** of)
infranchissable impossible to cross; *obstacle* insurmountable
infrarouge infrared
infrastructure *f* infrastructure
infroissable crease-resistant
infructueux, -euse unsuccessful
infusion *f* herb tea
ingénierie *f* engineering; **ingénieur** *m* engineer
ingéniosité *f* ingeniousness
ingrat ungrateful; *tâche* thankless; **ingratitude** *f* ingratitude
ingrédient *m* ingredient
ingurgiter gulp down
inhabitable uninhabitable; **inhabité** uninhabited
inhalateur *m* MÉD inhaler; **inhaler** inhale
inhérent inherent (***à*** in)
inhibé inhibited; **inhibition** *f* PSYCH inhibition
inhospitalier, -ère inhospitable
inhumain inhuman
ininflammable non-flammable
ininterrompu uninterrupted; *pluie, musique* non-stop
initial, ~e 1 *adj* initial **2** *f* initial (letter)
initiation *f* initiation; ***~ à*** *fig* introduction to
inimitié *f* enmity
initiative *f* initiative
initié, ~e *m/f* insider; **initier** initiate (***à*** in); *fig* introduce (***à*** to)
injecté: ***~ (de sang)*** blood-shot; **injecter** inject; **injection** *f* injection
injoignable unreachable, uncontactable
injure *f* insult; ***~s*** abuse; **injurier** insult, abuse
injuste unfair, unjust; **injustice** *f* injustice; *d'une décision aussi* unfairness
inlassable tireless
inné innate
innocence *f* innocence; **innocent** innocent; **innocenter** clear
innombrable countless; *auditoire, foule* vast
innovant innovative; **innovation** *f* innovation
inoccupé *personne* idle; *maison* unoccupied
inodore odorless, *Br* odourless

inoffensif, **-ive** harmless; *humour* inoffensive
inondation *f* flood; **inonder** flood; **~ de** *fig* inundate with
inopiné unexpected
inopportun ill-timed
inorganique inorganic
inoubliable unforgettable
inouï unheard-of
inoxydable stainless
inquiet, **-ète** anxious, worried (**de** about); **inquiéter** worry; **s'~** worry (**de** about); **inquiétude** *f* anxiety
insaisissable elusive; *différence* imperceptible
insatiable insatiable
insatisfaisant unsatisfactory; **insatisfait** unsatisfied; *mécontent* dissatisfied
inscription *f* inscription; (*immatriculation*) registration; **inscrire** (*noter*) write down, note; *dans registre* enter; *à examen* register; (*graver*) inscribe; **s'~** put one's name down; *à l'université* register; *à un cours* enroll, *Br* enrol (**à** for)
insecte *m* insect; **insecticide** *m* insecticide
insécurité *f* insecurity; POL security problem
insensé mad, insane
insensibiliser numb; **insensible** ANAT numb; *personne* insensitive (**à** to)
insérer insert; *annonce* put; **insertion** *f* insertion
insigne *m* (*emblème*) insignia; (*badge*) badge
insignifiant insignificant
insinuer insinuate; ***s'~ dans*** worm one's way into
insipide insipid
insistance *f* insistence; **insistant** insistent; **insister** insist; F (*persévérer*) persevere; ***~ pour faire qch*** insist on doing sth; ***~ sur qc*** (*souligner*) stress sth
insolation *f* sunstroke
insolence *f* insolence; **insolent** insolent
insolite unusual
insolvable insolvent
insomnie *f* insomnia
insonoriser soundproof
insouciant carefree
insoumis rebellious
insoutenable (*insupportable*) unbearable; *argument* untenable
inspecter inspect; **inspecteur**, **-trice** *m/f* inspector; **inspection** *f* inspection
inspiration *f* *fig* inspiration; **inspirer 1** *v/i* breathe in, inhale **2** *v/t* inspire; ***s'~ de*** be inspired by
installation *f* installation; ***~ électrique*** wiring; ***~s*** facilities; **installer** install; *appartement*: fit out; (*loger*, *placer*) put; **s'~** (*s'établir*) settle down; *à la campagne etc* settle; *d'un médecin*, *dentiste* set up
instant *m* instant, moment; ***à l'~*** just this minute; ***dans un***

~ in a minute; ***pour l'~*** for the moment; **instantané 1** *adj* immediate; *café* instant; *mort* instantaneous **2** *m* PHOT snap(shot)

instaurer establish

instinct *m* instinct; **instinctif, -ive** instinctive

instituer introduce; **institut** *m* institute; ***~ de beauté*** beauty salon; **instituteur, -trice** *m/f* (primary) school teacher; **institution** *f* institution

instructeur *m* MIL instructor; **instructif, -ive** instructive; **instruction** *f* (*enseignement, culture*) education; MIL training; JUR preliminary investigation; INFORM instruction; ***~s*** instructions; **instruire** ÉDU educate, teach; MIL train; JUR investigate; **instruit** (well-)educated

instrument *m* instrument

insu: ***à l'~ de*** unbeknownst to

insubordination *f* insubordination

insuffisance *f* deficiency; ***~ respiratoire*** respiratory problem; **insuffisant** *quantité* insufficient; *qualité* inadequate

insulaire 1 *adj* island *atr* **2** *m/f* islander

insuline *f* insulin

insulte *f* insult; **insulter** insult

insupportable unbearable

insurger: ***s'~ contre*** rise up against

insurrection *f* insurrection

intact intact

intégral full, complete; *texte* unabridged

intégration *f* (*assimilation*) integration

intègre of integrity

intégrer (*assimiler*) integrate; (*incorporer*) incorporate; **intégriste** *m/f & adj* fundamentalist

intégrité *f* (*honnêteté*) integrity

intellectuel, ~le *m/f & adj* intellectual

intelligence *f* intelligence; **intelligent** intelligent

intempéries *fpl* bad weather

intempestif, -ive untimely

intenable *situation, froid* unbearable

intense intense; **intensif, -ive** intensive; **intensification** *f* intensification; *d'un conflit* escalation; **intensifier** intensify; ***s'~*** intensify; *d'un conflit* escalate; **intensité** *f* intensity

intenter: ***~ un procès contre*** start proceedings against

intention *f* intention; ***avoir l'~ de faire qch*** intend to do sth; ***à l'~ de*** for; **intentionné**: ***bien ~*** well-meaning; ***mal ~*** ill-intentioned; **intentionnel, ~le** intentional

interactif, -ive interactive

intercéder: ***~ pour qn*** intercede for s.o.

intercepter intercept; *soleil* shut out
interchangeable interchangeable
interdiction *f* ban; **interdire** ban; **~ à qn de faire qc** forbid s.o. to do sth; **interdit** forbidden; (*très étonné*) taken aback
intéressant interesting; (*avide*) selfish; *prix* good; *situation* well-paid; **interéssé** interested; (*concerné*) concerned; **intéresser** interest; (*concerner*) concern; **s'~ à** be interested in; **intérêt** *m* interest; (*égoïsme*) self-interest; **~s** COMM interest
interface *f* interface
intérieur 1 *adj poche* inside; *porte, vie* inner; *politique, vol* domestic; *mer* inland **2** *m* inside; *d'une auto etc* interior; **à l'~** (**de**) inside
intérim *m* interim; *travail* temporary work; **intérimaire 1** *adj travail* temporary **2** *m/f* temp
interlocuteur, -trice *m/f*: **mon/son ~** the person I/she was talking to
intermédiaire 1 *adj* intermediate **2** *m/f* intermediary; COMM middleman
interminable interminable
intermittence *f*: **par ~** intermittently
international, ~e *m/f & adj* international
interne 1 *adj* internal; *oreille* inner; *d'une société* in-house **2** *m/f élève* boarder; *médecin* intern, *Br* houseman; **interner** intern
Internet *m* Internet; **sur ~** on the Internet
interpeller call out to; *de la police*, POL question
interphone *m* intercom; *d'un immeuble* entry phone
interposer interpose; **s'~** (*intervenir*) intervene
interprète *m/f* interpreter; (*porte-parole*) spokesperson; **interpréter** interpret; *rôle*, MUS play
interrogation *f* question; *d'un suspect* questioning, interrogation; **interrogatoire** *m par police* questioning; *par juge* cross-examination;
interroger question; *de la police* question, interrogate; *d'un juge* cross-examine
interrompre interrupt; **s'~** break off
interrupteur *m* switch; **interruption** *f* interruption; **sans ~** without stopping
intersection *f* intersection
intervalle *m* space, gap; *de temps* interval
intervenir intervene; *d'une rencontre* take place; **intervention** *f* intervention; MÉD operation; (*discours*) speech
interview *f* interview; **interviewer** interview
intestin 1 *adj* internal **2** *m* intestin

intime 1 *adj* intimate; *ami* close; *pièce* cozy, *Br* cosy; *vie* private **2** *m/f* close friend
intimider intimidate
intimité *f* intimacy; *vie privée* privacy
intituler call; ***s'~*** be called
intolérable intolerable; **intolérance** *f* intolerance; **intolérant** intolerant
intoxication *f* poisoning; ***~ alimentaire*** food poisoning; **intoxiquer** poison; *fig* brainwash
intransigeant intransigent
intrépide intrepid
intrigue *f* plot; ***~s*** scheming, plotting; **intriguer 1** *v/i* scheme, plot **2** *v/t* intrigue
introduction *f* introduction; **introduire** introduce; *visiteur* show in; (*engager*) insert; ***s'~ dans*** gain entry to
introuvable impossible to find
introverti, **~e** *m/f* introvert
intrus, **~e** *m/f* intruder
intuitif, **-ive** intuitive; **intuition** *f* intuition; (*pressentiment*) premonition
inusable hard-wearing
inutile *qui ne sert pas* useless; (*superflu*) pointless, unnecessary; **inutilisable** unuseable
invalide 1 *adj* (*infirme*) disabled **2** *m/f* disabled person; **invalider** JUR, POL invalidate; **invalidité** *f* disability
invariable invariable
invasion *f* invasion
invendable unsellable
inventaire *m* inventory; COMM *opération* stocktaking
inventer invent; *histoire* make up; **inventeur**, **-trice** *m/f* inventor; **invention** *f* invention
inverse 1 *adj* MATH inverse; *sens* opposite; ***dans l'ordre ~*** in reverse order **2** *m* opposite, reverse; **inverser** invert; *rôles* reverse
investigation *f* investigation
investir FIN invest; (*cerner*) surround; **investissement** *m* FIN investment
invétéré inveterate
investisseur, **-euse** *m* investor
invincible invincible; *obstacle* insuperable
invisible invisible
invitation *f* invitation; **invité**, **~e** *m/f* guest; **inviter** invite; ***~ qn à faire qch*** urge s.o. to do sth
invivable unbearable
involontaire unintentional; *témoin* unwilling; *mouvement* involuntary
invoquer *Dieu* call on, invoke; *aide* call on; *texte*, *loi* refer to; *solution* put forward
invraisemblable unlikely, improbable
Iran *m*: ***l'~*** Iran; **iranien**, **~ne** Iranian; **Iranien**, **~ne** *m/f* Iranian

Iraq *m*: **l'~** Iraq; **iraquien, ~ne** Iraqi; **Iraquien, ~ne** *m/f* Iraqi
irascible irascible
irlandais, ~e 1 *adj* Irish **2** *m langue* Irish (Gaelic); **Irlandais, ~e** *m/f* Irishman; Irishwoman; **Irlande** *f*: **l'~** Ireland
ironie *f* irony; **ironiser** be ironic
irraisonné irrational
irrationnel, ~le irrational
irréalisable *projet* impracticable; *rêve* unrealizable
irréaliste unrealistic
irréconciliable irreconcilable
irrécupérable beyond repair; *personne* beyond redemption; *données* irretrievable
irréductible indomitable; *ennemi* implacable
irréel, ~le unreal
irréfléchi thoughtless, reckless
irréfutable irrefutable
irrégulier, -ère irregular; *surface, terrain* uneven; *étudiant, sportif* erratic
irrémédiable *maladie* incurable; *erreur* irreparable
irremplaçable irreplaceable
irréparable *faute, perte* irreparable; *vélo* beyond repair
irréprochable irreproachable
irrésistible irresistible
irrésolu *personne* indecisive; *problème* unresolved
irrespirable unbreathable
irresponsable irresponsible
irrigation *f* AGR irrigation
irritable irritable; **irritation** *f* irritation; **irriter** irritate; **s'~** get irritated
islam, Islam *m* REL Islam; **islamique** Islamic; **islamiste** Islamic fundamentalist
islandais, ~e 1 *adj* Icelandic **2** *m langue* Islandic; **Islandais, ~e** *m/f* Icelander; **Islande**: **l'~** Iceland
isolation *f* insulation; *contre le bruit* soundproofing; **isolé** isolated; TECH insulated; **isolement** *m* isolation; **isoler** isolate; *prisonnier* place in solitary confinement; ÉL insulate
Israël *m* Israel; **israélien, ~ne** Israeli; **Israélien, ~ne** *m/f* Israeli
issu: ***être ~ de*** *parenté* come from; *résultat* stem from
issue *f* way out (*aussi fig*), exit; (*fin*) outcome; ***à l'~ de*** at the end of
Italie *f*: **l'~** Italy; **italien, ~ne 1** *adj* Italian **2** *m langue* Italian; **Italien, ~ne** *m/f* Italian
itinéraire *m* itinerary
IVG *f* (= ***interruption volontaire de grossesse***) termination, abortion
ivoire *m* ivory
ivre drunk; **~ *de*** *joie, colère* wild with; **ivresse** *f* drunkenness; **ivrogne** *m/f* drunk

J

jacasser chatter
jacinthe *f* BOT hyacinth
jade *m* jade
jaillir shoot out (***de*** from)
jalousie *f* jealousy; (*store*) Venetian blind; **jaloux, -ouse** jealous
jamais ◇ *positif* ever; ***à ~*** for ever, for good; ◇ *négatif* never; ***ne ... ~*** never; ***je ne lui ai ~ parlé*** I've never spoken to him
jambe *f* leg
jambon *m* ham
jante *f* rim
janvier *m* January
Japon: ***le ~*** Japan; **japonais, ~e 1** *adj* Japanese **2** *m langue* Japanese; **Japonais, ~e** *m/f* Japanese
jappement *m* yap
jaquette *f d'un livre* dust jacket
jardin *m* garden; ***~ botanique*** botanical gardens *pl*; ***~ publique*** park; **jardinage** *m* gardening; **jardiner** garden; **jardinier** *m* gardener; **jardinière** *f à fleurs* window box; *femme* gardener
jargon *m* jargon; *péj* (*charabia*) gibberish
jarret *m* back of the knee; CUIS shin
jaser gossip
jatte *f* bowl
jauge *f* gauge; **jauger** gauge
jaunâtre yellowish; **jaune 1** *adj* yellow **2** *m*: ***~ d'œuf*** egg yolk; **jaunir** go yellow; **jaunisse** *f* MÉD jaundice
jazz *m* jazz; **jazzman** *m* jazz musician
je I
jean *m* jeans *pl*; ***veste*** *m* ***en ~*** denim jacket
jeep *f* jeep
Jésus-Christ Jesus (Christ)
jet *m* (*lancer*) throw; (*jaillissement*) jet; *de sang* spurt; ***~ d'eau*** fountain
jetable disposable
jetée *f* MAR jetty
jeter throw; (*se défaire de*) throw away; ***~ un coup d'œil à qch*** glance at sth
jeton *m* token; *de jeu* chip
jeu *m* play (*aussi* TECH); *activité, en tennis* game; (*série, ensemble*) set; *de cartes* deck, *Br* pack; MUS playing; THÉÂT acting; ***le ~*** gambling; ***être en ~*** be at stake; ***~ de mots*** play on words
jeudi *m* Thursday
jeun: ***à ~*** on an empty stomach
jeune 1 *adj* young; ***~s mariés*** newly-weds **2** *m/f*: ***un ~*** a young man; ***les ~s*** young people *pl*, the young *pl*
jeûne *m* fast; **jeûner** fast

jeunesse *f* youth; *caractère jeune* youthfulness
J.O. *mpl* (= ***Jeux Olympiques***) Olympic Games
joaillerie *f magasin* jewelry store, *Br* jeweller's; *articles* jewelry, *Br* jewellery; **joaillier, -ère** *m/f* jeweler, *Br* jeweller
jogging *m* jogging; (*survêtement*) sweats *pl*, *Br* tracksuit; ***faire du ~*** go jogging
joie *f* joy; ***débordant de ~*** jubilant
joindre join; *efforts* combine; *à un courrier* enclose (***à*** with); *personne* contact, get in touch with; *mains* clasp; ***se ~ à qn pour faire qch*** join s.o. in doing sth
joint *m* joint; *d'étanchéité* seal, gasket; *de robinet* washer
joli pretty
joncher strew (***de*** with)
jonction *f* junction
jongler juggle; **jongleur** *m* juggler
joue *f* cheek
jouer 1 *v/t* play; *argent, réputation* gamble; THÉÂT *pièce* perform; *film* show; ***~ la comédie*** put on an act **2** *v/i* play; *d'un acteur* act; *parier* gamble; ***~ au football*** play football; ***~ d'un instrument*** play an instrument; ***~ sur cheval etc*** put money on
jouet *m* toy
joueur, -euse *m/f* player; *de jeux d'argent* gambler; ***être beau/mauvais ~*** be a good/bad loser
jouir have an orgasm, come; ***~ de qc*** enjoy sth; (*posséder*) have sth; **jouissance** *f* enjoyment; JUR possession
jour *m* day; (*lumière*) daylight; (*ouverture*) opening; ***au grand ~*** in broad daylight; ***de nos ~s*** these days; ***du ~ au lendemain*** overnight; ***être à ~*** be up to date; ***se faire ~*** *de problèmes* come to light; ***deux ans ~ pour ~*** two years to the day; ***il fait ~*** it's (getting) light; ***au petit ~*** at first light
journal *m* (news)paper; *intime* diary; TV, *à la radio* news *sg*; **journalisme** *m* journalism; **journaliste** *m/f* journalist
journée *f* day
jovial jovial
joyeux, -euse joyful; ***~ Noël!*** Merry Christmas!
jubilation *f* jubilation; **jubiler** be jubilant; *péj* gloat
jucher perch
judiciaire legal
judicieux, -euse sensible, judicious
judo *m* judo
juge *m* judge; ***~ d'instruction*** examining magistrate; ***~ de touche*** SP linesman; **jugement** *m* judg(e)ment; *en matière criminelle* sentence; ***porter un ~ sur*** pass judg(e)-

ment on; **juger 1** *v/t* JUR try; (*évaluer*) judge; **~ *qc/qn intéressant*** consider sth/s.o. interesting; **~ *que*** think that; **~ *de qn/qc*** judge s.o./sth **2** *v/i* judge

juif, **-ive** *adj* Jewish; **Juif**, **-ive** *m/f* Jew

juillet *m* July

juin *m* June

jumeau, **jumelle** *m/f & adj* twin; **jumeler** *villes* twin; **jumelles** *fpl* binoculars

jument *f* mare

jungle *f* jungle

jupe *f* skirt

juré *m* JUR juror; **jurer** swear (***de qch*** to sth)

juridiction *f* jurisdiction

juridique legal

juron *m* curse

jury *m* JUR jury; *d'un concours* panel, judges *pl*; ÉDU board of examiners

jus *m* juice

jusque 1 *prép*: ***jusqu'à*** *lieu* as far as, up to; *temps* until; ***jusqu'où vous allez?*** how far are you going? **2** *adv* even, including **3** *conj*: ***jusqu'à ce qu'il s'endorme*** (*subj*) until he falls asleep

juste 1 *adj* fair, just; *salaire, récompense* fair; (*précis*) right, correct; *vêtement* tight **2** *adv* just; *viser, tirer* accurately; ***chanter ~*** sing in tune; **justesse** *f* accuracy; ***de ~*** only just; **justice** *f* fairness, justice; JUR justice; ***la ~*** the law; ***faire ~ à qn*** do s.o. justice

justification *f* justification; **justifier** justify; **~ *de qc*** prove sth

juteux, **-euse** juicy

juvénile youthful; ***délinquance ~*** juvenile delinquency

juxtaposer juxtapose

K

kaki khaki

kamikaze *m/f* suicide bomber

kangourou *m* kangaroo

kébab *m* kabob, *Br* kebab

kermesse *f* fair

kérosène *m* kerosene

ketchup *m* ketchup

kg (= ***kilogramme***) kg (= kilogram)

kidnapping *m* kidnapping; **kidnapper** kidnap

kilo(gramme) *m* kilo(gram); **kilométrage** *m* mileage; **kilomètre** *m* kilometer, *Br* kilometre; **kilo-octet** *m* kilobyte, k

kinésithérapeute *m/f* physiotherapist

kiosque *m* pavilion; COMM kiosk; **~ *à journaux*** newsstand

kit *m*: ***en ~*** kit

klaxon *m* AUTO horn; **klaxonner** sound one's horn, hoot
km (= ***kilomètre***) km (= kilometer)
knock-out *m* knockout
K-O *m* (= ***knock-out***) KO
Ko *m* (= ***kilo-octet*** *m*) k (= kilobyte)

L

la[1] → ***le***
la[2] *pron personnel* her; *chose* it
là here; *dans un autre lieu qu'ici* there; *causal* hence; ***par*~** that way; **là-bas** (over) there
laboratoire *m* laboratory, lab
laborieux, **-euse** laborious; *personne* hardworking
labourer plow, *Br* plough
labyrinthe *m* labyrinth, maze
lac *m* lake
lacer tie
lacérer lacerate
lacet *m de chaussures* lace; *de la route* sharp turn
lâche 1 *adj* loose; *personne* cowardly **2** *m* coward
lâcher 1 *v/t* let go of; (*laisser tomber*) drop; (*libérer*) release; *ceinture* loosen; *juron, vérité* let out; SP leave behind **2** *v/i de freins* fail; *d'une corde* break
lâcheté *f* cowardice
lacrymogène *gaz* tear *atr*; *grenade* tear-gas *atr*
lacune *f* gap
là-dedans inside; **là-dessous** underneath; *derrière* behind it; **là-dessus** on it, on top; *à ce moment* at that instant; *sur ce point* about it;
là-haut up there
laid ugly; **laideur** *f* ugliness; (*bassesse*) meanness
lainage *m étoffe* woolen *ou Br* woollen fabric; *vêtement* woolen, *Br* woollen; **laine** *f* wool; **laineux**, **-euse** fleecy
laïque 1 *adj* REL secular; (*sans confession*) State *atr* **2** *m/f* lay person
laisse *f* leash
laisser leave; (*permettre*) let; ***se ~ aller*** let o.s. go
laisser-aller *m* casualness
laissez-passer *m* pass
lait *m* milk; **laitage** *m* dairy product; **laitier**, **-ère** dairy *atr*
laiton *m* brass
laitue *f* BOT lettuce
lambin, **~e** *m/f* F slowpoke F, *Br* slowcoach F
lambris *m* paneling, *Br* panelling
lame *f* blade; (*plaque*) strip; (*vague*) wave
lamentable deplorable; **lamenter**: ***se ~*** complain
lampadaire *m* floor lamp; *dans la rue* street light

lampe *f* lamp; **~ *de poche*** flashlight, *Br* torch
lancé established; **lancement** *m* launch; **lancer** throw; *avec force* hurl; *injure* shout, hurl (**à** at); *cri* give; *fusée*, COMM launch; INFORM *programme* run; *moteur* start; ***se ~ sur*** *marché* enter; *piste de danse* step out onto; ***se ~ dans*** *des activités* take up; *des explications* launch into; *des discussions* get involved in
langage *m* language
langouste *f* spiny lobster
langue *f* tongue; LING language; ***mauvaise ~*** gossip; ***~ maternelle*** mother tongue
languette *f d'une chaussure* tongue
languir languish; *d'une conversation* flag
lanière *f* strap
laper lap up
lapider stone
lapin *m* rabbit
laps *m*: ***~ de temps*** period of time
laque *f* lacquer
larcin *m* petty theft
lard *m* bacon
lardon *m* lardon, diced bacon
large 1 *adj* wide; *épaules, hanches* broad; *mesure, rôle* large; (*généreux*) generous **2** *adv*: ***voir ~*** think big **3** *m* MAR open sea; ***prendre le ~*** *fig* take off; **largesse** *f* generosity; **largeur** *f* width; ***~ d'esprit*** broad-mindedness
larme *f* tear; ***une ~ de*** a drop of; **larmoyer** *des yeux* water; (*se plaindre*) complain
laryngite *f* laryngitis
las, ~se weary
laser *m* laser
lasser weary, tire; ***se ~ de*** tire *ou* weary of
latent latent
latéral lateral, side *atr*
latitude *f* latitude
latte *f* lath; *de plancher* board
lauréat, ~e *m/f* prizewinner
laurier *m* laurel; ***feuille f de ~*** CUIS bayleaf
lavabo *m* (wash)basin; **~s** toilets
lavage *m* washing
lavande *f* lavender
laver wash; *tâche* wash away; **laverie** *f*: ***~ automatique*** laundromat, *Br* laundrette; **lavette** *f* dishcloth; *fig péj* spineless individual
lave-vaisselle *m* dishwasher
laxatif, -ive *adj & m* laxative
laxisme *m* laxness
le *complément d'objet direct* him; *chose* it; ***oui, je ~ sais*** yes, I know
le, *f* **la,** *pl* **les** *article défini* the; ***le garçon/les garçons*** the boy/the boys; ***je me suis cassé la jambe*** I broke my leg; ***j'aime le vin*** I like wine; ***les dinosaures avaient ...*** dinosaurs had ...; ***le premier mai*** May first, *Br* the first of May; ***ouvert le samedi***

open (on) Saturdays; ***10 euros les 5*** 10 euros for 5; ***tu connais la France?*** do you know France; ***le printemps est là*** spring is here; ***je ne parle pas l'italien*** I don't speak Italian
leader *m* POL leader
lécher lick
leçon *f* lesson
lecteur, **-trice** **1** *m/f* reader; *à l'université* foreign language assistant **2** *m* INFORM drive; ***~ de CDs*** CD player; **lecture** *f* reading
ledit, **ladite** the said
légal legal; **légaliser** *signature* authenticate; (*rendre légal*) legalize; **légalité** *f* legality
légende *f* legend; *sous image* caption; *d'une carte* key
léger, **-ère** light; *erreur, retard* slight; *mœurs* loose; (*frivole, irréfléchi*) thoughtless; ***à la légère*** lightly; **légèrement** lightly; (*un peu*) slightly; **légèreté** *f* lightness; (*frivolité, irréflexion*) thoughtlessness
légion *f* legion; ***~ étrangère*** Foreign Legion; **légionnaire** *m* legionnaire
législation *f* legislation
légitime legitimate
legs *m* legacy
léguer bequeath
légume *m* vegetable
lendemain *m*: ***le ~*** the next *ou* following day; ***le ~ de son élection*** the day after he was elected
lent slow; **lentement** slowly; **lenteur** *f* slowness
lentille *f* TECH lens; *légume sec* lentil
léopard *m* leopard
lequel, **laquelle** (*pl* lesquels, lesquelles) *interrogatif* which (one); *relatif, avec personne* who; *avec chose* which
les[1] → ***le***
les[2] *pron personnel* them
lesbien, **~ne** *adj & f* lesbian
léser injure; *intérêts* damage; *droits* infringe
lésiner skimp (***sur*** on)
lésion *f* MÉD lesion
lessive *f produit* laundry detergent, *Br* washing powder; *liquide* detergent; *linge* laundry; ***faire la ~*** do the laundry
leste agile; *propos* crude
léthargie *f* lethargy
lettre *f* letter; ***à la ~, au pied de la ~*** literally; ***en toutes ~s*** in full; *fig* in black and white; ***~s*** literature; *études* arts; **lettré** well-read
leucémie *f* MÉD leukemia, *Br* leukaemia
leur **1** *adj possessif* their **2** *pron personnel*: ***le/la ~, les ~s*** theirs **3** *complément d'objet indirect* (to) them
leurrer *fig* deceive
levé: ***être ~*** be up; **levée** *f* lifting; *d'une séance* adjournment; *du courrier* collec-

tion; *aux cartes* trick; **lever 1** *v/t* raise, lift; *poids, interdiction* lift; *impôts* collect **2** *v/i de la pâte* rise; ***se ~*** get up; *du soleil* rise; *du jour* break **3** *m*: ***~ du jour*** daybreak; ***~ du soleil*** sunrise

levier *m* lever; ***~ de vitesse*** gear shift, *surtout Br* gear lever

lèvre *f* lip

levure *f* yeast; ***~ chimique*** baking powder

lézard *m* lizard

lézarde *f* crack

liaison *f* connection; *amoureuse* affair; *de train* link; LING liaison

liant sociable

libellule *f* dragonfly

libéral liberal; ***profession f ~e*** profession; **libéralisme** *m* liberalism

libérateur, -trice 1 *adj* liberating **2** *m/f* liberator; **libération** *f* liberation; *d'un prisonnier* release; ***~ conditionnelle*** parole; **libérer** liberate; *prisonnier* release, free (***de*** from); *gaz, d'un engagement* release

liberté *f* freedom, liberty; ***mettre en ~*** set free, release

librairie *f* bookstore, *Br* bookshop

libre free (***de faire*** to do); **libre-service** *m* self-service; *magasin* self-service shop

Libye *f* Libya; **libien, ~ne** Libyan; **Libyen, ~ne** *m/f* Libyan

licence *f* license, *Br* licence; *diplôme* degree

licenciement *m* layoff; (*renvoi*) dismissal; **licencier** lay off; (*renvoyer*) dismiss

lié: ***être ~ par*** be bound by; ***être très ~ avec qn*** be very close to s.o.

lien *m* tie, bond; (*rapport*) connection; ***avoir un ~ de parenté*** be related

lier tie (up); *d'un contrat* be binding on; CUIS thicken; *pensées, personnes* connect; ***~ amitié avec qn*** make friends with s.o.

lierre *m* BOT ivy

lieu *m* place; ***~x*** premises; JUR scene; ***au ~ de (faire) qch*** instead of (doing) sth; ***avoir ~*** take place; ***donner ~ à*** give rise to; ***en premier ~*** in the first place; ***s'il y a ~*** if necessary

lièvre *m* hare

ligne *f* line; *d'autobus* number; ***garder la ~*** keep one's figure; ***entrer en ~ de compte*** be taken into consideration; ***pêcher à la ~*** go angling; ***en ~*** INFORM on line; ***achats en ~*** on-line shopping

liguer: ***se ~*** join forces (***pour faire*** to do)

lilas *m & adj inv* lilac

limace *f* slug

lime *f* file; ***~ à ongles*** nail file; **limer** file

limitation *f* limitation; ***~ de***

vitesse speed limit; **limite** *f* limit; (*frontière*) boundary; ***à la ~*** if absolutely necessary; ***date*** *f* **~** deadline; ***vitesse*** *f* **~** speed limit; **limiter** limit (**à** to)
limoger POL dismiss
limonade *f* lemonade
limousine *f* limousine
lin *m* BOT flax; *toile* linen
linéaire linear
linge *m* linen; (*lessive*) washing
lingerie *f* lingerie
linguiste *m/f* linguist
lion *m* lion; ASTROL ***Lion*** Leo; **lionne** *f* lioness
liposuccion *f* liposuction
liqueur *f* liqueur
liquidation *f* liquidation; *vente au rabais* sale
liquide 1 *adj* liquid; ***argent*** *m* **~** cash **2** *m* liquid; **~ *de freins*** brake fluid; **liquider** liquidate; *stock* sell off; *problème* dispose of
lire read
lis *m* BOT lily
lisible legible
lisse smooth; **lisser** smooth
liste *f* list; **~ *d'attente*** waiting list; **~ *de commissions*** shopping list; **lister** list; **listing** *m* printout
lit *m* bed; ***aller au ~*** go to bed; **~ *de camp*** cot, *Br* camp bed; **literie** *f* bedding
litige *m* dispute
litre *m* liter, *Br* litre
littéraire literary; **littérature** *f* literature
littoral 1 *adj* coastal **2** *m* coastline
livraison *f* delivery
livre[1] *m* book; **~ *de poche*** paperback
livre[2] *f poids, monnaie* pound
livrer *marchandises* deliver; *prisonnier* hand over; *secret* divulge; ***se ~*** (*se confier*) open up; (*se soumettre*) give o.s. up; ***se ~ à*** (*se confier*) confide in; *activité* indulge in; *l'abattement* give way to
livret *m* booklet; *d'opéra* libretto
livreur *m* delivery man; **~ *de journaux*** paper boy
lobby *m* lobby
lobe *m*: **~ *de l'oreille*** earlobe
local 1 *adj* local **2** *m* (*salle*) premises *pl*; ***locaux*** premises; **localisation** *f* location; *de software etc* localization; **localiser** locate; (*limiter*), *de software* localize
locataire *m/f* tenant; **location** *f par propriétaire* renting out; *par locataire* renting; (*loyer*) rent; *au théâtre* reservation
logement *m* accommodations, *Br* accommodation, *pl*; (*appartement*) apartment, *Br aussi* flat; **loger 1** *v/t* accommodate **2** *v/i* live; **logeur** *m* landlord; **logeuse** *f* landlady
logiciel *m* INFORM software
logique 1 *adj* logical **2** *f* logic

loi *f* law
loin far (***de*** from); *dans le passé* long ago; *dans l'avenir* a long way off; ***au ~*** in the distance
lointain 1 *adj* distant **2** *m* distance
loisir *m* leisure; ***~s*** leisure activities
Londres London
long, longue 1 *adj* long; ***à ~ terme*** in the long term; ***à la longue*** in time; ***être ~*** (***à faire qch***) take a long time (doing sth) **2** *adv*: ***en dire ~*** speak volumes **3** *m*: ***de deux mètres de ~*** two meters long; ***le ~ de*** along
longer follow
longitude *f* longitude
longtemps a long time
longuement for a long time; *parler* at length
longueur *f* length; ***sur la même ~ d'onde*** on the same wavelength
loquace talkative
loque *f* rag
loquet *m* latch
lorgner eye; *héritage, poste* have one's eye on
lors: ***dès ~*** from then on; ***~ de*** during
lorsque when
lot *m* (*destin*) fate; *à la loterie* prize; (*portion*) share; COMM batch
loterie *f* lottery
loti: ***bien/mal ~*** well/badly off
lotion *f* lotion
lotissement *m* (*parcelle*) plot; *terrain loti* housing development
louable praiseworthy; **louange** *f* praise
louche[1] *adj* sleazy
louche[2] *f* ladle
loucher squint
louer[1] rent
louer[2] (*vanter*) praise (***de, pour*** for)
loup *m* wolf
loupe *f* magnifying glass
louper F *travail* botch; *bus* miss
lourd heavy; *plaisanterie* clumsy; *temps* oppressive; **lourdaud, ~e 1** *adj* clumsy **2** *m/f* oaf; **lourdement** heavily
loyal honest; *adversaire* fair-minded; *ami* loyal
loyer *m* rent
lubie *f* whim
lubrifiant *m* lubricant; **lubrifier** lubricate
lucarne *f* skylight
lucide lucid; (*conscient*) conscious; **lucidité** *f* lucidity
lucratif, -ive lucrative
lueur *f* faint light; ***une ~ d'espoir*** a glimmer of hope
luge *f* toboggan; ***faire de la ~*** go tobogganing
lugubre gloomy, lugubrious
lui *complément d'objet indirect, masculin* (to) him; *féminin* (to) her; *chose, animal* (to) it; *après prép, masculin* him; *animal* it

lui-même himself; *de chose* itself
luire glint, glisten
lumière *f* light; ***à la ~ de*** in the light of
lumineux, **-euse** luminous; *ciel*, *couleur* bright; *affiche* illuminated; *idée* brilliant
lunaire lunar
lunatique lunatic
lundi *m* Monday
lune *f* moon; ***~ de miel*** honeymoon
lunette *f*: ***~s*** glasses; ***~s de soleil*** sunglasses; ***~s de ski*** ski goggles
lustre *m* (*lampe*) chandelier; *fig* luster, *Br* lustre; **lustrer** polish
lutte *f* fight, struggle; SP wrestling; **lutter** fight, struggle; SP wrestle
luxe *m* luxury; ***de ~*** luxury *atr*
Luxembourg: ***le ~*** Luxemburg; **luxembourgeois**, **~e** of/from Luxemburg, Luxemburg *atr*; **Luxembourgeois**, **~e** *m/f* Luxemburger
luxer: ***se ~ l'épaule*** dislocate one's shoulder
luxueux, **-euse** luxurious
luxuriant luxuriant
lycée *m* senior high, *Br* grammar school; **lycéen**, **~ne** *m/f* student (at a lycée)
lyophilisé freeze-dried
lyrique lyric; *qui a du lyrisme* lyrical; ***artiste ~*** opera singer

M

M. (= ***monsieur***) Mr
ma → ***mon***
macabre macabre
macédoine *f*: ***~ de légumes*** mixed vegetables *pl*; ***~ de fruits*** fruit salad
macérer CUIS: ***faire ~*** marinate
mâcher chew
machin *m* F thing
machinal mechanical
machine *f* machine; NAUT engine; *fig* machinery; ***~ à laver*** washing machine; ***~ à sous*** slot machine
machisme *m* machismo; **macho 1** *adj* male chauvinist **2** *m* macho type
mâchoire *f* jaw; **mâchonner** chew (on); (*marmonner*) mutter
maçon *m* bricklayer; *avec des pierres* mason; **maçonnerie** *f* masonry
maculer spatter
madame *f*: ***Madame Durand*** Mrs Durand; ***mesdames et messieurs*** ladies and gentlemen
mademoiselle *f*: ***Mademoiselle Durand*** Miss Durand
madone *f* Madonna
magasin *m* (*boutique*) store, *surtout Br* shop; (*dépôt*)

store room; **grand ~** department store; **magasinier** *m* storeman
magazine *m* magazine
mage *m*: ***les Rois ~s*** the Three Wise Men, the Magi
magicien, ~ne *m/f* magician; **magie** *f* magic; **magique** magic, magical
magistral *ton* magisterial; *fig* masterly; ***cours*** *m* **~** lecture
magistrat *m* JUR magistrate
magnanime magnanimous
magner: ***se ~*** F move it F
magnétique magnetic
magnétophone *m* tape recorder
magnétoscope *m* video (recorder)
magnifique magnificent
magouille *f* F scheming; ***~s électorales*** election shenanigans F
mai *m* May
maigre thin; *résultat, salaire* meager, *Br* meagre; **maigrir** get thin, lose weight
mailing *m* mailshot
maille *f* stitch
maillet *m* mallet
maillot *m* SP shirt, jersey; *de coureur* vest; **~ *(de bain)*** swimsuit
main *f* hand; ***fait à la ~*** handmade; ***prendre qc en ~*** *fig* take sth in hand; ***perdre la ~*** *fig* lose one's touch; ***sous la ~*** to hand, within reach
main-d'œuvre *f inv* manpower, labor, *Br* labour
maint *fml* many; ***à ~es reprises*** time and again
maintenance *f* maintenance
maintenant now; **~ *que*** now that
maintenir keep; *tradition* uphold; *(tenir fermement)* hold; *d'une poutre* hold up; *(soutenir)* maintain; ***se ~*** *d'un prix* hold steady; *d'une tradition, de la paix* last; ***se ~ au pouvoir*** stay in power; **maintien** *m* maintenance; **~ *de la paix*** peace keeping
maire *m* mayor; **mairie** *f* town hall
mais 1 *conj* but **2** *adv*: **~ *bien sûr!*** of course!; **~ *non!*** no!
maïs *m* BOT corn, *Br aussi* maize; *en boîte* sweet corn
maison *f* house; *(chez-soi)* home; COMM company; ***à la ~*** at home; ***pâté*** *m* **~** homemade pâté; **~ *de campagne*** country house
maître *m* master; *(professeur)* school teacher; *(peintre, écrivain)* maestro; **~ *chanteur*** blackmailer; **~ *d'hôtel*** maitre d', *Br* head waiter; **~ *nageur*** swimming instructor
maîtresse 1 *f* mistress *(aussi amante)*; *(professeur)* schoolteacher **2** *adj*: ***idée*** *f* **~** main idea
maîtrise *f* mastery; *diplôme* MA, master's (degree); **~ *de soi*** self-control; **maîtri-**

ser master; *cheval* gain control of; *incendie* bring under control
majestueux, **-euse** majestic
majeur 1 *adj* major; ***être ~*** JUR be of age **2** *m* middle finger; **majorité** *f* majority
majuscule *f & adj*: (***lettre*** *f*) ~ capital (letter)
mal 1 *m* evil; (*maladie*) illness; (*difficulté*) difficulty; ***faire ~*** hurt; ***avoir ~ aux dents*** have toothache; ***se donner du ~*** go to a lot of trouble; ***faire du ~ à qn*** hurt s.o.; ***~ de mer*** seasickness **2** *adv* badly; ***pas ~*** not bad; ***se sentir ~*** feel ill **3** *adj*: ***faire/dire qc de ~*** do/say sth bad
malade ill, sick; ***tomber ~*** fall ill; ***~ mental*** mentally ill; **maladie** *f* illness
maladresse *f* clumsiness; **maladroit** clumsy
malaise *m* discomfort; POL malaise; ***faire un ~*** faint
malavisé ill-advised
malchance *f* bad luck
mâle *m & adj* male
malédiction *f* curse
malencontreux, **-euse** unfortunate
malentendant hard of hearing
malfaiteur *m* malefactor
malgré in spite of
malheur *m* misfortune; (*malchance*) bad luck; ***par ~*** unfortunately; **malheureusement** unfortunately;
malheureux, **-euse** unfortunate; (*triste*) unhappy; (*insignifiant*) silly little
malhonnête dishonest; **malhonnêteté** *f* dishonesty
malice *f* malice; (*espièglerie*) mischief; **malicieux**, **-euse** malicious; (*coquin*) mischievous
malin, **-igne** (*rusé*) crafty, cunning; (*méchant*) malicious; MÉD malignant
malle *f* trunk; **mallette** *f* little bag
malodorant foul-smelling
malpoli impolite
malpropre dirty
malsain unhealthy
malt *m* malt
Malte *f* Malta; **maltais**, **~e** Maltese; **Maltais**, **~e** *m/f* Maltese
maltraiter mistreat, maltreat
malveillant malevolent
malvoyant, **~e 1** *adj* visually impaired **2** *m/f* visually impaired person
maman *f* Mom, *Br* Mum
mamelle *f de vache* udder; *de chienne* teat
mamie *f* F granny
mammifère *m* mammal
manager *m* manager
manche[1] *m d'outils* handle; *d'un violon* neck
manche[2] *f* sleeve; SP round; **la Manche** the English Channel
manchette *f* cuff; *d'un journal* headline

mandarine *f* mandarin (orange)
mandat *m* POL term of office, mandate; (*procuration*) proxy; *de la poste* postal order; **~ *d'arrêt*** arrest warrant; **mandataire** *m/f à une réunion* proxy
manège *m* riding school; (*carrousel*) carousel, *Br* roundabout; *fig* game
mangeable edible, eatable
mangeoire *f* manger
manger eat; *argent, temps* eat up; *mots* swallow
maniable *voiture* easy to handle
maniaque fussy; **manie** *f* mania
manier handle
manière *f* way, manner; **~*s*** manners; *affectées* airs and graces; ***à la ~ de*** in the style of; ***de cette ~*** (in) that way; ***de toute ~*** anyway; ***d'une ~ générale*** generally speaking; ***de ~ à faire qch*** so as to do sth; **maniéré** affected
manifestant, **~*e*** *m/f* demonstrator; **manifestation** *f de joie etc* expression; POL demonstration; *culturelle, sportive* event
manifeste 1 *adj* obvious **2** *m* POL manifesto; **manifester 1** *v/t* show; ***se ~*** *de maladie, problèmes* manifest itself/themselves **2** *v/i* demonstrate
manipulateur, -trice manipulative; **manipulation** *f d'un appareil* handling; *d'une personne* manipulation; **~ *génétique*** genetic engineering; **manipuler** handle; *personne* manipulate
mannequin *m dans magasin* dummy; *personne* model
manœuvre 1 *f* maneuver, *Br* manoeuvre; *d'un outil, une machine etc* operation **2** *m* unskilled laborer *ou Br* labourer; **manœuvrer** maneuver, *Br* manoeuvre
manoir *m* manor (house)
manque *m* lack; ***par ~ de*** for lack of; **manqué** unsuccessful; *rendez-vous* missed; **manquer 1** *v/i* (*être absent*) be missing; (*faire défaut*) be lacking; (*échouer*) fail; ***tu me manques*** I miss you; **~ *à*** *promesse* fail to keep; *devoir* fail in **2** *v/t* (*être absent à*) miss; *examen* fail; ***elle a manqué* (*de*) *se faire écraser*** she was almost run over **3** *impersonnel* ***il manque des preuves*** there's a lack of evidence
manteau *m* coat; *de neige* blanket; **~ *de cheminée*** mantelpiece
manucure *f* manicure
manuel, **~*le*** *adj & m* manual; **~ *d'utilisation*** instruction manual
manufacturé: ***produits*** *mpl* **~*s*** manufactured goods
manuscrit 1 *adj* handwritten

2 *m* manuscript
maquereau *m* ZO mackerel; F (*souteneur*) pimp
maquette *f* model
maquillage *m* make-up; **maquiller** make up; *crime, vérité* conceal; ***se ~*** put one's make-up on
marais *m* swamp
marathon *m* marathon
marbre *m* marble
marc *m*: ***~ de café*** coffee grounds *pl*
marchand, **~e 1** *adj valeur* market *atr*; *rue* shopping *atr*; *marine* merchant *atr* **2** *m/f* merchant, storekeeper, *Br* shopkeeper; **marchander** haggle, bargain; **marchandise** *f*: ***~s*** merchandise; ***train m de ~s*** freight train
marche *f* walking; *d'escalier* step; MUS, MIL march; *des événements* course; (*démarche*) walk; ***~ arrière*** AUTO reverse; ***mettre en ~*** start (up)
marché *m* market; (*accord*) deal; **(*à*) *bon ~*** cheap; ***par-dessus le ~*** into the bargain; ***~ boursier*** stock market; ***le Marché Commun*** POL the Common Market; ***~ noir*** black market
marcher walk; MIL march; *d'une machine* run, work; F (*réussir*) work; *d'un bus, train* run; ***faire ~ qn*** pull s.o.'s leg
mardi *m* Tuesday; ***Mardi gras*** Mardi Gras, *Br* Shrove Tuesday
mare *f* pond; ***~ de sang*** pool of blood
marécage *m* swamp; **marécageux**, **-euse** swampy
marée *f* tide; ***~ basse/haute*** low/high tide; ***~ noire*** oil slick
margarine *f* margarine
marge *f* margin; ***en ~ de*** on the fringes of
marguerite *f* daisy
mari *m* husband
mariage *m fête* wedding; *état* marriage
marié 1 *adj* married **2** *m* (bride)groom; **mariée** *f* bride; **marier** marry; ***se ~*** get married; ***se ~ avec*** marry, get married to
marijuana *f* marijuana
marin 1 *adj air* sea *atr*; *animaux* marine **2** *m* sailor
marine *f* MIL navy; **(*bleu*) *~*** navy (blue)
marionnette *f* puppet; *avec des ficelles aussi* marionnette
marmelade *f* marmalade
marmite *f* (large) pot
marmonner mutter
maroquinerie *f* leather goods shop; *articles* leather goods *pl*
marquant remarkable
marque *f* mark; COMM brand; *de voiture* make; COMM (*signe*) trademark; ***~ déposée*** registered trademark; ***de ~***

COMM branded; *fig: personne* distinguished; **marquer** mark; (*noter*) write down; *personnalité* leave its mark on; *d'un baromètre etc* show; (*accentuer*) *taille* emphasize; ***~ un but*** score (a goal); **marqueur** *m* marker pen

marraine *f* godmother

marrant F funny

marre F: ***j'en ai ~*** I've had enough

marrer F: ***se ~*** have a good laugh

marron 1 *m* chestnut **2** *adj inv* brown; **marronnier** *m* chestnut tree

mars *m* March

marteau *m* hammer; ***~ piqueur*** pneumatic drill; **marteler** hammer

martyr, ~e[1] *m/f* martyr; **martyre**[2] *m* martyrdom; **martyriser** abuse; *petit frère, camarade de classe* bully

masculin male; GRAM masculine

masque *m* mask; **masquer** mask

massacre *m* massacre; **massacrer** massacre

massage *m* massage

masse *f* masse; ÉL ground, *Br* earth,; ***en ~*** in large numbers, en masse; *manifestation* massive; ***une ~ de choses à faire*** masses *pl* (of things) to do

massif, -ive 1 *adj* massif; *or, chêne* solid **2** *m* massif; ***~ de fleurs*** flowerbed

massue *f* club

mastiquer *nourriture* chew

mat[1] matt; *son* dull

mat[2] *inv aux échecs* checkmated

mât *m* mast

match *m* game, *Br aussi* match; ***~ nul*** tied game, *Br* draw

matelas *m* mattress; ***~ pneumatique*** air bed

matelot *m* sailor

matérialiser: ***se ~*** materialize; **matériau** *m* material; **matériel, ~le 1** *adj* material **2** *m de camping*, SP equipment; INFORM hardware

maternel, ~le 1 *adj* maternal; ***langue f ~le*** mother tongue **2** *f* nursery school; **maternité** *f* motherhood; *établissement* maternity hospital; (*enfantement*) pregnancy

mathématicien, ~ne *m/f* mathematician; **mathématique 1** *adj* mathematical **2** *fpl*: ***~s*** mathematics

matière *f* material; PHYS, PHIL matter; (*sujet*) subject; ***entrée en ~*** introduction; ***en ~ de*** when it comes to; ***~ première*** raw material

matin *m* morning; ***le ~*** in the morning; ***tous les lundis ~s*** every Monday morning; **matinal** morning *atr*; ***être ~*** be an early riser; **matinée** *f* morning; (*spectacle*) matinée; ***faire la grasse ~*** sleep

late
matou *m* tom cat
matricule *m* number
matrimonial matrimonial
maturité *f* maturity
maudire curse; **maudit** F damn F
mauvais 1 *adj* bad; (*erroné*) wrong **2** *adv* bad; ***il fait ~*** the weather is bad
mauve mauve
maximum *adj & m* maximum; ***au ~*** at most, at the maximum
mayonnaise *f* mayonnaise, mayo F
me me; *complément d'objet indirect* (to) me; ***je ~ suis coupé*** I've cut myself; ***je ~ lève à ...*** I get up at ...
mec *m* F guy F
mécanicien *m* mechanic; **mécanique 1** *adj* mechanical **2** *f* mechanics; **mécanisme** *m* mechanism
méchanceté *f* nastiness; *action, parole* nasty thing to do/say; **méchant, ~e 1** *adj* nasty; *enfant* naughty **2** *m/f* F: ***les gentils et les ~s*** the goodies and the baddies
mèche *f de bougie* wick; *d'explosif* fuse; *de perceuse* bit; *de cheveux* strand
méconnaissable unrecognizable
mécontent unhappy, displeased (***de*** with); **mécontenter** displease
médaille *f* medal; **médaillon** *m* medallion
médecin *m* doctor
médecine *f* medicine; ***les ~s douces*** alternative medicines
média *m* media *pl*
médiateur, -trice *m/f* mediator
médiatique media *atr*
médical medical
médicament *m* medicine, drug
médiéval medieval, *Br* mediaeval
médiocre mediocre; ***~ en*** ÉDU poor at
médire: ***~ de qn*** run s.o. down
méditation *f* meditation; **méditer 1** *v/t* think about, reflect on **2** *v/i* meditate (***sur*** on)
Méditerranée: ***la ~*** the Mediterranean; **méditerranéen, ~ne** Mediterranean; **Méditerranéen, ~ne** *m/f* Mediterranean *atr*
méduse *f* ZO jellyfish
meeting *m* meeting
méfait *m* JUR misdemeanor, *Br* misdemeanour; ***~s*** *de la drogue* harmful effects
méfiance *f* mistrust, suspicion; **méfiant** suspicious; **méfier**: ***se ~ de*** mistrust, be suspicious of; (*se tenir en garde*) be wary of
mégaoctet *m* INFORM megabyte
mégarde *f*: ***par ~*** inadvertently

mégot *m* cigarette butt
meilleur 1 *adj* better; ***le ~ …*** the best … **2** *m*: ***le ~*** the best
mél *m* email
mélancolie *f* gloom, melancholy
mélange *m* mixture; *de thés* blend; *action* mixing; *de thés* blending; **mélanger** mix; *thés* blend; (*brouiller*) jumble up, mix up
mêlée *f* fray, melee; *en rugby* scrum; **mêler** mix; (*réunir*) combine; (*brouiller*) jumble up, mix up; ***~ qn à qc*** *fig* involve s.o. in sth; ***se ~ à qc*** get involved with sth; ***se ~ de qc*** interfere in sth
mélodie *f* tune, melody; **mélodieux, -euse** tuneful, melodious; *voix* melodious
mélodramatique melodramatic; **mélodrame** *m* melodrama
melon *m* BOT melon
membre *m* ANAT limb; *fig* member
même 1 *adj*: ***le/la ~, les ~s*** the same; ***la bonté ~*** kindness itself **2** *pron*: ***le/la ~*** the same one; ***les ~s*** the same ones; ***cela revient au ~*** it comes to the same thing **3** *adv* even; ***~ pas*** not even; ***faire de ~*** do the same; ***de ~!*** likewise!; ***être à ~ de faire*** be able to do; ***tout de ~*** all the same; ***quand ~*** all the same; ***moi de ~*** me too
mémoire 1 *f* memory; ***à la ~ de*** in memory of **2** *m* (*exposé*) report; (*dissertation*) thesis; ***~s*** memoirs; **mémorable** memorable; **mémoriser** memorize
menace *f* threat; **menacer** threaten (***de*** with; ***de faire*** to do)
ménage *m* (*famille*) household; (*couple*) (married) couple; ***faire le ~*** clean house, *Br* do the housework; **ménagement** *m* consideration; **ménager[1]** *v/t* treat with consideration; *temps, argent* use sparingly; (*arranger*) arrange; **ménager[2], -ère 1** *adj* household *atr* **2** *f* home-maker, housewife
mendiant, ~e *m/f* beggar; **mendier 1** *v/i* beg **2** *v/t* beg for
mener 1 *v/t* lead; (*amener, transporter*) take **2** *v/i*: ***~ à*** *d'un chemin* lead to; ***ne ~ à rien*** *des efforts* come to nothing; **meneur** *m* leader; *péj* ringleader
mensonge *m* lie; **mensonger, -ère** false
mensualité *f somme à payer* monthly payment; **mensuel, ~le** monthly
mental mental; ***calcul m ~*** mental arithmetic; **mentalité** *f* mentality
menteur, -euse *m/f* liar
menthe *f* BOT mint
mention *f* mention; *à un examen* grade, *Br aussi* mark;

mentionner mention
mentir lie (**à** to)
menton *m* chin
menu 1 *adj* slight; *morceaux* small **2** *adv* finely, fine **3** *m* menu (*aussi* INFORM); (*repas*) set meal; ***par le ~*** in minute detail
menuisier *m* carpenter
méprendre: ***se ~*** be mistaken (***sur*** about)
mépris *m* (*indifférence*) disdain; (*dégoût*) scorn; **méprisable** despicable; **méprisant** scornful; **mépriser** *argent, ennemi* despise; *conseil, danger* scorn
mer *f* sea; ***en ~*** at see; ***la Mer du Nord*** the North Sea
mercenaire *m* mercenary
mercerie *f magasin* notions store, *Br* haberdashery; *articles* notions, *Br* haberdashery *pl*
merci 1 *int* thanks, thank you (***de, pour*** for); ***~ bien*** thanks a lot, thank you very much **2** *f* mercy
mercredi *m* Wednesday
merde *f* P shit P; **merder** P screw up P
mère *f* mother
méridional southern
mérite *m* merit; **mériter** deserve; ***~ le détour*** be worth a visit
merle *m* blackbird
merveille *f* wonder, marvel; ***à ~*** wonderfully well; **merveilleux, -euse** wonderful
mes → ***mon***
mésaventure *f* mishap
mesquin mean
message *m* message; **messager, -ère** *m/f* messenger, courier; **messagerie** *f* parcels service; *électronique* electronic mail; ***~ vocale*** voicemail
messe *f* REL mass
mesure *f* measurement; *disposition* measure, step; MUS (*rythme*) time; ***à ~ que*** as; ***être en ~ de faire qch*** be in a position to do sth; ***outre ~*** excessive; ***sur ~*** *fig* tailor-made; **mesurer** measure; *risque, importance* gauge; *paroles* weigh; ***se ~ avec qn*** pit o.s. against s.o.
métal *m* metal; **métallique** metallic
métamorphoser: ***se ~*** metamorphose
météo *f* weather forecast
météore *m* meteor
météorologie *f* meteorology; *service* weather office
méthode *f* method
méticuleux, -euse meticulous
métier *m* profession; *manuel* trade; (*expérience*) experience; *machine* loom
métrage *m d'un film* footage; ***court ~*** short
mètre *m* meter, *Br* metre; (*règle*) tape measure
métrique metric
métro *m* subway, *Br* under-

ground; *à Paris* metro
métropole *f* metropolis; *de colonie* mother country
mettre put; *vêtements, lunettes, chauffage* put on; *réveil* set; *argent dans entreprise* put in; ***~ deux heures à faire qc*** take two hours to do sth; ***se ~ à faire*** start to do
meuble *m* piece of furniture; ***~s*** furniture; **meubler** furnish
meurtre *m* murder; **meurtrier**, **-ère** **1** *adj* deadly **2** *m/f* murderer
meurtrir bruise; **meurtrissure** *f* bruise
meute *f* pack; *fig* mob
mexicain, **~e** Mexican; **Mexicain**, **~e** *m/f* Mexican; **Mexique**: ***le ~*** Mexico
mi-… half; ***à mi-chemin*** half-way; (***à la***) ***mi-janvier*** mid-January
mi-bas *mpl* knee-highs, pop socks
miche *f* large round loaf
micro *m* mike; INFORM computer, PC; *d'espionnage* bug
microbe *m* microbe
microfilm *m* microfilm
micro-ondes *m* microwave
microphone *m* microphone
microscope *m* microscope
midi *m* noon, twelve o'clock; (*sud*) south; **le Midi** the South of France
mie *f de pain* crumb
miel *m* honey
mien: ***le mien, la mienne, les miens, les miennes*** mine
miette *f* crumb
mieux **1** *adv comparatif de bien* better; *superlatif de bien* best; ***le ~*** best; ***de ~ en ~*** better and better; ***tant ~*** so much the better; ***vous feriez ~ de*** … you would *ou* you'd do best to … **2** *m*: (*progrès*) progress; ***j'ai fait de mon ~*** I did my best; ***le ~, c'est de …*** the best thing is to …
mièvre insipid
mignon, **~ne** (*charmant*) cute; (*gentil*) nice
migraine *f* migraine
migration *f* migration; **migrer** migrate
mijoter CUIS simmer; *fig* hatch
milieu *m* (*centre*) middle; *biologique, social* environment; ***au ~ de*** in the middle of; ***le ~*** the underworld
militaire **1** *adj* military **2** *m* soldier; ***les ~s*** the military *sg ou pl*
militant active
militer: ***~ dans*** be an active member of; ***~ pour/contre*** *fig* militate for/against
mille **1** (a) thousand **2** *m mesure* mile; ***~ marin*** nautical mile
millénaire **1** *adj* thousand-year old **2** *m* millennium
milliard *m* billion; **milliardaire** *m* billionaire
millième thousandth

millier *m* thousand
milligramme *m* milligram
millimètre millimeter, *Br* millimetre
million *m* million; **millionnaire** *m/f* millionaire
minable mean, shabby; ***un salaire ~*** a pittance
mince thin; *personne* slim; *espoir* slight; *somme, profit* small; *argument* flimsy
mine[1] *f* appearance, look; ***avoir bonne/mauvaise ~*** look/not look well
mine[2] *f* mine (*aussi* MIL); *de crayon* lead; **miner** undermine; MIL mine
minéral *adj & m* mineral
minéralogique AUTO: ***plaque f ~*** license plate, *Br* number plate
mineur[1] *adj* JUR, MUS minor
mineur[2] *m* (*ouvrier*) miner
miniature *f* miniature
minimal minimum; **minime** minimal; *salaire* tiny; **minimiser** minimize; **minimum** *adj & m* minimum; ***au ~*** at the very least; ***un ~ de*** the least little bit of
ministère *m* department; (*gouvernement*) government; REL ministry; **ministre** *m* minister; ***~ des Affaires étrangères*** Secretary of State, *Br* Foreign Secretary; ***~ de l'Intérieur*** Secretary of the Interior, *Br* Home Secretary
minitel *m* small home terminal connected to a number of data banks
minorité *f* JUR, POL minority
minuit *m* midnight
minuscule 1 *adj* tiny, minuscule; *lettre* small, lower case **2** *f* small *ou* lower-case letter
minute *f* minute
minuterie *f* time switch
minutie *f* meticulousness; **minutieux, -euse** meticulous
miracle *m* miracle; **miraculeux, -euse** miraculous
mirage *m* mirage; *fig* illusion
miroir *m* mirror
miroiter sparkle
mise *f au jeu* stake; ***de ~*** acceptable; ***~ en bouteilles*** bottling; ***~ en marche*** *ou* ***route*** start-up; **miser** stake (***sur*** on)
misérable wretched; **misère** *f* destitution; (*chose pénible*) misfortune
miséricordieux, -euse merciful
misogyne *m* misogynist
missile *m* MIL missile
mission *f* mission; (*tâche*) task
mite *f* ZO (clothes) moth
mi-temps 1 *f* SP half-time **2** *m* part-time job; ***à ~*** *travail* part-time
mitigé moderate; *sentiments* mixed
mi-voix: ***à ~*** under one's breath
mixer, mixeur *m* CUIS blender; **mixte** mixed; **mixture** *f*

péj vile concoction
MM (= ***Messieurs***) Messrs.
Mme (= ***Madame***) Mrs
Mo *m* (= ***mégaoctet***) Mb (= megabyte)
mobile 1 *adj* mobile; (*amovible*) movable; *feuilles* loose; *ombres* moving **2** *m* motive; ART mobile
mobilier, -ère 1 *adj* JUR movable, personal **2** *m* furniture
mobilisation *f* mobilization; **mobilité** *f* mobility
mobylette® *f* moped
moche F ugly; (*méprisable*) mean
mode[1] *m* method; ***~ d'emploi*** instructions (for use); ***~ de vie*** life-style
mode[2] *f* fashion; ***être à la ~*** be fashionable, be in fashion
modèle *m* model; *tricot* pattern; **modeler** model
modem *m* INFORM modem
modération *f* moderation; **modéré** moderate; **modérer** moderate; ***se ~*** control o.s.
moderne modern; **modernisation** *f* modernization; **moderniser** modernize
modeste modest; **modestie** *f* modesty
modification *f* modification; **modifier** modify
modique modest
module *m* TECH module; **moduler** modulate
moelle *f* marrow; ***~ épinière*** spinal cord; **moelleux, -euse** *lit* soft; *chocolat, vin* smooth
mœurs *fpl* morals; (*coutumes*) customs
moi me; ***avec ~*** with me
moi-même myself
moindre lesser; *prix* lower; *quantité* smaller; ***le/la ~*** the least
moine *m* monk
moineau *m* sparrow
moins 1 *adv* less; ***au*** *ou* ***du ~*** at least; ***à ~ que ... ne*** (+ *subj*) unless; ***de ~ en ~*** less and less; ***20 euros de ~*** 20 euros less **2** *m*: ***le ~*** the least **3** *prép* MATH minus; ***dix heures ~ cinq*** it's five of ten , *Br* it's five to ten; ***il fait ~ deux*** it's 2 below zero
mois *m* month
moisi 1 *adj* moldy, *Br* mouldy **2** *m* BOT mold, *Br* mould; **moisir** go moldy *ou* *Br* mouldy; **moisissure** *f* BOT mold, *Br* mould
moisson *f* harvest; **moissonner** harvest
moite damp, moist
moitié *f* half; ***à ~ vide/endormi*** half-empty/-asleep; ***~ ~*** fifty-fifty
molaire *f* molar
molécule *f* molecule
molester rough up
molette *f de réglage* knob
mollesse *f* softness; *d'une personne, d'actions* lethargy
mollet[1], **~te** *adj* soft; *œuf* soft-boiled
mollet[2] *m* calf

môme *m/f* F kid F
moment *m* moment; ***d'un ~ à l'autre*** at any moment; ***par ~s*** at times, sometimes; ***pour le ~*** for the moment
momentané temporary; **momentanément** for a short while
mon *m*, **ma** *f*, **mes** *pl* my
monarchie *f* monarchy; **monarque** *m* monarch
monastère *m* monastery
monceau *m* mound
mondain *vie* society *atr*; **mondanités** *fpl* social niceties
monde *m* world; *gens* people *pl*; ***tout le ~*** everybody, everyone; ***mettre au ~*** bring into the world
mondial world *atr*, global; **mondialisation** *f* globalization
monétaire monetary; *marché* money *atr*
moniteur, -trice 1 *m/f* instructor **2** *m* INFORM monitor
monnaie *f* money; (*pièces*) change; (*unité monétaire*) currency
monologue *m* monolog, *Br* monologue
monopole *m* monopoly; **monopoliser** monopolize
monospace *m* people carrier, MPV
monotone monotonous; **monotonie** *f* monotony
monsieur *m* (*pl* messieurs) *dans lettre* Dear Sir; ***Monsieur Durand*** Mr Durand; ***bonjour ~*** good morning
monstre 1 *m* monster **2** *adj* colossal
mont *m* mountain
montage *m* TECH assembly; *d'un film* editing; *d'une photographie* montage; ÉL connecting
montagnard, ~e 1 *adj* mountain *atr* **2** *m/f* mountain dweller; **montagne** *f* mountain; ***à la ~*** in the mountains; ***~s russes*** roller coaster; **montagneux, -euse** mountainous
montant 1 *adj robe* high-necked; *mouvement* upward **2** *m somme* amount
montée *f sur montagne* ascent; (*pente*) slope; *de prix, de température* rise; **monter 1** *v/t* climb, go/come up; *valise* take/bring up; *machine* assemble; *tente* put up; THÉÂT put on; *film* edit; *entreprise* set up; *cheval* ride **2** *v/i* come/go upstairs; *d'avion, de route* climb; *des prix* rise, go up; *de baromètre, fleuve* rise; ***~ dans*** *avion, train* get on; *voiture* get in(to) **3**: ***se ~ à*** *de frais* amount to
montre *f* (wrist)watch
montrer show; ***~ qn/qc du doigt*** point at s.o./sth
monture *f* (*cheval*) mount; *de lunettes* frame; *d'un diamant* setting

monument *m* monument; **monumental** monumental
moquer: ***se ~ de*** (*railler*) make fun of; (*dédaigner*) not care about; (*tromper*) fool; **moquerie** *f* mockery
moquette *f* wall-to-wall carpet
moqueur, **-euse 1** *adj* mocking **2** *m/f* mocker
moral, **~e 1** *adj* moral; *souffrance*, *santé* spiritual **2** *m* morale **3** *f* morality, morals *pl*; *d'une histoire* moral
morbide morbid
morceau *m* piece; *d'un livre* passage
morceler divide up
mordant biting; **mordre** bite; *d'un acide* eat into
morfondre: ***se ~*** mope; (*s'ennuyer*) be bored
morgue *f lieu* mortuary, morgue
moribond dying
morne gloomy
morose morose
mors *m* bit
morsure *f* bite
mort[1] *f* death
mort[2], **~e 1** *adj* dead; *eau* stagnant; *yeux* lifeless; *membre* numb; ***ivre ~*** dead drunk; ***être ~ de rire*** F die laughing **2** *m/f* dead man; dead woman; ***les ~s*** the dead *pl*
mortalité *f* mortality; ***taux*** *m* ***de ~*** death rate, mortality; **mortel**, **~le** mortal; *blessure*, *dose*, *maladie* fatal; *péché* deadly
morue *f* cod
morveux, **-euse** *m/f* F squirt F
mosaïque *f* mosaic
Moscou Moscow
mosquée *f* mosque
mot *m* word; (*court message*) note; ***bon ~*** witticism; ***~ clé*** key word; ***~ de passe*** password; ***gros ~*** rude word, swearword; ***~ à ~*** word for word
motard *m* motorcyclist, biker; *de la gendarmerie* motorcycle policeman
moteur, **-trice 1** *m* engine, motor; *fig*: *personne* driving force (***de*** behind) **2** *adj arbre* drive; *force* driving
motif *m* motive, reason; (*forme*) pattern; MUS theme, motif; *en peinture* motif
motion *f* POL motion
motivation *f* motivation; **motiver** motivate; (*expliquer*) be the reason for, prompt; (*justifier par des motifs*) give a reason for
moto *f* motorbike, motorcycle; ***faire de la ~*** ride one's motorbike; **motocycliste** *m/f* motorcyclist
motoriser mechanize; ***je suis motorisé*** F I have a car
mou, **molle** soft; *caractère*, *résistance* weak
mouche *f* fly
moucher: ***se ~*** blow one's nose

moucheron *m* gnat
mouchoir *m* handkerchief
moudre grind
moue *f* pout; ***faire la ~*** pout
mouette *f* seagull
moufle *f* mitten
mouillé wet; **mouiller 1** *v/t* wet; (*humecter*) dampen; *liquide* water down **2** *v/i* MAR anchor
moule 1 *m* mold, *Br* mould; CUIS tin **2** *f* ZO mussel
mouler mold, *Br* mould
moulin *m* mill; ***~ (à vent)*** windmill; ***~ à café*** coffee grinder
mourir die (**de** of); ***~ de froid*** freeze to death
mousse *f* foam; BOT moss; CUIS mousse; **mousser** lather; **mousseux, -euse 1** *adj* foamy **2** *m* sparkling wine
moustache *f* mustache, *Br* moustache
moustique *m* mosquito
moutarde *f* mustard
mouton *m* sheep; *viande* mutton; *fourrure* sheepskin
mouvement *m* movement; *trafic* traffic; ***en ~*** moving; **mouvementé** eventful; *débat* lively
mouvoir: ***se ~*** move
moyen, ~ne 1 *adj* average; *classe* middle; ***Moyen Âge*** *m* Middle Ages *pl*; ***Moyen-Orient*** *m* Middle East **2** *m* (*façon, méthode*) means *sg*; ***~s*** (*argent*) means *pl*; *intellectuelles* faculties; ***au ~ de, par le ~ de*** by means of **3** *f* average; *statistique* mean; ***en ~ne*** on average; **moyenâgeux, -euse** medieval
moyennant for
Mt (= ***Mont***) Mt (= Mount)
muer *d'oiseau* molt, *Br* moult; *de voix* break
muet, ~te dumb; *fig* silent
mufle *m* muzzle; *fig* F boor
mugir moo; *du vent* moan
muguet *m* BOT lily of the valley
mule *f* mule
multicolore multicolored, *Br* multicoloured
multimédia *m & adj* multimedia
multinational, ~e 1 *adj* multinational **2** *f*: ***multinationale*** multinational
multiplication *f* multiplication; ***la ~ de*** (*augmentation*) the increase in the number of; **multiplier** multiply; ***se ~*** *d'une espèce* multiply
multitude *f*: ***une ~ de*** a host of; ***la ~*** *péj* the masses *pl*
multiusages versatile
municipal town *atr*, municipal; **municipalité** *f* (*commune*) municipality; *conseil* town council
munir: ***~ de*** fit with; *personne* provide with; ***se ~ de qc*** *d'un parapluie, de son passeport* take sth
mur *m* wall
mûr ripe
muraille *f* wall

mûre *f* BOT mulberry; *des ronces* blackberry
murer *enclos* wall in; *porte* wall up
mûrier *m* mulberry (tree)
mûrir ripen
murmure *m* murmur; **murmurer** murmur; (*médire*) talk
muscle *m* muscle; **musclé** muscular; **musculation** *f* body-building
museau *m* muzzle
musée *m* museum
museler muzzle (*aussi fig*); **muselière** *f* muzzle
musical musical; **musicien, ~ne 1** *adj* musical **2** *m/f* musician; **musique** *f* music; ***~ de fond*** piped music
must *m* must
musulman, ~e *m/f & adj* Muslim
mutation *f* change; BIOL mutation; *de fonctionnaire* transfer
mutiler mutilate
mutuel, ~le mutual
myope shortsighted
myrtille *f* bilberry
mystère *m* mystery; **mystérieux, -euse** mysterious
mystifier fool, take in
mystique 1 *adj* mystical **2** *m/f* mystic **3** *f* mystique
mythe *m* myth; **mythologie** *f* mythology
mythomane *m/f* pathological liar

N

nabot *m péj* midget
nacre *f* mother-of-pearl
nage *f* swimming; *style* stroke; ***être en ~*** *fig* be dripping with sweat
nageoire *f* fin
nager 1 *v/i* swim **2** *v/t*: ***~ la brasse*** do the breaststroke
naïf, naïve naive
nain, ~e *m/f & adj* dwarf
naissance *f* birth (*aussi fig*)
naître be born (*aussi fig*); ***faire ~*** *sentiment* give rise to
naïveté *f* naivety
nana *f* F chick F, girl
nantir provide (***de*** with)
nappe *f* tablecloth; *de gaz, pétrole* layer
narcotique *m & adj* narcotic
narguer taunt
narine *f* nostril
narquois taunting
narrateur, -trice *m/f* narrator; **narration** *f* narration
nasal nasal
natal *pays etc* of one's birth, native; **natalité** *f*: (***taux m de***) ***~*** birth rate
natation *f* swimming
natif, -ive native
nation *f* nation; **national, ~e 1** *adj* national **2** *mpl*: ***natio-***

naux nationals **3** *f* highway; **nationaliser** nationalize; **nationaliste 1** *adj* nationalist; *péj* nationalistic **2** *m/f* nationalist; **nationalité** *f* nationality

natte *f* (*tapis*) mat; *de cheveux* braid, plait

naturalisation *f* naturalization

nature 1 *adj yaourt* plain; *thé, café* without milk or sugar; *personne* natural **2** *f* nature; **~ *morte*** ART still life; **naturel, ~le 1** *adj* natural **2** *m* (*caractère*) nature; (*spontanéité*) naturalness; **naturellement** naturally

naufrage *m* shipwreck; ***faire ~*** be shipwrecked

nausée *f* nausea; ***j'ai la ~*** I'm nauseous, *Br* I feel sick; **nauséeux, -euse** nauseous

nautique nautical; *ski* water *atr*

nautisme *m* water sports and sailing

naval naval; *construction* ship *atr*

navet *m* rutabaga, *Br* swede; *fig* turkey F, *Br* flop

navette *f* shuttle; ***faire la ~*** shuttle

navigable navigable; **navigation** *f* sailing; (*pilotage*) navigation; **~ *aérienne*** air travel; **~ *spatiale*** space travel; **naviguer** *d'un navire, marin* sail; *d'un avion* fly; (*conduire*), INFORM navigate; **~ *sur Internet*** surf the Net

navire *m* ship

navrant upsetting; **navré**: ***je suis ~*** I am so sorry

ne: ***je ~ comprends pas*** I don't understand, I do not understand; ***ne ... guère*** hardly; ***ne ... jamais*** never; ***ne ... personne*** nobody; ***ne ... plus*** no longer; not any more; ***ne ... que*** only; ***ne ... rien*** nothing, not anything; → *aussi* **guère, jamais** *etc*

né born; ***~e Lepic*** nee Lepic

néanmoins nevertheless

néant *m* nothingness

nécessaire 1 *adj* necessary **2** *m* necessary; ***le strict ~*** the bare minimum; ***~ de toilette*** toiletries *pl*; **nécessité** *f* necessity; **nécessiter** require, necessitate

néerlandais, ~e 1 *adj* Dutch **2** *m langue* Dutch; **Néerlandais, ~e** *m/f* Dutchman; Dutchwoman

néfaste harmful

négatif, -ive *adj & m* negative; **négation** *f* negation; GRAM negative

négligé 1 *adj travail* careless; *tenue* untidy; *épouse, enfant* neglected **2** *f* negligee; **négligence** *f* negligence, carelessness; *d'une épouse, d'un enfant* neglect; (*nonchalance*) casualness; **négligent** careless, negligent; *parent* negligent; *geste* casual; **né-**

gliger neglect; *occasion* miss; *avis* disregard; ***~ de faire*** fail to do
négoce *m* trade; **négociant** *m* merchant; **négociateur, -trice** *m/f* negotiator; **négociation** *f* negotiation; **négocier** negotiate
neige *f* snow; **neiger** snow
néon *m* neon
nerf *m* nerve; (*vigueur*) energy; ***être à bout de ~s*** be at the end of one's tether
nerveux, -euse nervous; (*vigoureux*) full of energy; AUTO responsive; **nervosité** *f* nervousness
n'est-ce pas: ***il fait beau, ~?*** it's a fine day, isn't it?; ***tu la connais, ~?*** you know her, don't you?
net, ~te 1 *adj* (*propre*) clean; (*clair*) clear; *différence* distinct; COMM net **2** *adv* (*aussi* ***nettement***) *tué* outright; *refuser* flatly; *parler* plainly; **netteté** *f* cleanliness; (*clarté*) clarity
nettoyage *m* cleaning; ***~ ethnique*** ethnic cleansing; ***~ à sec*** dry cleaning; **nettoyer** clean; F (*ruiner*) clean out F; ***~ à sec*** dryclean
neuf[1] nine
neuf[2], **neuve** *adj* new; ***refaire à ~*** *maison etc* renovate; *moteur* recondition
neutraliser neutralize; **neutralité** *f* neutrality; **neutre** neutral
neuvième ninth
neveu *m* nephew
névralgie *f* MÉD neuralgia
névrosé, ~e *m/f* neurotic
nez *m* nose
ni neither, nor; ***je n'ai ~ intérêt ~ désir*** I have neither interest nor inclination; ***sans sucre ~ lait*** without sugar or milk, with neither sugar nor milk; ***~ moi non plus*** neither *ou* nor do I, me neither
niais stupid; **niaiserie** *f* stupidity
niche *f* *dans un mur* niche; *d'un chien* kennel; **nicher** nest; *fig* F live
nicotine *f* nicotine
nid *m* nest; ***~ de poule*** *fig* pothole
nièce *f* niece
nier: **~ (*avoir fait*)** deny (doing)
nigaud 1 *adj* silly **2** *m* idiot, fool
niveau *m* level; ÉDU standard; *outil* spirit level; ***~ de vie*** standard of living; **niveler** *terrain* level; *fig*: *différences* even out
noble noble; **noblesse** *f* nobility
noce *f* wedding; ***faire la ~*** F paint the town red
nocif, -ive harmful, noxious
nocturne 1 *adj* night *atr*; *zo* nocturnal **2** *f*: ***un match joué en ~*** an evening match
Noël *m* Christmas; ***joyeux ~!***

Merry Christmas!; ***le père ~*** Santa Claus, *Br aussi* Father Christmas

nœud *m* knot (*aussi* NAUT); *fig: d'un problème* nub; ***~ papillon*** bow tie

noir 1 *adj* black; (*sombre*) dark; ***il fait ~*** it's dark **2** *m* black; (*obscurité*) dark; ***travail*** *m* ***au ~*** moonlighting

Noir *m* black man

noircir blacken

Noire *f* black woman

noisetier *m* hazel; **noisette** *f & adj inv* hazelnut

noix *f* walnut

nom *m* name; GRAM noun; ***au ~ de qn*** in *ou Br* on behalf of s.o.; ***~ de famille*** surname, family name; ***~ de jeune fille*** maiden name

nombre *m* number; ***sans ~*** countless; **nombreux, -euse** numerous, many; *famille* large

nombril *m* navel

nomination *f* appointment; *à un prix* nomination

nommer name, call; *à une fonction* appoint; ***se ~*** be called

non no; ***j'espère que ~*** I hope not; ***moi ~ plus*** me neither; ***c'est normal, ~?*** that's normal, isn't it?

non-alcoolisé non-alcoholic

nonchalant nonchalant, casual

nonobstant notwithstanding

non-polluant environmentally friendly, non-polluting

nord 1 *m* north; ***au ~ de*** (to the) north of **2** *adj* north; *hémisphère* northern

nord-américain, ~e North-American; **Nord-Américain, ~e** *m/f* North-American

nord-est *m* north-east

nord-ouest *m* north-west

normal, ~e 1 *adj* normal **2** *f*: ***inférieur/supérieur à la ~e*** above/below average; **normalement** normally; **normalisation** *f* normalization; TECH standardization; **normalité** *f* normality

norme *f* norm; TECH standard

Norvège: ***la ~*** Norway; **norvégien, ~ne 1** *adj* Norwegian **2** *m langue* Norwegian; **Norvégien, ~ne** *m/f* Norwegian

nos → ***notre***

nostalgie *f* nostalgia; ***avoir la ~ de son pays*** be homesick

notaire *m* notary

notamment particularly

note *f* note; *à l'école* grade, *Br* mark; (*facture*) check, *Br* bill; ***~ de frais*** expense account; ***~ de service*** memo; **noter** (*écrire*) write down; (*remarquer*) note

notice *f* note; (*mode d'emploi*) instructions *pl*

notifier *v/t*: ***~ qch à qn*** notify s.o. of sth

notion *f* (*idée*) notion, con-

cept; **~s** basics *pl*
notre, *pl* **nos** our
nôtre: ***le/la ~, les ~s*** ours
nouer tie; *relations* establish
nougat *m* nougat
nouilles *fpl* noodles
nounou *f* F nanny
nounours *m* teddy bear
nourrice *f* child minder
nourrir feed; *fig*: *espoir* nurture
nourrisson *m* infant
nourriture *f* food
nous *sujet* we; *complément d'objet direct* us; *complément d'objet indirect* (to) us; ***~ ~ sommes levés tôt*** we got up early; ***~ ~ aimons*** we love each other
nouveau, **nouvelle** (*m* **nouvel** *before a vowel or silent h*; *mpl* **nouveaux**) **1** *adj* new; ***de*** *ou* ***à ~*** again; ***Nouvel An*** *m* New Year('s) **2** *m/f* new person
nouveau-né **1** *adj* newborn **2** *m* newborn baby
nouveauté *f* novelty
nouvelle *f* (*récit*) short story; ***une ~*** *dans les médias* a piece of news; **nouvelles** *fpl* news *sg*; **Nouvelle Zélande** *f* New Zealand
novembre *m* November
novice **1** *m/f* novice **2** *adj* inexperienced
noyade *f* drowning
noyau *m* pit, *Br* stone; PHYS nucleus; *fig* (small) group
noyer[1] *v/t* drown; AUTO flood; ***se ~*** drown; *se suicider* drown o.s.
noyer[2] *m arbre*, *bois* walnut
nu **1** *adj* naked; *arbre*, *bras*, *tête etc* bare **2** *m* ART nude
nuage *m* cloud; **nuageux**, **-euse** cloudy
nuance *f* shade; *fig* slight difference; (*subtilité*) nuance; **nuancé** subtle; **nuancer** qualify
nucléaire **1** *adj* nuclear **2** *m*: ***le ~*** nuclear power
nudiste *m/f* & *adj* nudist; **nudité** *f* nudity
nuée *f d'insectes* cloud; *de journalistes* horde
nuire: ***~ à*** hurt, harm
nuit *f* night; ***il fait ~*** it's dark
nul, **~le** **1** *adj* no; (*non valable*) invalid; (*sans valeur*) hopeless; (*inexistant*) nonexistent; ***~le part*** nowhere **2** *pron* no-one; **nullement** not in the least; **nullité** *f* JUR invalidity; *fig* hopelessness; *personne* loser
numérique numerical; INFORM digital
numéro *m* number; ***~ vert*** toll-free number, *Br* Freefone number; **numéroter** **1** *v/t* number **2** *v/i* TÉL dial
nuque *f* nape of the neck
nurse *f* nanny
nutritif, **-ive** nutritional; *aliment* nutritious; **nutrition** *f* nutrition
nylon *m* nylon

O

obéir obey; **~ à** obey; **obéissance** *f* obedience; **obéissant** obedient

obèse obese; **obésité** *f* obesity

objecter: **~ *qch*** *pour ne pas faire qch* give sth as a reason; **~ *que*** object that; **objectif, -ive 1** *adj* objective **2** *m* objective; PHOT lens; **objection** *f* objection; **objectivité** *f* objectivity

objet *m* object; *de réflexions, d'une lettre* subject

obligation *f* obligation; COMM bond; **obligatoire** compulsory, obligatory

obligeant obliging; **obliger** oblige; (*forcer*) force; ***être obligé de faire qc*** be obliged to do sth

oblique oblique

oblitérer *timbre* cancel

obscène obscene

obscur obscure; *nuit, rue* dark; **obscurcir** darken; ***s'~*** grow dark; **obscurité** *f* obscurity; *de la nuit, d'une rue* darkness

obséder obsess

obsèques *fpl* funeral

observateur, -trice *m/f* observer; **observation** *f* observation; *d'une règle* observance; **observatoire** *m* observatory; **observer** observe; *changement* notice; ***faire ~ qc à qn*** point sth out to s.o.

obsession *f* obsession

obstacle *m* obstacle; SP hurdle; *pour cheval* jump; ***faire ~ à qc*** stand in the way of sth

obstination *f* obstinacy; **obstiné** obstinate; **obstiner**: ***s'~ à faire qc*** persist in doing sth

obstruction *f* obstruction; *dans tuyau* blockage; **obstruer** obstruct, block

obtenir get, obtain

obturer seal; *dent* fill

obtus MATH, *fig* obtuse

obus *m* MIL shell

occasion *f* opportunity; *marché* bargain; ***d'~*** second-hand; ***à l'~*** when the opportunity arises; **occasionner** cause

Occident *m*: ***l'~*** the West; **occidental, ~e** western; **Occidental, ~e** *m/f* Westerner

occulte occult

occupant 1 *adj* occupying **2** *m* occupant; **occupation** *f* occupation; **occupé** busy; *pays, appartement* occupied; *chaise* taken; TÉL busy; **occuper** occupy; *personnel* employ; ***s'~ de*** *politique etc* take an interest in; *malade, organisation* look after

occurrence *f*: ***en l'~*** as it hap-

pens
océan *m* ocean
octet *m* INFORM byte
octobre *m* October
oculaire eye *atr*
oculiste *m/f* eye specialist
odeur *f* smell; ~ ***corporelle*** BO
odieux, -euse hateful, odious
odorant scented
odorat *m* sense of smell
œil *m* (*pl* yeux) eye; ***à vue d'~*** visibly
œillet *m* BOT carnation
œuf *m* egg; ***~s brouillés*** scrambled eggs; ***~ à la coque*** soft-boiled egg; ***~ sur le plat*** fried egg
œuvre 1 *f* work; ***~ d'art*** work of art; ***mettre en ~*** (*employer*) use; (*exécuter*) carry out **2** *m* ART, *littérature* works *pl*
offense *f* (*insulte*) insult; (*péché*) sin; **offenser** offend; ***s'~ de*** take offense *ou Br* offence at
office *m* office; REL service; ***d'~*** automatically; ***faire ~ de*** act as
officiel, ~le official
officier *m* officer
officieux, -euse semi-official
officinal *plante* medicinal
offre *f* offer; ***~ d'emploi*** job offer; **offrir** offer; *cadeau* give; ***s'~ qc*** treat o.s. to sth
offusquer offend
oie *f* goose
oignon *m* onion; BOT bulb
oiseau *m* bird; ***à vol d'~*** as the crow flies
oiseux, -euse idle
oisif, -ive idle; **oisiveté** *f* idleness
olive *f* olive; **olivier** *m* olive (tree)
olympique Olympic
ombrage *m* shade; **ombragé** shady; **ombrageux, -euse** *cheval* skittish; *personne* touchy; **ombre** *f* shade; (*silhouette*) shadow; *fig* (*anonymat*) obscurity; *de regret* hint
ombrelle *f* sunshade
omelette *f* omelet, *Br* omelette
omettre leave out, omit; ***~ de faire*** fail *ou* omit to do; **omission** *f* omission
omnibus *m*: (***train*** *m*) ~ slow train
on (*après* ***que, et, où, qui, si*** *souvent* **l'on**) (*nous*) we; (*tu, vous, indéterminé*) you; (*quelqu'un*) someone; (*eux, les gens*) they, people; *autorités* they; ***~ m'a dit que...*** I was told that …; ***~ ne sait jamais*** you never know, one never knows *fml*
oncle *m* uncle
onction *f* REL unction; **onctueux, -euse** smooth; *fig* smarmy F, unctuous
onde *f* wave; ***sur les ~s*** RAD on the air; ***grandes ~s*** long wave
ondée *f* downpour

on-dit *m* rumor, *Br* rumour
ondoyer *du blés* sway
ondulation *f de terrain* undulation; *de coiffure* wave; **onduler** *d'ondes* undulate; *de cheveux* be wavy
onéreux, -euse expensive
ongle *m* nail; zo claw
onguent *m* cream, salve
onze eleven; ***le ~*** the eleventh; **onzième** eleventh
opaque opaque
opéra *m* opera; *bâtiment* opera house
opérable MÉD operable; **opérateur, -trice** *m/f* operator; *en cinéma* cameraman; FIN trader; **opération** *f* operation; *action* working; FIN transaction; **opérer 1** *v/t* MÉD operate on; (*produire*) make; (*exécuter*) implement **2** *v/i* MÉD operate; (*avoir effet*) work; (*procéder*) proceed; ***se faire ~*** have an operation
opiner: ***~ de la tête*** nod in agreement
opiniâtre stubborn; **opiniâtreté** *f* stubbornness
opinion *f* opinion
opium *m* opium
opportun *ou* opportune; *moment* right; **opportuniste** *m/f* opportunist; **opportunité** *f* timeliness; (*occasion*) opportunity
opposant, ~e 1 *adj* opposing **2** *m/f* opponent; ***les ~s*** the opposition; **opposé 1** *adj pôles* opposite; *opinions* conflicting; ***être ~ à qc*** be opposed to sth **2** *m* opposite; ***à l'~ de qn*** unlike s.o.; **opposer** bring into conflict; *argument* put forward; ***s'~ à qn/à qc*** oppose s.o./sth; **opposition** *f* opposition; (*contraste*) contrast
oppresser oppress, weigh down; **oppression** *f* oppression
opprimer oppress
opter: ***~ pour*** opt for
opticien, ~ne *m/f* optician
optimisme *m* optimism; **optimiste 1** *adj* optimistic **2** *m/f* optimist
option *f* option
optique 1 *adj nerf* optic; *verre* optical **2** *f science* optics; *fig* viewpoint
opulent wealthy; *poitrine* ample
or[1] *m* gold
or[2] *conj* now
orage *m* storm; **orageux, -euse** stormy
oraison *f* REL prayer
oral *adj & m* oral
orange *f & adj inv* orange; **oranger** *m* orange tree
orateur, -trice *m/f* orator
orbital orbital
orbite *f* ANAT eyesocket; ASTR orbit (*aussi fig*)
orchestre *m* orchestra; *de théâtre* orchestra, *Br* stalls *pl*
orchidée *f* orchid
ordinaire 1 *adj* ordinary **2** *m*

essence regular; **d'~** ordinarily
ordinateur *m* computer
ordonnance *f* arrangement, layout; (*ordre*) order (*aussi* JUR); MÉD prescription; **ordonné** tidy; **ordonner** organize; (*commander*) order; MÉD prescribe
ordre *m* order; **~ du jour** agenda; **de premier ~** first-rate; **mettre en ~** tidy
ordures *fpl* (*détritus*) garbage, *Br* rubbish; *fig* filth
oreille *f* ear; *d'un bol* handle; **dur d'~** hard of hearing
oreiller *m* pillow
oreillons *mpl* MÉD mumps *sg*
orfèvre *m* goldsmith
organe *m* organ; (*voix, porte-parole*) voice; *d'un mécanisme* part
organisation *f* organization; **organiser** organize; **s'~** *d'une personne* get organized; **organiseur** *m* INFORM personal organizer
organisme *m* organism; ANAT system; (*organisation*) organization, body
orgue *m* organ
orgueil *m* pride; **orgueilleux, -euse** proud
Orient *m*: **l'~** the East; *Asie* the East, the Orient; **oriental, ~e** east, eastern; *d'Asie* eastern, Oriental; **Oriental, ~e** *m/f* Oriental
orientation *f* direction; *d'une maison* exposure; **orienter** orient, *Br* orientate; (*diriger*) direct; **s'~** get one's bearings; **s'~ vers** *fig* go in for
orifice *m* opening
originaire original; **être ~ de** come from; **original 1** *adj* original; *péj* eccentric **2** *m* *ouvrage* original; *personne* eccentric; **origine** *f* origin; **à l'~** originally; **originel, ~le** original
orme *m* BOT elm
ornement *m* ornament; **ornementer** ornament
orner decorate (**de** with)
orphelin, ~e *m/f* orphan; **orphelinat** *m* orphanage
orteil *m* toe
orthographe *f* spelling
ortie *f* BOT nettle
os *m* bone
osciller PHYS oscillate; *d'un pendule* swing; **~ entre** *fig* waver between
osé daring; **oser**: **~ faire** dare to do
osier *m* BOT osier; **en ~** wicker
ossements *mpl* bones; **osseux, -euse** ANAT bone *atr*; *visage, mains* bony
ostensible evident
otage *m* hostage
ôter remove; MATH take away
ou or; **~ bien** or (else); **~ … ~** … either … or
où where; **d'~ vient-il?** where does he come from?; **d'~ l'on peut déduire que …** from which it can be deduced that

...; ***le jour ~ ...*** the day when ...

ouate *f* absorbent cotton, *Br* cotton wool; **ouater** pad, quilt

oubli *m* forgetting; (*omission*) oversight; ***tomber dans l'~*** sink into oblivion; **oublier** forget; ***~ de faire*** forget to do

ouest 1 *m* west; ***à l'~ de*** (to the) west of **2** *adj* west, western

oui yes

ouï-dire: ***par ~*** by hearsay

ouïe *f* hearing; ***~s*** ZO gills

ouragan *m* hurricane

ourler hem; **ourlet** *m* hem

ours *m* bear; **ourse** *f* she-bear; ***la Grande Ourse*** ASTR the Great Bear

oursin *m* ZO sea urchin

outil *m* tool; **outillage** *m* tools *pl*

outrage *m* insult; **outrager** insult

outrance *f* excessiveness; ***à ~*** excessively

outre 1 *prép* in addition to **2** *adv*: ***en ~*** besides; ***passer ~*** ignore

outré: ***être ~ de** ou **par*** be outraged by

outre-Atlantique on the other side of the Atlantic

outre-Manche on the other side of the Channel

outre-mer: ***d'~*** overseas *atr*

ouvert open; **ouverture** *f* opening; MUS overture

ouvrable working; ***jour** m **~*** workday; **ouvrage** *m* work; **ouvragé** ornate

ouvre-boîtes *m* can opener, *Br aussi* tin opener; **ouvre-bouteilles** *m* bottle opener

ouvrier, **-ère 1** *adj* working-class **2** *m/f* worker

ouvrir 1 *v/t* open; *radio*, *gaz* turn on **2** *v/i d'un magasin* open; ***s'~*** open; *fig* open up

ovale *m & adj* oval

ovni *m* (= ***objet volant non identifié***) UFO (= unidentified flying object)

oxygène *m* oxygen

P

pacifier pacify; **pacifique 1** *adj personne* peace-loving; *coexistence* peaceful **2** *m* ***le Pacifique*** the Pacific; **pacifiste** *m/f & adj* pacifist

pacte *m* pact; **pactiser**: ***~ avec*** come to terms with

pagaie *f* paddle

pagaïe, pagaille *f* F mess

page *f* page; ***~ d'accueil*** INFORM home page

paie, paye *f* pay; **paiement** *m* payment

païen, **~ne** *m/f & adj* pagan

paillasson *m* doormat

paille *f* straw

pain *m* bread; ~ ***au chocolat*** chocolate croissant; ~ ***complet*** whole wheat *ou Br* wholemeal bread; ~ ***d'épice*** gingerbread; ***petit*** ~ roll
pair 1 *adj nombre* even **2** *m*: ***hors*** ~ unrivaled, *Br* unrivalled; ***fille*** *f* ***au*** ~ au pair
paire *f*: ***une*** ~ ***de*** a pair of
paisible peaceful; *personne* quiet
paître graze
paix *f* peace; (*calme*) peace and quiet
Pakistan: ***le*** ~ Pakistan; **pakistanais**, **~e** Pakistani; **Pakistanais**, **~e** *m/f* Pakistani
palais *m* **1** palace; ~ ***de justice*** law courts *pl* **2** ANAT palate
pale *f* blade
pâle pale; *fig*: *style* colorless, *Br* colourless; *imitation* pale
Palestine: ***la*** ~ Palestine; **palestinien**, **~ne** Palestinian; **Palestinien**, **~ne** *m/f* Palestinian
palette *f de peinture* palette
pâleur *f* paleness, pallor
palier *m d'un escalier* landing; TECH bearing; (*phase*) stage
pâlir go pale; *de couleurs* fade
palissade *f* fence
pallier alleviate; *manque* make up for
palme *f* BOT palm; *de natation* flipper; **palmier** *m* BOT palm tree
pâlot, **~te** pale
palper feel; MÉD palpate
palpitant *fig* exciting, thrilling; **palpitations** *fpl* palpitations; **palpiter** *du cœur* pound
pamplemousse *m* grapefruit
pan *m de vêtement* tail; *de mur* section
panache *m* plume; ***avoir du*** ~ have panache; **panaché** *m* shandy-gaff, *Br* shandy
pancarte *f* sign; *de manifestation* placard
pané breaded
panier *m* basket
panique *f* panic; **paniquer** panic
panne *f* breakdown; ~ ***en panne*** have a breakdown; ***tomber en*** ~ ***sèche*** run out of gas *ou Br* petrol; ~ ***d'électricité*** power outage, *Br* power failure
panneau *m* board; TECH panel; ~ ***de signalisation*** roadsign
panorama *m* panorama
pansement *m* dressing; **panser** *blessure* dress; *cheval* groom
pantalon *m* pants *pl*, *Br* trousers *pl*; ***un*** ~ a pair of pants
pantelant panting
pantois *inv*: ***rester*** ~ be speechless
pantoufle *f* slipper
paon *m* peacock
papa *m* dad
papal REL papal; **pape** *m* REL pope

paperasse *f* (*souvent au pl* **~s**) *péj* papers *pl*
papeterie *f magasin* stationery store, *Br* stationer's
papi, papy *m* F grandpa
papier *m* paper; **~ (d')aluminium** kitchen foil; **~ hygiénique** toilet tissue; **~s d'identité** identification, ID
papillon *m* butterfly; TECH wing nut; F (*contravention*) (parking) ticket
paquebot *m* liner
pâquerette *f* BOT daisy
Pâques *msg ou fpl* Easter; ***joyeuses ~!*** happy Easter
paquet *m* packet; *de sucre, café* bag; *de la poste* parcel
par *lieu* through; *passif, moyen* by; ***~ terre*** on the ground; ***~ beau temps*** in fine weather; ***~ curiosité*** out of curiosity; ***~ hasard*** by chance; ***diviser ~ quatre*** divide by four; ***~ an*** a year; ***finir ~ faire*** finish by doing
parabolique: ***antenne f ~*** satellite dish
paracétamol *m* paracetamol
parachute *m* parachute; **parachutiste** *m/f* parachutist; MIL para(trooper)
parade *f* parade; *en escrime* parry; *à un argument* counter
paradis *m* paradise
paradoxe *m* paradox
parages *mpl*: ; ***dans les ~*** around; ***dans les ~ de*** in the vicinity of
paragraphe *m* paragraph
paraître appear; *d'un livre* come out, be published; ***il paraît que*** it seems that, it would appear that; ***laisser ~*** show
parallèle 1 *adj* parallel (**à** to) **2** *f* MATH parallel (line) **3** *m* GÉOGR parallel (*aussi fig*)
paralyser paralyse; **paralysie** *f* paralysis
paramètre *m* parameter
paranoïaque *m/f & adj* paranoid
parapharmacie *f* (non-dispensing) pharmacy; *produits* toiletries *pl*
paraplégique *m/f & adj* paraplegic
parapluie *m* umbrella
parasite 1 *adj* parasitic **2** *m* parasite; **~s** *radio* interference
parasol *m* parasol; *de plage* beach umbrella
paratonnerre *m* lightning rod, *Br* lightning conductor
paravent *m* windbreak
parc *m* park; *pour enfant* playpen
parcelle *f de terrain* parcel
parce que because
par-ci *adv*: ***~, par-là*** *espace* here and there; *temps* now and then
parcimonie *f*: ***avec ~*** parcimoniously
parcourir *région* travel through; *distance* cover; *texte* read quickly

parcours *m* route; *course d'automobiles* circuit
par-derrière from behind
par-dessous underneath
pardessus *m* overcoat
par-dessus over
par-devant from the front
pardon *m* forgiveness; **~!** sorry!; **~?** excuse me?; **pardonner: ~ *qc à qn*** forgive s.o. sth
pare-brise *m* windshield, *Br* windscreen
pare-chocs *m* bumper
pareil, ~le 1 *adj* similar (**à** to); (*tel*) such; ***c'est toujours ~*** it's always the same **2** *adv*: ***habillés ~*** similarly dressed, dressed the same way
parent, ~e 1 *adj* related **2** *m/f* relative; **~s** (*mère et père*) parents; **parenté** *f* relationship
parenthèse *f* parenthesis, *Br* (round) bracket; ***entre ~s*** *fig* by the way
parer *attaque* ward off; *en escrime* parry
paresse *f* laziness; **paresseux, -euse** lazy
parfait 1 *adj* perfect; *avant le substantif* complete **2** *m* GRAM perfect (tense)
parfois sometimes
parfum *m* perfume; *d'une glace* flavor, *Br* flavour
pari *m* bet; **parier** bet
parisien, ~ne Parisian, of/from Paris; **Parisien, ~ne** *m/f* Parisian
parité *f* ÉCON parity
parking *m* parking lot, *Br* car park; *édifice* parking garage, *Br* car park
parlant *comparaison* striking; *preuves* decisive
Parlement *m* Parliament; **parlementaire 1** *adj* Parliamentary **2** *m/f* Parliamentarian
parler 1 *v/i* speak, talk; ***sans ~ de*** not to mention **2** *v/t*: ***~ affaires*** talk business; ***~ anglais*** speak English
parmi among
parodie *f* parody
paroi *f* partition
paroisse *f* REL parish
parole *f* word; *faculté* speech; ***donner la ~ à qn*** give s.o. the floor
parquer *bétail* pen; *réfugiés* dump
parquet *m* (parquet) floor; JUR public prosecutor's office
parrain *m* godfather; *dans un club* sponsor
parsemer sprinkle (***de*** with)
part *f* share; (*fraction*) part; ***faire ~ de qc à qn*** inform s.o. of sth; ***de la ~ de qn*** in *ou Br* on behalf of s.o.; ***d'une ~ … d'autre ~*** on the one hand … on the other hand; ***autre ~*** elsewhere; ***nulle ~*** nowhere; ***quelque ~*** somewhere; ***à ~*** *traiter etc* separately; ***à ~ cela*** apart from that
partage *m* division; **partager**

share; (*couper, diviser*) divide (up)
partenaire *m/f* partner
parterre *m de fleurs* bed; *au théâtre* rear orchestra, *Br* rear stalls *pl*
parti[1] *m* side; POL party; ***prendre ~ pour*** side with; ***tirer ~ de qc*** turn sth to good use; ***~ pris*** preconceived idea
parti[2] *adj* F: **être ~** (*ivre*) be tight
partial biassed
participant, **~e** *m/f* participant; **participer**: **~ à** participate in, take part in; *bénéfices* share; *frais* contribute to; *douleur, succès* share in
particularité *f* special feature; **particulier**, **-ère 1** *adj* particular, special; *privé* private; **~ à** peculiar to **2** *m* (private) individual; **particulièrement** particularly
partie *f* part; *d'un jeu* game; JUR party; *lutte* struggle; ***en ~*** partly; ***faire ~ de qch*** be part of sth
partiel, **~le** partial
partir leave (**à**, **pour** for); SP start; *de la saleté* come out; ***~ de qc*** (*provenir de*) come from sth; ***à ~ de*** (starting) from
partisan, **~e** *m/f* supporter; MIL *m* partisan
partition *f* MUS score; POL partition
partout everywhere
parure *f* finery; *de bijoux* set
parvenir arrive; ***faire ~ qc à qn*** forward sth to s.o.; ***~ à faire*** manage to do
parvenu, **~e** *m/f* upstart
pas[1] *m* step, pace; ***faux ~*** stumble; *fig* blunder, faux pas
pas[2] *adv* not; ***ne ... ~*** not; ***il ne pleut ~*** it's not raining; ***il n'a ~ plu*** it didn't rain
passable acceptable
passage *m* passage; *fig* (*changement*) changeover; ***~ à niveau*** grade crossing, *Br* level crossing; ***de ~*** passing
passager, **-ère 1** *adj* passing **2** *m/f* passenger
passant, **~e** *m/f* passerby
passe *f* SP pass
passé 1 *adj* past **2** *prép*: ***~ dix heures*** after ten o'clock **3** *m* past; ***~ composé*** GRAM perfect
passe-partout *m* skeleton key
passe-passe *m*: ***tour m de ~*** conjuring trick
passeport *m* passport
passer 1 *v/i* pass, go past; *d'un film* show; ***~ chez qn*** drop by at s.o.'s place; ***~ de mode*** go out of fashion; ***~ en seconde*** AUTO shift into second; ***~ pour qc*** pass as sth; ***faire ~*** *personne* let past; *plat, journal* pass; ***laisser ~*** *personne* let past; *lumière* let in; *chance* let slip **2** *v/t*

frontière cross; (*omettre*) miss (out); *temps* spend; *examen* take; *vêtement* slip on; *film* show; *contrat* enter into; **~ qc à qn** pass s.o. sth, pass sth to s.o. **3**: **se ~** (*se produire*) happen; **se ~ de qc** do without sth

passerelle *f* footbridge; MAR gangway; AVIAT steps *pl*

passe-temps *m* hobby, pastime

passif, **-ive 1** *adj* passive **2** *m* GRAM passive; COMM liabilities *pl*

passion *f* passion; **passionnant** exciting; **passionné**, **~e 1** *adj* passionate **2** *m/f* enthusiast; **passionner** excite; **se ~ pour** have a passion for

passivité *f* passiveness, passivity

passoire *f* sieve

pastel *m* pastel

pastèque *f* BOT watermelon

pasteur *m* REL pastor

pasteuriser pasteurize

pastille *f* pastille

patate *f* F potato, spud F

patauger flounder

pâte *f* paste; CUIS: *à pain* dough; *à tarte* pastry; **~s** pasta *sg*

pâté *m* paté; **~ de maisons** block of houses

patère *f* coat peg

paternaliste paternalistic

paternel, **~le** paternal

pâteux, **-euse** doughy; *bouche* dry

pathétique touching; F (*mauvais*) pathetic

pathologique pathological

patience *f* patience; **patient**, **~e** *m/f* & *adj* patient; **patienter** wait

patin *m*: **faire du ~** go skating; **~ à roulettes** roller skate; **patinage** *m* skating; **patiner** skate; AUTO skid; *de roues* spin; **patineur**, **-euse** *m/f* skater; **patinoire** *f* skating rink

pâtisserie *f* cake shop; *gâteaux* cakes; **pâtissier**, **-ère** *m/f* pastrycook

patois *m* dialect

patrie *f* homeland

patrimoine *m* heritage

patriote 1 *adj* patriotic **2** *m/f* patriot

patron *m* boss; (*propriétaire*) owner; *d'une auberge* landlord; REL patron saint; *de couture* pattern

patronne *f* boss; (*propriétaire*) owner; *d'une auberge* landlady; REL patron saint

patronner sponsor

patrouille *f* patrol

patte *f* paw; *d'un oiseau* foot; *d'un insecte* leg; F hand, paw *péj*

paume *f* palm

paumer F lose

paupière *f* eyelid

pause *f* (*silence*) pause; (*interruption*) break; **~ café** coffee break

pauvre 1 *adj* poor **2** *m/f* poor

person; ***les ~s*** the poor *pl*; **pauvreté** *f* poverty

pavé *m* paving; (*chaussée*) pavement, *Br* road surface; *pierres rondes* cobbles *pl*; ***un ~*** a paving stone; *rond* a cobblestone; **paver** pave

pavillon *m* (*maisonnette*) small house; MAR flag

pavot *m* BOT poppy

payable payable

payant *spectateur* paying; *parking* which charges; *fig* profitable

payer 1 *v/t* pay; ***~ qc dix euros*** pay ten euros for sth **2** *v/i* pay **3**: ***se ~ qc*** treat o.s. to sth

pays *m* country; ***mal m du ~*** homesickness

paysage *m* landscape

paysan, ~ne 1 *m/f* small farmer; HIST peasant **2** *adj mœurs* country *atr*

Pays-Bas *mpl*: ***les ~*** the Netherlands

PC *m* (= ***personal computer***) PC

PDG *m* (= ***président-directeur général***) President, CEO (= Chief Executive Officer),

péage *m d'une autoroute* tollbooth; ***autoroute à ~*** turnpike, toll road

peau *f* skin; *cuir* leather

pêche[1] *f* BOT peach

pêche[2] *f* fishing; *poissons* catch

péché *m* sin; **pécher** sin

pêcher[1] *m* BOT peach tree

pêcher[2] **1** *v/t* fish for; (*attraper*) catch **2** *v/i* fish; ***~ à la ligne*** go angling

pécheur, -eresse *m/f* sinner

pêcheur *m* fisherman; ***~ à la ligne*** angler

pédagogie *f* education, teaching; **pédagogique** educational; *méthode* teaching

pédale *f* pedal; **pédaler** *à vélo* pedal

pédéraste *m* homosexual

pédestre: ***sentier*** *m* ***~*** footpath; ***randonnée*** *f* ***~*** hike

pédiatre *m/f* MÉD pediatrician

pédicure *m/f* podiatrist, *Br* chiropodist

pègre *f* underworld

peigne *m* comb; **peigner** comb; ***se ~*** comb one's hair

peignoir *m* robe, *Br* dressing gown

peindre paint; (*décrire*) depict

peine *f* (*punition*) punishment; (*effort*) trouble; (*difficulté*) difficulty; (*chagrin*) sorrow; ***ce n'est pas la ~*** there's no point, it's not worth it; ***valoir la ~ de faire qc*** be worth doing sth; ***à ~*** scarcely, hardly

peiner 1 *v/t* upset **2** *v/i* labor, *Br* labour

peintre *m* painter

peinture *f* paint; *action, tableau* painting; *description* depiction

péjoratif, **-ive** pejorative
pelage *m* coat
peler peel
pèlerin *m* pilgrim
pelle *f* spade
pellicule *f* film; **~s** dandruff
pelote *f de fil* ball
peloter F grope, feel up
peloton *m* ball; MIL platoon; SP pack; **pelotonner** wind into a ball; ***se ~ contre qn*** snuggle up to s.o.
pelouse *f* lawn
peluche *f jouet* soft toy; ***ours m en ~*** teddy bear
pelure *f de fruit* peel
pénaliser penalize; **pénalité** *f* penalty
penchant *m* (*inclination*) liking, penchant
pencher 1 *v/t pot* tilt; ***penché*** *écriture* sloping; ***~ la tête en avant*** bend *ou* lean forward **2** *v/i* lean; *d'un plateau* tilt; *d'un bateau* list; ***se ~ sur un problème*** *fig* examine a problem
pendant[1] **1** *prép* during; *avec chiffre* for **2** *conj*: ***~ que*** while
pendant[2] *adj oreilles* pendulous; (*en instance*) pending
penderie *f* armoire, *Br* wardrobe
pendre hang; ***se ~*** hang o.s.
pendule 1 *m* pendulum **2** *f* (*horloge*) clock
pénétrer 1 *v/t* penetrate; *pensées*, *personne* fathom out **2** *v/i*: ***~ dans*** penetrate; *maison*, *bureaux* get into
pénible *travail*, *vie* hard; *nouvelle* painful; *caractère* difficult
pénicilline *f* penicillin
péninsule *f* peninsula
pénis *m* penis
pénitence *f* REL penitence; (*punition*) punishment; **pénitencier** *m* penitentiary, *Br* prison
pénombre *f* semi-darkness
pense-bête *m* reminder
pensée *f* thought; BOT pansy;
penser think; ***~ à*** (*réfléchir à*) think about; ***faire ~ à qn à faire qch*** remind s.o. to do sth; ***~ faire qch*** (*avoir l'intention*) be thinking of doing sth; **penseur** *m* thinker; **pensif**, **-ive** thoughtful
pension *f* (*allocation*) allowance; *logement* rooming house, *Br* boarding house; *école* boarding school; ***~ complète*** American plan, *Br* full board; **pensionnaire** *m/f d'un hôtel* guest; *écolier* boarder; **pensionnat** *m* boarding school
pente *f* slope; ***en ~*** sloping
Pentecôte: ***la ~*** Pentecost
pénurie *f* shortage
pépin *m de fruit* seed
perçant *regard*, *froid* piercing
percée *f* breakthrough
percepteur *m* tax collector
perception *f* perception; *des impôts* collection; *bureau* tax office

percer 1 *v/t* make a hole in; *porte* make; (*transpercer*) pierce **2** *v/i du soleil* break through; **perceuse** *f* drill

percevoir perceive; *impôts* collect

perche *f* ZO perch; *en bois, métal* pole

percher: (**se**) **~** *d'un oiseau* perch; F live; **perchoir** *m* perch

percolateur *m* percolator

percussion *f* MUS percussion

percuter crash into

perdant, ~e 1 *adj* losing **2** *m/f* loser

perdre 1 *v/t* lose; *occasion* miss; *son temps* waste; ***se ~*** *disparaître* disappear; *d'une personne* get lost **2** *v/i*: ***~ au change*** lose out

perdrix *f* partridge

père *m* father (*aussi* REL)

perfection *f* perfection; **perfectionnement** *m* perfecting; **perfectionner** perfect; ***se ~ en anglais*** improve one's English

perfide treacherous

perforer perforate; *cuir* punch

performance *f* performance; **performant** high-performance

péril *m* peril; **périlleux, -euse** perilous

périmé out of date

périmètre *m* MATH perimeter

période *f* period; ***en ~ de*** in times of; **périodique 1** *adj* periodic **2** *m* periodical

périphérie *f d'une ville* outskirts *pl*; **périphérique** *m* beltway, *Br* ringroad

périr perish; **périssable** *nourriture* perishable

péritel: ***prise*** *f* **~** scart

perle *f* pearl; (*boule percée*) bead; *fig*: *personne* gem; *de sang* drop; **perler**: ***la sueur perlait sur son front*** he had beads of sweat on his forehead

permanence *f* permanence; ***être de ~*** be on duty; ***en ~*** constantly; **permanent, ~e 1** *adj* permanent **2** *f coiffure* perm

perméable permeable

permettre allow, permit; ***~ à qn de faire qch*** allow s.o. to do sth; ***se ~ qc*** allow o.s. sth

permis *m* permit; ***passer son ~*** sit one's driving test; ***~ de conduire*** driver's license, *Br* driving licence; ***~ de séjour*** residence permit

permission *f* permission; MIL leave

perpendiculaire perpendicular (**à** to)

perpétrer JUR perpetrate

perpétuel, ~le perpetual; **perpétuer** perpetuate; **perpétuité** *f*: ***à ~*** in perpetuity; JUR *condamné* to life imprisonment

perplexe perplexed, puzzled

perron *m* steps *pl*

perroquet *m* parrot
perruque *f* wig
persécuter persecute
persévérance *f* perseverance; **persévérer** persevere (***dans*** in)
persienne *f* shutter
persil *m* BOT parsley
persistance *f* persistence; **persister** persist (***à faire*** in doing); ***~ dans sa décision*** stick to one's decision
personnage *m* character; (*dignitaire*) important person
personnalité *f* personality
personne[1] *f* person; ***deux ~s*** two people; ***par ~*** per person, each; ***les ~s âgées*** the old *pl*, old people *pl*
personne[2] *pron* no-one, nobody; ***il n'y avait ~*** no-one was there, there wasn't anyone there; ***je ne vois jamais ~*** I never see anyone; *qui que ce soit* anyone, anybody
personnel, **~le 1** *adj* personal; *conversation, courrier* private **2** *m* personnel *pl*, staff *pl*
perspective *f* perspective; *fig*: *pour l'avenir* prospect
perspicace shrewd; **perspicacité** *f* shrewdness
persuader persuade (***de faire*** to do); ***se ~*** convince o.s.
perte *f* loss; *fig* (*destruction*) ruin; ***à ~ de vue*** as far as the eye can see; ***une ~ de temps*** a waste of time
pertinent relevant
perturbateur, **-trice** disruptive; **perturber** *personne* upset; *trafic* disrupt
pervers perverse; **pervertir** pervert
pesant heavy; **pesanteur** *f* PHYS gravity
pèse-personne *f* scales *pl*
peser weigh; *fig* weigh up; *mots* weigh
pessimisme *m* pessimism; **pessimiste 1** *adj* pessimistic **2** *m/f* pessimist
pétale *f* petal
pétard *m* firecracker; F (*bruit*) racket
péter F fart F
pétillant sparkling; **pétiller** *du feu* crackle; *d'une boisson, d'yeux* sparkle
petit, **~e 1** *adj* small, little; ***~ à ~*** gradually, little by little; ***~ ami*** *m* boyfriend; ***~e amie*** *f* girlfriend **2** *m/f* child; ***une chatte et ses ~s*** a cat and her young; ***attendre des ~s*** be pregnant
petite-fille *f* granddaughter
petit-fils *m* grandson
pétition *f* petition
pétrifier turn to stone; *fig* petrify
pétrin *m fig* F mess
pétrir knead
pétrole *m* oil, petroleum; ***~ brut*** crude (oil); **pétrolier**, **-ère 1** *adj* oil *atr* **2** *m* tanker
peu 1 *adv*: ***~ gentil*** not very nice; ***~ après*** a little after;

j'ai ~ dormi I didn't sleep much; ***~ de pain*** not much bread; ***~ de choses à faire*** not many things to do; ***~ de gens*** few people; ***dans ~ de temps*** in a little while; ***un ~*** a little, a bit; ***un tout petit ~*** just a very little, just a little bit; ***un ~ de chocolat*** a little chocolate, a bit of chocolate; ***un ~ plus long*** a bit *ou* little longer; ***de ~*** *rater le bus etc* only just; ***~ à ~*** little by little; ***à ~ près*** (*plus ou moins*) more or less; (*presque*) almost

peuple *m* people; **peupler** *région* populate; *maison* live in

peuplier *m* BOT poplar

peur *f* fear (**de** of); ***avoir ~*** be frightened, be afraid (**de** of); ***faire ~ à qn*** frighten s.o.; ***de ~ que*** (*+subj*) in case; **peureux, -euse** fearful, timid

peut-être perhaps, maybe

phare *m* MAR lighthouse; AVIAT beacon; AUTO headlight; ***se mettre en*** (***pleins***) ***~s*** switch to full beam

pharmacie *f* pharmacy, *Br aussi* chemist's; *science* pharmacy; *médicaments* pharmaceuticals *pl*; **pharmacien, ~ne** *m/f* pharmacist

phénomène *m* phenomenon

philosophe *m* philosopher; **philosophie** *f* philosophy; **philosophique** philosophical

phobie *f* phobia

photo *f* photo; *l'art* photography; ***prendre qn en ~*** take a photo of s.o.

photocopie *f* photocopy; **photocopier** photocopy; **photocopieur** *m*, **photocopieuse** *f* photocopier

photographe *m/f* photographer; **photographie** *f* photograph; *l'art* photography; **photographier** photograph

phrase *f* GRAM sentence; MUS phrase; ***sans ~s*** straight out

physicien, ~ne *m/f* physicist

physique 1 *adj* physical **2** *m* physique **3** *f* physics

piailler *d'un oiseau* chirp; F *d'un enfant* scream

pianiste *m/f* pianist; **piano** *m* piano; ***~ à queue*** grand piano

pic *m* pick; *d'une montagne* peak; ***à ~*** *tomber* steeply

pichet *m* pitcher, *Br* jug

pickpocket *m* pickpocket

pick-up *m* pick-up (truck)

pie *f* ZO magpie

pièce *f* piece; *de machine* part; (*chambre*) room; (*document*) document; *de monnaie* coin; *de théâtre* play; ***cinq euros*** (***la***) ***~*** five euros each; ***mettre en ~s*** smash to smithereens; ***~ jointe*** enclosure

pied *m* foot; *d'un meuble* leg; *d'un champignon* stalk; ***à ~*** on foot; ***~s nus*** barefoot; ***au ~ de*** at the foot of; ***mettre***

sur ~ set up
piège *m* trap; **piégé**: ***voiture f ~e*** car bomb; **piéger** trap; *voiture* booby-trap
piercing *m* body piercing
pierre *f* stone; ***~ tombale*** gravestone; **pierreux, -euse** *sol* stony
piétiner 1 *v/t* trample; *fig* trample underfoot **2** *v/i fig* (*ne pas avancer*) mark time
piéton, ~ne 1 *m/f* pedestrian **2** *adj*: ***zone f ~ne*** pedestrianized zone, *Br* pedestrian precinct
pieu *m* stake; F pit F
pieuvre *f* octopus
pieux, -euse pious
pigeon *m* pigeon
piger F understand, get F
pigment *m* pigment
pile[1] *f* (*tas*) pile; ÉL battery; *monnaie* tails
pile[2] *adv*: ***s'arrêter ~*** stop dead; ***à deux heures ~*** at two o'clock on the dot
piler *ail* crush; *amandes* grind
pilier *m* pillar (*aussi fig*)
pillage *m* pillage, plunder; **piller** pillage
pilote 1 *m* pilot; AUTO driver **2** *adj*: ***usine f ~*** pilot plant; **piloter** pilot; AUTO drive
pilule *f* pill
piment *m* pimento; *fig* spice
pimenter spice up
pin *m* BOT pine
pinard *m* F wine
pince *f* pliers *pl*; *d'un crabe* pincer; ***~ à épiler*** tweezers *pl*; ***~ à linge*** clothespin, *Br* clothespeg
pinceau *m* brush
pincer pinch; MUS pluck
ping-pong *m* ping-pong
pinson *m* chaffinch
pintade *f* guinea fowl
pioche *f* pickax, *Br* pickaxe; **piocher** dig
pioncer F sleep, *Br* kip F
pipe *f* pipe
pipi *m* F pee F
pique *m aux cartes* spades
pique-nique *m* picnic
piquer *d'une abeille, des orties* sting; *d'un moustique, serpent* bite; *d'épine* prick; *fig*: *curiosité* excite; *fig* F (*voler*) pinch F; ***se ~*** prick o.s.; *se faire une piqûre* inject o.s.
piquet *m* stake; ***~ de tente*** tent peg; ***~ de grève*** picket line
piquette *f* cheap wine
piqûre *f d'abeille* sting; *de moustique* bite; MÉD injection
pirate *m* pirate; ***~ informatique*** hacker; ***~ de l'air*** hijacker; **pirater** pirate
pire worse; ***le/la ~*** the worst
piscine *f* (swimming) pool; ***~ couverte/en plein air*** indoor/outdoor pool
pisser F pee F, piss F
piste *f* track; AVIAT runway; *ski alpin* piste; *ski de fond* trail; ***~ cyclable*** cycle path
pistolet *m* pistol

piston *m* piston; **pistonner** F pull strings for
pitié *f* pity; ***avoir ~ de qn*** take pity on s.o.
pitoyable pitiful
pittoresque picturesque
pivot *m* pivot
pizza *f* pizza
PJ (= ***pièce(s) jointe(s)***) enclosure(s)
placard *m* (*armoire*) cabinet, *Br* cupboard; (*affiche*) poster; **placarder** *avis* stick up
place *f de ville* square; (*lieu*) place; (*siège*) seat; (*espace libre*) room, space; (*emploi*) position; ***sur ~*** on the spot; ***à la ~ de*** instead of; ***~ de place avec*** change places with
placement *m* (*emploi*) placement; FIN investment; ***agence f de ~*** employment agency; **placer** put, place; (*procurer emploi à*) find a job for; *argent* invest; *dans une famille etc* find a place for; ***se ~*** take one's place
plafond *m* ceiling
plage *f* beach; *lieu* seaside resort
plagiat *m* plagiarism
plaider 1 *v/i* JUR plead **2** *v/t*: ***~ la cause de qn*** defend s.o.; *fig* plead s.o.'s cause
plaidoyer *m* JUR speech for the defense *ou Br* defence; *fig* plea
plaie *f* cut; *fig* wound
plaignant, ~e *m/f* JUR plaintiff
plaindre pity; ***se ~*** complain (***de*** about; ***à*** to)
plaine *f* plain
plainte *f* complaint; (*lamentation*) moan
plaire: ***s'il vous plaît, s'il te plaît*** please; ***Paris me plaît*** I like Paris; ***ça me plairait d'aller ...*** I would like to go ...; ***se ~** de personnes* be attracted to each other
plaisance *f*: ***port m de ~*** marina
plaisanter joke; **plaisanterie** *f* joke
plaisir *m* pleasure; ***par ~, pour le ~*** for pleasure; ***faire ~ à*** please
plan 1 *adj* flat, level **2** *m* (*surface*) surface; (*projet, relevé*) plan; ***premier ~*** foreground; ***sur ce ~*** in that respect; ***sur le ~ économique*** in economic terms
planche *f* plank; ***~ à voile*** sailboard
plancher *m* floor
planer hover; *fig* live in another world
planète *f* planet
planeur *m* glider
planifier plan
planning *m*: ***~ familial*** family planning
planquer F hide; ***se ~*** hide
plant *m* AGR seedling; (*plantation*) plantation
plante[1] *f* plant
plante[2] *f*: ***~ du pied*** sole of the foot
planter plant; *jardin* plant up;

poteau hammer in; *tente* put up

plaque *f* plate; (*inscription*) plaque; **~ *électrique*** hotplate; **~ *tournante*** turntable; *fig* hub

plaquer *argent, or* plate; *meuble* veneer; *fig* pin (**contre** to, against); F (*abandonner*) dump F; *au rugby* tackle

plastique *adj & m* plastic

plat 1 *adj* flat; *eau* still **2** *m* dish

plateau *m* tray; *de théâtre* stage; TV, *d'un film* set; GÉOGR plateau; **~ *de fromages*** cheeseboard

plate-bande *f* flower bed

plate-forme *f* platform; **~ *de lancement*** launch pad

platine 1 *m* CHIM platinum **2** *f*: **~ *laser*** *ou* ***CD*** CD player

platitude *f* dullness; (*lieu commun*) platitude

plâtre *m* plaster; **plâtrer** plaster

plausible plausible

plein 1 *adj* full (**de** of); ***en ~ air*** in the open (air); ***en ~ Paris*** in the middle of Paris; ***en ~ jour*** in broad daylight **2** *adv*: **~ *de*** F lots of, a whole bunch of F **3** *m*: ***faire le ~*** AUTO fill up

pleurer 1 *v/i* cry; **~ *sur*** complain about **2** *v/t* (*regretter*) mourn

pleurnicher F snivel

pleuvoir rain; ***il pleut*** it's raining

pli *m* fold; *d'une jupe* pleat; *d'un pantalon* crease; (*enveloppe*) envelope; (*lettre*) letter; **plier 1** *v/t* (*rabattre*) fold; (*courber, ployer*) bend **2** *v/i* bend; *fig* (*céder*) give in; ***se ~ à*** (*se soumettre*) submit to

plomb *m* lead; ***sans ~*** *essence* unleaded

plombage *m* filling

plomberie *f* plumbing; **plombier** *m* plumber

plongée *f* diving; **plonger 1** *v/i* dive **2** *v/t* plunge; ***se ~ dans*** bury o.s. in; **plongeur, -euse** *m/f* diver

pluie *f* rain; *fig* shower

plumage *m* plumage; **plume** *f* feather; **plumer** pluck; *fig* fleece

plupart: ***la ~ d'entre nous*** most of us; ***pour la ~*** mostly; ***la ~ du temps*** most of the time

pluriel, ~le *adj & m* plural

plus 1 *adv* more (***que, de*** than); **~ *grand*** bigger; **~ *efficace*** more efficient; ***le ~ grand*** the biggest; ***le ~ efficace*** the most efficient; **~ *il vieillit ~ il dort*** the older he gets the more he sleeps; ***le ~*** the most; ***tu en veux ~?*** do you want some more?; ***20 euros de ~*** 20 euros more; ***nous n'avons ~ d'argent*** we have no more money, we don't have any more money; ***elle n'y habite ~***

she doesn't live there any more, she no longer lives there; ***je ne le reverrai ~ jamais*** I won't see him ever again; ***moi non ~*** me neither **2** *prép* MATH plus
plusieurs several
plutôt rather
pluvieux, **-euse** rainy
pneu *m* tire, *Br* tyre
pneumonie *f* pneumonia
poche *f* pocket; zo pouch; ***livre** m **de ~*** paperback; ***argent de ~*** pocket money
pocher *œufs* poach
pochette *f pour photos etc* folder; *d'un disque, CD* sleeve; (*sac*) bag
poêle 1 *m* stove **2** *f* frypan, *Br* frying pan
poème *m* poem
poésie *f* poetry; (*poème*) poem
poète *m* poet; **poétique** poetic; *atmosphère* romantic
poids *m* weight; *fig* (*charge, fardeau*) burden; (*importance*) weight; ***perdre/prendre du ~*** lose/gain weight
poignard *m* dagger; **poignarder** stab
poignée *f petit nombre* handful; *d'une valise etc* handle; ***~ de main*** handshake
poignet *m* wrist
poil *m* hair; ***à ~*** naked; **poilu** hairy
poinçonner *argent* hallmark; *billet* punch
poing *m* fist; ***coup** m **de ~*** punch
point¹ *m* point; *de couture* stitch; ***deux ~s*** colon; ***être sur le ~ de faire*** be on the point of doing; ***à ~*** *viande* medium; ***à ce ~*** so much; ***~ du jour*** dawn; ***~ de vue*** point of view
point² *adv litt*: ***il ne le fera ~*** he will not do it
pointe *f* point; *d'asperge* tip; ***en ~*** pointed; ***de ~*** *technologie* leading-edge; *secteur* high-tech; ***une ~ de*** a touch of
pointer 1 *v/t sur liste* check, *Br* tick off **2** *v/i d'un employé* clock in
pointillé *m*: ***les ~s*** the dotted line
pointilleux, **-euse** fussy
pointu pointed; *voix* high-pitched
pointure *f* (shoe) size
point-virgule *m* GRAM semi-colon
poire *f* pear
poireau *m* BOT leek
poirier *m* BOT pear (tree)
pois *m* BOT pea; ***petits ~*** garden peas
poison 1 *m* poison **2** *m/f fig* F nuisance, pest
poisson *m* fish; ***Poissons*** *mpl* ASTROL Pisces
poissonnerie *f* fish shop, *Br* fishmonger's
poitrine *f* chest; (*seins*) bosom
poivre *m* pepper; **poivrer**

pepper
poivron *m* bell pepper, *Br* pepper
polaire polar; **pôle** *m* pole; *fig* center, *Br* centre, focus; *~ Nord* North Pole; *~ Sud* South Pole
poli (*courtois*) polite; *métal, caillou* polished
police *f* police; *~ d'assurance* insurance policy
policier, -ère 1 *adj* police *atr*; *film, roman* detective *atr* **2** *m* police officer
polir polish
politesse *f* politeness
politicien, ~ne *m/f* politician
politique 1 *adj* political; *homme m ~* politician **2** *f d'un parti etc* policy; (*affaires publiques*) politics *sg*
pollen *m* pollen
polluer pollute; **pollution** *f* pollution; *~ atmosphérique* air pollution
Pologne: *la ~* Poland; **polonais, ~e 1** *adj* Polish **2** *m langue* Polish; **Polonais, ~e** *m/f* Pole
poltron, ~ne *m/f* coward
polyclinique *f* (general) hospital
polycopié *m* (photocopied) handout
polystyrène *m* polystyrene
polyvalence *f* versatility; **polyvalent** multipurpose; *personne* versatile
pommade *f* MÉD ointment
pomme *f* apple; *~ de terre* potato
pommette *f* ANAT cheekbone
pommier *m* BOT apple tree
pompe[1] *f faste* pomp; *~s funèbres* funeral director
pompe[2] *f* TECH pump; *~ à essence* gas pump, *Br* petrol pump; **pomper** pump; *fig* (*épuiser*) knock out
pompeux, -euse pompous
pompier *m* firefighter; *~s* fire department, *Br* fire brigade
pomponner F: *se ~* get dolled up F
poncer sand
ponctualité *f* punctuality; **ponctuel, ~le** *personne* punctual; *fig*: *action* one-off
ponctuer punctuate
pondération *f d'une personne* level-headedness; *de forces* balance; ÉCON weighting; **pondéré** *personne* level-headed; *forces* balanced; ÉCON weighted
pondre *œufs* lay; *fig* F come up with; *roman* churn out
poney *m* pony
pont *m* bridge; MAR deck; *faire le ~* make a long weekend of it
pontage *m*: *~ coronarien* (heart) bypass
pop *f* MUS pop
populaire popular; **populariser** popularize; **popularité** *f* popularity
population *f* population
porc *m* hog, pig; *fig* pig; *viande* pork

porcelaine *f* porcelain
porcherie *f* hog *ou* pig farm
pore *m* pore; **poreux**, **-euse** porous
pornographique pornographic
port[1] *m* port; **~ de pêche** fishing port
port[2] *m d'armes* carrying; *courrier* postage
portable **1** *adj* portable **2** *m ordinateur* laptop; *téléphone* cellphone, cell, *Br* mobile
portail *m* ARCH portal; *d'un parc* gate
portant *mur* load-bearing; ***à bout ~*** at point-blank range; ***bien ~*** well; ***mal ~*** not well
portatif, **-ive** portable
porte *f* door; *d'une ville* gate; ***mettre qn à la ~*** show s.o. the door
porte-bagages *m* AUTO roof rack; *filet* luggage rack; **porte-bonheur** *m* lucky charm; **porte-clés** *m* keyring; **porte-documents** *m* briefcase
portée *f* ZO litter; *d'une arme* range; (*importance*) significance; ***être à la ~ de qn*** *fig* be accessible to s.o.
portefeuille *m* portfolio (*aussi* POL, FIN); (*porte-monnaie*) billfold, *Br* wallet
portemanteau *m* coat rack; *sur pied* coatstand
porte-monnaie *m* coin purse, *Br* purse
porte-parole *m* spokesperson
porter **1** *v/t* carry; *un vêtement, des lunettes etc* wear; (*apporter*) take; bring; *yeux, attention* turn (***sur*** to); *toast* drink; *fruits, nom* bear; ***~ plainte*** make a complaint **2** *v/i d'une voix* carry; ***~ sur*** (*appuyer sur*) rest on; (*concerner*) be about **3**: ***il se porte bien/mal*** he's well/not well; ***se ~ candidat*** be a candidate, run
porteur *m d'un message* bearer
portier *m* doorman
portière *f de train, voiture* door
portion *f* portion
portrait *m* portrait
portugais, **~e** **1** *adj* Portuguese **2** *m langue* Portuguese; **Portugais**, **~e** *m/f* Portuguese; **Portugal**: ***le ~*** Portugal
pose *f d'un radiateur* installation; *de moquette* fitting; *de papier peint, rideaux* hanging; (*attitude*) pose; **posé** poised, composed; **poser** **1** *v/t* (*mettre*) put (down); *compteur, radiateur* install, *Br* instal; *moquette* fit; *papier peint, rideaux* hang; *problème* pose; *question* ask; ***se ~ en*** set o.s. up as **2** *v/i* pose
positif, **-ive** positive
position *f* position
possédé possessed (***de*** by); **posséder** own, possess;

possesseur *m* owner; **possession** *f* possession, ownership

possibilité *f* possibility; **possible 1** *adj* possible; ***le plus souvent*** ~ as often as possible; ***autant que*** ~ as far as possible **2** *m*: ***faire tout son*** ~ do everything one can

poste[1] *f* mail, *Br aussi* post; (***bureau*** *m* ***de***) ~ post office; ***mettre à la*** ~ mail, *Br aussi* post

poste[2] *m* post; (*profession*) position; RAD, TV set; TÉL extension; ~ ***de secours*** first-aid post; ~ ***de travail*** INFORM work station

poster *soldat* post; *lettre* mail, *Br aussi* post

postérieur 1 *adj dans l'espace* back *atr*, rear *atr*; *dans le temps* later; ~ ***à qch*** after sth **2** *m* F posterior F

postérité posterity

posthume posthumous

postier, **-ère** *m/f* post office employee

postillonner splutter

postuler apply for

posture *f* position, posture; *fig* position

pot *m* pot; ~ ***à eau*** water jug; ***prendre un*** ~ F have a drink; ***avoir du*** ~ F be lucky

potable fit to drink; ***eau*** ~ drinking water

potage *m* soup; **potager**, **-ère**: ***jardin*** *m* ~ kitchen garden

pot-au-feu *m* boiled beef dinner

pot-de-vin *m* F kickback F, bribe

poteau *m* post; ~ ***indicateur*** signpost

poterie *f* pottery; *objet* piece of pottery

potion *f* potion

potiron *m* BOT pumpkin

pou *m* louse

poubelle *f* trash can, *Br* dustbin

pouce *m* thumb

poudre *f* powder; ***chocolat*** *m* ***en*** ~ chocolate powder; **poudrier** *m* powder compact

pouffer: ~ ***de rire*** burst out laughing

poulailler *m* henhouse; *au théâtre* gallery, *Br* gods *pl*

poulain *m* ZO foal

poule *f* hen; **poulet** *m* chicken

poulpe *m* octopus

pouls *m* pulse

poumon *m* lung

poupée *f* doll (*aussi fig*)

poupon *m* little baby

pour 1 *prép* for; ~ ***20 euros de courses*** 20 euros' worth of shopping; ***je l'ai dit*** ~ ***te prévenir*** I said that to warn you **2** *conj*: ~ ***que*** (+ *subj*) so that; ***il parle trop vite*** ~ ***que je le comprenne*** he speaks too fast for me to understand **3** *m*: ***le*** ~ ***et le contre*** the pros and the cons *pl*

pourboire *m* tip

pourcentage *m* percentage
pourparlers *mpl* talks
pourpre purple
pourquoi why
pourri rotten (*aussi fig*); **pourrir 1** *v/i* rot; *fig: d'une situation* deteriorate **2** *v/t* rot; *fig* (*corrompre*) corrupt; (*gâter*) spoil; **pourriture** *f* rot (*aussi fig*)
poursuite *f* chase, pursuit; *fig* pursuit; **~s** JUR proceedings; **poursuivre** pursue, chase; *fig*: *bonheur* pursue; *de pensées* haunt; JUR sue; *malfaiteur* prosecute; (*continuer*) carry on with
pourtant yet
pourvoir 1 *v/t emploi* fill; **~ de** *voiture*, *maison* equip with **2** *v/i*: **~ à** *besoins* provide for; **se ~ de** provide o.s.
pourvu: **~ que** (+ *subj*) provided that; *exprimant désir* hopefully
pousse *f* AGR shoot; **poussée** *f* thrust; MÉD outbreak; *de fièvre* rise; *fig*: *de racisme etc* upsurge; **pousser 1** *v/t* push; *du vent* drive; *cri*, *soupir* give; *fig*: *recherches* pursue; **se ~** *d'une foule* push forward; *pour faire de la place* move over **2** *v/i* push; *de cheveux*, *plantes* grow; **poussette** *f pour enfants* stroller, *Br* pushchair
poussière *f* dust; *particule* speck of dust
poussin *m* chick
poutre *f* beam
pouvoir 1 *v/aux* be able to, can; ***je ne peux pas aider*** I can't *ou* cannot help; ***je ne pouvais pas accepter*** I couldn't accept, I wasn't able to accept; ***il se peut que*** (+ *subj*) it's possible that; ***tu aurais pu me prévenir!*** you could have *ou* might have warned me! **2** *m* power; *procuration* power of attorney; ***les ~s publics*** the authorities
prairie *f* meadow; *plaine* prairie
praline *f* praline
praticable *projet* feasible; *route* passable
pratique 1 *adj* practical **2** *f* practice; *expérience* practical experience; **pratiquement** (*presque*) practically; *dans la pratique* in practice; **pratiquer** practice, *Br* practise; *sports* play; *technique* use; TECH *trou*, *passage* make
pré *m* meadow
préado *m/f* pre-teen
préalable 1 *adj* (*antérieur*) prior; (*préliminaire*) preliminary **2** *m* condition; **au ~** beforehand
préavis *m* notice
précaire precarious
précaution *f* caution; *mesure* precaution; **par ~** as a precaution
précédent 1 *adj* previous **2** *m*

precedent; **précéder** precede
prêcher preach
précieux, -euse precious
précipice *m* precipice
précipitamment hastily, in a rush; **précipitation** *f* haste; **~s** *temps* precipitation; **précipiter** (*faire tomber*) plunge (**dans** into); (*pousser*) hurl; (*brusquer*) precipitate; *pas* hasten; **se ~** (*se jeter*) throw o.s.; (*se dépêcher*) rush
précis 1 *adj* precise **2** *m* precis, summary; **préciser** specify; **~ que** (*souligner*) make it clear that; **précision** *f* accuracy; *d'un geste* preciseness; **pour plus de ~s** for further details
précoce early; *enfant* precocious; **précocité** *f* earliness; *d'un enfant* precociousness
préconçu preconceived
précurseur 1 *m* precursor **2** *adj*: **signe** *m* **~** warning sign
prédateur, -trice 1 *adj* predatory **2** *m/f* predator
prédécesseur *m* predecessor
prédestiner predestine (**à qc** for sth; **à faire** to do)
prédiction *f* prediction
prédilection *f* predilection; **de ~** favorite, *Br* favourite
prédire predict
prédominer predominate
préfabriqué prefabricated
préface *f* preface
préférable preferable (**à** to);
préféré favorite, *Br* favourite; **préférence** *f* preference; **de ~** preferably; **préférer** prefer (**à** to); **~ faire qc** prefer to do sth; **je préfère que tu viennes** (*subj*) **demain** I would *ou* I'd prefer you to come tomorrow, I'd rather you came tomorrow
préfet *m* prefect; **~ de police** chief of police
préfixe *m* prefix
préjudice *m* harm; **porter ~ à** harm
préjugé *m* prejudice
prélever *échantillon* take; *montant* deduct (**sur** from)
préliminaire preliminary
préluder *fig*: **~ à** be the prelude to
prématuré premature
préméditer premeditate
premier, -ère 1 *adj* first; *rang* front; *objectif*, *cause* primary; *nombre* prime; **au ~ étage** on the second floor, *Br* on the first floor; **Premier ministre** Prime Minister; **le ~ août** August first, *Br* the first of August **2** *m/f*: **partir le ~** leave first **3** *m* second floor, *Br* first floor; **en ~** first **4** *f* THÉÂT first night; AUTO first (gear); *en train* first (class)
prémisse *f* premise
prémonition *f* premonition; **prémonitoire** *rêve* prophetic
prendre 1 *v/t* take; (*enlever*) take away; *froid* catch; *poids*

put on; **~ qch à qn** take sth (away) from s.o. **2** *v/i* (*durcir*) set; *de mode* catch on; *d'un feu* take hold; **~ à droite** turn right **3**: **se ~** (*se laisser attraper*) get caught; **se ~ d'amitié pour qn** take a liking to s.o.

prénom *m* first name; **deuxième ~** middle name

préoccuper preoccupy; (*inquiéter*) worry; **se ~ de** worry about

préparatifs *mpl* preparations; **préparation** *f* preparation; **préparer** prepare; (*organiser*) arrange; **~ qn à qch** prepare s.o. for sth; **~ un examen** prepare for an exam; **se ~** get ready; *de dispute, d'orage* be brewing

prépondérant predominant

préposé *m* (*facteur*) mailman, *Br* postman; *au vestiaire* attendant; *des douanes* official; **préposée** *f* (*factrice*) mailwoman, *Br* postwoman

préretraite *f* early retirement

près 1 *adv* close, near; **de ~** closely **2** *prép*: **~ de qch** near sth, close to sth; **~ de 500** nearly 500

présage *m* omen

presbyte farsighted, *Br* long-sighted

prescription *f* rule; MÉD prescription; **prescrire** stipulate; MÉD prescribe

présence *f* presence; **en ~ de** in the presence of; **présent 1** *adj* present **2** *m* present (*aussi* GRAM); **les ~s** those present; **à ~** at present; **à ~ que** now that; **jusqu'à ~** till now

présentateur, **-trice** *m/f* TV presenter; **~ météo** weatherman; **présentation** *f* presentation; **présenter** present; *chaise* offer; *personne* introduce; *pour un concours* put forward; *billet* show, present; *condoléances, félicitations* offer; *difficultés, dangers* involve; **se ~** introduce o.s.; *pour un poste, un emploi* apply; *aux élections* run; *de difficultés* come up

préservatif *m* condom

préserver protect (**de** from); *bois, patrimoine* preserve

présidence *f* chairmanship; POL presidency; **président**, **~e** *m/f d'une réunion* chair; POL president; **présidentiel**, **~le** presidential; **présider** *réunion* chair

présomption *f* presumption; **présomptueux**, **-euse** presumptuous

presque almost, nearly

presqu'île *f* peninsula

pressant *besoin* pressing, urgent; *personne* insistent

presse *f* press; **mise** *f* **sous ~** going to press

pressé *lettre, requête* urgent; *citron* fresh; **je suis ~** I'm in a hurry

pressentiment *m* foreboding, presentiment; **pressentir**: **~ *qch*** have a premonition that sth is going to happen; **~ *qn*** *pour un poste* approach s.o., sound s.o. out
presser 1 *v/t bouton* push, press; *fruit* squeeze; (*harceler*) press; *pas* quicken; *affaire* speed up; (*étreindre*) press, squeeze; ***se ~ contre*** press (o.s.) against **2** *v/i* be urgent; ***se ~*** hurry up
pressing *m magasin* dry cleaner
pression *f* pressure; *bouton* snap fastener, *Br aussi* press-stud fastener; (***bière f***) **~** draft beer, *Br* draught beer; ***faire ~ sur*** pressure, put pressure on
prestance *f* presence
prestation *f* (*allocation*) allowance; ***~s familiales*** child benefit
prestige *m* prestige
présumer 1 *v/t*: **~ *que*** presume *ou* assume that **2** *v/i*: **~ *de*** overrate
prêt[1] *adj* ready (**à** for; ***à faire*** to do)
prêt[2] *m* loan; **~ *immobilier*** mortgage
prêt-à-porter *m* ready-to--wear clothes *pl*
prétendre 1 *v/t* maintain; **~ *faire qch*** claim to do sth **2** *v/i*: **~ *à*** lay claim to; **prétendu** so-called
prétentieux, **-euse** pretentious
prêter 1 *v/t* lend **2** *v/i*: **~ *à*** give rise to; ***se ~ à*** *d'une chose* lend itself to; *d'une personne* be a party to
prétexte *m* pretext; ***sous ~ de faire*** on the pretext of doing
prêtre *m* priest; **prêtresse** *f* woman priest
preuve *f* proof, evidence; MATH proof; ***faire ~ de courage*** show courage
prévenance *f* consideration
prévenir (*avertir*) warn (***de*** of); (*informer*) inform (***de*** of); *besoin, question* anticipate; *crise, maladie* avert
préventif, **-ive** preventive; **prévention** *f* prevention; **~ *routière*** road safety
prévision *f* forecast; ***~s météorologiques*** weather forecast
prévoir (*pressentir*) foresee; (*planifier*) plan; ***comme prévu*** as expected; **prévoyance** *f* foresight; **prévoyant** farsighted
prier 1 *v/i* REL pray **2** *v/t* (*supplier*) beg; REL pray to; **~ *qn de faire qc*** ask s.o. to do sth; ***je vous en prie*** don't mention it
prière *f* REL prayer; (*demande*) entreaty; ***faire sa ~*** say one's prayers
primaire primary; *péj* narrow-minded
prime[1]: ***de ~ abord*** at first sight

prime² *f d'assurance* premium; *de fin d'année* bonus; (*cadeau*) free gift
primer 1 *v/i* take precedence **2** *v/t* take precedence over
primeur *f*: ***avoir la ~ de*** *nouvelle* be the first to hear *objet* have first use of; ***~s*** early fruit and vegetables
primitif, -ive primitive; *couleur, sens* original
primordial essential
prince *m* prince; **princesse** princess
principal, ~e 1 *adj* main, principal **2** *m*: ***le ~*** the main thing **3** *m/f* principal, *Br* head teacher
principe *m* principle; ***par ~*** on principle; ***en ~*** in principle
printemps *m* spring
priorité *f* priority (***sur*** over); *sur la route* right of way
pris *place* taken; *personne* busy
prise *f* hold; *d'un pion, une ville etc* capture, taking; *de poissons* catch; ÉL outlet, *Br* socket; *d'un film* take; ***être aux ~s avec*** be struggling with; ***~ de conscience*** awareness; ***~ de courant*** outlet, *Br* socket
prison *f* prison; **prisonnier, -ère** *m/f* prisoner
privation *f* deprivation
privatisation *f* privatization; **privatiser** privatize
privé 1 *adj* private **2** *m*: ***en ~*** in private; **priver**: ***~ qn de*** deprive s.o. of; ***se ~ de*** go without
privilège *m* privilege; **privilégier** favor, *Br* favour
prix *m* price; (*valeur*) value; (*récompense*) prize; ***à tout ~*** at all costs; ***hors de ~*** prohibitive; ***au ~ de*** at the cost of; ***~ fort*** full price; ***~ de revient*** cost price
probabilité *f* probability; **probable** probable
probant convincing
problème *m* problem
procédé *m* (*méthode*) method; TECH process; ***~s*** (*comportement*) behavior, *Br* behaviour
procéder proceed; ***~ à qc*** carry out sth
procès *m* JUR trial
processus *m* process
procès-verbal *m* minutes *pl*; (*contravention*) ticket
prochain, ~e 1 *adj* next **2** *m/f*: ***son ~*** one's neighbor *ou Br* neighbour
proche 1 *adj* close (**de** to), near; *ami* close; *événement* recent; ***~ de*** *fig* close to **2** *mpl*: ***~s*** family and friends
proclamer *roi, république* proclaim; *résultats, innocence* declare
procréer procreate
procuration *f* proxy, power of attorney; **procurer** get, procure *fml*
prodigieux, -euse enormous,

tremendous
prodigue extravagant; **prodiguer** lavish
producteur, **-trice 1** *adj* producing **2** *m/f* producer; **productif**, **-ive** productive; **production** *f* production; **produire** produce; ***se ~*** happen; **produit** *m* product; *d'un investissement* yield; ***~ d'entretien*** cleaning product; ***~ fini*** end product
profane 1 *adj art, musique* secular **2** *m/f fig* lay person; **profaner** desecrate, profane
proférer *menaces* utter
professeur *m* teacher; *d'université* professor
profession *f* profession; **professionnel**, **~le** *m/f & adj* professional
profil *m* profile
profit *m* COMM profit; (*avantage*) benefit; **profitable** beneficial; COMM profitable; **profiter**: ***~ de qc*** take advantage of sth; ***~ à qn*** be to s.o.'s advantage
profond deep; *personne, pensées* deep, profound; *influence* profound; **profondément** deeply, profoundly; **profondeur** *f* depth
programme *m* program, *Br* programme; INFORM program; ***~ télé*** TV program; **programmer** TV schedule; INFORM program; **programmeur**, **-euse** *m/f* programmer
progrès *m* progress; *d'un incendie, d'une épidémie* spread; **progresser** progress; *d'une incendie, d'une épidémie* spread; **progressif**, **-ive** progressive; **progression** *f* progress
prohiber ban, prohibit; **prohibition** *f* ban; ***la Prohibition*** HIST Prohibition
proie *f* prey (*aussi fig*); ***en ~ à*** prey to
projecteur *m* (*spot*) spotlight; *au cinéma* projector
projection *f* projection
projet *m* project; *personnel* plan; (*ébauche*) draft; ***~ de loi*** bill; **projeter** (*jeter*) throw; *film* screen; *travail, voyage* plan
proliférer proliferate
prologue *m* prologue
prolongation *f* extension; ***~s*** SP overtime, *Br* extra time; **prolonger** prolong; *mur, route* extend; ***se ~*** continue
promenade *f* walk; *en voiture* drive; **promener** take for a walk; ***se ~*** go for a walk; *en voiture* go for a drive; **promeneur**, **-euse** *m/f* stroller, walker
promesse *f* promise; **prometteur**, **-euse** promising; **promettre** promise (***qc à qn*** s.o. sth, sth to s.o., ***de faire*** to do); ***se ~ de faire qc*** make up one's mind to do sth
promiscuité *f* overcrowding;

sexuelle promiscuity
promontoire *m* promontory
promoteur, -trice 1 *m/f* (*instigateur*) instigator **2** *m*: **~ immobilier** property developer; **promotion** *f* promotion; *sociale* advancement; ÉDU class, *Br* year; **en ~** on special offer; **promouvoir** promote
prompt swift
pronom *m* GRAM pronoun
prononcé *fig* marked, pronounced; *accent, traits* strong; **prononcer** (*dire*) say, utter; (*articuler*) pronounce; *discours* give; JUR *sentence* pass, pronounce; **se ~** *d'un mot* be pronounced; (*se déterminer*) express an opinion; **se ~ pour/contre qch** come out in favor *ou Br* favour of /against sth; **prononciation** *f* pronunciation; JUR passing
propager *idée, nouvelle* spread; BIOL propagate; **se ~** spread; BIOL reproduce
propension *f* propensity (**à** for)
propice favorable, *Br* favourable; *moment* right
proportion *f* proportion; **toutes ~s gardées** on balance; **proportionnel, ~le** proportional (**à** to)
propos 1 *mpl* (*paroles*) words **2** *m* (*intention*) intention; **à ~** at the right moment; **mal à ~, hors de ~** at the wrong moment; **à ~!** by the way; **à ~ de** (*au sujet de*) about
proposer suggest, propose; (*offrir*) offer; **se ~ de faire** propose doing; **se ~** offer one's services; **proposition** *f* (*suggestion*) proposal, suggestion; (*offre*) offer; GRAM clause
propre 1 *adj* own; (*net*) clean; (*approprié*) suitable; **~ à** (*particulier à*) characteristic of **2** *m*: **mettre au ~** make a clean copy of; **propreté** *f* cleanliness
propriétaire *m/f* owner; *qui loue* landlord; *femme* landlady; **propriété** *f* ownership; (*caractéristique*) property
propulser propel; **propulsion** *f* propulsion
proscrire (*interdire*) ban; (*bannir*) banish
prospectus *m* brochure; FIN prospectus
prospère prosperous; **prospérer** prosper; **prospérité** *f* prosperity
prosterner: **se ~** prostrate o.s.
prostituée *f* prostitute; **prostitution** *f* prostitution
protecteur, -trice 1 *adj* protective; *péj*: *ton* patronizing **2** *m/f* protector; (*mécène*) sponsor, patron; **protection** *f* protection; **protéger** protect (**contre, de** from); *arts, artistes* be a patron of
protéine *f* protein

protestant, **~e** REL *m/f & adj* Protestant
protestation *f* (*plainte*) protest; (*déclaration*) protestation; **protester** protest
prothèse *f* prosthesis
protocole *m* protocol
prototype *m* prototype
prouesse *f* prowess
prouver prove
provenance *f* origin; ***en ~ de*** *avion, train* from
provenir: ***~ de*** come from
proverbe *m* proverb
providence *f* providence
province *f* province
proviseur *m* principal, *Br* head (teacher)
provision *f* supply; **~s** (*vivres*) provisions; (*achats*) shopping; *d'un chèque* funds *pl*; ***chèque*** *m* ***sans ~*** bad check *ou Br* cheque
provisoire provisional
provocant, **provocateur**, **-trice** provocative; **provoquer** provoke; *accident* cause
proximité *f* proximity; ***à ~ de*** near, in the vicinity of
prude prudish
prudence *f* caution, prudence; **prudent** cautious, prudent; *conducteur* careful
prune *f* BOT plum
pruneau *m* prune
prunier *m* plum (tree)
PS *m* (= ***Parti socialiste***) Socialist Party; (= ***Post Scriptum***) PS (= postscript)
psaume *m* psalm
pseudonyme *m* pseudonym
psychanalyser psychoanalyze; **psychanalyste** *m/f* psychoanalyst
psychiatre *m/f* psychiatrist
psychologie *f* psychology; **psychologique** psychological; **psychologue** *m/f* psychologist
psychopathe *m/f* psychopath
puant stinking; *fig* arrogant; **puanteur** *f* stink
pub *f*: ***une ~*** an ad; ***faire de la ~*** do some advertising
public, **publique 1** *adj* public **2** *m* public; *d'un spectacle* audience
publication *f* publication
publicitaire advertising *atr*; **publicité** *f* publicity; COMM advertising; (*affiche*) ad
publier publish
publipostage *m* mailshot
puce *f* ZO flea; INFORM chip
pudeur *f* modesty; **pudique** modest; *discret* discreet
puer 1 *v/i* stink; ***~ des pieds*** have smelly feet **2** *v/t* stink of
puéril childish
puis then
puiser draw (***dans*** from)
puisque since
puissance *f* power; *d'une armée* strength; **puissant** powerful; *musculature, médicament* strong
puits *m* well; *d'une mine* shaft; ***~ de pétrole*** oil well
pull(-over) *m* sweater, *Br*

aussi pullover
pulluler swarm
pulsation *f* beat, beating
pulsion *f* drive; **~s** *fpl* **de mort** death wish
pulvériser *solide* pulverize (*aussi fig*); *liquide* spray
punaise *f* ZO bug; (*clou*) thumbtack, *Br* drawing pin
punir punish; **punition** *f* punishment
pupille 1 *m/f* JUR ward **2** *f* ANAT pupil
pur pure; *whisky* straight
purée *f* puree; **~ (de pommes de terre)** mashed potatoes *pl*
pureté *f* purity
purge *f* purge; **purger** TECH bleed; POL purge; JUR *peine* serve
purification *f* purification; **purifier** purify
pur-sang *m* thoroughbred
pus *m* pus
pute *f* F slut
puzzle *m* jigsaw (puzzle)
P.-V. *m* (= ***procès-verbal***) ticket
pyjama *m* pajamas *pl*, *Br* pyjamas *pl*
pyramide *f* pyramid
Pyrénées *fpl* Pyrenees
pyromane *m* pyromaniac; JUR arsonist

Q

quadragénaire *m/f & adj* forty-year old
quadrillé *papier* squared; **quadriller** *fig*: *région* put under surveillance
quadruple quadruple
quai *m* *d'un port* quay; *d'une gare* platform
qualification *f* qualification; (*appellation*) name; **qualifier** qualify; **~ *qn d'idiot*** describe s.o. as an idiot; ***se ~*** SP qualify
qualité *f* quality; ***de ~*** quality *atr*; ***en ~ d'ambassadeur*** as ambassador, in his capacity as ambassador
quand when; ***~ je serai de retour*** when I'm back
quant à as for
quantifier quantify
quantité *f* quantity; ***une ~ de*** *grand nombre* a great many; *abondance* a great deal of
quarantaine *f* MÉD quarantine; ***une ~ de*** about forty, forty or so; ***avoir la ~*** be in one's forties; **quarante** forty
quart *m* quarter; *de vin* quarter liter, *Br* quarter litre; ***~ d'heure*** quarter of an hour; ***~ de finale*** quarter-final
quartier *m* (*quart*) quarter; *d'orange* segment; *d'une ville* area; ***~ général*** MIL headquarters *pl*
quasiment virtually
quatorze fourteen

quatre four; **quatre-vingt(s)** eighty; **quatre-vingt-dix** ninety; **quatrième** fourth
quatuor *m* MUS quartet
que 1 *pron relatif personne* who, that; *chose, animal* which, that; ***les étudiants ~ j'ai rencontrés*** the students (who *ou* that) I met **2** *pron interrogatif* what; ***qu'y a-t-il?*** what's the matter?; ***qu'est-ce que c'est?*** what's that? **3** *adv dans exclamations*: ***~ c'est beau!*** it's so beautiful!; ***~ de fleurs!*** what a lot of flowers! **4** *conj* that; ***je croyais ~ ...*** I thought (that) ...; ***plus grand ~ moi*** bigger than me; ***aussi petit ~ cela*** as small as that; ***ne ... ~*** only
quel, ~le what, which; ***~le femme!*** what a woman!
quelconque (*médiocre*) mediocre; ***un travail ~*** some sort of job
quelque some; ***~s*** some, a few; ***~ ... que*** (+ *subj*) whatever, whichever
quelque chose something; *avec interrogatif, conditionnel aussi* anything
quelquefois sometimes
quelques-uns, quelques-unes a few, some
quelqu'un someone, somebody; *avec interrogatif, conditionnel aussi* anyone, anybody
querelle *f* quarrel; **quereller**: ***se ~*** quarrel; **querelleur, -euse** quarrelsome
question *f* question; **questionnaire** *m* questionnaire; **questionner** question (***sur*** about)
quête *f* search; (*collecte*) collection
queue *f d'un animal* tail; *d'un fruit* stalk; *d'une casserole* handle; *d'un train* rear; *d'une classe* bottom; *d'une file* line, *Br* queue; ***faire la ~*** stand in line, *Br* queue (up); ***à la ~, en ~*** at the rear
qui *interrogatif* who; *relatif, personne* who, that; *relatif, chose, animal* which, that
quiconque whoever; (*n'importe qui*) anyone, anybody
quincaillerie *f* hardware; *magasin* hardware store
quinquagénaire *m/f & adj* fifty-year old
quintal *m* hundred kilos *pl*
quinte *f*: ***~ (de toux)*** coughing fit
quinzaine *f de jours* two weeks *pl*, *Br aussi* fortnight; ***une ~ de personnes*** about fifteen people *pl*; **quinze** fifteen; ***~ jours*** two weeks, *Br aussi* fortnight
quitte: ***être ~ envers qn*** be quits with s.o.
quitter leave; *vêtement* take off; ***se ~*** part; ***ne quittez pas*** TÉL hold the line please
quoi what; ***après ~, il ...*** after which he ...; ***à ~ bon?*** what's

the point?; ***il n'y a pas de ~!*** don't mention it; ***~ que*** (+ *subj*) whatever

quoique (+ *subj*) although, though

quotidien, ~ne 1 *adj* daily; *de tous les jours* everyday **2** *m* daily

R

rabâcher keep on repeating

rabais *m* discount, reduction; **rabaisser** *prix* reduce; *mérites* belittle

rabattre 1 *v/t siège* pull down; *couvercle* shut; *col* turn down **2** *v/i fig*: ***se ~ sur*** fall back on; *d'une voiture* pull back into

râblé stocky

rabot *m* plane

rabougri stunted

rabrouer snub

racaille *f* rabble

raccommoder mend; *chaussettes* darn

raccompagner: ***je vais vous ~ chez vous*** *à pied* I'll take you home

raccord *m* join; *d'un film* splice; **raccorder** join

raccourci *m* shortcut; ***en ~*** briefly; **raccourcir 1** *v/t* shorten **2** *v/i* get shorter

raccrocher 1 *v/t* put back up; ***~ le téléphone*** hang up; ***se ~ à*** cling to **2** *v/i* TÉL hang up

race *f* race; (*ascendance*) descent; ZO breed

rachat *m d'un otage* ransoming; *d'une société* buyout; **racheter** buy back; *otage* ransom; *fig*: *faute* make up for; ***se ~*** make amends

racine *f* root

racisme *m* racism; **raciste** *m/f & adj* racist

racler scrape; ***se ~ la gorge*** clear one's throat

raconter tell

radar *m* radar

radeau *m* raft

radiateur *m* radiator

radiation *f* radiation; *d'une liste* deletion

radical *adj & m* radical

radier strike out

radieux, -euse radiant; *temps* glorious

radin F mean, tight

radio *f* radio; (*radiographie*) X-ray

radioactif, -ive radioactive

radiocassette *f* radio cassette player

radiographie *f procédé* radiography; *photo* X-ray

radioréveil radio alarm

radis *m* BOT radish

radoter ramble

radoucir make milder; ***se ~*** *du temps* get milder

rafale *f de vent* gust; MIL burst

raffermir *chair* firm up; *auto-*

rité re-assert
raffinage *m* refining; **raffiné** refined; **raffiner** refine; **raffinerie** *f* refinery
raffoler: **~ de** adore
rafraîchir 1 *v/t* cool down; *mémoire* refresh **2** *v/i du vin* chill; **se ~** *de la température* get cooler; *d'une personne* have a drink (in order to cool down); **rafraîchissant** refreshing (*aussi fig*); **rafraîchissement** *m de la température* cooling; **~s** (*boissons*) refreshments
rage *f* rage; MÉD rabies *sg*; **rageur, -euse** furious
ragoût *m* CUIS stew
raide *personne, membres* stiff; *pente* steep; *cheveux* straight; (*ivre, drogué*) stoned; **raideur** *f* stiffness; *d'une pente* steepness; **raidir**: **se ~** *de membres* stiffen up
raie *f* (*rayure*) stripe; *des cheveux* part, *Br* parting; ZO skate
rail *m* rail; **~ de sécurité** crash barrier
railler mock; **raillerie** *f* mockery
raisin *m* grape; **~ sec** raisin
raison *f* reason; **avoir ~** be right; **avoir ~ de** get the better of; **à ~ de** at a rate of; **à plus forte ~** all the more so; **en ~ de** (*à cause de*) because of; **~ sociale** company name; **raisonnable** reasonable; **raisonnement** *m* reasoning; **raisonner 1** *v/i* reason **2** *v/t*: **~ qn** make s.o. see reason
rajeunir 1 *v/t thème* modernize; **~ qn** make s.o. look (years) younger **2** *v/i* look younger
rajouter add
rajuster adjust; *coiffure* put straight
ralenti *m* AUTO idle; *dans un film* slow motion; **au ~** *fig* at a snail's pace; **ralentir** slow down; **ralentissement** *m* slowing down; **ralentisseur** *m de circulation* speedbump
râler moan; F beef F; **râleur, -euse** F **1** *adj* grumbling **2** *m/f* grumbler
rallier rally; (*s'unir à*) join; **se ~ à** rally to
rallonger 1 *v/t* lengthen **2** *v/i* get longer
rallumer *télé, lumière* switch on again; *fig* revive
ramassage *m* collection; *de fruits* picking; **ramasser** collect; *ce qui est par terre* pick up; *fruits* pick; F *coup* get
rame *f* oar; *de métro* train
rameau *m* branch
ramener take back; (*rapporter*) bring back; *l'ordre* restore; **se ~ à** (*se réduire à*) come down to
ramer row; **rameur, -euse** *m/f* rower
ramification *f* ramification

ramollir soften; ***se ~*** soften; *fig* go soft
rampant crawling; BOT creeping; *fig*: *inflation* rampant
rampe *f* ramp; *d'escalier* bannisters *pl*; *au théâtre* footlights *pl*
ramper crawl; BOT creep
rance rancid
rancœur *f* resentment (***contre*** toward)
rançon *f* ransom; ***la ~ de*** *fig* the price of
rancune *f* resentment; **rancunier**, **-ère** resentful
randonnée *f* walk; *en montagne* hill walk; **randonneur** *m* walker; *en montagne* hillwalker
rang *m* row; (*niveau*) rank; ***être au premier ~*** be in the forefront
rangée *f* row
ranger put away; *chambre* tidy up; *voiture* park; (*classer*) arrange; ***se ~*** (*s'écarter*) move aside; AUTO pull over; *fig* (*assagir*) settle down; ***se ~ à une opinion*** come around to a point of view
ranimer *personne* bring around; *fig*: *force* revive
rap *m* MUS rap
rapace 1 *adj animal* predatory; *personne* greedy **2** *m* bird of prey
rapatrier repatriate
râpe *f* grater; TECH rasp; **râper** CUIS grate; *bois* file; ***râpé*** CUIS grated; *manteau* threadbare
rapide 1 *adj* fast, rapid; *coup d'œil*, *décision* quick **2** *m dans l'eau* rapid; *train* fast train; **rapidité** *f* speed, rapidity
rapiécer patch
rappel *m* reminder; *d'un ambassadeur*, *produit* recall; THÉÂT curtain call; MÉD booster; **rappeler** call back; *ambassadeur* recall; ***~ qc/qn à qn*** remind s.o. of sth/s.o.; ***se ~ qc*** remember sth
rapport *m écrit*, *oral* report; (*lien*) connection; (*proportion*) proportion; COMM return; MIL briefing; ***~s*** (***sexuels***) sexual relations; ***par ~ à*** compared with; ***être en ~ avec*** be in touch with; **rapporter** return, bring/take back; *d'un chien* fetch; COMM bring in; *relater* report; ***se ~ à*** be connected with; **rapporteur** *m* reporter; *enfant* sneak
rapprochement *m fig* reconciliation; POL rapprochement; *analogie* connection; **rapprocher** bring closer (***de*** to); *établir un lien* connect; ***se ~*** come closer
rapt *m* abduction
raquette *f* racket
rare rare; *marchandises* scarce; (*peu dense*) sparse; **raréfier**: ***se ~*** become rare; *de l'air* become rarefied; **rarement** rarely; **rareté** *f* rarity

ras short; ***rempli à ~ bord*** full to the brim; ***faire table ~e*** make a clean sweep
raser shave; *barbe* shave off; (*démolir*) raze to the ground; *murs* hug; F (*ennuyer*) bore
rasoir *m* razor; ***~ électrique*** electric shaver
rassasier satisfy
rassembler collect, assemble; ***se ~*** gather
rasseoir replace; ***se ~*** sit down again
rassis stale; *fig* sedate
rassurer reassure; ***rassurez-vous*** don't be concerned
rat *m* rat
ratatiner: ***se ~*** shrivel up
rate *f* ANAT spleen
raté, **~e 1** *adj* unsuccessful; *occasion* missed **2** *m/f personne* failure
râteau *m* rake
rater 1 *v/t* miss; *examen* fail **2** *v/i d'une arme* misfire; *d'un projet* fail
ration *f* ration; *fig* (fair) share
rationaliser rationalize; **rationnel**, **~le** rational; **rationner** ration
ratisser rake; (*fouiller*) search
rattacher *chien* tie up again; *cheveux* put up again; *lacets* do up again; *conduites d'eau* connect; *idées* connect; ***se ~ à*** be linked to
rattraper recapture; *objet qui tombe* catch; (*rejoindre*) catch up (with); *retard* make up; *imprudence* make up for; ***se ~*** make up for it; (*se raccrocher*) get caught
rature *f* deletion
rauque hoarse
ravages *mpl* devastation; ***les ~ du temps*** the ravages of time; **ravager** devastate
ravaler swallow; *façade* clean up
rave *f*: ***céléri ~*** celeriac
rave *f* rave
ravi delighted (***de*** with; ***de faire*** to do)
ravir (*enchanter*) delight
raviser: ***se ~*** change one's mind
ravissant delightful
ravisseur, **-euse** *m/f* abductor
ravitaillement *m* supplying; *en carburant* refueling, *Br* refuelling; **ravitailler** supply; *en carburant* refuel
raviver revive
rayé striped; *papier* lined; *verre*, *carrosserie* scratched; **rayer** scratch; *mot* score *ou* scratch out
rayon *m* ray; MATH radius; *d'une roue* spoke; (*étagère*) shelf; *de magasin* department; ***~ laser*** laser beam; **rayonner** *de chaleur* radiate; *d'un visage* shine; ***~ de*** *fig* radiate
rayure *f* stripe; *sur un meuble*, *du verre* scratch
raz *m*: ***~ de marée*** tidal wave

réacteur *m* reactor; AVIAT jet engine; **réaction** *f* reaction; ***avion** m* ***à ~*** jet (aircraft); **réactionnaire** *m/f & adj* reactionary
réagir react (***à*** to; ***contre*** against)
réalisable feasible; **réalisateur, -trice** *m/f* director; **réalisation** *f d'un projet* execution, realization; *création, œuvre* creation; *d'un film* direction; **réaliser** *projet* carry out; *rêve* fulfill, *Br* fulfil; *vente* make; *film* direct; *bien, capital* realize; (*se rendre compte*) realize; ***se ~*** *d'un rêve* come true; *d'un projet* be carried out
réalisme *m* realism; **réaliste 1** *adj* realistic **2** *m/f* realist; **réalité** *f* reality
réanimer resuscitate
rébarbatif, -ive off-putting, daunting
rebelle 1 *adj* rebellious **2** *m/f* rebel; **rebeller**: ***se ~*** rebel; **rébellion** *f* rebellion
rebondir bounce; (*faire un ricochet*) rebound; ***faire ~ qch*** *fig* get sth going again; **rebondissement** *m fig* unexpected development
rebord *m* edge; *d'une fenêtre* sill
rebours *m*: ***compte*** *m* ***à ~*** countdown
rebrousser: ***~ chemin*** retrace one's footsteps
rebut *m* dregs *pl*; ***mettre au ~*** get rid of
rebuter (*décourager*) dishearten; (*choquer*) offend
récapituler recap
récemment recently
recenser *population* take a census of
récent recent
récépissé *m* receipt
récepteur *m* receiver
réception *f* reception; *d'une lettre, de marchandises* receipt; **réceptionniste** *m/f* receptionist, desk clerk
récession *f* ÉCON recession
recette *f* COMM takings *pl*; CUIS, *fig* recipe
recevoir receive; ***être reçu à un examen*** pass an exam
rechange *m*: ***de ~*** spare *atr*
rechargeable *pile* rechargeable; **recharger** *camion, arme* reload; *accumulateur* recharge; *briquet* refill
réchaud *m* stove
réchauffement *m* warming; ***~ de la planète*** global warming; **réchauffer** warm up
recherche *f* search (***de*** for); *scientifique* research; ***~s*** *de la police* search; **rechercher** look for, search for; (*prendre*) fetch
rechute *f* MÉD relapse
récif *m* reef
récipient *m* container
réciproque reciprocal
récit *m* account; (*histoire*) story; **réciter** recite
réclamation *f* claim; (*protes-*

tation) complaint
réclame *f* advertisement
réclamer *secours, aumône* ask for; *son dû* claim; (*nécessiter*) call for
réclusion *f* imprisonment
récolte *f* harvesting; *de produits* harvest, crop; *fig* crop; **récolter** harvest
recommander recommend; *lettre* register
recommencer start again
récompense *f* reward; **récompenser** reward (**de** for)
réconcilier reconcile
reconduire: **~ qn** *chez lui* take s.o. home; *à la porte* see s.o. out
réconforter console, comfort
reconnaissance *f* recognition; *d'une faute* acknowledg(e)ment; (*gratitude*) gratitude; MIL reconnaissance; **reconnaissant** grateful (**de** for); **reconnaître** recognize; *faute* acknowledge; **se ~** *de deux personnes* recognize each other; **se ~ à** be recognizable by; **reconnu** known
reconstituer reconstitute; *ville, maison* restore; *événement* reconstruct
reconstruire rebuild
reconvertir: **se ~** retrain
recopier *notes* copy out
record *m* record; **recordman** *m* record holder; **recordwoman** *f* record holder
recourbé bent
recours *m* recourse, resort; **avoir ~ à** resort to
recouvrer recover; *santé* regain
recouvrir recover; *enfant* cover up again; (*couvrir entièrement*) cover (**de** with); (*cacher, embrasser*) cover
récréation *f* relaxation; ÉDU recess, *Br* recreation
récriminations *fpl* recriminations
recrudescence *f* new outbreak
recrue *f* recruit; **recruter** recruit
rectangle *m* rectangle; **rectangulaire** rectangular
rectifier rectify; (*ajuster*) adjust; (*corriger*) correct
recto *m d'une feuille* front
reçu *m* receipt
recueil *m* collection; **recueillir** collect; *personne* take in; **se ~** meditate
recul *m d'un fusil* recoil; *d'une armée* retreat; *de la production* drop; *fig* detachment; **reculer 1** *v/t* push back; *décision* postpone **2** *v/i* back away, recoil; MIL retreat; *d'une voiture* back, reverse; **~ devant** *fig* back away from; **reculons**: **à ~** backward, *Br* backwards
récupérer 1 *v/t* recover, retrieve; *ses forces* regain; *vieux matériel* salvage; *temps* make up **2** *v/i* recover
recyclable recyclable; **recyclage** *m du personnel* re-

training; TECH recycling; **recycler** retrain; TECH recycle
rédacteur, **-trice** *m/f* editor; (*auteur*) writer; **~ en chef** editor-in-chief; **rédaction** *f* editing; (*rédacteurs*) editorial team
redescendre **1** *v/i* come/go down again; **~ d'une voiture** get out of a car again **2** *v/t* bring/take down again; *montagne* come down again
redevable: **être ~ de qc à qn** owe s.o. sth; **redevance** *f d'un auteur* royalty; TV licence fee
rédiger write
redire repeat, say again; (*rapporter*) repeat; **trouver à ~ à** find fault with
redoubler **1** *v/t* double **2** *v/i* ÉDU repeat a class; *d'une tempête* intensify; **~ d'efforts** redouble one's efforts
redoutable formidable; *hiver* harsh; **redouter** dread (**de faire** doing)
redresser *ce qui est courbe* straighten; *ce qui est tombé* set upright; **se ~** *d'un pays* recover
réduction *f* reduction; MÉD setting; **réduire** reduce; *personnel* cut back; **se ~ à** amount to; **réduit** **1** *adj* reduced; *possibilités* limited **2** *m* small room
rééducation *f* MÉD rehabilitation
réel, **~le** real
refaire do again; *examen* retake; *erreur* repeat; *remettre en état*: *maison* do up
réfectoire *m* refectory
référence *f* reference; **~s** (*recommandation*) reference
référendum *m* referendum
référer: **en ~ à** consult; **se ~ à** refer to
réfléchir **1** *v/t* reflect **2** *v/i* think (**à**, **sur** about)
reflet *m de lumière* glint; *dans miroir* reflection (*aussi fig*)
réflexe *m* reflex
réflexion *f* reflection; (*remarque*) remark
réforme *f* reform; **la Réforme** REL the Reformation; **réformer** reform; MIL discharge
refouler push back; PSYCH repress
refrain *m* refrain, chorus
réfréner control
réfrigérateur *m* refrigerator
refroidir cool down; *fig* cool; **se ~** *du temps* get colder; MÉD catch a chill; **refroidissement** *m* cooling; MÉD chill
refuge *m* refuge, shelter; *pour piétons* traffic island; *en montagne* (mountain) hut; **réfugié**, **~e** *m/f* refugee; **réfugier**: **se ~** take shelter
refus *m* refusal; **refuser** refuse; **~ de** *ou* **se ~ à faire** refuse to do
réfuter refute
regagner win back, regain; *endroit* get back to
régal *m* treat; **régaler** regale

(**de** with)
regard *m* look; **regardant** *avec argent* careful with one's money; ***ne pas être ~ sur*** not be too worried about; **regarder 1** *v/t* look at; *télé* watch; (*concerner*) regard, concern; ***~ qn faire qch*** watch s.o. doing sth **2** *v/i* look; ***se ~*** look at o.s.; *de plusieurs personnes* look at each other
régate *f* regatta
régime *m* POL government, régime; MÉD diet; *fiscal* system
région *f* region; ***~ sinistrée*** disaster area; **régional** regional
régir govern
régisseur *m* THÉÂT stage manager; *dans le film* assistant director
réglage *m* adjustment
règle *f* rule; *instrument* ruler; ***en ~ générale*** as a rule; ***~s*** (*menstruation*) period
réglé *organisé* settled; *vie* well-ordered; *papier* ruled
règlement *m* settlement; (*règles*) regulations *pl*; **réglementaire** in accordance with the rules; *tenue* regulation *atr*; **réglementer** control, regulate
régler *affaire* settle; TECH adjust; COMM pay, settle; *épicier etc* pay, settle up with
règne *m* reign; **régner** reign
régression *f* regression
regret *m* regret (**de** about); ***à ~*** with regret, reluctantly; ***être au ~ de faire*** regret to do; **regrettable** regrettable; **regretter** regret; *personne absente* miss; ***~ d'avoir fait qc*** regret doing sth, regret having done sth; ***je ne regrette rien*** I have no regrets; ***je regrette mais ...*** I'm sorry (but) ...
régulariser put in order; *situation* regularize; TECH regulate; **régularité** *f* regularity; *d'élections* legality; **régulier, -ère** regular; *allure, progrès* steady; *écriture* even; (*réglementaire*) lawful; (*correct*) honest; **régulièrement** regularly
réhabiliter rehabilitate; *quartier* renovate, redevelop
rehausser raise; *fig* (*accentuer*) emphasize
rein *m* ANAT kidney; ***~s*** lower back
reine *f* queen
réitérer reiterate
rejaillir spurt
rejeter reject; (*relancer*) throw back; (*vomir*) bring up; *responsabilité, faute* lay (***sur*** on)
rejoindre *personne* join, meet; (*rattraper*) catch up with; MIL rejoin; *autoroute* get back onto; ***se ~*** meet
réjouir make happy, delight; ***se ~ de*** be delighted about; **réjouissance** *f* rejoicing

relâche *f*: ***sans ~*** without a break, nonstop
relâcher *corde, emprise* loosen; *prisonnier* release; ***se ~*** *d'un élève, de la discipline* become slack
relais *m* SP, ÉL relay; ***prendre le ~ de*** take over from
relancer *balle* throw back; *moteur* restart; *fig*: *économie* kickstart; *personne* contact again
relater relate
relatif, **-ive** relative; ***~ à*** relating to; **relation** *f* relationship; (*connaissance*) acquaintance; ***être en ~ avec qn*** be in touch with s.o.; ***~s*** relations; (*connaissances*) contacts; **relativement** relatively; ***~ à*** compared with; (*en ce qui concerne*) relating to; **relativiser** look at in context
relaxer: ***se ~*** relax
relayer take over from; TV, *radio* relay; ***se ~*** take turns
reléguer relegate
relève *f* relief; ***prendre la ~*** take over
relevé **1** *adj manche* turned up; *style* elevated; CUIS spicy **2** *m de compteur* reading; ***~ de compte*** bank statement; **relever** **1** *v/t* raise; (*remettre debout*) pick up; *col, chauffage* turn up; *manches* roll up; *siège* put up; *économie* improve; (*ramasser*) collect; *défi* take up; *faute* find; *adresse, date* copy; (*relayer*) take over from; ***se ~*** get up; *fig* recover **2** *v/i*: ***~ de*** (*dépendre de*) be answerable to; (*ressortir de*) be the responsibility of
relief *m* relief; ***mettre en ~*** *fig* highlight
relier connect (***à*** to); *livre* bind
religieux, **-euse** **1** *adj* religious **2** *m* monk **3** *f* nun; **religion** *f* religion
reliure *f* binding
reluire shine
remanier *texte* re-work; POL reshuffle
remarquable remarkable
remarque *f* remark; **remarquer** notice; (*dire*) remark; ***faire ~ qc à qn*** point sth out to s.o.; ***se faire ~*** *d'un acteur etc* get o.s. noticed; *d'un écolier* get into trouble; *se différencier* be conspicuous
rembourrer stuff
remboursement *m* refund; *de dettes* repayment; **rembourser** *frais* refund, reimburse; *dettes, emprunt* pay back
remède *m* remedy; **remédier**: ***~ à*** remedy
remerciement *m*: ***~s*** thanks; **remercier** thank (***de***, ***pour*** for); (*congédier*) dismiss
remettre put back; *vêtement* put on again; *peine* remit; *décision* postpone; (*ajouter*) add; ***~ qc à qn*** give sth to

s.o.; ***se ~ à qc*** take sth up again; ***se ~ à faire qc*** start doing sth again; ***se ~ de qc*** recover from sth; ***s'en ~ à qn*** rely on s.o.

remise *f* (*hangar*) shed; *d'une lettre* delivery; *de peine* remission; COMM discount; *d'une décision* postponement; ***~ à neuf*** reconditioning; ***~ en question*** questioning

rémission *f* MÉD remission

remonte-pente *m* ski lift

remonter 1 *v/i* come/go up again; *dans une voiture* get back in; *de prix, température* go up again; *d'un avion, chemin* climb, rise **2** *v/t choses* bring/take back up; *rue, escalier* come/go back up; *montre* wind; TECH reassemble; *col* turn up; *stores* raise

remords *mpl* remorse

remorque *f véhicule* trailer; *câble* towrope; **remorquer** *voiture* tow

remplaçant, **~e** *m/f* replacement; **remplacement** *m* replacement; **remplacer** replace (***par*** with)

remplir fill (***de*** with); *formulaire* fill out; *conditions* fulfill, *Br* fulfil; *tâche* carry out; **remplissage** *m* filling

remporter take away; *prix* win

remue-ménage *m* (*agitation*) commotion

remuer 1 *v/t* move (*aussi fig*); *sauce* stir; *salade* toss; *terre* turn over **2** *v/i* move; ***se ~*** move; *fig* F get a move on F

rémunération *f* pay, remuneration; **rémunérer** pay

renaître REL be born again; *fig* be reborn

renard *m* fox

renchérir go up; ***~ sur*** outdo

rencontre *f* meeting; ***aller à la ~ de*** go and meet; **rencontrer** meet; *accueil* meet with; *difficulté* encounter; *amour* find; (*heurter*) hit; ***se ~*** meet

rendement *m* AGR yield; *d'un employé, d'une machine* output; *d'un placement* return

rendez-vous *m* appointment; *amoureux* date; *lieu* meeting place; ***prendre ~*** make an appointment

rendre 1 *v/t* give back; *salut, invitation* return; (*donner*) give; (*traduire*) render; (*vomir*) bring up; MIL surrender; ***~ visite à*** visit **2** *v/i de terre, d'un arbre* yield; ***se ~ à un endroit*** go; MIL surrender; ***se ~ malade*** make o.s. sick

rêne *f* rein

renfermer (*contenir*) contain; ***se ~ dans le silence*** withdraw into silence

renforcer reinforce

renfort *m* reinforcements *pl*; ***à grand ~ de*** with copious amounts of

renier *qn* disown
renifler sniff
renne *m* reindeer
renom *m* (*célébrité*) fame, renown; (*réputation*) reputation; **renommée** *f* fame
renoncement *m* renunciation (**à** of); **renoncer**: **~ à qc** give sth up; **~ à faire** give up doing
renouer 1 *v/t amitié etc* renew **2** *v/i*: **~ avec** get back in touch with; *après brouille* get back together with
renouveler renew; *demande, promesse* repeat; **se ~** (*se reproduire*) happen again; **renouvellement** *m* renewal
rénovation *f* renovation; *fig* (*modernisation*) updating
renseignement *m* piece of information (**sur** about); **~s** information; MIL intelligence; **prendre des ~s sur** find out about; **renseigner**: **~ qn sur qc** tell *ou* inform s.o. about sth; **se ~** find out
rentabilité *f* profitability; **rentable** cost-effective; *entreprise* profitable; **ce n'est pas ~** there's no money in it
rente *f revenu d'un bien* private income; (*pension*) annuity; *versée à sa femme etc* allowance
rentrée *f* return; **~ des classes** beginning of the new school year; **~s** COMM takings
rentrer 1 *v/i* go/come in; *de nouveau* go/come back in; *chez soi* go/come home; *dans un récipient* go in, fit; *de l'argent* come in; **~ dans** (*heurter*) collide with; *serrure, sac* go into; *responsabilités* be part of **2** *v/t* bring/take in; *voiture* put away; *ventre* pull in
renversement *m d'un régime* overthrow; **renverser** *image* reverse; (*mettre à l'envers*) upturn; (*faire tomber*) knock over; *liquide* spill; *gouvernement* overthrow
renvoi *m de personnel* dismissal; *d'un élève* expulsion; *d'une lettre* return; *dans un texte* cross-reference (**à** to); **renvoyer** (*faire retourner*) send back; *ballon* return; *personnel* dismiss; *élève* expel; *rencontre, décision* postpone
repaire *m* den
répandre spread; (*renverser*) spill; **se ~** spread; (*être renversé*) spill; **répandu** widespread
réparation *f* repair; (*compensation*) reparation; **en ~** being repaired; **réparer** repair; *fig* make up for
répartie *f* retort; **avoir de la ~** have a gift for repartee
repartir set off again; **~ de zéro** start again from scratch
répartir share out; *chargement* distribute; *en catégories* divide; **répartition** *f* dis-

tribution; *en catégories* division
repas *m* meal
repassage *m* ironing; **repasser** **1** *v/i* come/go back again **2** *v/t linge* iron; *examen* take again
repentir **1**: ***se ~*** REL repent; ***se ~ de*** be sorry for **2** *m* penitence
répercussions *fpl* repercussions
repère *m* mark; (***point*** *m* ***de***) **~** landmark; **repérer** (*situer*) pinpoint; (*trouver*) find; (*marquer*) mark
répertoire *m* directory; THÉÂT repertoire
répéter repeat; THÉÂT rehearse; **répétition** *f* repetition; THÉÂT rehearsal
répit *m* respite
replacer put back, replace
repli *m* fold; *d'une rivière* bend; **replier** fold; *jambes* draw up; *journal* fold up; *manches* roll up; ***se ~ sur soi-même*** retreat into one's shell
répliquer retort; *d'un enfant* answer back
répondeur *m*: ***~ automatique*** answering machine; **répondre** **1** *v/t* answer, reply **2** *v/i* answer; (*réagir*) respond; ***~ à*** answer, reply to; (*réagir à*) respond to; *besoin* meet; *attente* come up to; *signalement* match; **réponse** *f* answer; (*réaction*) response
reportage *m* report; **reporter** *m/f* reporter
repos *m* rest; **reposer** **1** *v/t* (*remettre*) put back; *question* ask again; (*détendre*) rest; ***se ~*** rest **2** *v/i*: ***~ sur*** rest on
repoussant repulsive; **repousser** **1** *v/t* (*dégoûter*) repel; (*différer*) postpone; *pousser en arrière*, MIL push back; (*rejeter*) reject **2** *v/i* grow again
reprendre **1** *v/t* take back; (*prendre davantage de*) take more; *ville* recapture; (*recommencer*) start again; (*corriger*) correct; *entreprise* take over (***à*** from) **2** *v/i* (*recommencer*) start again; ***se ~*** (*se corriger*) correct o.s.; (*se maîtriser*) pull o.s. together
représailles *fpl* reprisals
représentant, **~e** *m/f* representative; **représentation** *f* representation; *au théâtre* performance; **représenter** represent; THÉÂT perform; ***se ~ qc*** imagine sth
répression *f* repression; ***mesures*** *fpl* ***de ~*** crackdown (***contre*** on)
réprimander reprimand
réprimer suppress
reprise *f de ville* recapture; *de marchandise* taking back; *de travail*, *de lutte* resumption; ***à plusieurs ~s*** on several occasions
repriser darn, mend

reproche *m* reproach; **reprocher** reproach; ~ ***qch à qn*** reproach s.o. for sth
reproduction *f* reproduction; **reproduire** reproduce; ***se*** ~ happen again; BIOL reproduce
républicain, ~**e** *m/f & adj* republican; **république** *f* republic
répugnant repugnant; **répugner**: ~ ***à*** be repelled by; ~ ***à faire*** be reluctant to do
répulsion *f* repulsion
réputation *f* reputation
requérir require
requête *f* request
requin *m* shark
requis necessary
réseau *m* network
réservation *f* booking, reservation
réserve *f* reserve; (*entrepôt*) storeroom; ***sans*** ~ unreservedly; ***sous*** ~ ***de*** subject to
réserver reserve; *dans hôtel, restaurant* book, reserve; (*mettre de côté*) put aside; ~ ***qc à qn*** keep *ou* save sth for s.o.
réservoir *m* tank; *lac etc* reservoir
résidence *f* residence; ~ ***universitaire*** dormitory, *Br* hall of residence; **résider** live; ~ ***dans*** *fig* lie in
résidu *m* residue; MATH remainder
résigner resign; ***se*** ~ resign o.s. (***à*** to)
resilier *contrat* cancel
résistance *f* resistance; (*endurance*) stamina; *d'un matériau* strength; ***la Résistance*** HIST the Resistance; **résister** resist; ~ ***à*** *tentation, personne* resist; *sécheresse* withstand
résolu determined (***à faire*** to do); **résolution** *f* (*décision*) resolution; (*fermeté*) determination; *d'un problème* solving
résonner echo, resound
résoudre 1 *v/t problème* solve **2** *v/i*: ~ ***de faire, se*** ~ ***à faire*** decide to do
respect *m* respect; **respecter** respect; ~ ***le(s) délai(s)*** meet the deadline; ***se*** ~ have some self-respect; *mutuellement* respect each other; ***se faire*** ~ command respect; **respectif**, **-ive** respective; **respectueux**, **-euse** respectful
respiration *f* breathing; ***retenir sa*** ~ hold one's breath; ~ ***artificielle*** MÉD artificial respiration; **respirer** breathe
resplendir glitter
responsabilité *f* responsibility (***de*** for); JUR liability; **responsable** responsible (***de*** for)
ressaisir: ***se*** ~ pull o.s. together
ressemblance *f* resemblance; **ressembler**: ~ ***à*** resemble, be like; ***se*** ~ resem-

ble each other, be like each other
ressemeler resole
ressentiment *m* resentment
ressentir feel; ***se ~ de*** still feel the effects of
resserrer tighten; *fig*: *amitié* strengthen
ressort *m* TECH spring; *fig* motive; (*énergie*) energy; (*compétence*) province; JUR jurisdiction
ressortir 1 come/go out again **2** (*se détacher*) stand out; ***faire ~*** bring out; ***~ à*** JUR fall within the jurisdiction of
ressource *f* resource
restant 1 *adj* remaining **2** *m* remainder
restaurant *m* restaurant
restauration *f* catering; ART restoration; ***~ rapide*** fast food; **restaurer** restore
reste *m* rest, remainder; ***~s*** CUIS leftovers; ***du ~, au ~*** moreover; **rester** (*subsister*) be left, remain; (*demeurer*) stay, remain; ***on en reste là*** we'll stop there; ***il reste du vin*** there's some wine left
restituer (*rendre*) return; (*reconstituer*) restore; **restitution** *f* restitution
restreindre restrict
restriction *f* restriction; ***sans ~*** unreservedly
résultat *m* result; **résulter** result (***de*** from)
résumé *m* summary
rétablir restore; ***se ~*** recover
retard *m* lateness; *dans travail*, *paiement* delay; ***avoir deux heures de ~*** be two hours late; ***avoir du ~ sur qn*** be behind s.o.; ***être en ~*** be late; **retarder 1** *v/t* delay, hold up; *montre* put back **2** *v/i d'une montre* be slow; ***~ de cinq minutes*** be five minutes slow; ***~ sur son temps*** *fig* be behind the times
retenir *personne* keep; *argent* withhold; (*rappeler*) remember; *proposition* accept; (*réserver*) reserve; ***se ~*** restrain o.s.
retentir sound; *du tonnerre* boom; ***~ sur*** impact on; **retentissant** resounding (*aussi fig*)
retenu (*réservé*) reserved; (*empêché*) delayed
retenue *f sur salaire* deduction; *fig* (*modération*) restraint
réticence *f* (*omission*) omission; (*hésitation*) hesitation
retirer withdraw; *vêtement* take off; *promesse* take back; *profit* derive; ***~ qch de*** remove sth from; ***se ~*** withdraw; (*prendre sa retraite*) retire
retombées *fpl* fallout; **retomber** fall again; (*tomber*) land; *de cheveux*, *d'un rideau* fall; ***~ dans qc*** sink back into sth

rétorsion POL: ***mesure** f **de ~*** retaliatory measure
retoucher *texte, vêtement* alter; *photographie* retouch
retour *m* return; ***être de ~*** be back; ***bon ~!*** have a good trip home!; **retourner 1** *v/i* return, go back; ***~ sur ses pas*** backtrack **2** *v/t matelas, tête* turn; *lettre* return; *vêtement* turn inside out; ***se ~*** *au lit* turn over (*aussi* AUTO); (*tourner la tête*) turn (around)
retrait *m* withdrawal; ***en ~*** set back
retraite *f* retirement; (*pension*) retirement pension; MIL retreat; ***prendre sa ~*** retire; **retraité, ~e** *m/f* pensioner, retired person
retrancher (*enlever*) remove, cut (**de** from); (*déduire*) deduct
rétrécir 1 *v/t* shrink; *fig* narrow **2** *v/i de tissu* shrink; ***se ~*** narrow
rétrograder 1 *v/t* demote **2** *v/i* retreat; AUTO downshift
rétrospectif, -ive 1 *adj* retrospective **2** *f*: ***rétrospective*** retrospective
retrousser *manches* roll up
retrouver (*trouver*) find; *de nouveau* find again; (*rejoindre*) meet; *santé* regain; ***se ~*** meet; ***se ~ seul*** find o.s. alone
rétroviseur *m* AUTO rear-view mirror
réunion *f* meeting; POL reunion; **réunir** bring together; *pays* reunite; *documents* collect; ***se ~*** meet
réussi successful; **réussir 1** *v/i* succeed; ***~ à faire*** manage to do, succeed in doing **2** *v/t vie, projet* make a success of; *examen* be successful in;
réussite *f* success; *aux cartes* solitaire, *Br aussi* patience
revanche *f* revenge; ***en ~*** on the other hand
rêve *m* dream
réveil *m* awakening; (*pendule*) alarm (clock); **réveiller** wake up; *fig* revive; ***se ~*** wake up
révélation *f* revelation; **révéler** reveal; ***se ~ faux*** prove to be false
revenant *m* ghost
revendeur, -euse *m/f* retailer
revendication *f* claim, demand; **revendiquer** claim
revendre resell
revenir come back, return (**à** to); ***~ sur*** *thème* go back to; *décision* go back on; ***~ à qn*** *d'une part* be due to s.o.; ***~ de*** *évanouissement* come around from; *étonnement* get over; *illusion* lose
revenu *m* income; ***~s*** revenue
rêver dream (**de**, **à** about)
réverbère *m* street lamp
rêverie *f* daydream
revers *m* back; *d'un pantalon* cuff, *Br* turn-up; *fig* (*échec*) reversal

revêtir *vêtement* put on; *forme, caractère* assume; *importance* take on
rêveur, -euse 1 *adj* dreamy **2** *m/f* dreamer
revirement *m*: **~ *d'opinion*** sudden change in the public's attitude
réviser *texte* revise; *machine* service; **révision** *f* revision; AUTO service
révocation *f* revocation; *d'un dirigeant etc* dismissal
revoir 1 *v/t* see again; *texte* review; ÉDU review, *Br* revise **2** *m*: ***au ~!*** goodbye!
révolte *f* revolt; **révolter** revolt; ***se ~*** rebel, revolt
révolution *f* revolution; **révolutionner** revolutionize
revolver *m* revolver
révoquer *fonctionnaire* dismiss; *contrat* revoke
revue *f* review; ***passer en ~*** *fig* review
rez-de-chaussée *m* first floor, *Br* ground floor
rhubarbe *f* rhubarb
rhum *m* rum
rhumatismes *mpl* rheumatism
rhume *m* cold; ***~ des foins*** hay fever
ricaner sneer; *bêtement* snigger
riche rich; *sol* fertile; *décoration* elaborate; **richesse** *f* wealth; *du sol* fertility
rictus *m* grimace
ride *f* wrinkle, line
rideau *m* drape, *Br* curtain
rider *peau* wrinkle; ***se ~*** become wrinkled
ridicule 1 *adj* ridiculous **2** *m* ridicule; (*absurdité*) ridiculousness; **ridiculiser** ridicule; ***se ~*** make a fool of o.s.
rien 1 *pron* nothing; *quelque chose* anything; ***de ~*** *comme réponse* you're welcome; ***ne … ~*** nothing, not anything **2** *m* trifle; ***en un ~ de temps*** in no time
rigide rigid
rigole *f* (*conduit*) channel
rigoler F (*plaisanter*) joke; (*rire*) laugh
rigolo, ~te F (*amusant*) funny
rigoureux, -euse rigorous; **rigueur** *f* rigor, *Br* rigour; ***à la ~*** if absolutely necessary; ***de ~*** compulsory
rincer rinse
riposte *f* riposte, response; *avec armes* return of fire; **riposter** reply, response; *avec armes* return fire
rire 1 *v/i* laugh (***de*** about, at); (*s'amuser*) have fun; ***~ aux éclats*** roar with laughter; ***~ de qn*** laugh at s.o. **2** *m* laugh; ***~s*** laughter
risque *m* risk; ***à tes ~s et périls*** at your own risk; **risqué** risky; *plaisanterie* risqué; **risquer** risk; ***~ de faire*** risk doing; ***se ~ dans*** venture into
rituel, ~le *adj & m* ritual
rivage *m* shore

rival, **~e** *m/f & adj* rival; **rivaliser** compete, vie; **rivalité** *f* rivalry
rive *f d'un fleuve* bank; *d'une mer, d'un lac* shore
riverain, **~e** *m/f* resident
rivet *m* TECH rivet
rivière *f* river
riz *m* BOT rice
robe *f* dress; *d'un juge* robe; ***~ de chambre*** robe, *Br* dressing gown
robinet *m* faucet, *Br* tap
robuste robust
roche *f* rock
rocher *m* rock; **rocheux**, **-euse** rocky
rôder prowl
rogne *f*: ***être en ~*** F be in a bad mood
rogner cut, trim
rognon *m* CUIS kidney
roi *m* king
rôle *m* role; (*registre*) roll; ***à tour de ~*** turn and turn about
roman *m* novel
romancier, **-ère** *m/f* novelist
romantique *m/f & adj* romantic; **romantisme** *m* romanticism
romarin *m* BOT rosemary
rompre 1 *v/i* break; ***~ avec*** *petit ami* break it off with; *tradition* break with; *habitude* break **2** *v/t* break; *négociations, fiançailles* break off
ronce *f* BOT: ***~s*** brambles
rond, **~e 1** *adj* round; *joues, personne* plump; F (*ivre*) drunk **2** *adv*: ***tourner ~*** run smoothly **3** *m figure* circle *m* **4** *f*: ***faire sa ronde*** do one's rounds; *de soldat, policier* be on patrol; ***à la ronde*** around
rondelle *f* disk, *Br* disc; *de saucisson* slice; TECH washer
rondement (*promptement*) briskly; (*carrément*) frankly
rond-point *m* traffic circle, *Br* roundabout
ronflement *m* snoring; *d'un moteur* purr; **ronfler** snore; *d'un moteur* purr
ronger gnaw at; *fig* torment; ***se ~ les ongles*** bite one's nails; **rongeur** *m* ZO rodent
ronronner purr
rosbif *m* CUIS roast beef
rose 1 *f* BOT rose **2** *m couleur* pink **3** *adj* pink
rosé 1 *m* rosé **2** *adj* pinkish
roseau *m* BOT reed
rosée *f* dew
rosier *m* rose bush
rossignol *m* ZO nightingale
rot *m* F belch; **roter** F belch
rôti *m* roast; **rôtir** roast; **rôtisserie** *f* grill-room
rouage *m* cogwheel; ***~s*** *d'une montre* works; *fig* machinery
roue *f* wheel; ***deux ~s*** *m* two-wheeler; ***quatre ~s motrices*** all-wheel drive
roué crafty
rouer: ***~ qn de coups*** beat s.o. black and blue
rouge 1 *adj* red **2** *adv fig*: ***voir ~*** see red **3** *m* red; ***~ à lèvres***

lipstick
rouge-gorge *m* robin (redbreast)
rougeole *f* MÉD measles *sg*
rougir go red; *d'une personne aussi* blush (***de*** with); *de colère* flush (***de*** with)
rouille *f* rust; **rouillé** rusty; **rouiller** rust; ***se ~*** rust; *fig* go rusty
rouleau *m* roller; *de pellicule etc* roll; CUIS rolling pin
rouler 1 *v/i* roll; *d'une voiture* travel; ***~ sur qc*** *d'une conversation* be about sth **2** *v/t* roll; ***~ qn*** F cheat s.o.
roulette *f de meubles* caster; *jeu* roulette
roumain, **~e 1** *adj* Romanian **2** *m langue* Romanian; **Roumain**, **~e** *m/f* Romanian; **Roumanie**: ***la ~*** Romania
rouspéter F complain
rousseur *f*: ***taches*** *fpl* ***de ~*** freckles
route *f* road; (*parcours*) route; *fig* (*chemin*) path; ***en ~*** on the way; ***se mettre en ~*** set off; *fig* get under way; ***faire ~ vers*** be heading for
routier, **-ère 1** *adj* road *atr* **2** *m* (*conducteur*) truck driver, *Br* long-distance lorry driver; *restaurant* truck stop, *Br aussi* transport café
routine *f* routine; ***de ~*** routine *atr*
roux, **rousse** *personne* red-haired; *cheveux* red
royal royal; *fig*: *pourboire*, *accueil* superb, right royal
royaume *m* kingdom; **le Royaume-Uni** the United Kingdom
R.-U. (= ***Royaume-Uni***) UK (= United Kingdom)
ruban *m* ribbon; ***~ adhésif*** adhesive tape
rubéole *f* MÉD German measles *sg*
rubrique *f* heading
ruche *f* hive
rude *manières* uncouth; (*sévère*) harsh; *travail*, *lutte* hard
rudimentaire rudimentary; **rudiments** *mpl* rudiments
rue *f* street; ***dans la ~*** on the street
ruée *f* rush
ruelle *f* alley
rugby *m* rugby
rugir roar; *du vent* howl
rugueux, **-euse** rough
ruine *f* ruin; **ruiner** ruin
ruisseau *m* stream; (*caniveau*) gutter
ruisseler run
rumeur *f* hum; *de personnes* murmuring; (*nouvelle*) rumor, *Br* rumour
ruminer 1 *v/i* chew the cud, ruminate **2** *v/t fig*: ***~ qch*** mull sth over
rupture *f* breaking; *fig* split; *de négociations* breakdown; *de relations* breaking off; *de contrat* breach
ruse *f* ruse; ***la ~*** cunning; **rusé** crafty, cunning

russe 1 *adj* Russian **2** *m langue* Russian; **Russe** *m/f* Russian; **Russie**: ***la ~*** Russia
rustique rustic
rustre *péj* **1** *adj* uncouth **2** *m* oaf
rythme *m* rhythm; (*vitesse*) pace; **rythmique** rhythmical

S

sa → ***son***[1]
S.A. *f* (= ***société anonyme***) Inc, *Br* plc
sable *m* sand; **sabler** sand; ***~ le champagne*** break open the champagne
sablier *m* CUIS eggtimer
sabot *m* clog; ZO hoof
sabotage *m* sabotage; **saboter** sabotage; F *travail* make a mess of
sac *m* bag; *de pommes de terre* sack; ***~ de couchage*** sleeping bag; ***~ à dos*** backpack; ***~ à main*** purse, *Br* handbag
saccadé *mouvements* jerky; *voix* breathless
saccager (*piller*) sack; (*détruire*) destroy
saccharine *f* saccharine
sachet *m* sachet; ***~ de thé*** teabag
sacoche *f* bag; *de vélo* saddlebag
sacré sacred; F damn F
sacrement *m* REL sacrament
sacrifice *m* sacrifice; **sacrifier** sacrifice; ***se ~*** sacrifice o.s.
sacrilège 1 *adj* sacrilegious **2** *m* sacrilege
sadique 1 *adj* sadistic **2** *m/f* sadist
safran *m* saffron
sagace shrewd; **sagacité** *f* shrewdness
sage 1 *adj* wise; *enfant* good **2** *m* sage, wise man; **sage-femme** *f* midwife; **sagesse** *f* wisdom; *d'un enfant* goodness
Sagittaire *m* ASTROL Sagittarius
saignant bleeding; CUIS rare; **saigner 1** *v/i* bleed **2** *v/t fig* bleed dry
saillant *pommettes* prominent; *fig* salient; **saillie** *f* ARCH projection; *fig* quip; **saillir** ARCH project
sain healthy; *gestion* sound; ***~ d'esprit*** sane
saint, **~e 1** *adj* holy **2** *m/f* saint; **sainteté** *f* holiness; **Saint-Sylvestre**: ***la ~*** New Year's Eve
saisie *f* seizure; ***~ de données*** INFORM data capture; **saisir** seize; *sens*, *intention* grasp; INFORM capture; **saisissant** striking; *froid* penetrating
saison *f* season; **saisonnier**,

-ère 1 *adj* seasonal 2 *m ouvrier* seasonal worker
salade *f* salad; **saladier** *m* salad bowl
salaire *m d'un ouvrier* wages *pl*; *d'un employé* salary; **~ net** take-home pay
salarié, ~e 1 *adj travail* paid 2 *m/f ouvrier* wage-earner; *employé* salaried employee
salaud *m* P bastard P
sale *après le substantif* dirty; *devant le substantif* nasty
salé *eau* salt; CUIS salted; *histoire* daring; *prix* steep; **saler** salt
saleté *f* dirtiness; **~s** *fig* (*grossièretés*) filthy remarks; F *choses sans valeur, mauvaise nourriture* junk
salière *f* salt cellar
salir: **~ qch** get sth dirty
salive *f* saliva
salle *f* room; **~ d'attente** waiting room; **~ d'eau** shower room; **~ à manger** dining room
salon *m* living room; *d'un hôtel* lounge; (*foire*) show; **~ de l'automobile** auto show, *Br* motor show; **~ de thé** tea room
salope *f* P bitch; **saloperie** *f* F *chose sans valeur* piece of junk; (*bassesse*) dirty trick
salopette *f* dungarees *pl*
salubre healthy
saluer greet; MIL salute; **~ qn (de la main)** wave to s.o.
salut *m* greeting; MIL salute; (*sauvegarde*) safety; REL salvation; **~!** F hi!; (*au revoir*) bye!
salutaire salutary
samedi *m* Saturday
sanction *f* sanction
sanctuaire *m* sanctuary
sandale *f* sandal
sandwich *m* sandwich
sang *m* blood; **sang-froid** *m* composure; **garder son ~** keep one's cool; **tuer qn de ~** kill s.o. in cold blood;
sanglant bloodstained; *combat, mort* bloody
sanglot *m* sob; **sangloter** sob
sanguin blood *atr*; *tempérament* sanguine; **groupe** *m* **~** blood group
sanitaire sanitary
sans without; **~ manger** without eating; **~ balcon** without a balcony
sans-abri *m/f*: **les ~** the homeless *pl*
sans-emploi *m*: **les ~** the unemployed *pl*
santé *f* health; **à votre ~!** cheers!, your very good health!
saper undermine
sapeur-pompier *m* firefighter
saphir *m* sapphire
sapin *m* BOT fir
sarcasme *m* sarcasm; **sarcastique** sarcastic
sardine *f* sardine
sardonique sardonic
S.A.R.L. *f* (= **société à res-**

***ponsabilité limitée*)** Inc, *Br* Ltd
satellite *m* satellite
satin *m* satin
satirique satirical
satisfaction *f* satisfaction; **satisfaire 1** *v/i*: **~ à 2** *v/t* satisfy; *attente* come up to; **satisfaisant** satisfactory; **satisfait** satisfied (**de** with)
saturer saturate
sauce *f* sauce
saucisse *f* sausage
saucisson *m* (dried) sausage
sauf[1] *prép* except; ***~ avis contraire*** unless you/I / *etc* hear to the contrary
sauf[2], **sauve** *adj* safe
sauf-conduit *m* safe-conduct
saugrenu ridiculous
saule *m* BOT willow; ***~ pleureur*** weeping willow
saumon *m* salmon
sauna *m* sauna
saupoudrer sprinkle (**de** with)
saut *m* jump; ***faire un ~ chez qn*** *fig* drop in briefly on s.o.; ***~ à l'élastique*** bungee jumping; ***~ en longueur*** broad jump, *Br* long jump; ***~ à la perche*** pole vault
sauter 1 *v/i* jump; (*exploser*) blow up; *d'un fusible* blow; *d'un bouton* come off; ***~ sur*** *personne* pounce on; *occasion, offre* jump at; ***cela saute aux yeux*** it's obvious **2** *v/t fossé* jump (over); *mot, repas* skip
sauterelle *f* grasshopper
sautiller hop
sauvage 1 *adj* wild; (*insociable*) unsociable; (*primitif, barbare*) savage; *pas autorisé* unauthorized **2** *m/f* savage; (*solitaire*) unsociable person
sauvegarde *f* safeguard; INFORM back-up
sauver save; *personne en danger* save, rescue; *navire* salvage; ***se ~*** run away; F (*partir*) be off; (*déborder*) boil over
sauvetage *m* rescue; *de navire* salvaging; **sauveteur** *m* rescuer
sauveur *m* savior, *Br* saviour
savant 1 *adj* (*érudit*) learned; (*habile*) skillful, *Br* skilful **2** *m* scientist
saveur *f* taste
savoir 1 *v/t & v/i* know; ***sais-tu nager?*** can you swim?, do you know how to swim? **2** *m* knowledge
savoir-faire *m* expertise, knowhow
savoir-vivre *m* good manners *pl*
savon *m* soap
savourer savor, *Br* savour; **savoureux, -euse** tasty; *fig*: *récit* spicy
saxophone *m* saxophone, sax
scandale *m* scandal; ***faire ~*** cause a scandal; ***faire tout un ~*** make a scene; **scanda-**

liser scandalize; ***se ~ de*** be shocked by
scanner 1 *v/t* scan **2** *m* scanner
scaphandrier *m* diver
scarlatine *f* scarlet fever
sceau *m* seal; *fig* (*marque, signe*) stamp
scellé *m* official seal; **sceller** seal
scénario *m* scenario; (*script*) screenplay; ***~ catastrophe*** worst-case scenario
scène *f* scene (*aussi fig*); (*plateau*) stage; ***mettre en ~*** *pièce, film* direct; *présenter* stage; ***~ de ménage*** domestic argument
sceptique 1 *adj* skeptical, *Br* sceptical **2** *m* skeptic, *Br* sceptic
schéma *m* diagram; **schématiser** oversimplify
sciatique *f* sciatica
scie *f* saw; *fig* F bore
sciemment knowingly
science *f* science; (*connaissance*) knowledge; **scientifique 1** *adj* scientific **2** *m/f* scientist
scier saw; *branche etc* saw off
scinder *fig* split; ***se ~*** split up
scintiller sparkle
scission *f* split
scolaire school *atr*; *succès, échec* academic; **scolarité** *f* education, schooling
scooter *m* (motor) scooter
score *m* SP score; POL share of the vote
scorpion *m* ZO scorpion; ASTROL ***Scorpion*** Scorpio
scotch® *m* Scotch tape®, *Br* sellotape®
scrupule *m* scruple; **scrupuleux, -euse** scrupulous
scruter scrutinize
scrutin *m* ballot; ***~ majoritaire*** majority vote system; ***~ proportionnel*** proportional representation
sculpter sculpt; *pierre* carve; **sculpteur** *m* sculptor; **sculpture** *f* sculpture
SDF *m/f* (= ***sans domicile fixe***) homeless person
se *réfléchi masculin* himself; *féminin* herself; *chose, animal* itself; *pluriel* themselves; *avec 'one'* oneself; *réciproque* each other; ***cela ne ~ fait pas*** that isn't done; ***ils ~ lèvent à ...*** they get up at ...
séance *f* session; *de cinéma* show, performance; ***~ tenante*** *fig* immediately
seau *m* bucket
sec, sèche 1 *adj* dry; *fruits, légumes* dried; (*maigre*) thin; *réponse, ton* curt **2** *m*: ***tenir au ~*** keep in a dry place **3** *adv boire* neat, straight
sèche-cheveux *m* hair dryer; **sèche-linge** *m* clothes dryer; **sécher** dry; *d'un lac* dry up; **sécheresse** *f* dryness; *manque de pluie* drought; *de réponse, ton* curtness

second, **~e 1** *adj* second **2** *m* *étage* third floor, *Br* second floor; (*adjoint*) second in command **3** *f* second; *en train* second class; **secondaire** secondary; **seconder** *personne* assist
secouer shake; *poussière* shake off
secouriste *m/f* first-aider; **secours** *m* help; *matériel* aid; ***au ~!*** help!; ***sortie** f **de ~*** emergency exit; ***premiers ~s*** first aid
secousse *f* jolt; *électrique* shock; *tellurique* tremor
secret, **-ète 1** *adj* secret **2** *m* secret; (*discrétion*) secrecy; ***en ~*** in secret
secrétaire 1 *m/f* secretary **2** *m* writing desk
secrétariat *m* secretariat; *profession* secretarial work
secte *f* REL sect
secteur *m* sector; (*zone*) area, district; ÉL mains *pl*
section *f* section; **sectionner** (*couper*) sever; *région etc* divide up
séculaire a hundred years old; *très ancien* centuries-old
séculier, **-ère** secular
sécurité *f* security; (*manque de danger*) safety; ***Sécurité sociale*** welfare, *Br* social security; ***être en ~*** be safe
sédatif *m* sedative
sédentaire sedentary; *population* settled
séduction *f* seduction; *fig* (*charme*) attraction; **séduire** seduce; *fig* (*charmer*) appeal to; *d'une personne* charm; **séduisant** appealing; *personne* attractive
ségrégation *f* segregation
seigle *m* AGR rye
seigneur *m* HIST the lord of the manor; REL: ***le Seigneur*** the Lord
sein *m* breast; *fig* bosom; ***au ~ de*** within
seize sixteen; **seizième** sixteenth
séjour *m* stay; (***salle** f **de***) **~** living room; **séjourner** stay
sel *m* salt
sélection *f* selection; **sélectionner** select
selle *f* saddle; MÉD stool
selon according to; ***~ moi*** in my opinion; ***c'est ~*** it all depends
semaine *f* week; ***à la ~*** by the week; ***en ~*** during the week, on weekdays
semblable 1 *adj* similar; *tel* such; ***~ à*** like, similar to **2** *m* (*être humain*) fellow human being
semblant *m* semblance; ***faire ~ de faire*** pretend to do
sembler seem
semelle *f* sole; *pièce intérieure* insole
semence *f* AGR seed
semer sow; *fig* (*répandre*) spread; ***~ qn*** F shake s.o. off
semestre *m* half-year

séminaire *m* seminar; REL seminary
semi-remorque *m* semi, *Br* articulated lorry
semonce *f* reproach
semoule *f* CUIS semolina
Sénat *m* POL Senate; **sénateur** *m* senator
sénile senile
sens *m* sense; (*direction*) direction; **~ *interdit*** no entry; **~ *dessus dessous*** upside down; **~ *de l'humour*** sense of humor *ou Br* humour; (***rue*** *f* ***à***) **~ *unique*** one-way street
sensation *f* feeling, sensation; *effet de surprise* sensation; ***faire* ~** cause a sensation; **sensationnel**, **~le** sensational
sensé sensible
sensibilité *f* sensitivity; **sensible** sensitive; (*notable*) appreciable; **sensiblement** appreciably; *plus ou moins* more or less
sensualité *f* sensuality; **sensuel**, **~le** sensual
sentence *f* JUR sentence
sentier *m* path
sentiment *m* feeling; **sentimental** *vie* love *atr*; *péj* sentimental
sentinelle *f* MIL guard
sentir 1 *v/t* feel; (*humer*) smell; (*dégager une odeur de*) smell of; ***se* ~ *bien*** feel well **2** *v/i*: **~ *bon*** smell good
séparable separable; **séparation** *f* separation; (*cloison*) partition; **séparatisme** *m* POL separatism; **séparé** separate; *époux* separated; **séparément** separately; **séparer** separate; ***se* ~** separate
sept seven
septembre *m* September
septennat *m* term of office (of French President)
septentrional northern
septième seventh
septique septic
séquelles *fpl* MÉD after-effects; *fig* aftermath
séquence *f* sequence
serein calm
sérénité *f* serenity
série *f* series *sg*; *de casseroles, timbres* set; SP (*épreuve*) heat; ***hors* ~** *numéro* special; ***fabriquer en* ~** mass-produce
sérieux, **-euse 1** *adj* serious; *entreprise, employé* professional; (*consciencieux*) conscientious **2** *m* seriousness; ***prendre au* ~** take seriously
seringue *f* MÉD syringe
serment *m* oath; ***prêter* ~** take the oath
sermon *m* sermon
séropositif, **-ive** HIV-positive
serpent *m* snake; **serpenter** wind, meander
serpillière *f* floor cloth
serre *f* greenhouse; **~s** ZO talons
serré tight; *pluie* heavy; *per-*

sonnes closely packed; *café* strong

serrer 1 *v/t* (*tenir*) clasp; *ceinture* tighten; *d'un vêtement* be too tight for **2** *v/i*: ***se ~*** (*s'entasser*) squeeze up; ***se ~ contre qn*** press against s.o.

serrure *f* lock; **serrurier** *m* locksmith

serveur *m dans un café* bartender, *Br* barman; *dans un restaurant* waiter; INFORM server

serveuse *f dans un café* bartender, *Br* barmaid; *dans un restaurant* server, waitress

serviable helpful

service *m* service; (*faveur*) favor, *Br* favour; *au tennis* service, serve; *d'une entreprise*, *d'un hôpital* department; ***être de ~*** be on duty; ***rendre ~ à qn*** do s.o. a favor; ***mettre en ~*** put into service; ***hors ~*** out of order

serviette *f* serviette; *de toilette* towel; *pour documents* briefcase; ***~ hygiénique*** sanitary napkin

servile servile

servir serve; (*être utile*) be useful; ***~ à qn*** be of use to s.o.; ***~ à qch/à faire qch*** be used for sth/for doing sth; ***~ de qc*** act as sth; ***se ~*** *à table* help o.s. (**en** to); ***se ~ de*** (*utiliser*) use

ses → ***son***[1]

seuil *m* doorstep; *fig* threshold

seul 1 *adj* alone; (*solitaire*) lonely; *devant le subst* only, sole **2** *adv* alone; ***faire qch tout ~*** do sth all by o.s. *ou* all on one's own

seulement only; ***non ~ ... mais encore*** *ou* ***mais aussi*** not only ... but also

sévère severe; **sévérité** *f* severity

sévices *mpl* abuse

sévir *d'une épidemie* rage; ***~ contre qn*** come down hard on s.o.; ***~ contre qc*** clamp down on sth

sexagénaire *m/f & adj* sixty--year old

sexe *m* sex; *organes* genitals *pl*; **sexiste** *m/f & adj* sexist; **sexualité** *f* sexuality; **sexuel, ~le** sexual

shampo(o)ing *m* shampoo

short *m* shorts *pl*

si 1 *conj* (**s'il, s'ils**) if; ***~ bien que*** with the result that **2** *adv* (*tellement*) so; *après négation* yes; ***de ~ bonnes vacances*** such a good vacation; ***~ riche qu'il soit*** (*subj*) however rich he may be; ***tu ne veux pas? - mais ~!*** you don't want to? - oh yes, I do

sida *m* MÉD Aids

sidéré F thunderstruck

siècle *m* century; *fig* (*époque*) age

siège *m* seat; *d'une entreprise* headquarters *pl*; MIL siege; ~

social COMM head office; **siéger** sit; ***~ à*** *d'une entreprise* be headquartered in

sien: ***le sien, la sienne, les siens, les siennes*** *d'homme* his; *de femme* hers; *de chose*, *d'animal* its; *avec 'one'* one's

sieste *f* siesta, nap

sifflement *m* whistle; **siffler** whistle; *d'un serpent* hiss; **sifflet** *m* whistle; ***coup de ~*** blow on the whistle

signal *m* signal; ***~ d'alarme*** alarm (signal); **signalement** *m* description; **signaler** *par un signal* signal; (*faire remarquer*) point out; (*dénoncer*) report; ***se ~ par*** distinguish o.s. by

signature *f* signature

signe *m* sign; ***faire ~ à*** gesture *ou* signal to s; (*contacter*) get in touch with; ***~ de ponctuation*** punctuation mark; **signer** sign

signet *m* bookmark

signification *f* meaning; **signifier** mean; ***~ qch à qn*** (*faire savoir*) notify s.o. of sth

silence *m* silence; **silencieux, -euse 1** *adj* silent **2** *m d'une arme* muffler, *Br* silencer

silhouette *f* outline, silhouette; (*figure*) figure

sillage *m* wake (*aussi fig*)

sillon *m dans un champ* furrow; *d'un disque* groove; **sillonner** (*parcourir*) criss-cross

similaire similar; **similitude** *f* similarity

simple 1 *adj* simple **2** *m au tennis* singles *pl*; **simplicité** *f* simplicity

simplifier simplify

simulateur, -trice 1 *m/f*: ***c'est un ~*** he's pretending **2** *m* TECH simulator; **simulation** *f* simulation; **simuler** simulate

simultané simultaneous

sincère sincere; **sincérité** *f* sincerity

singe *m* monkey; **singer** ape; **singerie** *f* imitation; ***~s*** F antics

singulier, -ère 1 *adj* odd, strange **2** *m* GRAM singular

sinistre 1 *adj* sinister; (*triste*) gloomy **2** *m* disaster; **sinistré 1** *adj* stricken **2** *m/f* disaster victim

sinon (*autrement*) or else, otherwise; (*sauf*) except; (*si ce n'est*) if not

sinueux, -euse *route* winding; *ligne* squiggly; *explication* complicated

sinus *m* sinus; **sinusite** *f* sinusitis

sirène *f* siren

sirop *m* syrup

siroter sip

sismique seismic

sitcom *m ou f* sitcom

site *m* site; (*paysage*) area; ***~ Web*** website

sitôt 1 *adv*: **~ *parti, il ...*** as soon as he had left he ... **2** *conj*: **~ *que*** as soon as
situation *f* situation; (*emplacement, profession*) position; **situé** situated
six six; **sixième** sixth
skateboard *m* skateboard; *activité* skateboarding
sketch *m* sketch
ski *m* ski; *activité* skiing; **~ *alpin*** downhill (skiing); **~ *de fond*** cross-country (skiing); **~ *nautique*** water-skiing; **skier** ski; **skieur, -euse** *m/f* skier
slip *m de femme* panties *pl*; *d'homme* briefs; **~ *de bain*** swimming trunks *pl*
slogan *m* slogan
slovaque *adj* Slovak(ian); **Slovaque** *m/f* Slovak(ian)
slovène Slovene, Slovenian; **Slovène** *m/f* Slovene, Slovenian
smoking *m* tuxedo, *Br* dinner jacket
SMS *m* text (message)
S.N.C.F. *f* (= ***Societé nationale des chemins de fer français***) French national railroad company
sobre sober; *style* restrained
sociable sociable
social social; COMM company *atr*; **socialiser** socialize; **socialisme** *m* socialism; **socialiste** *m/f & adj* socialist
société *f* society; *firme* company; **~ *anonyme*** corporation, *Br* public limited company, plc
sociologie *f* sociology
socquette *f* anklet, *Br* ankle sock
soda *m* soda, *Br* fizzy drink; ***un whisky* ~** a whiskey and soda
sœur *f* sister; REL nun
sofa *m* sofa
soi oneself; ***avec* ~** with one; ***ça va de* ~** that goes without saying
soi-disant *inv* so-called
soie *f* silk
soif *f* thirst; ***avoir* ~** be thirsty
soigné *personne* well-groomed; *travail* careful;
soigner look after, take care of; *d'un médecin* treat; ***se* ~** take care of o.s.; **soigneux, -euse** careful (***de*** about)
soi-même oneself
soin *m* care; **~*s*** care; MÉD care, treatment; ***prendre* ~ *de*** look after, take care of; ***être sans* ~** be untidy
soir *m* evening; ***le* ~** in the evening; **soirée** *f* evening; (*fête*) party
soit[1] *adv* very well, so be it
soit[2] *conj* **~ ..., ~ ...** either ..., or ...; (*à savoir*) that is, ie
soixantaine *f* about sixty; **soixante** sixty; **soixante-dix** seventy
soja *m* BOT soy bean, *Br* soya
sol *m* ground; (*plancher*) floor; (*patrie*), GÉOL soil
solaire solar

soldat *m* soldier
solde[1] *f* MIL pay
solde[2] *m* COMM balance; **~s** *marchandises* sale goods; *vente au rabais* sale; **solder** *compte* close, balance; *marchandises* sell off
sole *f* ZO sole
soleil *m* sun; ***il y a du ~*** it's sunny; ***coup*** *m* ***de ~*** sunburn
solennel, **~le** solemn
solidaire: ***être ~ de qn*** suport s.o.; **solidarité** *f* solidarity
solide **1** *adj* solid; *tissu* strong; *argument* sound; *personne* sturdy **2** *m* PHYS solid; **solidité** *f* solidity; *d'un matériau* strength; *d'un argument* soundness
solitaire **1** *adj* solitary **2** *m/f* loner **3** *m diamant* solitaire; **solitude** *f* solitude
sollicitation *f* plea; **solliciter** request; *attention* attract; *curiosité* arouse; ***~ un emploi*** apply for a job; **sollicitude** *f* solicitude
solstice *m* ASTR solstice
soluble soluble; ***café*** *m* ***~*** instant coffee
solution *f* solution
solvable solvent; *digne de crédit* creditworthy
sombre *couleur, salle* dark; *temps* overcast; *avenir, regard* somber, *Br* sombre
sommaire **1** *adj* brief; *exécution* summary **2** *m* summary
somme[1] *f* sum; (*quantité*) amount; ***en ~***, ***~ toute*** in short
somme[2] *m* nap, snooze
sommeil *m* sleep; ***avoir ~*** be sleepy; **sommeiller** doze
sommelier *m* wine waiter
sommer: ***~ qn de faire qc*** order s.o. to do sth
sommet *m d'une montagne* summit, top; *d'un arbre, d'une tour* top; *fig* pinnacle; POL summit
sommier *m* mattress
somnambule *m/f* sleepwalker
somnifère *m* sleeping tablet
somnolence *f* drowsiness, sleepiness; **somnoler** doze
somptueux, **-euse** sumptuous; **somptuosité** *f* sumptuousness
son[1] *m*, **sa** *f*, **ses** *pl d'homme* his; *de femme* her; *de chose, d'animal* its; *avec 'one'* one's
son[2] *m* sound
sondage *m* probe; TECH drilling; **~ (*d'opinion*)** opinion poll, survey
sonde *f* probe; **sonder** MÉD probe; *personne, atmosphère* sound out
songe *m litt* dream; **songer**: ***~ à*** **(*faire*)** ***qc*** think about (doing) sth; **songeur**, **-euse** thoughtful
sonner **1** *v/i de cloches, sonnette* ring; *d'un réveil* go off; *d'un instrument, d'une voix* sound; *d'une horloge* strike; ***midi a sonné*** it has struck noon; ***~ creux/faux***

fig ring hollow/false **2** *v/t cloches* ring; **sonnerie** *f de cloches* ringing; (*sonnette*) bell; **sonnette** *f* bell

sonore *voix* loud; *rire* resounding; *cuivres* sonorous; *onde*, *film* sound *atr*; **sonorité** *f* sound, tone; *d'une salle* acoustics *pl*

sophistiqué sophisticated

soporifique sleep-inducing, soporific

soprano 1 *f* soprano **2** *m* treble

sorcellerie *f* sorcery, witchcraft

sorcier *m* sorcerer; **sorcière** *f* witch

sordide filthy; *fig* sordid

sort *m* fate; (*condition*) lot; ***tirer au ~*** draw lots; ***jeter un ~ à*** *fig* cast a spell on

sorte *f* (*manière*) way; (*espèce*) sort, kind; ***en quelque ~*** in a way; ***de*** (***telle***) ***~ que*** and so

sortie *f* exit; (*promenade*, *excursion*) outing; *d'un livre* publication; *d'un disque* release; *d'une voiture* launch; TECH outlet; MIL sortie; ***~*** (***sur***) ***imprimante*** printout

sortir 1 *v/i* come/go out; *pour se distraire* go out (***avec*** with); *d'un livre*, *un disque* come out; *au loto* come up; ***~ de*** *endroit* leave; *accident*, *entretien* emerge from; (*provenir de*) come from **2** *v/t chose* bring/take out; *chien*, *personne* take out; COMM bring out; F *bêtises* come out with **3**: ***s'en ~*** *d'un malade* pull through

sot, **~te 1** *adj* silly, foolish **2** *m/f* fool; **sottise** *f* foolishness; *action/remarque* foolish thing to do/say

sou *m fig* penny; ***être sans le ~*** be penniless

souche *f d'un arbre* stump; *d'un carnet* stub

souci *m* worry, care; ***sans ~*** carefree; **soucier**: ***se ~ de*** worry about; **soucieux**, **-euse** anxious, concerned (***de*** about)

soucoupe *f* saucer

soudain 1 *adj* sudden **2** *adv* suddenly

souder TECH weld; *fig* bring closer together

soudoyer bribe

souffle *m* breath; *d'une explosion* blast; ***à bout de ~*** breathless, out of breath; **souffler 1** *v/i du vent* blow; (*haleter*) puff; (*respirer*) breathe; (*reprendre son souffle*) get one's breath back **2** *v/t chandelle* blow out; ÉDU, *au théâtre* prompt; ***~ qc à qn*** F (*dire*) whisper sth to s.o.; (*enlever*) steal sth from s.o.

souffrance *f* suffering; **souffrant** unwell; **souffrir 1** *v/i* be in pain; ***~ de*** suffer from **2** *v/t* suffer

soufre *m* CHIM sulfur, *Br* sul-

phur
souhait *m* wish; ***à vos ~s!*** bless you!; **souhaitable** desirable; **souhaiter** wish for; ***~ que*** (+ *subj*) hope that
souiller dirty, soil; *fig*: *réputation* tarnish
soûl drunk
soulagement *m* relief; **soulager** relieve; ***~ qn*** *au travail* help s.o. out
soûler F: ***~ qn*** get s.o. drunk; ***se ~*** get drunk
soulèvement *m* uprising; **soulever** raise; *enthousiasme* arouse; *protestations* generate; ***se ~*** raise o.s.; (*se révolter*) rise up
souligner underline
soumettre *pays*, *peuple* subdue; *à un examen* subject (***à*** to); (*présenter*) submit; ***se ~ à*** submit to; **soumis** *peuple* subject; (*obéissant*) submissive; **soumission** *f* submission; COMM tender
soupçon *m* suspicion; ***un ~ de*** a hint of; **soupçonner** suspect; **soupçonneux, -euse** suspicious
soupe *f* CUIS (thick) soup
souper 1 *v/i* have dinner *ou* supper **2** *m* dinner, supper
soupir *m* sigh; **soupirer** sigh
souple flexible; **souplesse** *f* flexibility
source *f* spring; *fig* source
sourcil *m* eyebrow
sourd deaf; *voix* low; *douleur*, *bruit* dull; *colère* repressed; ***~-muet*** deaf-and-dumb
souriant smiling
souricière *f* mousetrap; *fig* trap
sourire *v/i & m* smile
souris *f* mouse
sournois, ~e 1 *adj* underhanded **2** *m/f* underhanded person
sous under; ***~ peu*** soon; ***~ la pluie*** in the rain
souscription *f* subscription; **souscrire**: ***~ à*** subscribe to (*aussi fig*); *emprunt* approve
sous-entendre imply; **sous-entendu 1** *adj* implied **2** *m* implication
sous-estimer underestimate
sous-jacent underlying
sous-louer sublet
sous-marin 1 *adj* underwater **2** *m* submarine
sous-sol *m d'une maison* basement
sous-titre *m* subtitle
soustraire MATH subtract (***de*** from); *fig*: *au regard de* remove; *à un danger* protect (***à*** from)
sous-traitance *f* sub-contracting
sous-vêtements *mpl* underwear
soutane *f* REL cassock
soute *f* MAR , AVIAT hold
soutenir support; *pression* withstand; *conversation* keep going; *opinion* maintain; ***~ que*** maintain that;

***se* ~** support each other; **soutenu** *effort* sustained; *style* elevated
souterrain 1 *adj* underground, subterranean **2** *m* underground passage
soutien *m* support
soutien-gorge *m* brassiere, bra
souvenir 1: ***se* ~ *de qn/qch*** remember s.o./sth; ***se* ~ *que*** remember that **2** *m* memory; *objet* souvenir
souvent often; ***le plus* ~** most of the time
souverain, **~e** *m/f* sovereign
soyeux, **-euse** silky
spacieux, **-euse** spacious
spaghetti *mpl* spaghetti *sg*
sparadrap *m* Band-Aid®, *Br* Elastoplast®
spasme *m* MÉD spasm; **spasmodique** spasmodic
spatial spatial; ASTR space *atr*
spécial special; **spécialiser**: ***se* ~** specialize; **spécialiste** *m/f* specialist; **spécialité** *f* speciality
spécifier specify
spécifique specific
spécimen *m* specimen
spectacle *m* spectacle; *théâtre*, *cinéma* show, performance; **spectaculaire** spectacular
spectateur, **-trice** *m/f* (*témoin*) onlooker; SP spectator; *au théâtre* member of the audience
spectre *m* ghost; PHYS spectrum
spéculer speculate
spéléologie *f* caving
spermatozoïde *m* BIOL sperm
sperme *m* BIOL sperm
sphère *f* MATH sphere (*aussi fig*)
spirale *f* spiral
spirituel, **~le** spiritual; (*amusant*) witty
spiritueux *mpl* spirits
splendeur *f* splendor, *Br* splendour, magnificence; **splendide** splendid
sponsor *m* sponsor; **sponsoriser** sponsor
spontané spontaneous
sport 1 *m* sport; ***faire du* ~** do sport **2** *adj vêtements* casual *atr*
sportif, **-ive 1** *adj résultats*, *association* sports *atr*; *allure* sporty; (*fair-play*) sporting **2** *m* sportsman **3** *f* sportswoman
square *m* public garden
squash *m* SP squash
squatter squat; **squatteur**, **-euse** *m/f* squatter
squelette *m* skeleton
stabilisateur, **-trice 1** *adj* stabilizing **2** *m* stabilizer; **stabiliser** stabilize; **stabilité** *f* stability; **stable** stable
stade *m* SP stadium; *d'un processus* stage
stage *m* training period; (*cours*) training course; *pour professeur* teaching prac-

tice; (*expérience professionnelle*) work placement; **stagiaire** *m/f* trainee
stagnant *eau* stagnant
stalle *f d'un cheval* box; **~s** REL stalls
stand *m de foire* booth, *Br* stand; *de kermesse* stall
standard *m* standard; TÉL switchboard
standardiser standardize
standardiste *m/f* TÉL (switchboard) operator
starter *m* AUTO choke
station *f* station; *de bus* stop; *de vacances* resort; **~ *de taxis*** cab stand, *Br* taxi rank; **~ *thermale*** spa
stationnement *m* parking; **stationner** park
station-service *f* gas station, *Br* petrol station
statistique 1 *adj* statistical **2** *f* statistic; *science* statistics *sg*
statue *f* statue
stature *f* stature
statut *m* status; **~s** *d'une société* statutes
stéréo *f* stereo
stéréotype *m* stereotype; **stéréotypé** stereotype
stérile sterile; **stériliser** sterilize; **stérilité** *f* sterility
steward *m* flight attendant, steward
stigmate *m* mark; **~s** REL stigmata
stimuler stimulate
stipulation *f* stipulation; **stipuler** stipulate
stock *m* stock; **stocker** stock; INFORM store
stoïque stoical
stop *m* stop; *écriteau* stop sign; (***feu*** *m*) **~** AUTO brake light; ***faire du*** **~** F hitchhike; **stopper** stop
store *m d'une fenêtre* shade, *Br* blind; *d'un magasin, d'une terrasse* awning
strapontin *m* tip-up seat
stratagème *m* stratagem
stratégie *f* strategy
stress *m* stress; **stressant** stressful; **stressé** stressed-out
strict strict; ***le ~ nécessaire*** the bare minimum
strident strident
strip-tease *m* strip(tease)
structure *f* structure
studieux, -euse studious
stupéfait stupefied; **stupéfiant 1** *adj* stupefying **2** *m* drug; **stupéfier** stupefy
stupeur *f* stupor
stupide stupid
style *m* style; **styliste** *m de mode, d'industrie* stylist
stylo *m* pen; **~ *plume*** fountain pen
suave *voix, goût* sweet
subalterne 1 *adj* junior **2** *m/f* junior, subordinate
subir (*endurer*) suffer; (*se soumettre volontairement à*) undergo
subit sudden
subjectif, -ive subjective
subjuguer *fig* captivate

sublime sublime
submerger submerge; ***être submergé de*** *fig* be buried in
subordonné, **~e** *adj & m/f* subordinate; **subordonner** subordinate (***à*** to)
subrepticement surreptitiously
subsidiaire subsidiary
subsistance *f* subsistence; **subsister** survive; *d'une personne aussi* live
substance *f* substance; **substantiel**, **~le** substantial
substituer: ***~ X à Y*** substitute X for Y
subterfuge *m* subterfuge
subtil subtle; **subtilité** *f* subtlety
subvenir: ***~ à*** provide for
subvention *f* grant, subsidy; **subventionner** subsidize
subversif, **-ive** subversive
suc *m*: ***~s gastriques*** gastric juices
succéder: ***~ à*** follow; *personne* succeed; ***se ~*** follow each other
succès *m* success
successeur *m* successor; **succession** *f* succession; JUR (*biens dévolus*) inheritance
succomber (*mourir*) die, succumb; ***~ à*** succumb to
succulent succulent
succursale *f* COMM branch
sucer suck; **sucette** *f bonbon* lollipop; *de bébé* pacifier, *Br* dummy
sucre *m* sugar; **sucré** sweet; *au sucre* sugared; *péj* sugary; **sucrer** sweeten; *avec sucre* sugar; **sucreries** *fpl* sweet things
sud 1 *m* south; ***au ~ de*** (to the) south of **2** *adj* south; *hémisphère* southern
sud-américain, **~e** South American; **Sud-Américain**, **~e** *m/f* South American
sud-est *m* south-east
sud-ouest *m* south-west
Suède: ***la ~*** Sweden; **suédois**, **~e 1** *adj* Swedish **2** *m langue* Swedish; **Suédois**, **~e** *m/f* Swede
suer 1 *v/i* sweat **2** *v/t* sweat; *fig* (*dégager*) ooze; **sueur** *f* sweat
suffire be enough; ***il suffit que tu le lui dises*** (*subj*) all you have to do is tell her; ***ça suffit!*** that's enough!
suffisamment sufficiently, enough; ***~ intelligent*** sufficiently intelligent, intelligent enough; ***~ de ...*** enough ..., sufficient ...; **suffisance** *f* arrogance; **suffisant** sufficient, enough; (*arrogant*) arrogant
suffocant suffocating; *fig* breath-taking; **suffocation** *f* suffocation; **suffoquer** suffocate
suffrage *m* vote; ***~ universel*** universal suffrage

suggérer suggest (***à*** to); **suggestion** *f* suggestion
suicide *m* suicide; **suicider**: ***se ~*** commit suicide
suinter *d'un mur* ooze
suisse Swiss; **Suisse 1** *m/f* Swiss **2 la Suisse** Switzerland
suite *f* pursuit; (*série*) series *sg*; (*continuation*) continuation; *d'un film, un livre* sequel; MUS, *appartement* suite; ***la ~ de l'histoire*** the rest of the story; ***~s*** (*conséquences*) consequences; *d'un choc, d'une maladie* after-effects; ***trois fois de ~*** three times in a row; ***et ainsi de ~*** and so on; ***par ~ de*** as a result of; ***tout de ~*** immediately
suivant, ~e 1 *adj* next, following **2** *m/f* next person; ***au ~!*** next! **3** *prép* (*selon*) according to **4** *conj*: ***~ que*** depending on whether
suivi *effort* sustained; *relations* continuous; *argumentation* coherent
suivre 1 *v/t* follow; *cours* take **2** *v/i* follow; *à l'école* keep up; ***faire ~*** *lettre* please forward; ***à ~*** to be continued
sujet, ~te 1 *adj*: ***~ à*** subject to **2** *m* subject; ***au ~ de*** on the subject of
sulfureux, -euse sultry
super 1 *adj* F great F, neat F **2** *m essence* premium
superbe superb
supercherie *f* hoax
superficie *f fig* surface; (*surface, étendue*) (surface) area; **superficiel, ~le** superficial
superflu 1 *adj* superfluous **2** *m* surplus
supérieur, ~e 1 *adj* higher; *étages, mâchoire* upper; (*meilleur, dans une hiérarchie*) superior (*aussi péj*) **2** *m/f* superior; **supériorité** *f* superiority
supermarché *m* supermarket
superposer stack; *couches* superimpose; ***lits*** *mpl* ***superposés*** bunk beds
superstitieux, -euse superstitious; **superstition** *f* superstition
superviser supervise
supplanter supplant
suppléant, ~e 1 *adj* acting **2** *m/f* stand-in, replacement; **suppléer**: ***~ à*** make up for
supplément *m* supplement; ***un ~ de …*** additional *ou* extra …; **supplémentaire** additional
supplication *f* plea
supplice *m* torture; *fig* agony; **supplicier** torture
supplier: ***~ qn de faire*** beg s.o. to do
support *m* support; **supportable** bearable; **supporter**[1] *v/t* TECH, ARCH support, hold up; *conséquences* take; *frais, douleur, personne* bear; *chaleur, alcool* tolerate; **sup-**

porter² *m* SP supporter, fan
supposer suppose; (*impliquer*) presuppose; **supposition** *f* supposition
suppression *f* suppression; **supprimer** *institution, impôt* abolish; *emplois* cut; *mot* delete; *concert* cancel
suprême supreme
sur on; ***prendre qch ~ l'étagère*** take sth off the shelf; ***une fenêtre ~ la rue*** a window looking onto the street; ***tirer ~ qn*** shoot at s.o.; ***un film ~ ...*** a movie on *ou* about ...; ***un ~ dix*** one out of ten
sûr sure; (*non dangereux*) safe; (*fiable*) reliable; ***bien ~*** of course; ***à coup ~ il sera ...*** he's bound to be ...
surcharge *f* overloading; (*poids excédentaire*) excess weight
surchauffer overheat
surclasser outclass
surcroît *m*: ***un ~ de travail*** extra work; ***de ~, par ~*** moreover
surdité *f* deafness
surdoué extremely gifted
surélever raise
sûrement surely
surenchère *f dans vente aux enchères* higher bid
surestimer overestimate
sûreté *f* safety; MIL security; *de jugement* soundness
surexciter overexcite
surexposer overexpose
surface *f* surface; ***grande ~*** COMM supermarket
surfait overrated
surfer surf; ***~ sur Internet*** surf the Net
surgelé 1 *adj* deep-frozen **2** *mpl*: ***~s*** frozen food
surgir suddenly appear; *d'un problème* crop up
sur-le-champ at once, straightaway
surlendemain *m* day after tomorrow
surligner highlight
surmener overwork; ***se ~*** overwork, overdo it F
surmonter dominate; *fig* overcome, surmount
surnaturel, ~le supernatural
surnom *m* nickname; **surnommer** nickname
surpasser surpass
surpeuplé *pays* overpopulated; *endroit* overcrowded
surplomber overhang
surplus *m* surplus; ***au ~*** moreover
surprenant surprising; **surprendre** surprise; *voleur* catch (in the act); ***se ~ à faire qch*** catch o.s. doing sth; **surpris** surprised; **surprise** *f* surprise
sursaut *m* jump, start; **sursauter** jump
sursis *m fig* reprieve, stay of execution; ***peine avec ~*** JUR suspended sentence
surtaxe *f* surcharge
surtout especially; (*avant*

tout) above all; ~ ***que*** F especially since
surveillance *f* supervision; *par la police etc* surveillance; **surveillant**, **~e** *m/f* supervisor; *de prison* guard; **surveiller** watch; *élèves*, *employés* supervise; ***se*** ~ *comportement* watch one's step; *poids* watch one's figure
survenir *d'une personne* arrive unexpectedly; *d'un événement* happen; *d'un problème* come up, arise
survêtement *m* sweats *pl*, *Br* tracksuit
survie *f* survival; REL afterlife; **survivant**, **~e** **1** *adj* surviving **2** *m/f* survivor; **survivre**: ~ ***à*** survive
susceptible sensitive, touchy; ~ ***de faire qch*** likely to do sth
susciter arouse
suspect (*équivoque*) suspicious; (*d'une qualité douteuse*) suspect; ~ ***de qc*** suspected of sth; **suspecter** suspect
suspendre suspend; (*accrocher*) hang up; **suspendu** suspended
suspens: ***en*** ~ *personne* in suspense; *affaire* outstanding
suspense *m* suspense
suspension *f* suspension
suspicion *f* suspicion
svelte trim, slender
sweat(-shirt) *m* sweatshirt
syllabe *f* syllable
symbole *m* symbol; **symboliser** symbolize
symétrie *f* symmetry
sympathie *f* sympathy; (*amitié, inclination*) liking; **sympathique** nice, friendly; **sympathiser** get on
symphonie *f* symphony
symptôme *m* symptom
synagogue *f* synagogue
synchroniser synchronize
syndical labor *atr*, *Br* (trade) union *atr*
syndicat *m* (labor) union, *Br* (trade) union; ~ ***d'initiative*** tourist information office
syndiqué unionized
synonyme **1** *adj* synonymous (***de*** with) **2** *m* synonym
synthèse *f* synthesis; **synthétiseur** *m* MUS synthesizer
systématique systematic; **système** *m* system; ~ ***antidémarrage*** immobilizer; ~ ***d'exploitation*** INFORM operating system

T

ta → ***ton***[2]
tabac *m* tobacco; ***bureau*** *m* ***de*** ~ tobacco store, *Br* tobacconist's
table *f* table; ***se mettre à*** ~ sit down to eat
tableau *m à l'école* board; (*peinture*) painting; *fig* picture; (*liste*) list; (*schéma*) table; ~ ***de bord*** AVIAT instrument panel
tablette *f* shelf; ~ ***de chocolat*** chocolate bar
tablier *m* apron
tabouret *m* stool
tache *f* stain
tâche *f* task
tacher stain
tâcher: ~ ***de faire*** try to do
tacheté stained
tacite tacit
taciturne taciturn
tact *m* tact; ***avoir du*** ~ be tactful
tactique 1 *adj* tactical **2** *f* tactics *pl*
taie *f*: ~ (***d'oreiller***) pillowslip
taille[1] *f* BOT pruning; *de la pierre* cutting
taille[2] *f* (*hauteur*) height; (*dimension*) size; ANAT waist
taille-crayon(s) *m* pencil sharpener
tailler BOT prune; *vêtement* cut out; *crayon* sharpen; *pierre* cut; **tailleur** *m* (*couturier*) tailor; *vêtement* (woman's) suit
taire: ***se*** ~ keep quiet (***sur*** about); *s'arrêter de parler* stop talking; ***tais-toi!*** be quiet!, shut up!
talc *m* talc
talent *m* talent; **talentueux, -euse** talented
talon *m* heel; *d'un chèque* stub; **talonner** (*serrer de près*) follow close behind; (*harceler*) harass
talus *m* bank
tambour *m* MUS, TECH drum; **tambouriner** drum
Tamise: ***la*** ~ the Thames
tamiser sieve; *lumière* filter
tampon *m d'ouate* pad; *hygiène féminine* tampon; (*amortisseur*) buffer; (*cachet*) stamp; **tamponnement** *m* AUTO collision; **tamponner** *plaie* clean; (*cacheter*) stamp; AUTO collide with
tandis que while
tangente *f* MATH tangent
tangible tangible
tango *m* tango
tanière *f* lair, den (*aussi fig*)
tanné tanned; *peau* weather-beaten; **tanner** tan; *fig* F pester
tant 1 *adv* so much; ~ ***de vin*** so much wine; ~ ***d'erreurs*** so many errors; ~ ***mieux*** so

much the better; *~ **pis*** too bad, tough **2** *conj*: ***~ que** temps* as long as; ***en ~ que Français*** as a Frenchman; ***~ … que …*** both … and …
tante *f* aunt
tantôt this afternoon; ***à ~*** see you soon; ***~ … ~ …*** now … now …
taon *m* horsefly
tapage *m* racket; *fig* fuss; **tapageur, -euse** (*voyant*) flashy, loud; (*bruyant*) noisy
tape *f* pat
taper 1 *v/t personne* hit; *table* bang on; *~* (***à l'ordinateur***) F key, type **2** *v/i* hit; *à l'ordinateur* key; ***~ sur les nerfs de qn*** F get on s.o.'s nerves
tapir: ***se ~*** crouch
tapis *m* carpet; SP mat; ***~ roulant*** TECH conveyor belt; *pour personnes* traveling *ou Br* travelling walkway; ***~ de souris*** mouse mat
tapisser *avec du papier peint* (wall)paper; **tapisserie** *f* tapestry; (*papier peint*) wallpaper
tapoter tap; *personne* pat
taquiner tease; **taquinerie** *f* teasing
tard 1 *adv* late; ***plus ~*** later (on); ***au plus ~*** at the latest **2** *m*: ***sur le ~*** late in life
tarder delay; ***~ à faire*** take a long time doing; ***il me tarde de te revoir*** I'm longing to see you again
tardif, -ive late
targuer: ***se ~ de qc*** *litt* pride o.s. on sth
tarif *m* rate; ***~ unique*** flat rate
tarir dry up (*aussi fig*); ***se ~*** dry up
tartan *m* tartan
tarte *f* tart; **tartelette** *f* tartlet
tartine *f* slice of bread; ***~ de confiture*** slice of bread and jam
tas *m* heap, pile; ***un ~ de choses*** heaps *pl ou* piles *pl* of things
tasse *f* cup; ***une ~ de café*** a cup of coffee; ***une ~ à café*** a coffee cup
tasser (*bourrer*) cram; ***se ~*** settle
tâter 1 *v/t* feel **2** *v/i* F: ***~ de qc*** try sth
tatillon, ~ne fussy
tâtons: ***avancer à ~*** feel one's way forward
tatouage *m action* tattooing; *signe* tattoo
taudis *m* slum
taupe *f* ZO mole
taureau *m* bull; ASTROL ***Taureau*** Taurus
taux *m* rate; ***~ d'alcoolémie*** blood alcohol level; ***~ de change*** exchange rate; ***~ d'intérêt*** interest rate
taxe *f* duty; (*impôt*) tax; ***~ sur** ou **à la valeur ajoutée*** sales tax, *Br* value added tax, VAT; **taxer** tax; ***~ qn de qc*** *fig* (*accuser*) tax s.o. with sth
taxi *m* taxi, cab
tchèque 1 *adj* Czech **2** *m lan-*

gue Czech; **Tchèque** *m/f* Czech

te you; *complément d'objet indirect* (to) you; ***tu t'es coupé*** you've cut yourself; ***si tu ~ lèves à …*** if you get up at …

technicien, **~ne** *m/f* technician

technique 1 *adj* technical **2** *f* technique

technologie *f* technology; ***~ informatique*** computer technology; ***~ de pointe*** high-tech; **technologique** technological

tee-shirt *m* T-shirt

teindre dye

teint, **~e 1** *adj* dyed **2** *m* complexion; ***fond*** *m* ***de ~*** foundation (cream) **3** *f* tint; *fig* tinge; **teinter** tint; *bois* stain; **teinture** *f action* dyeing; *produit* dye; PHARM tincture

tel, **~le** such; ***une ~le surprise*** such a surprise; *de ce genre* a surprise like that; ***~(s)*** *ou* ***~le(s) que*** such as, like

télé *f* F TV, tube F, *Br* telly F

télécharger INFORM download

télécommande *f* remote control

télécommunications *fpl* telecommunications

téléconférence *f* teleconference

téléguidage *m* remote control

téléobjectif *m* telephoto lens

télépathie *f* telepathy

téléphone *m* phone, telephone; ***~ portable*** cellphone, *Br* mobile (phone); ***coup*** *m* ***de ~*** (phone) call; **téléphoner 1** *v/i* phone, telephone; ***~ à qn*** call s.o., *Br aussi* phone s.o. **2** *v/t* phone, telephone; **téléphonique** phone *atr*, telephone *atr*; ***appel*** *m* **~** phone *ou* telephone call

téléréalité *f* reality TV

télescope *m* telescope; **télescoper** crash into; ***se ~*** crash

télésiège *m* chair lift

téléski *m* ski lift

téléspectateur, **-trice** *m/f* (TV) viewer

téléthon *m* telethon

télévision *f* television; ***~ câblée*** cable (TV)

tellement so; *avec verbe* so much; ***pas ~*** not really; ***~ de chance*** so much good luck; ***~ de filles*** so many girls

téméraire reckless; **témérité** *f* recklessness

témoignage *m* JUR testimony, evidence; (*rapport*) account; *fig*: *d'estime* token; **témoigner** JUR testify, give evidence; ***~ de*** (*être le témoignage de*) show; **témoin** *m* witness; ***être (le) ~ de qch*** witness sth

tempe *f* ANAT temple

tempérament *m* temperament; ***à ~*** in installments *ou Br* instalments

température *f* temperature; ***avoir de la ~*** have a fever, *Br aussi* have a temperature
tempérer moderate
tempête *f* storm
temple *m* temple; *protestant* church
temporaire temporary
temporel, ~le temporal
temporiser stall, play for time
temps *m* time; *atmosphérique* weather; TECH stroke; ***à ~*** in time; ***de ~ en ~*** from time to time; ***il est ~ de partir*** it's time to go; ***il est ~ que tu t'en ailles*** (*subj*) it's time you left; ***en même ~*** at the same time; ***par beau ~*** in good weather; ***quel ~ fait-il?*** what's the weather like?
tenace tenacious
tenailles *fpl* pincers
tendance *f* trend; (*disposition*) tendency; ***avoir ~ à faire*** have a tendency to do, tend to do
tendon *m* ANAT tendon
tendre[1] **1** *v/t filet, ailes* spread; *piège* set; *bras, main* hold out; *muscles* tense; *corde* tighten; ***~ qch à qn*** hold sth out to s.o.; ***se ~*** *de rapports* become strained **2** *v/i*: ***~ à qc*** strive for sth; ***~ à faire qch*** tend to do sth
tendre[2] *adj* tender; *couleur* soft
tendresse *f* tenderness
tendu *corde* tight; *fig* tense; *relations* strained
ténèbres *fpl* darkness; **ténébreux, -euse** dark
teneur *f d'une lettre* contents *pl*; (*concentration*) content
tenir 1 *v/t* hold; (*maintenir*) keep; *registre, promesse* keep; *caisse* be in charge of; *restaurant* run; *place* take up; ***~ à qc/qn*** (*donner de l'importance à*) value sth/s.o.; *à un objet* be attached to sth; ***~ à faire qc*** really want to do sth; ***cela ne tient qu'à toi*** (*dépend de*) it's entirely up to you **2** *v/i* hold; ***~ dans*** fit into **3**: ***se ~*** *d'un spectacle* be held; (*être, se trouver*) stand; ***se ~ à qch*** hold on to sth; ***s'en ~ à*** confine o.s. to
tennis *m* tennis; *terrain* tennis court; ***~*** *pl* sneakers, *Br* trainers; SP tennis shoes
ténor *m* MUS tenor
tension *f* tension; MÉD blood pressure; ***faire de la ~*** F have high blood pressure
tentacule *m* tentacle
tentant tempting; **tentation** *f* temptation
tentative *f* attempt
tente *f* tent
tenter tempt; (*essayer*) attempt, try (***de faire*** to do)
tenture *f* wallhanging
tenu: ***être ~ de faire qc*** be obliged to do sth; ***bien ~*** well looked after; ***mal ~*** badly kept; *enfant* neglected

ténu fine; *espoir* slim
tenue *f de comptes* keeping; *de ménage* running; (*conduite*) behavior, *Br* behaviour; *du corps* posture; (*vêtements*) clothes *pl*; **~ de soirée** evening wear
tergiverser hum and haw
terme *m* (*fin*) end; (*échéance*) time limit; (*expression*) term; **à court/long ~** in the short/long term; *emprunt, projet* short-/long-term
terminaison *f* GRAM ending;
terminer finish; **se ~** end; **se ~ par** end with; *d'un mot* end in
terminus *m* terminus
ternir tarnish
terrain *m* ground; GÉOL, MIL terrain; SP field; **un ~** a piece of land; **sur le ~** *essai* field *atr*; *essayer* in the field; **~ d'aviation** airfield; **~ à bâtir** building lot; **~ de jeu** play park; **véhicule** *m* **tout ~** 4x4, off-road vehicle
terrasse *f* terrace; **terrasser** *adversaire* fell
terre *f* (*sol, surface*) ground; *matière* earth, soil; *opposé à mer, propriété* land; (*monde*) earth, world; *pays, région* land, country; ÉL ground, *Br* earth; **~ à ~** *personne* down to earth; **à** *ou* **par ~** on the ground; **tomber par ~** fall down; **sur ~** on earth; **sur la ~** on the ground
terre-plein *m*: **~ central** median strip, *Br* central reservation
terrestre *animaux* land *atr*; REL earthly; TV terrestrial
terreur *f* terror
terrible terrible; F (*extraordinaire*) terrific; **c'est pas ~** it's not that good
terrien, ~ne 1 *adj*: **propriétaire** *m* **~** landowner **2** *m/f* (*habitant de la Terre*) earthling
terrier *m de renard* earth; ZO terrier
terrifier terrify
territoire *m* territory
terroir *m viticulture* soil; **du ~** (*régional*) local
terroriser terrorize; **terrorisme** *m* terrorism; **terroriste** *m/f & adj* terrorist
tertre *m* mound
tes → **ton²**
test *m* test; **~ de résistance** endurance test
testament *m* JUR will; **Ancien/Nouveau Testament** REL Old/New Testament
tester test
testicule *m* testicle
tête *f* head; (*cheveux*) hair; (*visage*) face; SP header; **de ~** *calculer* in one's head; *répondre* without looking anything up; **avoir la ~ dure** be stubborn; **se casser la ~** *fig* rack one's brains; **n'en faire qu'à sa ~** do exactly as one likes; **tenir ~ à qn** stand up to s.o.; *péj* defy s.o.; **faire la ~** sulk; **il se paie ta ~** *fig*

he's making a fool of you; ***en ~*** in the lead
tête-à-queue *m* AUTO spin; **tête-à-tête** *m* tête-à-tête; ***en ~*** in private
têtu obstinate
texte *m* text; ***~s choisis*** selected passages
textile *m* textile; ***le ~ industrie*** the textile industry, textiles *pl*
texto *m* text (message); ***envoyer un ~ à qn*** send s.o. a text, text s.o.
texture *f* texture
T.G.V. *m* (= ***train à grande vitesse***) high-speed train
thé *m* tea
théâtre *m* theater, *Br* theatre; *fig*: *cadre* scene
théière *f* teapot
thème *m* theme; ÉDU translation (into a foreign language)
théorie *f* theory; **théorique** theoretical
thérapeute *m/f* therapist; **thérapeutique 1** *f* (*thérapie*) therapy **2** *adj* therapeutic; **thérapie** *f* therapy
thermal thermal
thermomètre *m* thermometer
thermos *f ou m* thermos®
thèse *f* thesis
thon *m* tuna
thym *m* BOT thyme
tic *m* tic, twitch; *fig* habit
ticket *m* ticket; ***~ de caisse*** receipt
tiède warm; *péj* tepid, lukewarm (*aussi fig*); **tiédir** cool down; *devenir plus chaud* warm up
tien, **~ne**: ***le tien, la tienne, les tiens, les tiennes*** yours
tiers, **tierce 1** *adj* third; ***le ~ monde*** the Third World **2** *m* MATH third; JUR third party
tige *f* BOT stalk; TECH stem
tigre *m* tiger; **tigresse** *f* tigress
tilleul *m* BOT lime (tree); *boisson* lime-blossom tea
timbre *m* stamp; (*sonnette*) bell; (*son*) timbre; (*tampon*) stamp; **timbre-poste** *m* postage stamp
timide timid; *en société* shy
timoré timid
tintement *m* tinkle; *de clochettes* ringing; **tinter** *de verres* clink; *de clochettes* ring
tir *m* fire; *action*, SP shooting; ***~ à l'arc*** archery
tirage *m à la loterie* draw; PHOT print; TYP printing; (*exemplaires de journal*) circulation; *d'un livre* print run; COMM *d'un chèque* drawing; F (*difficultés*) trouble; ***par un ~ au sort*** by drawing lots
tirailler pull; ***tiraillé entre*** *fig* torn between
tire *f* P AUTO car, jeep P; ***vol m à la ~*** pickpocketing
tiré *traits* drawn
tire-bouchon *m* corkscrew
tirelire *f* piggy bank

tirer 1 *v/t* pull; *chèque*, *ligne*, *conclusions* draw; *coup de fusil* fire; *oiseau*, *cible* fire at; PHOT, TYP print; *plaisir*, *satisfaction* derive **2** *v/i* pull (***sur*** on); *avec arme* shoot (***sur*** at); ***~ à sa fin*** draw to a close **3**: ***se ~ de*** *situation difficile* get out of; ***se ~*** F take off

tiret *m* dash; (*trait d'union*) hyphen

tiroir *m* drawer

tisane *f* herbal tea

tisser weave; *d'une araignée* spin; *fig* hatch

tissu *m* fabric, material; BIOL tissue

titre *m* title; *d'un journal* headline; FIN security; ***à ce ~*** therefore; ***à juste ~*** rightly; ***à ~ d'essai*** on a trial basis; ***au même ~*** on the same basis

tituber stagger

titulaire *m/f d'un document*, *d'une charge* holder

toast *m* (*pain grillé*) piece of toast; *de bienvenue* toast

toboggan *m* slide; *rue* flyover

tocsin *m* alarm bell

toi you

toile *f de lin* linen; (*peinture*) canvas; ***~ d'araignée*** spiderweb, *Br* spider's web; ***~ cirée*** oilcloth; ***~ de fond*** backcloth; *fig* backdrop

toilette *f* (*lavage*) washing; (*mise*) outfit; (*vêtements*) clothes *pl*; ***~s*** toilet; ***aller aux ~s*** go to the toilet; ***faire sa ~*** get washed

toi-même yourself

toiser *fig*: ***~ qn*** look s.o. up and down

toison *f de laine* fleece; (*cheveux*) mane of hair

toit *m* roof; ***~ ouvrant*** AUTO sun roof; **toiture** *f* roof

tôle *f* sheet metal; ***~ ondulée*** corrugated iron

tolérance *f aussi* TECH tolerance; **tolérant** tolerant; **tolérer** tolerate

tomate *f* tomato

tombe *f* grave

tombeau *m* tomb

tombée *f*: ***à la ~ de la nuit*** at nightfall

tomber fall; *de cheveux* fall out; *d'une colère* die down; *d'une fièvre*, *d'un prix*, *d'une demande* drop, fall; ***~ malade*** fall sick; ***laisser ~*** drop (*aussi fig*); ***~ sur*** MIL attack; (*rencontrer*) bump into; ***~ d'accord*** reach agreement

tome *m* volume

ton[1] *m* tone; MUS key; ***il est de bon ~*** it's the done thing

ton[2] *m*, **ta** *f*, **tes** *pl* your

tondeuse *f* lawnmower; *de coiffeur* clippers *pl*; AGR shears *pl*; **tondre** *mouton* shear; *haie* clip; *herbe* mow, cut; *cheveux* shave off

tonifier tone up

tonique 1 *m* tonic **2** *adj climat* bracing

tonitruant thunderous
tonne *f* (metric) ton
tonneau *m* barrel; MAR ton
tonner thunder; *fig* rage
tonnerre *m* thunder
tonton *m* F uncle
tonus *m d'un muscle* tone; (*dynamisme*) dynamism
toqué F mad (***de*** about)
torche *f* flashlight, *Br* torch
torchon *m* dishtowel
tordre twist; *linge* wring; ***se ~*** twist; ***se ~ le pied*** twist one's ankle
tornade *f* tornado
torpille *f* torpedo; **torpiller** torpedo (*aussi fig*)
torrent *m* torrent; *fig*: *de larmes* flood; *d'injures* torrent
torse *m* torso
tort *m* fault; (*préjudice*) harm; ***à ~*** wrongly; ***à ~ et à travers*** wildly; ***avoir ~*** be wrong (***de faire*** to do); ***donner ~ à qn*** prove s.o. wrong; (*désapprouver*) blame s.o.; ***faire du ~ à*** hurt, harm
torticolis *m* MÉD stiff neck
tortiller twist; ***se ~*** wriggle
tortue *f* tortoise; ***~ de mer*** turtle
tortueux, **-euse** winding; *fig* tortuous; *esprit*, *manœuvres* devious
torture *f* torture; **torturer** torture
tôt early; (*bientôt*) soon; ***le plus ~ possible*** as soon as possible; ***au plus ~*** at the soonest *ou* earliest; ***~ ou tard*** sooner or later
total 1 *adj* total **2** *m* total; ***au ~*** in all; *fig* on the whole; **totalement** totally; **totaliser** total; **totalité** *f*: ***la ~ de*** all of; ***en ~*** in full; **totalitaire** POL totalitarian
touchant touching
touche *f* touch; *de clavier* key; SP touchline; (*remise en jeu*) throw-in; *pêche* bite; ***être mis sur la ~*** *fig* F be sidelined
toucher[1] *v/t* touch; *but* hit; (*émouvoir*) touch, move; (*concerner*) concern; (*contacter*) contact, get in touch with; *argent* get; *réserves* break into; *d'une maison* adjoin; ***~ au but*** near one's goal; ***se ~*** touch; *de maisons*, *terrains* adjoin
toucher[2] *m* touch
touffu dense, thick
toujours always; (*encore*) still; ***pour ~*** for ever
toupet *m* F nerve
tour[1] *f* tower; (*immeuble*) high-rise
tour[2] *m* turn; (*circonférence*) circumference; (*circuit*) lap; (*promenade*) stroll, walk; (*excursion*, *voyage*) tour; (*ruse*) trick; TECH lathe; *de potier* wheel; ***à mon ~***, ***c'est mon ~*** it's my turn; ***en un ~ de main*** in no time at all
tourbe *f matière* peat
tourbillon *m de vent* whirl-

wind; *d'eau* whirlpool
tourelle *f* turret
tourisme *m* tourism; **~ écologique** ecotourism; **touriste** *m/f* tourist
tourment *m litt* torture, torment
tourmente *f litt* storm
tourmenter torment; **se ~** worry, torment o.s.
tournant 1 *adj* revolving **2** *m* turn; *fig* turning point
tournée *f* round; *d'un artiste* tour
tourner 1 *v/t* turn; *sauce* stir; *salade* toss; *difficulté* get around; *film* shoot; **bien tourné(e)** well-put **2** *v/i* turn; *du lait* turn; **j'ai la tête qui tourne** my head is spinning; **faire ~** *clé* turn; *entreprise* run **3**: **se ~** turn; **se ~ vers** *fig* turn to
tournesol *m* BOT sunflower
tournevis *m* screwdriver
tournoyer *d'oiseaux* wheel; *de feuilles* swirl
tournure *f* (*expression*) turn of phrase; *des événements* turn
tourterelle *f* turtledove
tous → ***tout***
Toussaint: **la ~** All Saints' Day
tousser cough
toussoter have a slight cough
tout *m*, **toute** *f*, **tous** *mpl*, **toutes** *fpl* **1** *adj* all; (*n'importe lequel*) any; **~ Français** every Frenchman, all Frenchmen; **tous les deux jours** every two days; **tous les ans** every year **2** *pron sg* **tout** everything; *pl* **tous, toutes** all of us/them; **après ~** after all; **facile comme ~** F as easy as anything; **nous tous** all of us; **3** *adv* **tout** very, quite; **c'est ~ comme un ...** it's just like a ...; **~ nu** completely naked; **c'est ~ près d'ici** it's just nearby; **je suis ~e seule** I'm all alone; **~ à fait** altogether; **oui, ~ à fait** yes, absolutely; **~ de suite** straight away; **~ pauvres qu'ils sont** (*ou* **soient** (*subj*) however poor they are **4** *m* **tout** the whole lot, everything; **pas du ~** not at all
toutefois however
toux *f* cough *m*
toxique 1 *adj* toxic **2** *m* poison
trac *m* nervousness; *pour un acteur* stage fright
traçabilité *f* traceablility
tracas *m*: **des ~** worries; **tracasser**: **~ qn** *d'une chose* worry s.o.; *d'une personne* pester s.o.; **se ~** worry
trace *f* (*piste*) track, trail; (*marque*) mark; *fig* impression; **~s** *de sang, poison* traces; **des ~s de pas** footprints; **tracer** *plan* draw
trachée *f* windpipe, trachea
tractation *f péj*: **~s** horsetrading
tracteur *m* tractor

tradition *f* tradition; **traditionaliste** *m/f & adj* traditionalist; **traditionnel, ~le** traditional

traducteur, -trice *m/f* translator; **traduction** *f* translation; **traduire** translate (**en** into); *fig* be indicative of; ***se ~ par*** result in

trafic *m* traffic; **trafiquant** *m* trafficker; ***~ de drogue(s)*** drug trafficker; **trafiquer** traffic in; *moteur* tinker with

tragédie *f* tragedy; **tragique 1** *adj* tragic **2** *m* tragedy

trahir betray; **trahison** *f* betrayal; *crime* treason

train *m* train; *fig*: *de lois, décrets etc* series *sg*; ***être en ~ de faire qc*** be doing sth; ***mettre en ~*** set in motion; ***au ~ où vont les choses*** at the rate things are going; ***~ d'atterrissage*** undercarriage, landing gear; ***~ de vie*** lifestyle

traîner 1 *v/t* drag; *d'une voiture* pull, tow **2** *v/i de vêtements, livres* lie around; *d'une discussion* drag on; ***~ dans les rues*** hang around street corners **3**: ***se ~*** drag o.s. along

train-train *m* F: ***le ~ quotidien*** the daily routine

traire milk

trait *m* (*ligne*) line; *du visage* feature; *de caractère* trait; *d'une œuvre, époque* feature, characteristic; ***avoir ~ à*** be about; ***~ d'esprit*** witticism; ***~ d'union*** hyphen

traite *f* COMM draft, bill of exchange; *d'une vache* milking; ***d'une seule ~*** in one go

traité *m* treaty

traitement *m* treatment; (*salaire*) pay; TECH, INFORM processing; **traiter 1** *v/t* treat; TECH, INFORM process; ***~ qn de menteur*** call s.o. a liar **2** *v/i* (*négocier*) negotiate; ***~ de qc*** deal with sth

traître, ~sse 1 *m/f* traitor **2** *adj* treacherous

trajet *m* (*voyage*) journey; (*chemin*) way

trame *f fig*: *d'une histoire* background; *de la vie* fabric

tramway *m* streetcar, *Br* tram

tranchant 1 *adj* cutting **2** *m d'un couteau* cutting edge

tranche *f* (*morceau*) slice; (*bord*) edge; ***~ d'âge*** age bracket

tranché *fig* clear-cut; *couleur* definite

tranchée *f* trench

trancher 1 *v/t* cut; *fig* settle **2** *v/i*: ***~ sur*** stand out against

tranquille quiet; (*sans inquiétude*) easy in one's mind; ***laisse-moi ~!*** leave me alone!; **tranquillisant** *m* tranquilizer, *Br* tranquillizer; **tranquilliser**: ***~ qn*** set s.o.'s mind at rest; **tranquillité** *f* quietness, tranquillity; *du sommeil* peacefulness; (*stabilité morale*) peace of mind

transaction *f* JUR compromise; COMM transaction

transatlantique 1 *adj* transatlantic **2** *m bateau* transatlantic liner; *chaise* deck chair

transcription *f* transcription; **transcrire** transcribe

transférer transfer; **transfert** *m* transfer; PSYCH transference

transformation *f* transformation; TECH processing; *en rugby* conversion; **transformer** transform; TECH process; *appartement*, *en rugby* convert

transfuge *m* defector

transfusion *f*: **~ (*sanguine*)** (blood) transfusion

transgénique genetically modified

transgresser *loi* break, transgress

transi: **~ (*de froid*)** frozen

transiger come to a compromise

transistor *m* transistor

transit *m*: ***en ~*** in transit

transition *f* transition

transmettre transmit; *message*, *talen*, *maladie* pass on; *tradition*, *titre* hand down; **transmissible**: ***sexuellement ~*** sexually transmitted; **transmission** *f* transmission; *d'un message* passing on; *d'une tradition*, *d'un titre* handing down; RAD, TV broadcast

transparence *f* transparency; **transparent** transparent

transpercer pierce; *de l'eau*, *de la pluie* go right through

transpiration *f* perspiration; **transpirer** perspire

transplant *m* transplant; **transplantation** *f* transplanting; MÉD transplant; **transplanter** transplant

transport *m* transport; ***~s publics*** mass transit, *Br* public transport; **transporter** transport, carry

transposer transpose

transversal cross *atr*

trapèze *m* trapeze

trappe *f* (*ouverture*) trapdoor

trapu stocky

traquer hunt

traumatiser PSYCH traumatize; **traumatisme** *m* MÉD, PSYCH trauma

travail *m* work; ***être sans ~*** be out of work; ***travaux*** (*construction*) construction work; **travailler 1** *v/i* work **2** *v/t* work on; *d'une pensée* trouble; **travailleur, -euse 1** *adj* hard-working **2** *m/f* worker

travers 1 *adv*: ***de ~*** crooked; *marcher* not straight; ***en ~*** across **2** *prép*: ***à ~ qc, au ~ de qc*** through sth **3** *m* shortcoming

traversée *f* crossing; **traverser** *rue*, *mer* cross; *forêt*, *crise* go through; (*percer*) go right through

travesti 1 *adj pour fête* fancy-dress **2** *m* (*déguisement*) fancy dress; (*homosexuel*) transvestite; **travestir** *vérité* distort; ***se ~*** dress up (***en*** as a)
trébucher trip (***sur*** over)
trèfle *m* BOT clover; *aux cartes* clubs *pl*
treize thirteen; **treizième** thirteenth
tremblant trembling, quivering; **tremblement** *m* trembling; ***~ de terre*** earthquake; **trembler** tremble, shake (***de*** with); *de la terre* shake
trémousser: ***se ~*** wriggle
trempe *f fig* caliber, *Br* calibre
trempé soaked; *sol* saturated; **tremper** soak; *pain dans café etc* dunk; *pied dans l'eau* dip; *acier* harden; ***~ dans*** *fig* be involved in
tremplin *m* springboard; *pour ski* ski jump; *fig* stepping stone
trentaine *f*: ***une ~ de personnes*** about thirty people *pl*; **trente** thirty; **trentième** thirtieth
trépied *m* tripod
trépigner stamp (one's feet)
très very; ***~ lu/visité*** much read/visited
trésor *m* treasure; ***Trésor*** Treasury; **trésorier, -ère** *m/f* treasurer
tressaillir jump
tresse *f de cheveux* braid, *Br* plait
trêve *f* truce; ***~ de …*** that's enough …; ***sans ~*** without respite
tri *m* sort; ***faire un ~ dans qc*** sort sth out
triangle *m* triangle
tribord *m* MAR starboard
tribu *f* tribe
tribulations *fpl* tribulations
tribunal *m* court
tribune *f* platform; (*débat*) discussion; ***~s*** *dans stade* bleachers, *Br* stands
tributaire: ***être ~ de*** be dependent on
tricher cheat; **tricheur, -euse** *m/f* cheat
tricolore: ***drapeau*** *m* ***~*** tricolor *ou Br* tricolour
tricot *m* knitting; *vêtement* sweater; **tricoter** knit
trier (*choisir*) pick through; (*classer*) sort
trimballer F hump F, lug
trimer F work like a dog F
trimestre *m* quarter; ÉDU trimester, *Br* term
trinquer (*porter un toast*) clink glasses; ***~ à*** *fig* F toast, drink to
triomphe *m* triumph; **triompher** triumph (***de*** over)
tripes *fpl* guts; CUIS tripe
triple triple; **triplés, -ées** *mpl, fpl* triplets
tripoter F *objet* play around with; *femme* feel up
triste sad; *temps, paysage* dreary; **tristesse** *f* sadness

trivial vulgar; *litt* (*banal*) trite
troc *m* barter
trognon *m d'un fruit* core; *d'un chou* stump
trois 1 *adj* three; ***le ~ mai*** May third, *Br* the third of May **2** *m* three; **troisième** third
trombe *f*: ***des ~s d'eau*** sheets of water; ***en ~*** *fig* at top speed
trombone *m* MUS trombone; *pour papiers* paper clip
trompe *f* MUS horn; *d'un éléphant* trunk
tromper deceive; *époux* be unfaithful to; *confiance* abuse; ***se ~*** be mistaken; ***se ~ de numéro*** get the wrong number; **tromperie** *f* deception
trompette 1 *f* trumpet **2** *m* trumpet player
trompeur, **-euse** deceptive; (*traître*) deceitful
tronc *m* BOT, ANAT trunk; *à l'église* collection box
tronçon *m* section
trône *m* throne
trop too; *avec verbe* too much; ***~ de lait/gens*** too much milk/too many people
tropical tropical; **tropique** *m* tropic
trot *m* trot; ***aller au ~*** trot; **trotter** *d'un cheval* trot; *d'une personne* run around
trottiner scamper
trottinette *f* scooter
trottoir *m* sidewalk, *Br* pavement
trou *m* hole; ***~ de mémoire*** lapse of memory
trouble 1 *adj eau, liquide* cloudy; *explication* unclear; *situation* murky **2** *m* (*désarroi*) trouble; (*émoi*) excitement; MÉD disorder; ***~s*** POL unrest; **trouble-fête** *m* party-pooper F
troubler *liquide* make cloudy; *silence, sommeil* disturb; *réunion* disrupt; (*inquiéter*) bother; ***se ~*** get flustered *d'un liquide* go cloudy
trouée *f* gap; **trouer** make a hole in
troupe *f* troop; *de comédiens* troupe
troupeau *m de vaches* herd; *de moutons* flock
trousse *f* kit; ***être aux ~s de qn*** *fig* be on s.o.'s heels; ***~ de toilette*** toilet bag
trousseau *m d'une mariée* trousseau; ***~ de clés*** bunch of keys
trouver find; *plan* come up with; (*rencontrer*) meet; ***~ que*** think that; ***se ~*** (*être*) be; ***il se trouve que*** it turns out that
truc *m* F (*chose*) thing, thingamajig F; (*astuce*) trick
truffe *f* BOT truffle; *d'un chien* nose; **truffé** with truffles; ***~ de*** *fig: citations* peppered with
truie *f* sow
truite *f* trout
truquage *m dans film* special

effect; *d'une photo* faking; **truquer** *élections, cartes* rig
tu you
tuba *m* snorkel; MUS tuba
tube *m* tube; F (*chanson*) hit
tuberculose *f* MÉD tuberculosis, TB
tuer kill; *fig* (*épuiser*) exhaust; (*peiner*) bother; ***se ~*** (*se suicider*) kill o.s.; (*trouver la mort*) be killed; **tue-tête**: ***à ~*** at the top of one's voice; **tueur** *m* killer
tulipe *f* tulip
tumeur *f* MÉD tumor, *Br* tumour
tumulte *m* uproar; *fig* (*activité*) hustle and bustle; **tumultueux**, **-euse** noisy; *passion* tumultuous, stormy
tunique *f* tunic
Tunisie: ***la ~*** Tunisia; **tunisien**, **~ne** Tunisian; **Tunisien**, **~ne** *m/f* Tunisian
tunnel *m* tunnel
turbo-réacteur *m* AVIAT turbojet
turbulence *f* turbulence; *d'un élève* unruliness; **turbulent** turbulent; *élève* unruly
turc, **turque 1** *adj* Turkish **2** *m langue* Turkish; **Turc**, **Turque** *m/f* Turk
turf *m* SP horseracing; *terrain* racecourse
Turquie: ***la ~*** Turkey
tutelle *f* JUR guardianship; *d'un état, d'une société* supervision, control; *fig* protection
tuteur, **-trice 1** *m/f* JUR guardian **2** *m* BOT stake
tutoyer address as 'tu'
tuyau *m* pipe; *flexible* hose; F (*information*) tip; ***~ d'arrosage*** garden hose; **tuyauter** F: ***~ qn*** tip s.o. off
T.V.A. *f* (= ***taxe sur*** *ou* ***à la valeur ajoutée***) sales tax, *Br* VAT (= value added tax)
type *m* type; F (*gars*) guy F; ***contrat*** *m* ***~*** standard contract
typhon *m* typhoon
typique typical (***de*** of)
tyran *m* tyrant; **tyrannie** *f* tyranny; **tyranniser** tyrannize; *petit frère etc* bully

U

U.E. *f* (= ***Union européenne***) EU (= European Union)
ulcère *m* MÉD ulcer; **ulcérer** *fig* aggrieve
ultérieur later, subsequent
ultimatum *m* ultimatum
ultime last
ultrason *m* PHYS ultrasound
ultraviolet, **~te** *adj & m* ultraviolet
un, **une 1** *article* a; *devant voyelle* an **2** *pron* one; ***à la une*** on the front page; ***l'un des touristes*** one of the

tourists; ***les uns avaient …*** some (of them) had …; ***elles s'aident les unes les autres*** they help each other; ***l'un et l'autre*** both of them **3** *chiffre* one

unanime unanimous; **unanimité** *f* unanimity; ***à l'~*** unanimously

uni *pays* united; *surface* smooth; *tissu* solid(-colored), *Br* self-coloured; *famille* close-knit

unification *f* unification; **unifier** unite, unify

uniforme 1 *adj* uniform; *existence* unchanging **2** *m* uniform; **uniformité** *f* uniformity

unilatéral unilateral

union *f* union; (*cohésion*) unity; **Union européenne** European Union

unique (*seul*) single; *fils* only; (*extraordinaire*) unique; **uniquement** only

unir POL unite; *par moyen de communication* link; *couple* marry; ***s'~*** unite; (*se marier*) marry

unité *f* unit

univers *m* universe; *fig* world; **universel, ~le** universal

universitaire 1 *adj* university *atr* **2** *m/f* academic; **université** *f* university

uranium *m* CHIM uranium

urbain urban; **urbaniser** urbanize; **urbanisme** *m* town planning

urgence *f* urgency; ***une ~*** an emergency; ***d'~*** emergency *atr*; **urgent** urgent

urine *f* urine; **uriner** urinate

urne *f*: ***aller aux ~s*** go to the polls

usage *m* use; (*coutume*) custom; *linguistique* usage; ***hors d'~*** out of use; ***à l'~ de qn*** for use by s.o.; ***d'~*** customary; **usager** *m* user

usé worn; *vêtement, personne* worn-out; **user** *du gaz, de l'eau* use, consume; *vêtement* wear out; *yeux* ruin; ***s'~*** wear out; *personne* wear o.s. out; ***~ de qc*** use sth

usine *f* plant, factory; **usiner** machine

usité *mot* common

ustensile *m* tool; ***~ de cuisine*** kitchen utensil

usuel, ~le usual; *expression* common

usure *f* (*détérioration*) wear; *du sol* erosion

utérus *m* ANAT womb, uterus

utile useful; ***en temps ~*** in due course

utilisateur, -trice *m/f* user; ***~ final*** end user; **utilisation** *f* use; **utiliser** use

utilitaire utilitarian

utilité *f* usefulness, utility; ***ça n'a aucune ~*** it's no use whatever

V

vacance *f poste* opening, *Br* vacancy; **~s** vacation, *Br* holiday(s); **vacancier, -ère** *m/f* vacationer, *Br* holiday-maker
vacarme *m* din, racket
vaccin *m* vaccine; **vaccination** *f* vaccination; **vacciner** vaccinate
vache 1 *f* cow **2** *adj* F mean
vachement F *bon, content* damn F, *Br* bloody F; *changer, vieillir* one helluva lot F
vaciller *sur ses jambes* sway; *d'une flamme* flicker; (*hésiter*) vacillate
vagabond, ~e 1 *adj* wandering **2** *m/f* hobo, *Br* tramp
vagin *m* vagina
vague[1] *f* wave (*aussi fig*); ***~ de froid*** cold snap
vague[2] **1** *adj* vague; *regard* faraway; ***terrain** m* **~** waste ground **2** *m* vagueness; ***regarder dans le ~*** stare into the middle distance
vaillant brave, valiant
vain vain; *mots* empty; ***en ~*** in vain
vaincre conquer; SP defeat; *fig*: *angoisse* overcome, conquer; *obstacle* overcome; **vaincu 1** *adj* conquered; SP defeated **2** *m* loser; **vainqueur** *m* winner, victor
vaisseau *m* ANAT, *litt* (*bateau*) vessel; ***~ spatial*** spaceship
vaisselle *f* dishes *pl*; ***laver** ou **faire la ~*** do *ou* wash the dishes
valable valid
valeur *f* value, worth; *d'une personne* worth; **~s** COMM securities; ***sans ~*** worthless; ***mettre en ~*** emphasize, highlight
valide (*sain*) fit; *passeport, ticket* valid; **valider** validate; *ticket* stamp; **validité** *f* validity
valise *f* bag, suitcase
vallée *f* valley
valoir be worth; (*coûter*) cost; ***~ mieux*** be better (***que*** than); ***faire ~*** *droits* assert; *capital* make work; (*mettre en valeur*) emphasize
valoriser enhance the value of; *personne* enhance the image of
valse *f* waltz
vandale *m/f* vandal; **vandaliser** vandalize
vanille *f* vanilla
vanité *f* (*fatuité*) vanity; (*inutilité*) futility; **vaniteux, -euse** vain
vanne *f* sluice gate; F dig F
vantard, ~e 1 *adj* boastful **2** *m/f* boaster; **vanter** praise; ***se ~ de qch*** pride o.s. on sth
vapeur *f* vapor, *Br* vapour; **~**

(***d'eau***) steam; ***cuire à la ~*** steam
vaporeux, **-euse** *paysage* misty; *tissu* filmy
vaporisateur *m* spray; **vaporiser** spray
varappe *f* rock-climbing
variable variable; *temps, humeur* changeable; **variante** *f* variant; **variation** *f* (*changement*) change; (*écart*) variation
varice *f* ANAT varicose vein
varicelle *f* MÉD chickenpox
varié varied; **varier** vary; **variété** *f* variety; ***~s*** *spectacle* vaudeville, *Br* variety show
variole *f* MÉD smallpox
vase[1] *m* vase
vase[2] *f* mud; **vaseux**, **-euse** muddy; F (*nauséeux*) off-color, *Br* off-colour; F *explication* muddled
vasistas *m* fanlight
vaurien, **~ne** *m/f* good-for-nothing
vautour *m* vulture
veau *m* calf; *viande* veal
vedette *f* star; (*bateau*) launch; ***mettre en ~*** highlight
végétal 1 *adj* plant *atr*; *huile* vegetable **2** *m* plant; **végétalien**, **~ne** *m/f & adj* vegan
végétarien, **~ne** *m/f & adj* vegetarian
végétation *f* vegetation; **végéter** vegetate
véhémence *f* vehemence; **véhément** vehement
véhicule *m* vehicle (*aussi fig*)
veille *f* previous day; *absence de sommeil* wakefulness; ***à la ~ de*** on the eve of; **veiller** stay up late; ***~ à faire qch*** see to it that sth is done; ***~ sur qn*** watch over s.o.
veinard, **~e** *m/f* F lucky devil F; **veine** *f* vein; F luck
vélo *m* bike; ***faire du ~*** go cycling; **vélomoteur** *m* moped
velours *m* velvet; ***~ côtelé*** corduroy
velouté velvety; (*soupe*) creamy
velu hairy
venaison *f* venison
vendable saleable
vendange *f* grape harvest
vendeur *m* sales clerk, *Br* shop assistant; **vendeuse** *f* sales clerk, *Br* shop assistant; **vendre** sell; *fig* betray; ***à ~*** for sale
vendredi *m* Friday; ***Vendredi saint*** Good Friday
vendu, **~e 1** *adj* sold **2** *m/f péj* traitor
vénéneux, **-euse** poisonous
vénérable venerable; **vénération** *f* veneration; **vénérer** revere
vénérien, **~ne**: ***maladie f ~ne*** venereal disease
vengeance *f* vengeance; **venger** avenge (***qn de qc*** s.o. for sth); ***se ~ de qn*** get one's revenge on s.o.; ***se ~ de qc sur qn*** get one's revenge for sth on s.o.

venimeux, **-euse** poisonous; **venin** *m* venom (*aussi fig*)
venir come; ***à ~*** to come; ***où veut-il en ~?*** what's he getting at?; ***~ de*** come from; ***je viens de faire la vaisselle*** I have just washed the dishes; ***faire ~*** *médecin* send for
vent *m* wind; ***coup*** *m* ***de ~*** gust of wind; ***il y a du ~*** it's windy
vente *f* sale; *activité* selling; ***~ à crédit*** installment plan, *Br* hire purchase
venteux, **-euse** windy
ventilateur *m* ventilator; *électrique* fan; **ventilation** *f* ventilation; **ventiler** *pièce* air; *montant* break down
ventre *m* stomach; ***~ à bière*** beer belly
ventriloque *m* ventriloquist
venu, **~e 1** *adj*: ***bien/mal ~*** appropriate/inappropriate **2** *m/f*: ***le premier ~, la première ~e*** the first to arrive; (*n'importe qui*) anybody; **venue** *f* arrival
ver *m* worm; ***~ de terre*** earthworm; ***~ à soie*** silkworm
verbal verbal; **verbe** *m* verb
verdâtre greenish
verdict *m* verdict
verdir turn green
verdure *f* (*feuillages*) greenery; (*salade*) greens *pl*
verge *f* ANAT penis; (*baguette*) rod
verger *m* orchard
verglas *m* black ice
vergogne *f*: ***sans ~*** shameless; *avec verbe* shamelessly
véridique truthful
vérification *f* check; **vérifier** check; ***se ~*** turn out to be true
véritable real; *amour* true
vérité *f* truth; ***en ~*** actually; ***à la ~*** to tell the truth
vermeil, **~le** bright red, vermillion
vermine *f* vermin
verni varnished; F lucky; **vernir** varnish; *céramique* glaze; **vernis** *m* varnish; *de céramique* glaze; ***~ à ongle*** nail polish, *Br aussi* nail varnish
verre *m* glass; ***prendre un ~*** have a drink; ***~s de contact*** contact lenses
verrerie *f* glassmaking; *fabrique* glassworks *sg*; *objets* glassware
verrière *f* (*vitrail*) stained-glass window; *toit* glass roof
verrou *m* bolt; **verrouillage** *m*: ***~ central*** AUTO central locking; **verrouiller** bolt; F lock up
verrue *f* wart
vers[1] *m* verse
vers[2] *prép* toward, *Br* towards; (*environ*) around
versant *m* slope
versatile changeable
Verseau *m* ASTROL Aquarius
versement *m* payment; **verser 1** *v/t* pour (out); *sang*,

larmes shed; *argent à un compte* pay in; *intérêts, pension* pay **2** *v/i* (*basculer*) overturn

version *f* version; (*traduction*) translation

verso *m d'une feuille* back

vert 1 *adj* green; *fruit* unripe; *vin* too young; *fig*: *personne âgée* spry; *propos* risqué **2** *m* green; ***les ~s*** POL *mpl* the Greens

vertébral vertebral; ***colonne*** *f* ***~e*** spine, spinal column; **vertèbre** *f* vertebra

vertical, ~e 1 *adj* vertical **2** *f* vertical (line)

vertige *m* vertigo, dizziness; *fig* giddiness; ***un ~*** a dizzy spell; ***j'ai le ~*** I feel dizzy

vertu *f* virtue; (*pouvoir*) property; ***en ~ de*** in accordance with; **vertueux, -euse** virtuous

verve *f* wit

vésicule *f* ANAT: ***~ biliaire*** gall bladder

vessie *f* ANAT bladder

veste *f* jacket

vestiaire *m de théâtre* checkroom, *Br* cloakroom; *d'un stade* locker room

vestibule *m* hall

vestiges *mpl* traces

veston *m* jacket, coat

vêtement *m* item of clothing, garment; ***~s*** clothes; (***industrie*** *f* ***du***) ***~*** clothing industry

vétérinaire 1 *adj* veterinary **2** *m/f* veterinarian, vet

vêtu dressed

vétuste *bâtiment* dilapidated, ramshackle

veuf 1 *adj* widowed **2** *m* widower

veuve 1 *adj* widowed **2** *f* widow

vexant humiliating; **vexation** *f* humiliation; **vexer**: ***~ qn*** hurt s.o.'s feelings; ***se ~*** get upset

viable *projet*, BIOL viable

viaduc *m* viaduct

viager, -ère: ***rente*** *f* ***viagère*** life annuity

viande *f* meat

vibration *f* vibration; **vibrer** vibrate

vice *m* (*défaut*) defect; (*péché*) vice

vice-président *m* COMM, POL vice-president; *Br* COMM vice-chairman

vicié *air* stale

vicieux, -euse lecherous; *cercle* vicious

victime *f* victim

victoire *f* victory; SP win, victory; **victorieux, -euse** victorious

vidange *f* emptying, draining; AUTO oil change

vide 1 *adj* empty **2** *m* (*néant*) emptiness; *physique* vacuum; (*espace non occupé*) (empty) space; ***avoir peur du ~*** be afraid of heights

vidéo *adj* & *f* video ***~ amateur*** home movie; **vidéocassette** *f* video cassette

vide-ordures *m* rubbish chute
vider empty (out); F *personne* throw out; CUIS *volaille* draw; *salle* vacate, leave; ***se ~*** empty; **videur** *m* F bouncer
vie *f* life; *moyens matériels* living; ***à ~*** for life; ***être en ~*** be alive; ***coût de la ~*** cost of living; ***gagner sa ~*** earn one's living
vieil → ***vieux***
vieillard *m* old man; ***les ~s*** old people *pl*, the elderly *pl*
vieille → ***vieux***
vieillesse *f* old age
vieillir 1 *v/t*: ***~ qn*** age s.o. **2** *v/i d'une personne* get old, age; *d'un visage* age; *d'une théorie, d'un livre* become dated; *d'un vin* age, mature
viennoiseries *fpl croissants and similar types of bread*
vierge 1 *f* virgin; ***Vierge*** ASTROL Virgo **2** *adj* virgin; *feuille* blank
Viêt-nam: ***le ~*** Vietnam; **vietnamien, ~ne 1** *adj* Vietnamese **2** *m langue* Vietnamese; **Vietnamien, ~ne** *m/f* Vietnamese
vieux, (*m* **vieil** *before a vowel or silent h*), **vieille** (*f*) **1** *adj* old **2** *m/f* old man/old woman; ***les ~*** old people *pl*, the aged *pl*
vif, vive 1 *adj* lively; (*en vie*) alive; *plaisir, satisfaction* great; *critique, douleur* sharp; *air* bracing; *froid* biting; *couleur* bright **2** *m* ***à ~*** *plaie* open; ***piqué au ~*** cut to the quick; ***le ~ du sujet*** the heart of the matter; ***avoir les nerfs à ~*** be on edge
vigilance *f* vigilance; **vigilant** vigilant
vigile *m* (*gardien*) security man, guard
vigne *f* (*arbrisseau*) vine; (*plantation*) vineyard
vigneron, ~ne *m/f* wine grower
vignoble *m plantation* vineyard; *région* wine-growing area
vigoureux, -euse robust, vigorous; **vigueur** *f* vigor, *Br* vigour, robustness; ***entrer en ~*** come into force
V.I.H. *m* (= ***Virus de l'Immunodéficience Humaine***) HIV (= human immunodeficiency virus)
vilain nasty; *enfant* naughty; (*laid*) ugly
villa *f* villa
village *m* village; **villageois, ~e 1** *adj* village *atr* **2** *m/f* villager
ville *f* town; *grande* city; ***aller en ~*** go into town
vin *m* wine; ***~ d'honneur*** reception; ***~ de pays*** regional wine
vinaigre *m* vinegar
vinaigrette *f* salad dressing
vingt twenty; **vingtaine**: ***une***

~ de personnes about twenty people *pl*; **vingtième** twentieth
viol *m* rape; *d'un lieu saint* violation; **violation** *f d'un traité* violation; *d'une église* desecration
violemment violently; *fig* intensely; **violence** *f* violence; *fig* intensity; **violent** violent; *fig* intense
violer *loi* break, *sexuellement* rape; (*profaner*) desecrate
violet, ~te violet
violette *f* BOT violet
violon *m* violin; *musicien* violinist
violoncelle *m* cello
virage *m de la route* curve, corner; *d'un véhicule* turn; *fig* change of direction; **virement** *m* COMM transfer; **virer 1** *v/i* (*changer de couleur*) change color *ou Br* colour; *d'un véhicule* corner **2** *v/t argent* transfer; ***~ qn*** F kick s.o. out
virginité *f* virginity
virgule *f* comma
viril male; (*courageux*) manly; **virilité** *f* manhood; (*vigueur sexuelle*) virility
virtuel, ~le virtual; (*possible*) potential
virulent virulent
virus *m* MÉD, INFORM virus
vis *f* screw; ***escalier** m **à ~*** spiral staircase
visa *m* visa
visage *m* face
vis-à-vis 1 *prép*: ***~ de*** opposite; (*envers*) toward, *Br* towards; (*en comparaison de*) compared with **2** *m* person sitting opposite; (*rencontre*) face-to-face meeting
viser 1 *v/t* aim at; (*s'adresser à*) be aimed at **2** *v/i* aim (***à*** at); ***~ à faire*** aim to do
viseur *m d'une arme* sights *pl*; PHOT viewfinder
visibilité *f* visibility; **visible** visible; (*évident*) clear
vision *f* sight; (*conception, apparition*) vision; **visionnaire** *m/f & adj* visionary
visite *f* visit; *d'une ville* tour; ***rendre ~ à qn*** visit s.o.; ***avoir droit de ~*** *d'un parent divorcé* have access; ***~ de douane*** customs inspection; ***~ médicale*** medical (examination);
visiter visit; (*faire le tour de*) tour; *bagages* inspect; **visiteur, -euse** *m/f* visitor
vison *m* mink
visqueux, -euse viscous; *péj* slimy
visser screw
visuel, ~le visual; ***champ** m **~*** field of vision
vital vital; **vitalité** *f* vitality
vitamine *f* vitamin
vite fast, quickly; (*sous peu, bientôt*) soon; ***~!*** quick!; **vitesse** *f* speed; AUTO gear; ***à toute ~*** at top speed
viticulture *f* wine-growing
vitrage *m cloison* glass partition; *action* glazing; *ensem-*

ble de vitres windows *pl*
vitrail *m* stained-glass window
vitre *f* window (pane); *de voiture* window; **vitrer** glaze; **vitrier** *m* glazier
vitrine *f* (*étalage*) (store) window; *meuble* display cabinet
vivace hardy; *haine, amour* lasting; **vivacité** *f* liveliness, vivacity
vivant 1 *adj* alive; (*plein de vie*) lively; (*doué de vie*) living; *langue* modern **2** *m* living person; ***de son ~*** in his lifetime
vivement (*d'un ton vif*) sharply; (*vite*) briskly; *ému, touché* deeply
vivoter just get by
vivre 1 *v/i* live **2** *v/t* experience **3** *mpl*: ***~s*** supplies
vocabulaire *m* vocabulary
vociférer shout
vodka *f* vodka
vœu *m* REL vow; (*souhait*) wish; ***tous mes ~x!*** best wishes!
voici here is *sg*, here are *pl*; ***me ~!*** here I am!; ***le livre que ~*** this book
voie *f* way; *de chemin de fer* track; *d'autoroute* lane; ***en ~ de développement*** developing; ***être en ~ de guérison*** be on the mend; ***par ~ aérienne*** by air; ***par la ~ hiérarchique*** through channels; ***~ d'eau*** leak; ***~ express*** expressway
voilà there is *sg*, there are *pl*; (***et***) ***~!*** there you are!; ***en ~ assez!*** that's enough!; ***~ tout*** that's all
voile 1 *m* veil **2** *f* MAR sail; SP sailing
voiler[1] *v/t* veil; ***se ~*** *d'une femme* wear the veil; *du ciel* cloud over
voiler[2]: ***se ~*** *du bois* warp; *d'une roue* buckle
voir see; ***faire ~*** show; ***se ~*** see each other; ***cela se voit*** that's obvious; ***je ne peux pas le ~*** I can't stand him
voisin, ~e 1 *adj* neighboring, *Br* neighbouring; (*similaire*) similar **2** *m/f* neighbor, *Br* neighbour; **voisinage** *m* neighborhood, *Br* neighbourhood; (*proximité*) vicinity
voiture *f* car; *d'un train* car, *Br* carriage; ***en ~*** by car; ***~ de fonction*** company car
voix *f* voice (*aussi* GRAM); POL vote; ***à haute ~*** in a loud voice, aloud; ***à ~ basse*** in a low voice, quietly
vol[1] *m* theft; ***~ à main armée*** armed robbery
vol[2] *m* flight; ***à ~ d'oiseau*** as the crow flies; ***au ~*** in flight; ***~ à voile*** gliding
volaille *f* poultry; (*poulet etc*) bird
volant *m* AUTO (steering) wheel; SP shuttlecock; *d'un vêtement* flounce
volcan *m* volcano

volée *f d'oiseaux* flock; *en tennis, de coups de feu* volley; ***à la ~*** in mid-air
voler[1] *v/t* steal; ***~ qch à qn*** steal sth from s.o.
voler[2] *v/i* fly
volet *m de fenêtre* shutter; *fig* part; ***trier sur le ~*** *fig* handpick
voleur, **-euse 1** *adj* thieving **2** *m/f* thief; ***~ à l'étalage*** shoplifter
volontaire 1 *adj* voluntary; (*délibéré*) deliberate; (*décidé*) headstrong **2** *m/f* volunteer
volonté *f* will; (*souhait*) wish; (*fermeté*) willpower; ***de l'eau à ~*** as much water as you like; ***faire preuve de bonne ~*** show willing
volontiers willingly, with pleasure
volt *m* ÉL volt; **voltage** *m* ÉL voltage
volte-face *f* about-turn (*aussi fig*)
volubilité *f* volubility
volume *m* volume; **volumineux, -euse** bulky
voluptueux, **-euse** voluptuous
vomir 1 *v/i* vomit, throw up **2** *v/t* bring up; *fig* spew out; **vomissement** *m* vomiting
vorace voracious
vos → ***votre***
vote *m* vote; *action* voting; **voter 1** *v/i* vote **2** *v/t loi* pass
votre, *pl* **vos** your
vôtre: ***le/la ~, les ~s*** yours
vouer dedicate (**à** to); ***se ~ à*** *fig* dedicate o.s. to
vouloir want; ***il veut que tu partes*** (*subj*) he wants you to leave; ***je voudrais*** I would like, I'd like; ***je veux bien*** I'd like to; ***veuillez ne pas fumer*** please do not smoke; ***~ dire*** mean; ***en ~ à qn*** have something against s.o.; ***veux-tu te taire!*** will you shut up!
voulu requisite; *délibéré* deliberate
vous *sg et pl* you; *complément d'objet indirect, sg et pl* (to) you; *avec verbe pronominal* yourself; *pl* yourselves; ***~ ~ êtes coupé*** you've cut yourself; ***si ~ ~ levez à …*** if you get up at …
vous-même, *pl* **vous-mêmes** yourself; *pl* yourselves
voûte *f* ARCH vault; **voûté** *personne* hunched; *dos* bent; ARCH vaulted
vouvoyer adress as 'vous'
voyage *m* trip, journey; *en paquebot* voyage; ***~ d'affaires*** business trip; ***~ de noces*** honeymoon; ***~ organisé*** package holiday; **voyager** travel; **voyageur**, **-euse** *m/f* traveler, *Br* traveller; *par train, avion* passenger; ***~ de commerce*** traveling *ou Br* travelling salesman
voyant, **~e 1** *adj couleur* garish **2** *m* (*signal*) light) **3** *m/f*

(*devin*) clairvoyant
voyelle *f* GRAM vowel
voyou *m jeune* lout
vrac *m*: ***en ~*** COMM loose; *fig* jumbled together
vrai 1 *adj* (*après le subst*) true; (*devant le subst*) real, genuine; *ami* true **2** *m*: ***à ~ dire, à dire ~*** to tell the truth; **vraiment** really
vraisemblable likely, probable; **vraisemblance** *f* likelihood, probability
vrombir throb
VTT *m* (= ***vélo tout terrain***) mountain bike
vu in view of
vue *f* view; *sens, faculté* sight; ***à première ~*** at first sight; ***connaître qn de ~*** know s.o. by sight; ***avoir la ~ basse*** be shortsighted; ***point** m **de ~*** viewpoint, point of view; ***en ~ de faire*** with a view to doing
vulgaire (*banal*) common; (*grossier*) common, vulgar
vulnérable vulnerable

W

wagon *m* car, *Br* carriage; *de marchandises* car, *Br* wagon; **wagon-lit** *m* sleeping car; **wagon-restaurant** *m* dining car
walkman *m* Walkman®
watt *m* ÉL watt
W.-C. *mpl* WC *sg*
week-end *m* weekend; ***ce ~*** on the weekend
whisky *m* whiskey, *Br* whisky

X, Y

xénophobe xenophobic; **xénophobie** *f* xenophobia
xérès *m* sherry
y there; ***on ~ va!*** let's go!; ***ça ~ est!*** that's it!; ***j'~ suis*** (*je comprends*) now I get it; ***~ compris*** including; ***j'~ travaille*** I'm working on it
yacht *m* yacht; **yachting** *m* yachting
yaourt *m* yoghurt
yeux *pl* → ***œil***

Z

zapper channel-hop, *Br aussi* zap
zèbre *m* zebra
zèle *m* zeal; ***faire du ~*** be overzealous; **zélé** zealous
zéro **1** *m* zero, *Br aussi* nought; SP *Br* nil; *fig* nonentity **2** *adj*: ***~ faute*** no mistakes; ***partir de ~*** start from nothing
zeste *m* peel, zest
zézayer lisp
zigouiller F bump off F
zigzag *m* zigzag; **zigzaguer** zigzag
zinc *m* zinc
zona *m* shingles *sg*
zone *f* area, zone; *péj* slums *pl*; ***~ euro*** euro zone; ***~ industrielle*** industrial park, *Br* industrial estate; ***~ interdite*** prohibited area
zoo *m* zoo
zoologie *f* zoology; **zoologiste** *m/f* zoologist
zut! F blast!

English – French
Anglais – Français

A

a [ə] un(e)
abandon [ə'bændən] abandonner
abbreviate [ə'briːvɪeɪt] abréger; **abbreviation** abréviation *f*
abduct [əb'dʌkt] enlever
ability [ə'bɪlətɪ] capacité *f*; *skill* faculté *f*
able ['eɪbl] (*skillful*) compétent; ***be ~ to do*** pouvoir faire
abnormal [æb'nɔːrml] anormal
aboard [ə'bɔːrd] à bord
abolish [ə'bɑːlɪʃ] abolir; **abolition** abolition *f*
abort [ə'bɔːrt] suspendre; **abortion** MED avortement *m*; ***have an ~*** se faire avorter; **abortive** avorté
about [ə'baʊt] **1** *prep* (*concerning*) à propos de; ***a book ~*** un livre sur; ***talk ~*** parler de; ***what's it ~?*** *of book, movie* de quoi ça parle? **2** *adv* (*roughly*) à peu près; ***~ noon*** aux alentours de midi; ***be ~ to do*** (*be going to*) être sur le point de faire
above [ə'bʌv] au-dessus de; ***on the floor ~*** à l'étage du dessus
abrasive [ə'breɪsɪv] *personality* abrupt
abreast [ə'brest]: ***three ~*** les trois l'un à côté de l'autre; ***keep ~ of*** se tenir au courant de
abridge [ə'brɪdʒ] abréger
abroad [ə'brɒːd] à l'étranger
abrupt [ə'brʌpt] brusque
abscess ['æbsɪs] abcès *m*
absence ['æbsəns] absence *f*; **absent** absent; **absentee** absent(e) *m*(*f*); **absenteeism** absentéisme *m*; **absent-minded** distrait
absolute ['æbsəluːt] absolu; **absolution** REL absolution *f*; **absolve** absoudre
absorb [əb'sɔːrb] absorber; **absorbent** absorbant; **absorbent cotton** coton *m* hydrophile; **absorbing** absorbant
abstain [əb'steɪn] *in vote* s'abstenir; **abstention** *in vote* abstention *f*
abstract ['æbstrækt] abstrait
absurd [əb'sɜːrd] absurde; **absurdity** absurdité *f*
abundance [ə'bʌndəns] abondance *f*; **abundant** abondant

abuse[1] [ə'bjuːs] *n verbal* insultes *fpl*; *physical* violences *fpl* physiques; *sexual* sévices *mpl* sexuels; *of power etc* abus *m*

abuse[2] [ə'bjuːz] *v/t verbally* insulter; *physically* maltraiter; *sexually* faire subir des sévices sexuels à; *power etc* abuser de

abysmal [ə'bɪʒml] (*very bad*) lamentable

academic [ækə'demɪk] **1** *n* universitaire *m/f* **2** *adj year*: *at school* scolaire; *at university* universitaire; *interests* intellectuel; **academy** académie *f*

accelerate [ək'seləreɪt] accélérer; **acceleration** accélération *f*; **accelerator** accélérateur *m*

accent ['æksənt] accent *m*; **accentuate** accentuer

accept [ək'sept] accepter; **acceptable** acceptable; **acceptance** acceptation *f*

access ['ækses] **1** *n* accès *m* **2** *v/t also* COMPUT accéder à; **accessible** accessible

accessory [ək'sesərɪ] *for wearing* accessoire *m*; LAW complice *m/f*

accident ['æksɪdənt] accident *m*; ***by ~*** par hasard; **accidental** accidentel; **accidentally** accidentellement

acclimate, acclimatize [ə'klaɪmət, ə'klaɪmətaɪz] s'acclimater

accommodate [ə'kɑːmədeɪt] loger; *needs* s'adapter à; **accommodations** logement *m*

accompaniment [ə'kʌmpənɪmənt] MUS accompagnement *m*; **accompany** *also* MUS accompagner

accomplice [ə'kʌmplɪs] complice *m/f*

accomplished [ə'kʌmplɪʃt] accompli; **accomplishment** *of task* accomplissement *m*; (*achievement*) réussite *f*; (*talent*) talent *m*

accord [ə'kɔːrd] accord *m*; ***of one's own ~*** de son plein gré

accordance [ə'kɔːrdəns]: ***in ~ with*** conformément à

according [ə'kɔːrdɪŋ]: ***~ to*** selon; **accordingly** (*consequently*) par conséquent; (*appropriately*) en conséquence

account [ə'kaʊnt] *financial* compte *m*; (*report*) récit *m*; ***give an ~ of*** faire le récit de; ***on no ~*** en aucun cas; ***on ~ of*** en raison de; ***take ... into ~*** tenir compte de; **accountable**: ***be held ~*** être tenu responsable; **accountant** comptable *m/f*; **accounts** comptabilité *f*

accumulate [ə'kjuːmjʊleɪt] **1** *v/t* accumuler **2** *v/i* s'accumuler; **accumulation** accumulation *f*

accuracy ['ækjʊrəsɪ] justesse *f*; **accurate** juste; **accurately** avec justesse

accusation [ækjuː'zeɪʃn] accusation *f*; **accuse**: ~ ***s.o. of doing sth*** accuser qn de faire qch; **accused** LAW accusé(e) *m(f)*; **accusing** accusateur

accustom [ə'kʌstəm]: ***get ~ed to*** s'accoutumer à

ace [eɪs] *in cards* as *m*; *tennis shot* ace *m*

ache [eɪk] **1** *n* douleur *f* **2** *v/i*: ***my arm ~s*** j'ai mal au bras

achieve [ə'ʧiːv] accomplir; **achievement** (*thing achieved*) accomplissement *m*; *of ambition* réalisation *f*

acid ['æsɪd] acide *m*

acknowledge [ək'nɑːlɪdʒ] reconnaître; ~ ***receipt of*** accuser réception de; **acknowledg(e)ment** reconnaissance *f*; *of a letter* accusé *m* de réception

acoustics [ə'kuːstɪks] acoustique *f*

acquaint [ə'kweɪnt]: ***be ~ed with*** connaître; **acquaintance** *person* connaissance *f*

acquire [ə'kwaɪr] acquérir; **acquisition** acquisition *f*

acquit [ə'kwɪt] LAW acquitter; **acquittal** LAW acquittement *m*

acre ['eɪkər] acre *m* (*4.047m²*)

across [ə'krɑːs] **1** *prep* de l'autre côté de; ***walk ~ the street*** traverser la rue; ~ ***Europe*** *all over* dans toute l'Europe; ~ ***from*** en face de **2** *adv*: ***swim ~*** traverser à la nage; ***10m ~*** 10 *m* de large

act [ækt] **1** *v/i* (*take action*) agir; THEA faire du théâtre **2** *n* (*deed*) fait *m*; *of play* acte *m*; *in vaudeville* numéro *m*; (*law*) loi *f*

action ['ækʃn] action *f*; ***take ~*** prendre des mesures

active ['æktɪv] actif; **activist** POL activiste *m/f*; **activity** activité *f*

actor ['æktər] acteur *m*

actress ['æktrɪs] actrice *f*

actual ['ækʧuəl] véritable; **actually** ['ækʧuəlɪ] en fait; *expressing surprise* vraiment

acute [ə'kjuːt] *pain* intense; *sense* très développé

AD [eɪ'diː] (= ***anno domini***) apr. J.-C. (= après Jésus Christ)

ad [æd] → ***advertisement***

adamant ['ædəmənt]: ***be ~ that …*** soutenir catégoriquement que …

adapt [ə'dæpt] **1** *v/t* adapter **2** *v/i* *of person* s'adapter; **adaptability** faculté *f* d'adaptation; **adaptable** adaptable; **adaptation** *of play etc* adaptation *f*; **adapter** ELEC adaptateur *m*

add [æd] **1** *v/t* ajouter; MATH additionner **2** *v/i of person* faire des additions

◆ **add on** *15% etc* ajouter

◆ **add up 1** *v/t* additionner **2** *v/i* avoir du sens

addict ['ædɪkt] (*drug ~*) drogué(e) *m(f)*; *of TV program* *etc* accro *m/f*; **addicted** *to drugs* drogué; *to TV program etc* accro F; **addiction** *to drugs* dépendance *f* (***to*** de); **addictive**: ***be ~*** entraîner une dépendance

addition [ə'dɪʃn] MATH addition *f*; *to list* ajout *m*; *to company* recrue *f*; ***in ~ to*** en plus de; **additional** supplémentaire; **additive** additif *m*; **add-on** accessoire *m*

address [ə'dres] **1** *n* adresse *f* **2** *v/t letter* adresser; *audience* s'adresser à; **addressee** destinataire *m/f*

adequate ['ædɪkwət] (*sufficient*) suffisant; (*satisfactory*) satisfaisant; **adequately** suffisamment

◆ **adhere to** [əd'hɪr] adhérer à

adhesive [əd'hi:sɪv] adhésif *m*

adjacent [ə'dʒeɪsnt] adjacent

adjective ['ædʒɪktɪv] adjectif *m*

adjoining [ə'dʒɔɪnɪŋ] attenant

adjourn [ə'dʒɜ:rn] ajourner; **adjournment** ajournement *m*

adjust [ə'dʒʌst] ajuster; **adjustable** ajustable; **adjustment** ajustement *m*

ad lib [æd'lɪb] **1** *adj* improvisé **2** *v/i* improviser

administer [əd'mɪnɪstər] *country* administrer; **administration** administration *f*; (*administrative work*) tâches *fpl* administratives; **administrative** administratif; **administrator** administrateur(-trice) *m(f)*

admirable ['ædmərəbl] admirable; **admiration** admiration *f*; **admire** admirer; **admirer** admirateur(-trice) *m(f)*; **admiring** admiratif; **admiringly** admirativement

admissible [əd'mɪsəbl] admis; **admission** (*confession*) aveu *m*; ***~ free*** entrée *f* gratuite; **admit** *to a place*, (*accept*) admettre; (*confess*) avouer; **admittance**: ***no ~*** entrée *f* interdite

adolescence [ædə'lesns] adolescence *f*; **adolescent** **1** *adj* adolescent **2** *n* adolescent(e) *m(f)*

adopt [ə'dɑ:pt] adopter; **adoption** adoption *f*

adorable [ə'dɔ:rəbl] adorable; **adoration** adoration *f*; **adore** adorer

adrenalin [ə'drenəlɪn] adrénaline *f*

adult ['ædʌlt] **1** *adj* adulte **2** *n* adulte *m/f*; **adultery** adultère *m*

advance [əd'væns] **1** *n money* avance *f*; *in science etc* avancée *f*; MIL progression *f*; ***in ~*** à l'avance; ***payment in ~*** paiement *m* anticipé; ***make ~s*** (*progress*) faire des progrès; *sexually* faire des avances **2** *v/i* MIL, (*make progress*)

avancer **3** *v/t theory, sum of money* avancer; *human knowledge, cause* faire avancer; **advanced** avancé
advantage [əd'væntɪdʒ] avantage *m*; ***take ~ of*** *opportunity* profiter de; **advantageous** avantageux
adventure [əd'ventʃər] aventure *f*; **adventurous** aventureux
adverb ['ædvɜːrb] adverbe *m*
adversary ['ædvərsərɪ] adversaire *m/f*
adverse ['ædvɜːrs] adverse
advertise ['ædvərtaɪz] *product* faire de la publicité pour; *job* mettre une annonce pour; **advertisement** *for product* publicité *f*, pub *f*; *for job* annonce *f*; **advertiser** annonceur(-euse) *m(f)*; **advertising** publicité *f*
advice [əd'vaɪs] conseils *mpl*; ***a bit of ~*** un conseil; **advisable** conseillé; **advise** conseiller
advocate ['ædvəkeɪt] recommander
aerial ['erɪəl] *Br* antenne *f*; **aerial photograph** photographie *f* aérienne
aerobics [e'roubɪks] aérobic *m*
aerodynamic [eroudaɪ'næmɪk] aérodynamique
aeroplane ['erouplеɪn] avion *m*
aerosol ['erəsɑːl] aérosol *m*
aesthetic *etc* → ***esthetic*** *etc*
affair [ə'fer] (*matter*) affaire *f*; (*love ~*) liaison *f*
affection [ə'fekʃn] affection *f*; **affectionate** affectueux; **affectionately** affectueusement
affirmative [ə'fɜːrmətɪv] affirmatif
affluence ['æfluəns] richesse *f*; **affluent** riche
afford [ə'fɔːrd]: ***be able to ~ sth*** *financially* pouvoir se permettre d'acheter qch
afloat [ə'flout] *boat* sur l'eau
afraid [ə'freɪd]: ***be ~*** avoir peur (***of*** de); ***I'm ~*** *expressing regret* je crains
afresh [ə'freʃ]: ***start ~*** recommencer
Africa ['æfrɪkə] Afrique *f*
African ['æfrɪkən] **1** *adj* africain **2** *n* Africain(e) *m(f)*; **African-American 1** *adj* afro-américain(e) **2** *n* Afro-Américain(e) *m(f)*
after ['æftər] **1** *prep* après; ***it's ten ~ two*** il est deux heures dix **2** *adv* (*afterward*) après; ***the day ~*** le lendemain
afternoon [æftər'nuːn] après-midi *m*; ***in the ~*** l'après-midi; ***this ~*** cet après-midi; ***good ~*** bonjour
'after sales service service *m* après-vente; **aftershave** lotion *f* après-rasage; **afterward** ensuite
again [ə'geɪn] encore; ***I never saw him ~*** je ne l'ai jamais revu

against [ə'genst] contre
age [eɪdʒ] âge *m*; ***she's five years of ~*** elle a cinq ans; **aged**: ***~ 16*** âgé de 16 ans; **age group** catégorie *f* d'âge; **age limit** limite *f* d'âge
agency ['eɪdʒənsɪ] agence *f*
agenda [ə'dʒendə] ordre *m* du jour
agent ['eɪdʒənt] COM agent *m*
aggravate ['ægrəveɪt] faire empirer; (*annoy*) agacer
aggression [ə'greʃn] agression *f*; **aggressive** agressif; **aggressively** agressivement
aghast [ə'gæst] horrifié
agile ['ædʒəl] agile; **agility** agilité *f*
agitated ['ædʒɪteɪtɪd] agité; **agitation** agitation *f*; **agitator** agitateur(-trice) *m*(*f*)
agnostic [æg'nɑːstɪk] agnostique *m*/*f*
ago [ə'goʊ]: ***two days ~*** il y a deux jours; ***long ~*** il y a longtemps
agonize ['ægənaɪz] se tourmenter (***over*** sur); **agonizing** terrible; **agony** ['ægənɪ] *mental* tourment *m*; *physical* grande douleur *f*
agree [ə'griː] **1** *v/i* être d'accord; *of figures* s'accorder; (*reach agreement*) s'entendre **2** *v/t price* s'entendre sur; **agreeable** (*pleasant*) agréable; **agreement** accord *m*
agricultural [ægrɪ'kʌltʃərəl] agricole; **agriculture** agriculture *f*
ahead [ə'hed] devant; ***plan/think ~*** prévoir/penser à l'avance
aid [eɪd] **1** *n* aide *f* **2** *v/t* aider
aide [eɪd] aide *m*/*f*
Aids [eɪdz] sida *m*
ailing ['eɪlɪŋ] *economy* mal en point
ailment ['eɪlmənt] mal *m*
aim [eɪm] **1** *n* (*objective*) but *m* **2** *v/i in shooting* viser; ***~ to do sth*** essayer de faire qch **3** *v/t*: ***be ~ed at*** *of remark* viser; *of gun* être pointé sur; **aimless** ['eɪmlɪs] sans but
air [er] **1** *n* air *m*; ***by ~*** par avion; ***in the open ~*** en plein air **2** *v/t room* aérer; *views* exprimer; **airbag** airbag *m*; **air-conditioned** climatisé; **air-conditioning** climatisation *f*; **aircraft** avion *m*; **aircraft carrier** porte-avions *m inv*; **air force** armée *f* de l'air; **air hostess** hôtesse *f* de l'air; **airline** compagnie *f* aérienne; **airliner** avion *m* de ligne; **airmail**: ***by ~*** par avion; **airplane** avion *m*; **airport** aéroport *m*; **air terminal** aérogare *f*; **air-traffic controller** contrôleur(-euse) aérien(ne) *m*(*f*)
aisle [aɪl] *in airplane* couloir *m*; *in theater* allée *f*
ajar [ə'dʒɑːr]: ***be ~*** être entrouvert
alarm [ə'lɑːrm] **1** *n* (*fear*) inquiétude *f*; *device* alarme *f*;

(~ *clock*) réveil *m* **2** *v/t* alarmer; **alarming** alarmant; **alarmingly** de manière alarmante
album ['ælbəm] album *m*
alcohol ['ælkəhɑːl] alcool *m*; **alcoholic 1** *adj drink* alcoolisé **2** *n* alcoolique *m/f*
alert [ə'lɜːrt] **1** *adj* vigilant **2** *n signal* alerte *f* **3** *v/t* alerter
alibi ['ælɪbaɪ] alibi *m*
alien ['eɪlɪən] **1** *adj* étranger (*to* à) **2** *n* étranger(-ère) *m(f)*; *from space* extra-terrestre *m/f*; **alienate** s'aliéner
align [ə'laɪn] aligner
alike [ə'laɪk] **1** *adj*: ***be ~*** se ressembler **2** *adv*: ***old and young ~*** les vieux comme les jeunes
alimony ['ælɪmənɪ] pension *f* alimentaire
alive [ə'laɪv]: ***be ~*** être en vie
all [ɒːl] **1** *adj* tout **2** *pron* tout; ***~ of us/them*** nous/eux tous; ***he ate ~ of it*** il l'a mangé en entier; ***for ~ I know*** pour autant que je sache; ***~ but him*** (*except*) tous sauf lui **3** *adv*: ***~ at once*** (*suddenly*) tout d'un coup; (*at the same time*) tous ensemble; ***~ but*** (*nearly*) presque; ***~ the better*** encore mieux; ***they're not at ~ alike*** ils ne se ressemblent pas du tout; ***not at ~!*** pas du tout!; ***two ~*** SP deux à deux
allegation [ælɪ'geɪʃn] allégation *f*; **allege** alléguer; **alleged** supposé; **allegedly**: ***he ~ killed two women*** il aurait assassiné deux femmes
allegiance [ə'liːdʒəns] loyauté *f* (*to* à)
allergic [ə'lɜːrdʒɪk] allergique (*to* à)
alleviate [ə'liːvɪeɪt] soulager
alley ['ælɪ] ruelle *f*
alliance [ə'laɪəns] alliance *f*
allocate ['æləkeɪt] assigner; **allocation** [ælə'keɪʃn] *action* assignation *f*; *amount allocated* part *f*
allot [ə'lɑːt] assigner
allow [ə'laʊ] (*permit*) permettre; (*calculate for*) compter
◆ **allow for** prendre en compte
allowance [ə'laʊəns] *money* allocation *f*; (*pocket money*) argent *m* de poche
alloy ['ælɔɪ] alliage *m*
'all-purpose universel; *vehicle* tous usages; **all-round** général; *athlete* complet;
◆ **allude to** [ə'luːd] faire allusion à
alluring [ə'luːrɪŋ] alléchant
all-wheel 'drive quatre roues motrices *fpl*; *vehicle* 4x4 *m*
ally ['ælaɪ] allié(e) *m(f)*
almond ['ɑːmənd] amande *f*
almost ['ɒːlmoʊst] presque
alone [ə'loʊn] seul
along [ə'lɒːŋ] **1** *prep* le long de; ***walk ~ this path*** prenez ce chemin **2** *adv*: ***bring ~*** amener; ***~ with*** *in addition to* ainsi que
alongside [əlɒːŋ'saɪd] *paral-*

lel to à côté de; *in cooperation with* aux côtés de
aloof [ə'luːf] distant
aloud [ə'laʊd] à haute voix
alphabet ['ælfəbet] alphabet *m*; **alphabetical** alphabétique
already [ɒːl'redɪ] déjà
alright [ɒːl'raɪt] (*permitted*) permis; (*acceptable*) convenable; ***be ~*** (*in working order*) fonctionner; ***she's ~*** *not hurt* elle n'est pas blessée; ***everything is ~*** tout va bien
altar ['ɒːltər] autel *m*
alter ['ɒːltər] modifier; *person* changer; **alteration** modification *f*
alternate 1 ['ɒːltərneɪt] *v/i* alterner **2** ['ɒːltərnət] *adj*: ***on ~ Mondays*** un lundi sur deux
alternative [ɒːl'tɜːrnətɪv] **1** *adj* alternatif **2** *n* alternative *f*; **alternatively** sinon; ***or ~*** ou bien
although [ɒːl'ðoʊ] bien que (*+subj*), quoique (*+subj*)
altitude ['æltɪtuːd] altitude *f*
altogether [ɒːltə'geðər] (*completely*) totalement; (*in all*) en tout
altruism ['æltruːɪzm] altruisme *m*; **altruistic** altruiste
aluminum [ə'luːmənəm] **aluminium** [æljʊ'mɪnɪəm] aluminium *m*
always ['ɒːlweɪz] toujours
a.m. ['eɪem] (= ***ante meridiem***) du matin
amass [ə'mæs] amasser
amateur ['æmətʃʊr] SP amateur *m*/*f*; **amateurish** *attempt* d'amateur; *painter* sans talent
amaze [ə'meɪz] étonner; **amazed** étonné; **amazement** étonnement *m*; **amazing** étonnant; (*very good*) impressionnant; **amazingly** étonnamment
ambassador [æm'bæsədər] ambassadeur(-drice) *m*(*f*)
amber ['æmbər]: ***at ~*** à l'orange
ambience ['æmbɪəns] ambiance *f*
ambiguity [æmbɪ'gjuːətɪ] ambiguïté *f*; **ambiguous** ambigu
ambition [æm'bɪʃn] ambition *f*; **ambitious** ambitieux
ambivalent [æm'bɪvələnt] ambivalent
amble ['æmbl] déambuler
ambulance ['æmbjʊləns] ambulance *f*
ambush ['æmbʊʃ] **1** *n* embuscade *f* **2** *v/t* tendre une embuscade à
amend [ə'mend] modifier; **amendment** modification *f*; **amends**: ***make ~*** se racheter
amenities [ə'miːnətɪz] facilités *fpl*
America [ə'merɪkə] (*United States*) États-Unis *mpl*; *continent* Amérique *f*; **American 1** *adj* américain **2** *n* Américain(e) *m*(*f*)

amicable ['æmɪkəbl] à l'amiable; **amicably** à l'amiable
ammunition [æmjʊ'nɪʃn] munitions *fpl*
amnesia [æm'ni:zɪə] amnésie *f*
amnesty ['æmnəstɪ] amnistie *f*
among(st) [ə'mʌŋ(st)] parmi
amoral [eɪ'mɔ:rəl] amoral
amount [ə'maʊnt] quantité *f*; (*sum of money*) somme *f*
◆ **amount to** s'élever à; (*be equivalent to*) revenir à
amphibian [æm'fɪbɪən] amphibien *m*
ample ['æmpl] beaucoup de
amplifier ['æmplɪfaɪr] amplificateur *m*; **amplify** amplifier
amputate ['æmpjʊ:teɪt] amputer; **amputation** amputation *f*
amuse [ə'mju:z] (*make laugh*) amuser; (*entertain*) distraire; **amusement** (*merriment*) amusement *m*; (*entertainment*) divertissement *m*; **amusement park** parc *m* d'attractions; **amusing** amusant
an [æn] → ***a***
anaemia *etc* → ***anemia*** *etc*
anaesthetic *etc* → ***anesthetic*** *etc*
analog ['ænəlɑ:g] analogique; **analogy** analogie *f*
analysis [ə'næləsɪs] PSYCH analyse *f*; **analyst** PSYCH analyste *m/f*; **analytical** analytique; **analyze** *also* PSYCH analyser
anarchy ['ænərkɪ] anarchie *f*
ancestor ['ænsestər] ancêtre *m/f*
anchor ['æŋkər] **1** *n* NAUT ancre *f*; TV présentateur(-trice) principal(e) *m(f)* **2** *v/i* NAUT ancrer
ancient ['eɪnʃənt] ancien; *Rome etc* antique
and [ænd] et
anemia [ə'ni:mɪə] anémie *f*; **anemic** anémique
anesthetic [ænəs'θetɪk] anesthésiant *m*
angel ['eɪndʒl] ange *m*
anger ['æŋgər] **1** *n* colère *f* **2** *v/t* mettre en colère
angle ['æŋgl] angle *m*
angry ['æŋgrɪ] *person* en colère; *mood, look* fâché
animal ['ænɪml] animal *m*
animated ['ænɪmeɪtɪd] animé; **animated cartoon** dessin *m* animé; **animation** animation *f*
animosity [ænɪ'mɑ:sətɪ] animosité *f*
ankle ['æŋkl] cheville *f*
annex ['æneks] **1** *n* annexe *f* **2** *v/t state* annexer
annihilate [ə'naɪəleɪt] anéantir; **annihilation** anéantissement *m*
anniversary [ænɪ'vɜ:rsərɪ] anniversaire *m*
announce [ə'naʊns] annoncer; **announcement** annonce *f*; **announcer** [ə'naʊnsər] TV, RAD speaker *m*, speakrine

f
annoy [ə'nɔɪ] agacer; **annoyance** (*anger*) agacement *m*; (*nuisance*) désagrément *m*; **annoying** agaçant
annual ['ænʊəl] annuel
annul [ə'nʌl] annuler; **annulment** annulation *f*
anonymous [ə'nɑːnɪməs] anonyme
anorexia [ænə'reksɪə] anorexie *f*
another [ə'nʌðər] **1** *adj* autre **2** *pron* un(e) autre *m(f)*; ***they know one ~*** ils se connaissent
answer ['ænsər] **1** *n* réponse *f*; (*solution*) solution *f* (***to*** à) **2** *v/t* répondre à **3** *v/i* répondre; **answerphone** répondeur *m*
ant [ænt] fourmi *f*
antagonism [æn'tægənɪzm] antagonisme *m*; **antagonistic** hostile; **antagonize** provoquer
Antarctic [ænt'ɑːrktɪk]: ***the ~*** l'Antarctique *m*
antenatal [æntɪ'neɪtl] prénatal
antenna [æn'tenə] antenne *f*
antibiotic [æntaɪbaɪ'ɑːtɪk] antibiotique *m*
anticipate [æn'tɪsɪpeɪt] prévoir; **anticipation** prévision *f*
antics ['æntɪks] singeries *fpl*
antidote ['æntɪdoʊt] antidote *m*
antifreeze ['æntaɪfriːz] antigel *m*
antipathy [æn'tɪpəθɪ] antipathie *f*
antiquated ['æntɪkweɪtɪd] antique
antique [æn'tiːk] antiquité *f*
antiseptic [æntaɪ'septik] **1** *adj* antiseptique **2** *n* antiseptique *m*
antisocial [æntaɪ'soʊʃl] asocial, antisocial
antivirus program [æntaɪ'vaɪrəs] COMPUT programme *m* antivirus
anxiety [æŋ'zaɪətɪ] inquiétude *f*; **anxious** inquiet; (*eager*) soucieux
any ['enɪ] **1** *adj*: ***are there ~ glasses?*** est-ce qu'il y a des verres?; ***is there ~ bread/improvement?*** est-ce qu'il y a du pain/une amélioration?; ***there isn't/aren't ~ ...*** il n'y a pas de ...; ***have you ~ idea at all?*** est-ce que vous avez une idée? **2** *pron*: ***do you have ~?*** est-ce que vous en avez?; ***there aren't/isn't ~ left*** il n'y en a plus; ***~ of them could be guilty*** ils pourraient tous être coupables
anybody ['enɪbɑːdɪ] quelqu'un; *with negatives* personne; *no matter who* n'importe qui; ***there wasn't ~ there*** il n'y avait personne
anyhow ['enɪhaʊ] (*anyway*) enfin; (*in any way*) de quelque façon que ce soit
anyone ['enɪwʌn] → ***anybody***

anything ['enɪθɪŋ] quelque chose; *with negatives* rien; ***I didn't hear ~*** je n'ai rien entendu ~ ***but …*** tout sauf …
anyway ['enɪweɪ] → ***anyhow***
anywhere ['enɪwer] quelque part; *with negative* nulle part; ***I can't find it ~*** je ne le trouve nulle part
apart [ə'pɑːrt] séparé; ~ ***from*** (*except*) à l'exception de; (*in addition to*) en plus de
apartment [ə'pɑːrtmənt] appartement *m*; **apartment block** immeuble *m*
ape [eɪp] singe *m*
aperitif [ə'perɪtiːf] apéritif *m*
apologize [ə'pɑːlədʒaɪz] s'excuser (***to s.o.*** auprès de qn); **apology** excuses *fpl*
appalling [ə'pɒːlɪŋ] scandaleux
apparatus [æpə'reɪtəs] appareils *mpl*
apparent [ə'pærənt] (*obvious*) évident; (*seeming*) apparent; **apparently** apparemment
appeal [ə'piːl] (*charm*) charme *m*; *for funds etc*, LAW appel *m*
◆ **appeal for** *calm etc* appeler à; *funds* demander
◆ **appeal to** (*be attractive to*) plaire à
appealing [ə'piːlɪŋ] séduisant
appear [ə'pɪr] apparaître; *in court* comparaître; (*seem*) paraître; ~ ***to be …*** avoir l'air d'être …; **appearance** apparition *f*; *in court* comparution *f*; (*look*) apparence *f*
appendicitis [əpendɪ'saɪtɪs] appendicite *f*
appendix [ə'pendɪks] MED, *of book etc* appendice *m*
appetite ['æpɪtaɪt] appétit *m*; **appetizer** *to drink* apéritif *m*; *to eat* amuse-gueule *m*; **appetizing** appétissant
applaud [ə'plɒːd] applaudir; **applause** applaudissements *mpl*
apple ['æpl] pomme *f*
appliance [ə'plaɪəns] appareil *m*
applicable [ə'plɪkəbl] applicable; **applicant** *for job* candidat(e) *m(f)*; **application** *for job* candidature *f*; *for passport etc* demande *f*; **apply 1** *v/t* appliquer **2** *v/i of rule, law* s'appliquer
◆ **apply for** *job* poser sa candidature pour; *passport etc* faire une demande de
◆ **apply to** (*contact*) s'adresser à; *of rules etc* s'appliquer à
appoint [ə'pɔɪnt] *to position* nommer; **appointment** *to position* nomination *f*; (*meeting*) rendez-vous *m*
appraisal [ə'preɪzəl] évaluation *f*
appreciable [ə'priːʃəbl] considérable; **appreciate 1** *v/t* apprécier; (*acknowledge*) reconnaître **2** *v/i* FIN s'apprécier; **appreciative** *grateful*

reconnaissant; *understanding* approbateur; *audience* réceptif
apprehensive [æprɪ'hensɪv] appréhensif
approach [ə'prouʧ] **1** *n* approche *f*; (*proposal*) proposition *f* **2** *v/t* (*get near to*) approcher; (*contact*) faire des propositions à; *problem* aborder; **approachable** *person* d'un abord facile
appropriate [ə'prouprɪət] approprié
approval [ə'pru:vl] approbation *f*; **approve 1** *v/i* être d'accord **2** *v/t plan* approuver
approximate [ə'prɑ:ksɪmət] approximatif; **approximately** approximativement
apricot ['eɪprɪkɑ:t] abricot *m*
April ['eɪprəl] avril *m*
apt [æpt] *remark* pertinent; **aptitude** aptitude *f*
aquarium [ə'kwerɪəm] aquarium *m*
Arab ['ærəb] **1** *adj* arabe **2** *n* Arabe *m/f*; **Arabic 1** *adj* arabe **2** *n* arabe *m*
arbitrary ['ɑ:rbɪtrərɪ] arbitraire
arbitrate ['ɑ:rbɪtreɪt] arbitrer; **arbitration** arbitrage *m*
arch [ɑ:rʧ] voûte *f*
archaeology *etc* → ***archeology*** *etc*
archaic [ɑ:r'keɪɪk] archaïque
archeological [ɑ:rkɪə'lɑ:dʒɪkl] archéologique; **archeologist** archéologue *m/f*; **archeology** archéologie *f*
architect ['ɑ:rkɪtekt] architecte *m/f*; **architectural** architectural; **architecture** architecture *f*
archives ['ɑ:rkaɪvz] archives *fpl*
Arctic ['ɑ:rktɪk]: ***the ~*** l'Arctique *m*
ardent ['ɑ:rdənt] fervent
arduous ['ɑ:rdjuəs] ardu
area ['erɪə] *of city* quartier *m*; *of country* région *f*; *of research* domaine *m*; *of room* surface *f*; GEOM, *of land* superficie *f*; **area code** TELEC indicatif *m* régional
arena [ə'ri:nə] SP arène *f*
Argentina [ɑ:rdʒən'ti:nə] Argentine *f*
Argentinian [ɑ:rdʒən'tɪnɪən] **1** *adj* argentin **2** *n* Argentin(e) *m(f)*
arguably ['ɑ:rgjuəblɪ]: ***it was ~ ...*** on peut dire que ...; **argue** (*quarrel*) se disputer; (*reason*) argumenter; **argument** (*quarrel*) dispute *f*; (*discussion*) discussion *f*; (*reasoning*) argument *m*
arid ['ærɪd] *land* aride
arise [ə'raɪz] *of situation* survenir
arithmetic [ə'rɪθmətɪk] arithmétique *f*
arm¹ [ɑ:rm] *n* bras *m*
arm² [ɑ:rm] *v/t* armer
armaments ['ɑ:rməmənts] armes *fpl*
'armchair fauteuil *m*

armed [ɑːrmd] armé; **armed forces** forces *fpl* armées; **armed robbery** vol *m* à main armée
'armpit aisselle *f*
arms [ɑːrmz] (*weapons*) armes *fpl*
army ['ɑːrmɪ] armée *f*
around [ə'raʊnd] **1** *prep* (*encircling*) autour de; ***it's ~ the corner*** c'est juste à côté **2** *adv* (*in the area*) dans les parages; (*encircling*) autour; (*roughly*) à peu près; *with expressions of time* à environ
arouse [ə'raʊz] susciter; *sexually* exciter
arrange [ə'reɪndʒ] arranger; *furniture* disposer; *meeting etc* organiser; *time* fixer; *appointment* prendre; ***I've ~d to meet her*** j'ai prévu de la voir; **arrangement** (*agreement*), *music* arrangement *m*; *of furniture* disposition *f*; *flowers* composition *f*
arrears [ə'rɪərz] arriéré *m*
arrest [ə'rest] **1** *n* arrestation *f*; ***be under ~*** être en état d'arrestation **2** *v/t* arrêter
arrival [ə'raɪvl] arrivée *f*; **arrive** arriver
◆ **arrive at** arriver à
arrogance ['ærəgəns] arrogance *f*; **arrogant** arrogant
arrow ['æroʊ] flèche *f*
arson ['ɑːrsn] incendie *m* criminel
art [ɑːrt] art *m*
artery ['ɑːrtərɪ] artère *f*
'art gallery galerie *f* d'art
arthritis [ɑːr'θraɪtɪs] arthrite *f*
artichoke ['ɑːrtɪtʃoʊk] artichaut *m*
article ['ɑːrtɪkl] article *m*
articulate [ɑːr'tɪkjʊlət] *person* qui s'exprime bien
artificial [ɑːrtɪ'fɪʃl] artificiel
artillery [ɑːr'tɪlərɪ] artillerie *f*
artist ['ɑːrtɪst] artiste *m/f*; **artistic** artistique
'arts degree licence *f* de lettres
as [æz] **1** *conj* (*while, when*) alors que; (*because*) comme; (*like*) comme; ***~ if*** comme si; ***~ usual*** comme d'habitude **2** *adv*: ***~ high ~ …*** aussi haut que …; ***~ much ~ that?*** autant que ça?; ***~ soon ~ possible*** aussi vite que possible **3** *prep* comme; ***work ~ a teacher*** travailler comme professeur; ***~ for*** quant à; ***~ from** or **of Monday*** à partir de lundi
ash [æʃ] cendres *fpl*
ashamed [ə'ʃeɪmd] honteux; ***be ~ of*** avoir honte de
'ash can poubelle *f*
ashore [ə'ʃɔːr] à terre; ***go ~*** débarquer
ashtray ['æʃtreɪ] cendrier *m*
Asia ['eɪʃə] Asie *f*; **Asian 1** *adj* asiatique **2** *n* Asiatique *m/f*; **Asian-American 1** *adj* américain(e) d'origine asiatique **2** *n* Américain(e) *m(f)* d'origine asiatique
aside [ə'saɪd] de côté; ***move ~***

please poussez-vous, s'il vous plaît; ***take s.o. ~*** prendre qn à part; ***~ from*** à part

ask [æsk] demander; *question* poser; (*invite*) inviter; ***~ s.o. for sth*** demander qch à qn

◆ **ask after** *person* demander des nouvelles de

◆ **ask for** demander; *person* demander à parler à

◆ **ask out**: ***he's asked me out*** il m'a demandé de sortir avec lui

asleep [ə'sliːp]: ***be*** (***fast***) ***~*** être (bien) endormi; ***fall ~*** s'endormir

asparagus [ə'spærəgəs] asperges *fpl*

aspect ['æspekt] aspect *m*

aspirations [æspə'reɪʃnz] aspirations *fpl*

aspirin ['æsprɪn] aspirine *f*

ass[1] [æs] (*idiot*) idiot(e) *m*(*f*)

ass[2] [æs] (*butt*) cul *m*

assassin [ə'sæsɪn] assassin *m*; **assassinate** assassiner

assassination assassinat *m*

assault [ə'sɒːlt] **1** *n* agression *f*; MIL attaque *f* (**on** contre) **2** *v/t* agresser

assemble [ə'sembl] **1** *v/t parts* assembler **2** *v/i of people* se rassembler; **assembly** POL assemblée *f*; *of parts* assemblage *m*; **assembly line** chaîne *f* de montage

assent [ə'sent] consentir

assertive [ə'sɜːrtɪv] *person* assuré

assess [ə'ses] *situation* évaluer; *value* estimer; **assessment** *of situation* évaluation *f*; *of value* estimation *f*

asset ['æset] FIN actif *m*; atout *m*

assign [ə'saɪn] assigner; **assignment** mission *f*; EDU devoir *m*

assimilate [ə'sɪmɪleɪt] assimiler

assist [ə'sɪst] aider; **assistance** aide *f*; **assistant** assistant(e) *m*(*f*); **assistant manager** sous-directeur *m*, sous-directrice *f*; *of department* assistant(e) *m*(*f*) du/de la responsable

associate 1 *v/t* [ə'soʊʃɪeɪt] associer **2** *n* [ə'soʊʃɪət] (*colleague*) collègue *m/f*; **association** association *f*

assortment [ə'sɔːrtmənt] assortiment *m*

assume [ə'suːm] (*suppose*) supposer; **assumption** supposition *f*

assurance [ə'ʃʊrəns] (*reassurance, confidence*) assurance *f*; **assure** (*reassure*) assurer

asthma ['æsmə] asthme *m*

astonish [ə'stɑːnɪʃ] étonner; **astonishing** étonnant; **astonishment** étonnement *m*

astound [ə'staʊnd] stupéfier

astride [ə'straɪd] à califourchon sur

astrology [ə'strɑːlədʒɪ] astrologie *f*

astronaut ['æstrənɒːt] astro-

naute *m/f*
astronomer [ə'strɑːnəmər] astronome *m/f*; **astronomical** *price etc* astronomique; **astronomy** astronomie *f*
astute [ə'stuːt] fin
asylum [ə'saɪləm] *political*, (*mental* ~) asile *m*
at [æt] *with places* à; ~ ***Joe's*** chez Joe; ~ ***10 dollars*** au prix de 10 dollars; ~ ***the age of 18*** à l'âge de 18 ans; ~ ***5 o'clock*** à 5 heures; ***be good/bad*** ~ ... être bon/mauvais en ...
atheist ['eɪθɪɪst] athée *m/f*
athlete ['æθliːt] athlète *m/f*; **athletic** d'athlétisme; (*strong*, *sporting*) sportif; **athletics** athlétisme *m*
Atlantic [ət'læntɪk]: ***the*** ~ l'Atlantique *m*
atlas ['ætləs] atlas *m*
ATM [eɪtiː'em](= ***automatic teller machine***) distributeur *m* automatique (de billets)
atmosphere ['ætməsfɪr] atmosphère *f*
atom ['ætəm] atome *m*; **atomic** atomique
◆ **atone for** [ə'toʊn] racheter
atrocious [ə'troʊʃəs] atroce; **atrocity** atrocité *f*
at-'seat TV *télévision que l'on regarde à sa place, par exemple en avion*
attach [ə'tæʧ] attacher; **attachment** *to e-mail* fichier *m* joint
attack [ə'tæk] **1** *n* attaque *f* **2** *v/t* attaquer
attempt [ə'tempt] **1** *n* tentative *f* **2** *v/t* essayer
attend [ə'tend] assister à; *school* aller à
◆ **attend to** s'occuper de
attendance [ə'tendəns] présence *f*; **attendant** *in museum etc* gardien(ne) *m(f)*
attention [ə'tenʃn] attention *f*; ***pay*** ~ faire attention; **attentive** attentif
attic ['ætɪk] grenier *m*
attitude ['ætɪtuːd] attitude *f*
attorney [ə'tɜːrnɪ] avocat *m*
attract [ə'trækt] attirer; **attraction** *of job*, *doing sth* attrait *m*; *romantic* attirance *f*; *touristic* attraction *f*; **attractive** *person* attirant; *idea*, *city* attrayant
auction ['ɒːkʃn] vente *f* aux enchères
audacity [ɒː'dæsətɪ] audace *f*
audible ['ɒːdəbl] audible
audience ['ɒːdɪəns] public *m*
audio ['ɒːdɪoʊ] audio; **audiovisual** audiovisuel
audit ['ɒːdɪt] **1** *n* audit *m* **2** *v/t* contrôler; *course* suivre en auditeur libre
audition [ɒː'dɪʃn] **1** *n* audition *f* **2** *v/i* passer une audition
auditor ['ɒːdɪtər] FIN auditeur(-trice) *m(f)*
auditorium [ɒːdɪ'tɔːrɪəm] *of theater etc* auditorium *m*
August ['ɒːgəst] août
aunt [ænt] tante *f*
au pair [oʊ'per] jeune fille *f* au pair

aura ['ɒːrə] aura *f*
auspicious [ɒː'spɪʃəs] favorable
austere [ɒː'stiːr] austère; **austerity** austérité *f*
Australia [ɒː'streɪlɪə] Australie *f*; **Australian 1** *adj* australien **2** *n* Australien(ne) *m*(*f*)
Austria ['ɒːstrɪə] Autriche *f*; **Austrian 1** *adj* autrichien **2** *n* Autrichien(ne) *m*(*f*)
authentic [ɒː'θentɪk] authentique; **authenticity** authenticité *f*
author ['ɒːtər] auteur *m*
authoritarian [əθɑːrɪ'terɪən] autoritaire; **authoritative** *source* qui fait autorité; *person, manner* autoritaire; **authority** [ə'θɑːrətɪ] autorité *f*; (*permission*) autorisation *f*; **authorization** autorisation *f*; **authorize** autoriser
autistic [ɒː'tɪstɪk] autiste
autobiography [ɒːtəbaɪ'ɑːgrəfɪ] autobiographie *f*
autocratic [ɒːtə'krætɪk] autocratique
autograph ['ɒːtəgræf] autographe *m*
automate ['ɒːtəmeɪt] automatiser; **automatic 1** *adj* automatique **2** *n car* automatique *f*; *gun* automatique *m*; **automatically** automatiquement; **automation** automatisation *f*
automobile ['ɒːtəmoʊbiːl] automobile *f*; **automobile industry** industrie *f* automobile
autonomous [ɒː'tɑːnəməs] autonome
autopilot ['ɒːtoʊpaɪlət] pilotage *m* automatique
autopsy ['ɒːtɑːpsɪ] autopsie *f*
autumn ['ɒːtəm] *Br* automne *m*
auxiliary [ɒːg'zɪljərɪ] auxiliaire
available [ə'veɪləbl] disponible
avalanche ['ævəlænʃ] avalanche *f*
avenue ['ævənuː] avenue *f*; ***explore all ~s*** explorer toutes les possibilités
average ['ævərɪdʒ] **1** *adj* moyen **2** *n* moyenne *f*; ***on ~*** en moyenne
◆ **average out at** faire une moyenne de
averse [ə'vɜːrs]: ***not be ~ to*** ne rien avoir contre; **aversion** aversion *f* (***to*** pour)
avid ['ævɪd] avide
avocado [ɑːvə'kɑːdoʊ] avocat *m*
avoid [ə'vɔɪd] éviter
await [ə'weɪt] attendre
awake [ə'weɪk] éveillé; ***it's keeping me ~*** ça m'empêche de dormir
award [ə'wɔːrd] **1** *n* (*prize*) prix *m* **2** *v/t* décerner; *damages* attribuer; **awards ceremony** cérémonie *f* de remise des prix; EDU cérémonie *f* de remise des diplômes

aware [ə'wer]: ***be ~ of sth*** avoir conscience de qch; ***become ~ of sth*** prendre conscience de qch; **awareness** conscience *f*

away [ə'weɪ]: ***be ~*** être absent, ne pas être là; ***walk ~*** s'en aller; ***look ~*** tourner la tête; ***it's 2 miles ~*** c'est à 2 miles d'ici; ***take sth ~ from s.o.*** enlever qch à qn; **away game** SP match *m* à l'extérieur

awesome ['ɒːsəm] F (*terrific*) super *inv*

awful ['ɒːfəl] affreux

awkward ['ɒːkwərd] (*clumsy*) maladroit; (*difficult*) difficile; (*embarrassing*) gênant; ***feel ~*** se sentir mal à l'aise

ax, *Br* **axe** [æks] **1** *n* hache *f* **2** *v/t project* abandonner; *budget* faire des coupures dans; *job* supprimer

axle ['æksl] essieu *m*

B

baby ['beɪbɪ] bébé *m*; **baby-sit** faire du baby-sitting

bachelor ['bætʃələr] célibataire *m*

back [bæk] **1** *n of person, clothes* dos *m*; *of chair* dossier *m*; *of drawer* fond *m*; *of house* arrière *m*; SP arrière *m*; ***in ~ (of the car)*** à l'arrière (de la voiture); ***at the ~ of the book*** à la fin du livre; ***~ to front*** à l'envers **2** *adj door* de derrière; *wheels, legs* arrière *inv* **3** *adv*: ***move ~*** se reculer; ***give sth ~ to s.o.*** rendre qch à qn; ***she'll be ~ tomorrow*** elle sera de retour demain **4** *v/t* (*support*) soutenir; *car* faire reculer; *horse* miser sur

◆ **back down** faire marche arrière

◆ **back out** *of commitment* se dégager

◆ **back up 1** *v/t* (*support*) soutenir; *file* sauvegarder **2** *v/i in car* reculer

'**backache** mal *m* de dos; **backbone** colonne *f* vertébrale; **backdate** antidater; **backdoor** porte *f* arrière; **backer** bailleur *m* de fonds; *for artist, show* producteur (-trice) *m*(*f*); **background** *of picture* arrière-plan *m*; *social* milieu *m*; *of crime* contexte *m*; ***his work ~*** son expérience professionnelle; **backhand** *in tennis* revers *m*; **backing** (*support*) soutien *m*; MUS accompagnement *m*; **backing group** groupe *m* d'accompagnement; **backlash** répercussion(s) *f*(pl); **backlog** retard *m* (***of*** dans); **backpack** sac *m* à dos; **back-**

packer randonneur(-euse) *m(f)*; **back seat** siège *m* arrière; **back streets** petites rues *fpl*; *poor area* quartiers *mpl* pauvres; **backstroke** SP dos *m* crawlé; **backtrack** retourner sur ses pas; **backup** (*support*) renfort *m*; COMPUT copie *f* de sauvegarde; **backyard** arrière-cour *f*

bacon ['beɪkn] bacon *m*

bacteria [bæk'tɪrɪə] bactéries *fpl*

bad [bæd] mauvais; *person* méchant; (*rotten*) avarié; ***go ~*** s'avarier; ***it's not ~*** c'est pas mal; ***that's really too ~*** (*shame*) c'est vraiment dommage

badge [bædʒ] insigne *f*

bad 'language grossièretés *fpl*; **badly** mal; *injured* grièvement; *damaged* sérieusement; ***he ~ needs ...*** il a grand besoin de ...

badminton ['bædmɪntən] badminton *m*

bad-tempered [bæd'tempərd] de mauvaise humeur

baffle ['bæfl] déconcerter; ***be ~d*** être perplexe

bag [bæg] sac *m*; (*piece of baggage*) bagage *m*

baggage ['bægɪdʒ] bagages *mpl*; **baggage check** contrôle *m* des bagages

baggy ['bægɪ] flottant; *fashionably* large

bail [beɪl] LAW caution *f*; ***be out on ~*** être en liberté provisoire sous caution

bait [beɪt] appât *m*

bake [beɪk] cuire au four; **baked potato** pomme *f* de terre au four; **baker** boulanger(-ère) *m(f)*; **bakery** boulangerie *f*

balance ['bæləns] **1** *n* équilibre *m*; (*remainder*) reste *m*; *of bank account* solde *m* **2** *v/t* mettre en équilibre **3** *v/i* rester en équilibre; *of accounts* équilibrer; **balanced** (*fair*) objectif; *diet, personality* équilibré; **balance sheet** bilan *m*

balcony ['bælkənɪ] balcon *m*

bald [bɒːld] chauve; **balding** qui commence à devenir chauve

ball [bɒːl] *for soccer etc* ballon *m*; *for tennis, golf* balle *f*

ballad ['bæləd] ballade *f*

ballet [bæ'leɪ] ballet *m*; **ballet dancer** danceur(-euse) *m(f)* de ballet

'ball game match *m* de baseball

ballistic missile [bə'lɪstɪk] missile *m* balistisque

balloon [bə'luːn] *child's* ballon *m*; *for flight* montgolfière *f*

ballot ['bælət] **1** *n* vote *m* **2** *v/t* *members* faire voter; **ballot box** urne *f*

'ballpark terrain *m* de baseball; **ballpark figure** chiffre *m* en gros; **ballpoint (pen)**

stylo *m* bille
balls [bɒːlz] V couilles *fpl*
bamboo [bæm'buː] bambou *m*
ban [bæn] **1** *n* interdiction *f* **2** *v/t* interdire
banal [bə'næl] banal
banana [bə'nænə] banane *f*
band [bænd] MUS orchestre *m*; *pop* groupe *m*; *of material* bande *f*
bandage ['bændɪdʒ] **1** *n* bandage *m* **2** *v/t* faire un bandage à
'Band-Aid® sparadrap *m*
bandit ['bændɪt] bandit *m*
bandy ['bændɪ] *legs* arqué
bang [bæŋ] **1** *n noise* boum *m*; (*blow*) coup *m* **2** *v/t door* claquer; (*hit*) cogner
bangle ['bæŋgl] bracelet *m*
bangs [bæŋʒ] frange *f*
banisters ['bænɪstərz] rampe *f*
banjo ['bændʒoʊ] banjo *m*
bank¹ [bæŋk] *of river* bord *m*, rive *f*
bank² [bæŋk] FIN banque *f*
◆ **bank on** compter sur
'bank account compte *m* en banque; **banker** banquier (-ière) *m*(*f*); **banker's card** carte *f* d'identité bancaire; **banking** banque *f*; **bank loan** emprunt *m* bancaire; **bank manager** directeur (-trice) *m*(*f*) de banque; **bank rate** taux *m* bancaire; **bankroll** financer; **bankrupt** en faillite; ***go ~*** faire faillite;
bankruptcy faillite *f*
banner ['bænər] bannière *f*
banquet ['bæŋkwɪt] banquet *m*
baptism ['bæptɪzm] baptême *m*; **baptize** baptiser
bar¹ [bɑːr] *n of iron, chocolate* barre *f*; *for drinks, counter* bar *m*
bar² [bɑːr] *v/t* exclure
barbaric [bɑːr'bærɪk] barbare
barbecue ['bɑːrbɪkjuː] **1** *n* barbecue *m* **2** *v/t* cuire au barbecue
barbed 'wire [bɑːrbd] fil *m* barbelé
barber ['bɑːrbər] coiffeur *m*
'bar code code *m* barre
bare [ber] nu; *room, shelves* vide; **barefoot**: ***be ~*** être pieds nus; **bare-headed** tête nue; **barely** à peine
bargain ['bɑːrgɪn] **1** *n* (*deal*) marché *m*; (*good buy*) bonne affaire *f* **2** *v/i* marchander
barge [bɑːrdʒ] NAUT péniche *f*
◆ **barge into** se heurter contre; (*enter noisily*) faire irruption dans
baritone ['bærɪtoʊn] baryton *m*
bark¹ [bɑːrk] **1** *n of dog* aboiement *m* **2** *v/i* aboyer
bark² [bɑːrk] *of tree* écorce *f*
barn [bɑːrn] grange *f*
barometer [bə'rɑːmɪtər] *also fig* baromètre *m*
barracks ['bærəks] MIL caserne *f*
barrel ['bærəl] tonneau *m*

barren ['bærən] *land* stérile
barrette [bə'ret] barrette *f*
barricade [bærɪ'keɪd] barricade *f*
barrier ['bærɪər] barrière *f*
'bar tender barman *m*, barmaid *f*
barter ['bɑːrtər] **1** *n* troc *m* **2** *v/t* troquer (***for*** contre)
base [beɪs] **1** *n* base *f* **2** *v/t* baser (***on*** sur); **baseball** baseball *m*; *ball* ballon *m* de baseball; **baseball cap** casquette *f* de baseball; **baseboard** plinthe *f*; **basement** sous-sol *m*
basic ['beɪsɪk] (*rudimentary*) rudimentaire; (*fundamental*), *salary* de base; **basically** au fond
basin ['beɪsn] *for washing dishes* bassine *f*; *in bathroom* lavabo *m*
basis ['beɪsɪs] base *f*; *of argument* fondement *m*
bask [bæsk] se dorer
basket ['bæskɪt] panier *m*; **basketball** *game* basket (-ball) *m*; *ball* ballon *m* de basket
bass [beɪs] basse *f*; ***double ~*** contrebasse *f*; ***~ guitar*** basse *f*
bastard ['bæstərd] salaud(e) *m(f)*
bat[1] [bæt] **1** *n for baseball* batte *f*; *for table tennis* raquette *f* **2** *v/i in baseball* batter
bat[2] [bæt] *animal* chauve-souris *f*
batch [bætʃ] *of students*, *data* lot *m*; *of bread* fournée *f*
bath [bæθ] (*~tub*) baignoire *f*
bathe [beɪð] (*have a bath*) se baigner
'bathrobe peignoir *m*; **bathroom** salle *f* de bains; *toilet* toilettes *fpl*; **bath towel** serviette *f* de bain; **bathtub** baignoire *f*
batter ['bætər] *for cakes*, *pancakes etc* pâte *f* lisse; *in baseball* batteur *m*; **battered** *wife*, *children* battu
battery ['bætərɪ] pile *f*; MOT batterie *f*
battle ['bætl] **1** *n* bataille *f*; *fig* lutte *f* **2** *v/i against illness etc* se battre, lutter; **battleship** cuirassé *m*
bawl [bɒːl] (*shout*, *weep*) brailler
bay [beɪ] (*inlet*) baie *f*
BC [biː'siː] (= ***before Christ***) av. J.-C.
be [biː] ◊ être; ***~ 15*** avoir 15 ans; ***it's me*** c'est moi; ***how much is...?*** combien coûte ...?; ***there is/are*** il y a; ***how are you?*** comment ça va? ◊ ***has the mailman been?*** est-ce que le facteur est passé?; ***I've never been to Japan*** je ne suis jamais allé au Japon ◊ *tags*: ***that's right, isn't it?*** c'est juste, n'est-ce pas?; ***she's American, isn't she?*** elle est américaine, n'est-ce pas?

◇ *passive*: ***he was killed*** il a été tué; ***it hasn't been decided*** on n'a encore rien décidé

beach [biːʧ] plage *f*; **beachwear** vêtements *mpl* de plage

beads [biːdz] collier *m* de perles

beak [biːk] bec *m*

beam [biːm] **1** *n in ceiling etc* poutre *f* **2** *v/i* (*smile*) rayonner

bean [biːn] haricot *m*; *of coffee* grain *m*

bear[1] [ber] *n animal* ours *m*

bear[2] [ber] **1** *v/t weight* porter; *costs* prendre en charge; (*tolerate*) supporter; **bearable** supportable

beard [bɪrd] barbe *f*

beat [biːt] **1** *n of heart* battement *m*; *of music* mesure *f* **2** *v/i of heart* battre; *of rain* s'abattre **3** *v/t in competition*, (*hit*) battre; (*pound*) frapper

◆ **beat up** tabasser

beaten ['biːtən]: ***off the ~ track*** à l'écart; **beating** *physical* raclée *f*; **beat-up** déglingué

beautiful ['bjuːtəfʊl] beau; **beautifully** admirablement; **beauty** beauté *f*

beaver ['biːvər] castor *m*

because [bɪ'kɑːz] parce que; ***~ of*** à cause de

become [bɪ'kʌm] devenir; ***what's ~ of her?*** qu'est-elle devenue?; **becoming** seyant

bed [bed] *also of sea* lit *m*; *of flowers* parterre *m*; ***go to ~*** aller se coucher; **bedding** literie *f*; **bedridden** cloué au lit; **bedroom** chambre *f* (à coucher); **bedtime** heure *f* du coucher

bee [biː] abeille *f*

beech [biːʧ] hêtre *m*

beef [biːf] bœuf *m*; **beefburger** steak *m* hâché

beep [biːp] **1** *n* bip *m* **2** *v/i* faire bip

beer [bɪr] bière *f*

beet [biːt] betterave *f*

beetle ['biːtl] coléoptère *m*, cafard *m*

before [bɪfɔːr] **1** *prep* avant; ***~ signing it*** avant de le signer; ***~ a vowel*** devant une voyelle **2** *adv* auparavant; (*already*) déjà; ***the week/day ~*** la semaine/le jour d'avant **3** *conj* avant que (*+subj*); ***I had a coffee ~ I left*** j'ai pris un café avant de partir; **beforehand** à l'avance

befriend [bɪ'frend] se lier d'amitié avec

beg [beg] **1** *v/i* mendier **2** *v/t*: ***~ s.o. to do sth*** prier qn de faire qch; **beggar** mendiant (e) *m* (*f*)

begin [bɪ'gɪn] **1** *v/i* commencer; **beginner** débutant(e) *m*(*f*); **beginning** début *m*

behalf [bɪ'hɑːf]: ***in*** *or* ***on ~ of*** de la part de

behave [bɪ'heɪv] se comporter; ***~ (yourself)!*** sois sage!; **behavior**, *Br* **behaviour**

comportement *m*
behind [bɪ'haɪnd] **1** *prep* derrière; ***be ~ …*** (*responsible for, support*) être derrière … **2** *adv* (*at the back*) à l'arrière; *leave, stay* derrière; ***be ~*** *in match* être derrière
beige [beɪʒ] beige
being ['bi:ɪŋ] (*creature*) être *m*; (*existence*) existence *f*
belated [bɪ'leɪtɪd] tardif
belch [beltʃ] **1** *n* éructation *f*, rot m **2** *v/i* éructer, roter
Belgian ['beldʒən] **1** *adj* belge **2** *n* Belge *m/f*; **Belgium** Belgique *f*
belief [bɪ'li:f] conviction *f*; REL *also* croyance *f*; *in person* foi *f* (***in*** en); **believe** croire
◆ **believe in** *God, person* croire en; *sth* croire à; cacher la vérité aux gens
believer [bɪ'li:vər] *in God* croyant(e) *m*(*f*); *in sth* partisan(e) *m*(*f*) (***in*** de)
bell [bel] *on bike, door* sonnette *f*; *in church* cloche *f*; *in school*: *electric* sonnerie *f*;
bellhop groom *m*
belligerent [bɪ'lɪdʒərənt] belligérant
bellow ['beloʊ] brailler; *of bull* beugler
belly ['belɪ] *of person* ventre *m*; *fat* bedaine *f*; *of animal* panse *f*
◆ **belong to** *of object* appartenir à; *club, organization* faire partie de
belongings [bɪ'lɒ:ŋɪŋz] affaires *fpl*
beloved [bɪ'lʌvɪd] bien-aimé
below [bɪ'loʊ] **1** *prep* au-dessous de **2** *adv* en bas, au-dessous; *in text* en bas; ***10 degrees ~*** moins dix
belt [belt] ceinture *f*
'**benchmark** référence *f*
bend [bend] **1** *n* tournant *m* **2** *v/t head* baisser; *arm, knees* plier; *metal, plastic* tordre **3** *v/i of road* tourner; *of person* se pencher
◆ **bend down** se pencher
beneath [bɪ'ni:θ] **1** *prep* sous **2** *adv* (au-)dessous
benefactor ['benɪfæktər] bienfaiteur(-trice) *m*(*f*)
beneficial [benɪ'fɪʃl] bénéfique
benefit ['benɪfɪt] **1** *n* bénéfice *m* **2** *v/t* bénéficier à **3** *v/i* bénéficier (***from*** de)
benevolent [bɪ'nevələnt] bienveillant
benign [bɪ'naɪn] doux; MED bénin
bequeath [bɪ'kwi:ð] léguer;
bequest legs *m*
beret [ber'eɪ] béret *m*
berry ['berɪ] baie *f*
berth [bɜ:rθ] couchette *f*; *for ship* mouillage *m*
beside [bɪ'saɪd] à côté de; ***be ~ o.s.*** être hors de soi; ***that's ~ the point*** c'est hors de propos
besides [bɪ'saɪdz] **1** *adv* d'ailleurs **2** *prep* (*apart from*) à part

best [best] **1** *adj* meilleur **2** *adv* le mieux; ***I like her ~*** c'est elle que j'aime le plus **3** *n*: ***do one's ~*** faire de son mieux; ***the ~*** le mieux; ***the ~*** (*outstanding thing or person*) le (la) meilleur(e) *m*(*f*); ***all the ~!*** meilleurs vœux!; **best before date** date *f* limite de consommation; **best man** *at wedding* garçon *m* d'honneur

bet [bet] **1** *n* pari *m* **2** *v/t & v/i* parier; ***you ~!*** évidemment!

betray [bɪ'treɪ] trahir; **betrayal** trahison *f*

better ['betər] **1** *adj* meilleur; ***get ~*** s'améliorer; ***he's ~*** *in health* il va mieux **2** *adv* mieux; ***I'd really ~not*** je ne devrais vraiment pas; ***I like her ~*** je l'aime plus; **better-off** (*richer*) plus aisé

between [bɪ'twiːn] entre

beware [bɪ'wer]: ***~ of*** attention à

bewilder [bɪ'wɪldər] confondre; **bewilderment** confusion *f*

beyond [bɪ'jɑːnd] au-delà de

bias ['baɪəs] parti *m* pris, préjugé *m*; **bias(s)ed** partial, subjectif

Bible ['baɪbl] Bible *f*; **biblical** biblique

bicentennial [baɪsen'teniəl] bicentenaire *m*

bicker ['bɪkər] se chamailler

bicycle ['baɪsɪkl] bicyclette *f*

bid [bɪd] **1** *n at auction* enchère *m*; (*attempt*) tentative *f*; *in takeover* offre *f* **2** *v/i at auction* faire une enchère; **bidder** enchérisseur(-euse) *m*(*f*)

biennial [baɪ'enɪəl] biennal

big [bɪg] **1** *adj* grand; *sum of money, mistake* gros; ***my ~ brother/sister*** mon grand frère/ma grande sœur **2** *adv*: ***talk ~*** se vanter

bigamist ['bɪgəmɪst] bigame *m/f*

'bighead crâneur(-euse) *m*(*f*)

bigot ['bɪgət] fanatique *m/f*, sectaire *m/f*

bike [baɪk] vélo *m*; (*motorbike*) moto *f*; **biker** ['baɪkər] motard(e) *m*(*f*)

bikini [bɪ'kiːnɪ] bikini *m*

bilingual [baɪ'lɪŋgwəl] bilingue

bill [bɪl] facture *f*; *money* billet *m* (de banque); POL projet *m* de loi; (*poster*) affiche *f*; **billboard** panneau *m* d'affichage; **billfold** portefeuille *m*

billion ['bɪljən] milliard *m*

bin [bɪn] *for storage* boîte *f*

bind [baɪnd] (*connect*) unir; (*tie*) attacher; LAW (*oblige*) obliger; **binding** *agreement* obligatoire

binoculars [bɪ'nɑːkjulərz] jumelles *fpl*

biodegradable [baɪoʊdɪ'greɪdəbl] biodégradable

biographer [baɪ'ɑːgrəfər] biographe *m/f*; **biography** biographie *f*

biological [baɪoʊ'lɑːdʒɪkl]

biologique; **biology** biologie *f*

bird [bɜːrd] oiseau *m*

biro® ['baɪroʊ] *Br* stylo *m* bille

birth [bɜːrθ] naissance *f*; (*labor*) accouchement *m*; ***give ~ to*** *child* donner naissance à; ***date of ~*** date *f* de naissance; **birth certificate** acte *m* de naissance; **birth control** contrôle *m* des naissances; **birthday** anniversaire *m* ***happy ~!*** bon anniversaire!

biscuit ['bɪskɪt] biscuit *m*

bisexual ['baɪseksjʊəl] **1** *adj* bisexuel **2** *n* bisexuel(le) *m*(*f*)

bishop ['bɪʃəp] évêque *m*

bit [bɪt] (*piece*) morceau *m*; (*part: of book*) passage *m*; (*part: of garden, road*) partie *f*; COMPUT bit *m*; ***a ~ of*** (*a little*) un peu de

bitch [bɪʧ] **1** *n dog* chienne *f*; F: *woman* garce *f* **2** *v/i* F (*complain*) rouspéter

bite [baɪt] **1** *of dog, snake* morsure *f*; *of flea, mosquito* piqûre *f*; *of food* morceau *m* **2** *v/t & v/i of dog, snake, person* mordre; *of flea, mosquito* piquer

bitter ['bɪtər] *taste, person* amer

black [blæk] **1** *adj* noir; *tea* nature; *future* sombre **2** *n color* noir *m*; *person* Noir(e) *m*(*f*)

◆ **black out** (*faint*) s'évanouir

'blackboard tableau *m* noir; **black coffee** café *m* noir; **black economy** économie *f* souterraine; **black eye** œil *m* poché; **blacklist** liste *f* noire; **blackmail 1** *n* chantage *m* **2** *v/t* faire chanter; **black market** marché *m* noir; **blackness** noirceur *f*; **blackout** ELEC panne *f* d'électricité; MED évanouissement *m*

bladder ['blædər] vessie *f*

blade [bleɪd] *of knife* lame *f*; *of propeller* ailette *f*; *of grass* brin *m*

blame [bleɪm] **1** *n* responsabilité *f* **2** *v/t*: ***~ s.o. for sth*** reprocher qch à qn

bland [blænd] fade

blank [blæŋk] **1** *adj paper, tape* vierge; *look* vide **2** *n* (*empty space*) espace *m* vide; **blank check**, *Br* **blank cheque** chèque *m* en blanc

blanket ['blæŋkɪt] couverture *f*

blast [blæst] **1** *n* (*explosion*) explosion *f*; (*gust*) rafale *f* **2** *v/t tunnel etc* percer (à l'aide d'explosifs); ***~!*** mince!; **blast-off** lancement *m*

blatant ['bleɪtənt] flagrant; *person* éhonté

blaze [bleɪz] **1** *n* (*fire*) incendie *m* **2** *v/i of fire* flamber

blazer ['bleɪzər] blazer *m*

bleach [bliːʧ] **1** *n for clothes* eau *f* de Javel; *for hair* décolorant *m* **2** *v/t hair* décolorer

bleak [bliːk] *countryside* désolé; *weather* morne; *future* sombre

bleary-eyed ['blɪrɪaɪd] aux yeux troubles

bleat [bli:t] *of sheep* bêler

bleed [bli:d] saigner; **bleeding** saignement *m*

bleep [bli:p] **1** *n* bip *m* **2** *v/i* faire bip

blemish ['blemɪʃ] tache *f*

blend [blend] **1** *n* mélange *m* **2** *v/t* mélanger; **blender** *machine* mixeur *m*

bless [bles] bénir; ~ ***you!*** *in response to sneeze* à vos souhaits!; **blessing** bénédiction *f*

blind [blaɪnd] **1** *adj* aveugle; ~ ***corner*** virage *m* masqué **2** *v/t of sun* aveugler; **blind alley** impasse *f*; **blind date** rendez-vous *m* arrangé; **blindfold 1** *n* bandeau *m* sur les yeux **2** *v/t* bander les yeux à; **blinding** *light* aveuglant; *headache* terrible; **blindly** sans rien voir; *fig* aveuglément; **blind spot** *in road* angle *m* mort

blink [blɪŋk] *of person* cligner des yeux; *of light* clignoter

blizzard ['blɪzərd] tempête *f* de neige

bloc [blɑ:k] POL bloc *m*

block [blɑ:k] **1** *n* bloc *m*; *buildings* pâté *m* de maisons; (*blockage*) obstruction *f m*; ***it's three ~s away*** c'est à trois rues d'ici **2** *v/t* bloquer; **blockage** obstruction *f*; **blockbuster** *movie* film *m* à grand succès; *novel* roman *m* à succès; **block letters** capitales *fpl*

blond [blɑ:nd] blond; **blonde** *woman* blonde *f*

blood [blʌd] sang *m*; **blood donor** donneur(-euse) *m*(*f*) de sang; **blood group** groupe *m* sanguin

'**blood poisoning** empoisonnement *m* du sang; **blood pressure** tension *f* (artérielle); **blood sample** prélèvement *m* sanguin; **bloodshed** carnage *m*; ***without ~*** sans effusion de sang; **bloodshot** injecté de sang; **bloodstained** taché de sang; **blood test** test *m* sanguin; **bloodthirsty** sanguinaire

bloom [blu:m] *also fig* fleurir

blossom ['blɑ:səm] **1** *n* fleur *f* **2** *v/i* fleurir; *fig* s'épanouir

blot [blɑ:t] tache *f*

◆ **blot out** effacer

blouse [blaʊz] chemisier *m*

blow[1] [bloʊ] *n also fig* coup *m*

blow[2] [bloʊ] **1** *v/t* souffler; ~ ***one's whistle*** donner un coup de sifflet **2** *v/i of wind, person* souffler; *of whistle* retentir; *of fuse* sauter; *of tire* éclater

◆ **blow out 1** *v/t candle* souffler **2** *v/i of candle* s'éteindre

◆ **blow over 1** *v/t* renverser **2** *v/i* se renverser; (*pass*) passer

◆ **blow up 1** *v/t with explosives* faire sauter; *balloon* gonfler; *photograph* agran-

dir **2** *v/i of boiler etc* sauter, exploser
'blow-dry sécher (au sèche--cheveux); **blow-out** *of tire* éclatement *m*
blue [blu:] bleu; *movie* porno; **blueberry** myrtille *f*; **blue chip** de premier ordre; **blues** MUS blues *m*; ***have the ~*** avoir le cafard
bluff [blʌf] **1** *n* (*deception*) bluff *m* **2** *v/i* bluffer
blunder ['blʌndər] **1** *n* gaffe *f* **2** *v/i* faire une gaffe
blunt [blʌnt] émoussé; *person* franc; **bluntly** franchement
blur [blɜːr] **1** *n* masse *f* confuse **2** *v/t* brouiller
◆ **blurt out** [blɜːrt] lâcher
blush [blʌʃ] **1** *n* rougissement *m* **2** *v/i* rougir; **blusher** *cosmetic* rouge *m*
blustery ['blʌstərɪ] à bourrasques
BO [biː'oʊ] (= ***body odor***) odeur *f* corporelle
board [bɔːrd] **1** *n of wood* planche *f*; *cardboard* carton *m*; *for game* plateau *m* de jeu; *for notices* panneau *m*; ~ (***of directors***) conseil *m* d'administration; ***on ~*** à bord **2** *v/t plane, ship* monter à bord de; *train, bus* monter dans **3** *v/i of passengers* embarquer; *on train, bus* monter (à bord)
◆ **board up** *windows* condamner
boarder ['bɔːrdər] pensionnaire *m/f*; EDU interne *m/f*; **board game** jeu *m* de société; **boarding card** carte *f* d'embarquement; **boarding school** internat *m*, pensionnat *m*; **board meeting** réunion *f* du conseil d'administration; **board room** salle *f* du conseil
boast [boʊst] se vanter (***about*** de)
boat [boʊt] bateau *m*; *small, for leisure* canot *m*
bodily ['bɑːdɪlɪ] **1** *adj* corporel **2** *adv*: ***they ~ ejected him*** ils l'ont saisi à bras-le-corps et l'ont mis dehors **body** corps *m*; *dead* cadavre *m*; **bodyguard** garde *m* du corps; **bodywork** MOT carrosserie *f*
bogus ['boʊgəs] faux
boil[1] [bɔɪl] *n* (*swelling*) furoncle *m*
boil[2] [bɔɪl] **1** *v/t* faire bouillir **2** *v/i* bouillir
◆ **boil down to** se ramener à
boiler ['bɔɪlər] chaudière *f*
boisterous ['bɔɪstərəs] bruyant
bold [boʊld] **1** *adj* courageux; *text* en caractères gras **2** *n print* caractères *mpl* gras
bolster ['boʊlstər] *confidence* soutenir
bolt [boʊlt] **1** *n* (*metal pin*) boulon *m*; *on door* verrou *m* **2** *adv*: ***~ upright*** tout droit **3** *v/t* (*fix with bolts*) boulonner; *close* verrouiller **4** *v/i* (*run off*) décamper; *of horse*

s'emballer

bomb [bɑːm] **1** *n* bombe *f* **2** *v/t* MIL bombarder; *of terrorist* faire sauter; **bombard** [bɑːm'bɑːrd] *also fig* bombarder; **bomb attack** attaque *f* à la bombe; **bomber** *airplane* bombardier *m*; *terrorist* poseur *m(f)* de bombes; **bomb scare** alerte *f* à la bombe; **bombshell**: ***come as a ~*** faire l'effet d'une bombe

bond [bɑːnd] **1** *n* (*tie*) lien *m*; FIN obligation *f* **2** *v/i of glue* se coller

bone [boʊn] os *m*; *in fish* arête *f*

bonnet ['bɑːnɪt] *Br of car* capot *m*

bonus ['boʊnəs] *money* prime *f*; (*something extra*) plus *m*

boob [buːb] P (*breast*) nichon *m*

booboo ['buːbuː] F bêtise *f*

book [bʊk] **1** *n* livre *m* **2** *v/t seat* réserver; *ticket* prendre; *of policeman* donner un P.V. à; **bookcase** bibliothèque *f*; **booked up** complet; *perso* complètement pris; **bookie** F bookmaker *m*; **booking** réservation *f*; **bookkeeper** comptable *m*

'bookkeeping comptabilité *f*; **booklet** livret *m*; **bookmaker** bookmaker *m*; **books** (*accounts*) comptes *mpl*; **bookseller** libraire *m/f*; **bookstore** librairie *f*

boom[1] [buːm] **1** *n* boum *m* **2** *v/i of business* aller très fort

boom[2] [buːm] *n noise* boum *m*

boost [buːst] **1** *n*: ***give sth a ~*** stimuler qc **2** *v/t* stimuler

boot [buːt] botte *f*; *for climbing, football* chaussure *f*

◆ **boot up** COMPUT **1** *v/i* démarrer **2** *v/t* faire démarrer

booth [buːð] *at market* tente *f* (de marché); *at fair* baraque *f*; *at trade fair* stand *m*; *in restaurant* alcôve *f*

booze [buːz] boisson *f* (alcoolique)

border ['bɔːrdər] **1** *n* frontière *f*; (*edge*) bordure *f* **2** *v/t country* avoir une frontière avec

◆ **border on** avoir une frontière avec; (*be almost*) friser

bore[1] [bɔːr] *v/t hole* percer

bore[2] [bɔːr] **1** *n person* raseur(-euse) *m(f)* **2** *v/t* ennuyer

bored [bɔːrd] ennuyé; ***be ~*** s'ennuyer; **boredom** ennui *m*; **boring** ennuyeux, chiant

born [bɔːrn]: ***be ~*** être né

borrow ['bɑːroʊ] emprunter

bosom ['bʊzm] poitrine *f*

boss [bɑːs] patron(-onne) *m(f)*

◆ **boss around** donner des ordres à

bossy ['bɑːsɪ] autoritaire

botanical [bə'tænɪkl] botanique

botch [bɑːtʃ] bâcler

both [boʊθ] **1** *adj & pron* les deux; **~ of them** tous(-tes) *m(f)* les deux **2** *adv*: **~ ... and ...** à la fois ... et ...
bother ['bɑːðər] **1** *n* problèmes *mpl* **2** *v/t* (*disturb*) déranger; (*worry*) ennuyer **3** *v/i* s'inquiéter (**with** de)
bottle ['bɑːtl] bouteille *f*; *for medicines* flacon *m*; *for baby* biberon *m*
◆ **bottle up** *feelings* réprimer
'**bottle bank** conteneur *m* à verre; **bottled water** eau *f* en bouteille; **bottleneck** rétrécissement *m*; *in production* goulet *m* d'étranglement; **bottle-opener** ouvre-bouteilles *m inv*
bottom ['bɑːtəm] **1** *adj* du bas **2** *n of drawer, pan, garden* fond *m*; (*underside*) dessous *m*; (*lowest part*) bas *m*; *of street* bout *m*; (*buttocks*) derrière *m*
◆ **bottom out** se stabiliser
bottom 'line *financial* résultat *m*; (*real issue*) la question principale
boulder ['boʊldər] rocher *m*
bounce [baʊns] **1** *v/t ball* faire rebondir **2** *v/i of ball* rebondir; *on sofa etc* sauter; *of check* être refusé; **bouncer** videur *m*
bound[1] [baʊnd] *adj*: **be ~ to do sth** (*sure to*) aller forcément faire qch
bound[2] [baʊnd] *adj*: **be ~ for** *of ship* être à destination de
bound[3] [baʊnd] *n* (*jump*) bond *m*
boundary ['baʊndərɪ] frontière *f*
bouquet [bʊ'keɪ] bouquet *m*
bourbon ['bɜːrbən] bourbon *m*
bout [baʊt] MED accès *m*; *in boxing* match *m*
bow[1] [baʊ] **1** *n as greeting* révérence *f* **2** *v/i* faire une révérence **3** *v/t head* baisser
bow[2] [boʊ] (*knot*) nœud *m*; MUS archet *m*; *for archery* arc *m*
bow[3] [baʊ] *of ship* avant *m*
bowels ['baʊəlz] intestins *mpl*
bowl[1] [boʊl] *n* bol *m*; *for soup etc* assiette *f* creuse; *for serving salad etc* saladier *m*; *for washing dishes* cuvette *f*
bowl[2] [boʊl] *v/i* jouer au bowling
bowling ['boʊlɪŋ] bowling *m*; **bowling alley** bowling *m*
bow 'tie [boʊ] (nœud *m*) papillon *m*
box[1] [bɑːks] *n container* boîte *f*; *on form* case *f*
box[2] [bɑːks] *v/i* boxer
boxer ['bɑːksər] boxeur *m*; **boxing** boxe *f*; **boxing glove** gant *m* de boxe; **boxing match** match *m* de boxe
'**box number** boîte *f* postale; **box office** bureau *m* de location
boy [bɔɪ] garçon *m*; (*son*) fils *m*
boycott ['bɔɪkɑːt] **1** *n* boycott

m **2** *v/t* boycotter
'boyfriend petit ami *m*; *younger* copain *m*
bra [brɑː] soutien-gorge *m*
bracelet ['breɪslɪt] bracelet *m*
bracket ['brækɪt] *for shelf* support *m* (d'étagère)
brag [bræg] se vanter (***about*** de)
braid [breɪd] *in hair* tresse *f*; *trimming* galon *m*
braille [breɪl] braille *m*
brain [breɪn] ANAT cerveau *m*; **brainless** écervelé; **brains** cerveau *m*; **brain surgeon** neurochirurgien(ne) *m(f)*; **brain tumor**, *Br* **brain tumour** tumeur *f* au cerveau; **brainwash** conditionner
brake [breɪk] **1** *n* frein *m* **2** *v/i* freiner
branch [bræntʃ] *of tree, company* branche *f*
brand [brænd] **1** *n* marque *f* **2** *v/t*: ***be ~ed a liar*** être étiqueté comme voleur; **brand image** image *f* de marque
brandish ['brændɪʃ] brandir
brand 'leader marque *f* dominante; **brand name** nom *m* de marque; **brand-new** flambant neuf
brandy ['brændɪ] brandy *m*
brassière [brə'zɪr] soutien-gorge *m*
brat [bræt] garnement *m*
brave [breɪv] courageux; **bravery** courage *m*
brawl [brɒːl] **1** *n* bagarre *f* **2** *v/i* se bagarrer
Brazil [brə'zɪl] Brésil *m*; **Brazilian 1** *adj* brésilien **2** *n* Brésilien(ne) *m(f)*
breach [briːtʃ] (*violation*) violation *f*; *in party* désaccord *m*; **breach of contract** rupture *f* de contrat
bread [bred] pain *m*
breadth [bredθ] largeur *m*; *of knowledge* étendue *f*
'breadwinner soutien *m* de famille
break [breɪk] **1** *n* fracture *f*; (*rest*) repos *m*; *in relationship* séparation *f* **2** *v/t* casser; *rules, law, promise* violer; *news* annoncer; *record* battre **3** *v/i* se casser; *of news, storm* éclater
◆ **break down 1** *v/i of vehicle, machine* tomber en panne; *of talks* échouer; *in tears* s'effondrer; *mentally* faire une dépression **2** *v/t door* défoncer; *figures* détailler
◆ **break even** rentrer dans ses frais
◆ **break in** (*interrupt*) interrompre qn; *of burglar* s'introduire par effraction
◆ **break up 1** *v/t into parts* décomposer; *fight* interrompre **2** *v/i of ice* se briser; *of couple, band* se séparer; *of meeting* se dissoudre
breakable ['breɪkəbl] cassable; **breakage** casse *f*; **breakdown** *of talks* échec *m*; (*nervous ~*) dépression *f* (nerveuse); *of figures* détail

m

breakfast ['brekfəst] petit déjeuner *m*; ***have ~*** prendre son petit déjeuner; **break-in** cambriolage *m*; **breakthrough** percée *f*; **breakup** *of partnership* échec *m*

breast [brest] *of woman* sein *m*; **breastfeed** allaiter; **breaststroke** brasse *f*

breath [breθ] souffle *m*; ***out of ~*** à bout de souffle

breathe [bri:ð] respirer

◆ **breathe in** inspirer

◆ **breathe out** expirer

breathing ['bri:ðɪŋ] respiration *f*

breathtaking ['breθteɪkɪŋ] à vous couper le souffle

breed [bri:d] **1** *n* race *f* **2** *v/t animals* élever; *plants, also fig* cultiver **3** *v/i of animals* se reproduire; **breeding** *of animals* élevage *m*; *of person* éducation *f*

breeze [bri:z] brise *f*; **breezy** venteux

brew [bru:] **1** *v/t beer* brasser **2** *v/i* couver; **brewery** brasserie *f*

bribe [braɪb] **1** *n* pot-de-vin *m* **2** *v/t* soudoyer; **bribery** corruption *f*

brick [brɪk] brique *m*

bride [braɪd] *about to be married* (future) mariée *f*; *married* jeune mariée *f*; **bridegroom** *about to be married* (futur) marié *m*; *married* jeune marié *m*; **bridesmaid** demoiselle *f* d'honneur

bridge [brɪdʒ] **1** *n* pont *m*; *of ship* passerelle *f* **2** *v/t gap* combler

bridle ['braɪdl] bride *f*

brief[1] [bri:f] *adj* bref, court

brief[2] [bri:f] **1** *n* (*mission*) instructions *fpl* **2** *v/t*: ***~ s.o. on sth*** (*give information*) informer qn de qch

'**briefcase** serviette *f*; **briefing** *session* séance *f* d'information; *instructions* instructions *fpl*; **briefly** brièvement; (*to sum up*) en bref; **briefs** slip *m*

bright [braɪt] *color* vif; *smile* radieux; *future* brillant; (*sunny*) clair; (*intelligent*) intelligent; **brightly** *smile* d'un air radieux; *colored* vivement; ***shine ~*** resplendir

brilliance ['brɪljəns] *of person* esprit *m* lumineux; *of color* vivacité *f*; **brilliant** *sunshine etc* resplendissant; (*very good*) génial; (*very intelligent*) brillant

brim [brɪm] *of container, hat* bord *m*

bring [brɪŋ] *object* apporter; *person, peace* amener; *hope, happiness* donner

◆ **bring back** (*return*) ramener; (*re-introduce*) réintroduire; ***it brought back memories of … childhood*** ça m'a rappelé …

◆ **bring down** *also fig: government* faire tomber; *air-*

plane abattre; *price* faire baisser
◆ **bring on** *illness* donner
◆ **bring out** (*produce*) sortir
◆ **bring up** *child* élever; *subject* soulever; (*vomit*) vomir
brink [brɪŋk] bord *m*
brisk [brɪsk] vif; (*businesslike*) énergique; *trade* florissant
bristles ['brɪslz] *on chin* poils *mpl* raides; *of brush* poils *mpl*
Britain ['brɪtn] Grande-Bretagne; **British 1** *adj* britannique **2** *npl*: ***the ~*** les Britanniques
brittle ['brɪtl] fragile
broad [brɒ:d] **1** *adj* large; *smile* grand; (*general*) général; ***in ~ daylight*** en plein jour **2** *n* F gonzesse *f*; **broadcast 1** *n* émission *f* **2** *v/t* transmettre; **broadcaster** présentateur(-trice) *m(f)* (radio/télé); **broad jump** saut *m* en longueur; **broadly**: ***~ speaking*** en gros; **broad-minded** large d'esprit
broccoli ['brɑ:kəlɪ] brocoli(s) *m(pl)*
brochure ['broʊʃər] brochure *f*
broil [brɔɪl] griller; **broiler** *on stove* grill *m*; *chicken* poulet *m* à rôtir
broke [broʊk] fauché; **broken** cassé; *home* brisé; **broker** courtier *m*
bronchitis [brɑ:ŋ'kaɪtɪs] bronchite *f*
bronze [brɑ:nz] bronze *m*
brooch [broʊʧ] broche *f*
brothel ['brɑ:θl] bordel *m*
brother ['brʌðər] frère *m*; **brother-in-law** beau-frère *m*; **brotherly** fraternel
brow [braʊ] (*forehead*) front *m*; *of hill* sommet *m*
brown [braʊn] **1** *adj* marron *inv*; (*tanned*) bronzé **2** *n* marron *m*; **brownie** brownie *m*
brown paper 'bag sac *m* en papier kraft
browse [braʊz] *in store* flâner; COMPUT surfer; ***~ through a book*** feuilleter un livre; **browser** COMPUT navigateur *m*
bruise [bru:z] bleu *m*; *on fruit* meurtrissure *f*
brunette [bru:'net] brune *f*
brush [brʌʃ] **1** *n* brosse *f*; (*conflict*) accrochage *m* **2** *v/t* brosser; (*touch lightly*) effleurer
◆ **brush aside** *person* mépriser; *remark, criticism* écarter
◆ **brush up** réviser
brusque [brʊsk] brusque
brutal ['bru:tl] brutal; **brutality** brutalité *f*; **brutally** brutalement; **brute** brute *f*
bubble ['bʌbl] bulle *f*
buck[1] [bʌk] *n* F (*dollar*) dollar *m*
buck[2] [bʌk] *v/i of horse* ruer
bucket ['bʌkɪt] seau *m*
buckle[1] ['bʌkl] **1** *n* boucle *f* **2** *v/t belt* boucler
buckle[2] ['bʌkl] *v/i of metal* dé-

former

bud [bʌd] BOT bourgeon *m*

buddy ['bʌdɪ] copain *m*, copine *f*; *form of address* mec

budge [bʌdʒ] **1** *v/t* (*move*) déplacer **2** *v/i* (*move*) bouger

budget ['bʌdʒɪt] budget *m*

buff [bʌf] passionné(e) *m(f)*

buffalo ['bʌfəloʊ] buffle *m*

buffer ['bʌfər] RAIL, COMPUT, *fig* tampon *m*

buffet ['bʊfeɪ] *meal* buffet *m*

bug [bʌg] **1** *n* (*insect*) insecte *m*; (*virus*) virus *m*; COMPUT bogue *f*; (*spying device*) micro *m* **2** *v/t room, telephone* mettre sur écoute; F (*annoy*) énerver

buggy ['bʌgɪ] *for baby* poussette *f*

build [bɪld] **1** *n of person* carrure *f* **2** *v/t* construire

◆ **build up 1** *v/t strength* développer; *relationship* construire **2** *v/i* s'accumuler; *fig* s'intensifier

builder ['bɪldər] constructeur(-trice) *m(f)*; **building** bâtiment *m*; *activity* construction *f*

'building site chantier *m*; **building society** *Br* caisse *f* d'épargne-logement; **building trade** (industrie *f* du) bâtiment *m*; **build-up** accumulation *f*; ***give s.o./sth a big ~*** faire beaucoup de battage autout de qn/qch; **built-in** encastré; *flash* incorporé

bulb [bʌlb] BOT bulbe *m*; (*light ~*) ampoule *f*

bulge [bʌldʒ] **1** *n* gonflement *m*, saillie *f* **2** *v/i* être gonflé, faire saillie

'bulky ['bʌlkɪ] encombrant; *sweater* gros

bull [bʊl] *animal* taureau *m*; **bulldozer** ['bʊldoʊzər] bulldozer *m*

bullet ['bʊlɪt] balle *f*

bulletin ['bʊlɪtɪn] bulletin *m*

'bulletin board tableau *m* d'affichage; COMPUT serveur *m* télématique

'bullet-proof protégé contre les balles; *vest* pare-balles

'bull's-eye mille *m*; ***hit the ~*** *also fig* mettre dans le mille; **bullshit** merde *f* V, conneries *fpl* P

bully ['bʊlɪ] **1** *n* brute *f* **2** *v/t* brimer; **bullying** brimades *fpl*

bum [bʌm] **1** *n* F (*worthless person*) bon à rien *m*; (*tramp*) clochard *m* **2** *v/t*: ***can I ~ a cigarette?*** est-ce que je peux vous taper une cigarette?

bump [bʌmp] **1** *n* bosse *f* **2** *v/t* se cogner; **bumper** MOT pare-chocs *mpl*; **bumpy** *road* cahoteux; ***we had a ~ flight*** nous avons été secoués pendant le vol

bunch [bʌntʃ] *of people* groupe *m*; *of keys* trousseau *m*; *of grapes* grappe *f*; *of flowers* bouquet *m*; ***thanks a ~*** merci beaucoup

bungle ['bʌŋgl] bousiller
bunk [bʌŋk] couchette *f*
buoy [bɔɪ] NAUT bouée *f*; **buoyant** *mood* jovial; *economy* prospère
burden ['bɜːrdn] **1** *n* fardeau *m* **2** *v/t*: **~ s.o. with sth** accabler qn de qch
bureau ['bjʊroʊ] bureau *m*; **bureaucrat** bureaucrate *m/f*; **bureaucratic** bureaucratique
burger ['bɜːrgər] steak *m* hâché; *in roll* hamburger *m*
burglar ['bɜːrglər] cambrioleur(-euse) *m(f)*; **burglar alarm** alarme *f* antivol; **burglarize** cambrioler; **burglary** cambriolage *m*
burial ['berɪəl] enterrement *m*
burn [bɜːrn] **1** *n* brûlure *f* **2** *v/t & v/i* brûler
◆ **burn down 1** *v/t* incendier **2** *v/i* être réduit en cendres
burp [bɜːrp] **1** *n* rot *m* **2** *v/i* roter
burst [bɜːrst] **1** *n in pipe* trou *m* **2** *adj tire* creuvé **3** *v/t & v/i* crever; *of pipe* éclater; **~ into tears** fondre en larmes; **~ out laughing** éclater de rire
bus [bʌs] (auto)bus *m*; *long distance* (auto)car *m*
bush [bʊʃ] *plant* buisson *m*
bushy ['bʊʃɪ] *beard* touffu
business ['bɪznɪs] commerce *m*; (*company*) entreprise *f*; (*work*) travail *m*; (*sector*) secteur *m*; (*matter*) affaire *f*; **on ~** en déplacement (professionnel); **mind your own ~!** occupe-toi de tes affaires!; **business card** carte *f* de visite; **business class** classe *f* affaires; **businesslike** sérieux; **businessman** homme *m* d'affaires; **business meeting** réunion *f* d'affaires; **business school** école *f* de commerce; **business studies** *course* études *fpl* de commerce; **business trip** voyage *m* d'affaires; **businesswoman** femme *f* d'affaires
'bus station gare *f* routière; **bus stop** arrêt *m* d'autobus
bust[1] [bʌst] *n of woman* poitrine *f*
bust[2] [bʌst] F (*broken*) cassé
'bust-up F brouille *f*; **busty** à la poitrine plantureuse
busy ['bɪzɪ] *person*, TELEC occupé; *day, life* bien rempli; *street, shop* plein de monde; **busybody** curieux(-se) *m(f)*
but [bʌt] **1** *conj* mais **2** *prep*: **all ~ him** tous sauf lui; **the last ~ one** l'avant-dernier; **~ for you** si tu n'avais pas été là; **nothing ~ the best** rien que le meilleur
butcher ['bʊtʃər] boucher (-ère) *m(f)*
butt [bʌt] **1** *n of cigarette* mégot *m*; F (*backside*) cul *m* **2** *v/t* donner un coup de tête à
butter ['bʌtər] beurre *m*; **butterfly** *also swimming* papillon *m*
buttocks ['bʌtəks] fesses *fpl*

button ['bʌtn] bouton *m*; (*badge*) badge *m*
buy [baɪ] acheter
◆ **buy out** COM racheter la part de
buyer ['baɪr] acheteur(-euse) *m* (*f*)
buzz [bʌz] **1** *n* bourdonnement *m* **2** *v/i of insect* bourdonner; **buzzer** sonnerie *f*
by [baɪ] *to show agent* par; (*near, next to*) près de; (*no later than*) pour; *mode of transport* en; **~ *bus*** en bus; **~ *day*** le jour; **~ *my watch*** selon ma montre; **~ *o.s.*** tout seul
bye(-bye) [baɪ] au revoir
'**bypass** *road* déviation *f*; MED pontage *m* (coronarien); **by-product** sous-produit *m*; **bystander** spectateur(-trice) *m*(*f*)

C

cab [kæb] taxi *m*; *of truck* cabine *f*; **cab driver** chauffeur *m* de taxi
cabin ['kæbɪn] *of plane, ship* cabine *f*; **cabin attendant** *male* steward *m*; *female* hôtesse *f* (de l'air); **cabin crew** équipage *m*
cabinet ['kæbɪnɪt] *furniture* meuble *m* (de rangement); POL cabinet *m*; ***display* ~** vitrine *f*
cable ['keɪbl] câble *m*; **cable car** téléphérique *m*; *on rail* funiculaire *m*; **cable television** (télévision *f* par) câble *m*
'**cab stand** station *f* de taxis
cactus ['kæktəs] cactus *m*
cadaver [kə'dævər] cadavre *m*
caddie ['kædɪ] *in golf* caddie *m*
Caesarean *Br* → ***Cesarean***
café ['kæfeɪ] café *m*; **cafeteria** cafétéria *f*
caffeine ['kæfiːn] caféine *f*
cage [keɪdʒ] cage *f*; **cagey** évasif
cake [keɪk] gâteau *m*
calculate ['kælkjʊleɪt] (*work out*) évaluer; *in arithmetic* calculer; **calculating** calculateur; **calculation** calcul *m*; **calculator** calculatrice *f*
calendar ['kælɪndər] calendrier *m*
calf[1] [kæf] (*young cow*) veau *m*
calf[2] [kæf] *of leg* mollet *m*
caliber, *Br* **calibre** ['kælɪbər] *of gun* calibre *m*
call [kɒːl] **1** *n* appel *m*; (*phone ~ also*) coup *m* de téléphone **2** *v/t on phone* appeler; ***be ~ed ...*** s'appeler ... **3** *v/i on phone* appeler; (*visit*) passer
◆ **call back 1** *v/t* rappeler **2** *v/i*

on phone rappeler; (*make another visit*) repasser
◆ **call for** (*collect*) venir chercher; (*demand, require*) demander
◆ **call off** annuler
caller ['kɒːlər] *on phone* personne *f* qui appelle; (*visitor*) visiteur *m*
callous ['kæləs] dur
calm [kɑːm] **1** *adj* calme, tranquille **2** *n* calme *m*
◆ **calm down 1** *v/t* calmer **2** *v/i* se calmer
calmly ['kɑːmlɪ] calmement
calorie ['kælərɪ] calorie *f*
camcorder ['kæmkɔːrdər] caméscope *m*
camera ['kæmərə] appareil *m* photo; TV caméra *f*; **cameraman** cadreur *m*, caméraman *m*
camouflage ['kæməflɑːʒ] **1** *n* camouflage *m* **2** *v/t* camoufler
camp [kæmp] **1** *n* camp *m* **2** *v/i* camper
campaign [kæm'peɪn] **1** *n* campagne *f* **2** *v/i* faire campagne
camper ['kæmpər] *person* campeur *m*; *vehicle* camping-car *m*; **camping** camping *m*; **campsite** (terrain *m* de) camping *m*
campus ['kæmpəs] campus *m*
can[1] [kæn] *v/aux* pouvoir; **~ *you hear me?*** tu m'entends?; **~ *she swim?*** sait-elle nager?; **~ *I help you?*** est-ce que je peux t'aider?
can[2] [kæn] *n for food* boîte *f*; *for drinks* canette *f*; *of paint* bidon *m*
Canada ['kænədə] Canada *m*; **Canadian 1** *adj* canadien **2** *n* Canadien *m*
canal [kə'næl] canal *m*
cancel ['kænsl] annuler; **cancellation** annulation *f*
cancer ['kænsər] cancer *m*
candid ['kændɪd] franc
candidacy ['kændɪdəsɪ] candidature *f*; **candidate** candidat *m*
candle ['kændl] bougie *f*; *in church* cierge *m*
candor, *Br* **candour** ['kændər] franchise *f*
candy ['kændɪ] (*sweet*) bonbon *m*; (*sweets*) bonbons *mpl*
cane [keɪn] (tige *f* de) bambou *m*
canister ['kænɪstər] boîte *f* (métallique); *for gas, spray* bombe *f*
canned [kænd] en conserve, en boîte; (*recorded*) enregistré
cannot ['kænɑːt] = ***can not***
canny ['kænɪ] (*astute*) rusé
canoe [kə'nuː] canoë *m*
'can opener ouvre-boîte *m*
can't [kænt] = ***can not***
canteen [kæn'tiːn] *in factory* cantine *f*
canvas ['kænvəs] toile *f*
canyon ['kænjən] canyon *m*
cap [kæp] *hat* bonnet *m*; *with peak* casquette *f*; *of soldier,*

policeman képi *m*
capability [keɪpə'bɪlətɪ] capacité *f*; **capable** capable
capacity [kə'pæsətɪ] capacité *f*
capital ['kæpɪtl] *of country* capitale *f*; *letter* majuscule *f*; *money* capital *m*; **capitalism** capitalisme *m*; **capitalist 1** *adj* capitaliste **2** *n* capitaliste *m/f*; **capital punishment** peine *f* capitale
capsize [kæp'saɪz] chavirer
capsule ['kæpsʊl] *of medicine* gélule *f*; (*space* **~**) capsule *f* spatiale
captain ['kæptɪn] capitaine *m*; *of aircraft* commandant *m* de bord
caption ['kæpʃn] légende *f*
captivate ['kæptɪveɪt] captiver, fasciner; **captive** captif; **captivity** captivité *f*; **capture 1** *n of city* prise *f*; *of person, animal* capture *f* **2** *v/t person, animal* capturer; *city, building* prendre; *market share* conquérir
car [kɑːr] voiture *f*, automobile *f*; *of train* wagon *m*, voiture *f*; ***by* ~** en voiture
carbon monoxide [kɑːrbənmən'ɑːksaɪd] monoxyde *m* de carbone
carbureter, carburetor [kɑːrbʊ'retər] carburateur *m*
carcass ['kɑːrkəs] carcasse *f*
card [kɑːrd] carte *f*; **cardboard box** carton *m*
cardiac ['kɑːrdɪæk] cardiaque
cardinal ['kɑːrdɪnl] REL cardinal *m*
care [ker] **1** *n of baby, pet* garde *f*; *of the elderly, sick* soins *mpl*; (*medical* **~**) soins *mpl* médicaux; (*worry*) souci *m* **care of** → ***c/o***; ***take* ~** (*be cautious*) faire attention; ***take* ~ *of*** s'occuper de **2** *v/i* se soucier; ***I don't* ~!** ça m'est égal!
◆ **care about** s'intéresser à
◆ **care for** (*look after*) s'occuper de
career [kə'rɪr] carrière *f*
careful ['kerfl] (*cautious*) prudent; (*thorough*) méticuleux; (***be***) **~!** (fais) attention!; **carefully** (*with caution*) prudemment; *worded etc* soigneusement; **careless** négligent; *work* négligé; **carelessly** négligemment
caress [kə'res] caresser
'car ferry (car-)ferry *m*, transbordeur
cargo ['kɑːrgoʊ] cargaison *f*
caricature ['kærɪkətʃər] caricature *f*
carnival ['kɑːrnɪvl] fête *f* foraine; *with processions etc* carnaval *m*
carpenter ['kɑːrpɪntər] charpentier *m*; *for smaller objects* menuisier *m*
carpet ['kɑːrpɪt] tapis *m*; *fitted* moquette *f*
'car phone téléphone *m* de voiture; **carpool** faire du co-voiturage; **car rental** location *f* de voitures

carrier ['kærɪər] *company* entreprise *f* de transport; *of disease* porteur(-euse) *m(f)*
carrot ['kærət] carotte *f*
carry ['kærɪ] **1** *v/t* porter; *of ship, bus etc* transporter **2** *v/i of sound* porter
◆ **carry on 1** *v/i* (*continue*) continuer (***with sth*** qch) **2** *v/t business* exercer
◆ **carry out** *survey etc* faire; *orders etc* exécuter
cart [kɑːrt] charrette *f*
carton ['kɑːrtn] carton *m*; *of cigarettes* cartouche *f*
cartoon [kɑːr'tuːn] dessin *m* humoristique; *on TV* dessin *m* animé; (*strip* ~) BD *f*, bande *f* dessinée
carve [kɑːrv] *meat* découper; *wood* sculpter
case[1] [keɪs] *for eyeglasses, camera* étui *m*; *for gadget* pochette *f*; *of wine etc* caisse *f*; *Br* (*suitcase*) valise *f*
case[2] [keɪs] (*instance*), MED cas *m*; *for police* affaire *f*; LAW procès *m*; ***in ~ .*** au cas où ...; ***in any ~*** en tout cas
cash [kæʃ] **1** *n* (*money*) argent *m*; (*coins and notes*) (argent *m*) liquide *m* **2** *v/t check* toucher; **cash desk** caisse *f*; **cash flow** COM trésorerie *f*; ***I've got ~ problems*** j'ai des problèmes d'argent; **cashier** *in store etc* caissier(-ère) *m(f)*; **cashpoint** *Br* distributeur *m* automatique (de billets); **cash register** caisse *f* enregistreuse
casino [kə'siːnoʊ] casino *m*
casket ['kæskɪt] (*coffin*) cercueil *m*
casserole ['kæsəroʊl] *meal* ragoût *m*; *container* cocotte *f*
cassette [kə'set] cassette *f*; **cassette player** lecteur *m* de cassettes
cast [kæst] **1** *n of play* distribution *f*; (*mold*) moule *m* **2** *v/t doubt* jeter; *metal* couler
cast 'iron fonte *f*
castle ['kæsl] chateau *m*
casual ['kæʒʊəl] (*chance*) fait au hasard; (*offhand*) désinvolte; (*not formal*) décontracté; **casually** *dressed* de manière décontractée; *say* de manière désinvolte; **casualty** victime *f*
cat [kæt] chat(te) *m(f)*
catalog, *Br* **catalogue** ['kætəlɑːg] catalogue *m*
catalyst ['kætəlɪst] catalyseur *m*
catastrophe [kə'tæstrəfɪ] catastrophe *f*; **catastrophic** catastrophique
catch [kætʃ] **1** *n* prise *f* (au vol); *of fish* pêche *f*; (*lock: on door*) loquet *m*; (*problem*) entourloupette *f* **2** *v/t ball, prisoner, bus, illness* attraper; (*get on: bus, train*) prendre; (*hear*) entendre; **catching** *also fig* contagieux; **catchy** facile à retenir
categoric [kætə'gɑːrɪk] catégorique; **category** catégorie

f
caterer ['keɪtərər] traiteur *m*
cathedral [kə'θiːdrl] cathédrale *f*
Catholic ['kæθəlɪk] **1** *adj* catholique **2** *n* catholique *m/f*; **Catholicism** catholicisme *m*
catty ['kætɪ] méchant
cause [kɒːz] **1** *n* cause *f*; (*grounds*) raison *f* **2** *v/t* causer
caution ['kɒːʃn] **1** *n* (*carefulness*) prudence *f* **2** *v/t* (*warn*) avertir; **cautious** prudent; **cautiously** prudemment
cave [keɪv] caverne *f*, grotte *f*
cavity ['kævətɪ] cavité *f*
CD [siː'diː] (= ***compact disc***) CD *m* (= compact-disc *m*, disque *m* compact)
C'D player lecteur *m* de CD; **CD-ROM** CD-ROM *m*
cease [siːs] cesser
'cease-fire cessez-le-feu *m*
ceiling ['siːlɪŋ] plafond *m*
celebrate ['selɪbreɪt] **1** *v/i* faire la fête **2** *v/t* fêter; *Christmas*, *event* célébrer; **celebrated** célèbre; **celebration** fête *f*; *of event*, *wedding* célébration *f*; **celebrity** célébrité *f*
cell [sel] *for prisoner*, *of spreadsheet*, BIO cellule *f*
cellar ['selər] cave *f*
cello ['tʃelou] violoncelle *m*
cell phone, cellular phone ['seljuːlər] (téléphone *m*) portable *m*
cement [sɪ'ment] ciment *m*
cemetery ['seməterɪ] cimetière *m*
censor ['sensər] censurer
census ['sensəs] recensement *m*
cent [sent] cent *m*
centenary [sen'tiːnərɪ] centenaire *m*
center ['sentər] **1** *n* centre *m* **2** *v/t* centrer
centigrade ['sentɪgreɪd] centigrade
centimeter, *Br* **centimetre** ['sentɪmiːtər] centimètre *m*
central ['sentrəl] central
central 'heating chauffage *m* central; **centralize** centraliser; **central locking** MOT verrouillage *m* centralisé
centre *Br* → ***center***
century ['sentʃərɪ] siècle *m*
CEO [siːiː'ou] (= ***Chief Executive Officer***) directeur *m* général
ceramic [sɪ'ræmɪk] en céramique
cereal ['sɪrɪəl] céréale *f*; (*breakfast* ~) céréales *fpl*
ceremonial [serɪ'mounɪəl] **1** *adj* de cérémonie **2** *n* cérémonial *m*; **ceremony** cérémonie *f*
certain ['sɜːrtn] (*sure*) certain, sûr; (*particular*) certain; **certainly** certainement; **certainty** certitude *f*
certificate [sər'tɪfɪkət] certificat *m*
certified public accountant ['sɜːrtɪfaɪd] expert *m* comp-

table; **certify** certifier

Cesarean [sɪ'zerɪən] césarienne *f*

CFO [siːef'oʊ] (= ***chief financial officer***) directeur *m* financier

chain [ʧeɪn] **1** *n also of stores etc* chaîne *f* **2** *v/t*: ***~ sth. to sth*** enchaîner qch à qch

chair [ʧer] **1** *n* chaise *f*; (*arm~*) fauteuil *m*; *at university* chaire *f* **2** *v/t meeting* présider; **chair lift** télésiège *m*; **chairman** président *m*; **chairmanship** présidence *f*; **chairperson** président(e) *m(f)*

chalk [ʧɒːk] craie *f*

challenge ['ʧælɪndʒ] **1** *n* défi *m*, challenge *m* **2** *v/t* (*defy*) défier; (*call into question*) mettre en doute; ***~ s.o. to a game*** proposer à qn de faire une partie; **challenger** challenger *m*; **challenging** *job, undertaking* stimulant

Chamber of 'Commerce Chambre *f* de commerce

champagne [ʃæm'peɪn] champagne *m*

champion ['ʧæmpɪən] **1** *n* SP, *of cause* champion(ne) *m(f)* **2** *v/t cause* être le (la) champion(ne) *m(f)* de; **championship** *event* championnat *m*; *title* titre *m* de champion(-ne)

chance [ʧæns] (*possibility*) chances *fpl*; (*opportunity*) occasion *f*; (*luck*) hasard *m*; ***by ~*** par hasard; ***take a ~*** prendre un risque

change [ʧeɪndʒ] **1** *n* changement *m*; (*money*) monnaie *f*; ***for a ~*** pour changer un peu **2** *v/t* changer; *bankbill* faire la monnaie sur **3** *v/i* changer; (*put on different clothes*) se changer; **changeover** changement *m*; **changing room** SP vestiaire *m*; *in shop* cabine *f* d'essayage

channel ['ʧænl] *on TV, radio* chaîne *f*; (*waterway*) chenal *m*

chant [ʧænt] **1** *n* slogans *mpl* scandés; REL chant *m* **2** *v/i of crowds etc* scander des slogans; REL psalmodier

chaos ['keɪɑːs] chaos *m*; **chaotic** chaotique

chapel ['ʧæpl] chapelle *f*

chapter ['ʧæptər] chapitre *m*

character ['kærɪktər] caractère *m*; (*person*) personne *f*; *in book* personnage *m*; **characteristic** **1** *n* caractéristique *f* **2** *adj* caractéristique; **characterize** caractériser

charge [ʧɑːrdʒ] **1** *n* (*fee*) frais *mpl*; LAW accusation *f*; ***free of ~*** gratuit; ***be in ~*** être responsable **2** *v/t sum of money* faire payer; LAW inculper (***with*** de); *battery* charger; ***can you ~ it?*** (*put on account*) pouvez-vous le mettre sur mon compte? **3** *v/i* (*attack*) charger; **charge account** compte *m*; **charge card** carte *f* de paiement

charitable ['tʃærɪtəbl] charitable; **charity** charité *f*; (*organization*) organisation *f* caritative
charm [tʃɑːrm] **1** *n also on bracelet* charme *m* **2** *v/t* (*delight*) charmer; **charming** charmant
charred [tʃɑːrd] carbonisé
chart [tʃɑːrt] diagramme *m*; (*map*) carte *f*
'**charter flight** (vol *m*) charter *m*
chase [tʃeɪs] **1** *n* poursuite *f* **2** *v/t* poursuivre
◆ **chase away** *v/t* chasser
chassis ['ʃæsɪ] *of car* châssis *m*
chat [tʃæt] **1** *n* causette *f* **2** *v/i* causer; **chatline** chat *m* téléphonique; **chat room** chat *m*
chatter ['tʃætər] **1** *n* bavardage *m* **2** *v/i* (*talk*) bavarder; ***my teeth were ~ing*** je claquais des dents
chauffeur ['ʃoʊfər] chauffeur *m*
chauvinist ['ʃoʊvɪnɪst] (*male ~*) machiste *m*
cheap [tʃiːp] bon marché, pas cher; (*nasty*) méchant; (*mean*) pingre
cheat [tʃiːt] **1** *n person* tricheur(-euse) *m*(*f*) **2** *v/t* tromper **3** *v/i* tricher
check[1] [tʃek] **1** *adj shirt* à carreaux **2** *n* carreaux *m*
check[2] [tʃek] *n* FIN chèque *m*; *in restaurant etc* addition *f*
check[3] [tʃek] **1** *n to verify sth* contrôle *m*, vérification *f* **2** *v/t* vérifier; *with a ~mark* cocher; *coat etc* mettre au vestiaire **3** *v/i* vérifier
◆ **check in** *v/i at airport* se faire enregistrer; *at hotel* s'inscrire
◆ **check out 1** *v/i of hotel* régler sa note **2** *v/t* (*look into*) enquêter sur; *club etc* essayer
◆ **check up on** se renseigner sur
'**checkbook** carnet *m* de chèques; **checked** *material* à carreaux
checkered ['tʃekərd] *pattern* à carreaux; *career* varié
'**check-in (counter)** enregistrement *m*; **checking account** compte *m* courant; **checklist** liste *f* (de contrôle); **check mark**: ***put a ~ against sth*** cocher qch; **check-out** caisse *f*; **checkpoint** contrôle *m*; **checkroom** *for coats* vestiaire *m*; *for baggage* consigne *f*; **checkup** *medical* examen *m* médical; *dental* examen *m* dentaire
cheek [tʃiːk] *on face* joue *f*
cheer [tʃɪr] **1** *n* hourra *m* **2** *v/t* acclamer **3** *v/i* pousser des hourras
◆ **cheer up 1** *v/i* reprendre courage; ***cheer up!*** courage! **2** *v/t* remonter le moral à
cheerful ['tʃɪrfəl] gai, joyeux; **cheering** acclamations *fpl*; **cheerleader** meneuse *f* de

ban
cheese [tʃiːz] fromage *m*
chef [ʃef] chef *m* (de cuisine)
chemical ['kemɪkl] **1** *adj* chimique **2** *n* produit *m* chimique; **chemist** *in laboratory* chimiste *m/f*; *Br* pharmacien(ne) *m(f)*; **chemistry** chimie *f*
chemotherapy [kiːmoʊ'θerəpɪ] chimiothérapie *f*
cheque [tʃek] *Br* → ***check²***
chess [tʃes] (jeu *m* d')échecs *mpl*; ***play*** ~ jouer aux échecs
chest [tʃest] poitrine *f*; (*box*) coffre *m*, caisse *f*
chew [tʃuː] mâcher; *of rat* ronger; **chewing gum** chewing-gum *m*
chick [tʃɪk] poussin *m*; F *girl* nana
chicken ['tʃɪkɪn] poulet *m*
chief [tʃiːf] **1** *n* chef *m* **2** *adj* principal; **chiefly** principalement
child [tʃaɪld] enfant *m/f*; **childhood** enfance *f*; **childish** puéril; **childlike** enfantin
children ['tʃɪldrən] *pl* → ***child***
Chile ['tʃɪlɪ] Chili *m*; **Chilean 1** *adj* chilien **2** *n* Chilien(ne) *m(f)*
◆ **chill out** se relaxer
chilly ['tʃɪlɪ] *also fig* froid
chimney ['tʃɪmnɪ] cheminée *f*
chin [tʃɪn] menton *m*
China ['tʃaɪnə] Chine *f*
china ['tʃaɪnə] **1** *n* porcelaine *f* **2** *adj* en porcelaine
Chinese [tʃaɪ'niːz] **1** *adj* chinois **2** *n language* chinois *m*; *person* Chinois(e) *m(f)*
chip [tʃɪp] **1** *n damage* brèche *f*; *in gambling* jeton *m*; COMPUT puce *f*; ~***s*** (*potato* ~*s*) chips *mpl*; *Br* pommes frites *fpl* **2** *v/t damage* ébrécher
chipmunk tamia *m* rayé
chisel ['tʃɪzl] ciseau *m*, burin *m*
chlorine ['klɔːriːn] chlore *m*
chocolate ['tʃɑːkələt] chocolat *m*
choice [tʃɔɪs] **1** *n* choix *m*; ***I had no*** ~ je n'avais pas le choix **2** *adj* (*top quality*) de choix
choir ['kwaɪr] chœur *m*
choke [tʃoʊk] **1** *v/i* s'étrangler **2** *v/t* (*strangle*) étrangler
cholesterol [kə'lestəroʊl] cholestérol *m*
choose [tʃuːz] choisir; **choosey** difficile
chop [tʃɑːp] **1** *n of meat* côtelette *f* **2** *v/t* couper
◆ **chop down** *tree* abattre
chore [tʃɔːr] ~***s*** travaux *mpl* domestiques
choreography [kɔːrɪ'ɑːgrəfɪ] chorégraphie *f*
chorus ['kɔːrəs] *singers* chœur *m*; *of song* refrain *m*
Christ [kraɪst] Christ *m*; ~***!*** mon Dieu!
christen ['krɪsn] baptiser
Christian ['krɪstʃən] **1** *n* chrétien(ne) *m(f)* **2** *adj* chrétien; **Christianity** christianisme *m*

Christmas ['krɪsməs] Noël *m*; ***Merry ~!*** Joyeux Noël!; **Christmas card** carte *f* de Noël; **Christmas Day** jour *m* de Noël; **Christmas Eve** veille *f* de Noël; **Christmas present** cadeau *m* de Noël; **Christmas tree** arbre *m* de Noël
chronic ['krɑːnɪk] chronique
chubby ['ʧʌbɪ] potelé
chuck [ʧʌk] lancer
chuckle ['ʧʌkl] **1** *n* petit rire *m* **2** *v/i* rire tout bas
chunk [ʧʌŋk] gros morceau *m*
church [ʧɜːrʧ] église *f*; **church service** office *m*; **churchyard** cimetière *m* (autour d'une église)
chute [ʃuːt] *for garbage* vide-ordures *m*; *for escape* toboggan *m*
cigar [sɪ'gɑːr] cigare *m*
cigarette [sɪgə'ret] cigarette *f*; **cigarette lighter** briquet *m*
cinema ['sɪnɪmə] *Br* cinéma *m*
circle ['sɜːrkl] **1** *n* cercle *m* **2** *v/i of plane* tournoyer
circuit ['sɜːrkɪt] circuit *m*; (*lap*) tour *m* (de circuit); **circuit board** COMPUT plaquette *f*; **circular** ['sɜːrkjʊlər] **1** *n* circulaire *f* **2** *adj* circulaire; **circulate** ['sɜːrkjʊleɪt] **1** *v/i* circuler **2** *v/t memo* faire circuler; **circulation** circulation *f*; *of newspaper* tirage *m*
circumstances ['sɜːrkəmstænsɪs] circonstances *fpl*; *financial* situation *f* financière
circus ['sɜːrkəs] cirque *m*
cistern ['sɪstərn] réservoir *m*; *of WC* réservoir *m* de chasse d'eau
citizen ['sɪtɪzn] citoyen(ne) *m*(*f*); **citizenship** citoyenneté *f*
city ['sɪtɪ] (grande) ville *f*
city 'center, *Br* **city 'centre** centre-ville *m*; **city hall** hôtel *m* de ville
civic ['sɪvɪk] municipal; *pride, responsibilities* civique
civil ['sɪvl] civil; (*polite*) poli; **civil ceremony** mariage *m* civil; **civil engineer** ingénieur *m* des travaux publics
civilian [sɪ'vɪljən] civil(e) *m*(*f*); **civilization** civilisation *f*; **civilize** civiliser; **civil rights** droits *mpl* civils; **civil servant** fonctionnaire *m/f*; **civil service** fonction *f* publique, administration *f*; **civil war** guerre *f* civile
claim [kleɪm] **1** *n* (*request*) demande *f*; (*assertion*) affirmation *f* **2** *v/t* (*ask for as a right*) demander, réclamer; (*assert*) affirmer; *lost property* réclamer; **claimant** ['kleɪmənt] demandeur(-euse) *m*(*f*)
clam [klæm] palourde *f*, clam *m*
clammy ['klæmɪ] moite
clamp [klæmp] *fastener* pince *f*, crampon *m*
◆ **clamp down on** sévir con-

tre

clandestine [klæn'destɪn] clandestin

clap [klæp] (*applaud*) applaudir

clarification [klærɪfɪ'keɪʃn] clarification *f*; **clarify** clarifier; **clarity** clarité *f*

clash [klæʃ] **1** *n between people* affrontement *m* **2** *v/i* s'affronter; *of colors* détonner; *of events* tomber en même temps

clasp [klæsp] **1** *n* agrafe *f* **2** *v/t in hand* serrer

class [klæs] **1** *n* (*lesson*) cours *m*; (*group of people, category*) classe *f*; ***the ~ of 2002*** la promo(tion) 2002 **2** *v/t* classer

classic ['klæsɪk] **1** *adj* classique **2** *n* classique *m*; **classical** *music* classique; **classification** classification *f*; **classified** *information* secret; **classified ad(vertisement)** petite annonce *f*; **classify** classifier; **classroom** salle *f* de classe; **classy** F *restaurant etc* chic *inv*; *person* classe

clause [klɒːz] (*in agreement*) clause *f*; GRAM proposition *f*

claustrophobia [klɔːstrə'foʊbɪə] claustrophobie *f*

claw [klɒː] *of cat* griffe *f*; *of lobster* pince *f*

clay [kleɪ] argile *f*, glaise *f*

clean [kliːn] **1** *adj* propre **2** *adv* (*completely*) complètement **3** *v/t* nettoyer; **cleaner** *male* agent *m* de propreté; *female* femme *f* de ménage; (*dry~*) teinturier(-ère) *m*(*f*)

cleanse [klenz] *skin* nettoyer; **cleanser** *for skin* démaquillant *m*

clear [klɪr] **1** *adj voice, photo* net; *to understand, sky, water* clair; *conscience* tranquille **2** *v/t roads etc* dégager; *place* (faire) évacuer; *table* débarrasser; *ball* dégager; (*acquit*) innocenter; (*authorize*) autoriser **3** *v/i of sky* se dégager; *of mist* se dissiper; *of face* s'éclairer

◆ **clear out 1** *v/t closet* vider **2** *v/i* ficher le camp

◆ **clear up 1** *v/i in room etc* ranger; *of weather* s'éclaircir; *of illness* disparaître **2** *v/t* (*tidy*) ranger; *problem* résoudre

clearance ['klɪrəns] (*space*) espace *m* (libre); (*authorization*) autorisation *f*; **clearance sale** liquidation *f*; **clearing** clairière *f*; **clearly** *speak, see* clairement; *hear* distinctement; (*evidently*) manifestement

cleavage ['kliːvɪdʒ] décolleté *m*

clench [klentʃ] serrer

clergy ['klɜːrdʒɪ] clergé *m*; **clergyman** ecclésiastique *m*; *Protestant* pasteur *m*

clerk [klɜːrk] *administrative* employé(e) *m*(*f*) de bureau; *in store* vendeur(-euse) *m*(*f*)

clever ['klevər] intelligent; *gadget* ingénieux; (*skillful*) habile
click [klɪk] **1** *n* COMPUT clic *m* **2** *v/i* cliqueter
◆ **click on** COMPUT cliquer sur
client ['klaɪənt] client(e) *m*(*f*); **clientele** clientèle *f*
climate ['klaɪmət] *also fig* climat *m*
climax ['klaɪmæks] point *m* culminant
climb [klaɪm] **1** *n up mountain* ascension *f f* **2** *v/t* monter sur; *mountain* escalader **3** *v/i* monter; **climber** alpiniste *m*/*f*
clinch [klɪntʃ] *deal* conclure
cling [klɪŋ] *of clothes* coller
◆ **cling to** s'accrocher à
clingy ['klɪŋɪ] *person* collant
clinic ['klɪnɪk] clinique *f*; **clinical** clinique
clip[1] [klɪp] **1** *n fastener* pince *f*; *for hair* barrette *f* **2** *v/t*: **~ *sth to sth*** attacher qch à qch
clip[2] [klɪp] **1** *n* (*extract*) extrait *m* **2** *v/t hair, grass* couper; **clipping** *from press* coupure *f* (de presse)
clock [klɑːk] horloge *f*; **clock radio** radio-réveil *m*; **clockwise** dans le sens des aiguilles d'une montre
clone [kloʊn] **1** *n* clone *m* **2** *v/t* cloner; **cloning** clonage *m*
close[1] [kloʊs] **1** *adj family, friend* proche **2** *adv* près; **~ *at hand***, **~ *by*** tout près; **~ *to*** près de
close[2] [kloʊz] *v/t* fermer
closed-circuit 'television télévision *f* en circuit fermé; **close-knit** très uni; **closely** *listen* attentivement; *watch* de près; *cooperate* étroitement
closet ['klɑːzɪt] armoire *f*, placard *m*
close-up ['kloʊsʌp] gros plan *m*
closing date ['kloʊzɪŋ] date *f* limite
closure ['kloʊʒər] fermeture *f*
clot [klɑːt] **1** *n of blood* caillot *m* **2** *v/i of blood* coaguler
cloth [klɑːθ] tissu *m*; *for drying* torchon *m*; *for washing* lavette *f*
clothes [kloʊðz] vêtements *mpl*; **clothing** vêtements *mpl*
cloud [klaʊd] nuage *m*; **cloudless** sans nuages; **cloudy** nuageux
clout [klaʊt] *fig* (*influence*) influence *f*
clove of 'garlic [kloʊv] gousse *f* d'ail
clown [klaʊn] *also pej* clown *m*
club [klʌb] club *m*; *weapon* massue *f*
clue [kluː] indice *m*
clumsiness ['klʌmzɪnɪs] maladresse *f*; **clumsy** maladroit
cluster ['klʌstər] groupe *m*
clutch [klʌtʃ] **1** *n* MOT embrayage *m* **2** *v/t* étreindre
◆ **clutch at** s'agripper à
c/o (= ***care of***) chez

Co. (= ***Company***) Cie (= Compagnie)
coach [koʊʧ] **1** *n* (*trainer*) entraîneur(-euse) *m*(*f*); *Br* (*bus*) (auto)car *m* **2** *v/t* SP entraîner; **coaching** entraînement *m*
coagulate [koʊ'ægjʊleɪt] *of blood* coaguler
coal [koʊl] charbon *m*
coalition [koʊə'lɪʃn] coalition *f*
'coalmine mine *f* de charbon
coarse [kɔːrs] *fabric* rugueux; *hair* épais; (*vulgar*) grossier; **coarsely** (*vulgarly*), *ground* grossièrement
coast [koʊst] côte *f*; **coastal** côtier; **coastguard** gendarmerie *f* maritime; *person* gendarme *m* maritime; **coastline** littoral *m*
coat [koʊt] **1** *n* veston *m*; (*over*~) pardessus *m*; *of animal* pelage *m*; *of paint etc* couche *f* **2** *v/t* (*cover*) couvrir (***with*** de); **coathanger** cintre *m*; **coating** couche *f*
coax [koʊks] cajoler
cocaine [kə'keɪn] cocaïne *f*
cock [kɑːk] *chicken* coq *m*; *any male bird* (oiseau *m*) mâle *m*; **cockpit** *of plane* poste *m* de pilotage, cockpit *m*; **cockroach** cafard *m*; **cocktail** cocktail *m*
cocoa ['koʊkoʊ] cacao *m*
coconut ['koʊkənʌt] noix *m* de coco; **coconut palm** cocotier *m*
code [koʊd] code *m*; ***in*** ~ codé
coeducational [koʊedʊ'keɪʃnl] mixte
coerce [koʊ'ɜːrs] forcer
coexist [koʊɪg'zɪst] coexister; **coexistence** coexistence *f*
coffee ['kɑːfɪ] café *m*; **coffee maker** machine *f* à café; **coffee pot** cafetière *f*; **coffee shop** café *m*
cohabit [koʊ'hæbɪt] cohabiter
coherent [koʊ'hɪrənt] cohérent
coil [kɔɪl] *of rope* rouleau *m*; *of snake* anneau *m*
coin [kɔɪn] pièce *f* (de monnaie)
coincide [koʊɪn'saɪd] coïncider; **coincidence** coïncidence *f*
Coke® [koʊk] coca® *m*
cold [koʊld] **1** *adj* froid; ***I'm*** ~ j'ai froid; ***it's*** ~ *of weather* il fait froid **2** *n* froid *m*; MED rhume *m*; **cold-blooded** à sang froid; *murder* commis de sang-froid; **coldly** froidement; **coldness** froideur *f*; **cold sore** bouton *m* de fièvre
collaborate [kə'læbəreɪt] collaborer; **collaboration** collaboration *f*; **collaborator** collaborateur(-trice) *m*(*f*)
collapse [kə'læps] s'effondrer; *of building* s'écrouler; **collapsible** pliant
collar ['kɑːlər] col *m*; *for dog* collier *m*

colleague ['kɑ:li:g] collègue *m/f*
collect [kə'lekt] **1** *v/t person, cleaning etc* aller/venir chercher; *as hobby* collectionner; (*gather together*) recueillir **2** *v/i* (*gather together*) s'assembler; **collect call** communication *f* en PCV; **collection** collection *f*; *in church* collecte *f*; **collective** collectif; **collector** collectionneur(-euse) *m(f)*
college ['kɑ:lɪdʒ] université *f*
collide [kə'laɪd] se heurter; **collision** collision *f*
colon ['koʊlən] *punctuation* deux-points *mpl*
colonel ['kɜ:rnl] colonel *m*
colonial [kə'loʊnɪəl] colonial; **colonize** coloniser; **colony** colonie *f*
color ['kʌlər] couleur *f*; **color-blind** daltonien; **colored** *person* de couleur; **colorful** *also fig* coloré
colossal [kə'lɑ:sl] colossal
colour *Br* → ***color***
colt [koʊlt] poulain *m*
column ['kɑ:ləm] *architectural, of text* colonne *f*; **columnist** chroniqueur(-euse) *m(f)*
coma ['koʊmə] coma *m*
comb [koʊm] **1** *n* peigne *m* **2** *v/t* peigner; *area* passer au peigne fin
combat ['kɑ:mbæt] **1** *n* combat *m* **2** *v/t* combattre
combination [kɑ:mbɪ'neɪʃn] *also of safe* combinaison *f*; **combine 1** *v/t* combiner; *ingredients* mélanger **2** *v/i* se combiner
come [kʌm] venir; *of train, bus* arriver
◆ **come across** (*find*) tomber sur
◆ **come along** (*come too*) venir (aussi); (*turn up*) arriver; (*progress*) avancer
◆ **come back** revenir
◆ **come down** descendre; *in price etc* baisser; *of rain, snow* tomber
◆ **come for** (*attack*) attaquer; (*to collect*) venir chercher
◆ **come forward** se présenter
◆ **come from** venir de
◆ **come in** entrer; *of train, in race* arriver; *of tide* monter
◆ **come in for** *criticism* recevoir
◆ **come off** *of handle etc* se détacher
◆ **come out** sortir; *of results* être communiqué; *of sun, product* apparaître; *of stain* partir
◆ **come to 1** *v/t* (*reach*) arriver à; ***that comes to $70*** ça fait 70 $ **2** *v/i* (*regain consciousness*) revenir à soi
◆ **come up** monter; *of sun* se lever
'**comeback** retour *m*, come-back *m*
comedian [kə'mi:dɪən] (*comic*) comique *m/f*; *pej* pitre *m/f*; **comedy** comédie *f*

comfort ['kʌmfərt] **1** *n* confort *m*; (*consolation*) réconfort *m* **2** *v/t* réconforter; **comfortable** confortable; ***be ~*** *of person* être à l'aise
comic ['kɑːmɪk] **1** *n to read* bande *f* dessinée; (*comedian*) comique *m/f* **2** *adj* comique; **comical** comique; **comic book** bande *f* dessinée, BD *f*; **comics** bandes *fpl* dessinées; **comic strip** bande *f* dessinée
comma ['kɑːmə] virgule *f*
command [kə'mænd] **1** *n* (*order*) ordre *m*; MIL commandement *m* **2** *v/t* commander
commandeer [kɑːmən'dɪr] réquisitionner
commander [kə'mændər] commandant(e) *m(f)*; **commander-in-chief** commandant(e) *m(f)* en chef
commemorate [kə'meməreɪt] commémorer
commence [kə'mens] commencer
commendable [kə'mendəbl] louable; **commendation** *for bravery* éloge *m*
comment ['kɑːment] **1** *n* commentaire *m* **2** *v/i*: ***~ on*** commenter; **commentary** commentaire *m*; **commentator** commentateur(-trice) *m(f)*
commerce ['kɑːmɜːrs] commerce *m*; **commercial 1** *adj* commercial **2** *n* (*ad*) publicité *f*; **commercial break** page *f* de publicité; **commercialize** commercialiser
commission [kə'mɪʃn] (*payment, committee*) commission *f*; (*job*) commande *f*
commit [kə'mɪt] *crime* commettre; *money* engager; **commitment** *in relationship* engagement *m*; (*responsibility*) responsabilité *f*; **committee** comité *m*
commodity [kə'mɑːdətɪ] marchandise *f*
common ['kɑːmən] courant; *species etc* commun; (*shared*) commun; ***have sth in ~ with s.o.*** avoir qch en commun; **commonly** communément; **common sense** bon sens *m*
commotion [kə'moʊʃn] agitation *f*
communal [kəm'juːnl] en commun
communicate [kə'mjuːnɪkeɪt] communiquer; **communication** communication *f*; **communicative** communicatif
Communion [kə'mjuːnjən] REL communion *f*
Communism ['kɑːmjʊnɪzəm] communisme *m*; **Communist 1** *adj* communiste **2** *n* communiste *m/f*
community [kə'mjuːnətɪ] communauté *f*
commute [kə'mjuːt] **1** *v/i* faire la navette (pour aller travailler) **2** *v/t* LAW commuer
compact 1 *adj* [kəm'pækt] compact **2** *n* ['kɑːmpækt]

MOT petite voiture *f*
companion [kəm'pænjən] compagnon *m*
company ['kʌmpənɪ] COM société *f*; (*companionship*) compagnie *f*; (*guests*) invités *mpl*
comparable ['kɑːmpərəbl] comparable; **comparative** comparativement; **compare** comparer; **comparison** comparaison *f*
compartment [kəm'pɑːrtmənt] compartiment *m*
compass ['kʌmpəs] compas *m*
compassion [kəm'pæʃn] compassion *f*; **compassionate** compatissant
compatibility [kəmpætə'bɪlɪtɪ] compatibilité *f*; **compatible** compatible
compel [kəm'pel] obliger
compensate ['kɑmpənseɪt] **1** *v/t* dédommager **2** *v/i*: ~ ***for*** compenser; **compensation** (*money*) dédommagement *m*; (*reward*) compensation *f*; (*comfort*) consolation *f*
compete [kəm'piːt] être en compétition; (*take part*) participer (***in*** à)
competence ['kɑːmpɪtəns] compétence *f*; **competent** *person* compétent, capable; *piece of work* (très) satisfaisant
competition [kɑːmpə'tɪʃn] (*contest*) concours *m*; SP compétition *f*; (*competing, competitors*) concurrence *f*; **competitive** compétitif; *price, offer* concurrentiel; **competitiveness** COM compétitivité *f*; *of person* esprit *m* de compétition; **competitor** concurrent *m*
complacent [kəm'pleɪsənt] complaisant, suffisant
complain [kəm'pleɪn] se plaindre; **complaint** plainte *f*; IN SHOP réclamation *f*; MED maladie *f*
complementary [kɑːmplɪ'mentərɪ] complémentaire
complete [kəm'pliːt] **1** *adj* complet; (*finished*) terminé **2** *v/t task, building etc* terminer, achever; *form* remplir; **completely** complètement; **completion** achèvement *m*
complex ['kɑːmpleks] **1** *adj* complexe **2** *n building*, PSYSCH complexe *m*; **complexion** *facial* teint *m*; **complexity** complexité *f*
compliance [kəm'plaɪəns] conformité *f*
complicate ['kɑːmplɪkeɪt] compliquer; **complicated** compliqué; **complication** complication *f*
complimentary [kɑːmplɪ'mentərɪ] élogieux, flatteur; (*free*) gratuit
comply [kəm'plaɪ] obéir; ~ ***with ...*** se conformer à
component [kəm'pounənt] composant *m*

compose [kəm'pouz] composer; **composed** (*calm*) calme; **composer** MUS compositeur *m*; **composition** composition *f*; **composure** calme *m*

compound ['kɑːmpaʊnd] CHEM composé *m*

comprehend [kɑːmprɪ'hend] comprendre; **comprehension** compréhension *f*; **comprehensive** complet

compress [kəm'pres] comprimer; *information* condenser

comprise [kəm'praɪz] comprendre; (*make up*) constituer; ***be ~d of*** se composer de

compromise ['kɑːmprəmaɪz] **1** *n* compromis *m* **2** *v/i* trouver un compromis **3** *v/t* compromettre

compulsion [kəm'pʌlʃn] PSYCH compulsion *f*; **compulsive** *behavior* compulsif; *reading* captivant; **compulsory** obligatoire

computer [kəm'pjuːtər] ordinateur *m*; **computer game** jeu *m* informatique; **computerize** informatiser; **computer science** informatique *f*; **computing** informatique *f*

comrade ['kɑːmreɪd] camarade *m/f*; **comradeship** camaraderie *f*

conceal [kən'siːl] cacher; **concealment** dissimulation *f*

conceit [kən'siːt] vanité *f*; **conceited** vaniteux

conceivable [kən'siːvəbl] concevable; **conceive** *of woman* concevoir

concentrate ['kɑːnsəntreɪt] **1** *v/i* se concentrer **2** *v/t energies* concentrer; **concentration** concentration *f*

concept ['kɑːnsept] concept *m*; **conception** *of child* conception *f*

concern [kən'sɜːrn] **1** *n* (*anxiety, care*) inquiétude *f*, souci *m*; (*business*) affaire *f*; (*company*) entreprise *f* **2** *v/t* (*involve*) concerner; (*worry*) préoccuper; **concerned** (*anxious*) inquiet; (*caring, involved*) concerné; **concerning** concernant, au sujet de

concert ['kɑːnsərt] concert *m*; **concerted** concerté

concession [kən'seʃn] concession *f*

concise [kən'saɪs] concis

conclude [kən'kluːd] conclure; ***~ sth from sth*** déduire qch de qch; **conclusion** conclusion *f*; **conclusive** concluant

concrete ['kɑːŋkriːt] **1** *n* béton *m* **2** *adj* concret

concussion [kən'kʌʃn] commotion *f* cérébrale

condemn [kən'dem] condamner; **condemnation** condamnation *f*

condescend [kɑːndɪ'send]

daigner (***to do*** faire); **condescending** condescendant
condition [kən'dɪʃn] **1** *n* (*state, requirement*) condition *f*; MED maladie *f* **2** *v/t* PSYCH conditionner; **conditioning** PSYCH conditionnement *m*
condo ['kɑːndoʊ] *building* immeuble *m* (en copropriété); *apartment* appart *m*
condolences [kən'doʊlənsɪz] condoléances *fpl*
condom ['kɑːndəm] préservatif *m*
condominium [kɑːndə'mɪnɪəm] → ***condo***
condone [kən'doʊn] excuser
conduct ['kɑːndʌkt] **1** *n* (*behavior*) conduite *f* **2** *v/t* [kən'dʌkt] (*carry out*) mener; ELEC conduire; MUS diriger; **conducted tour** visite *f* guidée; **conductor** MUS chef *m* d'orchestre; *on train* chef *m* de train
cone [koʊn] cône *m*; *for ice cream* cornet *m*; *of pine tree* pomme *f* de pin
conference ['kɑːnfərəns] conférence *f*; *discussion* réunion *f*; **conference room** salle *f* de conférences
confess [kən'fes] **1** *v/t* avouer, confesser **2** *v/i also to police* avouer; REL se confesser; **confession** confession *f*
confide [kən'faɪd] **1** *v/t* confier **2** *v/i*: **~ *in s.o.*** (*trust*) faire confiance à qn; **confidence** confiance *f*; (*in self*) assurance *f*; **confident** (*self-assured*) sûr de soi; (*convinced*) confiant; **confidential** confidentiel; **confidently** avec assurance
confine [kən'faɪn] (*imprison*) enfermer; (*restrict*) limiter; **confined** *space* restreint
confirm [kən'fɜːrm] confirmer; **confirmation** confirmation *f*
confiscate ['kɑːnfɪskeɪt] confisquer
conflict ['kɑːnflɪkt] **1** *n* conflit *m* **2** *v/i* [kən'flɪkt] être en conflit; *of dates* coïncider
confront [kən'frʌnt] (*face*) affronter; (*tackle*) confronter; **confrontation** confrontation *f*; (*clash, dispute*) affrontement *m*
confuse [kən'fjuːz] (*muddle*) compliquer; *person* embrouiller; **~ *s.o. with s.o.*** confondre qn avec qn; **confused** *person* désorienté; *ideas, situation* confus; **confusing** déroutant; **confusion** confusion *f*
congestion [kən'dʒestʃn] *on roads* encombrement *m*
congratulate [kən'grætʊleɪt] féliciter (***on*** pour); **congratulations** félicitations *fpl*
congregate ['kɑːŋgrɪgeɪt] se rassembler; **congregation** REL assemblée *f*
Congress ['kɑːŋgres] le Congrès; **Congressional** du

Congrès; **Congressman** membre *m* du Congrès; **Congresswoman** membre *m* du Congrès

conjecture [kən'dʒektʃər] conjecture *f*

con man ['kɑːnmæn] escroc *m*, arnaqueur *m*

connect [kə'nekt] raccorder, relier; TELEC passer; (*link*) associer; *to power supply* brancher; **connected**: ***be well-~*** avoir des relations; ***be ~ with*** être lié à; **connection** *in wiring* branchement *m*, connexion *f*; *causal etc* rapport *m*; *when traveling* correspondance *f*; (*personal contact*) relation *f*

connoisseur [kɑːnə'sɜːr] connaisseur *m*, connaisseuse *f*

conquer ['kɑːŋkər] conquérir; *fear etc* vaincre; **conqueror** conquérant *m*; **conquest** conquête *f*

conscience ['kɑːnʃəns] conscience *f*; **conscientious** consciencieux; **conscientiousness** conscience *f*

conscious ['kɑːnʃəs] conscient; (*deliberate*) délibéré; **consciously** (*knowingly*) consciemment; (*deliberately*) délibérément; **consciousness** conscience *f*; ***lose/regain ~*** perdre/reprendre connaissance

consecutive [kən'sekjʊtɪv] consécutif

consensus [kən'sensəs] consensus *m*

consent [kən'sent] **1** *n* consentement *m* **2** *v/i* consentir (***to*** à)

consequence ['kɑːnsɪkwəns] conséquence *f*; **consequently** par conséquent

conservation [kɑːnsər'veɪʃn] protection *f*; **conservationist** écologiste *m/f*; **conservative** conservateur; *clothes* classique; *estimate* prudent; **conserve 1** *n* (*jam*) confiture *f* **2** *v/t energy* économiser

consider [kən'sɪdər] considérer; (*show regard for*) prendre en compte; **considerable** considérable; **considerably** considérablement; **considerate** attentionné; **considerately** gentiment; **consideration** (*thought*) réflexion *f*; (*factor*) facteur *m*; (*thoughtfulness, concern*) attention *f*; ***take sth into ~*** prendre qch en considération

◆ **consist of** [kən'sɪst] consister en

consistency [kən'sɪstənsɪ] (*texture*) consistance *f*; (*unchangingness*) constance *f*; (*logic*) cohérence *f*; **consistent** (*unchanging*) constant; *logically etc* cohérent

consolidate [kən'sɑːlɪdeɪt] consolider

conspicuous [kən'spɪkjʊəs]

voyant; ***look~*** se faire remarquer

conspiracy [kən'spɪrəsɪ] conspiration *f*; **conspirator** conspirateur(-trice) *m(f)*; **conspire** conspirer

constant ['kɑːnstənt] constant; **constantly** constamment

constipated ['kɑːnstɪpeɪtɪd] constipé; **constipation** constipation *f*

constitute ['kɑːnstɪtuːt] constituer; **constitution** constitution *f*; **constitutional** POL constitutionnel

constraint [kən'streɪnt] (*restriction*) contrainte *f*

construct [kən'strʌkt] construire; **construction** construction *f*; (*trade*) bâtiment *m*; **constructive** constructif

consul ['kɑːnsl] consul *m*; **consulate** consulat *m*

consult [kən'sʌlt] consulter; **consultancy** *company* cabinet-conseil *m*; (*advice*) conseil *m*; **consultant** consultant *m*; **consultation** consultation *f*

consume [kən'suːm] consommer; **consumer** consommateur *m*; **consumption** consommation *f*

contact ['kɑːntækt] **1** *n* contact *m* **2** *v/t* contacter; **contact lens** lentille *f* de contact

contagious [kən'teɪdʒəs] contagieux

contain [kən'teɪn] contenir; **container** récipient *m*; COM conteneur *m*, container *m*

contaminate [kən'tæmɪneɪt] contaminer; **contamination** contamination *f*

contemporary [kən'tempərerɪ] **1** *adj* contemporain **2** *n* contemporain *m*

contempt [kən'tempt] mépris *m*; **contemptible** méprisable; **contemptuous** méprisant

contender [kən'tendər] *in sport* prétendant *m*; *in competition* concurrent *m*; POL candidat *m*

content[1] ['kɑːntent] *n* contenu *m*

content[2] [kən'tent] **1** *adj* content **2** *v/t*: ***~ o.s. with*** se contenter de

contented [kən'tentɪd] satisfait; **contentment** contentement *m*

contents ['kɑːntents] contenu *m*

contest[1] ['kɑːntest] *n* (*competition*) concours *m*; *in sport* compétition *f*; (*struggle for power*) lutte *f*

contest[2] [kən'test] *leadership etc* disputer; (*oppose*) contester; ***~ an election*** se présenter à une élection

contestant [kən'testənt] concurrent *m*

context ['kɑːntekst] contexte *m*

continent ['kɑːntɪnənt] continent *m*; **continental** continental

continual [kən'tɪnʊəl] continuel; **continually** continuellement; **continuation** continuation *f*; *of story* suite *f*; **continue** continuer; **continuous** continu; **continuously** continuellement

contort [kən'tɔːrt] *face* tordre; **~ *one's body*** se contorsionner

contraception [kɑːntrə'sepʃn] contraception *f*; **contraceptive** contraceptif *m*

contract[1] ['kɑːntrækt] *n* contrat *m*

contract[2] [kən'trækt] **1** *v/i* (*shrink*) se contracter **2** *v/t illness* contracter

contractor [kən'træktər] entrepreneur *m*

contractual [kən'træktʊəl] contractuel

contradict [kɑːntrə'dɪkt] contredire; **contradiction** contradiction *f*; **contradictory** contradictoire

contrary[1] ['kɑːntrərɪ] **1** *adj* contraire; **~ *to …*** contrairement à … **2** *n*: ***on the ~*** au contraire

contrary[2] [kən'trerɪ] *adj* (*perverse*) contrariant

contrast ['kɑːntræst] **1** *n* contraste *m* **2** *v/t* mettre en contraste **3** *v/i* contraster; **contrasting** contrastant; *views* opposé

contravene [kɑːntrə'viːn] enfreindre

contribute [kən'trɪbjuːt] **1** contribuer (***to*** à); *to magazine* collaborer (***to*** à) **2** *v/t money*, *suggestion* donner, apporter; **contribution** contribution *f*; *to political party, church* don *m*; **contributor** *of money* donateur *m*; *to magazine* collaborateur(-trice) *m*(*f*)

control [kən'troʊl] **1** *n* contrôle *m*; ***be in ~ of*** contrôler **2** *v/t* contrôler; *company* diriger

controversial [kɑːntrə'vɜːrʃl] controversé; **controversy** controverse *f*

convenience [kən'viːnɪəns] commodité *f*; ***at your ~*** à votre convenance; **convenience store** magasin *m* de proximité; **convenient** commode, pratique

convent ['kɑːnvənt] couvent *m*

convention [kən'venʃn] (*tradition*) conventions *fpl*; (*conference*) convention *f*; **conventional** conventionnel; *person* conformiste

conversation [kɑːnvər'seɪʃn] conversation *f*; **conversational** de conversation

conversion [kən'vɜːrʃn] conversion *f*; *of building* aménagement *m*; **convert 1** *n* converti *m* **2** *v/t* convertir; *building* aménager; **convertible** *car* (voiture *f*) décapotable *f*

convey [kən'veɪ] (*transmit*) transmettre; (*carry*) trans-

porter; **conveyor belt** convoyeur *m*, tapis *m* roulant
convict 1 ['kɑːnvɪkt] *n* détenu *m* **2** [kən'vɪkt] *v/t* LAW déclarer coupable; **conviction** LAW condamnation *f*; (*belief*) conviction *f*
convince [kən'vɪns] convaincre
convoy ['kɑːnvɔɪ] convoi *m*
cook [kʊk] **1** *n* cuisinier(-ière) *m(f)* **2** *v/t meal* préparer; *food* faire cuire **3** *v/i* faire la cuisine; *of food* cuire; **cookbook** livre *m* de cuisine; **cookery** cuisine *f*; **cookie** cookie *m*; **cooking** cuisine *f*
cool [kuːl] **1** *n*: ***keep one's ~*** garder son sang-froid **2** *adj* frais; *dress* léger; (*calm*) calme; (*unfriendly*) froid; F (*great*) cool **3** *v/i* refroidir; *of tempers* se calmer; *of interest* diminuer **4** *v/t* : ***~ it*** on se calme
◆ **cool down 1** *v/i* refroidir; *of weather* se rafraîchir; : *of tempers* se calmer **2** *v/t food* (faire) refroidir; *fig* calmer
cooperate [koʊ'ɑːpəreɪt] coopérer; **cooperation** coopération *f*; **cooperative 1** *n* COM coopérative *f* **2** *adj* coopératif
coordinate [koʊ'ɔːrdɪneɪt] coordonner; **coordination** coordination *f*
cop [kɑːp] F flic *m* F
cope [koʊp] se débrouiller; ***~ with ...*** faire face à ...
copier ['kɑːpɪər] *machine* photocopieuse *f*
copper ['kɑːpər] cuivre *m*
copy ['kɑːpɪ] **1** *n* copie *f*; *of book* exemplaire *m* **2** *v/t* copier; (*photocopy*) photocopier
cord [kɔːrd] (*string*) corde *f*; (*cable*) fil *m*, cordon *m*
cordon ['kɔːrdn] cordon *m*
cords [kɔːrdz] *pants* pantalon *m* en velours (côtelé)
core [kɔːr] **1** *n of fruit, problem* cœur *m*; *of party* noyau *m* **2** *adj issue* fondamental
cork [kɔːrk] *in bottle* bouchon *m*; *material* liège *m*; **corkscrew** tire-bouchon *m*
corn [kɔːrn] *grain* maïs *m*
corner ['kɔːrnər] **1** *n* coin *m*; *in road* virage *m*, tournant *m*; *in soccer* corner *m*; ***on the ~*** *of street* au coin **2** *v/t person* coincer; ***~ the market*** accaparer le marché **3** *v/i of driver, car* prendre le/les virage(s)
coronary ['kɑːrənerɪ] **1** *adj* coronaire **2** *n* infarctus *m* (du myocarde)
coroner ['kɑːrənər] coroner *m*
corporal ['kɔːrpərəl] caporal *m*; **corporal punishment** châtiment *m* corporel
corporate ['kɔːrpərət] COM d'entreprise; **corporation** (*business*) société *f*, entreprise *f*

corpse [kɔːrps] cadavre *m*, corps *m*
corral [kəˈræl] corral *m*
correct [kəˈrekt] **1** *adj* correct; ***the ~ answer*** la bonne réponse; ***that's ~*** c'est exact **2** *v/t* corriger; **correction** correction *f*; **correctly** correctement
correspond [kɑːrɪˈspɑːnd] correspondre (***to*** à); **correspondence** correspondance *f*; **correspondent** correspondant(e) *m(f)*
corridor [ˈkɔːrɪdər] couloir *m*
corroborate [kəˈrɑːbəreɪt] corroborer
corrosion [kəˈroʊʒn] corrosion *f*
corrupt [kəˈrʌpt] **1** *adj also* COMPUT corrompu; MORALS, YOUTH dépravé **2** *v/t* corrompre; **corruption** corruption *f*
cosmetic [kɑːzˈmetɪk] cosmétique; *fig* esthétique; **cosmetics** cosmétiques *mpl*; **cosmetic surgery** chirurgie *f* esthétique
cosmopolitan [kɑːzməˈpɑːlɪtən] cosmopolite
cost [kɑːst] **1** *n also fig* coût *m* **2** *v/t* coûter; ***how much does it ~?*** combien ça coûte?
ˈcost-effective rentable; **cost of living** coût *m* de la vie
costume [ˈkɑːstuːm] *for actor* costume *m*
cosy *Br* → ***cozy***
cot [kɑːt] (*camp-bed*) lit *m* de camp; *Br for child* lit *m* d'enfant
cottage [ˈkɑːtɪdʒ] cottage *m*
cotton [ˈkɑːtn] **1** *n* coton *m* **2** *adj* en coton; **cotton candy** barbe *f* à papa; **cotton wool** *Br* coton *m* hydrophile, ouate *f*
couch [kaʊʧ] canapé *m*; **couch potato** téléphage *m/f*
cough [kɑːf] **1** *n* toux *f* **2** *v/i* tousser; **cough medicine, cough syrup** sirop *m* contre la toux
could [kʊd]: ***~ I have my key?*** pourrais-je avoir ma clef?; ***~ you help me?*** pourrais-tu m'aider?; ***you ~ be right*** vous avez peut-être raison; ***you ~ have warned me!*** tu aurais pu me prévenir!
council [ˈkaʊnsl] (*assembly*) conseil *m*, assemblée *f*; **councilor** conseiller *m*
counsel [ˈkaʊnsl] **1** *n* (*advice*) conseil *m*; (*lawyer*) avocat *m* **2** *v/t* conseiller; **counseling**, *Br* **counselling** aide *f* (psychologique); **counselor**, *Br* **counsellor** (*adviser*) conseiller *m*; LAW maître *m*
count [kaʊnt] **1** *n* compte *m* **2** *v/t & v/i* compter
◆ **count on** compter sur
ˈcountdown compte *m* à rebours
counter [ˈkaʊntər] *in shop, café* comptoir *m*; *in game* pion *m*
ˈcounteract neutraliser, contrecarrer; **counter-attack 1**

n contre-attaque *f* **2** *v/i* contre-attaquer; **counterclockwise** dans le sens inverse des aiguilles d'une montre; **counterespionage** contre-espionnage *m*; **counterfeit** **1** *v/t* contrefaire **2** *adj* faux; **counterpart** *person* homologue *m/f*; **counterproductive** contre-productif
countless ['kauntlɪs] innombrable
country ['kʌntrɪ] pays *m*; *as opposed to town* campagne *f*
county ['kaʊntɪ] comté *m*
coup [kuː] POL coup *m* d'État; *fig* beau coup *m*
couple ['kʌpl] (*two people*) couple *m*; ***a ~ of*** (*a pair*) deux; (*a few*) quelques
courage ['kʌrɪdʒ] courage *m*; **courageous** courageux
courier ['kʊrɪər] (*messenger*) coursier *m*; *with tourist party* guide *m/f*
course [kɔːrs] *of lessons* cours *m*(*pl*); *of meal* plat *m*; *of ship, plane* route *f*; *for sports* piste *f*; *for golf* terrain *m*; ***of ~*** bien sûr; ***of ~ not*** bien sûr que non
court [kɔːrt] LAW tribunal *m*, cour *f*; FOR TENNIS court *m*; *for basketball* terrain *m*; ***take s.o. to ~*** faire un procès à qn; **court case** affaire *f*, procès *m*
courtesy ['kɜːrtəsɪ] courtoisie *f*
'courthouse palais *m* de justice, tribunal *m*; **courtroom** salle *f* d'audience; **courtyard** cour *f*
cousin ['kʌzn] cousin(e) *m*(*f*)
cover ['kʌvər] **1** *n protective* housse *f*; *of book, magazine* couverture *f*; (*shelter*) abri *m*; (*insurance*) couverture *f*, assurance *f* **2** *v/t* couvrir
◆ **cover up** **1** *v/t* couvrir; *scandal* dissimuler **2** *v/i* cacher la vérité
coverage ['kʌvərɪdʒ] *by media* couverture *f* (médiatique)
covert ['koʊvɜːrt] secret, clandestin
'cover-up black-out *m inv*
cow [kaʊ] vache *f*
coward ['kaʊərd] lâche *m/f*; **cowardice** lâcheté *f*
'cowboy cow-boy *m*
co-worker ['koʊwɜːrkər] collègue *m/f*
cozy ['koʊzɪ] confortable, douillet
crab [kræb] crabe *m*
crack [kræk] **1** *n* fissure *f*; *in cup, glass* fêlure *f*; (*joke*) vanne *f* **2** *v/t cup, glass* fêler; *nut* casser; (*solve*) résoudre; *code* décrypter **3** *v/i* se fêler; **crack** (**cocaine**) crack *m*; **cracked** *cup* fêlé; **cracker** *to eat* cracker *m*
cradle ['kreɪdl] berceau *m*
craft¹ [kræft] NAUT embarcation *f*
craft² (*trade*) métier *m*; *weaving, pottery etc* artisanat *m*;

(*craftsmanship*) art *m*; **craftsman** (*artisan*) artisan *m*; **crafty** malin, rusé

crag [kræg] (*rock*) rocher *m* escarpé

cram [kræm] fourrer; *food* enfourner; *people* entasser

cramps [kræmps] crampe *f*

crane [kreɪn] **1** *n* (*machine*) grue *f* **2** *v/t*: **~ *one's neck*** tendre le cou

crank [kræŋk] *person* allumé *m*; **cranky** (*bad-tempered*) grognon

crash [kræʃ] **1** *n noise* fracas *m*; *accident* accident *m*; COM faillite *f*; *of stock exchange* krach *m*; COMPUT plantage *m* **2** *v/i* s'écraser; *of car* avoir un accident; *of market* s'effondrer; COMPUT se planter **3** *v/t car* avoir un accident avec; **crash course** cours *m* intensif; **crash diet** régime *m* intensif; **crash helmet** casque *m*; **crash-land** atterrir en catastrophe

crate [kreɪt] caisse *f*

crater ['kreɪtər] cratère *m*

crave [kreɪv] avoir très envie de; **craving** envie *f* (irrépressible)

crawl [krɒːl] **1** *n in swimming* crawl *m* **2** *v/i on belly* ramper; *on hands and knees* marcher à quatre pattes; (*move slowly*) se traîner

crayon ['kreɪɑːn] crayon *m* de couleur

craze [kreɪz] engouement *m*; ***the latest ~*** la dernière mode; **crazy** fou

creak [kriːk] craquer, grincer; **creaky** qui craque, grinçant

cream [kriːm] **1** *n* crème *f*; *color* crème *m* **2** *adj* crème *inv*

crease [kriːs] **1** *n* pli *m* **2** *v/t accidentally* froisser

create [kriː'eɪt] créer; **creation** création *f*; **creative** créatif; **creator** créateur(-trice) *m*(*f*)

creature ['kriːʧər] animal *m*; (*person*) créature *f*

credibility [kredə'bɪlətɪ] crédibilité *f*; **credible** crédible

credit ['kredɪt] crédit *m*; (*honor*) honneur *m*, mérite *m*; **creditable** honorable; **credit card** carte *f* de crédit; **credit limit** limite *f* de crédit; **creditor** créancier *m*; **creditworthy** solvable

creep [kriːp] **1** *n pej* sale type *m* **2** *v/i* se glisser (en silence); (*move slowly*) avancer lentement; **creepy** F flippant F

cremate [krɪ'meɪt] incinérer; **cremation** incinération *f*, crémation *f*

crest [krest] crête *f*

crevice ['krevɪs] fissure *f*

crew [kruː] *of ship, airplane* équipage *m*; **crew cut** cheveux *mpl* en brosse

crib [krɪb] *for baby* lit *m* d'enfant

crime [kraɪm] crime *m*; **criminal** **1** *n* criminel *m* **2** *adj* cri-

minel; (*shameful*) honteux
crimson ['krɪmzn] cramoisi
cripple ['krɪpl] **1** *n* handicapé(e) *m(f)* **2** *v/t person* estropier; *fig* paralyser
crisis ['kraɪsɪs] crise *f*
crisp [krɪsp] *weather* vivifiant; *lettuce*, *apple* croquant; *bacon, toast* croustillant; **crisps** *Br* chips *fpl*
criterion [kraɪ'tɪrɪən] critère *m*
critic ['krɪtɪk] critique *m*; **critical** critique; **criticism** critique *f*; **criticize** critiquer
crocodile ['krɑːkədaɪl] crocodile *m*
crony ['kroʊnɪ] pote *m* , copain *m*
crook [krʊk] escroc *m*; **crooked** de travers; *streets* tortueux; (*dishonest*) malhonnête
crop [krɑːp] **1** *n* culture *f*; (*harvest*) récolte *f* **2** *v/t hair, photo* couper
◆ **crop up** surgir
cross [krɑːs] **1** *adj* (*angry*) fâché **2** *n* croix *f* **3** *v/t* (*go across*) traverser; ~ **o.s.** REL se signer **4** *v/i* (*go across*) traverser; *of lines* se croiser
◆ **cross off, cross out** rayer
'**crosscheck 1** *n* recoupement *m* **2** *v/t* vérifier par recoupement; **cross-examine** LAW faire subir un contre-interrogatoire à; **cross-eyed** qui louche; **crossing** NAUT traversée *f*; **crossroads** *also fig* carrefour *m*; **crosswalk** passage *m* (pour) piétons; **crossword** (**puzzle**) mots *mpl* croisés
crotch [krɑːtʃ] entrejambe *m*
crouch [kraʊtʃ] s'accroupir
crowd [kraʊd] foule *f*; *at sports event* public *m*; **crowded** bondé, plein (de monde)
crown [kraʊn] *also on tooth* couronne *f*
crucial ['kruːʃl] crucial
crucifix ['kruːsɪfɪks] crucifix *m*; **crucifixion** *of Christ* crucifixion *f*; **crucify** REL crucifier; *fig* assassiner
crude [kruːd] **1** *adj* (*vulgar*) grossier; (*unsophisticated*) rudimentaire **2** *n*: ~ (*oil*) pétrole *m* brut
cruel ['kruːəl] cruel; **cruelty** cruauté *f*
cruise [kruːz] **1** *n* croisière *f* **2** *v/i of people* faire une croisière; *of car* rouler (à une vitesse de croisière); *of plane* voler (à une vitesse de croisière)
crumb [krʌm] miette *f*
crumble ['krʌmbl] *of bread* s'émietter; *of stonework* s'effriter; *fig*: *of opposition etc* s'effondrer
crumple ['krʌmpl] **1** *v/t* (*crease*) froisser **2** *v/i* (*collapse*) s'écrouler
crush [krʌʃ] **1** *n* (*crowd*) foule *f* **2** *v/t* écraser; (*crease*) froisser

crust [krʌst] *on bread* croûte *f*
crutch [krʌʧ] *for injured person* béquille *f*
cry [kraɪ] **1** *n* (*call*) cri *m* **2** *v/i* (*weep*) pleurer
◆ **cry out** crier
cryptic ['krɪptɪk] énigmatique
crystal ['krɪstl] cristal *m*
cube [kjuːb] cube *m*; **cubic** cubique; **~ meter** mètre cube
cubicle ['kjuːbɪkl] (*changing room*) cabine *f*
cuddle ['kʌdl] câliner
cue [kjuː] *for actor etc* signal *m*; *for pool* queue *f*
cuff [kʌf] *of shirt* poignet *m*; *of pants* revers *m*; (*blow*) gifle *f*
culminate ['kʌlmɪneɪt]: **~ in** se terminer par; **culmination** apogée *f*
culprit ['kʌlprɪt] coupable *m/f*
cult [kʌlt] (*sect*) secte *f*
cultivate ['kʌltɪveɪt] *land*, *person* cultiver; **cultivated** *person* cultivé; **cultivation** *of land* culture *f*
cultural ['kʌlʧərəl] culturel; **culture** culture *f*; **cultured** cultivé
cumulative ['kjuːmjʊlətɪv] cumulatif
cunning ['kʌnɪŋ] **1** *n* ruse *f* **2** *adj* rusé
cup [kʌp] tasse *f*; (*trophy*) coupe *f*
cupboard ['kʌbərd] placard *m*
curb [kɜːrb] **1** *n of street* bord *m* du trottoir; *on powers etc* frein *m* **2** *v/t* réfréner
cure [kjʊr] **1** *n* MED remède *m* **2** *v/t* MED guérir; *meat* saurer
curiosity [kjʊrɪ'ɑːsətɪ] curiosité *f*; **curious** curieux
curl [kɜːrl] **1** *n in hair* boucle *f*; *of smoke* volute *f* **2** *v/t hair* boucler; (*wind*) enrouler **3** *v/i of hair* boucler; *of leaf*, *paper etc* se gondoler
◆ **curl up** se pelotonner
curly ['kɜːrlɪ] *hair* bouclé; *tail* en tire-bouchon
currency ['kʌrənsɪ] monnaie *f*; **foreign ~** devise *f* étrangère; **current 1** *n in sea*, ELEC courant *m* **2** *adj* actuel; **current affairs** actualité *f*
curse [kɜːrs] **1** *n* (*spell*) malédiction *f*; (*swearword*) juron *m* **2** *v/t* maudire **3** *v/i* (*swear*) jurer
cursor ['kɜːrsər] COMPUT curseur *m*
cursory ['kɜːrsərɪ] superficiel
curt [kɜːrt] abrupt
curtain ['kɜːrtn] *also* THEA rideau *m*
curve [kɜːrv] **1** *n* courbe *f* **2** *v/i* (*bend*) s'incurver; *of road* faire une courbe
cushion ['kʊʃn] **1** *n* coussin *m* **2** *v/t blow*, *fall* amortir
custody ['kʌstədɪ] *of children* garde *f*; **in ~** LAW en détention
custom ['kʌstəm] coutume *f*; COM clientèle *f*; **customer** client *m*; **customer service** service *m* clientèle
customs ['kʌstəmz] douane

f; **customs officer** douanier *m*

cut [kʌt] **1** *n with knife, scissors* entaille *f*; (*injury*) coupure *f*; *of garment, hair* coupe *f*; (*reduction*) réduction *f* **2** *v/t* couper; (*reduce*) réduire; ***get one's hair ~*** se faire couper les cheveux

◆ **cut down 1** *v/t tree* abattre **2** *v/i on smoking etc* réduire

◆ **cut off** couper; (*isolate*) isoler

◆ **cut up** *meat etc* découper

cutback réduction *f*

cute [kju:t] *in appearance* mignon; (*clever*) malin

'cutoff date date *f* limite; **cut-price** à prix *m* réduit; **cut-throat** *competition* acharné; **cutting 1** *n from newspaper* coupure *f* **2** *adj remark* blessant

cyber ... ['saɪbər] cyber...

cycle ['saɪkl] **1** *n* vélo *m*; *of events* cycle *m* **2** *v/i* aller en vélo; **cycling** cyclisme *m*; **cyclist** cycliste *m/f*

cylinder ['sɪlɪndər] *in engine* cylindre *m*; **cylindrical** cylindrique

cynic ['sɪnɪk] cynique *m/f*; **cynical** cynique; **cynicism** cynisme *m*

Czech [ʧek] **1** *adj* tchèque; ***the ~ Republic*** la République tchèque **2** *n person* Tchèque *m/f*; *language* tchèque *m*

D

DA [di:'eɪ] (= ***district attorney***) procureur *m*

◆ **dabble in** toucher à

dad [dæd] papa *m*

daily ['deɪlɪ] **1** *n paper* quotidien *m* **2** *adj* quotidien

'dairy products produits *mpl* laitiers

dam [dæm] *for water* barrage *m*

damage ['dæmɪdʒ] **1** *n* dommage(s) *m(pl)*; *to reputation* préjudice *m* **2** *v/t* endommager; *fig: reputation* nuire à; **damages** LAW dommages-intérêts *mpl*; **damaging** préjudiciable

damn [dæm] F **1** *interj* zut **2** *adj* sacré **3** *adv* (*very*) vachement F; **damning** *evidence, report* accablant

damp [dæmp] humide

dance [dæns] **1** *n* danse *f*; *social event* bal *m* **2** *v/i* danser; **dancer** danseur(-euse) *m(f)*; **dancing** danse *f*

Dane [deɪn] Danois(e) *m(f)*

danger ['deɪndʒər] danger *m*; **dangerous** dangereux

dangle ['dæŋgl] **1** *v/t* balancer **2** *v/i* pendre

Danish ['deɪnɪʃ] **1** *adj* danois **2** *n language* danois *m*

Danish (pastry) feuilleté *m*

(sucré)
dare [der] **1** *v/i* oser; **~ *to do sth*** oser faire qch **2** *v/t*: **~ *s.o. to do sth*** défier qn de faire qch; **daring** audacieux
dark [dɑːrk] **1** *n* noir *m* **2** *adj room* sombre, noir; *hair* brun; *eyes, color, clothes* foncé; **dark glasses** lunettes *fpl* noires; **darkness** obscurité *f*
darling ['dɑːrlɪŋ] chéri(e) *m(f)*
dart [dɑːrt] **1** *n for game* fléchette *f* **2** *v/i* se précipiter
dash [dæʃ] **1** *n punctuation* tiret *m*; ***a ~ of*** un peu de **2** *v/i* se précipiter **3** *v/t hopes* anéantir; **dashboard** tableau *m* de bord
data ['deɪtə] données *fpl*; **database** base *f* de données
date[1] [deɪt] *fruit* datte *f*
date[2] [deɪt] date *f*; *meeting, person* rendez-vous *m*; ***out of ~*** *clothes* démodé; *passport* périmé; ***up to ~*** *information* à jour; *style* à la mode; **dated** démodé
daughter ['dɒːtər] fille *f*; **daughter-in-law** belle-fille *f*
dawn [dɒːn] *also fig* aube *f*
day [deɪ] jour *m*; *stressing duration* journée *f*; ***the ~ after*** le lendemain; ***the ~ after tomorrow*** après-demain; ***the ~ before*** la veille; ***the ~ before yesterday*** avant-hier; ***in those ~s*** en ce temps-là, à l'époque; ***the other ~*** (*recently*) l'autre jour; **daybreak** aube *f*, point *m* du jour; **daydream 1** *n* rêverie *f* **2** *v/i* rêvasser; **daylight** jour *m*; **day spa** spa *m* urbain
dazed [deɪzd] *by news* hébété; *by blow* étourdi
dazzle ['dæzl] éblouir
dead [ded] **1** *adj* mort; *battery* à plat; ***the phone's ~*** il n'y a pas de tonalité **2** *adv* F (*very*) très; **~ *beat*, ~ *tired*** crevé **3** *npl*: ***the ~*** les morts *mpl*; **dead end** *street* impasse *f*; **dead heat** arrivée *f* ex æquo; **deadline** date *f* limite; heure *f* limite, délai *m*; *for newspaper* heure *f* de clôture; ***meet the ~*** respecter le(s) délai(s); **deadlock** *in talks* impasse *f*; **deadly** mortel
deaf [def] sourd; **deafening** assourdissant; **deafness** surdité *f*
deal [diːl] **1** *n* accord *m*, marché *m*; ***a great ~ of*** beaucoup de **2** *v/t cards* distribuer
◆ **deal in** COM être dans le commerce de; *drugs* dealer
◆ **deal with** (*handle*) s'occuper de; (*do business with*) traiter avec; (*be about*) traiter de
dealer ['diːlər] marchand *m*; (*drug ~*) dealer *m*, dealeuse *f*; *large-scale* trafiquant *m* de drogue; **dealing** (*drug ~*) trafic *m* de drogue; **dealings** (*business*) relations *fpl*
dear [dɪr] cher; ***Dear Sir*** Monsieur

death [deθ] mort *f*; **death toll** nombre *m* de morts

debatable [dɪ'beɪtəbl] discutable; **debate 1** *n* débat *m* **2** *v/i* débattre **3** *v/t* débattre de

debit ['debɪt] **1** *n* débit *m* **2** *v/t account* débiter; *amount* porter au débit; **debit card** carte *f* bancaire

debris [də'briː] débris *mpl*

debt [det] dette *f*; ***be in ~*** être endetté; **debtor** débiteur *m*

debug [diː'bʌg] COMPUT déboguer

decade ['dekeɪd] décennie *f*

decadent ['dekədənt] décadent

decaffeinated [dɪ'kæfɪneɪtɪd] décaféiné

decay [dɪ'keɪ] **1** *n* détérioration *f*; *in wood, plant* pourriture *f*; *in teeth* carie *f* **2** *v/i of wood, plant* pourrir; *of civilization* tomber en décadence; *of teeth* se carier

deceased [dɪ'siːst]: ***the ~*** le défunt/la défunte

deceit [dɪ'siːt] duplicité *f*; **deceitful** fourbe; **deceive** tromper

December [dɪ'sembər] décembre *m*

decency ['diːsənsɪ] décence *f*; **decent** *person* correct, honnête; *salary* correct, décent; *meal, sleep* bon

deception [dɪ'sepʃn] tromperie *f*; **deceptive** trompeur

decide [dɪ'saɪd] décider; **decided** (*definite*) décidé; *views* arrêté; *improvement* net

decimal ['desɪml] décimale *f*

decipher [dɪ'saɪfər] déchiffrer

decision [dɪ'sɪʒn] décision *f*; **decisive** décidé; (*crucial*) décisif

deck [dek] *of ship* pont *m*; *of cards* jeu *m* (de cartes)

declaration [deklə'reɪʃn] déclaration *f*; **declare** déclarer

decline [dɪ'klaɪn] **1** *n* baisse *f*; *of civilization, health* déclin *m* **2** *v/t invitation* décliner; ***~ to comment*** refuser de commenter **3** *v/i* (*refuse*) refuser; (*decrease*) baisser; *of health* décliner

decode [diː'koʊd] décoder

décor ['deɪkɔːr] décor *m*

decorate ['dekəreɪt] *room* refaire; *with paint* peindre; *with paper* tapisser; (*adorn*), *soldier* décorer; **decoration** décoration *f*; **decorator** (*interior ~*) décorateur *m* (d'intérieur)

decoy ['diːkɔɪ] appât *m*, leurre *m*

decrease ['diːkriːs] **1** *n* baisse *f*, diminution *f*; *in size* réduction *f* **2** *v/t & v/i* diminuer

dedicate ['dedɪkeɪt] *book etc* dédicacer; **dedicated** dévoué; **dedication** *in book* dédicace *f*; *to cause, work* dévouement *m*

deduce [dɪ'duːs] déduire

deduct [dɪ'dʌkt] déduire

(***from*** de); **deduction** *from salary* prélèvement *m*; (*conclusion*) déduction *f*
deed [diːd] (*act*) acte *m*; LAW acte *m* (notarié)
deep [diːp] profond; *voice* grave; *color* intense; **deepen 1** *v/t* creuser **2** *v/i* devenir plus profond; *of mystery* s'épaissir; **deep freeze** congélateur *m*
deer [dɪr] cerf *m*; *female* biche *f*
deface [dɪ'feɪs] abîmer
defamation [defə'meɪʃn] diffamation *f*; **defamatory** diffamatoire
defeat [dɪ'fiːt] **1** *n* défaite *f* **2** *v/t* battre
defect ['diːfekt] défaut *m*; **defective** défectueux
defence *Br* → ***defense***
defend [dɪ'fend] défendre; *decision* justifier; **defendant** défendeur *m*, défenderesse *f*; *in criminal case* accusé(e) *m*(*f*); **defense** défense *f*; **defenseless** sans défense; **Defense Secretary** POL ministre de la Défense; **defensive 1** *n*: ***go on*** (***to***) ***the*** ~ se mettre sur la défensive **2** *adj* défensif
deference ['defərəns] déférence *f*
defiance [dɪ'faɪəns] défi *m*; **defiant** [dɪ'faɪənt] provocant; *look* de défi
deficiency [dɪ'fɪʃənsɪ] manque *m*; MED carence *f*
deficit ['defɪsɪt] déficit *m*
define [dɪ'faɪn] définir
definite ['defɪnɪt] définitif; *improvement* net; (*certain*) catégorique; **definitely** sans aucun doute; ~ ***not*** certainement pas!
definition [defɪ'nɪʃn] définition *f*
deformity [dɪ'fɔːrmətɪ] difformité *f*
defrost [diː'frɒːst] *food* décongeler; *fridge* dégivrer
defuse [diː'fjuːz] *bomb*, *situation* désamorcer
defy [dɪ'faɪ] défier; *superiors* braver
degrading [dɪ'greɪdɪŋ] dégradant
degree [dɪ'griː] degré *m*; *from university* diplôme *m*
dehydrated [diːhaɪ'dreɪtɪd] déshydraté
deign [deɪn]: ~ ***to*** daigner
dejected [dɪ'dʒektɪd] déprimé
delay [dɪ'leɪ] **1** *n* retard *m* **2** *v/t* retarder; ***be*** ~***ed*** être en retard **3** *v/i* tarder
delegate ['delɪgət] **1** *n* délégué(e) *m*(*f*) **2** *v/t* déléguer; **delegation** délégation *f*
delete [dɪ'liːt] effacer; (*cross out*) rayer; **deletion** *act* effacement *m*; *that deleted* rature *f*
deliberate 1 [dɪ'lɪbərət] *adj* délibéré **2** [dɪ'lɪbəreɪt] *v/i* délibérer; (*reflect*) réfléchir; **deliberately** délibérément,

exprès
delicate ['delɪkət] délicat
delicatessen [delɪkə'tesn] traiteur *m*, épicerie *f* fine
delicious [dɪ'lɪʃəs] délicieux
delight [dɪ'laɪt] joie *f*, plaisir *m*; **delighted** ravi; **delightful** charmant
deliver [dɪ'lɪvər] livrer; *letters* distribuer; *parcel etc* remettre; *message* transmettre; *baby* mettre au monde; *speech* faire; **delivery** *of goods* livraison *f*; *of mail* distribution *f*; *of baby* accouchement *m*; *of speech* débit *m*; **delivery date** date *f* de livraison
de luxe [də'lʌks] de luxe; *model* haut de gamme *inv*
demand [dɪ'mænd] **1** *n also* COM demande *f*; *of terrorist, unions etc* revendication *f*; **in ~** demandé **2** *v/t* exiger; *pay rise etc* réclamer; **demanding** *job* éprouvant; *person* exigeant
demo ['demoʊ] (*protest*) manif *f*; *of video etc* démo *f*
democracy [dɪ'mɑːkrəsɪ] démocratie *f*; **democrat** démocrate *m/f*; **democratic** démocratique
demolish [dɪ'mɑːlɪʃ] *building, argument* démolir; **demolition** démolition *f*
demonstrate ['demənstreɪt] **1** *v/t* (*prove*) démontrer; *machine etc* faire une démonstration de **2** *v/i politically* manifester; **demonstration** démonstration *f*; (*protest*) manifestation *f*; **demonstrator** (*protester*) manifestant(e) *m(f)*
demoralized [dɪ'mɔːrəlaɪzd] démoralisé; **demoralizing** démoralisant
demote [diː'moʊt] rétrograder
den [den] *room* antre *f*
denial [dɪ'naɪəl] *of accusation* démenti *m*, dénégation *f*; *of request* refus *m*
denim ['denɪm] jean *m*
Denmark ['denmɑːrk] le Danemark
denomination [dɪnɑːmɪ'neɪʃn] *of money* coupure *f*; *religious* confession *f*
dense [dens] (*thick*) dense; **density** ['densɪtɪ] densité *f*
dent [dent] **1** *n* bosse *f* **2** *v/t* bosseler
dental ['dentl] dentaire
dented ['dentɪd] bosselé
dentist ['dentɪst] dentiste *m/f*; **dentures** dentier *m*
Denver boot ['denvər] sabot *m* de Denver
deny [dɪ'naɪ] *charge* nier; *right, request* refuser
deodorant [diː'oʊdərənt] déodorant *m*
department [dɪ'pɑːrtmənt] *of company* service *m*; *of university* département *m*; *of government* ministère *m*; *of store* rayon *m*; **Department of State** ministère *m* des Affaires étrangères; **depart-**

ment store grand magasin *m*
departure [dɪ'pɑːrtʃər] départ *m*; *from standard etc* entorse *f* (***from*** à); **departure lounge** salle *f* d'embarquement; **departure time** heure *f* de départ
depend [dɪ'pend] dépendre; ***that ~s*** cela dépend; **dependence, dependency** dépendance *f*
depict [dɪ'pɪkt] représenter
deplorable [dɪ'plɔːrəbl] déplorable; **deplore** déplorer
deploy [dɪ'plɔɪ] (*use*) faire usage de; (*position*) déployer
deport [dɪ'pɔːrt] expulser; **deportation** expulsion *f*
deposit [dɪ'pɑːzɪt] **1** *n in bank* dépôt *m*; *on purchase* acompte *m*; *security* caution *f*; *of mineral* gisement *m* **2** *v/t money, object* déposer; **deposition** LAW déposition *f*
depot ['depoʊ] *for storage* dépôt *m*, entrepôt *m*
depreciation [dɪpriːʃɪ'eɪʃn] FIN dépréciation *f*
depress [dɪ'pres] *person* déprimer; **depressed** déprimé; **depressing** déprimant; **depression** MED, *meteorological* dépression *f*; *economic* crise *f*, récession *f*
deprivation [deprɪ'veɪʃn] privation(s) *f(pl)*; **deprive**: ***~ s.o. of sth*** priver qn de qch; **deprived** défavorisé
depth [depθ] profondeur *f*; *of color* intensité *f*; ***in ~*** en profondeur
deputy ['depjʊtɪ] adjoint(e) *m(f)*; *of sheriff* shérif *m* adjoint
derail [dɪ'reɪl]: ***be ~ed*** *of train* dérailler
derelict ['derəlɪkt] délabré
deride [dɪ'raɪd] se moquer de; **derision** dérision *f*; **derisory** dérisoire
derivative [dɪ'rɪvətɪv] (*not original*) dérivé
derive [dɪ'raɪv] tirer (***from*** de); ***be ~d from*** dériver de
dermatologist [dɜːrmə'tɑːlədʒɪst] dermatologue *m/f*
derogatory [dɪ'rɑːgətɔːrɪ] désobligeant; *term* péjoratif
descendant [dɪ'sendənt] descendant(e) *m(f)*; **descent** descente *f*; (*ancestry*) descendance *f*
describe [dɪ'skraɪb] décrire; **description** description *f*; *of criminal* signalement *m*
desegregate [diː'segrəgeɪt] supprimer la ségrégation dans
desert[1] ['dezərt] *n* désert *m*
desert[2] [dɪ'zɜːrt] **1** *v/t* abandonner **2** *v/i of soldier* déserter; **deserted** désert; **deserter** MIL déserteur *m*; **desertion** abandon *m*; MIL désertion *f*
deserve [dɪ'zɜːrv] mériter
design [dɪ'zaɪn] **1** *n* (*subject*) design *m*; (*style*) style *m*; (*drawing, pattern*) dessin *m*

2 *v/t* (*draw*) dessiner; *building, car* concevoir
designate ['dezɪgneɪt] *person* désigner
designer [dɪ'zaɪnər] designer *m/f*; *of car, ship* concepteur(-trice) *m(f)*; *of clothes* styliste *m/f*; **designer clothes** vêtements *mpl* de marque
desirable [dɪ'zaɪrəbl] souhaitable; *sexually, change* désirable; *house* beau; **desire** désir *m*
desk [desk] bureau *m*; *in hotel* réception *f*; **desk clerk** réceptionniste *m/f*; **desktop publishing** publication *f* assistée par ordinateur
desolate ['desələt] *place* désolé
despair [dɪ'sper] **1** *n* désespoir *m*; ***in ~*** désespéré **2** *v/i* désespérer (***of*** de); **desperate** désespéré; ***be ~ for sth*** avoir très envie de qch; **desperation** désespoir *m*; ***in ~*** en désespoir de cause
despicable [dɪs'pɪkəbl] méprisable; **despise** mépriser
despite [dɪ'spaɪt] malgré, en dépit de
dessert [dɪ'zɜːrt] dessert *m*
destination [destɪ'neɪʃn] destination *f*
destroy [dɪ'strɔɪ] détruire; **destroyer** NAUT destroyer *m*; **destruction** destruction *f*; **destructive** *power* destructeur; ***a ~ child*** un enfant qui casse tout
detach [dɪ'tætʃ] détacher; **detached** (*objective*) neutre; **detachment** (*objectivity*) neutralité *f*
detail ['diːteɪl] détail *m*; **detailed** détaillé
detain [dɪ'teɪn] (*hold back*) retenir; *as prisoner* détenir; **detainee** détenu(e) *m(f)*; ***political ~*** prisonnier *m* politique
detect [dɪ'tekt] déceler; *of device* détecter; **detection** *of criminal* découverte *f*; *of smoke etc* détection *f*; **detective** inspecteur *m* de police; **detector** détecteur *m*
détente ['deɪtɑːnt] POL détente *f*
deter [dɪ'tɜːr] dissuader
detergent [dɪ'tɜːrdʒənt] détergent *m*
deteriorate [dɪ'tɪrɪəreɪt] se détériorer
determination [dɪtɜːrmɪ'neɪʃn] (*resolution*) détermination *f*; **determine** (*establish*) déterminer; **determined** déterminé, résolu; *effort* délibéré
detest [dɪ'test] détester; **detestable** détestable
detour ['diːtʊr] détour *m*; (*diversion*) déviation *f*
devaluation [diːvæljʊ'eɪʃn] dévaluation *f*; **devalue** dévaluer
devastate ['devəsteɪt] dévaster; *fig*: *person* anéantir

develop [dɪ'veləp] **1** *v/t film, business* développer; *site* aménager; *technique, vaccine* mettre au point; *illness* attraper **2** *v/i* (*grow*) se développer; **developing country** pays *m* en voie de développement; **development** *of film, business* développement *m*; *of site* aménagement *m*; (*event*) événement *m*; *of technique, vaccine* mise *f* au point

device [dɪ'vaɪs] (*tool*) appareil *m*

devil ['devl] diable *m*; ***a little~*** un petit monstre

devise [dɪ'vaɪz] concevoir

devote [dɪ'vout] consacrer; **devoted** *son etc* dévoué (***to*** à); **devotion** dévouement *m*

devour [dɪ'vaʊər] dévorer

devout [dɪ'vaʊt] pieux

diabetes [daɪə'biːtiːz] diabète *m*; **diabetic** diabétique *m/f*

diagnose ['daɪəgnouz] diagnostiquer; **diagnosis** diagnostic *m*

diagonal [daɪ'ægənl] diagonal; **diagonally** en diagonale

diagram ['daɪəgræm] diagramme *m*

dial ['daɪl] **1** *n* cadran *m* **2** *v/i* TELEC faire le numéro **3** *v/t* TELEC *number* composer

dialog, *Br* **dialogue** ['daɪəlɑːg] dialogue *m*

'dial tone tonalité *f*

diameter [daɪ'æmɪtər] diamètre *m*

diamond ['daɪmənd] diamant *m*; *shape* losange *m*

diaper ['daɪpər] couche *f*

diaphragm ['daɪəfræm] diaphragme *m*

diarrhea, *Br* **diarrhoea** [daɪə'riːə] diarrhée *f*

diary ['daɪrɪ] journal *m*; *for appointments* agenda *m*

dice [daɪs] dé *m*; *pl* dés *mpl*

dictate [dɪk'teɪt] dicter; **dictator** POL dictateur *m*; **dictatorship** dictature *f*

dictionary ['dɪkʃənerɪ] dictionnaire *m*

die [daɪ] mourir

◆ **die down** *of storm* se calmer; *of excitement* s'apaiser

◆ **die out** disparaître

diet ['daɪət] **1** *n* (*regular food*) alimentation *f*; *to lose weight, for health* régime *m* **2** *v/i* faire un régime

differ ['dɪfər] différer; (*disagree*) différer; **difference** différence *f*; **different** différent; **differently** différemment

difficult ['dɪfɪkəlt] difficile; **difficulty** difficulté *f*

dig [dɪg] creuser

digest [daɪ'dʒest] digérer; *information* assimiler; **digestion** digestion *f*

digit ['dɪdʒɪt] chiffre *m*; **digital** numérique; **digital camera** appareil *m* photo numérique; **digital photo** photo *f* numérique

dignified ['dɪgnɪfaɪd] digne; **dignity** dignité *f*

dilapidated [dɪ'læpɪdeɪtɪd] délabré
dilemma [dɪ'lemə] dilemme *m*
dilute [daɪ'luːt] diluer
dim [dɪm] **1** *adj room, prospects* sombre; *light* faible; *outline* vague; (*stupid*) bête **2** *v/i of lights* baisser
dime [daɪm] (pièce *f* de) dix cents *mpl*
dimension [daɪ'menʃn] dimension *f*
diminish [dɪ'mɪnɪʃ] diminuer
din [dɪn] brouhaha *m*
dine [daɪn] dîner
dinghy ['dɪŋgɪ] *small yacht* dériveur *m*; *rubber boat* canot *m* pneumatique
dining car ['daɪnɪŋ] RAIL wagon-restaurant *m*; **dining room** salle *f* à manger; *in hotel* salle *f* de restaurant
dinner ['dɪnər] dîner *m*; *at midday* déjeuner *f*; *gathering* repas *m*; **dinner party** dîner *m*, repas *m*
dip [dɪp] **1** *n for food* sauce *f* (*dans laquelle on trempe des aliments*); *in road* inclinaison *f* **2** *v/i of road* s'incliner
diploma [dɪ'ploumə] diplôme *m*
diplomacy [dɪ'ploumәsɪ] *also* (*tact*) diplomatie *f*; **diplomat** diplomate *m/f*; **diplomatic** diplomatique; (*tactful*) diplomate
direct [daɪ'rekt] **1** *adj* direct **2** *v/t to a place* indiquer (***to sth*** qch); *play* mettre en scène; *movie* réaliser; *attention* diriger
direction [dɪ'rekʃn] direction *f*; *of movie* réalisation *f*; **~s** (*instructions*) indications *fpl*; *for use* mode *m* d'emploi; *for medicine* instructions *fpl*; ***ask for ~s*** *to a place* demander son chemin; **directly** (*straight*) directement; (*soon*) dans très peu de temps; (*immediately*) immédiatement; **director** *of company* directeur(-trice) *m(f)*; *of movie* réalisateur(-trice) *m(f)*; *of play* metteur(-euse) *m(f)* en scène; **directory** répertoire *m* (d'adresses); TELEC annuaire *m* (des téléphones)
dirt [dɜːrt] saleté *f*; **dirty 1** *adj* sale; (*pornographic*) cochon **2** *v/t* salir
disability [dɪsə'bɪlətɪ] infirmité *f*; **disabled** handicapé
disadvantage [dɪsəd'væntɪdʒ] désavantage *m*; **disadvantaged** défavorisé
disagree [dɪsə'griː] *of person* ne pas être d'accord; **disagreeable** désagréable
disagreement désaccord *m*; (*argument*) dispute *f*
disappear [dɪsə'pɪr] disparaître; **disappearance** disparition *f*
disappoint [dɪsə'pɔɪnt] décevoir; **disappointing** décevant; **disappointment** dé-

ception *f*
disapproval [dɪsə'pru:vl] désapprobation *f*; **disapprove** désapprouver; ~ ***of*** *actions* désapprouver; *s.o.* ne pas aimer; **disapproving** désapprobateur
disarm [dɪs'ɑ:rm] désarmer; **disarmament** désarmement *m*
disaster [dɪ'zæstər] désastre *m*; **disastrous** désastreux
disband [dɪs'bænd] **1** *v/t* disperser **2** *v/i* se disperser
disbelief [dɪsbə'li:f] incrédulité *f*
disc [dɪsk] disque *m*; *CD* CD *m*
discard [dɪ'skɑ:rd] *old clothes etc* se débarrasser de; *boyfriend* abandonner
disciplinary [dɪsɪ'plɪnərɪ] disciplinaire; **discipline** discipline *f*
'disc jockey disc-jockey *m*
disclaim [dɪs'kleɪm] nier
disclose [dɪs'kloʊz] révéler
disco ['dɪskoʊ] discothèque *f*; *type of dance, music* disco *m*
discomfort [dɪs'kʌmfərt] gêne *f*; ***be in*** ~ être incommodé
disconcert [dɪskən'sɜ:rt] déconcerter
disconnect [dɪskə'nekt] *hose* détacher; *electrical appliance* débrancher; *supply, phones* couper
discontent [dɪskən'tent] mécontentement *m*
discontinue [dɪskən'tɪnu:] *product* arrêter; *bus service* supprimer
discotheque ['dɪskətek] discothèque *f*
discount ['dɪskaʊnt] remise *f*
discourage [dɪs'kʌrɪdʒ] décourager
discover [dɪ'skʌvər] découvrir; **discovery** découverte *f*
discredit [dɪs'kredɪt] discréditer
discreet [dɪ'skri:t] discret
discrepancy [dɪ'skrepənsɪ] divergence *f*
discretion [dɪ'skreʃn] discrétion *f*
discriminate [dɪ'skrɪmɪneɪt]: ~ ***against*** pratiquer une discrimination contre; **discriminating** avisé; **discrimination** *sexual etc* discrimination *f*
discuss [dɪ'skʌs] discuter de; *of article* traiter de; **discussion** discussion *f*
disease [dɪ'zi:z] maladie *f*
disembark [dɪsəm'bɑ:rk] débarquer
disentangle [dɪsən'tæŋgl] démêler
disfigure [dɪs'fɪgər] défigurer
disgrace [dɪs'greɪs] **1** *n* honte *f* **2** *v/t* faire honte à; **disgraceful** honteux
disguise [dɪs'gaɪz] **1** *n* déguisement *m* **2** *v/t* déguiser; *fear, anxiety* dissimuler
disgust [dɪs'gʌst] **1** *n* dégoût *m* **2** *v/t* dégoûter; **disgusting** dégoûtant

dish [dɪʃ] plat *m*; **~es** vaisselle *f*
disheartening [dɪs'hɑːrtnɪŋ] décourageant
dishonest [dɪs'ɑːnɪst] malhonnête; **dishonesty** malhonnêteté *f*
dishonor [dɪs'ɑːnər] déshonneur *m*; **dishonorable** dishonorant
dishonour *etc Br* → **dishonor** *etc*
disillusion [dɪsɪ'luːʒn] désillusionner; **disillusionment** désillusion *f*
disinfect [dɪsɪn'fekt] désinfecter; **disinfectant** désinfectant *m*
disinherit [dɪsɪn'herɪt] déshériter
disintegrate [dɪs'ɪntəgreɪt] se désintégrer; *of marriage* se désagréger
disjointed [dɪs'dʒɔɪntɪd] décousu
disk [dɪsk] *also* COMPUT disque *m*; *floppy* disquette *f*; **disk drive** COMPUT lecteur *m* de disque/disquette; **diskette** disquette *f*
dislike [dɪs'laɪk] **1** *n* aversion *f* **2** *v/t* ne pas aimer
dislocate ['dɪsləkeɪt] disloquer
disloyalty [dɪs'lɔɪəltɪ] déloyauté *f*
dismal ['dɪzməl] *weather* morne; *prospect* sombre; *person (sad)* triste; *person (negative)* lugubre; *failure* lamentable
dismantle [dɪs'mæntl] *object* démonter; *organization* démanteler
dismay [dɪs'meɪ] consternation *f*
dismiss [dɪs'mɪs] *employee* renvoyer; *suggestion* rejeter; *idea* écarter; **dismissal** *of employee* renvoi *m*
disobedience [dɪsə'biːdɪəns] désobéissance *f*; **disobedient** désobéissant; **disobey** désobéir à
disorganized [dɪs'ɔːrgənaɪzd] désorganisé
disoriented [dɪs'ɔːrɪəntɪd] désorienté
disparaging [dɪ'spærɪdʒɪŋ] désobligeant
disparity [dɪ'spærətɪ] disparité *f*
dispassionate [dɪ'spæʃənət] impartial, objectif
dispatch [dɪ'spætʃ] *(send)* envoyer
disperse [dɪ'spɜːrs] se disperser
display [dɪ'spleɪ] **1** *n of paintings etc* exposition *f*; *of emotion, in store window* étalage *m*; COMPUT affichage *m* **2** *v/t emotion* montrer; *at exhibition, for sale* exposer; COMPUT afficher
displease [dɪs'pliːz] déplaire à; **displeasure** mécontentement *m*
disposable [dɪ'spoʊzəbl] jetable; **disposal** *of waste* élimination *f*; *(sale)* cession *f*;

put sth at s.o.'s ~ mettre qch à la disposition de qn

◆ **dispose of** [dɪ'spoʊz] (*get rid of*) se débarrasser de

disprove [dɪs'pru:v] réfuter

dispute [dɪ'spju:t] **1** *n* contestation *f*; *between two countries* conflit *m*; ***industrial ~*** conflit *m* social **2** *v/t* contester; (*fight over*) se disputer

disqualification [dɪskwɑ:lɪfɪ'keɪʃn] disqualification *f*; **disqualify** disqualifier

disregard [dɪsrə'gɑ:rd] **1** *n* indifférence *f* (***for*** à l'égard de) **2** *v/t* ne tenir aucun compte de

disreputable [dɪs'repjʊtəbl] peu recommandable

disrespect [dɪsrə'spekt] manque *m* de respect, irrespect *m*; **disrespectful** irrespectueux

disrupt [dɪs'rʌpt] perturber; **disruption** perturbation *f*

dissatisfaction [dɪssætɪs'fækʃn] mécontentement *m*; **dissatisfied** mécontent

dissident ['dɪsɪdənt] dissident(e) *m(f)*

dissolve [dɪ'zɑ:lv] **1** *v/t* dissoudre **2** *v/i* se dissoudre

distance ['dɪstəns] distance *f*; ***in the ~*** au loin; **distant** éloigné; *fig* (*aloof*) distant

distaste [dɪs'teɪst] dégoût *m*; **distasteful** désagréable

distinct [dɪ'stɪŋkt] (*clear*) net; (*different*) distinct; **distinctive** distinctif; **distinctly** distinctement; (*decidedly*) vraiment

distinguish [dɪ'stɪŋgwɪʃ] distinguer; ***~ between X and Y*** distinguer X de Y; **distinguished** distingué

distort [dɪ'stɔ:rt] déformer

distract [dɪ'strækt] *person* distraire; *attention* détourner; **distraught** [dɪ'strɒ:t] angoissé

distress [dɪ'stres] **1** *n* douleur *f* **2** *v/t* (*upset*) affliger; **distressing** pénible

distribute [dɪ'strɪbju:t] *also* COM distribuer; **distribution** *also* COM distribution *f*; *of wealth* répartition *f*; **distributor** COM distributeur *m*

district ['dɪstrɪkt] *of town* quartier *m*; *of country* région *f*; **district attorney** procureur *m*

distrust [dɪs'trʌst] méfiance *f*

disturb [dɪ'stɜ:rb] (*interrupt*) déranger; (*upset*) inquiéter; **disturbance** (*interruption*) dérangement *m*; ***~s*** (*civil unrest*) troubles *mpl*; **disturbed** perturbé; *mentally* dérangé; **disturbing** perturbant

disused [dɪs'ju:zd] désaffecté

ditch [dɪtʃ] **1** *n* fossé *m* **2** *v/t* F (*get rid of*) se débarrasser de; *boyfriend*, *plan* laisser tomber

dive [daɪv] **1** *n* plongeon *m*; *underwater* plongée *f*; *of*

plane (vol *m*) piqué *m*; F *bar etc* bouge *m* **2** *v/i* plonger; *underwater* faire de la plongée sous-marine; *of plane* descendre en piqué; **diver** plongeur(-euse) *m(f)*
diverge [daɪ'vɜːrdʒ] diverger
diversification [daɪvɜːrsɪfɪ'keɪʃn] COM diversification *f*; **diversify** COM se diversifier
diversion [daɪ'vɜːrʃn] *for traffic* déviation *f*; *to distract attention* diversion *f*; **divert** *traffic* dévier; *attention* détourner
divide [dɪ'vaɪd] (*share*) partager; MATH, *country, family* diviser
dividend ['dɪvɪdend] FIN dividende *m*
diving ['daɪvɪŋ] *from board* plongeon *m*; *underwater* plongée *f* (sous-marine); **diving board** plongeoir *m*
division [dɪ'vɪʒn] division *f*
divorce [dɪ'vɔːrs] **1** *n* divorce *m* **2** *v/t* divorcer de **3** *v/i* divorcer; **divorced** divorcé; **divorcee** divorcé(e) *m(f)*
divulge [daɪ'vʌldʒ] divulguer
DIY [diːaɪ'waɪ] (= ***do-it-yourself***) bricolage *m*
dizziness ['dɪzɪnɪs] vertige *m*; **dizzy**: ***feel ~*** avoir un vertige des vertiges
DJ ['diːdʒeɪ] (= ***disc jockey***) D.J. *m/f* (= disc-jockey)
DNA [diːen'eɪ] (= ***deoxyribonucleic acid***) AND *m* (= acide *m* désoxyribonucléïque)
do [duː] **1** *v/t* faire; ***~ one's hair*** se coiffer **2** *v/i* (*be suitable, enough*) aller; ***that will ~!*** ça va!; ***~ well*** *in health, of business* aller bien; (*be successful*) réussir; ***well done!*** (*congratulations!*) bien!; ***how ~ you ~?*** enchanté
◆ **do away with** supprimer
◆ **do up** *building* rénover; *street* refaire; (*fasten*), *coat etc* fermer; *laces* faire
◆ **do with**: ***I could do with ...*** j'aurais bien besoin de ...
◆ **do without 1** *v/i* s'en passer **2** *v/t* se passer de
docile ['doʊsaɪl] docile
dock[1] [dɑːk] **1** *n* NAUT bassin *m* **2** *v/i of ship* entrer au bassin; *of spaceship* s'arrimer
dock[2] [dɑːk] *n* LAW banc *m* des accusés
doctor ['dɑːktər] MED docteur *m*, médecin *m*; *form of address* docteur; **doctorate** doctorat *m*
doctrine ['dɑːktrɪn] doctrine *f*
document ['dɑːkjʊmənt] document *m*; **documentary** documentaire *m*; **documentation** documentation *f*
dodge [dɑːdʒ] *blow, person* éviter; *question* éluder
dog [dɒːg] **1** *n* chien *m* **2** *v/t of bad luck* poursuivre
dogma ['dɒːgmə] dogme *m*; **dogmatic** dogmatique
'dog tag MIL plaque *f* d'identification; **dog-tired** F crevé
do-it-yourself [duːɪtjər'self]

bricolage *m*
doldrums ['douldrəmz]: ***be in the ~ of economy*** être dans le marasme; *of person* avoir le cafard
doll [dɑːl] *also* F *woman* poupée *f*
dollar ['dɑːlər] dollar *m*
dolphin ['dɑːlfɪn] dauphin *m*
dome [doum] *of building* dôme *m*
domestic [də'mestɪk] *chores* domestique; *news* national; *policy* intérieur; **domestic flight** vol *m* intérieur
dominant ['dɑːmɪnənt] dominant; **dominate** dominer; **domination** domination *f*; **domineering** dominateur
donate [dou'neɪt] faire don de; **donation** don *m*
donkey ['dɑːŋkɪ] âne *m*
donor ['dounər] *of money* donateur(-trice) *m(f)*; MED donneur(-euse) *m(f)*
donut ['dounʌt] beignet *m*
doom [duːm] (*fate*) destin *m*; (*ruin*) ruine *f*; **doomed** *project* voué à l'échec
door [dɔːr] porte *f*; *of car* portière *f*; **doorbell** sonnette *f*; **doorman** portier *m*; **doorway** embrasure *f* de porte
dope [doup] **1** *n* (*drugs*) drogue *f*; (*idiot*) idiot(e) *m(f)*
dormant ['dɔːrmənt]: ***~ volcano*** volcan *m* en repos
dormitory ['dɔːrmɪtɔːrɪ] résidence *f* universitaire; *Br* dortoir *m*
dose [dous] dose *f*
dot [dɑːt] point *m*
double ['dʌbl] **1** *n* double *m*; *of film star* doublure *f* **2** *adj* double **3** *adv* deux fois (plus); ***~ the size*** deux fois plus grand **4** *v/t & v/i* doubler; **double bed** grand lit *m*; **doublecheck** revérifier; **double-click** double-cliquer; **doublecross** trahir; **doublepark** stationner en double file; **double room** chambre *f* pour deux personnes; **doubles** *in tennis* double *m*
doubt [daut] **1** *n* doute *m*; ***be in ~*** être incertain; ***no ~*** (*probably*) sans doute **2** *v/t* douter de; **doubtful** *look* douteux; ***be ~ of person*** avoir des doutes; **doubtless** sans aucun doute
dough [dou] pâte *f*
dove [dʌv] colombe *f*
down [daun] **1** *adv* (*downward*) en bas, vers le bas; ***~ there*** là-bas; ***$200 ~*** (*as deposit*) 200 dollars d'acompte; ***~ south*** dans le sud; ***be ~ of*** *price, numbers* être en baisse; (*not working*) être en panne; F (*depressed*) être déprimé **2** *prep* (*along*) le long de; ***run ~ the stairs*** descendre les escaliers en courant; ***it's just ~ the street*** c'est à deux pas; **down-and-out** clochard(e) *m(f)*; **download** COMPUT **1** *v/t* télécharger **2** *n* fichier *m* teléchargé;

downmarket *Br* bas de gamme; **down payment** paiement *m* au comptant; **downplay** minimiser; **downpour** averse *f*; **downscale** bas de gamme; **downside** (*disadvantage*) inconvénient *m*; **downsize** *car etc* réduire la taille de; *company* réduire les effectifs de; **downstairs** **1** *adj neighbors etc* d'en bas **2** *adv* en bas; **down-town** **1** *adj* du centre-ville **2** *adv* en ville

doze [douz] sommeiller

dozen ['dʌzn] douzaine *f*

draft [dræft] **1** *n of air* courant *m* d'air; *of document* brouillon *m*; MIL conscription *f*; **~ beer** bière *f* à la pression **2** *v/t document* faire le brouillon de; MIL appeler; **draft dodger** réfractaire *m*; **draftsman** dessinateur(-trice) *m(f)*

drag [dræg] **1** *v/t* traîner, tirer; (*search*) draguer **2** *v/i of time* se traîner; *of show, movie* traîner en longueur

drain [dreɪn] **1** *n pipe* tuyau *m* d'écoulement; *under street* égout *m* **2** *v/t oil* vidanger; *vegetables* égoutter; *land* drainer; *glass, tank* vider; (*exhaust: person*) épuiser; **drainage** (*drains*) système *m* d'écoulement des eaux usées; *of water from soil* drainage *m*; **drainpipe** tuyau *m* d'écoulement

drama ['drɑːmə] drame *m*; **dramatic** dramatique; *scenery* spectaculaire; **dramatist** dramaturge *m/f*; **dramatize** *story* adapter (***for*** pour); *fig* dramatiser

drapes [dreɪps] rideaux *mpl*

drastic ['dræstɪk] radical; *measures also* drastique

draught [dræft] *Br* → ***draft***

draw [drɒː] **1** *n in competition* match *m* nul; *in lottery* tirage *m* (au sort); (*attraction*) attraction *f* **2** *v/t picture* dessiner; (*pull*), *in lottery, gun* tirer; (*attract*) attirer; (*lead*) emmener; *from bank account* retirer **3** *v/i of artist* dessiner; *in competition* faire match nul

◆ **draw back** **1** *v/i* (*recoil*) reculer **2** *v/t* (*pull back*) retirer; *drapes* ouvrir

◆ **draw out** *wallet, from bank* retirer

◆ **draw up** **1** *v/t document* rédiger; *chair* approcher **2** *v/i of vehicle* s'arrêter

'drawback désavantage *m*, inconvénient *m*

drawer [drɒːr] *of desk* tiroir *m*

drawing ['drɒːɪŋ] dessin *m*

drawl [drɒːl] voix *f* traînante

dread [dred]: **~ *doing*** redouter de faire; **dreadful** épouvantable

dream [driːm] **1** *n* rêve *m* **2** *v/i* rêver (***about, of*** de)

◆ **dream up** inventer

dreary ['drɪrɪ] morne

dress [dres] **1** *n for woman* robe *f*; (*clothing*) tenue *f* **2** *v/t person* habiller; *wound* panser; ***get ~ed*** s'habiller **3** *v/i* s'habiller

◆ **dress up** s'habiller chic; (*wear a disguise*) se déguiser (***as*** en)

'dress circle premier balcon *m*; **dresser** (*dressing table*) coiffeuse *f*; *in kitchen* buffet *m*; **dressing** *for salad* assaisonnement *m*; *for wound* pansement *m*; **dress rehearsal** (répétition *f*) générale *f*

dribble ['drɪbl] *of person* baver; *of water* dégouliner; SP dribbler

dried [draɪd] *fruit etc* sec

drier ['draɪr] → ***dryer***

drift [drɪft] *of snow* s'amonceler; *of ship* être à la dérive; (*go off course*) dériver; *of person* aller à la dérive; **drifter** personne qui vit au jour le jour

drill [drɪl] **1** *n tool* perceuse *f*; *exercise*, MIL exercice *m* **2** *v/t hole* percer **3** *v/i for oil* forer; MIL faire l'exercice

drily ['draɪlɪ] *say* d'un ton pince-sans-rire

drink [drɪŋk] **1** *n* boisson *f*; ***can I have a ~ of water*** est-ce que je peux avoir de l'eau? **2** *v/t* & *v/i* boire; ***I don't ~*** je ne bois pas; **drinkable** buvable; *water* potable

drinker ['drɪŋkər] buveur(-euse) *m*(*f*); **drinking water** eau *f* potable

drip [drɪp] **1** *n liquid* goutte *f*; MED goutte-à-goutte *m*, perfusion *f* **2** *v/i* goutter

drive [draɪv] **1** *n outing* promenade *f* (en voiture); (*energy*) dynamisme *m*; COMPUT unité *f*, lecteur *m*; (*campaign*) campagne *f* **2** *v/t vehicle* conduire; (*be owner of*) avoir; (*take in car*) amener; TECH actionner **3** *v/i* conduire; ***~ to work*** aller au travail en voiture; **drive-in** *movie theater* drive-in *m*

drivel ['drɪvl] bêtises *fpl*

driver ['draɪvər] conducteur (-trice) *m*(*f*); *of truck* camionneur(-euse) *m*(*f*); COMPUT pilote *m*; **driver's license** permis *m* de conduire

'driveway allée *f*; **drive-thru** drive-in *m inv*

drizzle ['drɪzl] **1** *n* bruine *f* **2** *v/i* bruiner

drop [drɑːp] **1** *n* goutte *f*; *in price*, *temperature* chute *f* **2** *v/t object* faire tomber; *bomb* lancer; *person from car* [illegible]poser; *person from te*[illegible] écarter; (*stop seeing*), *cha*[illegible]*ges*, *subject* laisser tombe[illegible] (*give up*) arrêter **3** *v/i* tombe[illegible]

◆ **drop in** (*visit*) passer

◆ **drop off 1** *v/t person*, *goods* déposer **2** *v/i* (*fall asleep*) s'endormir; (*decline*) diminuer

◆ **drop out** (*withdraw*) se re-

tirer (***of*** de); *of school* abandonner (***of sth*** qch)
drought [draʊt] sécheresse *f*
drown [draʊn] se noyer
drug [drʌg] **1** *n* MED médicament *m*; *illegal* drogue *f* **2** *v/t* droguer; **drug addict** toxicomane *m/f*; **drug dealer** dealer *m*, dealeuse *f*; *large-scale* trafiquant(e) *m*(*f*) de drogue; **druggist** pharmacien(ne) *m*(*f*); **drugstore** drugstore *m*; **drug trafficking** trafic *m* de drogue
drum [drʌm] MUS tambour *m*; *container* tonneau *m*; **~s** batterie *f*; **drumstick** MUS baguette *f* de tambour
drunk [drʌŋk] **1** *n* ivrogne *m/f*; *habitually* alcoolique *m/f* **2** *adj* ivre, soûl; ***get ~*** se soûler; **drunk driving** conduite *f* en état d'ivresse
dry [draɪ] **1** *adj* sec **2** *v/t clothes* faire sécher; *dishes*, *eyes* essuyer **3** *v/i* sécher; **dryclean** nettoyer à sec; **dry cleaner** pressing *m*; **dryer** *machine* sèche-linge *m*
dul ['duːəl] double
db [dʌb] *movie* doubler
dbious ['duːbɪəs] douteux; ***m still ~ about ...*** j'ai encore des doutes quant à ...
duck [dʌk] **1** *n* canard *m*; *female* cane *f* **2** *v/i* se baisser
dud [dʌd] F (*false bill*) faux *m*
due [duː] (*owed*) dû; ***the rent is ~ tomorrow*** il faut payer le loyer demain
dull [dʌl] *weather* sombre; *sound*, *pain* sourd; (*boring*) ennuyeux
duly ['duːlɪ] (*as expected*) comme prévu; (*properly*) dûment, comme il se doit
dumb [dʌm] (*mute*) muet; F (*stupid*) bête
dump [dʌmp] **1** *n for garbage* décharge *f*; (*unpleasant place*) trou *m*; *house*, *hotel* taudis *m* **2** *v/t* (*deposit*) déposer; (*throw away*) jeter; (*leave*) laisser; *waste* déverser
dune [duːn] dune *f*
duplex (**apartment**) ['duːpleks] duplex *m*
duplicate ['duːplɪkət] double *m*
durable ['dʊrəbl] *material* résistant
during ['dʊrɪŋ] pendant
dusk [dʌsk] crépuscule *m*
dust [dʌst] **1** *n* poussière *f* **2** *v/t* épousseter; **duster** chiffon *m* (à poussière); **dustpan** pelle *f* à poussière; **dusty** poussiéreux
duty ['duːtɪ] devoir *m*; (*task*) fonction *f*; *on goods* droit(s) *m*(*pl*); ***be on ~*** être de service; **dutyfree** hors taxe
DVD [diːviː'diː] (= ***digital versatile disk***) DVD *m*; **DVD-ROM** DVD-ROM *m*
dwarf [dwɔːrf] **1** *n* nain(e) *m*(*f*) **2** *v/t* rapetisser
dwindle ['dwɪndl] diminuer
dye [daɪ] **1** *n* teinture *f* **2** *v/t*

teindre
dying ['daɪɪŋ] *person* mourant; *industry* moribond; *tradition* qui se perd
dynamic [daɪ'næmɪk] dynamique; **dynamism** dynamisme *m*
dynasty ['daɪnəstɪ] dynastie *f*
dyslexic [dɪs'leksɪk] **1** *adj* dyslexique **2** *n* dyslexique *m/f*

E

each [i:tʃ] **1** *adj* chaque **2** *adv* chacun; ***they're $1.50 ~*** ils coûtent $1.50 chacun, ils sont 1,50 $ pièce **3** *pron* chacun(e) *m(f)*; ***~ of them*** chacun(e) d'entre eux(elles) *m(f)*; ***we know ~ other*** nous nous connaissons
eager ['i:gər] désireux; *look* avide; ***be ~ to do sth*** désirer vivement faire qch; **eagerly** avec empressement; *wait* impatiemment; **eagerness** empressement *m*
eagle ['i:gl] aigle *m*; **eagle-eyed**: ***be ~*** avoir des yeux d'aigle
ear¹ [ɪr] oreille *f*
ear² [ɪr] *of corn* épi *m*
'earache mal *m* d'oreilles
early ['3:rlɪ] **1** *adv* (*not late*) tôt; (*ahead of time*) en avance **2** *adj stages, Romans* premier; *arrival* en avance; *retirement* anticipé; *music* ancien; (*in the near future*) prochain; ***(in) ~ October*** début octobre; ***have an ~ supper*** dîner tôt *or* de bonne heure; **early bird**: ***be an ~*** (*early riser*) être matinal
earmark ['ɪrmɑ:rk] réserver
earn [3:rn] gagner; *interest* rapporter
earnest ['3:rnɪst] sérieux
earnings ['3:rnɪŋz] salaire *m*; *of company* profits *mpl*
'earphones écouteurs *mpl*; **earring** boucle *f* d'oreille
earth [3:rθ] terre *f*; **earthenware** poterie *f*; **earthly** terrestre; ***it's no ~ use doing that*** F ça ne sert strictement à rien de faire cela; **earthquake** tremblement *m* de terre; **earth-shattering** stupéfiant
ease [i:z] **1** *n* facilité *f*; ***feel at ~*** se sentir à l'aise **2** *v/t pain, mind* soulager; *suffering, shortage* diminuer **3** *v/i of pain* diminuer
easel ['i:zl] chevalet *m*
easily ['i:zəlɪ] facilement; (*by far*) de loin
east [i:st] **1** *n* est *m* **2** *adj* est *inv*; *wind* d'est **3** *adv travel* vers l'est
Easter ['i:stər] Pâques *fpl*; **Easter Day** (jour *m* de) Pâ-

ques *m*; **Easter egg** œuf *m* de Pâques
easterly ['i:stərlɪ] *wind* de l'est; *direction* vers l'est
Easter Monday lundi *m* de Pâques
eastern ['i:stərn] de l'est; (*oriental*) oriental; **easterner** habitant(e) *m*(*f*) de l'Est des États-Unis
Easter Sunday (jour *m* de) Pâques *m*
eastward ['i:stwərd] vers l'est
easy ['i:zɪ] facile; (*relaxed*) tranquille; **easy chair** fauteuil *m*; **easy-going** accommodant
eat [i:t] manger
◆ **eat out** manger au restaurant
eatable ['i:təbl] mangeable
eavesdrop ['i:vzdrɑ:p] écouter de façon indiscrète (***on s.o.*** qn)
ebb [eb] *of tide* descendre
e-book ['i:bʊk] livre *m* électronique; **e-business** commerce *m* électronique
eccentric [ɪk'sentrɪk] **1** *adj* excentrique **2** *n* original(e) *m*(*f*); **eccentricity** excentricité *f*
echo ['ekoʊ] **1** *n* écho *m* **2** *v/i* faire écho **3** *v/t words* répéter; *views* se faire l'écho de
eclipse [ɪ'klɪps] **1** *n* éclipse *f* **2** *v/t fig* éclipser
ecological [i:kə'lɑ:dʒɪkl] écologique; **ecologically** écologiquement; **ecologically friendly** écologique; **ecologist** écologiste *m/f*; **ecology** écologie *f*
economic [i:kə'nɑ:mɪk] économique; **economical** (*cheap*) économique; (*thrifty*) économe; **economics** économie *f*; *financial aspects* aspects *mpl* économiques; **economist** économiste *m/f*; **economize** économiser
◆ **economize on** économiser
economy [ɪ'kɑ:nəmɪ] économie *f*; **economy class** classe *f* économique
ecosystem ['i:koʊsɪstm] écosystème *m*; **ecotourism** tourisme *m* écologique
ecstasy ['ekstəsɪ] extase *f*; **ecstatic** extatique
eczema ['eksmə] eczéma *m*
edge [edʒ] **1** *n* bord *m*; *of knife* tranchant *m*; **on ~** énervé **2** *v/i* (*move slowly*) se faufiler; **edgewise**: ***I couldn't get a word in ~*** je n'ai pas pu en placer une F; **edgy** énervé
edible ['edɪbl] comestible
edit ['edɪt] *text* mettre au point; *book* préparer pour la publication; *newspaper* diriger; *TV program* réaliser; *film* monter; **edition** édition *f*; **editor** *of text, book* rédacteur(-trice) *m*(*f*); *of newspaper* rédacteur(-trice) *m*(*f*) en chef; *of TV program* réalisateur(-trice) *m*(*f*); *of film* monteur(-euse) *m*(*f*); **edito-**

rial 1 *adj* de la rédaction **2** *n* éditorial *m*

educate ['edʒəkeɪt] instruire (***about*** sur); ***she was ~d in France*** elle a fait sa scolarité en France; **educated** instruit; **education** éducation f; *as subject* pédagogie *f*; **educational** scolaire; (*informative*) instructif

eerie ['ɪrɪ] inquiétant

effect [ɪ'fekt] effet *m*; **effective** (*efficient*) efficace; (*striking*) frappant

effeminate [ɪ'femɪnət] efféminé

efficiency [ɪ'fɪʃənsɪ] efficacité *f*; *in motel* chambre *f* avec coin-cuisine; **efficient** efficace; **efficiently** efficacement

effort ['efərt] effort *m*; **effortless** aisé, facile

e.g. [iː'dʒiː] ex; *spoken* par example

egg [eg] œuf *m*; **eggcup** coquetier *m*; **egghead** F intello *m/f* F; **eggplant** aubergine *f*

ego ['iːgoʊ] PSYCH ego *m*; **egocentric** égocentrique; **egoism** égoïsme *m*; **egoist** égoïste *m/f*

eiderdown ['aɪdərdaʊn] (*quilt*) édredon *m*

eight [eɪt] huit; **eighteen** dix-huit; **eighteenth** dix-huitième; **eighth** huitième; **eightieth** quatre-vingtième; **eighty** quatre-vingts; ***~-two/four*** *etc* quatre-vingt-deux/-quatre *etc*

either ['iːðər] **1** *adj* l'un ou l'autre; (*both*) chaque **2** *pron* l'un(e) ou l'autre **3** *adv*: ***I won't go ~*** je n'irai pas non plus **4** *conj*: ***~ … or*** soit … soit …; *with negative* ni … ni …

eject [ɪ'dʒekt] **1** *v/t* éjecter **2** *v/i from plane* s'éjecter

◆ **eke out** [iːk] suppléer à l'insuffisance de; ***eke out a living*** vivoter

el [el] métro *m* aérien

elaborate [ɪ'læbərət] **1** *adj* compliqué **2** *v/i* [ɪ'læbəreɪt] donner des détails (***on*** sur)

elapse [ɪ'læps] (se) passer

elastic [ɪ'læstɪk] **1** *adj* élastique **2** *n* élastique *m*; **elasticated** élastique

elated [ɪ'leɪtɪd] transporté (de joie); **elation** exultation *f*

elbow ['elboʊ] coude *m*

elder ['eldər] **1** *adj* aîné **2** *n* aîné(e) *m(f)*; **elderly 1** *adj* âgé **2** *npl*: the ~ les personnes *fpl* âgées; **eldest 1** *adj* aîné **2** *n*: ***the ~*** l'aîné(e) *m(f)*

elect [ɪ'lekt] élire; **elected** élu; **election** élection *f*; **election campaign** campagne *f* électorale; **election day** jour *m* des élections; **electorate** électorat *m*

electric [ɪ'lektrɪk] *also fig* électrique; **electrical** électrique; **electric chair** chaise *f* électrique; **electrician** électricien(ne) *m(f)*; **electricity** électricité *f*; **electrify** électrifier; *fig* électriser

electrocute [ɪ'lektrəkju:t] électrocuter
electron [ɪ'lektrɑ:n] électron *m*; **electronic** électronique; **electronics** électronique *f*
elegance ['elɪgəns] élégance *f*; **elegant** élégant
element ['elɪmənt] élément *m*; **elementary** élémentaire; **elementary schoo** école *f* primaire
elephant ['elɪfənt] éléphant *m*
elevate ['elɪveɪt] élever; **elevated railroad** métro *m* aérien; **elevation** (*altitude*) altitude *f*; **elevator** ascenseur *m*
eleven [ɪ'levn] onze; **eleventh** onzième
eligible ['elɪdʒəbl]: ***be ~ to do sth*** avoir le droit de faire qch
eliminate [ɪ'lɪmɪneɪt] éliminer; **elimination** élimination *f*
elite [eɪ'li:t] **1** *n* élite *f* **2** *adj* d'élite
eloquence ['eləkwəns] éloquence *f*; **eloquent** éloquent
else [els]: ***anything ~?*** autre chose?; ***nothing ~*** rien d'autre; ***no one ~*** personne d'autre; ***everyone ~ is going*** tous les autres y vont; ***someone ~*** quelqu'un d'autre; ***something ~*** autre chose; ***let's go somewhere ~*** allons autre part; ***or ~*** sinon; **elsewhere** ailleurs
elude [ɪ'lu:d] (*escape from*) échapper à; (*avoid*) éviter;
elusive insaisissable
emaciated [ɪ'meɪsɪeɪtɪd] émacié
e-mail ['i:meɪl] **1** *n* e-mail *m*, courrier *m* électronique **2** *v/t person* envoyer un e-mail à; **e-mail address** adresse *f* e-mail, adresse *f* électronique
emancipation [ɪmænsɪ'peɪʃn] émancipation *f*
embalm [ɪm'bɑ:m] embaumer
embankment [ɪm'bæŋkmənt] *of river* berge *f*; RAIL remblai *m*
embargo [em'bɑ:rgoʊ] embargo *m*
embark [ɪm'bɑ:rk] (s')embarquer
embarrass [ɪm'bærəs] gêner, embarrasser; **embarrassed** gêné, embarrassé; **embarrassing** gênant, embarrassant; **embarrassment** gêne *f*, embarras *m*
embassy ['embəsɪ] ambassade *f*
embezzle [ɪm'bezl] détourner; **embezzlement** détournement *m* de fonds
emblem ['embləm] emblème *m*
embodiment [ɪm'bɑ:dɪmənt] personnification *f*; **embody** personnifier
embrace [ɪm'breɪs] **1** *n* étreinte *f* **2** *v/t* (*hug*) serrer dans ses bras, étreindre; (*take in*) embrasser **3** *v/i of two people* se

serrer dans les bras, s'étreindre
embroider [ɪm'brɔɪdər] broder; *fig* enjoliver
embryo ['embrɪoʊ] embryon *m*; **embryonic** *fig* embryonnaire
emerald ['emərəld] émeraude *f*
emerge [ɪ'mɜːrdʒ] sortir; *from mist, of truth* émerger
emergency [ɪ'mɜːrdʒənsɪ] urgence *f*; **emergency exit** sortie *f* de secours; **emergency landing** atterrissage *m* forcé; **emergency services** services *mpl* d'urgence
emigrate ['emɪgreɪt] émigrer; **emigration** émigration *f*
Eminence ['emɪnəns] REL: ***His ~*** son Éminence; **eminent** éminent
emission [ɪ'mɪʃn] *of gases* émission *f*; **emit** émettre
emotion [ɪ'moʊʃn] émotion *f*; **emotional** *problems* émotionnel, affectif; (*full of emotion*) ému; *reunion* émouvant
emphasis ['emfəsɪs] accent *m*; **emphasize** *syllable* accentuer; *fig* souligner; **emphatic** catégorique
empire ['empaɪr] *also fig* empire *m*
employ [ɪm'plɔɪ] employer; **employee** employé(e) *m(f)*; **employer** employeur(-euse) *m(f)*; **employment** (*jobs*) emplois *mpl*; (*work*) emploi *m*
emptiness ['emptɪnɪs] vide *m*; **empty 1** *adj* vide; *promises* vain **2** *v/t* vider **3** *v/i of room, street* se vider
emulate ['emjʊleɪt] imiter
enable [ɪ'neɪbl] permettre
enchanting [ɪn'ʧæntɪŋ] ravissant
encircle [ɪn'sɜːrkl] encercler
enclose [ɪn'kloʊz] *in letter* joindre; *area* entourer; **enclosure** *with letter* pièce *f* jointe
encore ['ɑːŋkɔːr] bis *m*
encounter [ɪn'kaʊntər] **1** *n* rencontre *f* **2** *v/t person* rencontrer; *problem, resistance* affronter
encourage [ɪn'kʌrɪdʒ] encourager; **encouragement** encouragement *m*; **encouraging** encourageant
encyclopedia [ɪnsaɪklə'piːdɪə] encyclopédie *f*
end [end] **1** *n* (*conclusion, purpose*) fin *f*; (*extremity*) bout *m*; ***in the ~*** à la fin **2** *v/t* terminer, finir **3** *v/i* se terminer, finir
◆ **end up** finir
endanger [ɪn'deɪndʒər] mettre en danger; **endangered species** espèce *f* en voie de disparition
endeavor, *Br* **endeavour** [ɪn'devər] **1** *n* effort *m* **2** *v/t* essayer (***to do sth*** de faire qch)
endemic [ɪn'demɪk] endémique

ending ['endɪŋ] fin *f*; GRAM terminaison *f*; **endless** sans fin

endorse [ɪn'dɔːrs] *candidacy* appuyer; *product* associer son image à; **endorsement** *of candidacy* appui *m*; *of product* association *f* de son image à

end 'product produit *m* fini

endurance [ɪn'dʊrəns] *of person* endurance *f*; *of car* résistance *f*; **endure 1** *v/t* endurer **2** *v/i* (*last*) durer; **enduring** durable

enemy ['enəmɪ] ennemi(e) *m(f)*

energetic [enərdʒetɪk] *also fig* énergique; **energy** énergie *f*; **energy supply** alimentation *f* en énergie

enforce [ɪn'fɔːrs] mettre en vigueur

engage [ɪn'geɪdʒ] **1** *v/t* (*hire*) engager **2** *v/i of machine part* s'engrener; **engaged** *to be married* fiancé; *Br* TELEC occupé; ***get ~*** se fiancer; **engagement** *to be married* fiançailles *fpl*; MIL engagement *m*; **engagement ring** bague *f* de fiançailles

engine ['endʒɪn] moteur *m*; **engineer** ingénieur *m/f*; NAUT, RAIL mécanicien(ne) *m(f)*; **engineering** ingénierie *f*

England ['ɪŋglənd] Angleterre *f*; **English 1** *adj* anglais **2** *n language* anglais *m*; ***the ~*** les Anglais *mpl*; **Englishman** Anglais *m*; **Englishwoman** Anglaise *f*

engrave [ɪn'greɪv] graver; **engraving** gravure *f*

engrossed [ɪn'groʊst]: ***~ in*** absorbé dans

engulf [ɪn'gʌlf] engloutir

enhance [ɪn'hæns] *flavor* rehausser; *reputation* accroître; *performance* améliorer; *enjoyment* augmenter

enigma [ɪ'nɪgmə] énigme *f*

enjoy [ɪn'dʒɔɪ] aimer; ***~ o.s.*** s'amuser; ***~!*** *said to s.o. eating* bon appétit!; **enjoyable** agréable; **enjoyment** plaisir *m*

enlarge [ɪn'lɑːrdʒ] agrandir; **enlargement** agrandissement *m*

enlighten [ɪn'laɪtn] éclairer

enlist [ɪn'lɪst] MIL enrôler

enmity ['enmətɪ] inimitié *f*

enormous [ɪ'nɔːrməs] énorme

enough [ɪ'nʌf] **1** *adj* assez de **2** *pron* assez; ***will $50 be ~?*** est-ce que $50 suffiront?; ***that's ~*** ça suffit **3** *adv* assez; ***big ~*** assez grand

enquire *etc* [ɪn'kwaɪr] → ***inquire*** *etc*

enroll, *Br* **enrol** [ɪn'roʊl] s'inscrire

en suite (bathroom) ['ɑːnswiːt] salle *f* de bains attenante

ensure [ɪn'ʃʊər] assurer; ***~ that ...*** s'assurer que ...

entail [ɪn'teɪl] entraîner

entangle [ɪn'tæŋgl] *in rope* empêtrer

enter ['entər] **1** *v/t room, house* entrer dans; *competition* entrer en; COMPUT entrer **2** *v/i* entrer; *in competition* s'inscrire **3** *n* COMPUT touche *f* entrée

enterprise ['entərpraɪz] (*initiative*) (esprit *m* d')initiative *f*; (*venture*) entreprise *f*; **enterprising** entreprenant

entertain [entər'teɪn] (*amuse*) amuser; (*consider: idea*) envisager; **entertainer** artiste *m/f* de variété; **entertaining** amusant, divertissant; **entertainment** divertissement *m*

enthusiasm [ɪn'θuːzɪæzəm] enthousiasme *m*; **enthusiast** enthousiaste *m/f*; **enthusiastic** enthousiaste; **enthusiastically** avec enthousiasme

entire [ɪn'taɪr] entier; **entirely** entièrement

entitle [ɪn'taɪtl]: **~ *s.o. to sth*** donner à qn droit à qch; ***be ~d to*** avoir droit à

entrance ['entrəns] entrée *f*

entranced [ɪn'trænst] enchanté

'entrance exam(ination) examen *m* d'entrée

entrant ['entrənt] inscrit(e) *m(f)*

entrepreneur [ɑːntrəprə'nɜːr] entrepreneur(-euse) *m(f)*; **entrepreneurial** *skills* d'entrepreneur

entrust [ɪn'trʌst] confier

entry ['entrɪ] entrée *f*; *for competition: person* participant(e) *m(f)*; **entryphone** interphone *m*

envelop [ɪn'veləp] envelopper

envelope ['envəloʊp] enveloppe *f*

enviable ['envɪəbl] enviable; **envious** envieux; ***be ~ of s.o.*** envier qn

environment [ɪn'vaɪrənmənt] environnement *m*; **environmental** écologique; **environmentalist** écologiste *m/f*; **environmentally friendly** écologique; **environs** environs *mpl*

envisage [ɪn'vɪzɪdʒ] envisager

envoy ['envɔɪ] envoyé(e) *m(f)*

envy ['envɪ] **1** *n* envie *f* **2** *v/t*: **~ *s.o. sth*** envier qch à qn

epic ['epɪk] **1** *n* épopée *f*; *movie* film *m* à grand spectacle **2** *adj journey* épique

epicenter, *Br* **epicentre** ['epɪsentər] épicentre *m*

epidemic [epɪ'demɪk] *also fig* épidémie *f*

episode ['epɪsoʊd] épisode *m*

epitaph ['epɪtæf] épitaphe *f*

equal ['iːkwl] **1** *adj* égal; ***be ~ to*** *task* être à la hauteur de **2** *n* égal *m* **3** *v/t* égaler; **equality** égalité *f*; **equalize** **1** *v/t* égaliser **2** *v/i Br* SP égaliser; **equalizer** *Br* SP but *m* égalisateur; **equally** *divide* de manière égale; *qualified*, *intelligent* tout aussi; **equal rights** égalité *f* des droits

equation [ɪ'kweɪʒn] MATH équation *f*

equator [ɪ'kweɪtər] équateur *m*

equip [ɪ'kwɪp] équiper; **equipment** équipement *m*

equity ['ekwətɪ] FIN capitaux *mpl* propres

equivalent [ɪ'kwɪvələnt] **1** *adj* équivalent **2** *n* équivalent *m*

era ['ɪrə] ère *f*

eradicate [ɪ'rædɪkeɪt] éradiquer

erase [ɪ'reɪz] effacer

erect [ɪ'rekt] **1** *adj* droit **2** *v/t* ériger, élever; **erection** *of building*, *penis* érection *f*

ergonomic [ɜːrgoʊ'nɑːmɪk] ergonomique

erode [ɪ'roʊd] éroder; *fig*: *power* miner; *rights* supprimer progressivement; **erosion** érosion *f*; *fig*: *of rights* suppression *f* progressive

errand ['erənd] commission *f*

erratic [ɪ'rætɪk] *performance*, *course* irrégulier; *driving* capricieux; *behavior* changeant

error ['erər] erreur *f*

erupt [ɪ'rʌpt] *of volcano* entrer en éruption; *of violence* éclater; *of person* exploser F; **eruption** *of volcano* éruption *f*; *of violence* explosion *f*

escalate ['eskəleɪt] s'intensifier; **escalation** intensification *f*; **escalator** escalier *m* mécanique, escalator *m*

escape [ɪ'skeɪp] **1** *n of prisoner* évasion *f*; *of animal*, *gas* fuite *f* **2** *v/i* s'échapper

escort ['eskɔːrt] **1** *n* cavalier (-ière) *m*(*f*); (*guard*) escorte *f* **2** *v/t* [ɪ'skɔːrt] *socially* accompagner; (*act as guard to*) escorter

especially [ɪ'speʃlɪ] particulièrement

espionage ['espɪənɑːʒ] espionnage *m*

espresso (**coffee**) [es'presoʊ] expresso *m*

essay ['eseɪ] *at school* rédaction *f*; *at university* dissertation *f*; *by writer* essai *m*

essential [ɪ'senʃl] essentiel

establish [ɪ'stæblɪʃ] *company* fonder; (*create*, *determine*) établir; **establishment** *firm*, *shop etc* établissement *m*

estate [ɪ'steɪt] *land* propriété *f*; *of dead person* biens *mpl*

esthetic [ɪs'θetɪk] esthétique

estimate ['estɪmət] **1** *n* estimation *f*; *from builder etc* devis *m* **2** *v/t* estimer

estuary ['estʃəwerɪ] estuaire *m*

etc [et'setrə] (= ***et cetera***) etc.

eternal [ɪ'tɜːrnl] éternel; **eternity** éternité *f*

ethical ['eθɪkl] *problem* éthique; (*morally right*) moral; **ethics** éthique *f*

ethnic ['eθnɪk] ethnique

EU [iː'juː] (= ***European Un-***

ion) U.E. *f* (= Union *f* européenne)
euphemism ['juːfəmɪzm] euphémisme *m*
euro ['jʊroʊ] FIN euro *m*
Europe ['jʊrəp] Europe *f*; **European 1** *adj* européen **2** *n* Européen(ne) *m(f)*
euthanasia [juθə'neɪzɪə] euthanasie *f*
evacuate [ɪ'vækjʊeɪt] (*clear people from*) faire évacuer; (*leave*) évacuer
evade [ɪ'veɪd] éviter; *question* éluder
evaluate [ɪ'væljʊeɪt] évaluer; **evaluation** évaluation *f*
evaporate [ɪ'væpəreɪt] *also fig* s'évaporer; **evaporation** évaporation *f*
evasion [ɪ'veɪʒn] fuite *f*; **evasive** évasif
eve [iːv] veille *f*
even ['iːvn] **1** *adj breathing* régulier; *distribution* égal; (*level*) plat; *surface* plan; *number* pair; ***get ~ with ...*** prendre sa revanche sur ... **2** *adv* même; ***~ bigger*** encore plus grand; ***not ~*** pas même; ***~ so*** quand même; ***~ if*** même si **3** *v/t*: ***~ the score*** égaliser
evening ['iːvnɪŋ] soir *m*; ***in the ~*** le soir; ***this ~*** ce soir; ***good ~*** bonsoir; **evening class** cours *m* du soir; **evening dress** *for woman* robe *f* du soir; *for man* tenue *f* de soirée
evenly ['iːvnlɪ] (*regularly*) de manière égale; *breathe* régulièrement
event [ɪ'vent] événement *m*; SP épreuve *f*; **eventful** mouvementé
eventually [ɪ'ventʃʊəlɪ] finalement
ever ['evər] jamais; ***have you ~ been to Japan?*** est-ce que tu es déjà allé au Japon?; ***for ~*** pour toujours; ***~ since*** depuis lors; ***~ since we ...*** depuis le jour où nous ...; **everlasting** éternel
every ['evrɪ]: ***~ day*** tous les jours, chaque jour; ***~ one of ...*** chacun de ...; **everybody** → ***everyone***; **everyday** de tous les jours; **everyone** tout le monde; ***~ who ...*** tous ceux qui ...; **everything** tout; **everywhere** partout; (*wherever*) partout où
evict [ɪ'vɪkt] expulser
evidence ['evɪdəns] preuve(s) *f(pl)*; LAW témoignage *m*; ***give ~*** témoigner; **evident** évident; **evidently** (*clearly*) à l'évidence; (*apparently*) de toute évidence
evil ['iːvl] **1** *adj* mauvais **2** *n* mal *m*
evolution [iːvə'luːʃn] évolution *f*; **evolve** évoluer
ex [eks] F *wife, husband* ex *m/f* F
exact [ɪg'zækt] exact; **exacting** exigeant; **exactly** exactement
exaggerate [ɪg'zædʒəreɪt]

exagérer; **exaggeration** exagération *f*

exam [ɪg'zæm] examen *m*; **examination** examen *m*; **examine** examiner

example [ɪg'zæmpl] exemple *m*; ***for ~*** par exemple

excavate ['ekskəveɪt] (*dig*) excaver; *of archeologist* fouiller; **excavation** excavation *f*; *archeological* fouille(s) *f(pl)*

exceed [ɪk'siːd] dépasser; *authority* outrepasser; **exceedingly** extrêmement

excel [ɪk'sel] **1** *v/i* exceller (***at*** en) **2** *v/t*: ***~ o.s.*** se surpasser; **excellence** excellence *f*; **excellent** excellent

except [ɪk'sept] sauf; ***~ for*** à l'exception de; **exception** exception *f*; **exceptional** exceptionnel

excerpt ['eksɜːrpt] extrait *m*

excess [ɪk'ses] **1** *n* excès *m* **2** *adj*: ***~ water*** excédent *m* d'eau; **excessive** excessif

exchange [ɪks'ʧeɪndʒ] **1** *n* échange *m* **2** *v/t* échanger; **exchange rate** FIN cours *m* du change

excite [ɪk'saɪt] (*make enthusiastic*) enthousiasmer; **excited** excité; ***get ~*** s'exciter; **excitement** excitation *f*; **exciting** passionnant

exclaim [ɪk'skleɪm] s'exclamer; **exclamation** exclamation *f*; **exclamation point** point *m* d'exclamation

exclude [ɪk'skluːd] exclure; **excluding** sauf; **exclusive** *hotel* huppé; *rights*, *interview* exclusif

excuse [ɪk'skjuːs] **1** *n* excuse *f* **2** *v/t* [ɪk'skjuːz] excuser; (*forgive*) pardonner; ***~ me*** excusez-moi

ex-directory *Br* : ***be ~*** être sur liste rouge

execute ['eksɪkjuːt] *criminal*, *plan* exécuter; **execution** *of criminal*, *plan* exécution *f*; **executive** cadre *m*

exempt [ɪg'zempt] exempt

exercise ['eksərsaɪz] **1** *n* exercice *m* **2** *v/t muscle* exercer; *dog* promener; *caution*, *restraint* user de **3** *v/i* prendre de l'exercice

exhale [eks'heɪl] exhaler

exhaust [ɪg'zɒːst] **1** *n fumes* gaz *m* d'échappement; *pipe* tuyau *m* d'échappement **2** *v/t* (*tire*, *use up*) épuiser; **exhausted** (*tired*) épuisé; **exhausting** épuisant; **exhaustion** épuisement *m*; **exhaustive** exhaustif

exhibit [ɪg'zɪbɪt] **1** *n in exhibition* objet *m* exposé **2** *v/t of artist* exposer; (*give evidence of*) montrer; **exhibition** exposition *f*; *of bad behavior* étalage *m*; *of skill* démonstration *f*

exhilarating [ɪg'zɪləreɪtɪŋ] *weather* vivifiant; *sensation* grisant

exile ['eksaɪl] **1** *n* exil *m*; *per-*

son exilé(e) *m(f)* **2** *v/t* exiler

exist [ɪg'zɪst] exister; **~ *on*** subsister avec; **existence** existence *f*; ***be in ~*** exister; **existing** existant

exit ['eksɪt] **1** *n* sortie *f* **2** *v/i* COMPUT sortir

exonerate [ɪg'zɑːnəreɪt] (*clear*) disculper

exotic [ɪg'zɑːtɪk] exotique

expand [ɪk'spænd] **1** *v/t* étendre **2** *v/i of population* s'accroître; *of business, city* se développer; *of metal, gas* se dilater; **expanse** étendue *f*; **expansion** *of population* accroissement *m*; *of business, city* développement *m*; *of metal, gas* dilatation *f*

expect [ɪk'spekt] **1** *v/t also baby* attendre; (*suppose*) penser; (*demand*) exiger **2** *v/i*: ***be ~ing*** attendre un bébé; ***I ~ so*** je pense que oui; **expectant mother** future maman *f*; **expectation** attente *f*, espérance *f*

expedition [ekspɪ'dɪʃn] expédition *f*

expel [ɪk'spel] expulser

expendable [ɪk'spendəbl] *person* pas indispensable

expenditure [ɪk'spendɪtʃər] dépenses *fpl* (***on*** de)

expense [ɪk'spens] dépense *f*; **expenses** frais *mpl*; **expensive** cher

experience [ɪk'spɪrɪəns] **1** *n* expérience *f* **2** *v/t pain, pleasure* éprouver; *difficulty* connaître; **experienced** expérimenté

experiment [ɪk'sperɪmənt] **1** *n* expérience *f* **2** *v/i* faire des expériences; **experimental** expérimental

expert ['ekspɜːrt] **1** *adj* expert **2** *n* expert(e) *m(f)*; **expertise** savoir-faire *m*

expiration date ['ekspɪ'reɪʃn] date *f* d'expiration; **expire** expirer; **expiry** expiration *f*; **expiry date** *Br* date *f* d'expiration

explain [ɪk'spleɪn] expliquer; **explanation** explication *f*; **explanatory** explicatif

explicit [ɪk'splɪsɪt] *instructions* explicite

explode [ɪk'sploʊd] **1** *v/i of bomb, fig* exploser **2** *v/t bomb* faire exploser

exploit[1] ['eksplɔɪt] *n* exploit *m*

exploit[2] [ɪk'splɔɪt] *v/t person, resources* exploiter

exploitation [eksplɔɪ'teɪʃn] *of person* exploitation *f*

exploration [eksplə'reɪʃn] exploration *f*; **explore** *country, possibility* explorer; **explorer** explorateur(-trice) *m(f)*

explosion [ɪk'sploʊʒn] *also in population* explosion *f*; **explosive** explosif *m*

export ['ekspɔːrt] **1** *n* exportation *f* **2** *v/t also* COMPUT exporter; **exporter** exportateur(-trice) *m(f)*

expose [ɪk'spoʊz] (*uncover*)

mettre à nu; *scandal* dévoiler; *person* démasquer; **~ *X to Y*** exposer X à Y; **exposure** exposition *f*; MED effets *mpl* du froid; *of dishonest behavior* dénonciation *f*; PHOT pose *f*; *in media* couverture *f*

express [ɪk'spres] **1** *adj* (*fast*) express; (*explicit*) explicite **2** *n train* express *m* **3** *v/t* exprimer; **expression** expression *f*; **expressive** expressif; **expressly** (*explicitly*) expressément; (*deliberately*) exprès; **expressway** voie *f* express

expulsion [ɪk'spʌlʃn] expulsion *f*

extend [ɪk'stend] **1** *v/t house, garden* agrandir; *search* étendre (***to*** à); *runway, contract, visa* prolonger **2** *v/i of garden etc* s'étendre; **extension** *to house* agrandissement *m*; *of contract, visa* prolongation *f*; TELEC poste *m*; **extensive** *search, knowledge* vaste, étendu; *damage* considérable; **extent** étendue *f*, ampleur *f*; ***to a certain ~*** jusqu'à un certain point

exterior [ɪk'stɪrɪər] **1** *adj* extérieur **2** *n of building* extérieur *m*; *of person* dehors *mpl*

exterminate [ɪk'stɜːrmɪneɪt] exterminer

external [ɪk'stɜːrnl] extérieur

extinct [ɪk'stɪŋkt] *species* disparu; **extinction** *of species* extinction *f*; **extinguish** *fire, cigarette* éteindre; **extinguisher** extincteur *m*

extortion [ɪk'stɔːrʃn] extortion *f*

extra ['ekstrə] **1** *n* extra *m* **2** *adj* (*spare*) de rechange; (*additional*) en plus; ***be ~*** (*cost more*) être en supplément **3** *adv* ultra-

extract¹ ['ekstrækt] *n* extrait *m*

extract² [ɪk'strækt] extraire; *tooth also* arracher; *information* arracher; **extraction** extraction *f*

extradite ['ekstrədaɪt] extrader; **extradition** extradition *f*

extramarital [ekstrə'mærɪtl] extraconjugal

extraordinary [ɪkstrə'ɔːrdɪnerɪ] extraordinaire

extra 'time *Br* SP prolongation(s) *f(pl)*

extravagance [ɪk'strævəgəns] dépenses *fpl* extravagantes; *single act* dépense *f* extravagante; **extravagant** *person* dépensier; *price* exorbitant; *claim* excessif

extreme [ɪk'striːm] **1** *n* extrême *m* **2** *adj* extrême; **extremely** extrêmement; **extremist** extrémiste *m/f*

extrovert ['ekstrəvɜːrt] **1** *n* extraverti(e) *m(f)* **2** *adj* extraverti

exuberant [ɪg'zuːbərənt] exubérant

eye [aɪ] **1** *n* œil *m* **2** *v/t* regarder; **eye-catching** accrocheur; **eyeglasses** lunettes *fpl*; **eyeliner** eye-liner *m*; **eyeshadow** ombre *f* à paupières; **eyesight** vue *f*; **eyewitness** témoin *m* oculaire

F

fabric ['fæbrɪk] tissu *m*
fabulous ['fæbjʊləs] fabuleux
façade [fə'sɑːd] façade *f*
face [feɪs] **1** *n* visage *m*, figure *f* **2** *v/t person, sea* faire face à
◆ **face up to** *bully* affronter; *responsibilities* faire face à
'**facecloth** gant *m* de toilette; **facelift** lifting *m*
facial ['feɪʃl] soin *m* du visage
facilitate [fə'sɪlɪteɪt] faciliter; **facilities** *of school, town etc* installations *fpl*; (*equipment*) équipements *mpl*
fact [fækt] fait *m*; ***in ~, as a matter of ~*** en fait
faction ['fækʃn] faction *f*
factor ['fæktər] facteur *m*
faculty ['fækəltɪ] faculté *f*
fad [fæd] lubie *f*
fade [feɪd] *of colors* passer; **faded** *color* passé
fag [fæg] *pej* F (*homosexual*) pédé *m* F
fail [feɪl] **1** *v/i* échouer **2** *v/t exam* être refusé à; **failing** défaut *m*, faiblesse *f*; **failure** échec *m*
faint [feɪnt] **1** *adj* faible, léger **2** *v/i* s'évanouir; **faintly** légèrement
fair[1] [fer] (*fun~*), COM foire *f*
fair[2] [fer] *hair* blond; *complexion* blanc
fairly ['ferlɪ] *treat* équitablement; (*quite*) assez; **fairness** *of treatment* équité *f*
faith [feɪθ] *also* REL foi *f*; **faithful** fidèle; **faithfully** fidèlement
fake [feɪk] **1** *n* (article *m*) faux *m* **2** *adj* faux; *suicide attempt* simulé **3** *v/t* (*forge*) falsifier; (*feign*) feindre; *suicide, kidnap* simuler
fall[1] [fɒːl] *n season* automne *m*
fall[2] [fɒːl] **1** *v/i* tomber; *of prices* baisser **2** *n* chute *f*; *in price, temperature* baisse *f*
◆ **fall behind** prendre du retard
◆ **fall for** *person* tomber amoureux de; (*be deceived by*) se laisser prendre à
◆ **fall through** *of plans* tomber à l'eau
fallible ['fæləbl] faillible
false [fɒːls] faux; **false start** *in race* faux départ *m*; **false teeth** fausses dents *fpl*; **falsify** falsifier
fame [feɪm] célébrité *f*
familiar [fə'mɪljər] familier; ***be ~ with sth*** bien connaître

qch; **familiarity** *with subject etc* (bonne) connaissance *f* (***with*** de); **familiarize**: ~ ***o.s. with*** se familiariser avec
family ['fæməlɪ] famille *f*; **family doctor** médecin *m* de famille; **family planning clinic** centre *m* de planning familial; **family tree** arbre *m* généalogique
famine ['fæmɪn] famine *f*
famous ['feɪməs] célèbre
fan[1] [fæn] *n in sport* fana *m/f* F; *of singer, band* fan *m/f*
fan[2] [fæn] **1** *n electric* ventilateur *m*; *handheld* évantail *m* **2** *v/t*: ~ ***o.s.*** s'éventer
fanatical [fə'nætɪkl] fanatique; **fanaticism** fanatisme *m*
fantasize ['fæntəsaɪz] fantasmer (***about*** sur); **fantastic** fantastique; **fantasy** *hopeful* rêve *m*; *unrealistic, sexual* fantasme *m*
fanzine ['fænziːn] fanzine *m*
far [fɑːr] loin; (*much*) bien; ~ ***away*** très loin; ***as ~ as the corner*** jusqu'au coin
farce [fɑːrs] farce *f*
fare [fer] *for ticket* prix *m* du billet; *for taxi* prix *m*
Far 'East Extrême-Orient *m*
farewell [fer'wel] adieu *m*
farfetched [fɑːr'fetʃt] tiré par les cheveux
farm [fɑːrm] ferme *f*; **farmer** fermier(-ière) *m(f)*; **farming** agriculture *f*; **farmworker** ouvrier(-ière) *m(f)* agricole; **farmyard** cour *f* de ferme
far-'off lointain, éloigné; **far-sighted** prévoyant; *visually* hypermétrope; **farther** plus loin; **farthest** le plus loin
fascinate ['fæsɪneɪt] fasciner; **fascinating** fascinant; **fascination** fascination *f*
fascism ['fæʃɪzm] fascisme *m*; **fascist 1** *n* fasciste *m/f* **2** *adj* fasciste
fashion ['fæʃn] mode *f*; (*manner*) manière *f*, façon *f*; ***in ~*** à la mode; ***out of ~*** démodé; **fashionable** à la mode; **fashionably** à la mode; **fashion-conscious** au courant de la mode; **fashion designer** créateur(-trice) *m(f)* de mode; **fashion show** défilé *m* de mode
fast[1] [fæst] **1** *adj* rapide; ***be ~ of clock*** avancer **2** *adv* vite; ***be ~ asleep*** dormir à poings fermés
fast[2] [fæst] *n* (*not eating*) jeûne *m*
fasten ['fæsn] **1** *v/t* attacher; *lid, window* fermer **2** *v/i of dress etc* s'attacher; **fastener** ['fæsnər] *for dress* agrafe *f*; *for lid* fermeture *f*
fast 'food fast-food *m*; **fast lane** voie *f* rapide; **fast train** train *m* rapide
fat [fæt] **1** *adj* gros **2** *n on meat* gras *m*; *for baking* graisse *f*
fatal ['feɪtl] *also error* fatal; **fatality** accident *m* mortel; **fatally** fatalement; ~ ***injured*** mortellement blessé

fate [feɪt] destin *m*
'fat free sans matières grasses; *yoghurt etc* 0%
father ['fɑːðər] père *m*; **fatherhood** paternité *f*; **father-in-law** beau-père *m*; **fatherly** paternel
fatigue [fə'tiːg] fatigue *f*
fatten ['fætn] *animal* engraisser; **fatty 1** *adj* adipeux **2** *n* F *person* gros(se) *m(f)*
faucet ['fɒːsɪt] robinet *m*
fault [fɒːlt] (*defect*) défaut *m*; ***it's your/my ~*** c'est de ta/ma faute; **faultless** impeccable; **faulty** défectueux
favor ['feɪvər] **1** *n* faveur *f*; ***do s.o. a ~*** rendre (un) service à qn **2** *v/t* (*prefer*) préférer; **favorable** favorable; **favorite 1** *n person* préféré(e) *m(f)*; *food* plat *m* préféré; *in race* **2** *adj* préféré; **favoritism** favoritisme *m*
favour *Br* → ***favor***
fax [fæks] **1** *n* fax *m* **2** *v/t* faxer
fear [fɪr] **1** *n* peur *f* **2** *v/t* avoir peur de; **fearless** sans peur; **fearlessly** sans peur
feasibility study [fiːzə'bɪlətɪ] étude *f* de faisabilité; **feasible** faisable
feast [fiːst] festin *m*
feat [fiːt] exploit *m*
feather ['feðər] plume *f*
feature ['fiːʧər] *on face* trait *m*; *of city, building, style* caractéristique *f*; *article in paper* chronique *f*; **feature film** long métrage *m*
February ['februərɪ] février *m*
federal ['fedərəl] fédéral; **federation** fédération *f*
fed 'up F: ***be ~ with*** en avoir ras-le-bol de F
fee [fiː] *of lawyer, doctor etc* honoraires *mpl*; *for membership* frais *mpl*
feeble ['fiːbl] faible
feed [fiːd] nourrir; **feedback** réactions *fpl*
feel [fiːl] **1** *v/t* (*touch*) toucher; (*sense*) sentir; *pain, pleasure* ressentir; (*think*) penser **2** *v/i*: ***it ~s like silk*** on dirait de la soie; ***do you ~ like a drink?*** est-ce que tu as envie de boire quelque chose?
◆ **feel up to** se sentir capable de
feeler ['fiːlər] *of insect* antenne *f*; **feeling** sentiment *m*; (*sensation*) sensation *f*
fellow 'citizen concitoyen(ne) *m(f)*
felony ['felənɪ] crime *m*
felt [felt] feutre *m*; **felt tip** stylo *m* feutre
female ['fiːmeɪl] **1** *adj* femelle; *relating to people* féminin **2** *n* femelle *f*; *person* femme *f*
feminine ['femɪnɪn] **1** *adj* féminin **2** *n* GRAM féminin *m*; **feminism** féminisme *m*; **feminist 1** *n* féministe *m/f* **2** *adj* féministe
fence [fens] barrière *f*, clôture *f*
fender ['fendər] MOT aile *f*
fermentation [fɜːrmen'teɪʃn]

fermentation *f*
ferocious [fə'roʊʃəs] féroce
ferry ['ferɪ] ferry *m*
fertile ['fɜːrtl] fertile; **fertility** fertilité *f*; **fertilize** féconder; **fertilizer** *for soil* engrais *m*
fervent ['fɜːrvənt] fervent
fester ['festər] *of wound* suppurer
festival ['festɪvl] festival *m*; **festive** de fête; **festivities** festivités *fpl*
fetal ['fiːtl] fœtal
fetch [fetʃ] (*go and* ~) aller chercher (***from*** à); (*come and* ~) venir chercher (***from*** à); *price* atteindre
fetus ['fiːtəs] fœtus *m*
feud [fjuːd] querelle *f*
fever ['fiːvər] fièvre *f*; **feverish** *also fig* fiévreux
few [fjuː] **1** *adj* (*not many*) peu de; ***a ~ …*** quelques; ***quite a ~, a good ~*** (*a lot*) beaucoup de **2** *pron* (*not many*) peu; ***a ~*** quelques-un(e)s *m(f)*; ***quite a ~, a good ~*** beaucoup; **fewer** moins de
fiancé [fɪ'ɑːnseɪ] fiancé *m*; **fiancée** fiancée *f*
fiber ['faɪbər] fibre *f*; **fiberglass** *n* fibre *f* de verre; **fiber optics** fibres *fpl* optiques
fibre *Br* → ***fiber***
fickle ['fɪkl] inconstant
fiction ['fɪkʃn] romans *mpl*; (*made-up story*) fiction *f*; **fictional** de roman; **fictitious** fictif
fiddle ['fɪdl] **1** *n* (*violin*) violon *m* **2** *v/i*: ***~ around with*** tripoter **3** *v/t accounts, results* truquer
fidgety ['fɪdʒɪtɪ] remuant
field [fiːld] champ *m*; *for sport* terrain *m*; (*competitors in race*) concurrent(e)s *m(f)pl*; **fielder** *in baseball* joueur *m* de champ
fierce [fɪrs] *animal* féroce; *wind, storm* violent; **fiercely** avec férocité
fiery ['faɪrɪ] ardent, fougueux
fifteen [fɪf'tiːn] quinze; **fifteenth** quinzième; **fifth** cinquième; **fiftieth** cinquantième; **fifty** cinquante; **fifty-fifty** moitié-moitié
fight [faɪt] **1** *n* combat *m*; (*argument*) dispute *f*; *for survival etc* lutte *f* **2** *v/t enemy, person* combattre; *in boxing* se battre contre; *injustice* lutter contre **3** *v/i* se battre; (*argue*) se disputer; **fighter** combattant(e) *m(f)*; *airplane* avion *m* de chasse; (*boxer*) boxeur *m*; **fighting** *physical* combat *m*; *verbal* dispute *f*
figure ['fɪgjər] **1** *n* (*digit*) chiffre *m*; *of person* ligne *f*; (*form, shape*) figure *f* **2** *v/t* F (*think*) penser:
◆ **figure on** F (*plan*) compter
◆ **figure out** comprendre; *calculation* calculer
file[1] [faɪl] **1** *n of documents* dossier *m*; COMPUT fichier *m* **2** *v/t documents* classer
file[2] [faɪl] *for wood etc* lime *f*

'file cabinet classeur *m*
fill [fɪl] remplir; *tooth* plomber; *prescription* préparer
◆ **fill in** *form* remplir; *hole* boucher
◆ **fill out 1** *v/t form* remplir **2** *v/i* (*get fatter*) grossir
fillet ['fɪlɪt] filet *m*
filling ['fɪlɪŋ] **1** *n in sandwich* garniture *f*; *in tooth* plombage *m* **2** *adj food* nourrissant; **filling station** station-service *f*
film [fɪlm] **1** *n* pellicule *f*; (*movie*) film *m* **2** *v/t* filmer; **film-maker** réalisateur(-trice) *m*(*f*) de films; **film star** star *f* de cinéma
filter ['fɪltər] **1** *n* filtre *m* **2** *v/t* filtrer
filth ['fɪlθ] saleté; **filthy** sale; *language etc* obscène
final ['faɪnl] **1** *adj* dernier; *decision* définitif, irrévocable **2** *n* SP finale *f*; **finale** apothéose *f*; **finalist** finaliste *m*/*f*; **finalize** finaliser, mettre au point; **finally** finalement, enfin
finance ['faɪnæns] **1** *n* finance *f*; (*funds*) financement *m* **2** *v/t* financer; **financial** financier; **financially** financièrement; **financier** financier (-ière) *m*(*f*)
find [faɪnd] trouver
◆ **find out** découvrir; (*enquire about*) se renseigner sur
findings ['faɪndɪŋz] *of report* constatations *fpl*
fine[1] [faɪn] *day* beau; (*good*) bon, excellent; *distinction* subtil; *line* fin; ***how's that? – that's ~*** que dites-vous de ça? – c'est bien
fine[2] [faɪn] **1** *n* amende *f* **2** *v/t* condamner à une amende de $5.000
finger ['fɪŋgər] **1** *n* doigt *m* **2** *v/t* toucher; **fingerprint** empreinte *f* digitale
finicky ['fɪnɪkɪ] *person* tatillon; *design* alambiqué
finish ['fɪnɪʃ] **1** *v/t* finir, terminer **2** *v/i* finir **3** *n of product* finition *f*; *of race* arrivée *f*
◆ **finish with** *boyfriend etc* en finir avec
fire ['faɪr] **1** *n* feu *m*; (*blaze*) incendie *m*; (*electric, gas*) radiateur *m*; ***be on ~*** être en feu; ***set ~ to sth*** mettre le feu à qch **2** *v/i* (*shoot*) tirer **3** *v/t* F (*dismiss*) virer F; **fire alarm** signal *m* d'incendie; **firearm** arme *f* à feu; **firecracker** pétard *m*; **fire department** sapeurs-pompiers *mpl*; **fire engine** *esp Br* voiture *f* de pompiers; **fire escape** *ladder* échelle *f* de secours; *stairs* escalier *m* de secours; **fire extinguisher** extincteur *m* (d'incendie); **fire fighter** pompier *m*; **fireplace** cheminée *f*; **fire station** caserne *f* de pompiers; **fire truck** voiture *f* de pompiers; **firework** pièce *f* d'artifice; **~s**

(*display*) feu *m* d'artifice
firm[1] [fɜːrm] *adj* ferme
firm[2] [fɜːrm] *n* COM firme *f*
first [fɜːrst] **1** *adj* premier **2** *n* premier(-ière) *m(f)* **3** *adv arrive, finish* le/la premier(-ière) *m(f)*; (*beforehand*) d'abord; ***at ~*** au début; **first aid** premiers secours *mpl*; **first class 1** *adj ticket* de première classe; (*very good*) de première qualité **2** *adv travel* en première classe; **first floor** rez-de-chaussée *m*; *Br* premier étage *m*; **First Lady** première dame *f*; **firstly** premièrement; **first name** prénom *m*; **first night** première *f*; **first-rate** de premier ordre
fiscal ['fɪskl] fiscal; **fiscal year** année *f* fiscale
fish [fɪʃ] **1** *n* poisson *m* **2** *v/i* pêcher; **fisherman** pêcheur *m*; **fishing** pêche *f*; **fishing boat** bateau *m* de pêche; **fish stick** bâtonnet *m* de poisson; **fishy** F (*suspicious*) louche
fist [fɪst] poing *m*
fit[1] [fɪt] *n* MED crise *f*, attaque *f*
fit[2] [fɪt] *adj physically* en forme; *morally* digne
fit[3] [fɪt] **1** *v/t of clothes* aller à; (*install, attach*) poser; ***it doesn't ~ me any more*** je ne rentre plus dedans **2** *v/i of clothes* aller
fitness ['fɪtnɪs] *physical* (bonne) forme *f*; **fitting** approprié; **fittings** installations *fpl*
five [faɪv] cinq
fix [fɪks] **1** *n* (*solution*) solution *f* **2** *v/t* (*attach*) attacher; (*repair*) réparer; *meeting etc* arranger; *lunch* préparer; *dishonestly*: *match etc* truquer; **fixed** fixe; **fixings** garniture *f*
flab [flæb] *on body* graisse *f*; **flabby** *muscles etc* mou
flag[1] [flæg] *n* drapeau *m*; NAUT pavillon *m*
flag[2] [flæg] *v/i* (*tire*) faiblir
'flagpole mât *m* (de drapeau)
flagrant ['fleɪgrənt] flagrant
flair [fler] (*talent*) flair *m*; ***have a natural ~ for*** avoir un don pour
flake [fleɪk] *of snow* flocon *m*; *of plaster* écaille *f*
flamboyant [flæm'bɔɪənt] extravagant; **flamboyantly** avec extravagance
flame [fleɪm] flamme *f*
flammable ['flæməbl] inflammable
flank [flæŋk] **1** *n* flanc *m* **2** *v/t*: ***be ~ed by*** être flanqué de
flap [flæp] **1** *n of envelope, pocket* rabat *m* **2** *v/t wings* battre **3** *v/i of flag etc* battre
◆ **flare up** [fler] *of violence, rash* éclater; *of fire* s'enflammer; (*get very angry*) s'emporter
flash [flæʃ] **1** *n of light* éclair *m*; PHOT flash *m*; ***in a ~*** F en un rien de temps; ***~ of lightning*** éclair *m* **2** *v/i of light* clignoter; **flashback** *in movie* flash-back *m*; **flashlight** lam-

pe *f* de poche; PHOT flash *m*; **flashy** *pej* voyant
flask [flæsk] (*hip* ~) fiole *f*
flat[1] [flæt] **1** *adj* plat; *beer* éventé; *battery*, *tire* à plat; bémol **2** *adv* MUS trop bas **3** *n* pneu *m* crevé
flat[2] [flæt] *n Br* (*apartment*) appartement *m*
flatly ['flætlɪ] *deny* catégoriquement; **flat rate** tarif *m* unique; **flatten** *land*, *road* aplanir; *by bombing*, *demolition* raser
flatter ['flætər] flatter; **flatterer** flatteur(-euse) *m*(*f*); **flattering** *comments* flatteur; *color*, *clothes* avantageux; **flattery** flatterie *f*
flavor ['fleɪvər] **1** *n* goût *m*; *of ice cream* parfum *m* **2** *v/t food* assaisonner; **flavoring** arôme *m*
flavour *Br* → ***flavor***
flaw [flɒː] défaut *m*; **flawless** parfait
flee [fliː] s'enfuir
fleet [fliːt] NAUT flotte *f*; *of vehicles* parc *m*
fleeting ['fliːtɪŋ] *visit etc* très court
flesh [fleʃ] *also of fruit* chair *f*
flex [fleks] *muscles* fléchir; **flexibility** flexibilité *f*; **flexible** flexible; **flextime** horaire *m* à la carte
flicker ['flɪkər] vaciller
flier ['flaɪr] (*circular*) prospectus *m*
flight [flaɪt] *in airplane* vol *m*; (*fleeing*) fuite *f*; ~ (***of stairs***) escalier *m*; **flight attendant** *male* steward *m*; *female* hôtesse *f* de l'air; **flight path** trajectoire *f* de vol; **flight recorder** enregistreur *m* de vol; **flight time** *departure* heure *f* de vol; *duration* durée *f* de vol; **flighty** frivole
flimsy ['flɪmzɪ] *furniture* fragile; *dress*, *material* léger; *excuse* faible
flinch [flɪntʃ] tressaillir
flipper ['flɪpər] nageoire *f*
flirt [flɜːrt] **1** *v/i* flirter **2** *n* flirteur(-euse) *m*(*f*); **flirtatious** flirteur
float [flout] *also* FIN flotter
flock [flɑːk] **1** *n of sheep* troupeau *m* **2** *v/i* venir en masse
flood [flʌd] **1** *n* inondation *f* **2** *v/t of river* inonder; **flooding** inondation(s) *f*(*pl*)
'floodlight projecteur *m*; **flood waters** inondations *fpl*
floor [flɔːr] sol *m*; *wooden* plancher *m*; (*story*) étage *m*
flop [flɑːp] **1** *v/i* s'écrouler; F (*fail*) faire un bide F **2** *n* F (*failure*) bide *m* F; **floppy** (**disk**) disquette *f*
florist ['flɔːrɪst] fleuriste *m*/*f*
flour ['flaʊr] farine *f*
flourish ['flʌrɪʃ] *of plants* fleurir; *fig* prospérer; **flourishing** *business* fleurissant, prospère
flow [flou] **1** *v/i of river* couler; *of electric current* passer; *of traffic* circuler; *of work* se

dérouler **2** *n of river* cours *m*; *of information* circulation *f*; **flowchart** organigramme *m*
flower ['flaʊr] **1** *n* fleur *f* **2** *v/i* fleurir
flu [flu:] grippe *f*
fluctuate ['flʌktʃʊeɪt] fluctuer; **fluctuation** fluctuation *f*
fluency ['flu:ənsɪ] *in a language* maîtrise *f* (**in** de); **fluent** *person* qui s'exprime avec aisance; ***he speaks ~ Spanish*** il parle couramment l'espagnol; **fluently** couramment; *in own language* avec aisance
fluid ['flu:ɪd] fluide *m*
flunk [flʌŋk] F *subject* rater
flush [flʌʃ] **1** *v/t*: ***~ the toilet*** tirer la chasse d'eau **2** *v/i* (*go red*) rougir
flutter ['flʌtər] *of bird* voleter; *of wings* battre; *of flag* s'agiter; *of heart* palpiter
fly[1] [flaɪ] *n* (*insect*) mouche *f*
fly[2] [flaɪ] *n on pants* braguette *f*
fly[3] [flaɪ] **1** *v/i* voler; *in airplane* prendre l'avion; *of flag* flotter **2** *v/t airplane* piloter, voler; *airline* voyager par; (*transport by air*) envoyer par avion
◆ **fly past** *of time* filer
flying ['flaɪɪŋ]: ***I hate ~*** je déteste prendre l'avion
foam [foʊm] *on sea* écume *f*; *on drink* mousse *f*; **foam rubber** caoutchouc *m* mousse
focus ['foʊkəs] *of attention* centre *m*; PHOT mise *f* au point
◆ **focus on** se concentrer sur; PHOT mettre au point sur
fodder ['fɑ:dər] fourrage *m*
fog [fɑ:g] brouillard *m*; **foggy** brumeux
foil[1] [fɔɪl] *n silver* feuille *f* d'aluminium
foil[2] [fɔɪl] *v/t* (*thwart*) faire échouer
fold [foʊld] **1** *v/t paper etc* plier; ***~ one's arms*** croiser les bras **2** *v/i of business* fermer (ses portes) **3** *n in cloth etc* pli *m*
◆ **fold up 1** *v/t* plier **2** *v/i of chair, table* se (re)plier
folder ['foʊlder] *for documents* chemise *f*; COMPUT dossier *m*; **folding** pliant
foliage ['foʊlɪɪdʒ] feuillage *m*
folk [foʊk] (*people*) gens *mpl*; **folk music** folk *m*; **folk singer** chanteur(-euse) *m(f)* de folk
follow ['fɑ:loʊ] **1** *v/t also* (*understand*) suivre **2** *v/i logically* s'ensuivre
◆ **follow up** *inquiry* donner suite à
follower ['fɑ:loʊər] *of politician etc* partisan(e) *m(f)*; *of football team* supporteur (-trice) *m(f)*; **following 1** *adj* suivant **2** *n people* partisans *mpl*
fond [fɑ:nd] (*loving*) aimant;

memory agréable; ***be ~ of*** beaucoup aimer
fondle ['fɑːndl] caresser
fondness ['fɑːndnɪs] *for s.o.* tendresse *f*; *for sth* penchant *m*
font [fɑːnt] *for printing* police *f*; *in church* fonts *mpl* baptismaux
food [fuːd] nourriture *f*; ***French ~*** la cuisine française; **food poisoning** intoxication *f* alimentaire
fool [fuːl] **1** *n* idiot(e) *m(f)* **2** *v/t* berner; **foolhardy** téméraire; **foolish** idiot, bête; **foolproof** à toute épreuve
foot [fʊt] *also measurement* pied *m*; *of animal* patte *f*; ***put one's ~ in it*** F mettre les pieds dans le plat F; **footage** séquences *fpl*; **football** football *m* américain; (*soccer*) football *m* F; (*ball*) ballon *m* de football; **football player** joueur(-euse) *m(f)* de football américain; *soccer* joueur(-euse) *m(f)* de football; **foothills** contreforts *mpl*; **footnote** note *f* (de bas de page); **footpath** sentier *m*; **footprint** trace *f* de pas; **footstep** pas *m*
for [fər], [fɔːr] pour; ***a train ~ ...*** un train à destination de ...; ***what is this ~?*** pour quoi est-ce que c'est fait?; ***what ~?*** pourquoi?; ***~ three days*** pendant trois jours; ***it lasted ~ three days*** ça a duré trois jours; ***I've been waiting ~ an hour*** j'attends depuis une heure
forbid [fər'bɪd] interdire; **forbidden** interdit; **forbidding** menaçant
force [fɔːrs] **1** *n* force *f*; ***come into ~*** *of law etc* entrer en vigueur **2** *v/t door, lock* forcer; ***~ s.o. to do sth*** forcer qn à faire qch; **forced** forcé; **forced landing** atterrissage *m* forcé; **forceful** *argument, speaker* puissant; *character* énergique
forceps ['fɔːrseps] MED forceps *m*
forcibly ['fɔːrsəblɪ] *restrain* par force
foreboding [fər'boudɪŋ] pressentiment *m*; **forecast 1** *n of results* pronostic *m*; *of weather* prévisions *fpl* **2** *v/t result* pronostiquer; *future, weather* prévoir; **forefathers** ancêtres *mpl*; **forefinger** index *m*; **foreground** premier plan *m*; **forehead** front *m*
foreign ['fɑːrən] étranger; **foreign affairs** affaires *fpl* étrangères; **foreign body** corps *m* étranger; **foreign currency** devises *fpl* étrangères; **foreigner** étranger (-ère) *m(f)*; **foreign exchange** devises *fpl* étrangères
'foreman chef *m* d'équipe; **foremost 1** *adv* (*uppermost*) le plus important **2** *adj* (*lead-*

ing) premier
forensic 'medicine [fə'rensɪk] médecine *f* légale; **forensic scientist** expert *m* légiste
'forerunner *person* prédécesseur *m*; *thing* ancêtre *m/f*; **foresee** prévoir; **foresight** prévoyance *f*
forest ['fɑːrɪst] forêt *f*; **forestry** sylviculture *f*
fore'tell prédire
forever [fə'revər] toujours
'foreword avant-propos *m*
forfeit ['fɔːrfət] (*lose*) perdre; (*give up*) renoncer à
forge [fɔːrdʒ] contrefaire; **forgery** *bank bill* faux billet *m*; *document* faux *m*; *signature* contrefaçon *f*
forget [fər'get] oublier; **forgetful**: ***you're so ~*** tu as vraiment mauvaise mémoire
forgive [fər'gɪv] **1** *v/t*: ***~ s.o. sth*** pardonner qch à qn **2** *v/i* pardonner; **forgiveness** pardon *m*
fork [fɔːrk] fourchette *f*; *for gardening* fourche *f*; *in road* embranchement *m*
form [fɔːrm] **1** *n* (*shape*) forme *f*; *document* formulaire *m* **2** *v/t* former; *friendship* développer; *opinion* se faire **3** *v/i* (*take shape, develop*) se former; **formal** *language* soutenu; *dress* de soirée; *manner, reception* cérémonieux; *recognition etc* officiel; **formality** *of language* caractère *m* soutenu; *of occasion* cérémonie *f*; ***it's just a ~*** c'est juste une formalité; **formally** *speak* cérémonieusement; *recognized* officiellement
format ['fɔːrmæt] **1** *v/t* formater **2** *n* format *m*
formation [fɔːr'meɪʃn] formation *f*
former ['fɔːrmər] ancien; ***the ~*** le premier, la première; **formerly** autrefois
formidable ['fɔːrmɪdəbl] redoutable
formula ['fɔːrmjʊlə] MATH, CHEM formule *f*; *fig* recette *f*
fort [fɔːrt] MIL fort *m*
forthcoming ['fɔːrθkʌmɪŋ] (*future*) futur; *personality* ouvert
'forthright franc
fortieth ['fɔːrtɪɪθ] quarantième
fortnight ['fɔːrtnaɪt] *Br* quinze jours *mpl*, quinzaine *f*
fortress ['fɔːrtrɪs] MIL forteresse *f*
fortunate ['fɔːrtʃnət] *decision* heureux; ***be ~*** avoir de la chance; **fortunately** heureusement; **fortune** (*fate*) destin *m*; (*luck*) chance *f*; (*lot of money*) fortune *f*
forty ['fɔːrtɪ] quarante
forward ['fɔːrwərd] **1** *adv* en avant **2** *adj pej*: *person* effronté **3** *n* SP avant *m* **4** *v/t letter* faire suivre; **forward-looking** moderne

fossil ['fɑːsl] fossile *m*
foster ['fɑːstər] *child* servir de famille d'accueil à; *attitude, belief* encourager
foul [faʊl] **1** *n* SP faute *f* **2** *adj smell* infect; *weather* sale **3** *v/t* SP commettre une faute contre
found [faʊnd] *school etc* fonder; **foundation** *of theory etc* fondement *m*; (*organization*) fondation *f*; **foundations** *of building* fondations *fpl*; **founder** fondateur(-trice) *m(f)*
fountain ['faʊntɪn] fontaine *f*; *with vertical spout* jet *m* d'eau
four [fɔːr] quatre; **four-star** quatre étoiles; **fourteen** quatorze; **fourteenth** quatorzième; **fourth** quatrième; **four-wheel drive** MOT quatre-quatre *m*
fox [fɑːks] **1** *n* renard *m* **2** *v/t* (*puzzle*) mystifier
foyer ['fɔɪər] hall *m* d'entrée
fraction ['frækʃn] fraction *f*; **fractionally** très légèrement
fracture ['fræktʃər] **1** *n* fracture *f* **2** *v/t* fracturer
fragile ['frædʒəl] fragile
fragment ['frægmənt] fragment *m*
fragrance ['freɪgrəns] parfum *m*; **fragrant** parfumé
frail [freɪl] frêle, fragile
frame [freɪm] **1** *n of picture, bicycle* cadre *m*; *of window* châssis *m*; *of eyeglasses* monture *f* **2** *v/t picture* encadrer; F *person* monter un coup contre; **framework** structure *f*; ***within the ~ of*** dans le cadre de
France [fræns] France *f*
franchise ['fræntʃaɪz] *for business* franchise *f*
frank [fræŋk] franc; **frankly** franchement; **frankness** franchise *f*
frantic ['fræntɪk] frénétique
fraternal [frə'tɜːrnl] fraternel
fraud [frɒːd] fraude *f*; *person* imposteur *m*; **fraudulent** frauduleux
frayed [freɪd] *cuffs* usé
freak [friːk] **1** *n* (*unusual event*) phénomène *m* étrange; (*two-headed animal etc*) monstre *m*; F (*strange person*) taré(e) *m(f)*F **2** *adj storm etc* anormalement violent
free [friː] **1** *adj* libre; *no cost* gratuit **2** *v/t prisoners* libérer; **freedom** liberté *f*; **free enterprise** libre entreprise *f*; **free kick** *in soccer* coup *m* franc; **freelance** indépendant, free-lance *inv*; **freely** *admit* volontiers; **free speech** libre parole *f*; **freeway** autoroute *f*
freeze [friːz] **1** *v/t* congeler; *bank account* bloquer; ***~ a video*** faire un arrêt sur image **2** *v/i of water* geler; **freeze-dried** lyophilisé; **freezer** congélateur *m*;

freezing 1 *adj* glacial **2** *n*: ***10 below ~*** 10 degrés au-dessous de zéro
freight [freɪt] fret *m*; **freighter** *ship*cargo *m*; *airplane* avion-cargo *m*
French [frentʃ] **1** *adj* français **2** *n language* français *m*; ***the ~*** les Français *mpl*; **French fries** frites *fpl*; **Frenchman** Français *m*; **Frenchwoman** Française *f*
frenzied ['frenzɪd] *attack, activity* forcené; *mob* déchaîné; **frenzy** frénésie *f*
frequency ['fri:kwənsɪ] *also of radio* fréquence *f*
frequent¹ *adj* fréquent
frequent² [frɪ'kwent] *v/t bar etc* fréquenter
frequently ['fri:kwəntlɪ] fréquemment
fresh [freʃ] frais; *start* nouveau; *sheets* propre; (*impertinent*) insolent; **fresh air** air *m*
◆ **freshen up 1** *v/i* se rafraîchir **2** *v/t paintwork* rafraîchir
freshly ['freʃlɪ] fraîchement; **freshman** étudiant(e) *m(f)* de première année; **freshwater** d'eau douce
fret [fret] s'inquiéter
friction ['frɪkʃn] friction *f*
Friday ['fraɪdeɪ] vendredi *m*
fridge [frɪdʒ] frigo *m* F
friend [frend] ami(e) *m(f)*; **friendliness** amabilité *f*; **friendly** amical; *hotel, city* sympathique; *argument* entre amis; **friendship** amitié *f*
fries [fraɪz] frites *fpl*
fright [fraɪt] peur *f*; **frighten** faire peur à; ***be ~ed*** avoir peur (***of*** de); **frightening** effrayant
frill [frɪl] *on dress etc*, (*extra*) falbala *m*
fringe [frɪndʒ] frange *f*; *of city* périphérie *f*; *of society* marge *f*; **fringe benefits** avantages *mpl* sociaux
frisk [frɪsk] fouiller
◆ **fritter away** ['frɪtər] *time, fortune* gaspiller
frivolity [frɪ'vɑ:lətɪ] frivolité *f*; **frivolous** frivole
frizzy ['frɪzɪ] *hair* crépu
frog [frɑ:g] grenouille *f*; **frogman** homme-grenouille *m*
from [frɑ:m] de; ***~ 9 to 5*** (***o'clock***) de 9 heures à 5 heures; ***~ the 18th century*** à partir du XVIIIe siècle; ***~ today on*** à partir d'aujourd'hui; ***~ here to there*** d'ici à là(-bas); ***I am ~ New Jersey*** je viens du New Jersey; ***tired ~ the journey*** fatigué par le voyage; ***it's ~ overeating*** c'est d'avoir trop mangé
front [frʌnt] **1** *n of building* façade *f*, devant *m*; *of book* devant *m*; (*cover organization*) façade *f*; MIL, *of weather* front *m*; ***in ~*** devant; ***in ~*** *in a race* en tête; ***in ~ of*** devant **2** *adj wheel, seat* avant **3** *v/t TV program* présenter; **front door** porte *f* d'entrée
frontier ['frʌntɪr] *also fig*

frontière *f*
'front line MIL front *m*; **front page** *of newspaper* une *f*; **front-wheel drive** traction *f* avant
frost [frɑːst] gel *m*; **frostbite** gelure *f*; **frosting** *on cake* glaçage *m*; **frosty** *also fig* glacial
froth [frɑːθ] écume *f*, mousse *f*
frown [fraʊn] froncer les sourcils
frozen ['froʊzn] gelé; *food* surgelé
fruit [fruːt] fruit *m*; *collective* fruits *mpl*; **fruitful** *discussions etc* fructueux; **fruit juice** jus *m* de fruit; **fruit salad** salade *f* de fruits
frustrate ['frʌstreɪt] *person* frustrer; *plans* contrarier; **frustrating** frustrant; **frustration** frustration *f*
fry [fraɪ] (faire) frire; **frypan** poêle *f* (à frire)
fuck [fʌk] V baiser V; ~ putain! V
fuel ['fjʊːəl] **1** *n* carburant *m* **2** *v/t fig* entretenir
fugitive ['fjuːdʒətɪv] fugitif (-ive) *m*(*f*)
fulfill, *Br* **fulfil** [fʊl'fɪl] *dreams* réaliser; *task* accomplir; *contract* remplir; **fulfillment**, *Br* **fulfilment** *of contract etc* exécution *f*; *moral, spiritual* accomplissement *m*
full [fʊl] plein (***of*** de); *hotel, account* complet; ***pay in ~*** tout payer; **full moon** pleine lune *f*; **full stop** *Br* point *m*; **full-time** à plein temps; **fully** complètement; *describe* en détail
fumble ['fʌmbl] *catch* mal attraper
fumes [fjuːmz] *s* fumée *f*
fun [fʌn] **1** *n* amusement *m*; ***it was great ~*** on s'est bien amusé; ***have ~!*** amuse-toi bien! **2** *adj* F marrant F
function ['fʌŋkʃn] **1** *n* fonction *f*; (*reception etc*) réception *f* **2** *v/i* fonctionner; ***~ as*** faire fonction de; **functional** fonctionnel
fund [fʌnd] **1** *n* fonds *m* **2** *v/t project etc* financer
fundamental [fʌndə'mentl] fondamental; **fundamentalist** fondamentaliste *m/f*; **fundamentally** fondamentalement
funding ['fʌndɪŋ] (*money*) financement *m*
funeral ['fjuːnərəl] enterrement *m*; **funeral home** établissement *m* de pompes funèbres
fungus ['fʌŋgəs] champignon *m*; *mold* moisissure *f*
funnies ['fʌnɪz] F pages *fpl* drôles; **funnily** (*oddly*) bizarrement; (*comically*) comiquement; ***~ enough*** chose curieuse; **funny** (*comical*) drôle; (*odd*) bizarre, curieux
fur [fɜːr] fourrure *f*
furious ['fjʊrɪəs] furieux
furnace ['fɜːrnɪs] four(neau)

m
furnish ['fɜːrnɪʃ] *room* meubler; (*supply*) fournir; **furniture** meubles *mpl*; ***a piece of ~*** un meuble
further ['fɜːrðər] **1** *adj* supplémentaire; (*more distant*) plus éloigné **2** *adv walk, drive* plus loin **3** *v/t cause etc* faire avancer, promouvoir; **furthermore** de plus, en outre
furtive ['fɜːrtɪv] furtif
fury ['fjʊrɪ] fureur *f*
fuse [fjuːz] **1** *n* ELEC fusible *m*, plomb *m* F **2** *v/i* ELEC: ***the lights have ~d*** les plombs ont sauté **3** *v/t* ELEC faire sauter; **fusebox** boîte *f* à fusibles
fusion ['fjuːʒn] fusion *f*
fuss [fʌs] agitation *f*; **fussy** *person* difficile; *design etc* trop compliqué
futile ['fjuːtl] futile; **futility** futilité *f*
future ['fjuːʧər] **1** *n* avenir *f*; GRAM futur *m* **2** *adj* futur; **futuristic** *design* futuriste
fuzzy ['fʌzɪ] *hair* crépu; (*out of focus*) flou

G

gadget ['gædʒɪt] gadget *m*
gag [gæg] **1** *n* bâillon *m*; (*joke*) gag *m* **2** *v/t also fig* bâillonner
gain [geɪn] acquérir; *victory* remporter; *advantage, sympathy* gagner
gala ['gælə] gala *m*
galaxy ['gæləksɪ] galaxie *f*
gale [geɪl] tempête *f*
gallery ['gælərɪ] *for art, in theater* galerie *f*
gallon ['gælən] gallon *m* (*0,785l, en GB 0,546l*)
gallop ['gæləp] galoper
gamble ['gæmbl] jouer; **gambler** joueur(-euse) *m(f)*; **gambling** jeu *m*
game [geɪm] *also in tennis* jeu *m*; ***have a ~ of tennis*** faire une partie de tennis
gang [gæŋ] gang *m*; *of friends* bande *f*; **gangster** gangster *m*; **gangway** passerelle *f*
gap [gæp] trou *m*; *in time* intervalle *m*; *between personalities* fossé *m*
gape [geɪp] rester bouche bée; **gaping** *hole* béant
garage [gə'rɑːʒ] garage *m*
garbage ['gɑːrbɪdʒ] ordures *fpl*; (*fig : nonsense*) bêtises *fpl*; **garbage can** poubelle *f*; **garbage truck** benne *f* à ordures
garbled ['gɑːrbld] *message* confus
garden ['gɑːrdn] jardin *m*; **gardening** jardinage *m*
garish ['gerɪʃ] criard
garlic ['gɑːrlɪk] ail *m*
garment ['gɑːrmənt] vête-

ment *m*
garnish ['gɑːrnɪʃ] garnir (***with*** de)
gas [gæs] gaz *m*; (*gasoline*) essence *f*
gash [gæʃ] entaille *f*
gasket ['gæskɪt] joint *m* d'étanchéité
gasoline ['gæsəliːn] essence *f*
gasp [gæsp] **1** *n in surprise* hoquet *m*; *with exhaustion* halètement *m* **2** *v/i with exhaustion* haleter; ***with surprise*** pousser une exclamation de surprise
'**gas pedal** accélérateur *m*; **gas pump** pompe *f* (à essence); **gas station** station-service *f*
gate [geɪt] *also at airport* porte *f*; **gateway** entrée *f*; *also fig* porte *f*
gather ['gæðər] **1** *v/t facts* recueillir; ~ ***speed*** prendre de la vitesse **2** *v/i of crowd* s'assembler; **gathering** (*group of people*) assemblée *f*
gaudy ['gɒːdɪ] voyant
gauge [geɪdʒ] **1** *n* jauge *f* **2** *v/t pressure* jauger; *opinion* mesurer
gaunt [gɒːnt] émacié
gawky ['gɒːkɪ] gauche
gawp [gɒːp] F rester bouche bée (***at*** devant)
gay [geɪ] gay
gaze [geɪz] **1** *n* regard *m* (fixe) **2** *v/i* regarder fixement
gear [gɪr] (*equipment*) équipement *m*; *in vehicles* vitesse *f*; **gearbox** MOT boîte *f* de vitesses; **gear shift** MOT levier *m* de vitesse
gel [dʒel] *for hair, shower* gel *m*
gem [dʒem] pierre *f* précieuse; *fig* perle *f*
gender ['dʒendər] genre *m*
gene [dʒiːn] gène *m*
general ['dʒenrəl] **1** *n* MIL général(e) *m(f)* **2** *adj* général; **generalization** généralisation *f*; **generalize** généraliser; **generally** généralement; ~ ***speaking*** de manière générale
generate ['dʒenəreɪt] produire; **generation** génération *f*; **generator** générateur *m*
generosity [dʒenə'rɑːsətɪ] générosité *f*; **generous** généreux
genetic [dʒɪ'netɪk] génétique; **genetically** génétiquement; **genetically engineered** transgénique; **genetically modified** génétiquement modifié; **genetic engineering** génie *m* génétique; **genetic fingerprint** empreinte *f* génétique; **genetics** génétique *f*
genial ['dʒiːnjəl] agréable
genitals ['dʒenɪtlz] organes *mpl* génitaux
genius ['dʒiːnjəs] génie *m*
genocide ['dʒenəsaɪd] génocide *m*
gentle ['dʒentl] doux; *breeze* léger; **gentleman** monsieur

m; ***he's a real ~*** c'est un vrai gentleman; **gentleness** douceur *f*; **gently** doucement; *blow* légèrement

genuine ['dʒenʊɪn] authentique; **genuinely** vraiment, sincèrement

geographical [dʒɪə'græfɪkl] géographique; **geography** géographie *f*

geological [dʒɪə'lɑːdʒɪkl] géologique; **geologist** géologue *m/f*; **geology** géologie *f*

geometric, geometrical [dʒɪə'metrɪk(l)] géométrique; **geometry** géométrie *f*

geriatric [dʒerɪ'ætrɪk] **1** *adj* gériatrique **2** *n* patient(e) *m(f)* gériatrique

germ [dʒɜːrm] *also of idea etc* germe *m*

German ['dʒɜːrmən] **1** *adj* allemand **2** *n person* Allemand(e) *m(f)*; *language* allemand *m*; **German shepherd** berger *m* allemand; **Germany** Allemagne *f*

gesture ['dʒestʃər] *also fig* geste *m*

get [get] (*obtain*) obtenir; (*buy*) acheter; (*fetch*) aller chercher; (*receive*: *letter*) recevoir; (*receive*: *knowledge, respect etc*) acquérir; (*catch*: *bus, train etc*) prendre; (*understand*) comprendre; (*become*) devenir; ***when we ~ home*** quand nous arrivons chez nous; ***~ old/tired*** vieillir/se fatiguer; ***~ sth done*** (*by s.o. else*) faire faire qch; ***~ s.o. to do sth*** faire faire qch à qn; ***~ one's hair cut*** se faire couper les cheveux; ***~ sth ready*** préparer qch; ***have got*** avoir; ***have got to*** devoir; ***I have got to study*** je dois étudier, il faut que j'étudie (subj); ***~ to know*** commencer à bien connaître

◆ **get at** (*criticize*) s'en prendre à; (*imply, mean*) vouloir dire

◆ **get by** (*pass*) passer; *financially* s'en sortir

◆ **get down 1** *v/i from ladder etc* descendre; (*duck*) se baisser **2** *v/t* (*depress*) déprimer

◆ **get in 1** *v/i* (*of train, plane*) arriver; (*come home*) rentrer; *to car* entrer **2** *v/t to suitcase etc* rentrer

◆ **get into** *house* entrar dans; *car* monter dans

◆ **get off 1** *v/i from bus etc* descendre; (*finish work*) finir; (*not be punished*) s'en tirer **2** *v/t* (*remove*) enlever

◆ **get on 1** *v/i to bike, bus* monter; (*be friendly*) s'entendre; (*advance*: *of time*) se faire tard; (*become old*) prendre de l'âge; (*progress*: *of book*) avancer **2** *v/t*: ***get on the bus*** monter dans le bus

◆ **get out 1** *v/i of car, prison*

etc sortir; ***get out!*** va-t-en! **2** *v/t nail, stain* enlever; *gun, pen* sortir
◆ **get through** *on telephone* obtenir la communication
◆ **get up 1** *v/i* se lever **2** *v/t* (*climb*: *hill*) monter
'getaway car voiture utilisée pour s'enfuir; **get-together** réunion *f*
ghastly ['gæstlı] horrible
ghetto ['getoʊ] ghetto *m*
ghost [goʊst] fantôme *m*, spectre *m*; **ghostly** spectral
ghoul [gu:l] personne *f* morbide
giant ['dʒaɪənt] **1** *n* géant(e) *m*(*f*) **2** *adj* géant
gibberish ['dʒɪbərɪʃ] F charabia *m*
gibe [dʒaɪb] moquerie *f*
giddiness ['gɪdɪnɪs] vertige *m*; **giddy**: ***feel ~*** avoir le vertige
gift [gɪft] cadeau *m*; *talent* don *m*; **gift card** carte *f* cadeau; **gifted** doué; **giftwrap**: ***~ sth*** faire un paquet-cadeau
gig [gɪg] F concert *m*
gigabyte ['gɪgəbaɪt] COMPUT gigaoctet *m*
gigantic [dʒaɪ'gæntɪk] gigantesque
giggle ['gɪgl] **1** *v/i* glousser **2** *n* gloussement *m*
gimmick ['gɪmɪk] truc F
gin [dʒɪn] gin *m*; ***~ and tonic*** gin *m* tonic
gipsy ['dʒɪpsɪ] gitan(e) *m*(*f*)
girder ['gɜ:rdər] poutre *f*
girl [gɜ:rl] (jeune) fille *f*; **girlfriend** *of boy* petite amie *f*; *younger also* copine *f*; *of girl* amie *f*, *younger also* copine *f*; **girlish** de jeune fille
gist [dʒɪst] essence *f*
give [gɪv] donner; *present* offrir; (*supply*: *electricity etc*) fournir; *talk, lecture* faire; *cry, groan* pousser
◆ **give away** *as present* donner; (*betray*) trahir
◆ **give back** rendre
◆ **give in 1** *v/i* (*surrender*) se rendre **2** *v/t* (*hand in*) remettre
◆ **give onto** (*open onto*) donner sur
◆ **give out 1** *v/t leaflets etc* distribuer **2** *v/i of supplies, strength* s'épuiser
◆ **give up 1** *v/t smoking etc* arrêter de **2** *v/i* (*stop making effort*) abandonner
◆ **give way** *of bridge etc* s'écrouler
give-and-'take concessions *fpl* mutuelles
gizmo ['gɪzmoʊ] F truc *m*
glad [glæd] heureux; **gladly** volontiers, avec plaisir
glamor ['glæmər] éclat *m*, fascination *f*; **glamorize** donner un aspect séduisant à; **glamorous** séduisant, fascinant; *job* prestigieux; **glamour** *Br* → ***glamor***
glance [glæns] **1** *n* regard *m* **2** *v/i* jeter un regard, lancer un coup d'œil

gland [glænd] glande *f*
glare [gler] **1** *n of sun, lights* éclat *m* (éblouissant) **2** *v/i of sun, lights* briller d'un éclat éblouissant
◆ **glare at** lancer un regard furieux à
glaring ['glerɪŋ] *mistake* flagrant
glass [glæs] *material, for drink* verre *m*; **glasses** lunettes *fpl*
glazed [gleɪzd] *expression* vitreux
gleam [gli:m] **1** *n* lueur *f* **2** *v/i* luire
glee [gli:] joie *f*; **gleeful** joyeux
glib [glɪb] désinvolte; **glibly** avec désinvolture
glide [glaɪd] glisser; *of bird, plane* planer; **glider** planeur *m*; **gliding** *sport* vol *m* à voile
glimpse [glɪmps] **1** *n*: ***catch a ~ of ...*** entrevoir **2** *v/t* entrevoir
glint [glɪnt] **1** *n* lueur *f* **2** *v/i of light, eyes* luire
glisten ['glɪsn] *of light* luire; *of water* miroiter; *of silk* chatoyer
glitter ['glɪtər] *of light, jewels* briller, scintiller
gloat [glout] jubiler
◆ **gloat over** se réjouir de
global ['gloubl] (*worldwide*) mondial; (*without exceptions*) global; **globalization** mondialisation *f*; **global warming** réchauffement *m* de la planète; **globe** globe *m*
gloom [glu:m] (*darkness*) obscurité *f*; *mood* tristesse *f*; **gloomy** sombre
glorious ['glɔ:rɪəs] *weather* magnifique; *victory* glorieux; **glory** gloire *f*
gloss [glɑ:s] (*shine*) brillant *m*; (*general explanation*) glose *f*; **glossary** glossaire *m*; **glossy 1** *adj paper* glacé **2** *n magazine* magazine *m* de luxe
glove [glʌv] gant *m*; **glove compartment** boîte *f* à gants
glow [glou] **1** *n of light* lueur *f*; *of fire* rougeoiement *m*; *in cheeks* couleurs *fpl* **2** *v/i of light* luire; *of fire* rougeoyer; *of cheeks* être rouge; **glowing** *description* élogieux
glucose ['glu:kous] glucose *m*
glue [glu:] **1** *n* colle *f* **2** *v/t* coller
glum [glʌm] morose
glut [glʌt] surplus *m*
glutton ['glʌtən] glouton(ne) *m(f)*
gnaw [nɒ:] *bone* ronger
go [gou] aller; (*leave*) partir; (*work, function*) marcher, fonctionner; (*come out: of stain etc*) s'en aller; (*cease: of pain etc*) partir, disparaître; (*match: of colors etc*) aller ensemble; ***hamburger to ~*** hamburger à emporter
◆ **go away** *of person* s'en aller, partir; *of rain* cesser; *of*

pain, *clouds* partir

◆ **go back** (*return*) retourner; (*date back*) remonter (***to*** à)

◆ **go by** *of car*, *time* passer

◆ **go down** descendre; *of sun* se coucher

◆ **go in** *to room*, *house* entrer; *of sun* se cacher; (*fit*: *of part etc*) s'insérer

◆ **go off** (*leave*) partir; *of bomb* exploser; *of gun* partir; *of alarm* se déclencher

◆ **go on** (*continue*) continuer; (*happen*) se passer

◆ **go out** *of person* sortir; *of light*, *fire* s'éteindre

◆ **go over** (*check*) revoir

◆ **go through** *hard times* traverser; *illness* subir; (*check*) revoir; (*read through*) lire en entier

◆ **go under** (*sink*) couler; *of company* faire faillite

◆ **go up** (*climb*) monter; *of prices* augmenter

◆ **go without 1** *v/t food etc* se passer de **2** *v/i* s'en passer

'go-ahead 1 *n* feu vert *m* **2** *adj* (*enterprising*, *dynamic*) entreprenant, dynamique

goal [goʊl] *in sport*, (*objective*) but *m*; **goalkeeper** gardien *m* de but; **goal kick** remise *f* en jeu; **goalpost** poteau *m* de but

goat [goʊt] chèvre *m*

gobble ['gɑːbl] dévorer

gobbledygook ['gɑːbldɪguːk] F charabia *m* F

'go-between intermédiaire *m/f*

god [gɑːd] dieu *m*; ***thank God!*** Dieu merci!

'godchild filleul(e) *m*(*f*); **godfather** *also in mafia* parrain *m*; **godmother** marraine *m*

gofer ['goʊfər] F coursier(-ière) *m*(*f*)

goggles ['gɑːgl] lunettes *fpl*

goings-on [goʊɪŋz'ɑːn] activités *fpl*

gold [goʊld] **1** *n* or *m* **2** *adj* en or; *ingot* d'or; **golden** *sky* doré; *hair also* d'or; **golden wedding** noces *fpl* d'or; **gold medal** médaille *f* d'or; **gold mine** *fig* mine *f* d'or

golf [gɑːlf] golf *m*; **golf ball** balle *f* de golf; **golf club** *organization*, *stick* club *m* de golf; **golf course** terrain *m* de golf; **golfer** golfeur(-euse) *m*(*f*)

good [gʊd] bon; *weather* beau; *child* sage; **goodbye** au revoir; **good-for-nothing** *n* bon(ne) *m*(*f*) à rien; **Good Friday** Vendredi *m* saint; **good-humored**, *Br* **good-humoured** jovial; **good-looking** beau; **good-natured** bon, au bon naturel; **goodness** *moral* bonté *f*; *of fruit etc* bonnes choses *fpl*; **goods** COM marchandises *fpl*; **goodwill** bonne volonté *f*

goof [guːf] F gaffer F

goose [guːs] oie *f*; **goose bumps** chair *f* de poule

gorgeous ['gɔːrdʒəs] magnifique, superbe
gospel ['gɑːspl] évangile *m*
gossip ['gɑːsɪp] **1** *n* potins *mpl*; *malicious* commérages *mpl*; *person* commère *f* **2** *v/i* bavarder; *maliciously* faire des commérages; **gossip column** échos *mpl*
gourmet ['gʊrmeɪ] gourmet *m*
govern ['gʌvərn] gouverner; **government** gouvernement *m*; **governor** gouverneur *m*
gown [gaʊn] robe *f*; *wedding dress* robe *f* de mariée; *of academic, judge* toge *f*; *of surgeon* blouse *f*
grab [græb] saisir; *food* avaler
grace [greɪs] *of dancer etc* grâce *f*; *before meals* bénédicité *m*; **graceful** gracieux; **gracious** *person* bienveillant; *style* élégant
grade [greɪd] **1** *n* (*quality*) qualité *f*; EDU classe *f*; (*mark*) note *f* **2** *v/t* classer; *school work* noter; **grade crossing** passage *m* à niveau; **grade school** école *f* primaire
gradient ['greɪdɪənt] pente *f*
gradual ['grædʒʊəl] graduel; **gradually** peu à peu, progressivement
graduate 1 ['grædʒʊət] *n* diplômé(e) *m(f)* **2** ['grædʒʊeɪt] *v/i* obtenir son diplôme (***from*** de); **graduation** obtention *f* du diplôme
graffiti [grə'fiːtiː] graffitis *mpl*; *single* graffiti *m*
graft [græft] **1** *n* BOT, MED greffe *f*; F (*corruption*) corruption *f* **2** *v/t* BOT, MED greffer
grain [greɪn] blé *m*; *of rice etc, in wood* grain *m*
gram [græm] gramme *m*
grammar ['græmər] grammaire *f*; **grammatical** grammatical
grand [grænd] **1** *adj* grandiose; F (*very good*) génial F **2** *n* F (*$1000*) mille dollars *mpl*; **grandchild** petit-fils *m*, petite-fille *f*; **granddaughter** petite-fille *f*; **grandeur** grandeur *f*; **grandfather** grand-père *m*; **grand jury** grand jury *m*; **grandmother** grand-mère *f*; **grandparents** grands-parents *mpl*; **grand piano** piano *m* à queue; **grandson** petit-fils *m*
granite ['grænɪt] granit *m*
grant [grænt] **1** *n money* subvention *f* **2** *v/t wish, visa* accorder
granule ['grænuːl] grain *m*
grape [greɪp] (grain *m* de) raisin *m*; ***some ~s*** du raisin; **grapefruit juice** jus *m* de pamplemousse
graph [græf] graphique *m*, courbe *f*; **graphic 1** *adj* (*vivid*) très réaliste **2** *n* COMPUT graphique *m*
◆ **grapple with** ['græpl] *attacker* en venir aux prises avec; *problem etc* s'attaquer

à
grasp [græsp] **1** *n physical* prise *f*; *mental* compréhension *f* **2** *v/t physically* saisir; (*understand*) comprendre
grass [græs] herbe *f*; **grasshopper** sauterelle *f*; **grass roots** *people* base *f*; **grassy** ['græsɪ] herbeux, herbu
grate¹ [greɪt] *n metal* grille *f*
grate² [greɪt] **1** *v/t in cooking* râper **2** *v/i*: **~ on the ear** faire mal aux oreilles
grateful ['greɪtful] reconnaissant; **gratefully** avec reconnaissance
gratify ['grætɪfaɪ] satisfaire
grating ['greɪtɪŋ] **1** *n* grille *f* **2** *adj sound, voice* grinçant
gratitude ['grætɪtu:d] gratitude *f*, reconnaissance *f*
grave¹ [greɪv] *n* tombe *f*
grave² [greɪv] *adj* grave
gravel ['grævl] gravier *m*
'gravestone pierre *f* tombale; **graveyard** cimetière *m*
gravity ['grævətɪ] PHYS, *of situation* gravité *f*
gray [greɪ] gris; **gray-haired** aux cheveux gris
graze¹ [greɪz] *v/i of cow etc* paître
graze² [greɪz] **1** *v/t arm etc* écorcher **2** *n* écorchure *f*
grease [gri:s] *for cooking* graisse *f*; *for car* lubrifiant *m*; **greasy** gras; (*covered in grease*) graisseux
great [greɪt] grand; *mistake, sum* gros; F (*very good*) super F; **Great Britain** Grande-Bretagne *f*; **greatly** beaucoup; ***not ~ different*** pas très différent; **greatness** grandeur *f*
Greece [gri:s] Grèce *f*
greed [gri:d] *for money* avidité *f*; *for food also* gourmandise *f*; **greedily** avec avidité; **greedy** *for money* avide; *for food also* gourmand
Greek [gri:k] **1** *n* Grec(que) *m(f)*; *language* grec *m* **2** *adj* grec
green [gri:n] vert; **green beans** haricots *mpl* verts; **green belt** ceinture *f* verte; **green card** (*work permit*) permis *m* de travail; **greenhouse effect** effet *m* de serre; **greens** légumes *mpl* verts
greet [gri:t] saluer; (*welcome*) accueillir; **greeting** salut *m*
grenade [grɪ'neɪd] grenade *f*
grey [greɪ] *Br* → ***gray***
grid [grɪd] grille *f*; **gridiron** SP terrain *m* de football; **gridlock** *in traffic* embouteillage *m*
grief [gri:f] chagrin *m*, douleur *f*; **grief-stricken** affligé; **grievance** grief *m*; **grieve** être affligé; ***~ for s.o.*** pleurer qn
grill [grɪl] **1** *n on window* grille *f* **2** *v/t* (*interrogate*) mettre sur la sellette
grille [grɪl] grille *f*
grim [grɪm] sinistre, sombre

grimace ['grɪməs] grimace *f*
grime [graɪm] crasse *f*; **grimy** crasseux
grin [grɪn] **1** *n* (large) sourire *m* **2** *v/i* sourire
grind [graɪnd] *coffee* moudre; *meat* hacher
grip [grɪp] saisir, serrer; **gripping** prenant, captivant
gristle ['grɪsl] cartilage *m*
grit [grɪt] **1** *n for roads* gravillon *m* **2** *v/t*: **~ *one's teeth*** grincer des dents; **gritty** F réaliste
groan [groʊn] **1** *n* gémissement *m* **2** *v/i* gémir
groceries ['groʊsərɪz] provisions *fpl*; **grocery store** épicerie *f* l'épicerie
groggy ['grɑːgɪ] F groggy F
groin [grɔɪn] ANAT aine *f*
groom [gruːm] **1** *n for bride* marié *m*; *for horse* palefrenier(-ère) *m(f)* **2** *v/t horse* panser; (*train*, *prepare*) préparer
groove [gruːv] rainure *f*; *on record* sillon *m*
grope [groʊp] **1** *v/i in the dark* tâtonner **2** *v/t sexually* peloter F
gross [groʊs] (*coarse*, *vulgar*) grossier; *exaggeration* gros; FIN brut
ground [graʊnd] **1** *n* sol *m*, terre *f*; *for football etc*, *fig* terrain; (*reason*) motif *m*; ELEC terre *f* **2** *v/t* ELEC mettre une prise de terre à; **grounding** *in subject* bases *fpl*; **groundless** sans fondement; **ground meat** viande *f* hachée; **groundwork** travail *m* préparatoire
group [gruːp] **1** *n* groupe *m* **2** *v/t* grouper
groupie ['gruːpɪ] F groupie *f* F
grouse [graʊs] **1** *n* F rouspéter F **2** *v/i* F plainte *f*
grovel ['grɑːvl] *fig* ramper (***to*** devant)
grow [groʊ] **1** *v/i* grandir; *of plants*, *hair* pousser; *of number* augmenter; *of business* se développer; (*become*) devenir **2** *v/t flowers* faire pousser
◆ **grow up** *of person* devenir adulte; *of city* se développer
growl [graʊl] **1** *n* grognement *m* **2** *v/i* grogner
'grown-up 1 *n* adulte *m/f* **2** *adj* adulte
growth [groʊθ] *of person*, *company* croissance *f*; (*increase*) augmentation *f*; MED tumeur *f*
grudge [grʌdʒ] rancune *f*; **grudging** accordé à contrecœur; *person* plein de ressentiment; **grudgingly** à contrecœur
grueling, *Br* **gruelling** ['gruːəlɪŋ] épuisant
gruff [grʌf] bourru, revêche
grumble ['grʌmbl] ronchonner; **grumbler** grognon(ne) *m(f)*
grunt [grʌnt] **1** *n* grognement *m* **2** *v/i* grogner

guarantee [gærən'tiː] **1** *n* garantie *f* **2** *v/t* garantir; **guarantor** garant(e) *m(f)*
guard [gɑːrd] **1** *n* gardien(ne) *m(f)*; MIL garde *f* **2** *v/t* garder; **guard dog** chien *m* de garde; **guarded** *reply* prudent; **guardian** LAW tuteur(-trice) *m(f)*
guerrilla [gə'rɪlə] guérillero *m*; **guerrilla warfare** guérilla *f*
guess [ges] **1** *n* conjecture *f* **2** *v/t answer* deviner **2** *v/i* deviner; ***I ~ so*** je crois; **guesswork** conjecture(s) *f(pl)*
guest [gest] invité(e) *m(f)*; *in hotel* hôte *m/f*; **guestroom** chambre *f* d'amis
guidance ['gaɪdəns] conseils *mpl*; **guide 1** *n person* guide *m/f*; *book* guide *m* **2** *v/t* guider; **guidebook** guide *m*; **guided missile** missile *m* téléguidé; **guided tour** visite *f* guidée; **guidelines** directives *fpl*
guilt [gɪlt] culpabilité *f*; **guilty** *also* LAW coupable
guinea pig ['gɪnɪpɪg] *also fig* cobaye *m*
guitar [gɪ'tɑːr] guitare *f*; **guitarist** guitariste *m/f*
gulf [gʌlf] golfe *m*; *fig* gouffre *m*
gull [gʌl] mouette *f*; *bigger* goéland *m*
gullet ['gʌlɪt] ANAT gosier *m*
gullible ['gʌlɪbl] crédule
gulp [gʌlp] **1** *n of drink* gorgée *f* **2** *v/i in surprise* dire en s'étranglant
◆ **gulp down** *drink* avaler à grosses gorgées; *food* avaler à grosses bouchées
gum¹ [gʌm] *in mouth* gencive *f*
gum² [gʌm] (*glue*) colle *f*; (*chewing gum*) chewing-gum *m*
gun [gʌn] arme *f* à feu; *pistol* pistolet *m*; *revolver* revolver *m*; *rifle* fusil *m*; *cannon* canon *m*
◆ **gun down** abattre
'**gunfire** coups *mpl* de feu; **gunman** homme *m* armé; **gunshot** coup *m* de feu; **gunshot wound** blessure *f* par balle
gurgle ['gɜːrgl] *of baby* gazouiller; *of drain* gargouiller
guru ['guːruː] *fig* gourou *m*
gush [gʌʃ] *of liquid* jaillir
gust [gʌst] rafale *f*, coup *m* de vent
gusto ['gʌstoʊ]: ***with ~*** avec enthousiasme
gusty ['gʌstɪ] *weather* très venteux
gut [gʌt] **1** *n* intestin *m*; F (*stomach*) bide *m* F **2** *v/t* (*destroy*) ravager; **guts** F (*courage*) cran *m* F; **gutsy** F (*brave*) qui a du cran F
gutter ['gʌtər] *on sidewalk* caniveau *m*; *on roof* gouttière *f*
guy [gaɪ] F type *m* F
guzzle ['gʌzl] *food* engloutir; *drink* avaler

gym [dʒɪm] *sports club* club *m* de gym; *in school* gymnase *m*; *activity* gym(nastique) *f*; **gymnast** gymnaste *m/f*; **gymnastics** gymnastique *f*

gynecology, *Br* **gynaecology** [gaɪnɪ'kɑːlədʒɪ] gynécologie

gypsy ['dʒɪpsɪ] gitan(e) *m(f)*

H

habit ['hæbɪt] habitude *f*

habitable ['hæbɪtəbl] habitable; **habitat** habitat *m*

habitual [hə'bɪʧʊəl] habituel; *smoker, drinker* invétéré

hacker ['hækər] COMPUT pirate *m* informatique

hackneyed ['hæknɪd] rebattu

haemorrhage *Br* → ***hemorrhage***

haggard ['hægərd] hagard, égaré

haggle ['hægl] chipoter

hail [heɪl] grêle *f*

hair [her] cheveux *mpl*; *single* cheveu *m*; *on body* poils *mpl*; *single* poil *m*; **hairbrush** brosse *f* à cheveux; **haircut** coupe *f* de cheveux; ***have a ~*** se faire couper les cheveux **'hairdo** coiffure *f*; **hairdresser** coiffeur(-euse) *m(f)*; **hairdryer** sèche-cheveux *m*; **hairpin** épingle *f* à cheveux; **hairpin curve** virage *m* en épingle à cheveux; **hair-raising** horrifique; **hair remover** crème *f* épilatoire; **hair-splitting** ergotage *m*; **hairstyle** coiffure *f*; **hairstylist** coiffeur(-euse) *m(f)*; **hairy** *arm, animal* poilu; F (*frightening*) effrayant

half [hæf] **1** *n* moitié *f*; ***~ past ten*** dix heures et demie; ***~ an hour*** une demi-heure **2** *adj* demi; ***at ~ price*** à moitié prix **3** *adv* à moitié; **half-hearted** tiède; **half time** SP mi-temps *f*; **halfway 1** *adj*: ***reach the ~ point*** être à la moitié **2** *adv in space, distance* à mi-chemin

hall [hɒːl] (*large room*) salle *f*; (*hallway in house*) vestibule *m*

Hallowe'en [hæloʊ'wiːn] halloween *f*

halo ['heɪloʊ] auréole *f*

halt [hɒːlt] **1** *v/i* faire halte, s'arrêter **2** *v/t* arrêter

halve [hæv] couper en deux; *input, costs* réduire de moitié

ham [hæm] jambon *m*; **hamburger** hamburger *m*

hammer ['hæmər] **1** *n* marteau *m* **2** *v/i* marteler; ***~ at the door*** frapper à la porte à coups redoublés

hammock ['hæmək] hamac *m*

hamper[1] ['hæmpər] *n for food* pannier *m*

hamper[2] ['hæmpər] *v/t* (*ob-*

struct) entraver, gêner

hand [hænd] **1** *n* main *f*; *of clock* aiguille *f*; (*worker*) ouvrier(-ère) *m*(*f*); ***at ~, to ~*** *thing* sous la main; ***at ~*** *person* à disposition; ***on the one ~ ..., on the other ~*** d'une part ..., d'autre part; ***on your right ~*** sur votre droite; ***give s.o. a ~*** donner un coup de main à qn

◆ **hand down** transmettre

◆ **hand out** distribuer

◆ **hand over** donner; *to authorities* livrer

'**handbag** *Br* sac *m* à main; **hand baggage** bagages *mpl* à main; **handcuff** menotter; **handcuffs** menottes *fpl*

handicap ['hændɪkæp] handicap *m*; **handicapped** handicapé; **handiwork** *object* ouvrage *m*

handkerchief ['hæŋkərtʃɪf] mouchoir *m*

handle ['hændl] **1** *n of door, suitcase* poignée *f*; *of knife, pan* manche *m* **2** *v/t goods* manier, manipuler; *case, deal* s'occuper de; **handlebars** guidon *m*

'**hand luggage** bagages *m* à main; **handmade** fait (à la) main; **hands-free** mains libres; **handshake** poignée *f* de main

handsome ['hænsəm] beau

'**handwriting** écriture *f*; **handwritten** écrit à la main; **handy** *device* pratique

hang ['hæŋ] **1** *v/t person* pendre **2** *v/i of dress, hair* tomber

◆ **hang on** (*wait*) attendre

◆ **hang up** TELEC raccrocher

hangar ['hæŋər] hangar *m*

hanger ['hæŋər] *for clothes* cintre *m*

'**hang glider** *person* libériste *m/f*; *device* deltaplane *m*; **hang gliding** deltaplane *m*; **hangover** gueule *f* de bois

hankie, hanky ['hæŋkɪ] F mouchoir *m*

haphazard [hæp'hæzərd] au hasard

happen ['hæpn] se passer, arriver

happily ['hæpɪlɪ] gaiement; *spend* volontiers; (*luckily*) heureusement; **happiness** bonheur *m*; **happy** heureux; **happy-go-lucky** insouciant

harass [hə'ræs] harceler; **harassed** surmené; **harassment** harcèlement *m*

harbor, *Br* **harbour** ['hɑːrbər] **1** *n* port *m* **2** *v/t criminal* héberger; *grudge* entretenir

hard [hɑːrd] **1** *adj* dur; *facts* brut; *evidence* concret **2** *adv work* dur; *rain, pull, push* fort; ***try ~*** faire tout son possible; **hardback** livre *m* cartonné; **hard-boiled** *egg* dur; **hard copy** copie *f* sur papier; **hard core** *pornography* (pornographie *f*) hard *m*; **hard currency** monnaie *f* forte; **hard disk** disque *m*

dur; **harden 1** *v/t* durcir **2** *v/i of glue, attitude* se durcir; **hard hat** casque *m*; (*construction worker*) ouvrier *m* du bâtiment; **hardheaded** réaliste; **hardhearted** au cœur dur; **hard line** ligne *f* dure; **hardliner** dur(e) *m(f)*
hardly ['hɑːrdlɪ] à peine; *see s.o. etc* presque pas
hardness ['hɑːrdnɪs] dureté *f*; (*difficulty*) difficulté *f*; **hardship** privation *f*; **hardware** COMPUT hardware *m*, matériel *m*; **hardware store** quincaillerie *f*; **hard-working** travailleur; **hardy** robuste
harm [hɑːrm] **1** *n* mal *m* **2** *v/t* faire du mal à; *non-physically* nuire à; **harmful** *substance* nocif; *influence* nuisible; **harmless** inoffensif
harmonious [hɑːr'moʊnɪəs] harmonieux; **harmonize** s'harmoniser; **harmony** harmonie *f*
harsh [hɑːrʃ] *words* dur; *color* criard; *light* cru; **harshly** durement
harvest ['hɑːrvɪst] moisson *f*
hash browns [hæʃ] pommes de terre *fpl* sautées; **hash mark** caractère *m* #, dièse *f*
haste [heɪst] hâte *f*; **hastily** à la hâte; **hasty** hâtif, précipité
hat [hæt] chapeau *m*
hatch [hætʃ] *for serving* guichet *m*; *on ship* écoutille *f*
◆ **hatch out** éclore
hatchet ['hætʃɪt] hachette *f*; ***bury the ~*** enterrer la hache de guerre
hate [heɪt] **1** *n* haine *f* **2** *v/t* détester, haïr; **hatred** haine *f*
haul [hɒːl] **1** *n of fish* coup *m* de filet **2** *v/t* (*pull*) tirer, traîner; **haulage** transports *mpl* (routiers)
haunch [hɒːntʃ] *of person* hanche *f*; *of animal* arrière-train *m*
haunt [hɒːnt] hanter; ***this place is ~ed*** ce lieu est hanté
have [hæv] **1** *v/t* (*own*) avoir; *breakfast, lunch* prendre; ***~ (got) to*** devoir; ***you don't ~ to do it*** tu n'es pas obligé de le faire; ***do I ~ to pay?*** est-ce qu'il faut payer?; ***I'll ~ it sent to you*** je vous le ferai envoyer; ***I had my hair cut*** je me suis fait couper les cheveux **2** *v/aux* (*past tense*): ***~ you seen her?*** l'as-tu vue?; ***they ~ arrived*** ils sont arrivés
◆ **have on** (*wear*) porter
haven ['heɪvn] *fig* havre *m*
hawk [hɒːk] *also fig* faucon *m*
hay [heɪ] foin *m*; **hay fever** rhume *m* des foins
hazard ['hæzərd] danger *m*; **hazard lights** MOT feux *mpl* de détresse; **hazardous** dangereux
haze [heɪz] brume *f*; **hazy** *view* brumeux; *image* flou; *memories* vague
he [hiː] il; ***there ~ is*** le voilà
head [hed] **1** *n* tête *f*; (*boss,*

leader) chef *m/f*; *Br* : *of school* directeur(-trice) *m(f)*; *on beer* mousse *f* **2** *v/t* (*lead*) être à la tête de; *ball* jouer de la tête

◆ **head for** se diriger vers

'**headache** mal *m* de tête; **headband** bandeau *m*; **header** *in soccer* (coup *m* de) tête *f*; *in document* en-tête *m*; **headhunter** COM chasseur *m* de têtes; **heading** *in list* titre *m*; **headlamp** phare *m*; **headline** *in newspaper* (gros) titre *m*; **head office** *of company* bureau *m* central; **head-on 1** *adv crash* de front **2** *adj* frontal; **headphones** écouteurs *mpl*; **headquarters** quartier *m* général; **headrest** appui-tête *m*; **headroom** *under bridge* hauteur *f* limite; *in car* hauteur *f* au plafond; **headscarf** foulard *m*; **headstrong** entêté; **head waiter** maître *m* d'hôtel; **heady** *wine etc* capiteux

heal [hi:l] guérir

health [helθ] santé *f*; **health food store** magasin *m* d'aliments diététiques; **health insurance** assurance *f* maladie; **healthy** *person* en bonne santé; *food*, *lifestyle*, *economy* sain

heap [hi:p] tas *m*

hear [hɪr] entendre

◆ **hear from** (*have news from*) avoir des nouvelles de

hearing ['hɪrɪŋ] ouïe *f*; LAW audience *f*; **hearing aid** appareil *m* acoustique, audiophone *m*

hearse [hɜ:rs] corbillard *m*

heart [hɑ:rt] *also fig* cœur *m*; ***know sth by ~*** connaître qch par cœur; **heart attack** crise *f* cardiaque; **heartbreaking** navrant; **heartbroken**: ***be ~*** avoir le cœur brisé; **heartburn** brûlures *fpl* d'estomac

hearth [hɑ:rθ] foyer *m*, âtre *f*

heartless ['hɑ:rtlɪs] insensible, cruel; **hearty** *appetite* gros; *meal* copieux; *person* jovial

heat [hi:t] chaleur *f*

◆ **heat up** réchauffer

heated ['hi:tɪd] *pool* chauffé; *discussion* passionné; **heater** radiateur *m*; *in car* chauffage *m*; **heating** chauffage *m*; **heatproof, heat-resistant** résistant à la chaleur; **heatwave** vague *f* de chaleur

heave [hi:v] (*lift*) soulever

heaven ['hevn] ciel *m*; **heavenly** F divin

heavy ['hevɪ] *also food*, *loss* lourd; *cold* grand; *rain*, *accent* fort; *traffic*, *smoker*, *bleeding* gros; **heavy-duty** très résistant; **heavyweight** SP poids lourd

hectic ['hektɪk] agité

hedge [hedʒ] haie *f*

heel [hi:l] talon *m*; **heel bar** talon-minute *m*

hefty ['heftɪ] gros; *person also*

costaud

height [haɪt] *of person* taille *f*; *of building* hauteur *f*; *of airplane* altitude *f*; **heighten** *tension* accroître

heir [er] héritier *m*; **heiress** héritière *f*

helicopter ['helɪkɑːptər] hélicoptère *m*

hell [hel] enfer *m*; ***what the ~ are you doing?*** F mais enfin qu'est-ce que tu fais?; ***go to ~!*** F va te faire foutre! P

hello [hə'loʊ] bonjour; TELEC allô

helmet ['helmɪt] casque *m*

help [help] **1** *n* aide *f* **2** *v/t* aider; ***~ o.s.*** *to food* se servir; ***I can't ~ it*** je ne peux pas m'en empêcher; **helper** aide *m/f*, assistant(e) *m(f)*; **helpful** *advice* utile; *person* serviable; **helping** *of food* portion *f*; **helpless** (*unable to cope*) sans défense; (*powerless*) impuissant; **helplessness** impuissance *f*

hem [hem] *of dress etc* ourlet *m*

hemisphere ['hemɪsfɪr] hémisphère *m*

'hemline ourlet *m*

hemorrhage ['hemərɪdʒ] **1** *n* hémorragie *f* **2** *v/i* faire une hémorragie

hen [hen] poule *f*; **hen party** soirée *f* entre femmes

hepatitis [hepə'taɪtɪs] hépatite *f*

her [hɜːr] **1** *adj* son, sa; *pl* ses **2** *pron object* la; *before vowel* l'; *indirect object* lui, à elle; *with prep* elle; ***I know ~*** je la connais; ***I gave ~ a dollar*** je lui ai donné un dollar; ***this is for ~*** c'est pour elle; ***who? – ~*** qui? – elle

herb [ɜːrb] herbe *f*; **herb(al) tea** tisane *f*

herd [hɜːrd] troupeau *m*

here [hɪr] ici; ***in ~, over ~*** ici; ***~'s to you!*** *as toast* à votre santé!; ***~ you are*** *giving sth* voilà

hereditary [hə'redɪterɪ] héréditaire; **heredity** hérédité *f*; **heritage** héritage *m*

hero ['hɪroʊ] héros *m*; **heroic** héroïque; **heroically** héroïquement

heroin ['heroʊɪn] héroïne *f*

heroine ['heroʊɪn] héroïne *f*

heroism ['heroʊɪzm] héroïsme *f*

herpes ['hɜːrpiːz] herpès *m*

hers [hɜːrz] le sien, la sienne; *pl* les siens, les siennes; ***it's ~*** c'est à elle

herself [hɜːr'self] elle-même; *reflexive* se; *after prep* elle; ***she hurt ~*** elle s'est blessée

hesitant ['hezɪtənt] hésitant; **hesitantly** avec hésitation; **hesitate** hésiter; **hesitation** hésitation *f*

heterosexual [hetəroʊ'sekʃʊəl] hétérosexuel

hi [haɪ] salut

hibernate ['haɪbərneɪt] hiberner

hiccup ['hɪkʌp] hoquet *m*; (*minor problem*) hic *m* F

hidden ['hɪdn] caché

hide[1] [haɪd] **1** *v/t* cacher **2** *v/i* se cacher

hide[2] [haɪd] *n of animal* peau *f*; *as product* cuir *m*

hide-and-'seek cache-cache *m*; **hideaway** cachette *f*

hideous ['hɪdɪəs] affreux, horrible

hiding ['haɪdɪŋ] (*beating*) rossée *f*; **hiding place** cachette *f*

hierarchy ['haɪrɑːrkɪ] hiérarchie *f*

high [haɪ] **1** *adj* haut; *salary, price, rent, temperature* élevé; *wind* fort; *speed* grand; *on drugs* défoncé F **2** *n* MOT quatrième *f*; cinquième *f*; *in statistics* pointe *f*; EDU collège *m*, lycée *m*; **highbrow** intellectuel; **highchair** chaise *f* haute; **high-class** de première class; **high-frequency** de haute fréquence; **high-grade** *ore* à haute teneur; **~ *gasoline*** supercarburant *m*; **high-handed** arbitraire; **high-heeled** à hauts talons; **high jump** saut *m* en hauteur; **high-level** à haut niveau; **highlight 1** *n* (*main event*) point *m* marquant; *in hair* reflets *mpl*, mèches *fpl* **2** *v/t with pen* surligner; COMPUT mettre en relief; **highlighter** *pen* surligneur *m*; **highly** *desirable, likely* fort, très; ***think ~ of s.o.*** penser beaucoup de bien de qn; **high performance** *drill, battery* haute performance; **high-pitched** aigu; **high point** *of career* point *m* culminant; **high-powered** *engine* très puissant; *intellectual* très compétent; **high pressure** *weather* anticyclone *m*; **high-pressure** TECH à haute pression; *salesman* de choc; *job, lifestyle* dynamique; **high school** collège *m*, lycée *m*; **high-strung** nerveux, très sensible; **high tech 1** *n* technologie *f* de pointe, high-tech *m* **2** *adj* de pointe, high-tech; **highway** grande route *f*

hijack ['haɪdʒæk] **1** *v/t* détourner **2** *n* détournement *m*; **hijacker** *of plane* pirate *m* de l'air; *of bus* pirate *m* de la route

hike[1] [haɪk] **1** *n* randonnée *f* à pied **2** *v/i* marcher à pied

hike[2] [haɪk] *n in prices* hausse *f*

hiker ['haɪkər] randonneur (-euse) *m*(*f*); **hiking** randonnée *f* (pédestre)

hilarious [hɪ'lerɪəs] hilarant, désopilant

hill [hɪl] colline *f*; (*slope*) côte *f*; **hilltop** sommet *m* de la colline; **hilly** montagneux; *road* vallonné

hilt [hɪlt] poignée *f*

him [hɪm] *object* le; *before vowel* l'; *indirect object, with* *prep* lui; ***I know ~*** je le connais; ***I gave ~ a dollar*** je lui ai donné un dollar; ***this is for ~*** c'est pour lui; ***who? – him*** qui? – lui; **himself** lui-même; *reflexive* se; *after prep* lui; ***he hurt ~*** il s'est blessé

hinder ['hɪndər] gêner, entraver; ***~ s.o. from doing sth*** empêcher qn de faire qch; **hindrance** obstacle *m*

hinge [hɪndʒ] charnière *f*

hint [hɪnt] (*clue*) indice *m*; (*piece of advice*) conseil *m*; (*suggestion*) allusion *f*; *of red, sadness etc* soupçon *m*

hip [hɪp] hanche *f*; **hip pocket** poche *f* revolver

hire ['haɪr] louer

his [hɪz] **1** *adj* son, sa; *pl* ses **2** *pron* le sien, la sienne; *pl* les siens, les siennes; ***it's ~*** c'est à lui

Hispanic [hɪ'spænɪk] **1** *n* Hispano-Américain(e) *m(f)* **2** *adj* hispano-américain

hiss [hɪs] siffler

historian [hɪ'stɔːrɪən] historien(ne) *m(f)*; **historic** historique; **historical** historique; **history** histoire *f*

hit [hɪt] **1** *v/t* frapper; (*collide with*) heurter; ***he was ~ by a bullet*** il a été touché par une balle **2** *n* (*blow*) coup *m*; MUS, (*success*) succès *m*; *on website* visiteur *m*

hitch [hɪʧ] **1** *n* (*problem*) anicroche *f*, accroc *m* **2** *v/t* attacher; **hitchhike** faire du stop; **hitchhiker** auto-stoppeur (-euse) *m(f)*

hi-'tech **1** *n* technologie *f* de pointe, high-tech *m* **2** *adj* de pointe, high-tech

'hitman tueur *m* à gages; **hit-or-miss** aléatoire

HIV [eɪʧaɪ'viː] (= ***human immunodeficiency virus***) V.I.H. *m* (= Virus de l'Immunodéficience Humaine); ***people with ~*** les séropositifs

hive [haɪv] *for bees* ruche *f*

HIV-'positive séropositif

hoard [hɔːrd] **1** *n* réserves *fpl* **2** *v/t money* amasser; *in times of shortage* faire des réserves de

hoarse [hɔːrs] rauque

hoax [hoʊks] canular *m*

hobble ['hɑːbl] boitiller

hobby ['hɑːbɪ] hobby *m*

hobo ['hoʊboʊ] F vagabond *m*

hockey ['hɑːkɪ] (*ice hockey*) hockey *m* (sur glace)

hog [hɑːg] (*pig*) cochon *m*

hoist [hɔɪst] **1** *n* palan *m* **2** *v/t* hisser

hold [hoʊld] **1** *v/t in hand* tenir; (*support, keep in place*) soutenir; *passport, license, prisoner* détenir; (*contain*) contenir; *job, post* occuper; ***~ the line*** TELEC ne quittez pas! **2** *n in ship* cale *f*; *in plane* soute *f*; ***take ~ of sth*** saisir qch

◆ **hold back** *crowds* contenir; *facts* retenir

◆ **hold out 1** *v/t hand* tendre; *prospect* offrir **2** *v/i of supplies* durer; (*survive*) tenir (bon)

◆ **hold up** *hand* lever; *bank etc* attaquer; (*make late*) retenir

holder ['houldər] (*container*) boîtier *m*; *of passport, ticket, record* détenteur(-trice) *m(f)*; **holding company** holding *m*; **holdup** (*robbery*) hold-up *m*; (*delay*) retard *m*

hole [houl] trou *m*

holiday ['hɑːlədeɪ] jour *m* de congé; *Br*: *period* vacances *fpl*

hollow ['hɑːlou] creux; *promise* faux

holocaust ['hɑːləkɒːst] holocauste *m*

hologram ['hɑːləgræm] hologramme *m*

holster ['houlstər] holster *m*

holy ['houlɪ] saint; **Holy Spirit** Saint-Esprit *m*

home [houm] **1** *n* maison *f*; (*native country, town*) patrie *f*; *for old people* maison *f* de retraite; ***at*** ~ chez moi/lui *etc*; (*in own country*) dans mon/son *etc* pays; SP à domicile; ***make o.s. at*** ~ faire comme chez soi **2** *adv* à la maison, chez soi; (*in own country*) dans son pays; (*in own town*) dans sa ville; ***go*** ~ rentrer; **home address** adresse *f* personnelle; **home banking** services *mpl* télématiques (bancaires); **homecoming** retour *m* (à la maison); **home computer** ordinateur *m* familial; **home game** match *m* à domicile; **homeless 1** *adj* sans abri **2** *npl*: ***the*** ~ les sans-abri *mpl*, les S.D.F. *mpl* (sans domicile fixe); **homeloving** casanier; **homely** (*homelike*) simple, comme à la maison; (*not good-looking*) sans beauté; **homemade** fait (à la) maison; **home page** COMPUT page *f* d'accueil; **homesick**: ***be*** ~ avoir le mal du pays; **home town** ville *f* natale; **homeward** *to own house* vers la maison; *to own country* vers son pays; **homework** EDU devoirs *mpl*

homicide ['hɑːmɪsaɪd] homicide *m*; *department* homicides *mpl*

homophobia [houmə'foubɪə] homophobie *f*

homosexual [houmə'sekʃuəl] **1** *adj* homosexuel **2** *n* homosexuel(le) *m(f)*

honest ['ɑːnɪst] honnête; **honestly** honnêtement; ~**!** vraiment!; **honesty** honnêteté *f*

honey ['hʌnɪ] miel *m*; F (*darling*) chéri(e) *m(f)*; **honeymoon** lune *f* de miel

honk [hɑːŋk] *horn* klaxonner

honor ['ɑːnər] **1** *n* honneur *f* **2** *v/t* honorer; **honorable** honorable; **honour** *Br* → ***honor***

hood [hʊd] *over head* capuche *f*; *over cooker* hotte *f*; MOT capot *m*; F (*gangster*) truand *m*

hook [hʊk] *to hang clothes on* patère *f*; *for fishing* hameçon *m*; ***off the ~*** TELEC décroché; **hooked** accro F; ***be ~ on sth*** être accro de qch; **hooker** F putain *f* P; *in rugby* talonneur *m*

hoot [huːt] **1** *v/t horn* donner un coup de **2** *v/i of car* klaxonner; *of owl* huer

hop [hɑːp] sauter, sautiller

hope [hoʊp] **1** *n* espoir *m* **2** *v/i* espérer; ***I ~ so*** je l'espère, j'espère que oui **2** *v/t*: ***~ that*** espérer que; **hopeful** plein d'espoir; (*promising*) prometteur; **hopefully** *say*, *wait* avec espoir; (*I/we hope*) avec un peu de chance; **hopeless** *position* sans espoir, désespéré; (*useless*: *person*) nul

horizon [hə'raɪzn] horizon *m*; **horizontal** horizontal

hormone ['hɔːrmoʊn] hormone *f*

horn [hɔːrn] *of animal* corne *f*; MOT klaxon *m*

hornet ['hɔːrnɪt] frelon *m*

horny ['hɔːrnɪ] F *sexually* excité

horrible ['hɑːrɪbl] horrible, affreux; **horrify** horrifier; **horrifying** horrifiant; **horror** horreur *f*

horse [hɔːrs] cheval *m*; **horse race** course *f* de chevaux; **horseshoe** fer *m* à cheval

horticulture horticulture *f*

hose [hoʊz] tuyau *m*

hospitable ['hɑːspɪtəbl] hospitalier

hospital ['hɑːspɪtl] hôpital *m*; **hospitality** hospitalité *f*

host [hoʊst] *at party* hôte *m/f*; *of TV program* présentateur(-trice) *m(f)*

hostage ['hɑːstɪdʒ] otage *m*; **hostage taker** preneur(-euse) *m(f)* d'otages

hostel ['hɑːstl] *for students* foyer *m*; (*youth ~*) auberge *f* de jeunesse

hostess ['hoʊstɪs] hôtesse *f*

hostile ['hɑːstl] hostile; **hostility** hostilité *f*; ***hostilities*** hostilités

hot [hɑːt] chaud; (*spicy*) épicé, fort; ***I'm ~*** j'ai chaud; ***it's ~*** *weather* il fait chaud; **hot dog** hot-dog *m*

hotel [hoʊ'tel] hôtel *m*

hour ['aʊr] heure *f*

house [haʊs] maison *f*; ***at your ~*** chez vous; **housebreaking** cambriolage *m*; **household** ménage *m*; **household name** nom *m* connu de tous; **housekeeper** femme *f* de ménage; **House of Representatives** Chambre *f* des Représentants; **housewarming (party)** pendaison *f* de crémaillère; **housewife** femme *f* au foyer; **housework** travaux *mpl* domestiques; **housing**

logement *m*; TECH boîtier *m*
hovel ['hɑːvl] taudis *m*
hover ['hɑːvər] planer
how [haʊ] comment; *~ are you?* comment allez-vous?; *~ about a drink?* et si on allait prendre un pot?; *~ much?* combien?; *~ much is it? cost* combien ça coûte?; *~ many?* combien?; *~ often?* tous les combien?; *~ sad!* comme c'est triste!; **however** cependant; *~ big they are* qu'ils soient grands ou non
howl [haʊl] hurler
hub [hʌb] *of wheel* moyeu *m*; **hubcap** enjoliveur *m*
◆ **huddle together** ['hʌdl] se blottir les uns contre les autres
hug [hʌg] serrer dans ses bras
huge [hjuːdʒ] énorme
hull [hʌl] coque *f*
hum [hʌm] fredonner
human ['hjuːmən] **1** *n* être *m* humain **2** *adj* humain; **human being** être *m* humain
humane [hjuː'meɪn] humain, plein d'humanité
humanitarian [hjuːmænɪ'terɪən] humanitaire
humanity [hjuː'mænətɪ] humanité *f*; **human race** race *f* humaine; **human resources** ressources *fpl* humaines
humble ['hʌmbl] modeste
humdrum ['hʌmdrʌm] monotone, banal
humid ['hjuːmɪd] humide; **humidifier** humidificateur *m*; **humidity** humidité *f*
humiliate [hjuː'mɪlɪeɪt] humilier; **humiliating** humiliant; **humiliation** humiliation *f*; **humility** humilité *f*
humor ['hjuːmər] humour *m*; (*mood*) humeur *f*; *sense of ~* sens *m* de l'humour; **humorous** drôle; **humour** *Br* → *humor*
hunch [hʌntʃ] (*idea*) intuition *f*, pressentiment *m*
hundred ['hʌndrəd] cent *m*; **hundredth** centième
hunger ['hʌŋgər] faim *f*
hung-'over: *be ~* avoir la gueule de bois F
hungry ['hʌŋgrɪ] affamé; *I'm ~* j'ai faim
hunk [hʌŋk] gros morceau *m*; F *man* beau mec F
hunt [hʌnt] **1** *n* chasse *f* (*for* à); *for new leader, missing child etc* recherche *f* (*for* de) **2** *v/t* chasser; **hunter** chasseur (-euse) *m*(*f*); **hunting** chasse *f*
hurdle ['hɜːrdl] SP haie *f*; *fig* obstacle *m*
hurl [hɜːrl] lancer, jeter
hurray [hʊ'reɪ] hourra
hurricane ['hʌrɪkən] ouragan *m*
hurried ['hʌrɪd] précipité; **hurry 1** *n* hâte *f*; *be in a ~* être pressé **2** *v/i* se dépêcher
◆ **hurry up 1** *v/i* se dépêcher; *hurry up!* dépêchez-vous! **2**

v/t presser
hurt [hɜːrt] **1** *v/i* faire mal **2** *v/t* faire mal à; *emotionally* blesser
husband ['hʌzbənd] mari *m*
hush [hʌʃ] silence *m*
◆ **hush up** *scandal etc* étouffer
husky ['hʌskɪ] *voice* rauque
hut [hʌt] cabane *f*, hutte *f*
hybrid ['haɪbrɪd] hybride *m*
hydrant ['haɪdrənt] prise *f* d'eau; (*fire* ~) bouche *f* d'incendie
hydraulic [haɪ'drɒːlɪk] hydraulique
hydroelectric [haɪdroʊɪ'lektrɪk] hydroélectrique
hydrogen ['haɪdrədʒən] hydrogène *m*
hygiene ['haɪdʒiːn] hygiène *f*; **hygienic** hygiénique
hymn [hɪm] hymne *m*
hype [haɪp] battage *m* publicitaire
hyperactive [haɪpər'æktɪv] hyperactif; **hypersensitive** hypersensible; **hypertext** COMPUT hypertexte *m*
hypnosis [hɪp'noʊsɪs] hypnose *f*; **hypnotize** hypnotiser
hypocrisy [hɪ'pɑːkrəsɪ] hypocrisie *f*; **hypocrite** hypocrite *m*/*f*; **hypocritical** hypocrite
hypothesis [haɪ'pɑːθəsɪs] hypothèse *f*; **hypothetical** hypothétique
hysterectomy [hɪstə'rektəmɪ] hystérectomie *f*
hysteria [hɪ'stɪrɪə] hystérie *f*; **hysterical** hystérique; F (*very funny*) à mourir de rire F; **hysterics** crise *f* de nerfs; *laughter* fou rire *m*

I

I [aɪ] je; *before vowel* j'; ***here ~ am*** me voici
ice [aɪs] glace *f*; *on road* verglas *m*; **icebox** glacière *f*; **ice cream** glace *f*; **ice cube** glaçon *m*; **iced** *drink* glacé; **ice hockey** hockey *m* sur glace; **ice rink** patinoire *f*; **ice skate** patin *m* (à glace); **ice skating** patinage *m* (sur glace)
icon ['aɪkɑːn] symbole *m*; COMPUT icône *f*
icy ['aɪsɪ] gelé; *welcome* glacial
ID [aɪ'diː] (= ***identity***) identité *f*
idea [aɪ'diːə] idée *f*; **ideal** idéal; **idealistic** idéaliste
identical [aɪ'dentɪkl] identique; **identification** identification *f*; (*papers etc*) papiers *mpl* d'identité; **identify** identifier; **identity** identité *f*; ***~ card*** carte *f* d'identité
ideological [aɪdɪə'lɑːdʒɪkl] idéologique; **ideology** idéologie *f*

idiomatic [ɪdɪə'mætɪk] (*natural*) idiomatique
idiot ['ɪdɪət] idiot(e) *m*(*f*); **idiotic** idiot, bête
idle ['aɪdl] **1** *adj* (*not working*) inoccupé; (*lazy*) paresseux; *threat* oiseux; *machinery* non utilisé **2** *v/i of engine* tourner au ralenti
idol ['aɪdl] idole *f*; **idolize** idolâtrer
if [ɪf] si
ignite [ɪg'naɪt] mettre le feu à; **ignition** *in car* allumage *m*; **~ key** clef *f* de contact
ignorance ['ɪgnərəns] ignorance *f*; **ignorant** ignorant; (*rude*) grossier; **ignore** ignorer
ill [ɪl] malade; ***fall ~, be taken ~*** tomber malade
illegal [ɪ'liːgl] illégal
illegible [ɪ'ledʒəbl] illisible
illegitimate [ɪlɪ'dʒɪtɪmət] *child* illégitime
illicit [ɪ'lɪsɪt] illicite
illiterate [ɪ'lɪtərət] illettré
illness ['ɪlnɪs] maladie *f*
illogical [ɪ'lɑːdʒɪkl] illogique
ill'treat maltraiter
illuminating [ɪ'luːmɪneɪtɪŋ] *remarks etc* éclairant
illusion [ɪ'luːʒn] illusion *f*
illustrate ['ɪləstreɪt] illustrer; **illustration** illustration *f*; **illustrator** illustrateur(-trice) *m*(*f*)
image ['ɪmɪdʒ] image *f*
imaginary [ɪ'mædʒɪnərɪ] imaginaire; **imagination** imagination *f*; **imaginative** imaginatif; **imagine** imaginer; ***you're imagining things*** tu te fais des idées
IMF [aɪem'ef] (= ***International Monetary Fund***) F.M.I. *m* (= Fonds *m* Monétaire International)
imitate ['ɪmɪteɪt] imiter; **imitation** imitation *f*
immaculate [ɪ'mækjʊlət] impeccable
immature [ɪmə'tur] immature
immediate [ɪ'miːdɪət] immédiat; **immediately** immédiatement
immense [ɪ'mens] immense
immerse [ɪ'mɜːrs] immerger, plonger
immigrant ['ɪmɪgrənt] immigrant(e) *m*(*f*); **immigrate** immigrer; **immigration** immigration *f*
imminent ['ɪmɪnənt] imminent
immobilize [ɪ'moʊbɪlaɪz] immobiliser
immoderate [ɪ'mɑːdərət] immodéré
immoral [ɪ'mɒːrəl] immoral; **immorality** immoralité *f*
immortal [ɪ'mɔːrtl] immortel; **immortality** immortalité *f*
immune [ɪ'mjuːn] *to illness* immunisé (***to*** contre); *from ruling* exempt (***from*** de); **immune system** MED système *m* immunitaire; **immunity** immunité *f*; *from ruling* exemption *f*

impact ['ɪmpækt] impact *m*
impair [ɪm'per] affaiblir
impartial [ɪm'pɑːrʃl] impartial
impassable [ɪm'pæsəbl] *road* impraticable
impassioned [ɪm'pæʃnd] *speech, plea* passionné
impatience [ɪm'peɪʃəns] impatience *f*; **impatient** impatient
impatiently impatiemment
impeccable [ɪm'pekəbl] impeccable
impede [ɪm'piːd] gêner, empêcher; **impediment** *obstacle* obstacle *m*; ***speech ~*** défaut *m* d'élocution
impending [ɪm'pendɪŋ] imminent
imperative [ɪm'perətɪv] **1** *adj* impératif **2** *n* GRAM impératif *m*
imperfect [ɪm'pɜːrfekt] **1** *adj* imparfait **2** *n* GRAM imparfait *m*
impersonal [ɪm'pɜːrsənl] impersonnel; **impersonate** *as a joke* imiter; *illegally* se faire passer pour
impertinence [ɪm'pɜːrtɪnəns] impertinence *f*; **impertinent** impertinent
impervious [ɪm'pɜːrvɪəs]: ***~ to*** insensible à
impetuous [ɪm'petʃuəs] impétueux
impetus ['ɪmpətəs] *of campaign etc* force *f*, élan *m*
implement ['ɪmplɪmənt] **1** *n* instrument *m*, outil *m* **2** *v/t* ['ɪmplɪment] appliquer
implicate ['ɪmplɪkeɪt] impliquer; **implication** implication *f*
implore [ɪm'plɔːr] implorer
imply [ɪm'plaɪ] impliquer; (*suggest*) suggérer
impolite [ɪmpə'laɪt] impoli
import ['ɪmpɔːrt] **1** *n* importation *f* **2** *v/t* importer
importance [ɪm'pɔː;rtəns] importance *f*; **important** important
importer [ɪm'pɔːrtər] importateur(-trice) *m(f)*
impose [ɪm'pouz] *tax* imposer; **imposing** imposant
impossibility [ɪmpɑːsɪ'bɪlɪtɪ] impossibilité *f*; **impossible** impossible
impotence ['ɪmpətəns] impuissance *f*; **impotent** impuissant
impractical [ɪm'præktɪkəl] dénué de sens pratique
impress [ɪm'pres] impressionner; **impression** impression *f*; (*impersonation*) imitation *f*; **impressive** impressionnant
imprint ['ɪmprɪnt] *of credit card* empreinte *f*
imprison [ɪm'prɪzn] emprisonner; **imprisonment** emprisonnement *m*
improbable [ɪm'prɑːbəbəl] improbable
improve [ɪm'pruːv] **1** *v/t* améliorer **2** *v/i* s'améliorer; **im-**

provement amélioration *f*
improvize ['ɪmprəvaɪz] improviser
impudent ['ɪmpjʊdənt] impudent
impulse ['ɪmpʌls] impulsion *f*; **impulsive** impulsif
in [ɪn] **1** *prep* dans; *with time* en; **~ *Rouen*** à Rouen; **~ *1999*** en 1999; **~ *the morning*** le matin; **~ *the summer*** l'été; **~ *August*** en août, au mois d'août; **~ *two hours*** *from now* dans deux heures; *over period of* en deux heures; **~ *English*** en anglais; **~ *yellow*** en jaune; **~ *crossing the road*** en traversant la route **2** *adv* (*at home, in the building etc*) là; (*arrived: train*) arrivé; (*in its position*) dedans; **~ *here*** ici **3** *adj* (*fashionable, popular*) à la mode
inability [ɪnə'bɪlɪtɪ] incapacité *f*
inaccurate [ɪn'ækjʊrət] inexact
inadequate [ɪn'ædɪkwət] insuffisant, inadéquat
inadvisable [ɪnəd'vaɪzəbl] peu recommandé
inanimate [ɪn'ænɪmət] inanimé
inappropriate [ɪnə'proʊprɪət] peu approprié
inaudible [ɪn'ɒːdəbl] inaudible
inaugural [ɪ'nɒːgjʊrəl] *speech* inaugural; **inaugurate** inaugurer
inborn ['ɪnbɔːrn] inné
inc. (= ***incorporated***) S.A. *f* (= Société *f* Anonyme)
incalculable [ɪn'kælkjʊləbl] *damage* incalculable
incapable [ɪn'keɪpəbl] incapable
incentive [ɪn'sentɪv] encouragement *m*, stimulation *f*
incessant [ɪn'sesnt] incessant; **incessantly** sans arrêt
incest ['ɪnsest] inceste *m*
inch [ɪntʃ] pouce *m*
incident ['ɪnsɪdənt] incident *m*; **incidental** fortuit; **~ *expenses*** frais *mpl* accessoires; **incidentally** soit dit en passant
incision [ɪn'sɪʒn] incision *f*; **incisive** incisif
incite [ɪn'saɪt] inciter
inclination [ɪnklɪ'neɪʃn] (*liking*) penchant *m*; (*tendency*) tendance *f*
inclose, inclosure → ***enclose, enclosure***
include [ɪn'kluːd] inclure, comprendre; **including** y compris; **~ *service*** service compris; **inclusive** **1** *adj price* tout compris **2** *prep*: **~ *of*** en incluant **3** *adv* tout compris; ***from Monday to Thursday* ~** du lundi au jeudi inclus
incoherent [ɪnkoʊ'hɪrənt] incohérent
income ['ɪnkəm] revenu *m*; **income tax** impôt *m* sur le revenu

incomparable [ɪn'kɑːmpərəbl] incomparable

incompatibility [ɪnkəmpætɪ'bɪlɪtɪ] incompatibilité *f*; **incompatible** incompatible

incompetence [ɪn'kɑːmpɪtəns] incompétence *f*; **incompetent** incompétent

incomplete [ɪnkəm'pliːt] incomplet

incomprehensible [ɪnkɑːmprɪ'hensɪbl] incompréhensible

inconceivable [ɪnkən'siːvəbl] inconcevable

inconsiderate [ɪnkən'sɪdərət] *action* inconsidéré; ***be ~ of person*** manquer d'égards

inconsistent [ɪnkən'sɪstənt] incohérent; *person* inconstant

inconspicuous [ɪnkən'spɪkjʊəs] discret

inconvenience [ɪnkən'viːnɪəns] inconvénient *m*; **inconvenient** *time* inopportun; *place, arrangement* peu commode

incorporate [ɪn'kɔːrpəreɪt] incorporer

incorrect [ɪnkə'rekt] incorrect

increase 1 [ɪn'kriːs] *v/t & v/i* augmenter **2** ['ɪnkriːs] *n* augmentation *f*; **increasing** croissant; **increasingly** de plus en plus

incredible [ɪn'kredɪbl] incroyable

incur [ɪn'kɜːr] *costs* encourir; *debts* contracter; *s.o.'s anger* s'attirer

incurable [ɪn'kjʊrəbl] *also fig* incurable

indecent [ɪn'diːsnt] indécent

indecisive [ɪndɪ'saɪsɪv] *argument* peu concluant; *person* indécis; **indecisiveness** indécision *f*

indeed [ɪn'diːd] (*in fact*) vraiment; (*yes, agreeing*) en effet; ***very much ~*** beaucoup

indefinable [ɪndɪ'faɪnəbl] indéfinissable

indefinite [ɪn'defɪnɪt] indéfini; **indefinitely** indéfiniment

indelicate [ɪn'delɪkət] indélicat

independence [ɪndɪ'pendəns] indépendance *f*; **Independence Day** fête *f* de l'Indépendance; **independent** indépendant

indescribable [ɪndɪ'skraɪbəbl] indescriptible; (*very bad*) inqualifiable

index ['ɪndeks] *for book* index *m*

India ['ɪndɪə] Inde *f*; **Indian 1** *adj* indien **2** *n also American* Indien(ne) *m*(*f*)

indicate ['ɪndɪkeɪt] **1** *v/t* indiquer **2** *v/i when driving* mettre ses clignotants; **indication** indication *f*, signe *m*

indict [ɪn'daɪt] accuser

indifference [ɪn'dɪfrəns] indifférence *f*; **indifferent** indifférent; (*mediocre*) médio-

cre
indigestion [ɪndɪ'dʒestʃn] indigestion *f*
indignant [ɪn'dɪgnənt] indigné; **indignation** indignation *f*
indirect [ɪndɪ'rekt] indirect; **indirectly** indirectement
indiscreet [ɪndɪ'skriːt] indiscret
indiscriminate [ɪndɪ'skrɪmɪnət] aveugle; *accusations* à tort et à travers
indispensable [ɪndɪ'spensəbl] indispensable
indisposed [ɪndɪ'spoʊzd] (*not well*) indisposé
indisputable [ɪndɪ'spjuːtəbl] incontestable
indistinct [ɪndɪ'stɪŋkt] indistinct
indistinguishable [ɪndɪ'stɪŋgwɪʃəbl] indifférenciable
individual [ɪndɪ'vɪdʒuəl] **1** *n* individu *m* **2** *adj* (*separate*) particulier; (*personal*) individuel; **individually** individuellement
indoctrinate [ɪn'dɑːktrɪneɪt] endoctriner
Indonesia [ɪndə'niːʒə] Indonésie *f*; **Indonesian 1** *adj* indonésien **2** *n person* Indonésien(ne) *m*(*f*)
indoor ['ɪndɔːr] *activities, games* d'intérieur; *sport* en salle; *arena* couvert; **indoors** à l'intérieur; (*at home*) à la maison
indorse → ***endorse***
indulgent [ɪn'dʌldʒənt] (*not strict enough*) indulgent
industrial [ɪn'dʌstrɪəl] industriel; **industrial dispute** conflit *m* social; **industrialist** industriel(le) *m*(*f*); **industrious** travailleur; **industry** industrie *f*
ineffective [ɪnɪ'fektɪv] inefficace
inefficient [ɪnɪ'fɪʃənt] inefficace
inept [ɪ'nept] inepte
inequality [ɪnɪ'kwɑːlɪtɪ] inégalité *f*
inescapable [ɪnɪ'skeɪpəbl] inévitable
inevitable [ɪn'evɪtəbl] inévitable; **inevitably** inévitablement
inexcusable [ɪnɪk'skjuːzəbl] inexcusable
inexhaustible [ɪnɪg'zɒːstəbl] inépuisable
inexpensive [ɪnɪk'spensɪv] bon marché, pas cher
inexperienced [ɪnɪk'spɪrɪənst] inexpérimenté
inexplicable [ɪnɪk'splɪkəbl] inexplicable
infallible [ɪn'fælɪbl] infaillible
infamous ['ɪnfəməs] infâme
infancy ['ɪnfənsɪ] *of person* petite enfance *f*; *of state, institution* débuts *mpl*; **infant** petit(e) enfant *m*(*f*); **infantile** *pej* infantile
infantry ['ɪnfəntrɪ] infanterie *f*
infect [ɪn'fekt] contaminer;

become ~ed *of wound* s'infecter; **infection** contamination *f*; *(disease)*, *of wound* infection *f*; **infectious** *disease* infectieux; *laughter* contagieux

infer [ɪn'fɜːr]: ***~ X from Y*** déduire X de Y

inferior [ɪn'fɪrɪər] inférieur; **inferiority** infériorité *f*; **inferiority complex** complexe *m* d'infériorité

infertile [ɪn'fɜːrtl] stérile; **infertility** stérilité *f*

infidelity [ɪnfɪ'delɪtɪ] infidélité *f*

infinite ['ɪnfɪnət] infini; **infinitive** infinitif *m*

infinity [ɪn'fɪnətɪ] infinité *f*; MATH infini *m*

inflammable [ɪn'flæməbl] inflammable; **inflammation** MED inflammation *f*

inflatable [ɪn'fleɪtəbl] *dinghy* gonflable; **inflate** *tire*, *dinghy* gonfler; **inflation** inflation *f*; **inflationary** inflationniste

inflexible [ɪn'fleksɪbl] *attitude*, *person* inflexible

inflict [ɪn'flɪkt] infliger (***on*** à)

influence ['ɪnflʊəns] **1** *n* influence *f* **2** *v/t* influencer; **influential** influent

inform [ɪn'fɔːrm] **1** *v/t* informer **2** *v/i*: ***~ on*** dénoncer

informal [ɪn'fɔːrməl] *meeting*, *agreement* non-officiel; *form of address* familier; *conversation*, *dress* simple; **informality** *of meeting*, *agreement* caractère *m* non officiel; *of form of address* familiarité *f*; *of conversation*, *dress* simplicité *f*

informant [ɪn'fɔːrmənt] informateur(-trice) *m(f)*; **information** renseignements *mpl*; **information technology** informatique *f*; **informative** instructif; **informer** dénonciateur(-trice) *m(f)*

infra-red [ɪnfrə'red] infrarouge

infrastructure ['ɪnfrəstrʌkʧər] infrastructure *f*

infrequent [ɪn'friːkwənt] rare

infuriate [ɪn'fjʊrɪeɪt] rendre furieux; **infuriating** exaspérant

ingenious [ɪn'dʒiːnɪəs] ingénieux

ingot ['ɪŋgət] lingot *m*

ingratitude [ɪn'grætɪtuːd] ingratitude *f*

ingredient [ɪn'griːdɪənt] *for cooking* ingrédient *m*; *for success* recette *f*

inhabit [ɪn'hæbɪt] habiter; **inhabitant** habitant(e) *m(f)*

inhale [ɪn'heɪl] **1** *v/t* inhaler **2** *v/i when smoking* avaler la fumée

inherit [ɪn'herɪt] hériter; **inheritance** héritage *m*

inhibited [ɪn'hɪbɪtɪd] inhibé; **inhibition** inhibition *f*

inhospitable [ɪnhɑː'spɪtəbl] inhospitalier

inhuman [ɪn'hjuːmən] inhumain

initial [ɪ'nɪʃl] **1** *adj* initial **2** *n* initiale *f* **3** *v/t* (*write initials on*) parapher; **initially** au début; **initiate** *procedure* lancer; *person* initier; **initiation** lancement *m*; *of person* initiation *f*; **initiative** initiative *f*

inject [ɪn'dʒekt] injecter; **injection** injection *f*

injure ['ɪndʒər] blesser; **injury** blessure *f*

injustice [ɪn'dʒʌstɪs] injustice *f*

ink [ɪŋk] encre *f*

inland ['ɪnlənd] intérieur

in-laws ['ɪnlɒːz] belle-famille *f*

inmate ['ɪnmeɪt] *of prison* détenu(e) *m(f)*; *of mental hospital* interné(e) *m(f)*

inn [ɪn] auberge *f*

innate [ɪ'neɪt] inné

inner ['ɪnər] *courtyard* intérieur; *thoughts* intime; *ear* interne

innocence ['ɪnəsəns] innocence *f*; **innocent** innocent

innocuous [ɪ'nɑːkjʊəs] inoffensif

innovation [ɪnə'veɪʃn] innovation *f*; **innovative** innovant; **innovator** innovateur(-trice) *m(f)*

inoculate [ɪ'nɑːkjʊleɪt] inoculer; **inoculation** inoculation *f*

inoffensive [ɪnə'fensɪv] inoffensif

'in-patient patient(e) hospitalisé(e) *m(f)*

input ['ɪnpʊt] **1** *n into project etc* apport *m*, contribution *f*; COMPUT entrée *f* **2** *v/t into project* apporter; COMPUT entrer

inquest ['ɪnkwest] enquête *f* (***into*** sur)

inquire [ɪn'kwaɪr] se renseigner; **inquiry** demande *f* de renseignements; ***government ~*** enquête *f* officielle

inquisitive [ɪn'kwɪzətɪv] curieux

insane [ɪn'seɪn] fou

insanitary [ɪn'sænɪterɪ] insalubre

insanity [ɪn'sænɪtɪ] folie *f*

inscription [ɪn'skrɪpʃn] inscription *f*

insect ['ɪnsekt] insecte *m*; **insecticide** insecticide *m*

insecure [ɪnsɪ'kjʊr]: ***be ~*** *not safe* ne pas se sentir en sécurité; *not sure of self* manquer d'assurance; **insecurity** *psychological* manque *m* d'assurance

insensitive [ɪn'sensɪtɪv] insensible (***to*** à)

insert **1** ['ɪnsɜːrt] *n in magazine etc* encart *m* **2** [ɪn'sɜːrt] *v/t* insérer

inside [ɪn'saɪd] **1** *n* intérieur *m*; ***~ out*** à l'envers **2** *prep* à l'intérieur de; ***~ of 2 hours*** en moins de 2 heures **3** *adv* à l'intérieur **4** *adj*: ***~ information*** informations *fpl* internes; ***~ lane*** SP couloir *m* intérieur

inside pocket poche *f* intérieure; **insider** initié(e) *m(f)*; **insider trading** FIN délit *m* d'initié; **insides** (*stomach*) ventre *m*
insignificant [ɪnsɪg'nɪfɪkənt] insignifiant
insincere [ɪnsɪn'sɪr] peu sincère; **insincerity** manque *f* de sincérité
insinuate [ɪn'sɪnjʊeɪt] insinuer
insist [ɪn'sɪst] insister (***on*** sur); **insistent** insistant
insolent ['ɪnsələnt] insolent
insolvent [ɪn'sɑːlvənt] insolvable
insomnia [ɪn'sɑːmnɪə] insomnie *f*
inspect [ɪn'spekt] *work, tickets, baggage* contrôler; *factory, school* inspecter; **inspection** *of work, tickets, baggage* contrôle *m*; *of factory, school* inspection *f*; **inspector** *in factory* inspecteur(-trice) *m(f)*
inspiration [ɪnspə'reɪʃn] inspiration *f*; **inspire** inspirer
instability [ɪnstə'bɪlɪtɪ] instabilité *f*
install [ɪn'stɒːl] installer; **installation** installation *f*; **installment**, *Br* **instalment** *of story etc* épisode *m*; (*payment*) versement *m*; **installment plan** vente *f* à crédit
instance ['ɪnstəns] (*example*) exemple *m*; ***for ~*** par exemple
instant ['ɪnstənt] **1** *adj* instantané **2** *n* instant *m*; **instantaneous** instantané; **instant coffee** café *m* soluble; **instantly** immédiatement
instead [ɪn'sted] à la place; ***~ of me*** à ma place; ***~ of going home*** au lieu de rentrer à la maison
instinct ['ɪnstɪŋkt] instinct *m*; **instinctive** instinctif
institute ['ɪnstɪtuːt] **1** *n* institut *m*; (*special home*) établissement *m* **2** *v/t new law, inquiry* instituer; **institution** institution *f*
instruct [ɪn'strʌkt] (*order*) ordonner; (*teach*) instruire; **instruction** instruction *f*; ***~s for use*** mode *m* d'emploi; **instructive** instructif; **instructor** moniteur(-trice) *m(f)*
instrument ['ɪnstrʊmənt] instrument *m*
insubordinate [ɪnsə'bɔːrdɪneɪt] insubordonné
insufficient [ɪnsə'fɪʃnt] insuffisant
insulate ['ɪnsəleɪt] ELEC, *against cold* isoler; **insulation** isolation *f*; *material* isolement *m*
insulin ['ɪnsəlɪn] insuline *f*
insult 1 ['ɪnsʌlt] *n* insulte *f* **2** [ɪn'sʌlt] *v/t* insulter
insurance [ɪn'ʃʊrəns] assurance *f*; **insurance company** compagnie *f* d'assurance; **insurance policy** police *f* d'as-

surance; **insurance premium** prime *f* d'assurance; **insure** assurer
insurmountable [ɪnsər'mauntəbl] insurmontable
intact [ɪn'tækt] (*not damaged*) intact
integrate ['ɪntɪgreɪt] intégrer; **integrity** (*honesty*) intégrité *f*
intellect ['ɪntəlekt] intellect *m*; **intellectual 1** *adj* intellectuel **2** *n* intellectuel(le) *m(f)*
intelligence [ɪn'telɪdʒəns] intelligence *f*; (*information*) renseignements *mpl*; **intelligent** intelligent
intelligible [ɪn'telɪdʒəbl] intelligible
intend [ɪn'tend] *v/i*: **~ *to do sth*** avoir l'intention de
intense [ɪn'tens] intense; *personality* passionné; **intensify 1** *v/t* intensifier **2** *v/i of pain, fighting* s'intensifier; **intensity** intensité *f*; **intensive** intensif; **intensive care** MED service *m* de soins intensifs
intention [ɪn'tenʃn] intention *f*; **intentional** intentionnel; **intentionally** délibérément
interaction [ɪntər'ækʃn] interaction *f*; **interactive** interactif
intercept [ɪntər'sept] intercepter
interchange ['ɪntərʧeɪndʒ] *of highways* échangeur *m*; **interchangeable** interchangeable
intercom ['ɪntərkɑːm] interphone *m*
intercourse ['ɪntərkɔːrs] *sexual* rapports *mpl*
interdependent [ɪntərdɪ'pendənt] interdépendant
interest ['ɪntrəst] **1** *n* intérêt *m*; *financial* intérêt(s) *m(pl)* **2** *v/t* intéresser; **interested** intéressé; **interesting** intéressant; **interest rate** taux *m* d'intérêt
interface ['ɪntərfeɪs] **1** *n* interface *f* **2** *v/i* avoir une interface (**with** avec)
interfere [ɪntər'fɪr] se mêler (**with** de); **interference** ingérence *f*; *on radio* interférence *f*
interior [ɪn'tɪrɪər] **1** *adj* intérieur **2** *n* intérieur *m*; **interior design** design *m* d'intérieurs; **interior designer** designer *m/f* d'intérieurs
interlude ['ɪntərluːd] intermède *m*
intermediary [ɪntər'miːdɪerɪ] intermédiaire *m/f*; **intermediate** *level* intermédiaire; *course* (de niveau) moyen
intermission [ɪntər'mɪʃn] *in theater* entracte *m*
internal [ɪn'tɜːrnl] interne; *trade* intérieur; **internally** *in organization* en interne; ***not to be taken* ~** à usage externe; **Internal Revenue (Service)** direction *f* générale des) impôts *mpl*
international [ɪntər'næʃnl]

international; **internationally** internationalement
Internet ['ɪntərnet] Internet *m*; ***on the ~*** sur Internet
interpret [ɪn'tɜːrprɪt] interpréter; **interpretation** interprétation *f*; **interpreter** interprète *m/f*
interrogate [ɪn'terəgeɪt] interroger; **interrogation** interrogatoire *m*; **interrogator** interrogateur(-trice) *m(f)*
interrupt [ɪntə'rʌpt] interrompre; **interruption** interruption *f*
intersect [ɪntər'sekt] **1** *v/t* couper, croiser **2** *v/i* s'entrecouper, s'entrecroiser; **intersection** *of roads* carrefour *m*
interstate ['ɪntərsteɪt] autoroute *f*
interval ['ɪntərvl] intervalle *m*; *in theater* entracte *m*
intervene [ɪntər'viːn] intervenir; **intervention** intervention *f*
interview ['ɪntərvjuː] **1** *n* interview *f*; *for job* entretien *m* **2** *v/t* interviewer; *for job* faire passer un entretien à; **interviewer** intervieweur (-euse) *m(f)*; *for job* personne *f* responsable d'un entretien
intimate ['ɪntɪmət] intime
intimidate [ɪn'tɪmɪdeɪt] intimider; **intimidation** intimidation *f*
into ['ɪntʊ] dans; ***translate ~ English*** traduire en anglais; ***be ~ sth*** F (*like*) aimer qch; *politics etc* être engagé dans qch
intolerable [ɪn'tɑːlərəbl] intolérable; **intolerant** intolérant
intoxicated [ɪn'tɑːksɪkeɪtɪd] ivre
intravenous [ɪntrə'viːnəs] intraveineux
intricate ['ɪntrɪkət] compliqué, complexe
intrigue 1 ['ɪntriːg] *n* intrigue *f* **2** [ɪn'triːg] *v/t* intriguer; **intriguing** intrigant
introduce [ɪntrə'duːs] *new technique etc* introduire; ***~ s.o. to s.o.*** présenter qn à qn; **introduction** *to person* présentations *fpl*; *in book, of new techniques* introduction *f*
intrude [ɪn'truːd] déranger; **intruder** intrus(e) *m(f)*; **intrusion** intrusion *f*
intuition [ɪntuː'ɪʃn] intuition *f*
invade [ɪn'veɪd] envahir
invalid[1] [ɪn'vælɪd] *adj* non valable
invalid[2] ['ɪnvəlɪd] *n* MED invalide *m/f*
invalidate [ɪn'vælɪdeɪt] *claim, theory* invalider
invaluable [ɪn'væljʊbl] inestimable
invariably [ɪn'veɪrɪəblɪ] (*always*) invariablement
invasion [ɪn'veɪʒn] invasion *f*
invent [ɪn'vent] inventer; **invention** invention *f*; **inventive** inventif; **inventor** inven-

teur(-trice) *m(f)*
inventory ['ɪnvəntoʊrɪ] inventaire *m*
invert [ɪn'vɜːrt] inverser
invest [ɪn'vest] investir
investigate [ɪn'vestɪgeɪt] *crime* enquêter sur; *scientific phenomenon* étudier; **investigation** *of crime* enquête *f*; *in science* étude *f*
investment [ɪn'vestmənt] investissement *m*; **investor** investisseur *m*
invincible [ɪn'vɪnsəbl] invincible
invisible [ɪn'vɪzɪbl] invisible
invitation [ɪnvɪ'teɪʃn] invitation *f*; **invite** inviter
invoice ['ɪnvɔɪs] **1** *n* facture *f* **2** *v/t customer* facturer
involuntary [ɪn'vɑːlənterɪ] involontaire
involve [ɪn'vɑːlv] *work* nécessiter; *expense* entraîner; (*concern*) concerner; ***what does it ~?*** qu'est-ce que cela implique?; **involved** (*complex*) compliqué; **involvement** *in project, crime etc* participation *f*; *in politics* engagement *m*
invulnerable [ɪn'vʌlnərəbl] invulnérable
inward ['ɪnwərd] **1** *adj* intérieur **2** *adv* vers l'intérieur; **inwardly** intérieurement
IQ [aɪ'kjuː] (= ***intelligence quotient***) Q.I. *m* (= Quotient *m* intellectuel)
Iran [ɪ'rɑːn] Iran *m*; **Iranian 1** *adj* iranien **2** *n* Iranien(ne) *m(f)*
Iraq [ɪ'ræːk] Iraq *m*; **Iraqi 1** *adj* irakien **2** *n* Irakien(ne) *m(f)*
Ireland ['aɪrlənd] Irlande *f*; **Irish 1** *adj* irlandais **2** *npl*: ***the ~*** les Irlandais
iron ['aɪərn] **1** *n* fer *m*; *for clothes* fer *m* à repasser **2** *v/t shirts etc* repasser
ironic(al) [aɪ'rɑːnɪk(l)] ironique
'ironing board planche *f* à repasser
irony ['aɪrənɪ] ironie *f*
irrational [ɪ'ræʃənl] irrationnel
irreconcilable [ɪrekən'saɪləbl] *people* irréconciliable; *positions* inconciliable
irregular [ɪ'regjʊlər] irrégulier
irrelevant [ɪ'reləvənt] hors de propos
irreplaceable [ɪrɪ'pleɪsəbl] irremplaçable
irrepressible [ɪrɪ'presəbl] *sense of humor* à toute épreuve; *person* qui ne se laisse pas abattre
irresistible [ɪrɪ'zɪstəbl] irrésistible
irresponsible [ɪrɪ'spɑːnsəbl] irresponsable
irreverent [ɪ'revərənt] irrévérencieux
irrevocable [ɪ'revəkəbl] irrévocable
irrigate ['ɪrɪgeɪt] irriguer; **irrigation** irrigation *f*

irritable ['ɪrɪtəbl] irritable; **irritate** irriter; **irritating** irritant; **irritation** irritation *f*
Islam ['ɪzlɑːm] *religion* islam *m*; *peoples, civilization* Islam *m*; **Islamic** islamique
island ['aɪlənd] île *f*
isolate ['aɪsəleɪt] isoler; **isolated** isolé; **isolation** isolement *m*
ISP [aɪes'piː] (= ***Internet service provider***) fournisseur *m* Internet
Israel ['ɪzreɪl] Israël *m*; **Israeli** **1** *adj* israélien **2** *n person* Israélien(ne) *m(f)*
issue ['ɪʃuː] **1** *n* (*matter*) question *f*, problème *m*; *of magazine* numéro *m* **2** *v/t supplies* distribuer; *coins, warning* émettre; *passport* délivrer
IT [aɪ'tiː] (= ***information technology***) informatique *f*
it [ɪt] *as subject* il, elle; *as object* le, la; ***~'s through there*** c'est par là; ***give ~ to him*** donne-le lui; ***on top of ~*** dessus; ***let's talk about ~*** parlons-en; ***~'s raining*** il pleut; ***~'s me/him*** c'est moi/lui; ***that's ~!*** (*that's right*) c'est ça!; (*finished*) c'est fini!
Italian [ɪ'tæljən] **1** *adj* italien **2** *n person* Italien(ne) *m(f)*; *language* italien *m*
italics [ɪ'tælɪks] italique *m*
Italy ['ɪtəlɪ] Italie *f*
itch [ɪtʃ] **1** *n* démangeaison *f* **2** *v/i*: ***it ~es*** ça me démange
item ['aɪtəm] article *m*; *on agenda* point *m*; ***~ of news*** nouvelle *f*; **itemize** *invoice* détailler
itinerary [aɪ'tɪnərerɪ] itinéraire *m*
its [ɪts] son, sa; *pl* ses
it's [ɪts] → ***it is, it has***
itself [ɪt'self] *reflexive* se; *stressed* lui-même; elle-même; ***by ~*** (*automatically*) tout(e) seul(e)

J

jab [dʒæb]: ***~ a stick into s.o.*** donner un coup de bâton à qn
jack [dʒæk] MOT cric *m*; *in cards* valet *m*
jacket ['dʒækɪt] veste *f*; *of book* couverture *f*
'jackpot jackpot *m*
jagged ['dʒægɪd] découpé
jail [dʒeɪl] prison *f*
jam[1] [dʒæm] *n for bread* confiture *f*
jam[2] [dʒæm] **1** *n* MOT embouteillage *m*; F (*difficulty*) pétrin *m* F **2** *v/t* (*ram*) fourrer; (*cause to stick*) bloquer; *broadcast* brouiller **3** *v/i* (*stick*) se bloquer
janitor ['dʒænɪtər] concierge *m/f*

January ['dʒænjʊerɪ] janvier *m*
Japan [dʒə'pæn] Japon *m*; **Japanese 1** *adj* japonais **2** *n person* Japonais(e) *m(f)*; *language* japonais *m*; ***the ~*** les Japonais *mpl*
jar [dʒɑːr] *container* pot *m*
jargon ['dʒɑːrgən] jargon *m*
jaw [dʒɒː] mâchoire *f*
jaywalker ['dʒeɪwɒːkər] piéton(ne) *m(f)* imprudent(e)
jazz [dʒæz] jazz *m*
jealous ['dʒeləs] jaloux; **jealousy** jalousie *f*
jeans [dʒiːnz] jean *m*
jeep [dʒiːp] jeep *f*
jeer [dʒɪr] **1** *n* raillerie *f*; *of crowd* huée *f* **2** *v/i of crowd* huer
Jello® ['dʒeloʊ] gelée *f*
jelly ['dʒelɪ] *jam* confiture *f*; **jellyfish** méduse *f*
jeopardize ['dʒepərdaɪz] mettre en danger
jerk¹ [dʒɜːrk] **1** *n* saccade *f* **2** *v/t* tirer d'un coup sec
jerk² [dʒɜːrk] *n* F couillon *m* F
jerky ['dʒɜːrkɪ] *movement* saccadé
Jesus ['dʒiːzəs] Jésus
jet [dʒet] (*airplane*) avion *m* à réaction, jet *m*; *of water* jet *m*; (*nozzle*) bec *m*; **jetlag** (troubles *mpl* dus au) décalage *m* horaire
jettison ['dʒetɪsn] jeter par-dessus bord; *fig* abandonner
jetty ['dʒetɪ] jetée *f*
Jew [dʒuː] Juif(-ive) *m(f)*
jewel ['dʒuːəl] bijou *m*; *fig : person* perle *f*; **jeweler**, *Br* **jeweller** bijoutier(-ère) *m(f)*; **jewelry**, *Br* **jewellery** bijoux *mpl*
Jewish ['dʒuːɪʃ] juif
jigsaw (puzzle) ['dʒɪgsɒː] puzzle *m*
jilt [dʒɪlt] laisser tomber
jingle ['dʒɪŋgl] **1** *n song* jingle *m* **2** *v/i of keys, coins* cliqueter
jinx [dʒɪŋks] *person* porte-malheur *m/f*; ***there's a ~ on this project*** ce projet porte malheur
jittery ['dʒɪtərɪ] F nerveux
job [dʒɑːb] travail *m*; **jobless** sans travail
jockey ['dʒɑːkɪ] jockey *m*
jog [dʒɑːg] *as exercise* faire du footing *or* jogging; **jogger** *person* joggeur(-euse) *m(f)*; **jogging** jogging *m*
john [dʒɑːn] F (*toilet*) petit coin *m* F
join [dʒɔɪn] **1** *n* joint *m* **2** *v/i of roads, rivers* se rejoindre; (*become a member*) devenir membre **3** *v/t* (*connect*) relier; *person, of road* rejoindre; *club* devenir membre de
◆ **join in** participer
joint [dʒɔɪnt] ANAT articulation *f*; *in woodwork* joint *m*; *of meat* rôti *m*; **joint account** compte *m* joint; **joint venture** entreprise *f* commune
joke [ʒoʊk] **1** *n* plaisanterie *f*,

blague *f* F; (*practical* ~) tour *m* **2** *v/i* plaisanter; **joker** farceur(-euse) *m(f)*, blagueur (-euse) *m(f)* F; *in cards* joker *m*; **jokingly** en plaisantant
jostle ['dʒɑːsl] bousculer
journal ['dʒɜːrnl] (*magazine*) revue *f*; (*diary*) journal *m*; **journalism** journalisme *m*; **journalist** journaliste *m/f*
journey ['dʒɜːrnɪ] voyage *m*; *across town etc* trajet *m*
joy [dʒɔɪ] joie *f*
jubilant ['dʒuːbɪlənt] débordant de joie; **jubilation** jubilation *f*
judge [dʒʌdʒ] **1** *n* juge *m/f* **2** *v/t* juger; *measurement*, *age* estimer **3** *v/i* juger; **judg(e)ment** jugement *m*; (*opinion*) avis *m*; **Judg(e)ment Day** le Jugement dernier
judicial [dʒuː'dɪʃl] judiciaire
juggle ['dʒʌgl] *also fig* jongler avec
juice [dʒuːs] jus *m*; **juicy** juteux; *gossip* croustillant
July [dʒʊ'laɪ] juillet *m*
jumbo (jet) ['dʒʌmboʊ] jumbo-jet *m*; **jumbo-sized** F géant
jump [dʒʌmp] **1** *n* saut *m*; (*increase*) bond *m* **2** *v/i* sauter; *in surprise* sursauter; (*increase*) faire un bond **3** *v/t fence etc* sauter; F (*attack*) attaquer; ~ ***the lights*** griller un feu (rouge)
◆ **jump at** *opportunity* sauter sur
jumper ['dʒʌmpər] *dress* robe-chasuble *f*; **jumpy** nerveux
June [dʒuːn] juin *m*
jungle ['dʒʌŋgl] jungle *f*
junior ['dʒuːnjər] **1** *adj* subalterne; (*younger*) plus jeune **2** *n in rank* subalterne *m/f*; ***she is ten years my*** ~ elle est ma cadette de dix ans; **junior high** collège *m*
junk [dʒʌŋk] camelote *f* F; **junk food** cochonneries *fpl*; **junkie** F drogué(e) *m(f)*; **junk mail** prospectus *mpl*
jurisdiction [dʒʊrɪs'dɪkʃn] LAW juridiction *f*
juror ['dʒʊrər] juré(e) *m(f)*; **jury** jury *m*
just [dʒʌst] **1** *adj cause* juste **2** *adv* (*barely*, *only*) juste; ~ ***as intelligent*** tout aussi intelligent; ***I've*** ~ ***seen her*** je viens de la voir; ~ ***about*** (*almost*) presque; ***I was*** ~ ***about to leave when …*** j'étais sur le point de partir quand …; ~ ***now*** (*a few moments ago*) tout à l'heure; (*at this moment*) en ce moment
justice ['dʒʌstɪs] justice *f*
justifiable [dʒʌstɪ'faɪəbl] justifiable; **justifiably** à juste titre; **justification** justification *f*; **justify** *also text* justifier
justly ['dʒʌstlɪ] (*fairly*) de manière juste; (*rightly*) à juste titre
◆ **jut out** [dʒʌt] être en saillie
juvenile ['dʒuːvənəl] *crime* ju-

vénile; *court* pour enfants; *pej* puéril; **juvenile delinquent** mineur(e) délinquant(e) *m(f)*

K

k [keɪ] (= ***kilobyte***) Ko *m* (= kilo-octet *m*); (= ***thousand***) mille
keel [kiːl] NAUT quille *f*
keen [kiːn] (*intense*) vif
keep [kiːp] **1** *v/t* garder; (*detain*) retenir; *in specific place* mettre; *family* entretenir; *dog etc* avoir; *bees, cattle* élever; *promise* tenir; ***~ sth from s.o.*** cacher qch à qn; ***~ s.o. from doing sth*** empêcher qn de faire qch; ***~ trying!*** essaie encore!; ***don't ~ interrupting!*** arrête de m'interrompre tout le temps! **2** *v/i* (*remain*) rester; *of food, milk* se conserver
◆ **keep back** (*hold in check*) retenir; *information* cacher
◆ **keep down** *costs etc* réduire; *food* garder
◆ **keep to** *path* rester sur; *rules* s'en tenir à
◆ **keep up 1** *v/i when walking, running etc* suivre; ***keep up with*** aller au même rythme que **2** *v/t pace, payments* continuer; *bridge, pants* soutenir
'keepsake souvenir *m*
kennel ['kenl] niche *f*; **kennels** chenil *m*
kerosene ['kerəsiːn] AVIA kérosène *m*; *for lamps* pétrole *m* (lampant)
ketchup ['ketʃʌp] ketchup *m*
kettle ['ketl] bouilloire *f*
key [kiː] **1** *n* clef *f*, clé *f*; COMPUT, MUS touche *f* **2** *adj* (*vital*) clef *inv*, clé *inv* **3** *v/t & v/i* COMPUT taper
◆ **key in** *data* taper
'keyboard COMPUT, MUS clavier *m*; **keyboarder** COMPUT claviste *m/f*; **keycard** carte-clef *f*; **keyed-up** tendu; **keyring** porte-clefs *m*
kick [kɪk] **1** *n* coup *m* de pied **2** *v/t* donner un coup de pied dans **3** *v/i of horse* ruer
◆ **kick around** *ball* taper dans; F (*discuss*) débattre
◆ **kick off** donner le coup d'envoi; F (*start*) démarrer F
◆ **kick out** mettre à la porte; ***be kicked out of the company*** être mis à la porte de la société
'kickback F (*bribe*) dessous-de-table *m* F
'kickoff SP coup *m* d'envoi
kid [kɪd] **1** *n* F (*child*) gamin(e) *m(f)* **2** *v/t* F taquiner **3** *v/i* F plaisanter
kidnap ['kɪdnæp] kidnapper; **kidnap(p)er** kidnappeur (-euse) *m(f)*; **kidnap(p)ing**

kidnapping *m*
kidney ['kɪdnɪ] ANAT rein *m*; *in cooking* rognon *m*
kill [kɪl] *also time* tuer; **killer** (*murderer*) tueur(-euse) *m(f)*; **killing** meurtre *m*
kiln [kɪln] four *m*
kilo ['kiːloʊ] kilo *m*; **kilobyte** kilo-octet *m*; **kilogram** kilogramme *m*; **kilometer**, *Br* **kilometre** kilomètre *m*
kind[1] [kaɪnd] *adj* gentil
kind[2] [kaɪnd] *n* (*sort*) sorte *f*, genre *m*; (*make, brand*) marque *f*; *~ of sad/strange* F plutôt triste/bizarre
kind-hearted [kaɪnd'hɑːrtɪd] bienveillant, bon; **kindly** gentil, bon; **kindness** bonté *f*, gentillesse *f*
king [kɪŋ] roi *m*; **kingdom** royaume *m*
kinky ['kɪŋkɪ] F bizarre
kiosk ['kiːɑːsk] kiosque *m*
kiss [kɪs] **1** *n* baiser *m* **2** *v/t* embrasser **3** *v/i* s'embrasser
kit [kɪt] (*equipment*) trousse *f*; *for assembly* kit *m*
kitchen ['kɪtʃɪn] cuisine *f*
kitten ['kɪtn] chaton(ne) *m(f)*
kitty ['kɪtɪ] *money* cagnotte *f*
klutz [klʌts] F (*clumsy person*) empoté(e) *m(f)* F
knack [næk]: ***have the ~ of doing*** avoir le chic pour faire; ***there's a ~ to it*** il y a un truc F
knee [niː] genou *m*; **kneecap** rotule *f*
kneel [niːl] s'agenouiller
'knee-length à la hauteur du genou
knife [naɪf] couteau *m*
knit [nɪt] tricoter; **knitwear** tricot *m*
knob [nɑːb] *on door* bouton *m*; *of butter* noix *f*
knock [nɑːk] **1** *n on door*, (*blow*) coup *m* **2** *v/t* (*hit*) frapper; *knee etc* se cogner; F (*criticize*) débiner F **3** *v/i on door* frapper
◆ **knock down** renverser; *wall, building* abattre; F (*reduce the price of*) solder
◆ **knock out** assommer; *boxer* mettre knock-out; *power lines etc* détruire; (*eliminate*) éliminer
◆ **knock over** renverser
'knockout *in boxing* knock-out *m*
knot [nɑːt] **1** *n* nœud *m* **2** *v/t* nouer
know [noʊ] **1** *v/t* savoir; *person, place, language* connaître; (*recognize*) reconnaître **2** *v/i* savoir; ***~ about sth*** être au courant de qch; **know-how** F savoir-faire *m*; **knowing** *smile* entendu; **knowingly** (*wittingly*) sciemment; *smile etc* d'un air entendu; **know-it-all** F je-sais-tout *m/f*; **knowledge** savoir *m*; *of a subject* connaissance(s) *f(pl)*; ***to the best of my ~*** autant que je sache
knuckle ['nʌkl] articulation *f* du doigt

Koran [kə'ræn] Coran *m*
Korea [kə'ri:ə] Corée *f*; **Korean** **1** *adj* coréen **2** *n* Coréen(ne) *m*(*f*); *language* coréen *m*
kosher ['kouʃər] REL casher *inv*; F réglo *inv* F
kudos ['kju:dɑ:s] prestige *m*

L

lab [læb] labo *m*
label ['leɪbl] **1** *n* étiquette *f* **2** *v/t also fig* étiqueter
labor ['leɪbər] *also in pregnancy* travail *m*
laboratory ['læbrətɔ:rɪ] laboratoire *m*
labored ['leɪbərd] *style, speech* laborieux; **laborer** travailleur *m* manuel; **laborious** laborieux; **labor union** syndicat *m*
labour *Br* → ***labor***
lace [leɪs] dentelle *f*; *for shoe* lacet *m*
lack [læk] **1** *n* manque *m* **2** *v/t* manquer de **3** *v/i*: ***be ~ing*** manquer
lacquer ['lækər] laque *f*
ladder ['lædər] échelle *f*
laden ['leɪdn] chargé (***with*** de)
ladies room ['leɪdi:z] toilettes *fpl* (pour dames)
lady ['leɪdɪ] dame *f*; **ladybug** coccinelle *f*; **ladylike** distingué
lager ['lɑ:gər] *Br* bière *f* blonde
laidback [leɪd'bæk] relax F
lake [leɪk] lac *m*
lamb [læm] agneau *m*
lame [leɪm] boîteux; *excuse* mauvais,
laminated ['læmɪneɪtɪd] *flooring, paper* stratifié; *wood* contreplaqué; *with plastic* plastifié; **~ *glass*** verre *m* feuilleté
lamp [læmp] lampe *f*; **lamppost** réverbère *m*; **lampshade** abat-jour *m inv*
land [lænd] **1** *n* terre *f*; (*country*) pays *m*; ***by ~*** par (voie de) terre **2** *v/t airplane* faire atterrir; *job* décrocher F **3** *v/i of airplane* atterrir; *of ball* tomber; **landing** *of airplane* atterrissage *m*; (*top of staircase*) palier *m*; **landing strip** piste *f* d'atterrissage; **landlady** propriétaire *f*; *of rented room* logeuse *f*; *Br of bar* patronne *f*; **landlord** propriétaire *m*; *of rented room* logeur *m*; *Br of bar* patron *m*; **landmark** point *m* de repère; ***be a ~ in*** *fig* faire date dans; **land owner** propriétaire *m* foncier; **landscape** **1** *n* paysage *m* **2** *adv print* en format paysage; **landslide** glissement *m* de terrain; **landslide victory** victoire *f* écrasante

lane [leɪn] *in country* petite route *f* (de campagne); (*alley*) ruelle *f*; MOT voie *f*
language ['læŋgwɪdʒ] langue *f*; (*style, code etc*) langage *m*; **language lab** laboratoire *m* de langues
lap[1] [læp] *of track* tour *m*
lap[2] [læp] *of water* clapotis *m*
lap[3] [læp] *of person* genoux *mpl*
lapel [lə'pel] revers *m*
lapse [læps] **1** *n* (*mistake*) erreur *f*; *in behavior* écart *m* (de conduite); *of time* intervalle *m* **2** *v/i* expirer
laptop ['læptɑːp] COMPUT portable *m*
larceny ['lɑːrsənɪ] vol *m*
larder ['lɑːrdər] garde-manger *m inv*
large [lɑːrdʒ] grand; *sum of money, head* gros; **largely** (*mainly*) en grande partie
laryngitis [lærɪn'dʒaɪtɪs] laryngite *f*
laser ['leɪzər] laser *m*; **laser printer** imprimante *f* laser
lash[1] [læʃ] *v/t with whip* fouetter
lash[2] [læʃ] *n* (*eyelash*) cil *m*
last[1] [læst] **1** *adj* dernier; **~ *night*** hier soir **2** *adv arrive, leave* en dernier; ***at* ~** enfin
last[2] [læst] *v/i* durer; **lasting** durable; **lastly** pour finir
late [leɪt] **1** *adj* (*behind time*) en retard; *in day* tard; ***it's getting* ~** il se fait tard **2** *adv arrive, leave* tard; **lately** récemment; **later** plus tard; **latest** dernier
Latin A'merica Amérique *f* latine; **Latin American 1** *n* Latino-Américain *m* **2** *adj* latino-américain
latitude ['lætɪtuːd] *also* (*freedom*) latitude *f*
latter ['lætər] dernier
laugh [læf] **1** *n* rire *m* **2** *v/i* rire
◆ **laugh at** rire de; (*mock*) se moquer de
laughter ['læftər] rires *mpl*
launch [lɒːntʃ] **1** *n boat* vedette *f*; *of rocket, product* lancement *m*; *of ship* mise *f* à l'eau **2** *v/t rocket, product* lancer; *ship* mettre à l'eau
launder ['lɒːndər] *clothes, money* blanchir; **laundromat** laverie *f* automatique; **laundry** *place* blanchisserie *f*; *clothes* lessive *f*
lavatory ['lævətərɪ] W.-C. *mpl*
lavish ['lævɪʃ] somptueux
law [lɒː] loi *f*; *subject* droit *m*; ***be against the* ~** être contraire à la loi; **law-abiding** respectueux des lois; **law court** tribunal *m*; **lawful** légal; *wife, child* légitime; **lawless** anarchique
lawn [lɒːn] pelouse *f*; **lawn mower** tondeuse *f* (à gazon)
'lawsuit procès *m*; **lawyer** avocat *m*
lax [læks] laxiste; *security* relâché
laxative ['læksətɪv] laxatif *m*

lay [leɪ] (*put down*) poser; *eggs* pondre; V *sexually* s'envoyer V

◆ **lay off** *workers* licencier; *temporarily* mettre au chômage technique

◆ **lay out** *objects* disposer; *page* faire la mise en page de

layer ['leɪr] couche *f*

'layman REL laïc *m*; *fig* profane *m*

'lay-out agencement *m*; *of page* mise *f* en page

lazy ['leɪzɪ] *person* paresseux; *day* tranquille

lb (= ***pound***) livre *f*

lead[1] [li:d] **1** *v/t* mener; *company* être à la tête de **2** *v/i in race, competition* mener; (*provide leadership*) diriger

lead[2] [li:d] *for dog* laisse *f*

lead[3] [led] *substance* plomb *m*; **leaded** *gas* au plomb

leader ['li:dər] *of state* dirigeant *m*; *in race* leader *m*; *of group* chef *m*; **leadership** *of party etc* direction *f*

lead-free ['ledfri:] *gas* sans plomb

leading ['li:dɪŋ] *runner* en tête (de la course); *company, product* premier; **leading-edge** *company, technology* de pointe

leaf [li:f] feuille *f*

◆ **leaf through** feuilleter

leaflet ['li:flət] dépliant *m*

league [li:g] ligue *f*

leak [li:k] **1** *n also of information* fuite *f* **2** *v/i of pipe* fuir; *of boat* faire eau **3** *v/t information* divulguer

lean[1] [li:n] **1** *v/i* (*be at an angle*) pencher; ~ ***against sth*** s'appuyer contre qch **2** *v/t* appuyer

lean[2] [li:n] *adj meat* maigre

leap [li:p] **1** *n* saut *m* **2** *v/i* sauter; **leap year** année *f* bissextile

learn [lɜ:rn] apprendre; **learner** apprenant(e) *m(f)*; **learning** (*knowledge*) savoir *m*; *act* apprentissage *m*

lease [li:s] **1** *n for apartment* bail *m*; *for equipment* location *f* **2** *v/t* louer

◆ **lease out** louer

leash [li:ʃ] *for dog* laisse *f*

least [li:st] **1** *adj* (*slightest*) (le ou la) moindre; *smallest quantity of* le moins de **2** *adv* (le) moins **3** *n* le moins; ***at*** ~ au moins

leather ['leðər] **1** *n* cuir *m* **2** *adj* de cuir

leave [li:v] **1** *n* (*vacation*) congé *m* **2** *v/t* quitter; *food, scar, memory* laisser; (*forget, leave behind*) oublier; ~ ***sth alone*** ne pas toucher à qch; ~ ***s.o. alone*** laisser qn tranquille; ***be left*** rester **2** *v/i of person, plane etc* partir

◆ **leave behind** *intentionally* laisser; (*forget*) oublier

◆ **leave out** omettre; (*not put away*) ne pas ranger

leaving party ['li:vɪŋ] soirée *f* d'adieu

lecture ['lektʃər] **1** *n* conférence *f*; *at university* cours *m* **2** *v/i at university* donner des cours; **lecturer** conférencier *m*; *at university* maître *m* de conférences

ledge [ledʒ] *of window* rebord *m*; *on rock face* saillie *f*; **ledger** COM registre *m* de comptes

left [left] **1** *adj* gauche **2** *n also* POL gauche *f*; ***on/to the ~*** à gauche **3** *adv turn, look* à gauche; **left-hand** gauche; **left-handed** gaucher; **left luggage (office)** *Br* consigne *f*; **left-overs** *food* restes *mpl*; **left-wing** POL de gauche

leg [leg] jambe *f*; *of animal* patte *f*; *of table etc* pied *m*

legacy ['legəsɪ] héritage *m*, legs *m*

legal ['liːgl] (*allowed*) légal; *relating to the law* juridique; **legal adviser** conseiller (-ère) *m*(*f*) juridique; **legality** légalité *f*; **legalize** légaliser

legend ['ledʒənd] légende *f*; **legendary** légendaire

legible ['ledʒəbl] lisible

legislate ['ledʒɪsleɪt] légiférer; **legislation** (*laws*) législation *f*; **legislative** législatif; **legislature** POL corps *m* législatif

legitimate [lɪ'dʒɪtɪmət] légitime

'leg room place *f* pour les jambes

leisure ['liːʒər] loisir *m*; (*free time*) temps *m* libre; **leisurely** tranquille

lemon ['lemən] citron *m*; **lemonade** citronnade *f*; *carbonated* limonade *f*

lend [lend] prêter

length [leŋθ] longueur *f*; (*piece*: *of material*) pièce *f*; *of piping, road* tronçon *m*; ***at ~*** *describe, explain* en détail; (*eventually*) finalement; **lengthen** *sleeve etc* allonger; *contract* prolonger; **lengthy** long

lenient ['liːnɪənt] indulgent

lens [lenz] *of microscope etc* lentille *f*; *of eyeglasses* verre *m*; *of camera* objectif *m*; *of eye* cristallin *m*

Lent [lent] REL Carême *m*

leotard ['liːoutɑːrd] justaucorps *m*

lesbian ['lezbɪən] **1** *n* lesbienne *f* **2** *adj* lesbien

less [les] **1** *adv* moins; ***~ than $200*** moins de 200 dollars **2** *adj money, salt* moins de; **lessen 1** *v/t* réduire **2** *v/i* diminuer

lesson ['lesn] leçon *f*; *at school* cours *m*

let [let] (*allow*) laisser; *Br house* louer; ***~'s stay here*** restons ici; ***~ go of sth*** lâcher qch

◆ **let down** *hair* détacher; *blinds* baisser; (*disappoint*) décevoir

◆ **let in** *to house* laisser entrer

◆ **let out** *from room, building* laisser sortir; *jacket etc* agrandir; *groan,yell* laisser échapper; *Br* (*rent*) louer
◆ **let up** (*stop*) s'arrêter
lethal ['li:θl] mortel
lethargic [lɪ'θɑ:rdʒɪk] léthargique; **lethargy** léthargie *f*
letter ['letər] *of alphabet, in mail* lettre *f*; **letterbox** *Br* boîte *f* aux lettres; **letterhead** (*heading*) en-tête *m*; (*headed paper*) papier *m* à en-tête
lettuce ['letɪs] laitue *f*
leukemia [lu:'ki:mɪə] leucémie *f*
level ['levl] **1** *adj surface* plat; *in competition* à égalité **2** *n* niveau *m*; *on scale, in hierarchy* échelon *m*; ***on the ~*** F (*honest*) réglo F; **level-headed** pondéré
lever ['levər] levier *m*; **leverage** effet *m* de levier; (*influence*) poids *m*
levy ['levɪ] *taxes* lever
liability [laɪə'bɪlətɪ] (*responsibility*) responsabilité *f*; (*likeliness*) disposition *f* (***to*** à); **liable** responsable (***for*** de); ***be ~ to*** (*likely*) être susceptible de
◆ **liaise with** [lɪ'eɪz] assurer la liaison avec
liaison [lɪ'eɪzɑ:n] (*contacts*) communication(s) *f*
liar [laɪr] menteur(-euse) *m*(*f*)
libel ['laɪbl] **1** *n* diffamation *f* **2** *v/t* diffamer
liberal ['lɪbərəl] large d'esprit; *portion etc* généreux; POL libéral
liberate ['lɪbəreɪt] libérer; **liberated** libéré; **liberation** libération *f*; **liberty** liberté *f*
librarian [laɪ'brerɪən] bibliothécaire *m*/*f*; **library** bibliothèque *f*
Libya ['lɪbɪə] Libye *f*; **Libyan** **1** *adj* libyen **2** *n* Libyen(ne) *m*(*f*)
lice [laɪs] *pl* → ***louse***
licence ['laɪsns] *Br* → ***license* 1** *n*
license ['laɪsns] **1** *n* permis *m* **2** *v/t company* accorder une licence à (***to do*** pour faire); ***be ~d*** *equipment* être autorisé; **license number** numéro *m* d'immatriculation; **license plate** *of car* plaque *f* d'immatriculation
lick [lɪk] lécher
lid [lɪd] couvercle *m*
lie[1] [laɪ] **1** *n* (*untruth*) mensonge *m* **2** *v/i* mentir
lie[2] [laɪ] *v/i of person* (*lie down*) s'allonger; (*be lying down*) être allongé; *of object* être; (*be situated*) être, se trouver
◆ **lie down** se coucher
lieutenant [lʊ'tenənt] lieutenant *m*
life [laɪf] vie *f*; **life expectancy** espérance *f* de vie; **lifeguard** maître nageur *m*; **life imprisonment** emprisonnement *m* à vie; **life insurance** assurance-vie *f*; **life jacket** gilet *m* de

sauvetage; **lifeless** *body* inanimé; *personality* mou; *town* mort; **lifelike** réaliste; **lifelong** de toute une vie; **lifesized** grandeur nature; **life support** (équipement *m* de) maintien *m* artificiel; **life-threatening** *illness* extrêmement grave; **lifetime** vie *f*; ***in my ~*** de mon vivant
lift [lɪft] **1** *v/t* soulever **2** *v/i of fog* se lever **3** *n Br* (*elevator*) ascenseur *m*; ***give s.o. a ~*** *in car* emmener qn en voiture; **lift-off** *of rocket* décollage *m*
ligament ['lɪgəmənt] ligament *m*
light[1] [laɪt] **1** *n* lumière *f*; ***do you have a ~?*** vous avez du feu? **2** *v/t fire, cigarette* allumer; (*illuminate*) éclairer **3** *adj* (*not dark*) clair
light[2] [laɪt] *adj* (*not heavy*) léger
◆ **light up 1** *v/t* éclairer **2** *v/i* (*start to smoke*) s'allumer une cigarette
'**light bulb** ampoule *f*
lighten[1] ['laɪtn] *color* éclaircir
lighten[2] ['laɪtn] *load* alléger
lighter ['laɪtər] *for cigarettes* briquet *m*; **light-headed** étourdi; **lighting** éclairage *m*
lightness *of room, color* clarté *f*; *in weight* légèreté *f*; **lightning** éclair *m*, foudre *f*; **lightweight** *in boxing* poids *m* léger; **light year** année-lumière *f*
like[1] [laɪk] **1** *prep* comme; ***be ~ s.o./sth*** ressembler à qn/qch; ***what is she ~?*** comment est-elle?; ***it's not ~ him*** *not his character* ça ne lui ressemble pas **2** *conj* F (*as*) comme; ***~ I said*** comme je l'ai dit
like[2] [laɪk] *v/t* aimer; ***I ~ it*** ça me plaît (bien); ***I ~ Susie*** j'aime bien Susie; *romantically* Susie me plaît (bien); ***I would ~ …*** je voudrais, j'aimerais …; ***I would ~ to leave*** je voudrais *or* j'aimerais partir; ***would you ~ …?*** voulez-vous…?; ***would you ~ to …?*** as-tu envie de …?; ***~ to do sth*** aimer faire qch; ***if you ~*** si vous voulez; **likeable** agréable, plaisant; **likelihood** probabilité *f*; **likely** probable; **likeness** ressemblance *f*; **likewise** de même, aussi; **liking** *for person* affection *f*; *for sth* penchant *m*
limb [lɪm] membre *m*
lime[1] [laɪm] *fruit* citron *m* vert; *tree* limettier *m*
lime[2] [laɪm] *substance* chaux *f*
limit ['lɪmɪt] **1** *n* limite *f* **2** *v/t* limiter; **limitation** limitation *f*; **limited company** *Br* société *f* à responsabilité limitée
limousine ['lɪməziːn] limousine *f*
limp[1] [lɪmp] *adj* mou
limp[2] [lɪmp] **1** *n* claudication *f*; ***he has a ~*** il boite **2** *v/i* boiter
line[1] [laɪn] *n* ligne *f*; RAIL voie

f; *of people* file *f*; *of trees* rangée *f*; *of poem* vers *m*; ***stand in ~*** faire la queue
line² [laɪn] *v/t with material* recouvrir, garnir; *clothes* doubler
linear ['lɪnɪər] linéaire
linen ['lɪnɪn] *material* lin *m*; (*sheets etc*) linge *m*
liner ['laɪnər] *ship* paquebot *m* de grande ligne
linesman ['laɪnzmən] SP juge *m* de touche; *tennis* juge *m* de ligne
linger ['lɪŋgər] *of person* s'attarder; *of pain* persister
lingerie ['læn ʒəriː] lingerie *f*
linguist ['lɪŋgwɪst] linguiste *m*; **linguistic** linguistique
lining ['laɪnɪŋ] *of clothes* doublure *f*; *of brakes*, *pipes* garniture *f*
link [lɪŋk] **1** *n* lien *m*; *in chain* maillon *m* **2** *v/t* lier, relier
lion ['laɪən] lion *m*
lip [lɪp] lèvre *f*
liposuction ['lɪpoʊsʌkʃən] liposuccion *f*
'lipread lire sur les lèvres; **lipstick** rouge *m* à lèvres
liqueur [lɪ'kjʊr] liqueur *f*
liquid ['lɪkwɪd] **1** *n* liquide *m* **2** *adj* liquide; **liquidate** liquider; **liquidation** liquidation *f*; ***go into ~*** entrer en liquidation; **liquidity** FIN liquidité *f*; **liquidize** passer au mixeur; **liquidizer** mixeur *m*
liquor ['lɪkər] alcool *m*; **liquor store** magasin *m* de vins et spiritueux
lisp [lɪsp] **1** *n* zézaiement *m* **2** *v/i* zézayer
list [lɪst] **1** *n* liste *f* **2** *v/t* faire la liste de; (*enumerate*) énumérer
listen ['lɪsn] écouter
◆ **listen to** écouter
listener ['lɪsnər] *to radio* auditeur(-trice) *m*(*f*)
listless ['lɪstlɪs] amorphe
liter ['liːtər] litre *m*
literal ['lɪtərəl] littéral; **literally** littéralement
literary ['lɪtərerɪ] littéraire; **literature** littérature *f*; *about a product* documentation *f*
litre ['liːtər] *Br* → ***liter***
litter ['lɪtər] détritus *mpl*, ordures *fpl*; *of animal* portée *f*
little ['lɪtl] **1** *adj* petit **2** *n* peu *m*; ***a ~ wine*** un peu de vin **3** *adv* peu; ***a ~ bigger*** un peu plus gros
live¹ [lɪv] *v/i* vivre
live² [laɪv] *adj broadcast* en direct; *bomb* non désamorcé
◆ **live up to** être à la hauteur de
livelihood ['laɪvlɪhʊd] gagne-pain *m inv*; **liveliness** vivacité *f*; **lively** *person*, *city* plein de vie; *party* animé; *music* entraînant
liver ['lɪvər] foie *m*
livestock ['laɪvstɑːk] bétail *m*
livid ['lɪvɪd] (*angry*) furieux
living ['lɪvɪŋ] **1** *adj* vivant **2** *n* vie *f*; **living room** salle *f* de séjour

lizard ['lɪzərd] lézard *m*
load [loʊd] **1** *n* charge *f* **2** *v/t* charger
loaf [loʊf]: ***a ~ of bread*** un pain
◆ **loaf around** F traîner
loafer ['loʊfər] *shoe* mocassin *m*
loan [loʊn] **1** *n* prêt *m* **2** *v/t*: ***~ s.o. sth*** prêter qch à qn
loathe [loʊð] détester; **loathing** dégoût *m*
lobby ['lɑːbɪ] *in hotel* hall *m*; *in theater* vestibule *m*; POL lobby *m*
lobe [loʊb] *of ear* lobe *m*
lobster ['lɑːbstər] homard *m*
local ['loʊkl] **1** *adj* local **2** *n* habitant *m* de la région/du quartier; **local call** TELEC appel *m* local; **local elections** élections *fpl* locales; **local government** autorités *f* locales; **locality** endroit *m*; **localize** localiser; **locally** *live, work* dans le quartier, dans la région; **local time** heure *f* locale
locate [loʊ'keɪt] *new factory etc* établir; (*identify position of*) localiser; ***be ~d*** se trouver; **location** (*siting*) emplacement *m*; (*identifying position of*) localisation *f*; ***on ~ movie*** en extérieur
lock[1] [lɑːk] *n of hair* mèche *f*
lock[2] [lɑːk] **1** *n on door* serrure *f* **2** *v/t door* fermer à clef
◆ **lock up** *in prison* mettre sous les verrous
locker ['lɑːkər] casier *m*; **locker room** vestiaire *m*
locust ['loʊkəst] locuste *f*, sauterelle *f*
lodge [lɑːdʒ] **1** *v/t complaint* déposer **2** *v/i of bullet* se loger
lofty ['lɑːftɪ] *heights* haut; *ideals* élevé
log [lɑːg] bûche *f*; (*written record*) journal *m* de bord
◆ **log in** se connecter (***to*** à)
◆ **log off** se déconnecter
◆ **log on** se connecter (***to*** à)
◆ **log out** se déconnecter
log 'cabin cabane *f* en rondins
logic ['lɑːdʒɪk] logique *f*; **logical** logique; **logically** logiquement
logistics [lə'dʒɪstɪks] logistique *f*
logo ['loʊgoʊ] logo *m*, sigle *m*
loiter ['lɔɪtər] traîner
lollipop ['lɑːlɪpɑːp] sucette *f*
London ['lʌndən] Londres
loneliness ['loʊnlɪnɪs] *of person* solitude *f*; *of place* isolement *m*; **lonely** *person* seul, solitaire; *place* isolé; **loner** solitaire *m/f*
long[1] [lɑːŋ] **1** *adj* long; ***it's a ~ way*** c'est loin **2** *adv* longtemps; ***how ~ will it take?*** combien de temps cela va-t-il prendre?; ***he no ~er works here*** il ne travaille plus ici; ***so ~ as*** (*provided*) pourvu que; ***so ~!*** à bientôt!
long[2] [lɑːŋ] *v/i*: ***~ for sth*** avoir très envie de qch; ***be ~ing to***

do sth avoir très envie de faire qch

long-'distance *phonecall* longue distance; *race* de fond; *flight* long-courrier; **longevity** longévité *f*; **longing** désir *m*, envie *f*; **longitude** longitude *f*; **long jump** saut *m* en longueur; **long-range** *missile* à longue portée; *forecast* à long terme; **long-sleeved** à manches longues; **long-standing** de longue date; **long-term** à long terme; *unemployment* de longue durée

loo [lu:] *Br* F toilettes *fpl*

look [lʊk] **1** *n* (*appearance*) air *m*; (*glance*) coup *m* d'œil, regard *m*; **~s** (*beauty*) beauté *f* **2** *v/i* regarder; (*search*) chercher, regarder; (*seem*) avoir l'air

◆ **look after** s'occuper de

◆ **look ahead** *fig* regarder en avant

◆ **look around** jeter un coup d'œil

◆ **look at** regarder; (*examine*) examiner; (*consider*) envisager

◆ **look back** regarder derrière soi

◆ **look down on** mépriser

◆ **look for** chercher

◆ **look into** (*investigate*) examiner

◆ **look onto** *garden etc* donner sur

◆ **look out** *of window etc* regarder dehors; (*pay attention*) faire attention

◆ **look over** *house, translation* examiner

◆ **look through** *magazine, notes* parcourir, feuilleter

◆ **look up 1** *v/i from paper etc* lever les yeux; (*improve*) s'améliorer **2** *v/t word, phone number* chercher; (*visit*) passer voir

◆ **look up to** (*respect*) respecter

'lookout *person* sentinelle *f*; ***be on the ~ for*** être à l'affût de

loop [lu:p] boucle *f*; **loophole** *in law etc* lacune *f*

loose [lu:s] *knot* lâche; *connection, screw* desserré; *clothes* ample; *morals* relâché; *wording* vague; **~ change** petite monnaie *f*; **loosely** *worded* de manière approximative; **loosen** desserrer

loot [lu:t] **1** *n* butin *m* **2** *v/i* se livrer au pillage; **looter** pilleur(-euse) *m(f)*

lop-sided [lɑ:p'saɪdɪd] déséquilibré, disproportionné

Lord [lɔ:rd] (*god*) Seigneur *m*

lorry ['lɑ:rɪ] *Br* camion *m*

lose [lu:z] **1** *v/t* perdre **2** *v/i* SP perdre; *of clock* retarder; **loser** perdant(e) *m(f)*

loss [lɑ:s] perte *f*

lost [lɑ:st] perdu; **lost-and-found**, *Br* **lost property (office)** (bureau *m* des) objets

mpl trouvés
lot [lɑːt]: ***a ~*** (***of***), ***~s*** (***of***) beaucoup (de)
lotion ['loʊʃn] lotion *f*
lottery ['lɑːtərɪ] loterie *f*
loud [laʊd] *music, voice* fort; *noise* grand; *color* criard; **loudspeaker** haut-parleur *m*
louse [laʊs] pou *m*; **lousy** F minable F, mauvais
lout [laʊt] rustre *m*
lovable ['lʌvəbl] sympathique, adorable; **love 1** *n* amour *m*; *in tennis* zéro *m*; ***fall in ~*** tomber amoureux (***with*** de); ***make ~*** faire l'amour (***to*** avec) **2** *v/t* aimer; *wine, music* adorer; **love affair** aventure *f*; **lovely** beau; *house, wife* ravissant; *character* charmant; *meal* délicieux; **lover** *man* amant *m*; *woman* maîtresse *f*; *person in love* amoureux(-euse) *m*(*f*); **loving** affectueux; **lovingly** avec amour
low [loʊ] **1** *adj* bas; *quality* mauvais **2** *n in weather* dépression *f*; *in statistics* niveau *m* bas; **lowbrow** peu intellectuel; **low-calorie** hypocalorique; **low-cut** *dress* décolleté; **lower** baisser; *to the ground* faire descendre; **low-fat** allégé; **lowkey** discret, mesuré
loyal ['lɔɪəl] fidèle, loyal; **loyally** fidèlement; **loyalty** loyauté *f*
lozenge ['lɑːzɪndʒ] *shape* losange *m*; *tablet* pastille *f*
Ltd (= ***limited***) *company* à responsabilité limitée
lubricant ['luːbrɪkənt] lubrifiant *m*; **lubricate** lubrifier; **lubrication** lubrification *f*
lucid ['luːsɪd] (*clear*) clair; (*sane*) lucide
luck [lʌk] chance *f*; ***good ~!*** bonne chance!; **luckily** heureusement; **lucky** *person* chanceux; *number* porte-bonheur *inv*; *coincidence* heureux; ***you were ~*** tu as eu de la chance
lucrative ['luːkrətɪv] lucratif
ludicrous ['luːdɪkrəs] ridicule
lug [lʌg] F traîner
luggage ['lʌgɪdʒ] bagages *mpl*
lukewarm ['luːkwɔːrm] *also fig* tiède
lull [lʌl] *in storm, fighting* accalmie *f*; *in conversation* pause *f*
lumber ['lʌmbər] (*timber*) bois *m* de construction
luminous ['luːmɪnəs] lumineux
lump [lʌmp] *of sugar* morceau *m*; (*swelling*) grosseur *f*; **lump sum** forfait *m*; **lumpy** *liquid, sauce* grumeleux; *mattress* défoncé
lunacy ['luːnəsɪ] folie *f*
lunar ['luːnər] lunaire
lunatic ['luːnətɪk] fou *m*, folle *f*
lunch [lʌntʃ] déjeuner *m*; ***have ~*** déjeuner; **lunch box** panier-repas *m*; **lunch**

break pause-déjeuner *f*; **lunchtime** heure *f* du déjeuner, midi *m*
lung [lʌŋ] poumon *m*
lurch [lɜːrʧ] *of person* tituber; *of ship* tanguer
lure [lʊr] **1** *n* appât *m* **2** *v/t* attirer
lurid ['lʊrɪd] *color* cru; *details* choquant
lurk [lɜːrk] *of person* se cacher
lush [lʌʃ] *vegetation* luxuriant
lust [lʌst] désir *m*
luxurious [lʌg'ʒʊrɪəs] luxueux; **luxuriously** luxueusement; **luxury 1** *n* luxe *m* **2** *adj* de luxe
lynch [lɪnʧ] lyncher
lyrics ['lɪrɪks] paroles *fpl*

M

ma'am [mæm] madame
machine [mə'ʃiːn] machine *f*; **machine gun** mitrailleuse *f*; **machinery** machines *fpl*
machismo [mə'kɪzmoʊ] machisme *m*
macho ['mæʧoʊ] macho *inv*; **~ *type*** macho *m*
macro ['mækroʊ] COMPUT macro *f*
mad [mæd] (*insane*) fou; F (*angry*) furieux; **madden** (*infuriate*) exaspérer; **maddening** exaspérant; **madhouse** *fig* maison *f* de fous; **madman** fou *m*; **madness** folie *f*
Madonna [mə'dɑːnə] Madone *f*
Mafia ['mɑːfɪə]: ***the* ~** la Mafia
magazine [mægə'ziːn] *printed* magazine *m*
Magi ['meɪdʒaɪ] REL: ***the* ~** les Rois *mpl* mages
magic ['mædʒɪk] **1** *adj* magique **2** *n* magie *f*; **magical** magique; **magician** *performer* prestidigitateur(-trice) *m*(*f*)
magnanimous [mæg'nænɪməs] magnanime
magnet ['mægnɪt] aimant *m*; **magnetic** *also fig* magnétique; **magnetism** *also fig* magnétisme *m*
magnificence [mæg'nɪfɪsəns] magnificence *f*; **magnificent** magnifique
magnify ['mægnɪfaɪ] grossir; *difficulties* exagérer; **magnifying glass** loupe *f*
magnitude ['mægnɪtuːd] ampleur *f*
maid [meɪd] *servant* domestique *f*; *in hotel* femme *f* de chambre
maiden name ['meɪdn] nom *m* de jeune fille
mail [meɪl] **1** *n* courrier *m*, poste *f* **2** *v/t letter* poster; **mailbox** boîte *f* aux lettres; **mailing list** fichier *m* d'adresses; **mailman** facteur *m*; **mailshot** mailing *m*, pu-

blipostage *m*
maim [meɪm] estropier, mutiler
main [meɪn] principal; **main course** plat *m* principal; **mainframe** ordinateur *m* central; **mainly** principalement; **main road** route *f* principale; **main street** rue *f* principale
maintain [meɪn'teɪn] *peace, law and order* maintenir; *speed* soutenir; *relationship, machine, building* entretenir; *innocence, guilt* affirmer; **maintenance** *of machine, building* entretien *m*; *Br money* pension *f* alimentaire; *of law and order* maintien *m*
majestic [mə'dʒestɪk] majestueux
major ['meɪdʒər] **1** *adj (significant)* important, majeur **2** *n* MIL commandant *m*
◆ **major in** se spécialiser en
majority [mə'dʒɑːrətɪ] *also* POL majorité *f*
make [meɪk] **1** *n (brand)* marque *f* **2** *v/t* faire; *(manufacture)* fabriquer; *(earn)* gagner; *decision* prendre; ***3 and 3 ~ 6*** 3 et 3 font 6; ***~ it*** *(catch bus, train)* arriver à temps; *(come)* venir; *(succeed)* réussir; *(survive)* s'en sortir; ***what time do you ~ it?*** quelle heure as-tu?; ***~ believe*** prétendre; ***~ do with*** se contenter de, faire avec; ***what do you ~ of it?*** qu'en dis-tu?; ***~ s.o. do sth*** *(force to)* forcer qn à faire qch; *(cause to)* faire faire qch à qn; ***~ s.o. happy/angry*** rendre qn heureux/furieux
◆ **make out** *list, check* faire; *(see)* distinguer; *(imply)* prétendre
◆ **make up 1** *v/i of woman, actor* se maquiller; *after quarrel* se réconcilier **2** *v/t story* inventer; *face* maquiller; *(constitute)* constituer
◆ **make up for** compenser
'make-believe: ***it's just ~*** c'est juste pour faire semblant
maker ['meɪkər] *(manufacturer)* fabricant *m*; **makeshift** de fortune; **make-up** *(cosmetics)* maquillage *m*
maladjusted [mælə'dʒʌstɪd] inadapté
male [meɪl] **1** *adj* masculin; *animal* mâle **2** *n (man)* homme *m*; *animal, bird* mâle *m*; **male chauvinism** machisme *m*; **male chauvinist pig** macho *m*
malevolent [mə'levələnt] malveillant
malfunction [mæl'fʌŋkʃn] **1** *n* mauvais fonctionnement *m*, défaillance *f* **2** *v/i* mal fonctionner
malice ['mælɪs] méchanceté *f*, malveillance *f*; **malicious** méchant, malveillant
malignant [mə'lɪgnənt] *tumor* malin

mall [mɒ:l] (*shopping ~*) centre *m* commercial

malnutrition [mælnu:'trɪʃn] malnutrition *f*

maltreat [mæl'tri:t] maltraiter; **maltreatment** mauvais traitement *m*

mammal ['mæml] mammifère *m*

man [mæn] **1** *n* (*pl* ***men*** [men]) homme *m*; (*humanity*) l'homme *m*; *in checkers* pion *m* **2** *v/t telephones* être de permanence à; *front desk* être de service à

manage ['mænɪdʒ] **1** *v/t business* diriger; *money* gérer; *bags* porter; ***~ to …*** réussir à … **2** *v/i* (*cope*) se débrouiller; **manageable** gérable; *vehicle* maniable; *task* faisable; **management** (*managing*) gestion *f*, direction *f*; (*managers*) direction *f*; **management consultant** conseiller(-ère) *m(f)* en gestion; **manager** directeur(-trice) *m(f)*; *of store*, *restaurant*, *hotel* gérant(e) *m(f)*; *of department* responsable *m/f*; *of singer*, *band*, *team* manageur(-euse) *m(f)*; **managerial** de directeur, de gestionnaire; **managing director** directeur(-trice) *m(f)* général(e)

mandate ['mændeɪt] mandat *m*; **mandatory** obligatoire

maneuver [mə'nu:vər] **1** *n* manœuvre *f* **2** *v/t* manœuvrer

mangle ['mæŋgl] (*crush*) broyer

manhandle ['mænhændl] *person* malmener; *object* déplacer manuellement

manhood ['mænhʊd] (*maturity*) âge *m* d'homme; (*virility*) virilité *f*; **manhunt** chasse *f* à l'homme

mania ['meɪnɪə] (*craze*) manie *f*; **maniac** F fou *m*, folle *f*

manicure ['mænɪkjʊr] manucure *f*

manifest ['mænɪfest] **1** *adj* manifeste **2** *v/t* manifester

manipulate [mə'nɪpjəleɪt] manipuler; **manipulation** manipulation *f*; **manipulative** manipulateur

mankind humanité *f*; **manly** viril; **man-made** synthétique

manner ['mænər] *of doing sth* manière *f*, façon *f*; (*attitude*) comportement *m*; **manners** manières *fpl*

manoeuvre [mə'nu:vər] *Br* → ***maneuver***

'manpower main-d'œuvre *f*

manual ['mænjʊəl] **1** *adj* manuel **2** *n* manuel *m*; **manually** manuellement

manufacture [mænjʊ'fæktʃər] **1** *n* fabrication *f* **2** *v/t equipment* fabriquer; **manufacturer** fabricant *m*; **manufacturing** *industry* industrie *f*

manure [mə'nʊr] fumier *m*

manuscript ['mænjʊskrɪpt] manuscrit *m*

many ['menɪ] **1** *adj* beaucoup de; **~ *times*** bien des fois; ***too ~ problems*** trop de problèmes; ***as ~ as possible*** autant que possible **2** *pron* beaucoup; ***a great ~, a good ~*** un bon nombre; ***how ~ do you need?*** combien en veux-tu?
map [mæp] carte *f*; *of town* plan *m*
maple ['meɪpl] érable *m*
mar [mɑːr] gâcher
marathon ['mærəθɑːn] *race* marathon *m*
marble ['mɑːrbl] *material* marbre *m*
March [mɑːrʧ] mars *m*
march [mɑːrʧ] **1** *n also* (*demonstration*) marche *f* **2** *v/i* marcher au pas; *in protest* défiler; **marcher** manifestant(e) *m*(*f*)
Mardi Gras ['mɑːrdɪgrɑː] mardi *m* gras
margin ['mɑːrdʒɪn] *of page*, COM marge *f*; **marginal** (*slight*) léger; **marginally** (*slightly*) légèrement
marihuana, marijuana [mærɪ'hwɑːnə] marijuana *f*
marina [mə'riːnə] port *m* de plaisance
marine [mə'riːn] **1** *adj* marin **2** *n* MIL marine *m*
marital ['mærɪtl] conjugal; **marital status** situation *f* de famille
maritime ['mærɪtaɪm] maritime
mark [mɑːrk] **1** *n* marque *f*; (*stain*) tache *f*; (*sign, token*) signe *m*; (*trace*) trace *f*; *Br* EDU note *f* **2** *v/t* marquer; (*stain*) tacher; *Br* EDU noter **3** *v/i of fabric* se tacher; **marked** (*definite*) marqué; **marker** (*highlighter*) marqueur *m*
market ['mɑːrkɪt] **1** *n* marché *m* **2** *v/t* commercialiser; **marketable** commercialisable; **market economy** économie *f* de marché; **marketing** marketing *m*; **market leader** *product* produit *m* vedette; *company* leader *m* du marché; **market place** *in town* place *f* du marché; *for commodities* marché *m*; **market research** étude *f* de marché; **market share** part *f* du marché
mark-up ['mɑːrkʌp] majoration *f*
marriage ['mærɪdʒ] mariage *m*; **marriage certificate** acte *m* de mariage; **married** marié; ***be ~ to*** être marié à; **married life** vie *f* conjugale; **marry** épouser, se marier avec; *of priest* marier; ***get married*** se marier
marsh [mɑːrʃ] *Br* marais *m*
marshal ['mɑːrʃl] *in police* chef *m* de la police; *in security service* membre *m* du service d'ordre
martial 'law loi *f* martiale
martyr ['mɑːrtər] *also fig* mar-

tyr(e) *m(f)*
marvel ['mɑːrvl] merveille *f*; **marvelous**, *Br* **marvellous** merveilleux
Marxism ['mɑːrksɪzm] marxisme *m*; **Marxist 1** *adj* marxiste **2** *n* marxiste *m/f*
mascara [mæ'skærə] mascara *m*
mascot ['mæskət] mascotte *f*
masculine ['mæskjʊlɪn] *also* GRAM masculin; **masculinity** masculinité *f*
mash [mæʃ] réduire en purée
mask [mæsk] **1** *n* masque *m* **2** *v/t feelings* masquer
masochism ['mæsəkɪzm] masochisme *m*; **masochist** masochiste *m/f*
mass[1] [mæs] **1** *n* (*great amount*) masse *f*; **~es of** F des tas de F **2** *v/i* se masser
mass[2] [mæs] *n* REL messe *f*
massacre ['mæsəkər] **1** *n also fig* F massacre *m* **2** *v/t also fig* F massacrer
massage ['mæsɑːʒ] **1** *n* massage *m* **2** *v/t* masser; *figures* manipuler
massive ['mæsɪv] énorme; *heart attack* grave
mass 'media médias *mpl*; **mass-produce** fabriquer en série; **mass production** fabrication *f* en série
mast [mæst] *of ship* mât *m*; *for radio signal* pylône *m*
master ['mæstər] **1** *n of dog* maître *m*; *of ship* capitaine *m* **2** *v/t* maîtriser; **master bedroom** chambre *f* principale; **master key** passe-partout *m inv*; **masterly** magistral; **mastermind 1** *n* cerveau *m* **2** *v/t* organiser; **masterpiece** chef-d'œuvre *m*; **master's (degree)** maîtrise *f*; **mastery** maîtrise *f*
mat [mæt] *for floor* tapis *m*; *for table* napperon *m*
match[1] [mætʃ] *n for cigarette* allumette *f*
match[2] [mætʃ] **1** *n* (*competition*) match *m*, partie *f* **2** *v/t* (*be the same as*) être assorti à; (*equal*) égaler **3** *v/i of colors, patterns* aller ensemble; **matching** assorti; **match stick** allumette *f*
mate [meɪt] **1** *n of animal* mâle *m*, femelle *f*; NAUT second *m* **2** *v/i* s'accoupler
material [mə'tɪrɪəl] **1** *n* (*fabric*) tissu *m*; (*substance*) matériau *m*, matière *f* **2** *adj* matériel; **materialism** matérialisme *m*; **materialist** matérialiste *m/f*; **materialistic** matérialiste; **materialize** (*appear*) apparaître; (*happen*) se concrétiser
maternal [mə'tɜːrnl] maternel; **maternity** maternité *f*; **maternity leave** congé *m* de maternité
math [mæθ] maths *fpl*; **mathematical** mathématique; **mathematician** mathématicien(ne) *m(f)*; **maths** *Br* → ***math***

matinée ['mætɪneɪ] matinée *f*
matriarch ['meɪtrɪɑːrk] femme *f* chef de famille
matrimony ['mætrəmounɪ] mariage *m*
matt [mæt] mat
matter ['mætər] **1** *n* (*affair*) affaire *f*, question *f*; PHYS matière *f*; ***what's the ~?*** qu'est-ce qu'il y a? **2** *v/i* importer; ***it doesn't ~*** cela ne fait rien; **matter-of-fact** impassible
mattress ['mætrɪs] matelas *m*
mature [mə'tjʊr] **1** *adj* mûr **2** *v/i of person* mûrir; *of insurance policy* arriver à échéance; **maturity** maturité *f*
maximize ['mæksɪmaɪz] maximiser; **maximum 1** *adj* maximal, maximum **2** *n* maximum *m*
May [meɪ] mai *m*
may [meɪ] ◇ *possibility*: ***it ~ rain*** il va peut-être pleuvoir; ***it ~ not happen*** cela n'arrivera peut-être pas
◇ *permission*: pouvoir; ***~ I help?*** puis-je aider?
maybe ['meɪbiː] peut-être
mayo, mayonnaise ['meɪoʊ, meɪə'neɪz] mayonnaise *f*
mayor ['meɪər] maire *m*
maze [meɪz] labyrinthe *m*
MB (= ***megabyte***) Mo (= mégaoctet)
MBA [embiː'eɪ] (= ***master of business administration***) MBA *m*
MD [em'diː] (= ***Doctor of Medicine***) docteur *m* en médecine; (= ***managing director***) DG *m* (= directeur général)
me [miː] me; *before vowel* m'; *after prep* moi; ***he knows ~*** il me connaît; ***she gave ~ a dollar*** elle m'a donné un dollar; ***it's for ~*** c'est pour moi; ***it's ~*** c'est moi
meadow ['medoʊ] pré *m*
meager, *Br* **meagre** ['miːgər] maigre
meal [miːl] repas *m*; ***enjoy your ~!*** bon appétit!
mean[1] [miːn] *adj with money* avare; (*nasty*) mesquin
mean[2] [miːn] *v/t* (*signify*) signifier, vouloir dire; ***be ~t for*** être destiné à; *of remark* être adressé à; **meaning** *of word* sens *m*; **meaningful** (*comprehensible*) compréhensible; (*constructive*) significatif; *glance* éloquent; **meaningless** *sentence etc* dénué de sens; *gesture* insignifiant
means [miːnz] *financial* moyens *mpl*; (*way*) moyen *m*; ***by all ~*** (*certainly*) bien sûr; ***by ~ of*** au moyen de
meantime ['miːntaɪm] entre-temps
measles ['miːzlz] rougeole *f*
measure ['meʒər] **1** *n* (*step*) mesure *f* **2** *v/t & v/i* mesurer
◆ **measure up to** être à la hauteur de
measurement ['meʒərmənt] *action* mesure *f*; (*dimension*)

dimension *f*; **measuring tape** mètre *m* ruban

meat [miːt] viande *f*; **meatball** boulette *f* de viande

mechanic [mɪ'kænɪk] mécanicien(ne) *m(f)*; **mechanical** *device* mécanique; *gesture etc also* machinal; **mechanical engineer** ingénieur *m* mécanicien; **mechanically** mécaniquement; *do sth* machinalement; **mechanism** mécanisme *m*; **mechanize** mécaniser

medal ['medl] médaille *f*; **medalist**, *Br* **medallist** médaillé *m*

meddle ['medl] se mêler (***in*** de)

media ['miːdɪə]: ***the ~*** les médias *mpl*; **media coverage** couverture *f* médiatique

median strip [miːdɪən'strɪp] terre-plein *m* central

'media studies études *fpl* de communication

mediate ['miːdɪeɪt] arbitrer; **mediation** médiation *f*; **mediator** médiateur(-trice) *m(f)*

medical ['medɪkl] **1** *adj* médical **2** *n* visite *f* médicale; **medicated** pharmaceutique, traitant; **medication** médicaments *mpl*; **medicinal** médicinal

medicine *science* médecine *f*; (*medication*) médicament *m*

medieval [medɪ'iːvl] médiéval

mediocre [miːdɪ'oʊkər] médiocre; **mediocrity** *of work etc* médiocrité *f*; *person* médiocre *m/f*

meditate ['medɪteɪt] méditer; **meditation** méditation *f*

Mediterranean [medɪtə'reɪnɪən] **1** *adj* méditerranéen **2** *n*: ***the ~*** la Méditerranée

medium ['miːdɪəm] **1** *adj* (*average*) moyen; *steak* à point **2** *n in size* taille *f* moyenne; (*vehicle*) moyen *m*; (*spiritualist*) médium *m*

medley ['medlɪ] (*assortment*) mélange *m*

meet [miːt] **1** *v/t* rencontrer; (*be introduced to*) faire la connaissance de; (*collect*) (aller/venir) chercher; *in competition* affronter; *of eyes* croiser; (*satisfy*) satisfaire **2** *v/i* se rencontrer; *by appointment* se retrouver; *of committee etc* se réunir **3** *n* SP rencontre *f*; **meeting** *by accident* rencontre *f*; *in business*, *of committee* réunion *f*; ***he's in a ~*** il est en réunion

megabyte ['megəbaɪt] COMPUT méga-octet *m*

mellow ['meloʊ] **1** *adj* doux **2** *v/i of person* s'adoucir

melodious [mɪ'loʊdɪəs] mélodieux

melodramatic [melədrə'mætɪk] mélodramatique

melody ['melədɪ] mélodie *f*

melon ['melən] melon *m*

melt [melt] **1** *v/i* fondre **2** *v/t*

faire fondre; **melting pot** *fig* creuset *m*

member ['membər] membre *m*; **Member of Congress** membre *m* du Congrès; **membership** adhésion *f*; *number of members* membres *mpl*

membrane ['membreɪn] membrane *f*

memento [me'mentoʊ] souvenir *m*

memo ['memoʊ] note *f* (de service)

memoirs ['memwɑːrz] mémoires *fpl*

memorable ['memərəbl] mémorable

memorial [mɪ'mɔːrɪəl] **1** *adj* commémoratif **2** *n* mémorial *m*; **Memorial Day** *jour commémoration des soldats américains morts à la guerre*

memorize ['meməraɪz] apprendre par cœur; **memory** mémoire *f*; *sth remembered* souvenir *m*

men [men] *pl* → ***man***

menace ['menɪs] **1** *n* menace *f*; *person* danger *m* **2** *v/t* menacer; **menacing** menaçant

mend [mend] réparer; *clothes* raccommoder

menial ['miːnɪəl] subalterne

menopause ['menoʊpɒːz] ménopause *f*

'men's room toilettes *fpl* pour hommes

menstruate ['menstrʊeɪt] avoir ses règles

mental ['mentl] mental; *ability, powers* intellectuel; *health, suffering* moral; F (*crazy*) malade F; **mental hospital** hôpital *m* psychiatrique; **mental illness** maladie *f* mentale; **mentality** mentalité *f*; **mentally** (*inwardly*) intérieurement; *calculate etc* mentalement

mention ['menʃn] **1** *n* mention *f* **2** *v/t* mentionner; ***don't ~ it*** (*you're welcome*) il n'y a pas de quoi!

mentor ['mentɔːr] mentor *m*

menu ['menjuː] *also* COMPUT menu *m*

mercenary ['mɜːrsɪnerɪ] **1** *adj* intéressé **2** *n* MIL mercenaire *m*

merchandise ['mɜːrʧəndaɪz] marchandises *fpl*

merchant ['mɜːrʧənt] négociant *m*, commerçant *m*

merciful ['mɜːrsɪfl] clément; *God* miséricordieux; **mercifully** (*thankfully*) heureusement; **merciless** impitoyable; **mercy** clémence *f*, pitié *f*

mere [mɪr] simple; **merely** simplement, seulement

merge [mɜːrdʒ] *of two lines etc* se rejoindre; *of companies* fusionner; **merger** COM fusion *f*

merit ['merɪt] **1** *n* mérite *m* **2** *v/t* mériter

mesh [meʃ] *of net* maille(s) *f(pl)*; *of grid* grillage *m*

mess [mes] (*untidiness*) désordre *m*, pagaille *f*; (*trouble*) gâchis *m*
message ['mesɪdʒ] *also of movie etc* message *m*
messenger ['mesɪndʒər] (*courier*) messager *m*
messy ['mesɪ] *room* en désordre; *person* désordonné; *job* salissant; *divorce* pénible
metabolism [mə'tæbəlɪzm] métabolisme *m*
metal ['metl] **1** *adj* en métal **2** *n* métal *m*; **metallic** métallique; *paint* métallisé
metaphor ['metəfər] métaphore *f*
meteor ['miːtɪɔːr] météore *m*; **meteoric** *fig* fulgurant; **meteorite** météorite *m* or *f*
meteorological [miːtɪərə'lɑːdʒɪkl] météorologique; **meteorologist** météorologiste *m/f*; **meteorology** météorologie *f*
meter[1] ['miːtər] *for gas, electricity* compteur *m*; (*parking* ~) parcmètre *m*
meter[2] ['miːtər] *unit of length* mètre *m*
method ['meθəd] méthode *f*; **methodical** méthodique
meticulous [mə'tɪkjʊləs] méticuleux
metre ['miːtə(r)] *Br* → ***meter[2]***
metropolis [mə'trɑːpəlɪs] métropole *f*; **metropolitan** citadin; *area* urbain
mew [mjuː] → ***miaow***
Mexican ['meksɪkən] **1** *adj* mexicain **2** *n* Mexicain(e) *m(f)*; **Mexico** Mexique *m*
miaow [mɪaʊ] **1** *n* miaou *m* **2** *v/i* miauler
mice [maɪs] *pl* → ***mouse***
'microchip puce *f*; **microclimate** microclimat *m*; **microcosm** microcosme *m*; **microorganism** micro-organisme *m*; **microphone** microphone *m*; **microprocessor** microprocesseur *m*; **microscope** microscope *m*; **microscopic** microscopique; **microwave** *oven* micro-ondes *m inv*
midday [mɪd'deɪ] midi *m*
middle ['mɪdl] **1** *adj* du milieu **2** *n* milieu *m*; ***be in the ~ of doing sth*** être en train de faire qch; **middle-aged** entre deux âges; **middle-class** bourgeois; **middle class(es)** classe(s) moyenne(s) *f(pl)*; **Middle East** Moyen-Orient *m*; **middleman** intermédiaire *m*; **middle name** deuxième prénom *m*; **middleweight** *boxer* poids moyen *m*
midfielder [mɪd'fiːldər] *in soccer* milieu *m* de terrain
midget ['mɪdʒɪt] miniature
'midnight minuit *m*; **midsummer** milieu *m* de l'été; **midweek** en milieu de semaine; **Midwest** Middle West *m*; **midwife** sage-femme *f*; **midwinter** milieu *m* de l'hiver
might[1] [maɪt] *v/aux*: ***I ~ be late*** je serai peut-être en retard; ***you ~ have told me!***

vous auriez pu m'avertir!
might[2] [maɪt] *n* (*power*) puissance *f*
mighty ['maɪtɪ] **1** *adj* puissant **2** *adv* F (*extremely*) vachement F, très
migraine ['mi:greɪn] migraine *f*
migrant worker ['maɪgrənt] travailleur *m* itinérant; **migrate** migrer; **migration** migration *f*
mike [maɪk] F micro *m*
mild [maɪld] doux; *taste* léger; **mildly** doucement; *spicy* légèrement; **mildness** douceur *f*; *of taste* légèreté *f*
mile [maɪl] mile *m*; **milestone** *fig* événement *m* marquant, jalon *m*
militant ['mɪlɪtənt] **1** *adj* militant **2** *n* militant(e) *m(f)*
military ['mɪlɪterɪ] **1** *adj* militaire **2** *n*: ***the ~*** l'armée *f*
militia [mɪ'lɪʃə] milice *f*
milk [mɪlk] **1** *n* lait *m* **2** *v/t* traire; **milk chocolate** chocolat *m* au lait; **milkshake** milk-shake *m*
mill [mɪl] *for grain* moulin *m*; *for textiles* usine *f*
millennium [mɪ'lenɪəm] millénaire *m*
milligram ['mɪlɪgræm] milligramme *m*
millimeter, *Br* **millimetre** ['mɪlɪmi:tər] millimètre *m*
million ['mɪljən] million *m*
millionaire [mɪljə'ner] millionnaire *m/f*
mime [maɪm] mimer
mimic ['mɪmɪk] **1** *n* imitateur(-trice) *m(f)* **2** *v/t* imiter
mince [mɪns] hacher
mind [maɪnd] **1** *n* esprit *m*; ***bear** or **keep sth in ~*** ne pas oublier qch; ***change one's ~*** changer d'avis; ***make up one's ~*** se décider; ***have sth on one's ~*** être préoccupé par qch; ***keep one's ~ on sth*** se concentrer sur qch **2** *v/t* (*look after*) surveiller; (*heed*) faire attention à; ***I don't ~ what he thinks*** il peut penser ce qu'il veut, cela m'est égal; ***do you ~ if I smoke?*** cela ne vous dérange pas si je fume?; ***~ the step!*** attention à la marche! **3** *v/i*: ***~!*** (*be careful*) fais attention!; ***never ~!*** peu importe!; ***I don't ~*** cela m'est égal; **mind-boggling** ahurissant; **mindless** *violence* gratuit
mine[1] [maɪn] *pron* le mien *m*, la mienne *f*; *pl* les miens, les miennes; ***it's ~*** c'est à moi
mine[2] [maɪn] *n for coal etc* mine *f*
mine[3] [maɪn] **1** *n explosive* mine *f* **2** *v/t* miner; **minefield** MIL champ *m* de mines; *fig* poudrière *f*; **miner** mineur *m*
mineral ['mɪnərəl] minéral *m*; **mineral water** eau *f* minérale
'minesweeper NAUT dragueur *m* de mines
mingle ['mɪŋgl] *of sounds* se

mélanger; *at party* se mêler (aux gens)
mini ['mɪnɪ] *skirt* minijupe *f*
miniature ['mɪnɪtʃər] miniature
minimal ['mɪnɪməl] minime; **minimalism** minimalisme *m*; **minimize** réduire au minimum; (*downplay*) minimiser; **minimum 1** *adj* minimal, minimum **2** *n* minimum *m*
mining ['maɪnɪŋ] exploitation *f* minière
'miniskirt minijupe *f*
minister ['mɪnɪstər] POL, REL ministre *m*; **ministerial** ministériel
mink [mɪŋk] vison *m*
minor ['maɪnər] **1** *adj* mineur; *pain* léger **2** *n* LAW mineur(e) *m(f)*; **minority** minorité *f*
mint [mɪnt] *herb* menthe *f*; *chocolate* chocolat *m* à la menthe; *hard candy* bonbon *m* à la menthe
minus ['maɪnəs] **1** *n* (~ *sign*) moins *m* **2** *prep* moins
minuscule ['mɪnəskju:l] minuscule
minute¹ ['mɪnɪt] *n of time* minute *f*
minute² [maɪ'nu:t] *adj* (*tiny*) minuscule; (*detailed*) minutieux
'minute hand ['mɪnɪt] grande aiguille *f*
minutely [maɪ'nu:tlɪ] (*in detail*) minutieusement; (*very slightly*) très légèrement
minutes ['mɪnɪts] *of meeting* procès-verbal *m*
miracle ['mɪrəkl] miracle *m*; **miraculous** miraculeux; **miraculously** par miracle
mirror ['mɪrər] **1** *n* miroir *m*; MOT rétroviseur *m* **2** *v/t* refléter
misanthropist [mɪ'zænθrəpɪst] misanthrope *m/f*
misbehave [mɪsbə'heɪv] se conduire mal
misbehavior, *Br* **misbehaviour** mauvaise conduite *f*
miscalculate [mɪs'kælkjʊleɪt] mal calculer; **miscalculation** erreur *f* de calcul; *fig* mauvais calcul *m*
miscarriage ['mɪskærɪdʒ] MED fausse couche *f*
miscellaneous [mɪsə'leɪnɪəs] divers; *collection* varié
mischief ['mɪstʃɪf] (*naughtiness*) bêtises *fpl*; **mischievous** (*naughty*) espiègle; (*malicious*) malveillant
misconception [mɪskən'sepʃn] idée *f* fausse
misconduct [mɪs'kɑ:ndʌkt] mauvaise conduite *f*
misconstrue [mɪskən'stru:] mal interpréter
misdemeanor, *Br* **misdemeanour** [mɪsdə'mi:nər] délit *m*
miser ['maɪzər] avare *m/f*
miserable ['mɪzrəbl] (*unhappy*) malheureux; *weather, performance* épouvantable
miserly ['maɪzərlɪ] avare; *sum* dérisoire

misery ['mɪzərɪ] (*unhappiness*) tristesse *f*; (*wretchedness*) misère *f*
misfire [mɪs'faɪr] *of scheme* rater; *of joke* tomber à plat
misfit ['mɪsfɪt] *in society* marginal(e) *m(f)*
misfortune [mɪs'fɔːrtʃən] malheur *m*, malchance *f*
misguided [mɪs'gaɪdɪd] malavisé, imprudent
mishandle [mɪs'hændl] *situation* mal gérer
misinform [mɪsɪn'fɔːrm] mal informer
misinterpret [mɪsɪn'tɜːrprɪt] mal interpréter; **misinterpretation** mauvaise interprétation *f*
misjudge [mɪs'dʒʌdʒ] mal juger
mislay [mɪs'leɪ] égarer
mislead [mɪs'liːd] induire en erreur, tromper; **misleading** trompeur
mismanage [mɪs'mænɪdʒ] mal gérer; **mismanagement** mauvaise gestion *f*
misprint ['mɪsprɪnt] faute *f* typographique
mispronounce [mɪsprə'naʊns] mal prononcer; **mispronunciation** mauvaise prononciation *f*
misread [mɪs'riːd] *word, figures* mal lire; *situation* mal interpréter
misrepresent [mɪsreprɪ'zent] présenter sous un faux jour
miss¹ [mɪs]: ***Miss Smith*** mademoiselle Smith; ***~!*** mademoiselle!
miss² [mɪs] **1** *n* SP coup *m* manqué **2** *v/t* manquer, rater; *bus, train etc*, (*not notice*) rater; ***I ~ you*** tu me manques **3** *v/i* rater son coup
misshapen [mɪs'ʃeɪpən] déformé; *person, limb* difforme
missile ['mɪsəl] *mil* missile *m*; *stone etc* projectile *m*
missing ['mɪsɪŋ]: ***be ~*** *have disappeared* avoir disparu; *member of school party, one of a set etc* ne pas être là
mission ['mɪʃn] mission *f*
misspell [mɪs'spel] mal orthographier
mist [mɪst] brume *f*
mistake [mɪ'steɪk] **1** *n* erreur *f*, faute *f*; ***make a ~*** faire une erreur, se tromper **2** *v/t* se tromper de; ***~ s.o./sth for s.o./sth*** prendre qn/qch pour qn/qch d'autre; **mistaken** erroné, faux; ***be ~*** faire erreur, se tromper
mister ['mɪstər] → ***Mr***
mistress ['mɪstrɪs] maîtresse *f*
mistrust [mɪs'trʌst] **1** *n* méfiance *f* **2** *v/t* se méfier de
misunderstand [mɪsʌndər'stænd] mal comprendre; **misunderstanding** malentendu *m*
misuse **1** [mɪs'juːs] *n* mauvais usage *m* **2** [mɪs'juːz] *v/t* faire mauvais usage de; *word* employer à tort

mitigating circumstances ['mɪtɪgeɪtɪŋ] circonstances *fpl* atténuantes

mitt [mɪt] *in baseball* gant *m*; **mitten** moufle *f*

mix [mɪks] **1** *n* mélange *m*; *in cooking*: *ready to use* préparation *f* **2** *v/t* mélanger; *cement* malaxer **3** *v/i socially* être sociable

◆ **mix up** confondre; *get out of order* mélanger; ***be mixed up in*** être mêlé à; **mixed** *economy, school, races* mixte; *reactions* mitigé; **mixer** *for food* mixeur *m*; *drink* boisson non-alcoolisée que l'on mélange avec certains alcools; **mixture** mélange *m*; *medicine* mixture *f*; **mix-up** confusion *f*

moan [moʊn] **1** *n of pain* gémissement *m* **2** *v/i in pain* gémir

mob [mɑːb] **1** *n* foule *f* **2** *v/t* assaillir

mobile ['moʊbəl] **1** *adj* mobile; ***be ~*** *have car* être motorisé **2** *n for decoration* mobile *m*; *Br phone* portable *m*; **mobile home** mobile home *m*; **mobile phone** *Br* téléphone *m* portable; **mobility** mobilité *f*

mobster ['mɑːbstər] gangster *m*

mock [mɑːk] **1** *adj* faux, feint **2** *v/t* se moquer de; **mockery** (*derision*) moquerie *f*; (*travesty*) parodie *f*

mode [moʊd] mode *m*

model ['mɑːdl] **1** *adj employee, husband* modèle; *boat, plane* modèle réduit *inv* **2** *n* (*miniature*) maquette *f*; (*pattern*) modèle *m*; (*fashion ~*) mannequin *m* **3** *v/i for designer* être mannequin; *for artist, photographer* poser

modem ['moʊdem] modem *m*

moderate 1 ['mɑːdərət] *adj also* POL modéré **2** ['mɑːdərət] *n* POL modéré *m* **3** ['mɑːdəreɪt] *v/t* modérer; **moderately** modérément; **moderation** (*restraint*) modération *f*

modern ['mɑːdərn] moderne; **modernization** modernisation *f*; **modernize 1** *v/t* moderniser **2** *v/i* se moderniser

modest ['mɑːdɪst] modeste; *wage, amount* modique; **modesty** *of apartment* simplicité *f*; *of wage* modicité *f*; (*lack of conceit*) modestie *f*

modification [mɑːdɪfɪ'keɪʃn] modification *f*; **modify** modifier

module ['mɑːdʒuːl] module *m*

moist [mɔɪst] humide; **moisten** humidifier; **moisture** humidité *f*; **moisturizer** *for skin* produit *m* hydratant

molasses [mə'læsɪz] mélasse *f*

mold¹ [moʊld] *n on food* moisi *m*, moisissure(s) *f(pl)*

mold² [moʊld] **1** *n* moule *m* **2**

v/t clay modeler; *character* façonner
moldy ['mouldɪ] *food* moisi
molecule ['mɑːlɪkjuːl] molécule *f*
molest [mə'lest] *child, woman* agresser (sexuellement)
mollycoddle ['mɑːlɪkɑːdl] F dorloter
molten ['moultən] en fusion
mom [mɑːm] F maman *f*
moment ['moumənt] instant *m*, moment *m*; **at the ~** en ce moment; **momentarily** (*for a moment*) momentanément; (*in a moment*) dans un instant; **momentary** momentané; **momentous** capital
momentum [mə'mentəm] élan *m*
monarch ['mɑːnərk] monarque *m*
monastery ['mɑːnəstrɪ] monastère *m*; **monastic** monastique
Monday ['mʌndeɪ] lundi *m*
monetary ['mɑːnəterɪ] monétaire
money ['mʌnɪ] argent *m*; **money belt** sac *m* banane; **money market** marché *m* monétaire; **money order** mandat *m* postal
mongrel ['mʌŋgrəl] bâtard *m*
monitor ['mɑːnɪtər] **1** *n* COMPUT moniteur *m* **2** *v/t* surveiller, contrôler
monk [mʌŋk] moine *m*
monkey ['mʌŋkɪ] singe *m*; F *child* polisson *m*; **monkey wrench** clef *f* anglaise
monolog, *Br* **monologue** ['mɑːnəlɑːg] monologue *m*
monopolize [mə'nɑːpəlaɪz] exercer un monopole sur; *fig* monopoliser; **monopoly** monopole *m*
monotonous [mə'nɑːtənəs] monotone; **monotony** monotonie *f*
monster ['mɑːnstər] monstre *m*; **monstrosity** horreur *f*
month [mʌnθ] mois *m*; **monthly 1** *adj* mensuel **2** *adv* mensuellement **3** *n magazine* mensuel *m*
monument ['mɑːnjumənt] monument *m*
mood [muːd] (*frame of mind*) humeur *f*; (*bad ~*) mauvaise humeur *f*; *of meeting, country* état *m* d'esprit; **moody** *changing moods* lunatique; (*bad-tempered*) maussade
moon [muːn] lune *f*; **moonlight** clair *m* de lune; **moonlit** éclairé par la lune
moor [mur] *boat* amarrer
moose [muːs] orignal *m*
mop [mɑːp] **1** *n for floor* balai *m* lave-sol; *for dishes* éponge *f* à manche **2** *v/t floor* laver; *eyes, face* éponger, essuyer
◆ **mop up** éponger; MIL balayer
moral ['mɔːrəl] **1** *adj* moral **2** *n of story* morale *f*; **~s** moralité *f*
morale [mə'ræl] moral *m*

morality [mə'rælətɪ] moralité *f*
morbid ['mɔːrbɪd] morbide
more [mɔːr] **1** *adj* plus de; ***some ~ tea?*** encore un peu de thé?; ***there's no ~ coffee*** il n'y a plus de café; ***~ and ~ students*** de plus en plus d'étudiants **2** *adv* plus; ***~ important*** plus important; ***~ and ~*** de plus en plus; ***~ or less*** plus ou moins; ***once ~*** une fois de plus; ***I don't live there any ~*** je n'habite plus là-bas **3** *pron* plus; ***do you want some ~?*** est-ce que tu en veux encore *or* davantage?; ***a little ~*** un peu plus; **moreover** de plus
morgue [mɔːrg] morgue *f*
morning ['mɔːrnɪŋ] matin *m*; ***in the ~*** le matin; (*tomorrow*) demain matin; ***tomorrow ~*** demain matin; ***good ~*** bonjour
moron ['mɔːrɑːn] F crétin *m*
morphine ['mɔːrfiːn] morphine *f*
mortal ['mɔːrtl] **1** *adj* mortel **2** *n* mortel *m*; **mortality** condition *f* mortelle; (*death rate*) mortalité *f*
mortar ['mɔːrtər] MIL, *cement* mortier *m*
mortgage ['mɔːrgɪdʒ] **1** *n* prêt *m* immobilier; *on own property* hypothèque *f* **2** *v/t* hypothéquer
mosaic [moʊ'zeɪk] mosaïque *f*
Moscow ['mɑːskaʊ] Moscou
Moslem ['mʊzlɪm] **1** *adj* musulman **2** *n* Musulman(e) *m*(*f*)
mosque [mɒsk] mosquée *f*
mosquito [mɑːs'kiːtoʊ] moustique *m*
moss [mɑːs] mousse *f*
most [moʊst] **1** *adj* la plupart de **2** *adv* (*very*) extrêmement, très; *play, swim, eat etc* le plus; ***the ~ beautiful*** le plus beau; ***~ of all*** surtout **3** *pron*: ***~ of*** la plupart de; ***at (the) ~*** au maximum; ***make the ~ of*** profiter au maximum de; **mostly** surtout
motel [moʊ'tel] motel *m*
moth [mɑːθ] papillon *m* de nuit
mother ['mʌðər] **1** *n* mère *f* **2** *v/t* materner; **motherhood** maternité *f*; **Mothering Sunday** → ***Mother's Day***; **mother-in-law** belle-mère *f*; **motherly** maternel; **Mother's Day** la fête des Mères; **mother tongue** langue *f* maternelle
motif [moʊ'tiːf] motif *m*
motion ['moʊʃn] **1** *n* (*movement*) mouvement *m*; (*proposal*) motion *f*; **motionless** immobile
motivate ['moʊtɪveɪt] motiver; **motivation** motivation *f*; **motive** *for crime* mobile *m*
motor ['moʊtər] moteur *m*; **motorbike** moto *f*; **motorcycle** moto *f*; **motorcyclist**

motocycliste *m/f*; **motor home** camping-car *m*; **motor mechanic** mécanicien(ne) *m(f)*; **motor racing** course *f* automobile; **motor vehicle** véhicule *m* à moteur

motto ['mɑːtoʊ] devise *f*

mould *etc Br* → ***mold*** *etc*

mound [maʊnd] (*hillock*) monticule *m*; (*pile*) tas *m*

mount [maʊnt] **1** *n* (*mountain*) mont *m*; (*horse*) monture *f* **2** *v/t steps, photo* monter; *horse, bicycle* monter sur; *campaign* organiser **3** *v/i* monter

◆ **mount up** s'accumuler

mountain ['maʊntɪn] montagne *f*; **mountaineer** alpiniste *m/f*; **mountaineering** alpinisme *m*; **mountainous** montagneux

mourn [mɔːrn] pleurer; **mourner** parent/ami *m* du défunt; **mournful** triste, mélancolique

mouse [maʊs] (*pl* ***mice*** [maɪs]) *also* COMPUT souris *f*; **mouse mat** tapis *m* de souris

moustache *Br* → ***mustache***

mouth [maʊθ] bouche *f*; *of animal* gueule *f*; *of river* embouchure *f*; **mouthful** *of food* bouchée *f*; *of drink* gorgée *f*; **mouthpiece** *of instrument* embouchure *f*; (*spokesperson*) porte-parole *m inv*; **mouthwash** bain *m* de bouche; **mouthwatering** alléchant

move [muːv] **1** *n* mouvement *m*; *in chess etc* coup *m*; (*step, action*) action *f*; (*change of house*) déménagement *m* **2** *v/t object* déplacer; *limbs* bouger; (*transfer*) transférer; *emotionally* émouvoir; **~ *house*** déménager **3** *v/i* bouger; (*transfer*) être transféré

◆ **move around** bouger, remuer; *from place to place* bouger, déménager

◆ **move in** emménager

movement ['muːvmənt] *also organization*, MUS mouvement *m*; **movers** déménageurs *mpl*

movie ['muːvɪ] film *m*; ***go to a/the ~s*** aller au cinéma; **moviegoer** amateur *m* de cinéma, cinéphile *m/f*; **movie theater** cinéma *m*

moving ['muːvɪŋ] *parts* mobile; *emotionally* émouvant

mow [moʊ] *grass* tondre; **mower** tondeuse *f* (à gazon)

mph [empiː'eɪtʃ] (= ***miles per hour***) miles à l'heure

Mr ['mɪstər] Monsieur, M.

Mrs ['mɪsɪz] Madame, Mme

Ms [mɪz] Madame, Mme

much [mʌtʃ] **1** *adj* beaucoup de; ***so ~ money*** tant d'argent; ***as ~ … as …*** autant (de)… que… **2** *adv* beaucoup; ***very ~*** beaucoup; ***too ~*** trop **3** *pron* beaucoup; ***nothing ~*** pas grand-chose; ***as ~ as …*** autant que…

mud [mʌd] boue *f*
muddle ['mʌdl] **1** *n* (*mess*) désordre *m*; (*confusion*) confusion *f* **2** *v/t* embrouiller
muddy ['mʌdɪ] boueux
muffin ['mʌfɪn] muffin *m*
muffle ['mʌfl] étouffer; **muffler** MOT silencieux *m*
mug[1] [mʌg] *n for coffee* chope *f*; F (*face*) gueule *f* F
mug[2] *v/t* (*attack*) agresser
mugger ['mʌgər] agresseur *m*; **mugging** agression *f*; **muggy** lourd, moite
mule [mju:l] *animal* mulet *m*, mule *f*; *slipper* mule *f*
multicultural [mʌltɪ'kʌltʃərəl] multiculturel; **multilateral** POL multilatéral; **multimedia 1** *adj* multimédia **2** *n* multimédia *m*; **multinational 1** *adj* multinational **2** *n* COM multinationale *f*
multiple ['mʌltɪpl] multiple; **multiple sclerosis** sclérose *f* en plaques
multiplex ['mʌltɪpleks] (cinéma *m*) multiplex *m*
multiplication [mʌltɪplɪ'keɪʃn] multiplication *f*; **multiply 1** *v/t* multiplier **2** *v/i* se multiplier
multitasking [mʌltɪ'tæskɪŋ] multitâche *m*; *for persons* multiplicité *f* des tâches
mumble ['mʌmbl] **1** *n* marmonnement *m* **2** *v/t* & *v/i* marmonner
munch [mʌntʃ] mâcher
municipal [mju:'nɪsɪpl] municipal
mural ['mjʊrəl] peinture *f* murale
murder ['mɜ:rdər] **1** *n* meurtre *m* **2** *v/t person* assassiner; *song* massacrer; **murderer** meurtrier(-ière) *m*(*f*)
murky ['mɜ:rkɪ] *also fig* trouble
murmur ['mɜ:rmər] **1** *n* murmure *m* **2** *v/t* murmurer
muscle ['mʌsl] muscle *m*; **muscular** *pain* musculaire; *person* musclé
museum [mju:'zɪəm] musée *m*
mushroom ['mʌʃrʊm] **1** *n* champignon *m* **2** *v/i fig* proliférer
music ['mju:zɪk] musique *f*; *in written form* partition *f*; **musical 1** *adj* musical; *person* musicien **2** *n* comédie *f* musicale; **musician** musicien(ne) *m*(*f*)
mussel ['mʌsl] moule *f*
must [mʌst] **1** *v/aux* ◇ *necessity* devoir; ***I ~ be on time*** je dois être à l'heure, il faut que je sois (subj) à l'heure; ***I ~n't be late*** je ne dois pas être en retard, il ne faut pas que je sois en retard
◇ *probability* devoir; ***it ~ be about 6 o'clock*** il doit être environ six heures
mustache [mə'stæʃ] moustache *f*
mustard ['mʌstərd] moutarde *f*

musty ['mʌstɪ] *room* qui sent le renfermé; *smell* de renfermé
mutilate ['mjuːtɪleɪt] mutiler
mutiny ['mjuːtɪnɪ] **1** *n* mutinerie *f* **2** *v/i* se mutiner
mutter ['mʌtər] marmonner
mutual ['mjuːʧʊəl] (*reciprocal*) mutuel; (*common*) commun
muzzle ['mʌzl] **1** *n of animal* museau *m*; *for dog* muselière *f* **2** *v/t*: **~ *the press*** bâillonner la presse
my [maɪ] mon *m*, ma *f*; *pl* mes; **myself** moi-même; *reflexive* me; *before vowel* m'; *after prep* moi; ***I hurt* ~** je me suis blessé
mysterious [mɪ'stɪrɪəs] mystérieux; **mysteriously** mystérieusement; **mystery** mystère *m*; **mystify** rendre perplexe; *of tricks* mystifier
myth [mɪθ] *also fig* mythe *m*; **mythical** mythique

N

nag [næg] **1** *v/i of person* faire des remarques continuelles **2** *v/t* harceler; **nagging** *pain* obsédant; ***I have this* ~ *doubt that …*** je n'arrive pas à m'empêcher de penser que …
nail [neɪl] *for wood* clou *m*; *on finger, toe* ongle *m*; **nail polish** vernis *m* à ongles; **nail polish remover** dissolvant *m*
naive [naɪ'iːv] naïf
naked ['neɪkɪd] nu
name [neɪm] **1** *n* nom *m*; ***what's your* ~?** comment vous appelez-vous? **2** *v/t* appeler; **namely** à savoir; **namesake** homonyme *m/f*
nanny ['nænɪ] nurse *f*
nap [næp] sieste *f*
napkin ['næpkɪn] (*table* ~) serviette *f* (de table); (*sanitary* ~) serviette *f* hygiénique
narcotic [nɑːr'kɑːtɪk] stupéfiant *m*
narrate ['næreɪt] raconter; **narrative 1** *adj poem, style* narratif **2** *n* (*story*) récit *m*; **narrator** narrateur(-trice) *m(f)*
narrow ['næroʊ] étroit; *victory* serré; **narrowly** *win* de justesse; *escape* de peu; **narrow-minded** étroit d'esprit
nasty ['næstɪ] *person, thing to say* méchant; *smell* nauséabond; *weather, cut, wound, disease* mauvais
nation ['neɪʃn] nation *f*; **national 1** *adj* national **2** *n* national *m*, ressortissant *m*; **national anthem** hymne *m* national; **national debt** dette *f* publique; **nationalism** nationalisme *m*; **nationality** nationalité *f*; **nationalize** *in-*

dustry etc nationaliser

native ['neɪtɪv] **1** *adj* natal **2** *n* natif(-ive) *m(f)*; (*tribesman*) indigène *m*; **Native American 1** *adj* amérindien **2** *n* Amérindien(ne) *m(f)*

NATO ['neɪtoʊ] (= ***North Atlantic Treaty Organization***) OTAN *f* (= Organisation du traité de l'Atlantique Nord)

natural ['nætʃrəl] naturel; **naturalist** naturaliste *m/f*; **naturalize**: ***become ~d*** se faire naturaliser; **naturally** (*of course*) bien entendu; *behave, speak* naturellement, avec naturel; (*by nature*) de nature; **nature** nature *f*; **nature reserve** réserve *f* naturelle

naughty ['nɒːtɪ] vilain; *photograph , word etc* coquin

nausea ['nɒːzɪə] nausée *f*; **nauseate** *fig* écœurer; **nauseating** écœurant; **nauseous**: ***feel ~*** avoir la nausée

nautical ['nɒːtɪkl] nautique, marin

naval ['neɪvl] naval, maritime; *history* de la marine

navel ['neɪvl] nombril *m*

navigate ['nævɪgeɪt] *also* COMPUT naviguer; *in car* diriger; **navigation** navigation *f*; *in car* indications *fpl*; **navigator** navigateur *m*

navy ['neɪvɪ] marine *f*; **navy blue 1** *adj* bleu marine *inv* **2** *n* bleu *m* marine

near [nɪr] **1** *adv* près; ***come ~er*** approche-toi **2** *prep* près de **3** *adj* proche; ***in the ~ future*** dans un proche avenir; **nearby** tout près; **nearly** presque; ***I ~ lost it*** j'ai failli le perdre; **near-sighted** myope

neat [niːt] *room, desk* bien rangé; *person* ordonné; *in appearance* soigné; *whiskey etc* sec; *solution* ingénieux; F (*terrific*) super *inv* F

necessarily ['nesəserəlɪ] nécessairement, forcément; **necessary** nécessaire; ***it is ~ to …*** il faut …; **necessity** nécessité *f*

neck [nek] cou *m*; *of clothing* col *m*; **necklace** collier *m*; **neckline** *of dress* encolure *f*; **necktie** cravate *f*

née [neɪ] née

need [niːd] **1** *n* besoin *m*; ***if ~ be*** si besoin est; ***in ~*** dans le besoin **2** *v/t* avoir besoin de; ***you don't ~ to wait*** vous n'êtes pas obligés d'attendre; ***I ~ to talk to you*** il faut que je te parle

needle ['niːdl] aiguille *f*; **needlework** travaux *mpl* d'aiguille

needy ['niːdɪ] nécessiteux

negative ['negətɪv] négatif

neglect [nɪ'glekt] **1** *n* négligence *f*; *state* abandon *m* **2** *v/t* négliger; **neglected** négligé

negligence ['neglɪdʒəns] né-

gligence *f*; **negligent** négligent; **negligible** *quantity* négligeable
negotiable [nɪ'goʊʃəbl] négociable; **negotiate 1** *v/i* négocier **2** *v/t deal* négocier; *obstacles* franchir; *bend in road* négocier, prendre; **negotiation** négociation *f*; **negotiator** négociateur(-trice) *m(f)*
neighbor ['neɪbər] voisin(e) *m(f)*; **neighborhood** *in town* quartier *m*; **neighboring** *house, state* voisin; **neighborly** aimable
neighbour *etc Br* → **neighbor** *etc*
neither ['niːðər] **1** *adj*: **~ *player*** aucun(e) des deux joueurs **2** *pron* ni l'un ni l'autre **3** *adv*: **~ ... *nor* ...** ni ... ni ... **4** *conj*: **~ *do/can I*** moi non plus
neon light ['niːɑːn] néon *m*
nephew ['nefjuː] neveu *m*
nerve [nɜːrv] nerf *m*; (*courage*) courage *m*; (*impudence*) culot *m* F; **nerve-racking** angoissant, éprouvant; **nervous** nerveux; **nervous breakdown** dépression *f* nerveuse; **nervousness** nervosité *f*; **nervy** (*fresh*) effronté, culotté F
nest [nest] nid *m*
net[1] [net] *n for fishing, tennis etc* filet *m*; *Internet* Net *m*
net[2] [net] *adj price etc* net
nettle ['netl] ortie *f*
'network *also* COMPUT réseau *m*
neurologist [nʊ'rɑːlədʒɪst] neurologue *m/f*
neurosis [nʊ'roʊsɪs] névrose *f*; **neurotic** névrosé, obsédé
neuter ['nuːtər] *animal* castrer; **neutral 1** *adj* neutre **2** *n gear* point *m* mort; **neutrality** neutralité *f*; **neutralize** neutraliser
never ['nevər] jamais; ***I've ~ been to New York*** je ne suis jamais allé à New York; **nevertheless** néanmoins
new [nuː] nouveau; (*not used*) neuf; **newborn** nouveau-né; **newcomer** nouveau venu *m*, nouvelle venue *f*; **newly** (*recently*) récemment, nouvellement; **newly-weds** jeunes mariés *mpl*
news [nuːz] nouvelle(s) *f(pl)*; *on TV, radio* informations *fpl*; **newscast** TV journal *m* télévisé; **newscaster** TV présentateur(-trice) *m(f)*; **news flash** flash *m* d'information; **newspaper** journal *m*; **newsreader** TV *etc* présentateur(-trice) *m(f)*; **news report** reportage *m*; **newsstand** kiosque *m* à journaux; **newsvendor** vendeur(-euse) *m(f)* de journaux
'New Year nouvel an *m*; ***Happy ~!*** Bonne année!; **New Year's Day** jour *m* de l'an; **New Year's Eve** la Saint-Sylvestre
next [nekst] **1** *adj* prochain; ***the ~ month*** le mois suivant

2 *adv* (*after*) ensuite, après; **~ to** à côté de; **next-door 1** *adj neighbor* d'à côté **2** *adv live* à côté; **next of kin** parent *m* le plus proche

nibble ['nɪbl] *cheese* grignoter; *ear* mordiller

nice [naɪs] agréable; *person also* sympathique; *house, hair* beau; ***that's very ~ of you*** c'est très gentil de votre part; **nicely** *written, presented* bien; (*pleasantly*) agréablement

niche [niːʃ] *in market* créneau *m*; (*special position*) place *f*

nick [nɪk] (*cut*) coupure *f*

nickel ['nɪkl] MIN nickel *m*; *coin* pièce *f* de cinq cents

'nickname surnom n

niece [niːs] nièce *f*

night [naɪt] nuit *f*; (*evening*) soir *m*; ***11 o'clock at ~*** onze heures du soir; ***during the ~*** pendant la nuit; ***good ~*** *going to bed* bonne nuit; *leaving office, friends' house etc* bonsoir; **nightcap** *drink* boisson *f* du soir; **nightclub** boîte *f* de nuit; **nightdress** chemise *f* de nuit; **night flight** vol *m* de nuit; **nightlife** vie *f* nocturne; **nightly 1** *adj* de toutes les nuits; *in evening* de tous les soirs **2** *adv* toutes les nuits; *in evening* tous les soirs; **nightmare** *also fig* cauchemar *m*; **night porter** gardien *m* de nuit; **night school** cours *mpl* du soir; **night shift** équipe *f* de nuit; **nightshirt** chemise *f* de nuit (d'homme); **nightspot** boîte *f* (de nuit); **nighttime**: ***at ~, in the ~*** la nuit

nimble ['nɪmbl] agile; *mind* vif

nine [naɪn] neuf; **nineteen** dix-neuf; **nineteenth** dix-neuvième; **ninetieth** quatre-vingt-dixième; **ninety** quatre-vingt-dix; **ninth** neuvième

nip [nɪp] (*pinch*) pincement *m*; (*bite*) morsure *f*

nipple ['nɪpl] mamelon *m*

nitrogen ['naɪtrədʒn] azote *m*

no [noʊ] **1** *adv* non **2** *adj* aucun, pas de; ***there's ~ coffee left*** il ne reste plus de café; ***I have ~ money*** je n'ai pas d'argent; ***~ smoking*** défense de fumer

noble ['noʊbl] noble

nobody ['noʊbədɪ] personne; ***~ knows*** personne ne le sait; ***there was ~ at home*** il n'y avait personne

no-brainer [noʊ'breɪnər] jeu *m* d'enfant; ***the math test was a ~*** le devoir de maths était super facile

nod [nɑːd] **1** *n* signe *m* de tête **2** *v/i* faire un signe de tête

noise [nɔɪz] bruit *m*; **noisy** bruyant; ***be ~*** *of person* faire du bruit

nominal ['nɑːmɪnl] nominal; (*token*) symbolique

nominate ['nɑːmɪneɪt] (*ap-*

point) nommer; **nomination** (*appointment*) nomination *f*; (*person proposed*) candidat *m*; **nominee** candidat *m*
nonalco'holic non alcoolisé
noncommissioned 'officer ['nɑːnkəmɪʃnd] sous-officier *m*
noncommittal [nɑːnkə'mɪtl] évasif
nondescript ['nɑːndɪskrɪpt] quelconque; *color* indéfinissable
none [nʌn] aucun(e); ***there is/are ~ left*** il n'en reste plus
nonentity [nɑːn'entətɪ] être *m* insignifiant
none'xistent inexistant
non'fiction ouvrages *mpl* non littéraires
noninter'ference non-ingérence *f*
noninter'vention non-intervention *f*
no-'nonsense *approach* pragmatique
non'payment non-paiement *m*
nonpol'luting non polluant
non'resident non-résident *m*; *in hotel* client *m* de passage
nonre'turnable non remboursable
nonsense ['nɑːnsəns] absurdité(s) *f*(*pl*); ***don't talk ~*** ne raconte pas n'importe quoi
non'smoker non-fumeur (-euse) *m*(*f*)
non'standard non standard *inv*; *use of word* impropre
non'stop 1 *adj flight, train* direct; *chatter* incessant **2** *adv fly, travel* sans escale; *chatter, argue* sans arrêt
non'union non syndiqué
non'violence non-violence *f*; **nonviolent** non-violent
noodles ['nuːdlz] nouilles *fpl*
noon [nuːn] midi *m*
no-one → ***nobody***
noose [nuːs] nœud *m* coulant
nor [nɔːr] ni; ***~ do I*** moi non plus
norm [nɔːrm] norme *f*; **normal** normal; **normality** normalité *f*; **normally** normalement
north [nɔːrθ] **1** *n* nord *m* **2** *adj* nord *inv*; *wind* du nord **3** *adv travel* vers le nord; **North America** Amérique *f* du Nord; **North American 1** *adj* nord-américain **2** *n* Nord-Américain(e) *m*(*f*); **northeast** nord-est *m*; **northerly** *wind* du nord; *direction* vers le nord; **northern** du nord; **northerner** habitant *m* du Nord; **North Korea** Corée *f* du Nord; **North Korean 1** *adj* nord-coréen **2** *n* Nord-Coréen(ne) *m*(*f*); **North Pole** pôle *m* Nord; **northward** *travel* vers le nord; **northwest** nord-ouest *m*
nose [noʊz] nez *m*
◆ **nose around** F fouiner
nostalgia [nɑː'stældʒə] nostalgie *f*; **nostalgic** nostalgi-

que
nostril ['nɑːstrəl] narine *f*
nosy ['noʊzɪ] F curieux
not [nɑːt] pas; *~ now* pas maintenant; *~ there* pas là; *~ a lot* pas beaucoup *with verbs* ne … pas; *it's ~ allowed* ce n'est pas permis; *he didn't help* il n'a pas aidé
notable ['noʊtəbl] notable
notch [nɑːʧ] entaille *f*
note [noʊt] MUS, *written* note *f*; (*short letter*) mot *m*; **notebook** carnet *m*; COMPUT ordinateur *m* bloc-notes; **noted** célèbre; **notepad** bloc-notes *m*; **notepaper** papier *m* à lettres
nothing ['nʌθɪŋ] rien; *she said ~* elle n'a rien dit; *~ but* rien que; *~ much* pas grand-chose; *for ~* (*for free*) gratuitement; (*for no reason*) pour un rien
notice ['noʊtɪs] **1** *n on bulletin board, in street* affiche *f*; (*advance warning*) préavis *m*; *in newspaper* avis *m*; *to leave job* démission *f*; *to leave house* préavis *m*; *at short ~* dans un délai très court; *until further ~* jusqu'à nouvel ordre; *hand in one's ~ to employer* donner sa démission; *take no ~ of* ne pas faire attention à **2** *v/t* remarquer; **noticeable** visible
notify ['noʊtɪfaɪ]: *~ s.o. of sth* signaler qch à qn
notion ['noʊʃn] idée *f*
notorious [noʊ'tɔːrɪəs] notoire
noun [naʊn] substantif *m*, nom *m*
nourishing ['nʌrɪʃɪŋ] nourrissant; **nourishment** nourriture *f*
novel ['nɑːvl] roman *m*; **novelist** romancier(-ière) *m*(*f*); **novelty** nouveauté *f*
November [noʊ'vembər] novembre *m*
novice ['nɑːvɪs] (*beginner*) novice *m*, débutant *m*
now [naʊ] maintenant; *~ and again, ~ and then* de temps à autre; *by ~* maintenant; **nowadays** aujourd'hui, de nos jours
nowhere ['noʊwer] nulle part; *it's ~ near finished* c'est loin d'être fini
nuclear ['nuːklɪər] nucléaire; **nuclear energy** énergie *f* nucléaire; **nuclear power** énergie *f* nucléaire; POL puissance *f* nucléaire; **nuclear power station** centrale *f* nucléaire; **nuclear reactor** réacteur *m* nucléaire; **nude** [nuːd] **1** *adj* nu **2** *n painting* nu *m*; *in the ~* tout nu
nudge [nʌdʒ] *person* donner un coup de coude à; *parked car* pousser (un peu)
nudist ['nuːdɪst] nudiste *m/f*
nuisance ['nuːsns] peste *f*, plaie *f* F; *event, task* ennui *m*; *make a ~ of o.s.* être embêtant F

null and 'void [nʌl] nul et non avenu
numb [nʌm] engourdi; *emotionally* insensible
number ['nʌmbər] **1** *n* nombre *m*; *symbol* chiffre *m*; *of hotel room, phone ~ etc* numéro *m* **2** *v/t* (*put a ~ on*) numéroter
numeral ['nu:mərəl] chiffre *m*
numerous ['nu:mərəs] nombreux
nun [nʌn] religieuse *f*
nurse [nɜ:rs] infirmier(-ière) *m*(*f*); **nursery** maternelle *f*; *for plants* pépinière *f*; **nursery rhyme** comptine *f*; **nursery school** école *f* maternelle; **nursing** profession *f* d'infirmier; **nursing home** *for old people* maison *f* de retraite
nut [nʌt] (*walnut*) noix *f*; (*Brazil*) noix *f* du Brésil; (*hazelnut*) noisette *f*; (*peanut*) cacahuète *f*; *for bolt* écrou *m*; **nutcrackers** casse-noisettes *m inv*
nutrient ['nu:triənt] élément *m* nutritif; **nutrition** nutrition *f*; **nutritious** nutritif
nuts [nʌts] F (*crazy*) fou

O

oar [ɔ:r] aviron *m*, rame *f*
oasis [oʊ'eɪsɪs] *also fig* oasis *f*
oath [oʊθ] LAW serment *m*; (*swearword*) juron *m*
oats [oʊts] *npl* avoine *f*
obedience [oʊ'bi:dɪəns] obéissance *f*; **obedient** obéissant; **obediently** docilement
obese [oʊ'bi:s] obèse; **obesity** obésité *f*
obey [oʊ'beɪ] obéir à
obituary [oʊ'bɪtʃuerɪ] nécrologie *f*
object[1] ['ɑ:bdʒɪkt] *n* (*thing*) objet *m*; (*aim*) objectif *m*; GRAM complément *m* d'objet
object[2] [əb'dʒekt] *v/i* protester; ***if nobody ~s*** si personne n'y voit d'objection
objection [əb'dʒekʃn] objection *f*; **objectionable** (*unpleasant*) désagréable; **objective** **1** *adj* objectif **2** *n* objectif *m*; **objectively** objectivement; **objectivity** objectivité *f*
obligation [ɑ:blɪ'geɪʃn] obligation *f*; **obligatory** obligatoire; **obliging** serviable, obligeant
oblique [ə'bli:k] **1** *adj reference* indirect; *line* oblique **2** *n in punctuation* barre *f* oblique
obliterate [ə'blɪtəreɪt] *city* détruire; *memory* effacer
oblivion [ə'blɪvɪən] oubli *m*
oblong ['ɑ:blɑ:ŋ] **1** *adj* oblong **2** *n* rectangle *m*

obscene [ɑːb'siːn] obscène; *salary, poverty* scandaleux; **obscenity** obscénité *f*

obscure [əb'skjʊr] obscur; *village* inconnu; **obscurity** obscurité *f*

observant [əb'zɜːrvnt] observateur; **observation** observation *f*; **observe** observer; **observer** observateur(-trice) *m(f)*

obsess [ɑːb'ses]: ***be ~ed with*** être obsédé par; **obsession** obsession *f* (***with*** de)

obsolete ['ɑːbsəliːt] obsolète

obstacle ['ɑːbstəkl] *also fig* obstacle *m*

obstetrician [ɑːbstə'trɪʃn] obstétricien(ne) *m(f)*; **obstetrics** obstétrique *f*

obstinacy ['ɑːbstɪnəsɪ] entêtement *m*, obstination *f*; **obstinate** obstiné

obstruct [ɑːb'strʌkt] *road* bloquer, obstruer; *investigation* entraver; *police* gêner; **obstruction** *on road etc* obstacle *m*; **obstructive** *behavior* qui met des bâtons dans les roues; *tactics* obstructionniste

obtain [əb'teɪn] obtenir; **obtainable** *products* disponible

obtuse [əb'tuːs] *fig* obtus

obvious ['ɑːbvɪəs] évident, manifeste; **obviously** manifestement; ***~!*** évidemment!

occasion [ə'keɪʒn] occasion *f*; **occasional** occasionnel; **occasionally** de temps en temps, occasionnellement

occupant ['ɑːkjʊpənt] occupant(e) *m(f)*; **occupation** (*job*) métier *m*; *of country* occupation *f*; **occupy** occuper

occur [ə'kɜːr] avoir lieu, se produire; **occurrence** (*event*) fait *m*

ocean ['oʊʃn] océan *m*

o'clock [ə'klɑːk]: ***at five ~*** à cinq heures

October [ɑːk'toʊbər] octobre *m*

odd [ɑːd] (*strange*) bizarre; (*not even*) impair; **oddball** F original *m*; **odds and ends** petites choses *fpl*, bricoles *fpl*; **odds-on**: ***the ~ favorite*** le grand favori

odometer [oʊ'dɑːmətər] odomètre *m*

odor, *Br* **odour** ['oʊdər] odeur *f*

of [ɑːv] de; ***the name ~ the street/hotel*** le nom de la rue/de l'hôtel; ***the color ~ the paper*** la couleur du papier; ***five minutes ~ ten*** dix heures moins cinq; ***die ~ cancer*** mourir d'un cancer; ***love ~ money*** l'amour de l'argent

off [ɑːf] **1** *prep*: ***~ the main road*** *away from* en retrait de la route principale; *near* près de la route principale; ***$20 ~ the price*** 20 dollars de réduction **2** *adv*: ***be ~*** *of light, TV, machine* être éteint; *of brake* être des-

serré; *of lid* ne pas être mis; *not at work* ne pas être là; *canceled* être annulé; ***we're ~ tomorrow*** *leaving* nous partons demain; ***take a day ~*** prendre un jour de congé; ***it's 3 miles ~*** c'est à 3 miles; ***it's a long way ~*** c'est loin **3** *adj*: ***the ~ switch*** le bouton d'arrêt
offence *Br* → ***offense***
offend [ə'fend] (*insult*) offenser; **offender** LAW délinquant(e) *m(f)*; **offense** LAW *minor* infraction *f*; *serious* délit *m*; ***take ~ at sth*** s'offenser de qch; **offensive 1** *adj behavior, remark* offensant; *smell* repoussant **2** *n* MIL offensive *f*
offer ['ɑːfər] **1** *n* offre *f* **2** *v/t* offrir
off'hand *attitude* désinvolte
office ['ɑːfɪs] bureau *m*; (*position*) fonction *f*; **officer** MIL officier *m*; *in police* agent *m* de police; **official 1** *adj* officiel **2** *n civil servant etc* fonctionnaire *m/f*; **officially** officiellement; (*strictly speaking*) en théorie; **officious** trop zélé
'off-line *work* hors connexion; ***go ~*** se déconnecter
'off-peak *rates* en période creuse
'off-season basse saison *f*
'offset *losses* compenser
'offshore offshore
'offside SP hors jeu
'offspring progéniture *f*
'off-the-record officieux
often ['ɑːfn] souvent; ***how ~ do you go there?*** vous y allez tous les combien?
oil [ɔɪl] **1** *n* huile *f*; *petroleum* pétrole *m* **2** *v/t* lubrifier, huiler; **oil change** vidange *f*; **oil company** compagnie *f* pétrolière; **oilfield** champ *m* pétrolifère; **oil painting** peinture *f* à l'huile; **oil refinery** raffinerie *f* de pétrole; **oil rig** *at sea* plate-forme *f* de forage; *on land* tour *f* de forage; **oil slick** marée *f* noire; **oil tanker** *ship* pétrolier *m*; **oil well** puits *m* de pétrole; **oily** graisseux
ointment ['ɔɪntmənt] pommade *f*
ok [oʊ'keɪ]: ***can I? – ~*** je peux? – d'accord; ***is it ~ with you if ...?*** ça te dérange si ...?; ***does that look ~?*** est-ce que ça va?; ***that's ~ by me*** ça me va; ***are you ~?*** (*well, not hurt*) ça va?
old [oʊld] vieux; (*previous*) ancien; ***how ~ is he?*** quel âge a-t-il?; **old age** vieillesse *f*; **old-fashioned** démodé
olive ['ɑːlɪv] olive *f*; **olive oil** huile *f* d'olive
Olympic Games [ə'lɪmpɪk] Jeux *mpl* Olympiques
omelet, *Br* **omelette** ['ɑːmlət] omelette *f*
ominous ['ɑːmɪnəs] inquiétant

omission [oʊ'mɪʃn] omission *f*; **omit** [oʊ'mɪt] omettre

on [ɑːn] **1** *prep* sur; **~ *the table*** sur la table; **~ *the bus*** dans le bus; **~ *the third floor*** au deuxième étage; **~ *TV*** à la télé; **~ *Sunday*** dimanche; **~ *Sundays*** le dimanche; **~ *the 1st of …*** le premier…; ***this is ~ me*** (*I'm paying*) c'est moi qui paie; ***have you any money ~ you?*** as-tu de l'argent sur toi?; **~ *his arrival*** à son arrivée; **~ *his departure*** au moment de son départ; **~ *hearing this*** en entendant ceci **2** *adv*: ***be ~*** *of light, TV, computer etc* être allumé; *of brake* être serré; *of lid* être mis; *of program: being broadcast* passer; *of meeting etc: be scheduled to happen* avoir lieu; ***what's ~ tonight?*** *on TV etc* qu'est-ce qu'il y a ce soir?; (*what's planned?*) qu'est-ce qu'on fait ce soir?; ***you're ~*** (*I accept*) c'est d'accord; **~ *you go*** (*go ahead*) vas-y; ***talk ~*** continuer à parler; ***and so ~*** et ainsi de suite; **~ *and ~ talk etc*** pendant des heures **3** *adj*: ***the ~ switch*** le bouton marche

once [wʌns] **1** *adv* (*one time*) une fois; (*formerly*) autrefois; **~ *again***, **~ *more*** encore une fois; ***at ~*** (*immediately*) tout de suite **2** *conj* une fois que; **~ *you have finished*** une fois que tu auras terminé

one [wʌn] **1** *n number* un *m* **2** *adj* un(e); **~ *day*** un jour **3** *pron*: **~ *is bigger than the other*** l'un(e) est plus grand(e) que l'autre; ***which ~?*** lequel/laquelle?; **~ *by ~*** *enter, deal with* un(e) à la fois; ***the little ~s*** les petits *mpl*; ***I for ~*** pour ma part; ***what can ~ say?*** qu'est-ce qu'on peut dire?; **one-parent family** famille *f* monoparentale; **oneself**: ***hurt ~*** se faire mal; ***for ~*** pour soi *or* soi-même; ***do sth by ~*** faire qch tout seul; **one-way street** rue *f* à sens unique; **one-way ticket** aller *m* simple

onion ['ʌnjən] oignon *m*

'on-line en ligne; ***go ~ to*** se connecter à; **on-line banking** (services *mpl* de) banque *f* en ligne; **on-line dating** rencontres *fpl* en ligne; **on-line shopping** shopping *m* en ligne

onlooker ['ɑːnlʊkər] spectateur(-trice) *m(f)*

only ['oʊnlɪ] **1** *adv* seulement; ***he's ~ six*** il n'a que six ans **2** *adj* unique

'onset début *m*

on-the-job 'training formation *f* sur le tas

opaque [oʊ'peɪk] *glass* opaque

open ['oʊpən] **1** *adj* ouvert; ***in the ~ air*** en plein air **2** *v/t* ouvrir **3** *v/i of shop, flower* s'ouvrir; **open-air** *meeting, concert* en plein air; *pool* découvert; **open day** journée *f* portes ouvertes; **open-ended** *contract etc* flexible; **opening** *in wall etc* ouverture *f*; *of film, novel etc* début *m*; (*job*) poste *m* (vacant); **openly** (*honestly, frankly*) ouvertement; **open-minded** à l'esprit ouvert, ouvert; **open ticket** billet *m* open

opera ['ɑːpərə] opéra *m*; **opera house** opéra *m*; **opera singer** chanteur(-euse) *m(f)* d'opéra

operate ['ɑːpəreɪt] **1** *v/i of company* opérer; *of airline, bus service* circuler; *of machine* fonctionner; MED opérer **2** *v/t machine* faire marcher

◆ **operate on** MED opérer

'operating room MED salle *f* d'opération; **operating system** COMPUT système *m* d'exploitation; **operation** MED opération *f* (chirurgicale); *of machine* fonctionnement *m*; ***have an ~*** MED se faire opérer; **operator** *of machine* opérateur(-trice) *m(f)*; (*tour ~*) tour-opérateur *m*, voyagiste *m*; TELEC standardiste *m/f*

opinion [ə'pɪnjən] opinion *f*; **opinion poll** sondage *m* d'opinion

opponent [ə'pounənt] adversaire *m/f*

opportunist [ɑːpər'tuːnɪst] opportuniste *m/f*; **opportunity** occasion *f*

oppose [ə'pouz] s'opposer à; ***be ~d to*** être opposé à

opposite ['ɑːpəzɪt] **1** *adj* opposé; *meaning* contraire **2** *adv* en face; ***the house ~*** la maison d'en face **3** *prep* en face de; **opposite 'number** homologue *m/f*

opposition [ɑːpə'zɪʃn] opposition *f*

oppress [ə'pres] *people* opprimer; **oppressive** *rule* oppressif; *weather* oppressant

optician [ɑːp'tɪʃn] opticien (-ne) *m(f)*

optimism ['ɑːptɪmɪzəm] optimisme *m*; **optimist** optimiste *m/f*; **optimistic** optimiste; **optimistically** avec optimisme

optimum ['ɑːptɪməm] optimal

option ['ɑːpʃn] option *f*; **optional** facultatif

or [ɔːr] ou; ***~ else!*** sinon …

oral ['ɔːrəl] *exam* oral; *hygiene* dentaire

orange ['ɔːrɪndʒ] **1** *adj color* orange *inv* **2** *n fruit* orange *f*; *color* orange *m*; **orange juice** jus *m* d'orange

orator ['ɔːrətər] orateur(-trice) *m(f)*

orbit ['ɔːrbɪt] **1** *n of earth* orbite *f* **2** *v/t the earth* décrire une orbite autour de

orchard ['ɔːrtʃərd] verger *m*

orchestra ['ɔːrkəstrə] orchestre *m*
orchid ['ɔːrkɪd] orchidée *f*
ordain [ɔːr'deɪn] ordonner
ordeal [ɔːr'diːl] épreuve *f*
order ['ɔːrdər] **1** *n* ordre *m*; *for goods, in restaurant* commande *f*; ***an ~ of fries*** une portion de frites; ***in ~ to*** pour; ***out of ~*** (*not functioning*) hors service; ***out of ~*** (*not in sequence*) pas dans l'ordre **2** *v/t* (*put in sequence, proper layout*) ranger; *goods, meal* commander; ***~ s.o. to do sth*** ordonner à qn de faire qch **3** *v/i in restaurant* commander; **orderly 1** *adj lifestyle* bien réglé **2** *n in hospital* aide-soignant *m*
ordinarily [ɔːrdɪ'nerɪlɪ] (*as a rule*) d'habitude; **ordinary** ordinaire
ore [ɔːr] minerai *m*
organ ['ɔːrgən] ANAT organe *m*; MUS orgue *m*; **organic** *food, fertilizer* biologique; **organically** *grown* biologiquement; **organism** organisme *m*
organization [ɔːrgənaɪ'zeɪʃn] organisation *f*; **organize** organiser; **organizer** *person* organisateur(-trice) *m*(*f*)
Orient ['ɔːrɪənt] Orient *m*; **Oriental** oriental
origin ['ɑːrɪdʒɪn] origine *f*; **original 1** *adj* (*not copied*) original; (*first*) d'origine, initial **2** *n painting etc* original *m*; **originality** originalité *f*; **originally** à l'origine; (*at first*) au départ; **originate 1** *v/t idea* être à l'origine de **2** *v/i of idea, belief* émaner (***from*** de); *of family* être originaire (***from*** de)
ornamental [ɔːrnə'mentl] décoratif
ornate [ɔːr'neɪt] *architecture* chargé; *prose style* fleuri
orphan ['ɔːrfn] orphelin(e) *m*(*f*)
orthodox ['ɔːrθədɑːks] orthodoxe
orthopedic [ɔːrθə'piːdɪk] orthopédique
ostensibly [ɑː'stensəblɪ] en apparence
ostentatious [ɑːsten'teɪʃəs] prétentieux, tape-à-l'œil *inv*
ostracize ['ɑːstrəsaɪz] frapper d'ostracisme
other ['ʌðər] **1** *adj* autre; ***the ~ day*** (*recently*) l'autre jour; ***every ~ day*** un jour sur deux; ***~ people*** d'autres **2** *n*: ***the ~*** l'autre *m/f*
otherwise ['ʌðərwaɪz] **1** *conj* sinon **2** *adv* (*differently*) autrement
ought [ɒːt]: ***I/you ~ to know*** je/tu devrais le savoir; ***you ~ to have done it*** tu aurais dû le faire
ounce [aʊns] once *f*
our ['aʊər] notre; *pl* nos; **ours** le nôtre, la nôtre; *pl* les nôtres; ***it's ~*** c'est à nous; **ourselves** nous-mêmes; *reflex-*

ive nous; *after prep* nous; ***we enjoyed*** nous nous sommes amusé(e)s

oust [aʊst] *from office* évincer

out [aʊt]: ***be ~*** *of light, fire* être éteint; *of flower* être en fleur; *of sun* briller; (*not at home, not in building*) être sorti; *of calculations* être faux; (*be published*) être sorti; *of secret* être connu; (*no longer in competition*) être éliminé; (*no longer in fashion*) être passé de mode; ***~ here in Dallas*** ici à Dallas; (***get***) ***~!*** dehors!; (***get***) ***~ of my room!*** sors de ma chambre!; ***that's ~!*** (*~ of the question*) hors de question!; ***he's ~ to win*** (*fully intends to*) il est bien décidé à gagner; **outbreak** *of war* déclenchement *m*; *of violence* éruption *f*

'outcast exclu(e) *m*(*f*)

'outcome résultat *m*

'outcry tollé *m*

out'dated démodé

out'do surpasser

out'door *activities* de plein air; *life* au grand air; *toilet* extérieur; **outdoors** dehors

outer ['aʊtər] *wall etc* extérieur

'outfit (*clothes*) tenue *f*, ensemble *m*; (*company, organization*) boîte *f* F

out'last durer plus longtemps que

'outlet *of pipe* sortie *f*; *for sales* point *m* de vente; ELEC prise *f* de courant

'outline 1 *n* silhouette *f*; *of plan, novel* esquisse *f* **2** *v/t plans* ébaucher

out'live survivre à

'outlook (*prospects*) perspective *f*

out'number être plus nombreux que

out of ◇ *motion* de, hors de; ***run ~ the house*** sortir de la maison en courant

◇ *position*: ***20 miles ~ Detroit*** à 32 kilomètres de Détroit

◇ *cause* par; ***~ jealousy*** par jalousie

◇ *without*: ***we're ~ gas*** nous n'avons plus d'essence

◇ *from a group* sur; ***5 ~ 10*** 5 sur 10

out-of-'date dépassé; (*expired*) périmé

'output 1 *n of factory* production *f*, rendement *m*; COMPUT sortie *f* **2** *v/t* (*produce*) produire

'outrage 1 *n feeling* indignation *f*; *act* outrage *m* **2** *v/t* faire outrage à; **outrageous** *acts* révoltant; *prices* scandaleux

'outright 1 *adj winner* incontesté **2** *adv kill* sur le coup; *refuse* catégoriquement

'outset début *m*

out'shine éclipser

'outside 1 *adj* extérieur **2** *adv* dehors, à l'extérieur **3** *prep* à

l'extérieur de; (*apart from*) en dehors de **4** *n of building, case etc* extérieur *m*
'outsize *clothing* grande taille
'outskirts *of town* banlieue *f*
out'smart → ***outwit***
'outsource externaliser
out'standing exceptionnel, remarquable; FIN impayé
outstretched ['aʊtstretʃt] *hands* tendu
outward ['aʊtwərd] *appearance* extérieur; ***~ journey*** voyage *m* aller; **outwardly** en apparence
out'weigh l'emporter sur
out'wit se montrer plus malin que
oval ['oʊvl] ovale
oven ['ʌvn] four *m*
over ['oʊvər] **1** *prep* (*above*) au-dessus de; (*across*) de l'autre côté de; (*more than*) plus de; (*during*) pendant; ***she walked ~ the street*** elle traversa la rue; ***travel all ~ Brazil*** voyager à travers le Brésil; ***we're ~ the worst*** le pire est passé; ***~ and above*** en plus de **2** *adv*: **be ~** (*finished*) être fini; (*left*) rester; ***there were just 6 ~*** il n'en restait que 6; ***~ in Japan*** au Japon; ***~ here*** ici; ***~ there*** là-bas; ***it hurts all ~*** ça fait mal partout; ***painted white all ~*** peint tout en blanc; ***it's all ~*** c'est fini; ***~ and ~ again*** maintes et maintes fois; ***do sth ~*** (***again***) refaire qch; **overall** *measure* en tout; (*in general*) dans l'ensemble;
overalls bleu *m* de travail
over'awe impressionner, intimider
over'balance *of person* perdre l'équilibre
over'bearing dominateur
'overcast *sky* couvert
over'charge faire payer trop cher à
'overcoat pardessus *m*
over'come *difficulties* surmonter
over'crowded *city* surpeuplé; *train* bondé
over'do (*exaggerate*) exagérer; *in cooking* trop cuire; **over'done** *meat* trop cuit
'overdose overdose *f*
'overdraft découvert *m*; ***have an ~*** être à découvert; **over'draw** *account* mettre à découvert
overdressed trop habillé
over'estimate surestimer
overex'pose surexposer
'overflow[1] *n pipe* trop-plein *m inv*
over'flow[2] *v/i of water* déborder
over'haul *engine etc* remettre à neuf; *plans* remanier
'overhead 1 *adj* au-dessus *m* **2** *n* FIN frais *mpl* généraux
over'hear entendre (par hasard)
over'heated *room* surchauffé; *engine* qui chauffe
overjoyed [oʊvər'dʒɔɪd] ravi,

enchanté

'overland 1 *adj transport* par terre **2** *adv travel* par voie de terre

over'lap *of tiles, periods etc* se chevaucher; *of theories* se recouper

over'load surcharger

over'look *of tall building etc* surplomber, dominer; *of window* donner sur; (*not see*) laisser passer

overly ['ouvərlı] trop

'overnight *travel* la nuit; *fig: change etc* du jour au lendemain

'overpass pont *m*

over'power *physically* maîtriser

overpriced [ouvər'praıst] trop cher

overrated [ouvə'reıtıd] surfait

over'ride *decision etc* annuler; *technically* forcer; **overriding** *concern* principal

over'rule *decision* annuler

over'seas à l'étranger

over'see superviser

over'shadow *fig* éclipser

'oversight omission *f*

over'sleep se réveiller en retard

over'state exagérer; **overstatement** exagération *f*

over'take *also Br* MOT dépasser

over'throw[1] *v/t government* renverser

'overthrow[2] *n of government* renversement *m*

'overtime 1 *n* SP temps *m* supplémentaire **2** *adv*: ***work ~*** faire des heures supplémentaires

over'turn 1 *v/t also government* renverser **2** *v/i of vehicle* se retourner

'overview vue *f* d'ensemble

overwhelming [ouvər'welmıŋ] *feeling* irrépressible; *relief* énorme; *majority* écrasant

over'work 1 *n* surmenage *m* **2** *v/i* se surmener

owe [ou] devoir (***s.o.*** à qn); **owing to** à cause de

owl [aul] hibou *m*, chouette *f*

own[1] [oun] *v/t* posséder

own[2] [oun] *pron*: ***an apartment of my ~*** un appartement à moi; ***on my/his ~*** tout seul

◆ **own up** avouer

owner ['ounər] propriétaire *m/f*; **ownership** possession *f*, propriété *f*

oxygen ['ɑːksıdʒən] oxygène *m*

oyster ['ɔıstər] huître *f*

ozone ['ouzoun] ozone *m*; **ozone layer** couche *f* d'ozone

P

PA [piː'eɪ] (= ***personal assistant***) secrétaire *m/f*

pace [peɪs] (*step*) pas *m*; (*speed*) allure *f*; **pacemaker** MED stimulateur *m* cardiaque, pacemaker *m*; SP lièvre *m*

Pacific [pə'sɪfɪk]: ***the ~ (Ocean)*** le Pacifique, l'océan *m* Pacifique

pacifier ['pæsɪfaɪər] *for baby* sucette *f*; **pacifism** pacifisme *m*; **pacifist** pacifiste *m/f*; **pacify** calmer, apaiser

pack [pæk] **1** *n* (*back~*) sac *m* à dos; *of cereal, cigarettes etc* paquet *m*; *of cards* jeu *m* **2** *v/t item of clothing etc* mettre dans ses bagages; *goods* emballer; ***~ one's bag*** faire sa valise **3** *v/i* faire ses bagages; **package 1** *n* (*parcel*) paquet *m*; *of offers etc* forfait *m* **2** *v/t in packs* conditionner; *idea, project* présenter; **packaging** *of product* conditionnement *m*; *material* emballage *m*; *of idea* présentation *f*; **packet** paquet *m*

pact [pækt] pacte *m*

pad[1] [pæd] **1** *n protective* tampon *m* de protection; *over wound* tampon *m*; *for writing* bloc *m* **2** *v/t with material* rembourrer; *speech, report* délayer

pad[2] [pæd] *v/i* (*move quietly*) marcher à pas feutrés

padding ['pædɪŋ] *material* rembourrage *m*; *in speech etc* remplissage *m*

paddle ['pædl] **1** *n for canoe* pagaie *f* **2** *v/i in canoe* pagayer

paddock ['pædək] paddock *m*

padlock ['pædlɑːk] cadenas *m*

page[1] [peɪdʒ] *n of book etc* page *f*

page[2] [peɪdʒ] (*call*) (faire) appeler

pager ['peɪdʒər] pager *m*, radiomessageur *m*; *for doctor* bip *m*

paid em'ployment travail *m* rémunéré

pain [peɪn] douleur *f*; ***be in ~*** souffrir; **painful** *arm, leg etc* douloureux; (*distressing*) pénible; (*laborious*) difficile; **painfully** (*extremely, acutely*) terriblement; **painkiller** analgésique *m*; **painstaking** minutieux

paint [peɪnt] **1** *n* peinture *f* **2** *v/t* peindre; **paintbrush** pinceau *m*; **painter** peintre *m*; **painting** *activity* peinture *f*; *picture* tableau *m*; **paintwork** peinture *f*

pair [per] paire *f*; *of people, animals* couple *m*; ***a ~ of pants*** un pantalon

pajamas [pə'dʒɑːməz] pyjama *m*
Pakistan [pækɪ'stɑːn] Pakistan *m*; **Pakistani 1** *adj* pakistanais **2** *n* Pakistanais(e) *m(f)*
pal [pæl] F (*friend*) copain *m*, copine *f*
palace ['pælɪs] palais *m*
palate ['pælət] ANAT, *fig* palais *m*
palatial [pə'leɪʃl] somptueux
pale [peɪl] pâle; ***go ~*** pâlir
Palestine ['pæləstaɪn] Palestine *f*; **Palestinian 1** *adj* palestinien **2** *n* Palestinien(ne) *m(f)*
pallet ['pælɪt] palette *f*
pallor ['pælər] pâleur *f*
palm [pɑːm] *of hand* paume *f*
palm tree palmier *m*
paltry ['pɒːltrɪ] dérisoire
pamper ['pæmpər] gâter
pamphlet ['pæmflɪt] *for information* brochure *f*; *political* tract *m*
pan [pæn] casserole *f*; *for frying* poêle *f*
pancake ['pænkeɪk] crêpe *f*
pandemonium [pændɪ'moʊnɪəm] désordre *m*
pane [peɪn]: ***a ~ of glass*** un carreau
panel ['pænl] panneau *m*; *people* comité *m*; *on TV program* invités *mpl*
paneling, *Br* **panelling** lambris *m*
panic ['pænɪk] **1** *n* panique *f* **2** *v/i* paniquer; **panic-stricken** affolé, pris de panique
panorama [pænə'rɑːmə] panorama *m*; **panoramic** panoramique
pant [pænt] *of person* haleter
panties ['pæntɪz] culotte *f*
pantihose → ***pantyhose***
pants [pænts] pantalon *m*
pantyhose ['pæntɪhoʊz] collant *m*
papal ['peɪpəl] papal
paparazzi [pæpə'rætsiː] paparazzi *m/f*
paper ['peɪpər] **1** *n* papier *m*; (*news~*) journal *m*; (*wall~*) papier *m* peint; *academic* article *m*, exposé *m*; (*examination ~*) épreuve *f*; ***~s*** (*documents*) documents *mpl*; (*identity ~s*) papiers *mpl* **2** *adj* (*made of ~*) en papier **3** *v/t room* tapisser; **paperback** livre *m* de poche; **paper clip** trombone *m*; **paperwork** tâches *fpl* administratives
parachute ['pærəʃuːt] **1** *n* parachute *m* **2** *v/i* sauter en parachute **3** *v/t troops*, *supplies* parachuter
parade [pə'reɪd] **1** *n* (*procession*) défilé *m* **2** *v/i of soldiers* défiler; *showing off* parader
paradise ['pærədaɪs] REL, *fig* paradis *m*
paradox ['pærədɑːks] paradoxe *m*; **paradoxical** paradoxal; **paradoxically** paradoxalement
paragraph ['pærəgræf] para-

graphe *m*
parallel ['pærəlel] **1** *n* parallèle *f*; GEOG, *fig* parallèle *m* **2** *adj also fig* parallèle **3** *v/t* (*match*) égaler
paralysis [pə'ræləsɪs] *also fig* paralysie *f*; **paralyze** paralyser
paramedic [pærə'medɪk] auxiliaire *m/f* médical(e)
parameter [pə'ræmɪtər] paramètre *m*
paramilitary [pærə'mɪlɪterɪ] **1** *adj* paramilitaire **2** *n* membre *m* d'une organisation paramilitaire
paranoia [pærə'nɔɪə] paranoïa *f*; **paranoid** paranoïaque
paraphrase ['pærəfreɪz] paraphraser
parasite ['pærəsaɪt] *also fig* parasite *m*
parasol ['pærəsɑːl] parasol *m*
paratrooper ['pærətruːpər] parachutiste *m*, para *m* F
parcel ['pɑːrsl] colis *m*, paquet *m*
pardon ['pɑːrdn] **1** *n* LAW grâce *f*; ***I beg your ~?*** (*what did you say?*) comment?; (*I'm sorry*) je vous demande pardon **2** *v/t* pardonner; LAW gracier; ***~ me?*** pardon?
parent ['perənt] père *m*; mère *f*; ***my ~s*** mes parents; **parental** parental; **parent company** société *f* mère
parent-'teacher association association *f* de parents d'élèves
parish ['pærɪʃ] paroisse *f*
park[1] [pɑːrk] *n* parc *m*
park[2] [pɑːrk] MOT **1** *v/t* garer **2** *v/i* stationner, se garer; **parking** MOT stationnement *m*; **parking brake** frein *m* à main; **parking garage** parking *m* couvert; **parking lot** parking *m*; **parking meter** parcmètre *m*; **parking ticket** contravention *f*
parliament ['pɑːrləmənt] parlement *m*
parole [pə'roʊl] **1** *n* libération *f* conditionnelle **2** *v/t* mettre en liberté conditionnelle
parrot ['pærət] perroquet *m*
part [pɑːrt] **1** *n* partie *f*; *of machine* pièce *f*; *in movie* rôle *m*; *in hair* raie *f*; ***take ~ in*** participer à, prendre part à **2** *adv* (*partly*) en partie **3** *v/i of two people* se quitter, se séparer; **partial** (*incomplete*) partiel; **partially** partiellement
participant [pɑːr'tɪsɪpənt] participant(e) *m*(*f*); **participate** participer (***in*** à); **participation** participation *f*
particular [pər'tɪkjələr] particulier; (*fussy*) à cheval (***about*** sur), exigeant; **particularly** particulièrement
partition [pɑːr'tɪʃn] (*screen*) cloison *f*; *of country* partage *m*, division *f*
partly ['pɑːrtlɪ] en partie
partner ['pɑːrtnər] partenaire

m; COM associé *m*; *in relationship* compagnon(ne) *m(f)*; **partnership** COM, *in relationship* association *f*; *in particular activity* partenariat *m*
'part-time à temps partiel
party ['pɑːrtɪ] **1** *n* (*celebration*) fête *f*; *for adults in the evening also* soirée *f*; POL parti *m*; (*group of people*) groupe *m* **2** *v/i* F faire la fête
pass [pæs] **1** *n for entry* laissez-passer *m inv*; SP passe *f*; *in mountains* col *m* **2** *v/t* (*go past*) passer devant; *another car* doubler, dépasser; *competitor* dépasser; (*go beyond*); (*approve*) approuver; ***~ an exam*** réussir (à) un examen **3** *v/i of time* passer; *in exam* être reçu; SP faire une passe; (*go away*) passer
◆ **pass away** (*euph*: *die*) s'éteindre
◆ **pass on 1** *v/t information*, *book* passer **2** *v/i* (*euph*: *die*) s'éteindre
◆ **pass out** (*faint*) s'évanouir
◆ **pass up** *opportunity* laisser passer
passable ['pæsəbl] *road* praticable; (*acceptable*) passable
passage ['pæsɪdʒ] (*corridor*) couloir *m*; *from book*, *of time* passage *m*
passenger ['pæsɪndʒər] passager(-ère) *m(f)*
passer-by [pæsər'baɪ] passant(e) *m(f)*
passion ['pæʃn] passion *f*;
passionate *lover* passionné; (*fervent*) fervent, véhément
passive ['pæsɪv] **1** *adj* passif **2** *n* GRAM passif *m*; **passive smoking** tabagisme *m* passif
'passport passeport *m*; **passport control** contrôle *m* des passeport; **password** mot *m* de passe
past [pæst] **1** *adj* (*former*) passé; ***the ~ few days*** ces derniers jours **2** *n* passé *m*; ***in the ~*** autrefois **3** *prep* après; ***it's ~ 7 o'clock*** il est plus de 7 heures; ***it's half ~ two*** il est deux heures et demie **4** *adv*: ***run ~*** passer en courant
pasta ['pæstə] pâtes *fpl*
paste [peɪst] **1** *n* (*adhesive*) colle *f* **2** *v/t* (*stick*) coller
pastime ['pæstaɪm] passe-temps *m inv*
past par'ticiple GRAM participe *m* passé
pastry ['peɪstrɪ] *for pie* pâte *f*; *small cake* pâtisserie *f*
'past tense GRAM passé *m*
pasty ['peɪstɪ] *complexion* blafard
pat [pæt] **1** *n* petite tape *f* **2** *v/t* tapoter
patch [pætʃ] **1** *n on clothing* pièce *f*; (*period of time*) période *f*; (*area*) tache *f*; ***go through a bad ~*** traverser une mauvaise passe **2** *v/t clothing* rapiécer
◆ **patch up** (*repair*) rafistoler F; *quarrel* régler

patchy ['pætʃɪ] inégal
patent ['peɪtnt] **1** *adj* (*obvious*) manifeste **2** *n for invention* brevet *m* **3** *v/t invention* breveter
paternal [pə'tɜːrnl] paternel; **paternalism** paternalisme *m*; **paternalistic** paternaliste; **paternity** paternité *f*
path [pæθ] chemin *m*; *surfaced* allée *f*; *fig* voie *f*
pathetic [pə'θetɪk] touchant; F (*very bad*) pathétique
pathological [pæθə'lɑːdʒɪkl] pathologique
patience ['peɪʃns] patience *f*; **patient 1** *adj* patient **2** *n* patient *m*; **patiently** patiemment
patio ['pætɪoʊ] *Br* patio *m*
patriot ['peɪtrɪət] patriote *m/f*; **patriotic** *person* patriote; *song* patriotique; **patriotism** patriotisme *m*
patrol [pə'troʊl] **1** *n* patrouille *f* **2** *v/t streets, border* patrouiller dans/à; **patrol car** voiture *f* de police; **patrolman** agent *m* de police; **patrol wagon** fourgon *m* cellulaire
patron ['peɪtrən] *of store, movie theater* client(e) *m(f)*; *of artist, charity etc* protecteur(-trice) *m(f)*; **patronize** *person* traiter avec condescendance; **patronizing** condescendant; **patron saint** patron(ne) *m(f)*
pattern ['pætərn] *on fabric* motif *m*; *for sewing* patron *m*; (*model*) modèle *m*; *in events* scénario *m*
paunch [pɒːntʃ] ventre *m*
pause [pɒːz] **1** *n* pause *f* **2** *v/i* faire une pause **3** *v/t tape* mettre en mode pause
pave [peɪv] paver; **pavement** (*roadway*) chaussée *f*; *Br* (*sidewalk*) trottoir *m*
paw [pɒː] **1** *n* patte *f* **2** *v/t* F tripoter
pawn [pɒːn] *in chess, fig* pion *m*
pay [peɪ] **1** *n* paye *f*, salaire *m* **2** *v/t* payer; **~ *attention*** faire attention **3** *v/i* payer; (*be profitable*) être rentable; **~ *for*** *purchase* payer
◆ **pay back** rembourser; (*get revenge on*) faire payer à
◆ **pay off 1** *v/t debt* rembourser; *corrupt official* acheter **2** *v/i* (*be profitable*) être rentable
◆ **pay up** payer
payable ['peɪəbl] payable; **pay check**, *Br* **pay cheque** chèque *m* de paie; **payday** jour *m* de paie; **payee** bénéficiaire *m/f*; **payment** paiement *m*; **pay phone** téléphone *m* public
PC [piː'siː] (= ***personal computer***) P.C. *m*; (= ***politically correct***) politiquement correct
pea [piː] petit pois *m*
peace [piːs] paix *f*; **peaceful** paisible, tranquille; *demonstration* pacifique; **peace-**

fully paisiblement
peach [piːʧ] pêche *f*
peak [piːk] **1** *n of mountain* pic *m*; *fig* apogée *f* **2** *v/i* culminer; **peak hours** *of electricity consumption* heures *fpl* pleines; *of traffic* heures *fpl* de pointe
peanut ['piːnʌt] cacahuète *f*; ***get paid ~s*** F être payé trois fois rien; **peanut butter** beurre *m* de cacahuètes
pear [per] poire *f*
pearl [pɜːrl] perle *f*
pecan ['piːkən] pécan *m*
peck [pek] **1** *n* (*bite*) coup *m* de bec; (*kiss*) bise *f* (rapide) **2** *v/t* (*bite*) donner un coup de bec à; (*kiss*) embrasser rapidement
peculiar [pɪ'kjuːljər] (*strange*) bizarre; **peculiarity** bizarrerie *f*; (*special feature*) particularité *f*
pedal ['pedl] **1** *n of bike* pédale *f* **2** *v/i* pédaler; ***he ~ed off home*** il est rentré chez lui à vélo
peddle ['pedl] *drugs* faire du trafic de
pedestrian [pɪ'destrɪən] piéton(ne) *m(f)*
pediatric [piːdɪ'ætrɪk] pédiatrique; **pediatrician** pédiatre *m/f*; **pediatrics** pédiatrie *f*
pedicure ['pedɪkjʊr] soins *mpl* des pieds
pedigree ['pedɪgriː] **1** *adj* avec pedigree **2** *n of dog, racehorse* pedigree *m*; *of person* arbre *m* généalogique
pee [piː] F faire pipi F
peek [piːk] **1** *n* coup *m* d'œil (furtif) **2** *v/i* jeter un coup d'œil, regarder furtivement
peel [piːl] **1** *n* peau *f* **2** *v/t fruit, vegetables* éplucher, peler **3** *v/i of nose, shoulders* peler; *of paint* s'écailler
peep [piːp] → ***peek***
'**peephole** judas *m*
peer[1] [pɪr] *n* (*equal*) pair *m*; *of same age group* personne *f* du même âge
peer[2] [pɪr] *v/i* regarder
peg [peg] *for hat, coat* patère *f*; *for tent* piquet *m*; ***off the ~*** de confection
pejorative [pɪ'dʒɑːrətɪv] péjoratif
pellet ['pelɪt] boulette *f*; *for gun* plomb *m*
pen[1] [pen] stylo *m*
pen[2] [pen] (*enclosure*) enclos *m*
pen[3] [pen] → ***penitentiary***
penalize ['piːnəlaɪz] pénaliser
penalty ['penəltɪ] sanction *f*; JUR peine *f*; *fine* amende *f*; SP pénalisation *f*; *soccer* penalty *m*; **penalty area** *soccer* surface *f* de réparation; **penalty clause** LAW clause *f* pénale; **penalty kick** *soccer* penalty *m*
pencil ['pensɪl] crayon *m* (de bois); **pencil sharpener** taille-crayon *m inv*
pendant ['pendənt] *necklace* pendentif *m*

penetrate ['penɪtreɪt] pénétrer; **penetration** pénétration *f*
penguin ['peŋgwɪn] manchot *m*
penicillin [penɪ'sɪlɪn] pénicilline *f*
peninsula [pə'nɪnsʊlə] presqu'île *f*
penitence ['penɪtəns] pénitence *f*, repentir *m*; **penitentiary** pénitencier *m*
'pen name nom *m* de plume
pennant ['penənt] fanion *m*
penniless ['penɪlɪs] sans le sou
'pen pal correspondant(e) *m(f)*
pension ['penʃn] retraite *f*, pension *f*
◆ **pension off** mettre à la retraite
pensive ['pensɪv] pensif
Pentagon ['pentəgɑːn]: ***the ~*** le Pentagone
pentathlon [pen'tæθlən] pentathlon *m*
penthouse ['penthaʊs] penthouse *m*, appartement *m* luxueux (édifié sur le toit d'un immeuble)
pent-up ['pentʌp] refoulé
penultimate [pe'nʌltɪmət] avant-dernier
people ['piːpl] gens *mpl*; (*race, tribe*) peuple *m*; ***10 ~*** 10 personnes; ***the ~*** le peuple; ***~ say …*** on dit…
pepper ['pepər] *spice* poivre *m*; *vegetable* poivron *m*; **peppermint** *candy* bonbon *m* à la menthe; *flavoring* menthe *f* poivrée
per [pɜːr] par; ***~ annum*** par an
perceive [pər'siːv] percevoir
percent [pər'sent] pour cent; **percentage** pourcentage *m*
perceptible [pər'septəbl] perceptible; **perceptibly** sensiblement; **perception** perception *f*; (*insight*) perspicacité *f*; **perceptive** perspicace
percolate ['pɜːrkəleɪt] *of coffee* passer; **percolator** cafetière *f* à pression
perfect **1** ['pɜːrfɪkt] *adj* parfait **2** ['pɜːrfɪkt] *n* GRAM passé *m* composé **3** [pər'fekt] *v/t* perfectionner; **perfection** perfection *f*; **perfectionist** perfectionniste *m/f*; **perfectly** parfaitement; (*totally*) tout à fait
perforated ['pɜːrfəreɪtɪd] perforé; ***~ line*** pointillé *m*
perform [pər'fɔːrm] **1** *v/t* (*carry out*) exécuter; *of actor etc* jouer **2** *v/i of actor, musician, dancer* jouer; *of machine* fonctionner; **performance** *by actor, musician etc* interprétation *f*; (*event*) représentation *f*; *of employee, company etc* résultats *mpl*; *of machine* performances *fpl*, rendement *m*; **performer** interprète *m/f*
perfume ['pɜːrfjuːm] parfum *m*
perfunctory [pər'fʌŋktərɪ]

sommaire
perhaps [pər'hæps] peut-être
peril ['perəl] péril *m*
perimeter [pə'rɪmɪtər] périmètre *m*
period ['pɪrɪəd] période *f*; (*menstruation*) règles *fpl*; *punctuation mark* point *m*; **periodic** périodique; **periodical** périodique *m*
peripheral [pə'rɪfərəl] **1** *adj* (*not crucial*) secondaire **2** *n* COMPUT périphérique *m*; **periphery** périphérie *f*
perish ['perɪʃ] *of rubber* se détériorer; *of person* périr; **perishable** *food* périssable
perjure ['pɜːrdʒər]: **~ *o.s.*** faire un faux témoignage; **perjury** faux témoignage *m*
perm [pɜːrm] **1** *n* permanente *f* **2** *v/t*: ***have one's hair ~ed*** se faire faire une permanente
permanent ['pɜːrmənənt] permanent; *address* fixe; **permanently** en permanence
permeate ['pɜːrmɪeɪt] *also fig* imprégner
permissible [pər'mɪsəbl] permis; **permission** permission *f*; **permissive** permissif; **permit 1** *n* permis *m* **2** *v/t* permettre (***s.o. to do*** à qn de faire)
perpendicular [pɜːrpən'dɪkjʊlər] perpendiculaire
perpetual [pər'petʃʊəl] perpétuel; **perpetually** perpétuellement
perplex [pər'pleks] laisser perplexe; **perplexity** perplexité *f*
persecute ['pɜːrsɪkjuːt] persécuter; **persecution** persécution *f*; **persecutor** persécuteur(-trice) *m*(*f*)
perseverance [pɜːrsɪ'vɪrəns] persévérance *f*; **persevere** persévérer
persist [pər'sɪst] persister; **persistent** *person* tenace, têtu; *questions* incessant; *rain, unemployment etc* persistant; **persistently** (*continually*) continuellement
person ['pɜːrsn] personne *f*; **personal** personnel; **personal computer** ordinateur *m* individuel; **personality** personnalité *f*; **personally** personnellement; *come, intervene* en personne; **personal organizer** organiseur *m*, agenda *m* électronique; *in book form* agenda *m*; **personal stereo** baladeur *m*; **personify** *of person* personnifier
personnel [pɜːrsə'nel] (*employees*) personnel *m*; *department* service *m* du personnel
perspective [pər'spektɪv] *in art* perspective *f*; ***get sth into ~*** relativiser qch
perspiration [pɜːrspɪ'reɪʃn] transpiration *f*; **perspire** transpirer
persuade [pər'sweɪd] *person*

persuader; **persuasion** persuasion *f*; **persuasive** *person* persuasif; *argument* convaincant
perturb [pər'tɜːrb] perturber; **perturbing** perturbant
pervasive [pər'veɪsɪv] *influence, ideas* envahissant
perversion [pər'vɜːrʃn] *sexual* perversion *f*; **pervert** *sexual* pervers(e) *m(f)*
pessimism ['pesɪmɪzm] pessimisme *m*; **pessimist** pessimiste *m/f*; **pessimistic** pessimiste
pest [pest] parasite *m*; F *person* peste *f*
pester ['pestər] harceler
pesticide ['pestɪsaɪd] pesticide *m*
pet [pet] **1** *n animal* animal *m* domestique; (*favorite*) chouchou *m* F **2** *adj* préféré, favori **3** *v/t animal* caresser **4** *v/i of couple* se peloter F
petite [pə'tiːt] menu
petition [pə'tɪʃn] pétition *f*
petrify ['petrɪfaɪ] pétrifier
petrochemical [petroʊ'kemɪkl] pétrochimique
petrol ['petrl] *Br* essence *f*
petroleum [pɪ'troʊlɪəm] pétrole *m*
petting ['petɪŋ] pelotage *m* F
petty ['petɪ] *person, behavior* mesquin; *details* insignifiant
pew [pjuː] banc *m* d'église
pharmaceutical [fɑːrmə'suːtɪkl] pharmaceutique; **pharmaceuticals** produits *mpl* pharmaceutiques
pharmacist ['fɑːrməsɪst] pharmacien(ne) *m(f)*; **pharmacy** *store* pharmacie *f*
phase [feɪz] phase *f*
phenomenal [fə'nɑːmɪnl] phénoménal; **phenomenon** phénomène *m*
philanthropic [fɪlən'θrɑːpɪk] *person* philanthrope; *action* philanthropique; **philanthropist** philanthrope *m/f*; **philanthropy** philanthropie *f*
Philippines ['fɪlɪpiːnz]: ***the ~*** les Philippines *fpl*
philosopher [fɪ'lɑːsəfər] philosophe *m/f*; **philosophical** philosophique; *attitude etc* philosophe; **philosophy** philosophie *f*
phobia ['foʊbɪə] phobie *f* (***about*** de)
phone [foʊn] **1** *n* téléphone *m* **2** *v/t* téléphoner à **3** *v/i* téléphoner; **phone book** annuaire *m*; **phone booth** cabine *f* téléphonique; **phonecall** coup *m* de fil *or* de téléphone; **phone card** télécarte *f*; **phone number** numéro *m* de téléphone
phon(e)y ['foʊnɪ] F faux
photo ['foʊtoʊ] photo *f*; **photocopier** photocopieuse *f*; **photocopy 1** *n* photocopie *f* **2** *v/t* photocopier; **photogenic** photogénique; **photograph 1** *n* photographie *f* **2** *v/t* photographier; **photog-**

rapher photographe *m/f*; **photography** photographie *f*

phrase [freɪz] **1** *n* expression *f*; *in grammar* syntagme *m* **2** *v/t* formuler

physical ['fɪzɪkl] **1** *adj* physique **2** *n* MED visite *f* médicale; **physically** physiquement

physician [fɪ'zɪʃn] médecin *m*

physicist ['fɪzɪsɪst] physicien(ne) *m(f)*; **physics** physique *f*

physiotherapist [fɪzɪoʊ'θerəpɪst] kinésithérapeute *m/f*; **physiotherapy** kinésithérapie *f*

physique [fɪ'zi:k] physique *m*

pianist ['pɪənɪst] pianiste *m/f*; **piano** piano *m*

pick [pɪk] (*choose*) choisir; *flowers*, *fruit* cueillir

◆ **pick up 1** *v/t* prendre; *phone* décrocher; *from ground* ramasser; (*collect*) passer prendre; *information* recueillir; *in car* prendre; *in sexual sense* lever F; *language*, *skill* apprendre; *illness* attraper; (*buy*) acheter **2** *v/i of business*, *economy* reprendre; *of weather* s'améliorer

picket ['pɪkɪt] **1** *n of strikers* piquet *m* de grève **2** *v/t*: ***~ a factory*** faire le piquet de grève devant une usine

'pickpocket voleur *m* à la tire, pickpocket *m*

pick-up (truck) ['pɪkʌp] pick-up *m*, camionnette *f*

picky ['pɪkɪ] F difficile

picnic ['pɪknɪk] **1** *n* pique-nique *m* **2** *v/i* pique-niquer

picture ['pɪktʃər] **1** *n* (*photo*) photo *f*; (*painting*) tableau *m*; (*illustration*) image *f*; (*movie*) film *m* **2** *v/t* imaginer

picturesque [pɪktʃə'resk] pittoresque

pie [paɪ] tarte *f*; *with top* tourte *f*

piece [pi:s] morceau *m*; (*component*) pièce *f*; *in board game* pion *m*; ***a ~ of advice*** un conseil; ***take to ~s*** démonter

◆ **piece together** *broken plate* recoller; *evidence* regrouper

piecemeal ['pi:smi:l] petit à petit

pier [pɪr] *Br at seaside* jetée *f*

pierce [pɪrs] (*penetrate*) transpercer; *ears* percer; **piercing** *noise*, *eyes* perçant; *wind* pénétrant

pig [pɪg] cochon *m*, porc *m*; (*unpleasant person*) porc *m*

pigeon ['pɪdʒɪn] pigeon *m*; **pigeonhole** casier *m*

pigheaded ['pɪghedɪd] obstiné; **pigpen** *also fig* porcherie *f*

pile [paɪl] *of books*, *plates etc* pile *f*; *of sand etc* tas *m*; ***a ~ of work*** F un tas de boulot F

◆ **pile up 1** *v/i of work*, *bills*

s'accumuler **2** *v/t* empiler
'pile-up MOT carambolage *m*
pilfering ['pɪlfərɪŋ] chapardage *m* F
pill [pɪl] pilule *f*
pillar ['pɪlər] pilier *m*
pillow ['pɪloʊ] oreiller *m*; **pillowcase** taie *f* d'oreiller
pilot ['paɪlət] **1** *n* AVIA, NAUT pilote *m* **2** *v/t airplane* piloter
pimp [pɪmp] maquereau *m*, proxénète *m*
pimple ['pɪmpl] bouton *m*
PIN [pɪn] (= ***personal identification number***) code *m* confidentiel
pin [pɪn] **1** *n for sewing* épingle *f*; *in bowling* quille *f*; (*badge*) badge *m*; fiche *f* **2** *v/t* (*hold down*) clouer; (*attach*) épingler
◆ **pin up** *notice* accrocher
pincers ['pɪnsərz] *of crab* pinces *fpl*; *tool* tenailles *fpl*
pinch [pɪntʃ] **1** *n* pincement *m*; *of salt etc* pincée *f* **2** *v/t* pincer **3** *v/i of shoes* serrer
pine [paɪn] *tree, wood* pin *m*; **pineapple** ananas *m*
pink [pɪŋk] rose
pinnacle ['pɪnəkl] *fig* apogée *f*
'pinpoint indiquer précisément; *find* identifier; **pins and needles** fourmillements *mpl*; **pin-up (girl)** pin-up *f inv*
pioneer [paɪə'nɪr] **1** *n fig* pionnier(-ière) *m(f)* **2** *v/t* lancer; **pioneering** *work* innovateur
pious ['paɪəs] pieux
pip [pɪp] *Br of fruit* pépin *m*
pipe [paɪp] **1** *n* tuyau *m*; *for smoking* pipe *f* **2** *v/t* transporter par tuyau; **pipeline** *for oil* oléoduc *m*; *for gas* gazoduc *m*
pirate ['paɪrət] **1** *n* pirate *m* **2** *v/t software* pirater
pissed [pɪst] P (*annoyed*) en rogne F; *Br* P (*drunk*) bourré
pistol ['pɪstl] pistolet *m*
piston ['pɪstən] piston *m*
pit [pɪt] (*hole*) fosse *f*; (*coal-mine*) mine *f*
pitch[1] [pɪtʃ] *n* ton *m*
pitch[2] [pɪtʃ] **1** *v/i in baseball* lancer **2** *v/t tent* planter; *ball* lancer
pitcher[1] ['pɪtʃər] *in baseball* lanceur *m*
pitcher[2] ['pɪtʃər] *container* pichet *m*
pitfall ['pɪtfɒːl] piège *m*
pitiful ['pɪtɪfl] pitoyable; **pitiless** impitoyable
pittance ['pɪtns] somme *f* dérisoire
pity ['pɪtɪ] **1** *n* pitié *f*; ***what a ~!*** quel dommage! **2** *v/t person* avoir pitié de
pizza ['piːtsə] pizza *f*
placard ['plækɑːrd] pancarte *f*
place [pleɪs] **1** *n* endroit *m*; *in race, competition* place *f*; (*seat*) place *f*; ***at my/his ~*** chez moi/lui; ***in ~ of*** à la place de; ***take ~*** avoir lieu **2** *v/t* (*put*) mettre, poser; *order* passer

placid ['plæsɪd] placide
plagiarism ['pleɪdʒərɪzm] plagiat *m*; **plagiarize** plagier
plain[1] [pleɪn] *n* plaine *f*
plain[2] [pleɪn] **1** *adj* (*clear, obvious*) clair, évident; (*not ornate*) simple; (*not patterned*) uni; (*not pretty*) ordinaire; (*blunt*) franc **2** *adv* tout simplement; **plainly** (*clearly*) manifestement; (*bluntly*) franchement; (*simply*) simplement; **plain-spoken** direct
plaintive ['pleɪntɪv] plaintif
plan [plæn] **1** *n* plan *m*, projet *m*; (*drawing*) plan *m* **2** *v/t* (*prepare*) organiser, planifier; (*design*) concevoir **3** *v/i* faire des projets
plane[1] [pleɪn] AVIA avion *m*
plane[2] [pleɪn] *tool* rabot *m*
planet ['plænɪt] planète *f*
plank [plæŋk] *of wood* planche *f*; *fig*: *of policy* point *m*
planning ['plænɪŋ] organisation *f*, planification *f*
plant[1] [plænt] **1** *n* BOT plante *f* **2** *v/t* planter
plant[2] [plænt] (*factory*) usine *f*; (*equipment*) installation *f*, matériel *m*
plantation [plæn'teɪʃn] plantation *f*
plaque [plæk] *on wall* plaque *f*; *on teeth* plaque *f* dentaire
plaster ['plæstər] **1** *n* plâtre *m* **2** *v/t wall, ceiling* plâtrer
plastic ['plæstɪk] **1** *adj* en plastique **2** *n* plastique *m*; **plastic money** cartes *fpl* de crédit; **plastic surgeon** spécialiste *m* en chirurgie esthétique; **plastic surgery** chirurgie *f* esthétique
plate [pleɪt] *for food* assiette *f*; (*sheet of metal*) plaque *f*
plateau ['plætoʊ] plateau *m*
platform ['plætfɔːrm] (*stage*) estrade *f*; *of railroad station* quai *m*; *fig*: *political* plateforme *f*
platinum ['plætɪnəm] **1** *adj* en platine **2** *n* platine *m*
platonic [plə'tɑːnɪk] platonique
platoon [plə'tuːn] *of soldiers* section *f*
plausible ['plɒːzəbl] plausible
play [pleɪ] **1** *n* jeu *m*; *in theater, on TV* pièce *f* **2** *v/i* jouer **3** *v/t musical instrument* jouer de; *piece of music* jouer; *game* jouer à; *opponent* jouer contre; (*perform*: *Macbeth etc*) jouer
◆ **play around** F (*be unfaithful*) coucher à droite et à gauche
◆ **play down** minimiser
player ['pleɪr] SP joueur(-euse) *m*(*f*); (*musician*) musicien (-ne) *m*(*f*); (*actor*) acteur (-trice) *m*(*f*); **playful** enjoué; **playground** aire *f* de jeu; **playing card** carte *f* à jouer; **playwright** dramaturge *m/f*
plaza ['plaːzə] *for shopping* centre *m* commercial
plc [piːel'siː] *Br* (= ***public lim-***

ited company) S.A. *f* (= société anonyme)

plea [pliː] appel

plead [pliːd]: ~ ***guilty/not guilty*** plaider coupable/non coupable; ~ ***with*** supplier

pleasant ['pleznt] agréable

please [pliːz] **1** *adv* s'il vous plaît, s'il te plaît; ~ ***do*** je vous en prie **2** *v/t* plaire à; ~ ***yourself*** comme tu veux; **pleased** content, heureux; ~ ***to meet you*** enchanté; **pleasing** agréable; **pleasure** plaisir *m*; ***with*** ~ avec plaisir

pleat [pliːt] *in skirt* pli *m*

pledge [pledʒ] **1** *n* (*promise*) promesse *f*; *as guarantee* gage *m*; ***Pledge of Allegiance*** serment *m* d'allégeance **2** *v/t* (*promise*) promettre; *money* mettre en gage

plentiful ['plentɪfl] abondant; ***be*** ~ abonder; **plenty** (*abundance*) abondance *f*; ~ ***of*** beaucoup de

pliable ['plaɪəbl] flexible

pliers ['plaɪərz] pinces *fpl*

plight [plaɪt] détresse *f*

plod [plɑːd] (*walk*) marcher d'un pas lourd

plot¹ [plɑːt] *of land* parcelle *f*

plot² [plɑːt] **1** *n* (*conspiracy*) complot *m*; *of novel* intrigue *f* **2** *v/t* & *v/i* comploter

plotter ['plɑːtər] conspirateur(-trice) *m(f)*; COMPUT traceur *m*

plow, *Br* **plough** [plaʊ] **1** *n* charrue *f* **2** *v/t* & *v/i* labourer

◆ **plow back** *profits* réinvestir

pluck [plʌk] *chicken* plumer; ~ ***one's eyebrows*** s'épiler les sourcils

plug [plʌg] **1** *n for sink, bath* bouchon *m*; *electrical* prise *f*; (*spark* ~) bougie *f* **2** *v/t hole* boucher; *new book etc* faire de la pub pour F

◆ **plug in** brancher

plumage ['pluːmɪdʒ] plumage *m*

plumber ['plʌmər] plombier *m*; **plumbing** plomberie *f*

plummet ['plʌmɪt] *of airplane* plonger, piquer; *of share prices* dégringoler

plump [plʌmp] *person, chicken* dodu; *hands, feet* potelé; *face, cheek* rond

plunge [plʌndʒ] **1** *n* plongeon *m*; *in prices* chute *f* **2** *v/i* tomber; *of prices* chuter **3** *v/t* plonger; *knife* enfoncer; **plunging** *neckline* plongeant

plural ['plʊrəl] pluriel *m*

plus [plʌs] **1** *prep* plus **2** *adj* plus de **3** *n sign* signe *m* plus; (*advantage*) plus *m* **4** *conj* (*moreover, in addition*) en plus

plush [plʌʃ] luxueux

plywood ['plaɪwʊd] contreplaqué *m*

PM [piː'em] *Br* (= ***Prime Minister***) Premier ministre

p.m. [piː'em] (= ***post meridiem***) *afternoon* de l'après-midi; *evening* du soir

pneumonia [nuːˈmoʊnɪə] pneumonie *f*
poach[1] [poʊʧ] *cook* pocher
poach[2] [poʊʧ] *salmon etc* braconner
poached egg [poʊʧtˈeg] œuf *m* poché
P.O. Box [piːˈoʊbɑːks] boîte *f* postale, B. P. *f*
pocket [ˈpɑːkɪt] **1** *n* poche *f* **2** *adj* (*miniature*) de poche **3** *v/t* empocher; **pocketbook** *purse* pochette *f*; (*billfold*) portefeuille *m*; *book* livre *m* de poche; **pocket calculator** calculatrice *f* de poche
podium [ˈpoʊdɪəm] estrade *f*; *for winner* podium *m*
poem [ˈpoʊɪm] poème *m*; **poet** poète *m*, poétesse *f*; **poetic** poétique; **poetry** poésie *f*
poignant [ˈpɔɪnjənt] poignant
point [pɔɪnt] **1** *n of pencil, knife* pointe *f*; *in competition, exam* point *m*; (*purpose*) objet *m*; (*moment*) moment *m*; *in argument, discussion* point *m*; *in decimals* virgule *f*; ***that's beside the ~*** là n'est pas la question; ***be on the ~ of doing sth*** être sur le point de faire qch; ***get to the ~*** en venir au fait; ***the ~ is …*** le fait est (que)…; ***there's no ~ in waiting*** ça ne sert à rien d'attendre **2** *v/i* montrer (du doigt)
◆ **point out** *sights* montrer; *advantages etc* faire remarquer
◆ **point to** *with finger* montrer du doig; *fig* (*indicate*) indiquer
pointed [ˈpɔɪntɪd] *remark* acerbe, mordant; **pointer** *for teacher* baguette *f*; (*hint*) conseil *m*; (*sign, indication*) indice *m*; **pointless** inutile; **point of view** point *m* de vue
poise [pɔɪz] assurance *f*, aplomb *m*; **poised** *person* posé
poison [ˈpɔɪzn] **1** *n* poison *m* **2** *v/t* empoisonner; **poisonous** *snake, spider* venimeux; *plant* vénéneux
poke [poʊk] **1** *n* coup *m* **2** *v/t* (*prod*) pousser; (*stick*) enfoncer
◆ **poke around** F fouiner F
poker [ˈpoʊkər] *card game* poker *m*
polar [ˈpoʊlər] polaire
pole[1] [poʊl] *of wood, metal* perche *f*
pole[2] [poʊl] *of earth* pôle *m*
police [pəˈliːs] police *f*; **police car** voiture *f* de police; **policeman** gendarme *m*; *criminal* policier *m*; **police state** État *m* policier; **police station** gendarmerie *f*; *for criminal matters* commissariat *m*; **policewoman** femme *f* gendarme; *criminal* femme *f* policier
policy[1] [ˈpɑːləsɪ] politique *f*
policy[2] [ˈpɑːləsɪ] (*insurance ~*) police *f* (d'assurance)
polio [ˈpoʊlɪoʊ] polio *f*

polish ['pɑːlɪʃ] **1** *n for furniture* cire *f*; *for shoes* cirage *m*; *for metal* produit *m* lustrant; (*nail* ~) vernis *m* (à ongles) **2** *v/t* faire briller, lustrer; *shoes* cirer; *speech* parfaire; **polished** *performance* impeccable
polite [pə'laɪt] poli; **politely** poliment; **politeness** politesse *f*
political [pə'lɪtɪkl] politique; **politically correct** politiquement correct; **politician** politicien *m*, homme *m*/femme *f* politique; **politics** politique *f*
poll [poʊl] **1** *n* (*survey*) sondage *m*; ***go to the*~*s*** (*vote*) aller aux urnes **2** *v/t people* faire un sondage auprès de; *votes* obtenir
pollen ['pɑːlən] pollen *m*
pollster ['pɑːlstər] sondeur *m*
pollutant [pə'luːtənt] polluant *m*; **pollute** polluer; **pollution** pollution *f*
'polo shirt polo *m*
polyester [pɑːlɪ'estər] polyester *m*
polystyrene [pɑːlɪ'staɪriːn] polystyrène *m*
polyunsaturated [pɑːlɪʌn-'sæʧəreɪtɪd] polyinsaturé
pond [pɑːnd] étang *m*; *artificial* bassin *m*
pontiff ['pɑːntɪf] pontife *m*
pony ['pounɪ] poney *m*; **ponytail** queue *f* de cheval
pool[1] [puːl] (*swimming* ~) piscine *f*; *of water, blood* flaque *f*
pool[2] [puːl] *game* billard *m* américain
pool[3] [puːl] **1** *n* (*common fund*) caisse *f* commune **2** *v/t resources* mettre en commun
'pool hall salle *f* de billard; **pool table** table *f* de billard
poop [puːp] F caca *m* F
pooped [puːpt] F crevé F
poor [pur] **1** *adj* pauvre; *quality etc* médiocre, mauvais **2** *npl*: ***the*** ~ les pauvres *mpl*; **poorly 1** *adj* (*unwell*) malade **2** *adv* mal
pop[1] [pɑːp] MUS pop *f*
pop[2] [pɑːp] F (*father*) papa *m*
'popcorn pop-corn *m*
pope [poup] pape *m*
Popsicle® ['pɑːpsɪkl] glace *f* à l'eau
popular ['pɑːpjələr] populaire; **popularity** popularité *f*
populate ['pɑːpjəleɪt] peupler; **population** population *f*
porch [pɔːrʧ] porche *m*
pork [pɔːrk] porc *m*
porn [pɔːrn] F porno F; **pornographic** pornographique; **pornography** pornographie *f*
port[1] [pɔːrt] *n* port *m*
port[2] [pɔːrt] *adj* (*left-hand*) de bâbord
portable ['pɔːrtəbl] **1** *adj* portable, portatif **2** *n* COMPUT portable *m*; *TV* téléviseur

m portable *or* portatif

porter ['pɔːrtər] (*doorman*) portier *m*

portion ['pɔːrʃn] partie *f*, part *f*; *of food* portion *f*

portrait ['pɔːrtreɪt] **1** *n* portrait *m* **2** *adv print* en mode portrait, à la française; **portray** *of artist* représenter; *of actor* interpréter; *of author* décrire

Portugal ['pɔːrtʃəgl] le Portugal; **Portuguese** **1** *adj* portugais **2** *n person* Portugais(e) *m(f)*; *language* portugais *m*

pose [pouz] **1** *n* attitude *f* **2** *v/i for artist* poser; ~ **as** se faire passer pour **3** *v/t problem* poser; *threat* constituer

position [pə'zɪʃn] **1** *n* position *f* **2** *v/t* placer

positive ['pɑːzətɪv] positif; **be ~** (*sure*) être sûr; **positively** vraiment

possess [pə'zes] posséder; **possession** possession *f*; **possessive** possessif

possibility [pɑːsə'bɪlətɪ] possibilité *f*; **possible** possible; **possibly** (*perhaps*) peut-être

post¹ [poust] **1** *n of wood, metal* poteau *m* **2** *v/t notice* afficher; *profits* enregistrer

post² [poust] **1** *n* (*place of duty*) poste *m* **2** *v/t soldier, employee* affecter; *guards* poster

post³ [poust] *Br* **1** *n* (*mail*) courrier *m* **2** *v/t letter* poster

postage ['poustɪdʒ] affranchissement *m*; **postage stamp** *fml* timbre *m*; **postal** postal; **postcard** carte *f* postale; **postdate** postdater

poster ['poustər] poster *m*, affiche *f*

postgraduate ['poustgrædʒuət] étudiant(e) *m(f)* de troisième cycle

posthumous ['pɑːstʃəməs] posthume

posting ['poustɪŋ] (*assignment*) affectation *f*

'postmark cachet *m* de la poste

post-mortem [poust'mɔːrtəm] autopsie *f*

'post office poste *f*

postpone [poust'poun] remettre (à plus tard), reporter; **postponement** report *m*

pot¹ [pɑːt] *for cooking* casserole *f*; *for coffee* cafetière *f*; *for tea* théière *f*; *for plant* pot *m*

pot² [pɑːt] F (*marijuana*) herbe *f*

potato [pə'teɪtou] pomme *f* de terre; **potato chips**, *Br* **potato crisps** chips *fpl*

potent ['poutənt] puissant

potential [pə'tenʃl] **1** *adj* potentiel **2** *n* potentiel *m*; **potentially** potentiellement

'pothole *in road* nid-de-poule *m*

potter ['pɑːtər] potier(-ière) *m(f)*; **pottery** poterie *f*; *items* poteries *fpl*

pouch [pautʃ] *bag* petit sac *m*

poultry ['poʊltrɪ] volaille *f*

pound[1] [paʊnd] *weight* livre *f* (0,453kg)

pound[2] [paʊnd] *n for strays, cars* fourrière *f*

pound[3] [paʊnd] *v/i of heart* battre (la chamade)

pour [pɔːr] **1** *v/t liquid* verser **2** *v/i*: ***it's ~ing*** (***with rain***) il pleut à verse

◆ **pour out** *liquid* verser; *troubles* déballer F

poverty ['pɑːvərtɪ] pauvreté *f*

powder ['paʊdər] **1** *n* poudre *f* **2** *v/t*: **~ *one's face*** se poudrer le visage

power ['paʊər] **1** *n* (*strength*) puissance *f*, force *f*; (*authority*) pouvoir *m*; (*energy*) énergie *f*; (*electricity*) courant *m*; **power drill** perceuse *f*; **power failure** panne *f* d'électricité; **powerful** puissant; **powerless** impuissant; **power line** ligne *f* électrique; **power outage** coupure *f* de courant; **power station** centrale *f* électrique; **power steering** direction *f* assistée

PR [piː'ɑːr] (= ***public relations***) relations *fpl* publiques

practical ['præktɪkl] pratique; **practically** d'une manière pratique; (*almost*) pratiquement

practice ['præktɪs] **1** *n* pratique *f*; *training also* entraînement *m*; (*rehearsal*) répétition *f*; (*custom*) coutume *f* **2** *v/i* s'entraîner **3** *v/t* travailler; *law, medicine* exercer

practise *Br* → ***practice*** *v/i & v/t*

prairie ['prerɪ] prairie *f*

praise [preɪz] **1** *n* louange *f*, éloge *m* **2** *v/t* louer; **praiseworthy** méritoire, louable

pray [preɪ] prier; **prayer** prière *f*

preach [priːʧ] prêcher; **preacher** pasteur *m*

precaution [prɪ'kɒːʃn] précaution *f*; **precautionary** *measure* préventif, de précaution

precede [prɪ'siːd] précéder; **precedent** précédent *m*; **preceding** précédent

precious ['preʃəs] précieux

precise [prɪ'saɪs] précis; **precisely** précisément; **precision** précision *f*

preconceived ['prɪkənsiːvd] *idea* préconçu

precondition [prɪkən'dɪʃn] condition *f* requise

predator ['predətər] prédateur *m*; **predatory** prédateur

predecessor ['priːdɪsesər] prédécesseur *m*

predicament [prɪ'dɪkəmənt] situation *f* délicate

predict [prɪ'dɪkt] prédire, prévoir; **prediction** prédiction *f*

predominant [prɪ'dɑːmɪnənt] prédominant; **predominantly** principalement

prefabricated [priː'fæbrɪkeɪtɪd] préfabriqué

preface ['prefɪs] préface *f*

prefer [prɪ'fɜːr] préférer; **preferable** préférable; **preferably** de préférence; **preference** préférence *f*; **preferential** préférentiel

pregnancy ['pregnənsɪ] grossesse *f*; **pregnant** enceinte; *animal* pleine

prehistoric [priːhɪs'tɑːrɪk] *also fig* préhistorique

prejudice ['predʒʊdɪs] **1** *n* (*bias*) préjugé *m* **2** *v/t person* influencer; *chances* compromettre; **prejudiced** partial

preliminary [prɪ'lɪmɪnerɪ] préliminaire

premarital [priː'mærɪtl] *sex* avant le mariage

premature [priːmə'tʊr] prématuré

premier ['premɪr] POL Premier ministre *m*

première ['premɪer] première *f*

premises ['premɪsɪz] locaux *mpl*

premium ['priːmɪəm] *in insurance* prime *f*

prenatal [priː'neɪtl] prénatal

preoccupied [prɪ'ɑːkjʊpaɪd] préoccupé

preparation [prepə'reɪʃn] préparation *f*; **~s** préparatifs *mpl*; **prepare** [prɪ'per] **1** *v/t* préparer; ***be ~d to do sth*** *willing, ready* être prêt à faire qch **2** *v/i* se préparer

preposition [prepə'zɪʃn] préposition *f*

prerequisite [priː'rekwɪzɪt] condition *f* préalable

prescribe [prɪ'skraɪb] *of doctor* prescrire; **prescription** MED ordonnance *f*

presence ['prezns] présence *f*; ***in the ~ of*** en présence de

present[1] ['preznt] **1** *adj* (*current*) actuel; ***be ~*** être présent **2** *n*: ***the ~*** *also* GRAM le présent

present[2] ['preznt] *n* (*gift*) cadeau *m*

present[3] [prɪ'zent] *v/t award, bouquet* remettre; *program* présenter

presentation [prezn'teɪʃn] présentation *f*; **present-day** actuel; **presenter** présentateur(-trice) *m*(*f*); **presently** (*at the moment*) à présent; (*soon*) bientôt

preservative [prɪ'zɜːrvətɪv] conservateur *m*; **preserve 1** *n* (*domain*) domaine *m* **2** *v/t standards, peace etc* maintenir; *wood etc* préserver; *food* conserver

preside [prɪ'zaɪd] *at meeting* présider; **presidency** présidence *f*; **president** POL président(e) *m*(*f*); *of company* président-directeur *m* général, PDG *m*; **presidential** présidentiel

press [pres] **1** *n*: ***the ~*** la presse **2** *v/t button* appuyer sur; *hand* serrer; *grapes, olives* presser; *clothes* repasser; **pressing** pressant; **pressure 1** *n* pression *f* **2** *v/t* faire pression sur

prestige [pre'stiːʒ] prestige *m*; **prestigious** prestigieux

presumably [prɪ'zuːməblɪ] sans doute; **presume** présumer; **presumption** *of innocence, guilt* présomption *f*

presuppose [priːsə'pouz] présupposer

pre-tax ['priːtæks] avant impôts

pretence *Br* → ***pretense***

pretend [prɪ'tend] **1** *v/t* prétendre **2** *v/i* faire semblant; **pretense** semblant *m*; ***under the ~ of cooperation*** sous prétexte de coopération; **pretentious** prétentieux

pretext ['priːtekst] prétexte *m*

pretty ['prɪtɪ] **1** *adj* joli **2** *adv* (*quite*) assez

prevail [prɪ'veɪl] (*triumph*) prévaloir, l'emporter; **prevailing** *wind* dominant; *opinion* prédominant; (*current*) actuel

prevent [prɪ'vent] empêcher; *disease* prévenir; ***~ s.o. (from) doing sth*** empêcher qn de faire qch; **prevention** prévention *f*; **preventive** préventif

preview ['priːvjuː] **1** *n* avant-première *f* **2** *v/t* voir en avant-première

previous ['priːvɪəs] (*earlier*) antérieur; (*the one before*) précédent; **previously** auparavant, avant

prey [preɪ] proie *f*

price [praɪs] **1** *n* prix *m* **2** *v/t* COM fixer le prix de; **priceless** sans prix

prick[1] [prɪk] **1** *n pain* piqûre *f* **2** *v/t* (*jab*) piquer

prick[2] [prɪk] V (*penis*) bite *f* V; *person* con *m* F

prickle ['prɪkl] *on plant* épine *f*, piquant *m*; **prickly** *beard, plant* piquant; (*irritable*) irritable

pride [praɪd] fierté *f*; (*self-respect*) amour-propre *m*, orgueil *m*

priest [priːst] prêtre *m*

primarily [praɪ'merɪlɪ] principalement; **primary** **1** *adj* principal **2** *n* POL (élection *f*) primaire *f*

prime 'minister Premier ministre *m*

primitive ['prɪmɪtɪv] primitif; *conditions* rudimentaire

prince [prɪns] prince *m*; **princess** princesse *f*

principal ['prɪnsəpl] **1** *adj* principal **2** *n of school* directeur(-trice) *m*(*f*); **principally** principalement

principle ['prɪnsəpl] principe *m*; ***on ~*** par principe; ***in ~*** en principe

print [prɪnt] **1** *n in book etc* texte *m*; (*photograph*) épreuve *f*; ***out of ~*** épuisé **2** *v/t* imprimer; (*use block capitals*) écrire en majuscules; **printer** ['prɪntər] *person* imprimeur *m*; *machine* imprimante *f*; **printout** impression *f*

prior ['praɪr] **1** *adj* préalable, antérieur **2** *prep*: ~ **to** avant **prioritize** (*put in order of priority*) donner un ordre de priorité à; (*give priority to*) donner la priorité à; **priority** priorité *f*

prison ['prɪzn] prison *f*; **prisoner** prisonnier(-ière) *m*(*f*); ***take s.o.*** ~ faire qn prisonnier; **prisoner of war** prisonnier(-ière) *m*(*f*) de guerre

privacy ['prɪvəsɪ] intimité *f*; **private 1** *adj* privé; *letter* personnel; *secretary* particulier **2** *n* MIL simple soldat *m*; **privately** *talk to s.o.* en privé; (*inwardly*) intérieurement; ~ ***owned*** privé

privilege ['prɪvəlɪdʒ] privilège *m*; **privileged** privilégié

prize [praɪz] **1** *n* prix *m* **2** *v/t* priser, faire (grand) cas de; **prizewinner** gagnant *m*; **prizewinning** gagnant

probability [prɑːbə'bɪlətɪ] probabilité *f*; **probable** probable; **probably** probablement

probation [prə'beɪʃn] *in job* période *f* d'essai; LAW probation *f*

probe [proʊb] **1** *n* (*investigation*) enquête *f*; *scientific* sonde *f* **2** *v/t* sonder; (*investigate*) enquêter sur

problem ['prɑːbləm] problème *m*; ***no*** ~ pas de problème; *it doesn't worry me* c'est pas grave

procedure [prə'siːdʒər] procédure *f*; **proceed** (*go*: *of people*) se rendre; *of work etc* avancer, se dérouler; **proceedings** (*events*) événements *mpl*; **proceeds** bénéfices *mpl*

process ['prɑːses] **1** *n* processus *m* **2** *v/t food, raw materials* transformer; *data, application* traiter; **procession** procession *f*; **processor** processeur *m*

prod [prɑːd] **1** *n* (petit) coup *m* **2** *v/t* donner un (petit) coup à, pousser

prodigy ['prɑːdɪdʒɪ]: prodige *m*; (***child***) ~ enfant *m*/*f* prodige

produce[1] ['prɑːduːs] *n* produits *mpl* (agricoles)

produce[2] [prə'duːs] *v/t* produire; (*bring about*) provoquer; (*bring out*) sortir

producer [prə'duːsər] producteur *m*; *of play, movie, TV program* producteur *m*; **product** produit *m*; **production** production *f*; **productive** productif; **productivity** productivité *f*

profess [prə'fes] prétendre; **profession** profession *f*; **professional 1** *adj* professionnel **2** *n* (*doctor, lawyer etc*) personne *f* qui exerce une profession libérale; *not amateur* professionnel(le) *m*(*f*); **professionally** *play sport* professionnellement;

(*well, skillfully*) de manière professionnelle
professor [prə'fesər] professeur *m*
proficient [prə'fɪʃnt] excellent, compétent
profile ['proufaɪl] profil *m*
profit ['prɑːfɪt] **1** *n* bénéfice *m*, profit *m* **2** *v/i*: **~ *from*** profiter de; **profitability** rentabilité *f*; **profitable** rentable
profound [prə'faund] profond
prognosis [prɑːg'nousɪs] MED pronostic *m*
program ['prougræm] **1** *n* programme *m*; *on radio, TV* émission *f* **2** *v/t* programmer; **programme** *Br* → ***program***; **programmer** programmeur(-euse) *m(f)*
progress 1 ['prɑːgres] *n* progrès *m(pl)* **2** [prə'gres] *v/i* (*in time*) avancer; (*move on*) passer à; (*make ~*) faire des progrès, progresser; **progressive** (*enlightened*) progressiste; (*which progresses*) progressif; **progressively** progressivement
prohibit [prə'hɪbɪt] défendre, interdire; **prohibitive** *prices* prohibitif
project[1] ['prɑːdʒekt] *n* projet *m*; EDU étude *f*; (*housing area*) cité *f* (H.L.M.)
project[2] [prə'dʒekt] **1** *v/t figures, sales* prévoir; *movie* projeter **2** *v/i* (*stick out*) faire saillie
projection [prə'dʒekʃn] (*forecast*) projection *f*, prévision *f*; **projector** *for slides* projecteur *m*
prolog, *Br* **prologue** ['prouləːg] prologue *m*
prolong [prə'lɒːŋ] prolonger
prominent ['prɑːmɪnənt] *nose, chin* proéminent; *visually* voyant; (*significant*) important
promiscuity [prɑːmɪ'skjuːətɪ] promiscuité *f*; **promiscuous** dévergondé
promise ['prɑːmɪs] **1** *n* promesse *f* **2** *v/t & v/i* promettre; **promising** prometteur
promote [prə'mout] *employee, idea* promouvoir; COM *also* faire la promotion de; **promoter** *of sports event* organisateur *m*; **promotion** promotion *f*
prompt [prɑːmpt] **1** *adj* (*on time*) ponctuel; (*speedy*) prompt **2** *v/t* (*cause*) provoquer; *actor* souffler à; **promptly** (*on time*) ponctuellement; (*immediately*) immédiatement
prone [proun]: ***be ~ to*** être sujet à
pronoun ['prounaun] pronom *m*
pronounce [prə'nauns] prononcer
pronto ['prɑːntou] F illico (presto) F
pronunciation [prənʌnsɪ'eɪʃn] prononciation *f*

proof [pruːf] preuve *f*; *of book* épreuve *f*

prop [prɑːp] THEA accessoire *m*

◆ **prop up** soutenir

propaganda [prɑːpəˈgændə] propagande *f*

propel [prəˈpel] propulser; **propeller** hélice *f*

proper [ˈprɑːpər] (*real*) vrai; (*correct*) bon, correct; (*fitting*) convenable; **properly** (*correctly*) correctement; (*fittingly also*) convenablement; **property** propriété *f*

proportion [prəˈpɔːrʃn] proportion *f*; **proportional** proportionnel

proposal [prəˈpoʊzl] proposition *f*; *of marriage* demande *f* en mariage; **propose 1** *v/t* (*suggest*) proposer; **~ *to do sth*** (*plan*) se proposer de faire qch **2** *v/i* (*make offer of marriage*) faire sa demande en mariage (***to*** à); **proposition 1** *n* proposition *f* **2** *v/t woman* faire des avances à

proprietor [prəˈpraɪətər] propriétaire *m*

prosecute [ˈprɑːsɪkjuːt] LAW poursuivre (en justice); **prosecution** LAW poursuites *fpl* (judiciaires); *lawyers* accusation *f*

prospect [ˈprɑːspekt] (*chance, likelihood*) chance(s) *f(pl)*; (*thought of something in the future*) perspective *f*; **~*s*** perspectives *fpl* (d'avenir); **prospective** potentiel

prosper [ˈprɑːspər] prospérer; **prosperity** prospérité *f*; **prosperous** prospère

prostitute [ˈprɑːstɪtuːt] prostituée *f*; ***male* ~** prostitué *m*; **prostitution** prostitution *f*

protect [prəˈtekt] protéger; **protection** protection *f*; **protective** protecteur; **protector** protecteur(-trice) *m(f)*

protein [ˈproʊtiːn] protéine *f*

protest [ˈproʊtest] **1** [ˈproʊtest] *n* protestation *f*; (*demonstration*) manifestation *f* **2** [prəˈtest] *v/t* (*object to*) protester contre **3** [prəˈtest] *v/i* protester; (*demonstrate*) manifester

Protestant [ˈprɑːtɪstənt] **1** *adj* protestant **2** *n* protestant(e) *m(f)*

protester [prəˈtestər] manifestant(e) *m(f)*

prototype [ˈproʊtətaɪp] prototype *m*

protrude [prəˈtruːd] *of eyes, ear* être saillant; *from pocket etc* sortir; **protruding** saillant; *ears* décollé; *chin* avancé; *teeth* en avant

proud [praʊd] fier; **proudly** fièrement, avec fierté

prove [pruːv] prouver

proverb [ˈprɑːvɜːrb] proverbe *m*

provide [prəˈvaɪd] fournir; **~*d that*** (*on condition that*) pour-

vu que (*+subj*), à condition que (*+subj*)
province ['prɑːvɪns] province *f*; **provincial** *also pej* provincial; *city* de province
provision [prə'vɪʒn] (*supply*) fourniture *f*; *of services* prestation *f*; *in a law, contract* disposition *f*; **provisional** provisoire
provocation [prɑːvə'keɪʃn] provocation *f*; **provocative** provocant; **provoke** provoquer
prowl [praʊl] *of tiger etc* chasser; *of burglar* rôder; **prowler** rôdeur(-euse) *m*(*f*)
proximity [prɑːk'sɪmətɪ] proximité *f*
proxy ['prɑːksɪ] (*authority*) procuration *f*; *person* mandataire *m*/*f*
prudence ['pruːdns] prudence *f*; **prudent** prudent
pry [praɪ] être indiscret
PS ['piːes] (= ***postscript***) P.-S. *m*
pseudonym ['suːdənɪm] pseudonyme *m*
psychiatric [saɪkɪ'ætrɪk] psychiatrique; **psychiatrist** psychiatre *m*/*f*; **psychiatry** psychiatrie *f*
psychoanalysis [saɪkoʊən'æləsɪs] psychanalyse *f*; **psychoanalyst** psychanalyste *m*/*f*; **psychoanalyze** psychanalyser
psychological [saɪkə'lɑːdʒɪkl] psychologique; **psychologist** psychologue *m*/*f*
psychology psychologie *f*
psychopath ['saɪkoʊpæθ] psychopathe *m*/*f*
psychosomatic [saɪkoʊsə'mætɪk] psychosomatique
pub [pʌb] *Br* pub *m*
public ['pʌblɪk] **1** *adj* public **2** *n*: ***the ~*** le public
publication [pʌblɪ'keɪʃn] publication *f*
public 'holiday jour *m* férié
publicity [pʌb'lɪsətɪ] publicité *f*; **publicize** (*make known*) faire connaître, rendre public; COM faire de la publicité pour
publicly ['pʌblɪklɪ] en public, publiquement
'public school école *f* publique; *Br* école privée (du secondaire)
publish ['pʌblɪʃ] publier; **publisher** éditeur(-trice) *m*(*f*); maison *f* d'édition; **publishing** édition *f*; **publishing company** maison *f* d'édition
puff [pʌf] **1** *n of wind* bourrasque *f*; *of smoke* bouffée *f* **2** *v/i* (*pant*) souffler, haleter; **puffy** *eyes, face* bouffi
pull [pʊl] **1** *n on rope* coup *m*; F (*appeal*) attrait *m*; F (*influence*) influence *f* **2** *v/t* tirer; *tooth* arracher; *muscle* se déchirer **3** *v/i* tirer
◆ **pull ahead** *in race, competition* prendre la tête

◆ **pull down** (*lower*) baisser; (*demolish*) démolir
◆ **pull in** *of bus, train* arriver
◆ **pull up 1** *v/t* (*raise*) remonter; *plant* arracher **2** *v/i of car etc* s'arrêter
pulley ['pʊlɪ] poulie *f*
pulsate [pʌl'seɪt] *of heart, blood* battre; *of rhythm* vibrer
pulse [pʌls] pouls *m*
pulverize ['pʌlvəraɪz] pulvériser
pump [pʌmp] **1** *n* pompe *f* **2** *v/t* pomper
pumpkin ['pʌmpkɪn] potiron *m*
pun [pʌn] jeu *m* de mots
punch [pʌntʃ] **1** *n blow* coup *m* de poing; *implement* perforeuse *f* **2** *v/t with fist* donner un coup de poing à; *hole* percer; *ticket* composter
punctual ['pʌŋktʃʊəl] ponctuel; **punctuality** ponctualité *f*
punctuation [pʌŋktʃʊ'eɪʃn] ponctuation *f*
puncture ['pʌŋktʃər] **1** *n* piqûre *f* **2** *v/t* percer, perforer
punish ['pʌnɪʃ] punir; **punishing** *pace, schedule* éprouvant, épuisant; **punishment** punition *f*
puny ['pju:nɪ] *person* chétif
pup [pʌp] chiot *m*
pupil[1] ['pju:pl] *of eye* pupille *f*
pupil[2] ['pju:pl] (*student*) élève *m/f*
puppet ['pʌpɪt] *also fig* marionnette *f*
purchase[1] ['pɜ:rtʃəs] **1** *n* achat *m* **2** *v/t* acheter
purchase[2] ['pɜ:rtʃəs] *n* (*grip*) prise *f*
purchaser ['pɜ:rtʃəsər] acheteur(-euse) *m(f)*
pure [pjʊr] pur; *white* immaculé; **purely** purement
purge [pɜ:rdʒ] **1** *n* POL purge *f* **2** *v/t* POL épurer
purify ['pjʊrɪfaɪ] *water* épurer
puritan ['pjʊrɪtən] puritain(e) *m(f)*
purity ['pjʊrɪtɪ] pureté *f*
purpose ['pɜ:rpəs] (*aim, object*) but *m*; ***on ~*** exprès; **purposely** exprès
purr [pɜ:r] *of cat* ronronner
purse [pɜ:rs] (*pocketbook*) sac *m* à main; *Br for money* porte-monnaie *m inv*
pursue [pər'su:] poursuivre; **pursuer** poursuivant(e) *m(f)*; **pursuit** poursuite *f*; (*activity*) activité *f*
push [pʊʃ] **1** *n* (*shove*) poussée *f* **2** *v/t* (*shove, pressure*) pousser; *button* appuyer sur; F *drugs* revendre, trafiquer **3** *v/i* pousser; **pusher** F *of drugs* dealer(-euse) *m(f)*; **push-up**: ***do ~s*** faire des pompes; **pushy** F qui se met en avant
puss, pussy (cat) [pʊs, 'pʊsɪ (kæt)] F minou *m*
put [pʊt] mettre; *question* poser; ***~ the cost at*** estimer le prix à

◆ **put across** *idea etc* faire comprendre
◆ **put aside** *money, work* mettre de côté
◆ **put away** *in closet etc* ranger; *in institution* enfermer; *in prison* emprisonner; F (*consume*) s'enfiler F; *animal* faire piquer
◆ **put back** (*replace*) remettre
◆ **put down** poser; *deposit* verser; *rebellion* réprimer; (*belittle*) rabaisser
◆ **put forward** *idea etc* soumettre, suggérer
◆ **put in for** (*apply for*) demander
◆ **put off** *light, TV* éteindre; (*postpone*) repousser; (*deter*) dissuader; (*repel*) dégoûter
◆ **put on** *light, TV* allumer; *music, jacket etc* mettre; (*perform*) monter; *accent etc* prendre
◆ **put out** *hand* tendre; *fire, light* éteindre
◆ **put together** (*assemble*) monter; (*organize*) organiser
◆ **put up** *hand* lever; *person* héberger; (*erect*) ériger; *prices* augmenter; *poster* accrocher; *money* fournir
◆ **put up with** supporter, tolérer

putty ['pʌtɪ] mastic *m*
puzzle ['pʌzl] **1** *n* (*mystery*) énigme *f*, mystère *m*; *game* jeu *m*, casse-tête *m*; (*jigsaw* ~) puzzle *m* **2** *v/t* laisser perplexe; **puzzling** curieux
PVC [pi:vi:'si:] (= ***polyvinyl chloride***) P.V.C. *m* (= polychlorure de vinyle)
pyjamas *Br* → ***pajamas***
pylon ['paɪlən] pylône *m*

Q

quadrangle ['kwɑ:dræŋgl] *figure* quadrilatère *m*; *courtyard* cour *f*
quadruped ['kwɑ:druped] quadrupède *m*
quail [kweɪl] flancher
quaint [kweɪnt] *cottage* pittoresque; (*eccentric: ideas etc*) curieux
quake [kweɪk] **1** *n* (*earthquake*) tremblement *m* de terre **2** *v/i of earth, with fear* trembler
qualification [kwɑ:lɪfɪ'keɪʃn] *from university etc* diplôme *m*; **qualified** *doctor, engineer etc* qualifié; (*restricted*) restreint; **qualify 1** *v/t of degree, course etc* qualifier; *remark etc* nuancer **2** *v/i* (*get degree etc*) obtenir son diplôme; *in competition* se qualifier
quality ['kwɑ:lətɪ] qualité *f*; **quality control** contrôle *m* de qualité
quandary ['kwɑ:ndərɪ] di-

lemme *m*
quantify ['kwɑːntɪfaɪ] quantifier
quantity ['kwɑːntətɪ] quantité *f*
quarantine ['kwɑːrəntiːn] quarantaine *f*
quarrel ['kwɑːrəl] **1** *n* dispute *f*, querelle *f* **2** *v/i* se disputer
quarry[1] ['kwɑːrɪ] *in hunt* gibier *m*
quarry[2] ['kwɑːrɪ] *for mining* carrière *f*
quart [kwɔːrt] quart *m* de gallon (*0,946 litre*)
quarter ['kwɔːrtər] quart *m*; *25 cents* vingt-cinq cents *mpl*; *part of town* quartier *m*; ***a ~ of an hour*** un quart d'heure; ***a ~ of 5*** cinq heures moins le quart; ***a ~ after 5*** cinq heures et quart; **quarterfinal** quart *m* de finale; **quarterfinalist** quart de finaliste *m*, quart-finaliste *m*; **quarterly 1** *adj* trimestriel **2** *adv* trimestriellement; **quarters** MIL quartiers *mpl*; **quartet** MUS quatuor *m*
quartz [kwɑːrts] quartz *m*
quash [kwɑːʃ] *rebellion* réprimer, écraser; *court decision* casser, annuler
quaver ['kweɪvər] **1** *n in voice* tremblement *m* **2** *v/i of voice* trembler
queasy ['kwiːzɪ] nauséeux; ***feel ~*** avoir la nausée
queen [kwiːn] reine *f*
queer [kwɪr] (*peculiar*) bizarre
quell [kwel] réprimer
quench [kwentʃ] *thirst* étancher, assouvir; *flames* éteindre
query ['kwɪrɪ] **1** *n* question *f* **2** *v/t* (*express doubt about*) mettre en doute; (*check*) vérifier
quest [kwest] quête *f*
question ['kwestʃn] **1** *n* question *f* **2** *v/t person* questionner, interroger; (*doubt*) mettre en question; **questionable** contestable; **questioning 1** *adj look* interrogateur **2** *n* interrogatoire *m*; **question mark** point *m* d'interrogation; **questionnaire** questionnaire *m*
queue [kjuː] *Br* **1** *n* queue *f* **2** *v/i* faire la queue
quibble ['kwɪbl] chipoter, chercher la petite bête
quick [kwɪk] rapide; ***be ~!*** fais vite!; **quickly** vite, rapidement; **quickwitted** à l'esprit vif
quiet ['kwaɪət] *street, life* tranquille; *music* doux; *engine* silencieux; *voice* bas; ***~!*** silence!; **quietly** doucement, sans bruit; (*unassumingly, peacefully*) tranquillement; **quietness** calme *m*, tranquillité *f*
quilt [kwɪlt] *on bed* couette *f*
quinine ['kwɪniːn] quinine *f*
quip [kwɪp] **1** *n* trait *m* d'esprit **2** *v/i* plaisanter
quirk [kwɜːrk] manie *f*, lubie

f; **quirky** bizarre, excentrique

quit [kwɪt] **1** *v/t job* quitter **2** *v/i* (*leave job*) démissionner; COMPUT quitter

quite [kwaɪt] (*fairly*) assez; (*completely*) tout à fait; **~ *a lot*** pas mal, beaucoup

quiver ['kwɪvər] trembler

quiz [kwɪz] **1** *n on TV* jeu *m* télévisé; *on radio* jeu *m* radiophonique; *at school* interrogation *f* **2** *v/t* interroger

quota ['kwoʊtə] quota *m*

quotation [kwoʊ'teɪʃn] *from author* citation *f*; *price* devis *m*; **quotation marks** guillemets *mpl*; **quote 1** *n from author* citation *f*; *price* devis *m*; (*quotation mark*) guillemet *m*; ***in ~s*** entre guillemets **2** *v/t text* citer; *price* proposer

R

rabbit ['ræbɪt] lapin *m*

rabble ['ræbl] cohue *f*, foule *f*; **rabble-rouser** agitateur(-trice) *m*(*f*)

rabies ['reɪbiːz] rage *f*

raccoon [rə'kuːn] raton *m* laveur

race[1] [reɪs] *n of people* race *f*

race[2] [reɪs] **1** *n* SP course *f* **2** *v/i* (*run fast*) courir à toute vitesse **3** *v/t*: ***I'll ~ you*** le premier arrivé a gagné

'racecourse champ *m* de courses, hippodrome *m*; **racehorse** cheval *m* de course; **race riot** émeute *f* raciale; **racetrack** *for cars* circuit *m*, piste *f*; *for horses* hippodrome *m*

racial ['reɪʃl] racial

racing ['reɪsɪŋ] course *f*

racism ['reɪsɪzm] racisme *m*; **racist 1** *adj* raciste **2** *n* raciste *m/f*

rack [ræk] **1** *n for bags on train* porte-bagages *m inv*; *for CDs* range-CD *m inv* **2** *v/t*: ***~ one's brains*** se creuser la tête

racket[1] ['rækɪt] SP raquette *f*

racket[2] ['rækɪt] (*noise*) vacarme *m*; *criminal activity* escroquerie *f*

radar ['reɪdɑːr] radar *m*

radiance ['reɪdɪəns] éclat *m*; **radiant** *smile* radieux; **radiate** *of heat, light* irradier, rayonner; **radiation** *nuclear* radiation *f*; **radiator** radiateur *m*

radical ['rædɪkl] **1** *adj* radical **2** *n* POL radical(e) *m*(*f*); **radicalism** POL radicalisme *m*; **radically** radicalement

radio ['reɪdɪoʊ] radio *f*; **radioactive** radioactif; **radioactivity** radioactivité *f*; **radio alarm** radio-réveil *m*; **radiographer** radiologue *m/f*; **radiography** radiographie *f*;

radio station station *f* de radio
radius ['reɪdɪəs] rayon *m*
raft [ræft] radeau *m*
rafter ['ræftər] chevron *m*
rag [ræg] *for cleaning etc* chiffon *m*
rage [reɪdʒ] **1** *n* colère *f*, rage *f* **2** *v/i of storm* faire rage
ragged ['rægɪd] *edge* irrégulier; *appearance* négligé; *clothes* en loques
raid [reɪd] **1** *n by troops*, FIN raid *m*; *by police* descente *f*; *by robbers* hold-up *m* **2** *v/t of troops* attaquer; *of police* faire une descente dans; *of robbers* attaquer; *fridge* faire une razzia dans; **raider** (*robber*) voleur *m*
rail [reɪl] *on track* rail *m*; (*hand~*) rampe *f*; *for towel* porte-serviettes *m inv*; ***by ~*** en train; **railings** *around park etc* grille *f*; **railroad** chemin *m* de fer; *track* voie *f* ferrée; **railroad station** gare *f*; **railway** *Br* chemin *m* de fer; *track* voie *f* ferrée
rain [reɪn] **1** *n* pluie *f* **2** *v/i* pleuvoir; ***it's ~ing*** il pleut; **rainbow** arc-en-ciel *m*; **raincheck**: ***can I take a ~ on that?*** F peut-on remettre cela à plus tard?; **raincoat** imperméable *m*; **raindrop** goutte *f* de pluie; **rainfall** précipitations *fpl*; **rain forest** forêt *f* tropicale (humide); **rainproof** *fabric* imperméable; **rainstorm** pluie *f* torrentielle; **rainy** pluvieux
raise [reɪz] **1** *n in salary* augmentation *f* (de salaire) **2** *v/t shelf etc* surélever; *offer* augmenter; *children* élever; *question* soulever; *money* rassembler
rake [reɪk] *for garden* râteau *m*
rally ['rælɪ] (*meeting, reunion*) rassemblement *m*; MOT rallye *m*; *in tennis* échange *m*
RAM [ræm] COMPUT (= ***random access memory***) RAM *f*, mémoire *f* vive
ram [ræm] **1** *n* bélier *m* **2** *v/t ship, car* heurter, percuter
ramble ['ræmbl] **1** *n walk* randonnée *f* **2** *v/i walk* faire de la randonnée; *when speaking* discourir; (*talk incoherently*) divaguer; **rambling** **1** *adj speech* décousu **2** *n walking* randonnée *f*; *in speech* digression *f*
ramp [ræmp] rampe *f* (d'accès), passerelle *f*; *for raising vehicle* pont *m* élévateur
rampant ['ræmpənt] *inflation* galopant
rampart ['ræmpɑːrt] rempart *m*
ramshackle ['ræmʃækl] délabré
ranch [ræntʃ] ranch *m*; **rancher** propriétaire *m/f* de ranch; **ranchhand** employé *m* de ranch
rancid ['rænsɪd] rance

rancor, *Br* **rancour** ['ræŋkər] rancœur *f*
R & D [ɑːrən'diː] (= ***research and development***) R&D *f* (= recherche et développement)
random ['rændəm] **1** *adj* aléatoire, au hasard; ~ ***sample*** échantillon *m* pris au hasard **2** *n*: ***at*** ~ au hasard
range [reɪndʒ] **1** *n of products* gamme *f*; *of gun* portée *f*; *of airplane* autonomie *f*; *of voice, instrument* registre *m*; *of mountains* chaîne *f*; ***at close*** ~ de très près **2** *v/i*: ~ ***from X to Y*** aller de X à Y;
ranger garde *m* forestier
rank [ræŋk] **1** *n* MIL grade *m*; *in society* rang *m* **2** *v/t* classer
◆ **rank among** compter parmi
ransack ['rænsæk] *searching* fouiller; *plundering* saccager
ransom ['rænsəm] *money* rançon *f*
rap [ræp] **1** *n at door etc* petit coup *m* sec; MUS rap *m* **2** *v/t table etc* taper sur
rape[1] [reɪp] **1** *n* viol *m* **2** *v/t* violer
rape[2] [reɪp] *n* BOT colza *m*
rapid ['ræpɪd] rapide; **rapidity** rapidité *f*; **rapidly** rapidement; **rapids** rapides *mpl*
rapist ['reɪpɪst] violeur *m*
rare [rer] rare; *steak* saignant, bleu; **rarely** rarement; **rarity** rareté *f*
rash[1] [ræʃ] *n* MED éruption *f* (cutanée)
rash[2] [ræʃ] *adj action*, imprudent, impétueux; **rashly** sans réfléchir
rat [ræt] rat *m*
rate [reɪt] taux *m*; (*price*) tarif *m*; (*speed*) rythme *m*; ***at this*** ~ (*at this speed*) à ce rythme; (*carrying on like this*) si ça continue comme ça; ***at any*** ~ en tout cas
rather ['ræðər] (*fairly, quite*) plutôt; ***I would*** ~ ***stay here*** je préfèrerais rester ici
ratification [rætɪfɪ'keɪʃn] *of treaty* ratification *f*; **ratify** ratifier
ratings ['reɪtɪŋz] indice *m* d'écoute
ratio ['reɪʃɪoʊ] rapport *m*, proportion *f*
ration ['ræʃn] **1** *n* ration *f* **2** *v/t supplies* rationner
rational ['ræʃənl] rationnel; **rationality** rationalité *f*; **rationalization** rationalisation *f*; **rationalize 1** *v/t* rationaliser **2** *v/i* (se) chercher des excuses; **rationally** rationnellement
rattle ['rætl] **1** *n of bottles, chains* cliquetis *m*; *in engine* bruit *m* de ferraille; *toy* hochet *m* **2** *v/t chains etc* entrechoquer **3** *v/i* faire du bruit; *of engine* faire un bruit de ferraille; *of crates* s'entrechoquer; *of chains* cliqueter; **rattlesnake** serpent *m* à sonnette

raucous ['rɒːkəs] bruyant
rave [reɪv] **1** *n party* rave *f*, rave-party *f* **2** *v/i* délirer; **~ *about sth*** (*be very enthusiastic*) s'emballer pour qch
ravenous ['rævənəs] affamé
ravine [rə'viːn] ravin *m*
raw [rɒː] *meat, vegetable* cru; *sugar, iron* brut; **raw materials** matières *fpl* premières
ray [reɪ] rayon *m*
razor ['reɪzər] rasoir *m*; **razor blade** lame *f* de rasoir
re [riː] COM en référence à
reach [riːʧ] **1** *n*: ***within ~*** à portée; ***out of ~*** hors de portée **2** *v/t* atteindre; *destination* arriver à; *decision* parvenir à
react [rɪ'ækt] réagir; **reaction** réaction *f*; **reactionary 1** *adj* POL réactionnaire **2** *n* POL réactionnaire *m/f*; **reactor** *nuclear* réacteur *m*
read [riːd] lire
◆ **read out** *aloud* lire à haute voix
readable ['riːdəbl] lisible; **reader** *person* lecteur(-trice) *m(f)*
readily ['redɪlɪ] *admit, agree* volontiers, de bon cœur
reading ['riːdɪŋ] *activity* lecture *f*; *from meter etc* relevé *m*
readjust [riːə'dʒʌst] **1** *v/t* régler (de nouveau) **2** *v/i to conditions* se réadapter (***to*** à)
ready ['redɪ] (*prepared, willing*) prêt; ***get sth ~*** préparer qch; **ready cash** (argent *m*) liquide *m*; **ready-made** *stew etc* cuisiné; *solution* tout trouvé; **ready-to-wear** de confection; **~ *clothing*** prêt-à-porter *m*
real [riːl] *not imaginary* réel; *not fake* vrai; **real estate** immobilier *m*, biens *mpl* immobiliers; **real estate agent** agent *m* immobilier; **realism** réalisme *m*; **realist** réaliste *m/f*; **realistic** réaliste; **realistically** de façon réaliste; **reality** réalité *f*; **realize** se rendre compte de; FIN réaliser; **really** vraiment; **real time** COMPUT temps *m* réel; **real-time** COMPUT en temps réel
realtor ['riːltər] agent *m* immobilier; **realty** immobilier *m*
reappear [riːə'pɪr] réapparaître
reappearance réapparition *f*
rear [rɪr] **1** *adj* arrière *inv*, de derrière **2** *n* arrière *m*
rearm [riː'ɑːrm] réarmer
rearrange [riːə'reɪndʒ] *flowers* réarranger; *furniture* déplacer; *schedule, meetings* réorganiser
rear-view 'mirror rétroviseur *m*, rétro *m* F
reason ['riːzn] **1** *n* (*cause*), *faculty* raison *f*; **reasonable** raisonnable; **reasonably** *act, behave* raisonnablement; (*quite*) relativement; **reasoning** raisonnement *m*
reassure [riːə'ʃʊr] rassurer;

reassuring rassurant
rebate ['ri:beɪt] (*refund*) remboursement *m*
rebel 1 ['rebl] *n* rebelle *m/f* **2** [rɪ'bel] *v/i* se rebeller; **rebellion** rébellion *f*; **rebellious** rebelle; **rebelliousness** esprit *m* de rébellion
rebound [rɪ'baʊnd] *of ball etc* rebondir
rebuild ['ri:bɪld] reconstruire
recall [rɪ'kɒ:l] *goods, ambassador* rappeler; (*remember*) se rappeler
recap ['ri:kæp] récapituler
recapture [ri:'kæptʃər] reprendre
recede [rɪ'si:d] *of flood waters* baisser
receipt [rɪ'si:t] *for purchase* reçu *m* (***for*** de), ticket *m* de caisse; **~s** FIN recette(s) *f(pl)*; **receive** recevoir; **receiver** TELEC combiné *m*; *for radio* (poste *m*) récepteur *m*; **receivership**: ***be in ~*** être en liquidation judiciaire
recent ['ri:snt] récent; **recently** récemment
reception [rɪ'sepʃn] réception *f*; (*welcome*) accueil *m*; **reception desk** réception *f*; **receptionist** réceptionniste *m/f*; **receptive**: ***be ~ to sth*** être réceptif à qch
recess ['ri:ses] *in wall etc* renfoncement *m*, recoin *m*; EDU récréation *f*; *of legislature* vacances *fpl* judiciaires; **recession** *economic* récession *f*
recharge [ri:'tʃɑ:rdʒ] *battery* recharger
recipe ['resəpɪ] recette *f*
recipient [rɪ'sɪpɪənt] *of parcel etc* destinataire *m/f*; *of payment* bénéficiaire *m/f*
reciprocal [rɪ'sɪprəkl] réciproque
recite [rɪ'saɪt] *poem* réciter; *details, facts* énumérer
reckless ['reklɪs] imprudent; **recklessly** imprudemment
reckon ['rekən] (*think, consider*) penser
◆ **reckon on** compter sur
reclaim [rɪ'kleɪm] *land from sea* gagner sur la mer; *lost property* récupérer
recline [rɪ'klaɪn] s'allonger; **recliner** *chair* chaise *f* longue, relax *m*
recluse [rɪ'klu:s] reclus *m*
recognition [rekəg'nɪʃn] reconnaissance *f*; **recognizable** reconnaissable; **recognize** reconnaître
recoil [rɪ'kɔɪl] reculer
recollect [rekə'lekt] se souvenir de; **recollection** souvenir *m*
recommend [rekə'mend] recommander; **recommendation** recommandation *f*
recompense ['rekəmpens] compensation *f*, dédommagement *m*
reconcile ['rekənsaɪl] réconcilier; *differences* concilier; *facts* faire concorder; **reconciliation** réconciliation *f*; *of*

differences, facts conciliation *f*
recondition [riːkən'dɪʃn] refaire, remettre à neuf
reconnaissance [rɪ'kɑːnɪsəns] MIL reconnaissance *f*
reconsider [riːkən'sɪdər] **1** *v/t* reconsidérer **2** *v/i* reconsidérer la question
reconstruct [riːkən'strʌkt] reconstruire; *crime* reconstituer
record[1] ['rekərd] *n* MUS disque *m*; SP *etc* record *m*; *written document etc* rapport *m*; *in database* article *m*, enregistrement *m*; **~s** (*archives*) archives *fpl*, dossiers *mpl*; ***have a criminal ~*** avoir un casier judiciaire
record[2] [rɪ'kɔːrd] *v/t electronically* enregistrer; *in writing* consigner
'record-breaking qui bat tous les records; **record holder** recordman *m*, recordwoman *f*
recording [rɪ'kɔːrdɪŋ] enregistrement *m*
recount [rɪ'kaʊnt] (*tell*) raconter
re-count ['riːkaʊnt] **1** *n of votes* recompte *m* **2** *v/t* recompter
recoup [rɪ'kuːp] *financial losses* récupérer
recover [rɪ'kʌvər] **1** *v/t* retrouver **2** *v/i from illness* se remettre; *of business* reprendre; **recovery** *of sth lost* récupération *f*; *from illness* rétablissement *m*
recreation [rekrɪ'eɪʃn] récréation *f*; **recreational** *done for pleasure* de loisirs
recruit [rɪ'kruːt] **1** *n* recrue *f* **2** *v/t* recruter; **recruitment** recrutement *m*
rectangle ['rektæŋgl] rectangle *m*; **rectangular** rectangulaire
rectify ['rektɪfaɪ] rectifier
recuperate [rɪ'kuːpəreɪt] récupérer
recur [rɪ'kɜːr] *of error, event* se reproduire; *of symptoms* réapparaître; **recurrent** récurrent
recycle [riː'saɪkl] recycler; **recycling** recyclage *m*
red [red] **1** *adj* rouge **2** *n*: ***in the ~*** FIN dans le rouge; **Red Cross** Croix-Rouge *f*
redecorate [riː'dekəreɪt] refaire
redeem [rɪ'diːm] *debt* rembourser; *sinners* racheter
redevelop [riːdɪ'veləp] *part of town* réaménager
'redhead roux *m*, rousse *f*; **red light** *for traffic* feu *m* rouge; **red light district** quartier *m* chaud; **red meat** viande *f* rouge; **redneck** F plouc *m* F; **red tape** F paperasserie *f*
reduce [rɪ'duːs] réduire; **reduction** réduction *f*
reek [riːk] empester (***of sth*** qch)
reel [riːl] *of film, thread* bobi-

ne *f*
re-e'lect réélire; **re-election** réélection *f*
re-'entry *of spacecraft* rentrée *f*
ref [ref] F arbitre *m*
◆ **refer to** faire allusion à; *dictionary etc* se reporter à
referee [refə'riː] SP arbitre *m*; *for job*: *personne qui fournit des références*; **reference** (*allusion*) allusion *f*; *for job* référence *f*; (~ *number*) (numéro *m* de) référence *f*; **reference book** ouvrage *m* de référence; **reference number** numéro *m* de référence
referendum [refə'rendəm] référendum *m*
refill ['riːfɪl] remplir
refine [rɪ'faɪn] *oil*, *sugar* raffiner; *technique* affiner; **refinement** *to process*, *machine* perfectionnement *m*; **refinery** raffinerie *f*
reflect [rɪ'flekt] **1** *v/t* refléter **2** *v/i* (*think*) réfléchir; **reflection** *also fig* reflet *m*; (*consideration*) réflexion *f*
reflex ['riːfleks] *in body* réflexe *m*
reform [rɪ'fɔːrm] **1** *n* réforme *f* **2** *v/t* réformer; **reformer** réformateur(-trice) *m*(*f*)
refresh [rɪ'freʃ] rafraîchir; *of sleep*, *rest* reposer; *of meal* redonner des forces à; **refreshing** *drink* rafraîchissant; *experience* agréable; **refreshments** rafraîchissements *mpl*
refrigerate [rɪ'frɪdʒəreɪt] réfrigérer; **refrigerator** réfrigérateur *m*
refuel [riː'fjuəl] **1** *v/t airplane* ravitailler **2** *v/i of airplane* se ravitailler (en carburant)
refuge ['refjuːdʒ] refuge *m*; ***take*** ~ *from storm etc* se réfugier; **refugee** réfugié(e) *m*(*f*)
refund 1 ['riːfʌnd] *n* remboursement *m* **2** [rɪ'fʌnd] *v/t* rembourser
refusal [rɪ'fjuːzl] refus *m*; **refuse** refuser; ~ ***to do sth*** refuser de faire qch
regain [rɪ'geɪn] *control*, *territory*, *the lead* reprendre; *composure* retrouver
regard [rɪ'gɑːrd] **1** *n*: ***with*** ~ ***to*** en ce qui concerne; (***kind***) ~***s*** cordialement; ***with no*** ~ ***for*** sans égard pour **2** *v/t*: ~ ***as*** considérer comme; **regarding** en ce qui concerne; **regardless** quand même; ~ ***of*** sans se soucier de
regime [reɪ'ʒiːm] (*government*) régime *m*
regiment ['redʒɪmənt] régiment *m*
region ['riːdʒən] région *f*; **regional** régional
register ['redʒɪstər] **1** *n* registre *m* **2** *v/t birth*, *death* déclarer; *vehicle* immatriculer; *letter* recommander; *emotion* exprimer **3** *v/i for a course* s'inscrire; *with police* se déclarer (***with*** à); **regis-**

tered letter lettre *f* recommandée; **registration** *of birth, death* déclaration *f*; *of vehicle* immatriculation *f*; *for a course* inscription *f*
regret [rɪ'gret] **1** *v/t* regretter **2** *n* regret *m*; **regretful** plein de regrets; **regrettable** regrettable
regular ['regjʊlər] **1** *adj* régulier; (*normal*) normal **2** *n at bar etc* habitué(e) *m(f)*; **regularity** régularité *f*; **regularly** régulièrement
regulate ['regjʊleɪt] régler; *expenditure* contrôler; **regulation** (*rule*) règlement *m*
rehabilitate [riːhə'bɪlɪteɪt] *ex-criminal* réinsérer; *disabled person* rééduquer
rehearsal [rɪ'hɜːrsl] répétition *f*; **rehearse** répéter
reign [reɪn] **1** *n* règne *m* **2** *v/i* régner
reimburse [riːɪm'bɜːrs] rembourser
reinforce [riːɪn'fɔːrs] renforcer; *argument* étayer; **reinforced concrete** béton *m* armé; **reinforcements** MIL renforts *mpl*
reinstate [riːɪn'steɪt] *person in office* réintégrer, rétablir dans ses fonctions; *paragraph etc* réintroduire
reject [rɪ'dʒekt] rejeter; **rejection** rejet *m*
relapse ['riːlæps] MED rechute *f*
related [rɪ'leɪtɪd] *by family* apparenté; *events, ideas etc* associé; **relation** *in family* parent(e) *m(f)*; (*connection*) rapport *m*, relation *f*; **relationship** relation *f*; *sexual* liaison *f*; **relative 1** *adj* relatif **2** *n* parent(e) *m(f)*; **relatively** relativement
relax [rɪ'læks] **1** *v/i* se détendre; **~!** du calme! **2** *v/t muscle* relâcher; **relaxation** détente *f*, relaxation *f*; **relaxed** détendu, décontracté; **relaxing** reposant, relaxant
relay 1 *v/t* [riː'leɪ] *message* transmettre; *radio, TV signals* relayer, retransmettre **2** *n* ['riːleɪ]: **~** (***race***) (course *f* de) relais *m*
release [rɪ'liːs] **1** *n from prison* libération *f*; *of CD, movie etc* sortie *f*; *CD, record* nouveauté *f* **2** *v/t prisoner* libérer; *CD, record, movie* sortir; *parking brake* desserrer; *information* communiquer
relegate ['relɪgeɪt] reléguer
relent [rɪ'lent] se calmer; *of person* s'adoucir; **relentless** (*determined*) acharné; *rain etc* incessant
relevance ['reləvəns] pertinence *f*; **relevant** pertinent
reliability [rɪlaɪə'bɪlətɪ] fiabilité *f*; **reliable** fiable; **reliance** [rɪ'laɪəns] confiance *f* (***on*** en); *on equipment* dépendance *f* (***on*** vis-à-vis de)
relic ['relɪk] relique *f*
relief [rɪ'liːf] soulagement *m*;

relieve *pain* soulager; (*take over from*) relayer, relever
religion [rɪ'lɪdʒən] religion *f*; **religious** religieux; *person* croyant
relinquish [rɪ'lɪŋkwɪʃ] abandonner
relish ['relɪʃ] **1** *n sauce* relish *f*; (*enjoyment*) délectation *f* **2** *v/t idea, prospect* se réjouir de
relive [riː'lɪv] *event* revivre
relocate [riːlə'keɪt] *of business* se réimplanter; *of employee* être muté
reluctance [rɪ'lʌktəns] réticence *f*; **reluctant** réticent; ***be ~ to do sth*** hésiter à faire qch
◆ **rely on** [rɪ'laɪ] compter sur; ***rely on s.o. to do sth*** compter sur qn pour faire qch
remain [rɪ'meɪn] rester; ***~ silent*** garder le silence; **remainder** *also* MATH reste *m*; **remaining** restant; ***the ~ refugees*** le reste des réfugiés; **remains** *of body* restes *mpl*
remake ['riːmeɪk] *of movie* remake *m*, nouvelle version *f*
remark [rɪ'mɑːrk] **1** *n* remarque *f* **2** *v/t* (*comment*) faire remarquer; **remarkable** remarquable; **remarkably** remarquablement
remarry [riː'mærɪ] se remarier
remedy ['remədɪ] MED, *fig* remède *m*
remember [rɪ'membər] **1** *v/t* se souvenir de, se rappeler **2** *v/i* se souvenir
remind [rɪ'maɪnd]: ***~ s.o. to do sth*** rappeler à qn de faire qch; ***~ X of Y*** rappeler Y à X; ***~ s.o. of sth*** (*bring to their attention*) rappeler qch à qn; **reminder** rappel *m*
reminisce [remɪ'nɪs] évoquer le passé
remission [rɪ'mɪʃn] MED rémission *f*; ***go into ~*** *of patient* être en sursis
remnant ['remnənt] vestige *m*, reste *m*
remorse [rɪ'mɔːrs] remords *m*; **remorseless** impitoyable; *demands* incessant
remote [rɪ'mout] *village* isolé; *possibility* vague; *ancestor* lointain; **remote control** télécommande *f*; **remotely** *related, connected* vaguement
removable [rɪ'muːvəbl] amovible; **removal** enlèvement *m*; *of demonstrators* expulsion *f*; *of doubt* dissipation *f*; **remove** enlever; *demonstrators* expulser; *doubt* dissiper
rename [riː'neɪm] rebaptiser; *file* renommer
rendez-vous ['rɑːndeɪvuː] rendez-vous *m*
renew [rɪ'nuː] *contract* renouveler; *discussion* reprendre; **renewal** *of contract etc* renouvellement *m*; *of discussion* reprise *f*
renounce [rɪ'nauns] renoncer à

renovate ['renəveɪt] rénover; **renovation** rénovation *f*
rent [rent] **1** *n* loyer *m*; ***for ~*** à louer **2** *v/t* louer; **rental** *for apartment* loyer *m*; *for TV, car* location *f*; **rental car** voiture *f* de location; **rent-free** sans payer de loyer
reopen [riː'oʊpn] **1** *v/t* rouvrir; *negotiations* reprendre **2** *v/i of store etc* rouvrir
reorganization [riːɔːrgənaɪ'zeɪʃn] réorganisation *f*; **reorganize** réorganiser
repaint [riː'peɪnt] repeindre
repair [rɪ'per] **1** *v/t* réparer **2** *n* réparation *f*; **repairman** réparateur *m*
repatriate [riː'pætrɪeɪt] rapatrier; **repatriation** rapatriement *m*
repay [riː'peɪ] rembourser; **repayment** remboursement *m*
repeal [rɪ'piːl] *law* abroger
repeat [rɪ'piːt] **1** *v/t* répéter **2** *n TV program etc* rediffusion *f*; **repeatedly** à plusieurs reprises
repel [rɪ'pel] repousser; (*disgust*) dégoûter; **repellent 1** *adj* repoussant, répugnant **2** *n* (*insect ~*) répulsif *m*
repercussions [riːpər'kʌʃnz] répercussions *fpl*
repertoire ['repərtwɑːr] répertoire *m*
repetition [repɪ'tɪʃn] répétition *f*; **repetitive** répétitif
replace [rɪ'pleɪs] (*put back*) remettre; (*take the place of*) remplacer; **replacement** *person* remplaçant *m*; *product* produit *m* de remplacement; **replacement part** pièce *f* de rechange
replay ['riːpleɪ] **1** *n recording* relecture *f*, replay *m*; *match* nouvelle rencontre *f*, replay *m* **2** *v/t match* rejouer
replenish [rɪ'plenɪʃ] *container* remplir (de nouveau); *supplies* refaire
replica ['replɪkə] réplique *f*
reply [rɪ'plaɪ] **1** *n* réponse *f* **2** *v/t & v/i* répondre
report [rɪ'pɔːrt] **1** *n* (*account*) rapport *m*, compte-rendu *m*; *in newspaper* bulletin *m* **2** *v/t facts* rapporter; *to authorities* déclarer **3** *v/i* (*present o.s.*) se présenter; **reporter** reporter *m/f*
repossess [riːpə'zes] COM reprendre possession de
represent [reprɪ'zent] représenter; **representative 1** *adj* (*typical*) représentatif **2** *n* représentant(e) *m(f)*
repress [rɪ'pres] réprimer; **repression** POL répression *f*; **repressive** POL répressif
reprieve [rɪ'priːv] **1** *n* LAW sursis *m*; *fig also* répit *m* **2** *v/t prisoner* accorder un sursis à
reprimand ['reprɪmænd] réprimander
reprint ['riːprɪnt] **1** *n* réimpression *f* **2** *v/t* réimprimer
reprisal [rɪ'praɪzl] représailles

fpl

reproach [rɪ'proʊʧ] **1** *n* reproche *m* **2** *v/t*: **~ *s.o. for sth*** reprocher qch à qn; **reproachful** réprobateur

reproduce [riːprə'duːs] **1** *v/t* reproduire **2** *v/i* BIO se reproduire; **reproduction** reproduction *f*

reproductive reproducteur

reptile ['reptaɪl] reptile *m*

republic [rɪ'pʌblɪk] république *f*; **Republican 1** *adj* républicain **2** *n* Républicain(e) *m(f)*

repulsive [rɪ'pʌlsɪv] repoussant

reputable ['repjʊtəbl] de bonne réputation; **reputation** réputation *f*

request [rɪ'kwest] **1** *n* demande *f*; ***on ~*** sur demande **2** *v/t* demander

require [rɪ'kwaɪr] (*need*) avoir besoin de; **required** (*necessary*) requis; **requirement** (*need*) besoin *m*, exigence *f*; (*condition*) condition *f* (requise)

requisition [rekwɪ'zɪʃn] réquisitionner

re-route [riː'ruːt] *airplane etc* dérouter

rerun ['riːrʌn] **1** *n of TV program* rediffusion *f* **2** *v/t tape* repasser

reschedule [riː'skedjuːl] changer l'heure/la date de

rescue ['reskjuː] **1** *n* sauvetage *m* **2** *v/t* sauver, secourir

research [rɪ'sɜːrʧ] recherche *f*; **research and development** recherche *f* et développement; **researcher** chercheur(-euse) *m(f)*

resemblance [rɪ'zembləns] ressemblance *f*; **resemble** ressembler à

resent [rɪ'zent] ne pas aimer; *person also* en vouloir à; **resentful** plein de ressentiment; **resentment** ressentiment *m* (***of*** par rapport à)

reservation [rezər'veɪʃn] réservation *f*; *mental*, (*special area*) réserve *f*; **reserve 1** *n* (*store*, *aloofness*) réserve *f*; SP remplaçant(e) *m(f)* **2** *v/t seat*, *judgment* réserver; **reserved** *table*, *manner* réservé

reservoir ['rezərvwɑːr] *for water* réservoir *m*

residence ['rezɪdəns] *fml*: *house etc* résidence *f*; (*stay*) séjour *m*; **resident** résident(e) *m(f)*; *on street* riverain(e) *m(f)*; *in hotel* client(e) *m(f)*; **residential** résidentiel

residue ['rezɪduː] résidu *m*

resign [rɪ'zaɪn] **1** *v/t position* démissionner de; **~ *o.s. to*** se résigner à **2** *v/i from job* démissionner; **resignation** *from job* démission *f*; *mental* résignation *f*

resilient [rɪ'zɪlɪənt] *personality* fort; *material* résistant

resist [rɪ'zɪst] **1** *v/t* résister à; *new measures* s'opposer à **2** *v/i* résister; **resistance** résistance *f*; **resistant** *material* résistant

resolution [rezə'luːʃn] résolution *f*

resort [rɪ'zɔːrt] *place* lieu *m* de vacances; *at seaside* station *f* balnéaire; *for health cures* station *f* thermale; ***as a last ~*** en dernier ressort

◆ **resort to** avoir recours à, recourir à

◆ **resound with** [rɪ'zaʊnd] résonner de

resounding [rɪ'zaʊndɪŋ] *success, victory* retentissant

resource [rɪ'sɔːrs] ressource *f*; **resourceful** ingénieux

respect [rɪ'spekt] **1** *n* respect *m*; ***in this/that ~*** à cet égard; ***in many ~s*** à bien des égards **2** *v/t* respecter; **respectability** respectabilité *f*; **respectable** respectable; **respectful** respectueux; **respective** respectif; **respectively** respectivement

respiration [respɪ'reɪʃn] respiration *f*; **respirator** MED respirateur *m*

respond [rɪ'spɑːnd] répondre; (*react also*) réagir; **response** réponse *f*; (*reaction also*) réaction *f*,

responsibility [rɪspɑːnsɪ'bɪlətɪ] responsabilité *f*; **responsible** responsable (***for*** de); ***a ~ job*** un poste à responsabilités

rest[1] [rest] **1** *n* repos *m*; *during walk, work* pause *f* **2** *v/i* se reposer **3** *v/t* (*lean, balance*) poser

rest[2] [rest]: ***the ~*** *objects* le reste; *people* les autres

restaurant ['restərɑːnt] restaurant *m*

restful ['restfl] reposant; **rest home** maison *f* de retraite; **restless** agité; **restlessly** nerveusement

restoration [restə'reɪʃn] *of building* restauration *f*; **restore** *building etc* restaurer; (*bring back*) restituer; *confidence* redonner

restrain [rɪ'streɪn] retenir; **restraint** (*moderation*) retenue *f*

restrict [rɪ'strɪkt] restreindre; ***I'll ~ myself to …*** je me limiterai à …; **restriction** restriction *f*

'rest room toilettes *fpl*

result [rɪ'zʌlt] résultat *m*; ***as a ~ of this*** par conséquent

resume [rɪ'zuːm] reprendre

résumé ['rezʊmeɪ] *of career* curriculum vitæ *m inv*, C.V. *m inv*

resumption [rɪ'zʌmpʃn] reprise *f*

resurface [riː'sɜːrfɪs] **1** *v/t roads* refaire (le revêtement de) **2** *v/i* (*reappear*) refaire surface

Resurrection [rezə'rekʃn] REL Résurrection *f*

retail ['riːteɪl] **1** *adv*: ***sell sth ~*** vendre qch au détail **2** *v/i*: ***~ at*** se vendre à; **retailer** détail-

lant(e) *m*(*f*)
retain [rɪ'teɪn] conserver; **retainer** FIN provision *f*
retaliate [rɪ'tælɪeɪt] riposter, se venger; **retaliation** riposte *f*
rethink [riː'θɪŋk] repenser
reticence ['retɪsns] réserve *f*; **reticent** réservé
retire [rɪ'taɪr] *from work* prendre sa retraite; **retired** à la retraite; **retirement** retraite *f*; **retiring** réservé
retort [rɪ'tɔːrt] **1** *n* réplique *f* **2** *v/t* répliquer
retract [rɪ'trækt] *claws, undercarriage* rentrer; *statement* retirer
're-train se recycler
retreat [rɪ'triːt] **1** *v/i also* MIL battre en retraite **2** *n* MIL, *place* retraite *f*
retrieve [rɪ'triːv] récupérer
retroactive [retroʊ'æktɪv] *law etc* rétroactif; **retroactively** rétroactivement, par rétroaction
retrograde ['retrəgreɪd] rétrograde
retrospective [retrə'spektɪv] rétrospective *f*
return [rɪ'tɜːrn] **1** *n* retour *m*; (*profit*) bénéfice *m*; **~** (*ticket*) *Br* aller *m* retour; ***many happy ~s*** (***of the day***) bon anniversaire; ***in ~ for*** en échange de; contre **2** *v/t* (*give back*) rendre; (*send back*) renvoyer; (*put back*) remettre **3** *v/i* (*go back*) retourner; (*come back*) revenir
reunification [riːjuːnɪfɪ'keɪʃn] réunification *f*
reunion [riː'juːnjən] réunion *f*; **reunite** réunir; *country* réunifier
reusable [riː'juːzəbl] réutilisable; **reuse** réutiliser
◆ **rev up** [rev] *engine* emballer
revaluation [riːvæljʊ'eɪʃn] réévaluation *f*
reveal [rɪ'viːl] révéler; (*make visible*) dévoiler; **revealing** *remark* révélateur; *dress* suggestif; **revelation** révélation *f*
revenge [rɪ'vendʒ] vengeance *f*; ***take one's ~*** se venger
revenue ['revənuː] revenu *m*
reverberate [rɪ'vɜːrbəreɪt] *of sound* retentir, résonner
revere [rɪ'vɪr] révérer; **reverence** déférence *f*, respect *m*; **reverent** respectueux
reverse [rɪ'vɜːrs] **1** *adj sequence* inverse **2** *n* (*opposite*) contraire *m*; (*back*) verso *m*; MOT *gear* marche *f* arrière **3** *v/i* MOT faire marche arrière
review [rɪ'vjuː] **1** *n of book, movie* critique *f*; *of troops* revue *f*; *of situation etc* bilan *m* **2** *v/t book, movie* faire la critique de; *troops* passer en revue; *situation etc* faire le bilan de; EDU réviser; **reviewer** *of book, movie* critique *m*
revise [rɪ'vaɪz] *opinion* revenir sur; *text* réviser; **revision**

of text révision *f*
revival [rɪ'vaɪvl] *of custom, old style* renouveau *m*; *of patient* rétablissement *m*; **revive 1** *v/t custom, old style* faire renaître; *patient* ranimer **2** *v/i of business* reprendre
revoke [rɪ'voʊk] *law* abroger; *license* retirer
revolt [rɪ'voʊlt] **1** *n* révolte *f* **2** *v/i* se révolter; **revolting** répugnant; **revolution** révolution *f*; **revolutionary 1** *adj* révolutionnaire **2** *n* révolutionnaire *m/f*; **revolutionize** révolutionner
revolve [rɪ'vɑːlv] tourner (***around*** autour de); **revolver** revolver *m*
revulsion [rɪ'vʌlʃn] répugnance *f*
reward [rɪ'wɔːrd] **1** *n financial* récompense *f*; (*benefit derived*) gratification *f* **2** *v/t financially* récompenser; **rewarding** *experience* gratifiant, valorisant
rewind [riː'waɪnd] *film, tape* rembobiner
rewrite [riː'raɪt] réécrire
rhetoric ['retərɪk] rhétorique *f*
rhyme [raɪm] **1** *n* rime *f* **2** *v/i* rimer (***with*** avec)
rhythm ['rɪðm] rythme *m*
rib [rɪb] ANAT côte *f*
ribbon ['rɪbən] ruban *m*
rice [raɪs] riz *m*
rich [rɪʧ] **1** *adj person, food* riche **2** *npl*: ***the ~*** les riches *mpl*
ricochet ['rɪkəʃeɪ] ricocher (***off*** sur)
rid [rɪd]: ***get ~ of*** se débarrasser de
ride [raɪd] **1** *n on horse* promenade *f* (à cheval); *excursion in vehicle* tour *m*; (*journey*) trajet *m*; ***do you want a ~ into town?*** est-ce que tu veux que je t'emmène en ville? **2** *v/t horse* monter; *bike* se déplacer en; ***can I ~ your bike?*** est-ce que je peux monter sur ton vélo? **3** *v/i on horse* monter à cheval; *on bike* rouler (à vélo); **rider** *on horse* cavalier(-ière) *m(f)*; *on bike* cycliste *m/f*
ridge [rɪdʒ] (*raised strip*) arête *f* (saillante); *of mountain* crête *f*; *of roof* arête *f*
ridicule ['rɪdɪkjuːl] **1** *n* ridicule *m* **2** *v/t* ridiculiser; **ridiculous** ridicule; **ridiculously** ridiculement
riding ['raɪdɪŋ] *on horseback* équitation *f*
rifle ['raɪfl] fusil *m*, carabine *f*
rift [rɪft] *in earth* fissure *f*; *in party etc* scission *f*
rig [rɪg] **1** *n* (*oil ~*) tour *f* de forage; *at sea* plateforme *f* de forage; (*truck*) semi-remorque *m* **2** *v/t elections* truquer
right [raɪt] **1** *adj* bon; (*not left*) droit; ***be ~*** *of answer* être juste; *of person* avoir raison; *of clock* être à l'heure; ***it's not ~ to …*** ce n'est pas bien de …;

put things ~ arranger les choses; ***that's ~!*** c'est ça!; ***that's all ~*** (*doesn't matter*) ce n'est pas grave; *when s.o. says thank you* je vous en prie; ***it's all ~*** (*is acceptable*) ça me va; ***I'm all ~*** *not hurt* je vais bien; *have enough* ça ira pour moi **2** *adv* (*directly*) directement, juste; (*correctly*) correctement, bien; (*not left*) à droite; ***~ now*** (*immediately*) tout de suite; (*at the moment*) en ce moment; ***it's ~ here*** c'est juste là **3** *n civil, legal* droit *m*; (*not left*), POL droite *f*; ***be in the ~*** avoir raison; **right-angle** angle *m* droit; **rightful** *owner etc* légitime; **right-handed** *person* droitier; **right-hand man** bras *m* droit; **right of way** *in traffic* priorité *f*; *across land* droit *m* de passage; **right wing** POL droite *f*; SP ailier *m* droit; **right-wing** POL de droite

rigid ['rɪdʒɪd] *also fig* rigide

rigor ['rɪgər] *of discipline* rigueur *f*; **rigorous** rigoureux; **rigorously** *check* rigoureusement

rigour *Br* → ***rigor***

rile [raɪl] F agacer

rim [rɪm] *of wheel* jante *f*; *of cup* bord *m*; *of eyeglasses* monture *f*

ring¹ [rɪŋ] *n* (*circle*) cercle *m*; *on finger* anneau *m*; *in boxing* ring *m*; *at circus* piste *f*

ring² [rɪŋ] **1** *n of bell* sonnerie *f*; *of voice* son *m* **2** *v/t bell* (faire) sonner; *Br* TELEC téléphoner à **3** *v/i of bell* sonner, retentir

'ringleader meneur(-euse) *m*(*f*); **ring-pull** anneau *m* (d'ouverture)

rink [rɪŋk] patinoire *f*

rinse [rɪns] **1** *n for hair color* rinçage *m* **2** *v/t* rincer

riot ['raɪət] **1** *n* émeute *f* **2** *v/i* participer à une émeute; *start to ~* créer une émeute; **rioter** émeutier(-ière) *m*(*f*); **riot police** police *f* anti-émeute

rip [rɪp] **1** *n in cloth etc* accroc *m* **2** *v/t cloth etc* déchirer
◆ **rip-off** F *customers* arnaquer F

ripe [raɪp] *fruit* mûr; **ripen** *of fruit* mûrir; **ripeness** *of fruit* maturité *f*

'rip-off F arnaque *f* F

ripple ['rɪpl] *on water* ride *f*

rise [raɪz] **1** *v/i from chair, bed, of sun* se lever; *of rocket, price, temperature* monter **2** *n in price, temperature* hausse *f*; *in water level* élévation *f*; *Br: in salary* augmentation *f*

risk [rɪsk] **1** *n* risque *m*; ***take a ~*** prendre un risque **2** *v/t* risquer; **risky** risqué

ritual ['rɪtʊəl] **1** *adj* rituel **2** *n* rituel *m*

rival ['raɪvl] **1** *n* rival(e) *m*(*f*) **2**

v/t (*match*) égaler; (*compete with*) rivaliser avec; **rivalry** rivalité *f*

river ['rɪvər] rivière *f*; *bigger* fleuve *m*; **riverbank** rive *f*; **riverbed** lit *m* de la rivière/du fleuve; **riverside 1** *adj* en bord de rivière **2** *n* berge *f*, bord *m* de l'eau

riveting ['rɪvɪtɪŋ] fascinant

road [roʊd] route *f*; *in city* rue *f*; **roadblock** barrage *m* routier; **road-holding** *of vehicle* tenue *f* de route; **road map** carte *f* routière; **road safety** sécurité *f* routière; **roadsign** panneau *m* (de signalisation); **roadway** chaussée *f*; **roadworthy** en état de marche

roam [roʊm] errer

roar [rɔːr] **1** *n* rugissement *m*; *of traffic* grondement *m*; *of engine* vrombissement *m* **2** *v/i* rugir; *of traffic* gronder; *of engine* vrombir

roast [roʊst] **1** *n of beef etc* rôti *m* **2** *v/t* rôtir **3** *v/i of food* rôtir; **roast beef** rosbif *m*

rob [rɑːb] *person* voler, dévaliser; *bank* cambrioler, dévaliser; **robber** voleur(-euse) *m(f)*; **robbery** vol *m*

robe [roʊb] *of judge, priest* robe *f*; (*bath~*) peignoir *m*; (*dressing gown*) robe *f* de chambre

robot ['roʊbɑːt] robot *m*

robust [roʊ'bʌst] robuste

rock [rɑːk] **1** *n* rocher *m*; MUS rock *m* **2** *v/t baby* bercer; *cradle* balancer; (*surprise*) secouer **3** *v/i on chair, of boat* se balancer; **rock-bottom** *price* le plus bas possible; **rock climber** varappeur(-euse) *m(f)*; **rock climbing** varappe *f*

rocket ['rɑːkɪt] **1** *n* fusée *f* **2** *v/i of prices etc* monter en flèche

rocking chair ['rɑːkɪŋ] rocking-chair *m*; **rock 'n' roll** rock-and-roll *m inv*; **rocky** *beach* rocheux

rod [rɑːd] baguette *f*; *for fishing* canne *f* à pêche

rodent ['roʊdnt] rongeur *m*

rogue [roʊg] vaurien *m*

role [roʊl] rôle *m*; **role model** modèle *m*

roll [roʊl] **1** *n* (*bread ~*) petit pain *m*; *of film* pellicule *f*; (*list, register*) liste *f* **2** *v/i of ball, boat* rouler

◆ **roll over 1** *v/i* se retourner **2** *v/t person, object* tourner; (*renew*) renouveler; (*extend*) prolonger

'roll call appel *m*; **roller** *for hair* rouleau *m*; **roller blade®** roller *m* (en ligne); **roller coaster** montagnes *fpl* russes; **roller skate** patin *m* à roulettes

ROM [rɑːm] COMPUT (= ***read only memory***) ROM *f*, mémoire *f* morte

Roman 'Catholic 1 *adj* REL catholique **2** *n* catholique *m/f*

romance ['roʊmæns] (*affair*)

idylle *f*; *novel, movie* histoire *f* d'amour; **romantic** romantique
roof [ruːf] toit *m*; **roof-rack** MOT galerie *f*
rookie ['rʊkɪ] F bleu *m* F
room [ruːm] pièce *f*, salle *f*; (*bed~*) chambre *f*; (*space*) place *f*; **room clerk** réceptionniste *m/f*; **roommate** *in apartment* colocataire *m/f*; *in room* camarade *m/f* de chambre; **room service** service *m* en chambre; **room temperature** température *f* ambiante; **roomy** spacieux; *clothes* ample
root [ruːt] racine *f*
rope [roʊp] corde *f*
rosary ['roʊzərɪ] REL rosaire *m*, chapelet *m*
rose [roʊz] BOT rose *f*
roster ['rɑːstər] tableau *m* de service
rostrum ['rɑːstrəm] estrade *f*
rosy ['roʊzɪ] *also fig* rose
rot [rɑːt] **1** *n* pourriture *f* **2** *v/i* pourrir
rotate [roʊ'teɪt] **1** *v/i* tourner **2** *v/t* (*turn*) (faire) tourner; *crops* alterner; **rotation** rotation *f*
rotten ['rɑːtn] *also* F *weather, luck* pourri
rough [rʌf] **1** *adj surface* rugueux; *hands, skin* rêche; *voice* rude; (*violent*) brutal; *crossing, seas* agité; (*approximate*) approximatif; ***~ draft*** brouillon *m* **2** *n in golf* rough *m*; **roughage** *in food* fibres *fpl*; **roughly** (*approximately*) environ; (*harshly*) brutalement
roulette [ruː'let] roulette *f*
round [raʊnd] **1** *adj* rond **2** *n of mailman, doctor, drinks* tournée *f*; *of competition* manche *f*, tour *m*; *in boxing* round *m* **3** *v/t corner* tourner **4** *adv & prep* → ***around***
◆ **round up** *figure* arrondir; *suspects* ramasser
roundabout ['raʊndəbaʊt] **1** *adj* détourné, indirect **2** *n Br*: *on road* rond-point *m*;
round-the-world autour du monde; **round trip** aller-retour *m*; **round-up** *of cattle* rassemblement *m*; *of suspects* rafle *f*; *of news* résumé *m*
rouse [raʊz] *from sleep* réveiller; *emotions* soulever; **rousing** exaltant
route [raʊt] itinéraire *m*
routine [ruː'tiːn] **1** *adj* de routine; *behavior* routinier **2** *n* routine *f*
row¹ [roʊ] *n* (*line*) rangée *f*; *of troops* rang *m*; ***5 days in a ~*** 5 jours de suite
row² [roʊ] *v/i in boat* ramer
rowboat ['roʊboʊt] bateau *m* à rames
rowdy ['raʊdɪ] tapageur, bruyant
royal ['rɔɪəl] royal; **royalty** (membres *mpl* de) la famille royale; *on book, recording*

droits *mpl* d'auteur
rub [rʌb] frotter
rubber ['rʌbər] **1** *n material* caoutchouc *m* **2** *adj* en caoutchouc; **rubber band** élastique *m*
rubble ['rʌbl] *from building* gravats *mpl*, décombres *mpl*
ruby ['ruːbɪ] *jewel* rubis *m*
rudder ['rʌdər] gouvernail *m*
ruddy ['rʌdɪ] *complexion* coloré
rude [ruːd] impoli; *language, gesture* grossier; **rudely** (*impolitely*) impoliment; **rudeness** impolitesse *f*
rudimentary [ruːdɪ'mentərɪ] rudimentaire; **rudiments** rudiments *mpl*
rueful ['ruːfl] contrit, résigné; **ruefully** avec regret; *smile* d'un air contrit
ruffian ['rʌfɪən] voyou *m*, brute *f*
ruffle ['rʌfl] **1** *n on dress* ruche *f* **2** *v/t hair* ébouriffer; *person* énerver
rug [rʌg] tapis *m*; *blanket* couverture *f*
rugby ['rʌgbɪ] rugby *m*
rugged ['rʌgɪd] *scenery, cliffs* escarpé; *face* aux traits rudes; *resistance* acharné
ruin ['ruːɪn] **1** *n* ruine *f* **2** *v/t* ruiner; *party, plans* gâcher
rule [ruːl] **1** *n* règle *f*; *of monarch* règne *m*; ***as a ~*** en règle générale **2** *v/t country* gouverner **3** *v/i of monarch* régner; **ruler** *for measuring* règle *f*; *of state* dirigeant(e) *m(f)*; **ruling 1** *n* décision *f* **2** *adj party* dirigeant, au pouvoir
rum [rʌm] *drink* rhum *m*
rumble ['rʌmbl] *of stomach* gargouiller; *of thunder* gronder
rumor, *Br* **rumour** ['ruːmər] **1** *n* bruit *m*, rumeur *f* **2** *v/t*: ***it is ~ed that …*** le bruit court que …
rump [rʌmp] *of animal* croupe *f*
rumple ['rʌmpl] *clothes, paper* froisser
'rumpsteak rumsteck *m*
run [rʌn] **1** *n on foot* course *f*; *in pantyhose* échelle *f*; ***go for a ~*** *for exercise* aller courir; ***in the short/long ~*** à court/long terme **2** *v/i* courir; *of river, paint, makeup* couler; *of trains, buses* passer, circuler; *of play* être à l'affiche; *of engine, machine* marcher, tourner; *of software* fonctionner; *in election* se présenter; ***~ for President*** être candidat à la présidence **3** *v/t race* courir; *business, hotel etc* diriger; *software* exécuter, faire tourner; *car* entretenir
◆ **run away** s'enfuir; *from home for a while* faire une fugue; *for good* s'enfuir de chez soi
◆ **run down 1** *v/t* (*knock down*) renverser; (*criticize*)

critiquer; *stocks* diminuer **2** *v/i of battery* se décharger
◆ **run off 1** *v/i* s'enfuir **2** *v/t* (*print off*) tirer
◆ **run out** *of contract* expirer; *of time* s'écouler; *of supplies* s'épuiser
◆ **run out of** ne plus avoir de
◆ **run over 1** *v/t* (*knock down*) renverser **2** *v/i of water etc* déborder
◆ **run up** *debts* accumuler
'runaway fugueur(-euse) *m(f)*; **run-down** *person* épuisé; *area* délabré
rung [rʌŋ] *of ladder* barreau *m*
runner ['rʌnər] *athlete* coureur(-euse) *m(f)*; **runner beans** haricots *mpl* d'Espagne; **runner-up** second(e) *m(f)*; **running 1** *n* SP course *f*; *of business* gestion *f* **2** *adj*: ***for two days*** **~** pendant deux jours de suite; **running water** eau *f* courante; **runny** *substance* liquide; *nose* qui coule; **run-up** SP élan *m*; ***in the ~ to*** pendant la période qui précède; **runway** AVIA piste *f*
rupture ['rʌptʃər] **1** *n also fig* rupture *f* **2** *v/i of pipe* éclater
rural ['rʊrəl] rural
ruse [ru:z] ruse *f*
rush [rʌʃ] **1** *n* ruée *f*; ***do sth in a ~*** faire qch à la hâte; ***be in a ~*** être pressé **2** *v/t person* presser; *meal* avaler (à toute vitesse) **3** *v/i* se presser; **rush hour** heures *fpl* de pointe
Russia ['rʌʃə] Russie *f*; **Russian** ['rʌʃən] **1** *adj* russe **2** *n* Russe *m/f*; *language* russe *m*
rust [rʌst] **1** *n* rouille *f* **2** *v/i* se rouiller; **rust-proof** antirouille *inv*; **rusty** *also fig* rouillé
rut [rʌt] *in road* ornière *f*; ***be in a ~*** *fig* être tombé dans la routine
ruthless ['ru:θlɪs] impitoyable, sans pitié; **ruthlessly** impitoyablement; **ruthlessness** dureté *f* (impitoyable)
rye [raɪ] seigle *m*; **rye bread** pain *m* de seigle

S

sabotage ['sæbətɑ:ʒ] **1** *n* sabotage *m* **2** *v/t* saboter; **saboteur** saboteur(-euse) *m(f)*
sachet ['sæʃeɪ] sachet *m*
sack [sæk] **1** *n bag* sac *m* **2** *v/t* F virer F
sacred ['seɪkrɪd] sacré
sacrifice ['sækrɪfaɪs] **1** *n* sacrifice *m* **2** *v/t also fig* sacrifier
sacrilege ['sækrɪlɪdʒ] REL, *fig* sacrilège *m*
sad [sæd] triste
saddle ['sædl] **1** *n* selle *f* **2** *v/t*

horse seller

sadism ['seɪdɪzm] sadisme *m*; **sadist** sadique *m/f*; **sadistic** sadique

sadly ['sædlɪ] tristement; (*regrettably*) malheureusement; **sadness** tristesse *f*

safe [seɪf] **1** *adj* (*not dangerous*) pas dangereux; *driver* prudent; (*not in danger*) en sécurité **2** *n* coffre-fort *m*; **safeguard 1** *n*: ***as a ~ against*** par mesure de protection contre **2** *v/t* protéger; **safely** *arrive, drive, assume* sans risque; **safety** sécurité *f*; *of investment, prediction* sûreté *f*; **safety pin** épingle *f* de nourrice

sag [sæg] *of ceiling* s'affaisser; *of rope* se détendre; *fig*: *of output* fléchir

saga ['sɑːgə] saga *f*

sage [seɪdʒ] *herb* sauge *f*

sail [seɪl] **1** *n of boat* voile *f*; *trip* voyage *m* (en mer) **2** *v/i* faire de la voile; (*depart*) partir; **sailboard 1** *n* planche *f* à voile **2** *v/i* faire de la planche à voile; **sailboarding** planche *f* à voile; **sailboat** bateau *m* à voiles; **sailing** SP voile *f*; **sailor** marin *m*

saint [seɪnt] saint(e) *m(f)*

sake [seɪk]: ***for my ~*** pour moi

salad ['sæləd] salade *f*

salary ['sælərɪ] salaire *m*

sale [seɪl] vente *f*; *reduced prices* soldes *mpl*; ***for ~*** *sign* à vendre; ***be on ~*** être en vente; *at reduced prices* être en solde; **sales department** vente *f*; **sales clerk** *in store* vendeur(-euse) *m(f)*; **sales figures** chiffre *m* d'affaires; **salesman** vendeur *m*; (*rep*) représentant *m*; **saleswoman** vendeuse *f*

salient ['seɪlɪənt] marquant

saliva [sə'laɪvə] salive *f*

salmon ['sæmən] saumon *m*

saloon [sə'luːn] (*bar*) bar *m* *Br* MOT berline *f*

salt [sɒːlt] sel *m*; **salty** salé

salute [sə'luːt] **1** *n* MIL salut *m* **2** *v/t* MIL saluer **3** *v/i* MIL faire un salut

salvage ['sælvɪdʒ] *from wreck* sauver

salvation [sæl'veɪʃn] *also fig* salut *m*

same [seɪm] **1** *adj* même **2** *pron*: ***the ~*** le/la même; *pl* ***the ~*** les mêmes; ***Happy New Year – the ~ to you*** Bonne année – à vous aussi; ***all the ~*** (*even so*) quand même **3** *adv*: ***look/sound the ~*** se ressembler, être pareil

sample ['sæmpl] *of work, cloth* échantillon *m*; *of blood* prélèvement *m*

sanction ['sæŋkʃn] **1** *n* (*approval*) approbation *f*; (*penalty*) sanction *f* **2** *v/t* (*approve*) approuver

sand [sænd] **1** *n* sable *m* **2** *v/t* *with sandpaper* poncer au papier de verre

sandal ['sændl] sandale *f*

'sandbag sac *m* de sable; **sand dune** dune *f*; **sander** *tool* ponçeuse *f*; **sandpaper** **1** *n* papier *m* de verre **2** *v/t* poncer au papier de verre
sandwich ['sænwɪtʃ] sandwich *m*
sandy ['sændɪ] *beach* de sable; *soil* sablonneux; *feet, towel* plein de sable; *hair* blond roux
sane [seɪn] sain (d'esprit)
sanitarium [sænɪ'terɪəm] sanatorium *m*
sanitary ['sænɪterɪ] sanitaire; (*clean*) hygiénique; **sanitary napkin** serviette *f* hygiénique; **sanitation** installations *fpl* sanitaires; (*removal of waste*) système *m* sanitaire
sanity ['sænətɪ] santé *f* mentale
Santa Claus ['sæntəklɒːz] le Père Noël
sap [sæp] **1** *n in tree* sève *f* **2** *v/t s.o.'s energy* saper
sapphire ['sæfaɪr] saphir *m*
sarcasm ['sɑːrkæzm] sarcasme *m*; **sarcastic** sarcastique; **sarcastically** sarcastiquement
sardine [sɑːr'diːn] sardine *f*
sardonic [sɑːr'dɑːnɪk] sardonique
satellite ['sætəlaɪt] satellite *m*; **satellite dish** antenne *f* parabolique; **satellite TV** télévision *f* par satellite
satin ['sætɪn] satin *m*
satire ['sætaɪr] satire *f*; **satirical** satirique; **satirize** satiriser
satisfaction [sætɪs'fækʃn] satisfaction *f*; **satisfactory** satisfaisant; (*just good enough*) convenable; **satisfy** satisfaire; *conditions* remplir
Saturday ['sætərdeɪ] samedi *m*
sauce [sɒːs] sauce *f*; **saucepan** casserole *f*; **saucer** soucoupe *f*
Saudi Arabia [saudɪə'reɪbɪə] Arabie *f* saoudite; **Saudi Arabian** **1** *adj* saoudien **2** *n* Saoudien(ne) *m(f)*
sausage ['sɒːsɪdʒ] saucisse *f*; *dried* saucisson *m*
savage ['sævɪdʒ] **1** *adj* féroce **2** *n* sauvage *m/f*; **savagery** férocité *f*
save [seɪv] **1** *v/t* (*rescue*), SP sauver; (*economize, put aside*) économiser; (*collect*) faire collection de; COMPUT sauvegarder **2** *v/i* (*put money aside*) faire des économies; SP arrêter le ballon **3** *n* SP arrêt *m*; **saver** *person* épargneur (-euse) *m(f)*; **savings** économies *fpl*; **savings account** compte *m* d'épargne; **savings and loan** caisse *f* d'épargne-logement; **savings bank** caisse *f* d'épargne
savior, *Br* **saviour** ['seɪvjər] REL sauveur *m*
savor ['seɪvər] savourer; **savory** *not sweet* salé
savour *etc Br* → ***savor*** *etc*

saw [sɒː] **1** *n tool* scie *f* **2** *v/t* scier; **sawdust** sciure *f*
saxophone ['sæksəfoʊn] saxophone *m*
say [seɪ] dire; ***that is to ~*** c'est-à-dire; **saying** dicton *m*
scab [skæb] *on wound* croûte *f*
scaffolding ['skæfəldɪŋ] échafaudage *m*
scald [skɒːld] ébouillanter
scale[1] [skeɪl] *n on fish* écaille *f*
scale[2] [skeɪl] **1** *n of project, map etc, on thermometer* échelle *f*; MUS gamme *f* **2** *v/t cliffs etc* escalader
scales [skeɪlz] *for weighing* balance *f*
scallop ['skæləp] *shellfish* coquille *f* Saint-Jacques
scalp [skælp] cuir *m* chevelu
scalpel ['skælpl] scalpel *m*
scam [skæm] F arnaque *m* F
scampi ['skæmpɪ] scampi *m*
scan [skæn] **1** *n* MED scanner *m*; *during pregnancy* échographie *f* **2** *v/t horizon, page* parcourir du regard; MED faire un scanner de; COMPUT scanner
◆ **scan in** COMPUT scanner
scandal ['skændl] scandale *m*; **scandalize** scandaliser; **scandalous** scandaleux
scanner ['skænər] MED, COMPUT scanner *m*
scanty ['skæntɪ] *dress* réduit au minimum
scapegoat ['skeɪpgoʊt] bouc *m* émissaire
scar [skɑːr] **1** *n* cicatrice *f* **2** *v/t* marquer d'une cicatrice
scarce [skers] rare; **scarcely** ['skerslɪ] à peine; ***~ anything*** presque rien; **scarcity** manque *m*
scare [sker] **1** *v/t* faire peur à; ***be ~d of*** avoir peur de **2** *n* (*panic, alarm*) rumeurs *fpl* alarmantes; **scaremonger** alarmiste *m/f*
scarf [skɑːrf] *around neck* écharpe *f*; *over head* foulard *m*
scarlet ['skɑːrlət] écarlate
scary ['skerɪ] effrayant
scathing ['skeɪðɪŋ] cinglant
scatter ['skætər] **1** *v/t leaflets, seed* éparpiller **2** *v/i of people* se disperser; **scattered** *showers* intermittent; *villages* éparpillé
scavenge ['skævɪndʒ]: ***~ for sth*** fouiller pour trouver qch; **scavenger** charognard *m*; *person* fouilleur(euse) *m(f)*
scenario [sɪ'nɑːrɪoʊ] scénario *m*
scene [siːn] scène *f*; *of accident, crime etc* lieu *m*; ***make a ~*** faire une scène; ***behind the ~s*** dans les coulisses; **scenery** paysage *m*; THEA décor(s) *m*(pl)
scent [sent] odeur *f*; *Br* (*perfume*) parfum *m*
sceptic *etc Br* → ***skeptic*** *etc*
schedule ['skedjuːl] **1** *n of*

events calendrier *m*; *for trains* horaire *m*; *of lessons, work* programme *m*; ***be on ~** of work, workers* être dans les temps; *of train* être à l'heure; ***be behind ~*** être en retard **2** *v/t* (*put on ~*) prévoir; **scheduled flight** vol *m* régulier

scheme [ski:m] **1** *n* plan *m* **2** *v/i* (*plot*) comploter; **scheming** intrigant

schizophrenia [skɪtsə'fri:nɪə] schizophrénie *f*; **schizophrenic 1** *adj* schizophrène **2** *n* schizophrène *m/f*

scholar ['skɑ:lər] érudit(e) *m(f)*; **scholarly** savant, érudit; **scholarship** (*learning*) érudition *f*; *financial award* bourse *f*

school [sku:l] école *f*; (*university*) université *f*; **school bag** cartable *m*; **schoolchildren** écoliers *mpl*

science ['saɪəns] science *f*; **scientific** scientifique; **scientist** scientifique *m/f*

scissors ['sɪzərz] ciseaux *mpl*

scoff[1] [skɑ:f] *food* engloutir

scoff[2] [skɑ:f] (*mock*) se moquer

scold [skoʊld] réprimander

scoop [sku:p] *for ice-cream* cuiller *f* à glace; *of ice cream* boule *f*; *story* scoop *m*

scooter ['sku:tər] *with motor* scooter *m*; *child's* trottinette *f*

scope [skoʊp] ampleur *f*; (*freedom, opportunity*) possibilités *fpl*

scorch [skɔ:rʧ] brûler; **scorching** très chaud

score [skɔ:r] **1** *n* SP score *m*; (*written music*) partition *f*; *of movie etc* musique *f* **2** *v/t goal, point* marquer; (*cut: line*) rayer **3** *v/i* SP marquer; (*keep the ~*) marquer les points; **scoreboard** tableau *m* des scores; **scorer** marqueur(-euse) *m(f)*

scorn [skɔ:rn] **1** *n* mépris *m* **2** *v/t idea* mépriser; **scornful** méprisant; **scornfully** avec mépris

Scot [skɑ:t] Écossais(e) *m(f)*; **Scotch** *whiskey* scotch *m*; **Scotch tape®** scotch *m*; **Scotland** Écosse *f*; **Scottish** écossais

scoundrel ['skaʊndrəl] gredin *m*

scour ['skaʊər] (*search*) fouiller

scowl [skaʊl] **1** *n* air *m* renfrogné **2** *v/i* se renfrogner

scramble ['skræmbl] **1** *n* (*rush*) course *f* folle **2** *v/t message* brouiller **3** *v/i*: ***he ~d to his feet*** il se releva d'un bond; **scrambled eggs** œufs *mpl* brouillés

scrap [skræp] **1** *n metal* ferraille *f*; (*fight*) bagarre *f*; *of food, paper* bout *m* **2** *v/t idea, plan* abandonner

scrape [skreɪp] **1** *n on paint, skin* éraflure *f* **2** *v/t paint-*

work, arm etc érafler
'scrap metal ferraille *f*
scrappy ['skræpɪ] *work, essay* décousu
scratch [skrætʃ] **1** *n mark* égratignure *f*; ***start from ~*** partir de zéro; ***not up to ~*** pas à la hauteur **2** *v/t* (*mark: skin, paint*) égratigner; *of cat* griffer; *because of itch* se gratter **3** *v/i of cat* griffer
scrawl [skrɒːl] **1** *n* gribouillis *m* **2** *v/t* gribouiller
scrawny ['skrɒːnɪ] décharné
scream [skriːm] **1** *n* cri *m* **2** *v/i* pousser un cri
screech [skriːtʃ] **1** *n of tires* crissement *m*; (*scream*) cri *m* strident **2** *v/i of tires* crisser; (*scream*) pousser un cri strident
screen [skriːn] **1** *n in room, hospital* paravent *m*; *in movie theater, of TV, computer* écran *m* **2** *v/t* (*protect, hide*) cacher; *movie* projeter; *for security reasons* passer au crible; **screenplay** scénario *m*; **screen saver** COMPUT économiseur *m* d'écran; **screen test** *for movie* bout *m* d'essai
screw [skruː] **1** *n* vis *m* **2** *v/t attach* visser (***to*** à); F (*cheat*) rouler F; V (*have sex with*) baiser V; **screwdriver** tournevis *m*; **screwed up** F *psychologically* paumé F; **screwy** F déjanté F
scribble ['skrɪbl] **1** *n* griffonnage *m* **2** *v/t* (*write quickly*) griffonner **3** *v/i* gribouiller
script [skrɪpt] *for movie* scénario *m*; *for play* texte *m*; *form of writing* script *m*; **Scripture**: ***the*** (***Holy***) ***~s*** les Saintes Écritures *fpl*; **scriptwriter** scénariste *m/f*
◆ **scroll down** [skroʊl] COMPUT faire défiler vers le bas
◆ **scroll up** COMPUT faire défiler vers le haut
scrounge [skraʊndʒ] se faire offrir; **scrounger** profiteur(-euse) *m(f)*
scrub [skrʌb] *floor* laver à la brosse
scruples ['skruːplz] scrupules *mpl*; **scrupulous** *morally*, (*thorough*) scrupuleux; **scrupulously** (*meticulously*) scrupuleusement
scrutinize ['skruːtɪnaɪz] (*examine closely*) scruter; **scrutiny** examen *m* minutieux
scuba diving ['skuːbə] plongée *f* sous-marine autonome
scuffle ['skʌfl] bagarre *f*
sculptor ['skʌlptər] sculpteur(-trice) *m(f)*; **sculpture** sculpture *f*
scum [skʌm] *on liquid* écume *f*; *pej*: *people* bande *f* d'ordures F
sea [siː] mer *f*; **seabird** oiseau *m* de mer; **seafood** fruits *mpl* de mer; **seagull** mouette *f*
seal[1] [siːl] *n animal* phoque *m*
seal[2] [siːl] **1** *n on document*

sceau *m*; TECH étanchéité *f* **2** *v/t container* sceller
'sea level: ***above/below ~*** au-dessus/au-dessous du niveau de la mer
seam [si:m] *on garment* couture *f*; *of ore* veine *f*
'seaman marin *m*; **seaport** port *m* maritime
search [sɜ:rʧ] **1** *n* recherche *f* (***for*** de) **2** *v/t* chercher dans
◆ **search for** chercher
searching ['sɜ:rʧɪŋ] *look, question* pénétrant; **searchlight** projecteur *m*
'seashore plage *f*; **seasick**: ***get ~*** avoir le mal de mer; **seaside**: ***at the ~*** au bord de la mer
season ['si:zn] saison *f*; **seasonal** *vegetables, employment* saisonnier; **seasoned** *wood* sec; *traveler, campaigner* expérimenté; **seasoning** assaisonnement *m*; **season ticket** carte *f* d'abonnement
seat [si:t] place *f*; *chair* siège *m*; *of pants* fond *m*; ***please take a ~*** veuillez vous asseoir; **seat belt** ceinture *f* de sécurité
'seaweed algues *fpl*
secluded [sɪ'klu:dɪd] retiré
second ['sekənd] **1** *n of time* seconde *f* **2** *adj* deuxième **3** *adv come in* deuxième **4** *v/t motion* appuyer; **secondary** secondaire; **second floor** premier étage *m*, *Br* deuxième étage *m*; **second-hand** d'occasion; **secondly** deuxièmement; **second-rate** de second ordre
secrecy ['si:krəsɪ] secret *m*;
secret 1 *n* secret *m* **2** *adj* secret
secretarial [sekrə'terɪəl] *job* de secrétariat; **secretary** secrétaire *m/f*; POL ministre *m/f*; **Secretary of State** secrétaire *m/f* d'État
secretive ['si:krətɪv] secret; **secretly** en secret
sect [sekt] secte *f*
section ['sekʃn] section *f*
sector ['sektər] secteur *m*
secular ['sekjʊlər] séculier
secure [sɪ'kjʊr] **1** *adj shelf etc* bien fixé; *job, contract* sûr **2** *v/t shelf etc* fixer; *s.o.'s help, finances* se procurer; **securities market** FIN marché *m* des valeurs; **security** sécurité *f*; *for investment* garantie *f*; **security alert** alerte *f* de sécurité; **security forces** forces *fpl* de sécurité; **security guard** garde *m* de sécurité; **security risk** *menace potentielle à la sécurité de l'État ou d'une organisation*
sedan [sɪ'dæn] MOT berline *f*
sedate [sɪ'deɪt] donner un calmant à; **sedative** calmant *m*
sedentary ['sedənterɪ] *job* sédentaire
sediment ['sedɪmənt] sédiment *m*

seduce [sɪ'duːs] séduire; **seduction** séduction *f*; **seductive** *dress, offer* séduisant

see [siː] *with eyes, (understand)* voir; ~ ***you!*** F à plus! F

◆ **see off** *at airport etc* raccompagner; (*chase away*) chasser

seed [siːd] *single* graine *f*; *collective* graines *fpl*; *of fruit* pépin *m*; *in tennis* tête *f* de série; **seedy** miteux

seeing 'eye dog chien *m* d'aveugle; **seeing (that)** étant donné que

seek [siːk] chercher

seem [siːm] sembler; **seemingly** apparemment

seesaw ['siːsɒː] bascule *f*

'see-through transparent

segment ['segmənt] segment *m*; *of orange* morceau *m*

segregate ['segrɪgeɪt] séparer; **segregation** ségrégation *f*; *of sexes* séparation *f*

seismology [saɪz'mɑːlədʒɪ] sismologie *f*

seize [siːz] *opportunity, arm, of police etc* saisir; *power* s'emparer de; **seizure** MED crise *f*; *of drugs etc* saisie *f*

seldom ['seldəm] rarement

select [sɪ'lekt] **1** *v/t* sélectionner **2** *adj group of people* choisi; *hotel etc* chic *inv*; **selection** sélection *f*; **selective** sélectif

self [self] moi *m*; **self-assurance** confiance *f* en soi; **self-assured** sûr de soi; **self-centered**, *Br* **self-centred** égocentrique; **self-confidence** confiance en soi; **self-confident** sûr de soi; **self-conscious** intimidé; *about sth* gêné (**about** par); **self-consciousness** timidité *f*; *about sth* gêne *f* (**about** par rapport à); **self-control** contrôle *m* de soi; **self-defense**, *Br* **self-defence** autodéfense *f*; LAW légitime défense *f*; **self-employed** indépendant; **self-evident** évident; **self-expression** expression *f*; **self-government** autonomie *f*; **self-interest** intérêt *m* (personnel); **selfish** égoïste; **selfless** désintéressé; **self-made man** self-made man *m*; **self-pity** apitoiement *m* sur soi-même; **self-portrait** autoportrait *m*; **self-reliant** autonome; **self-respect** respect *m* de soi; **self-satisfied** *pej* suffisant; **self-service** libre-service; **self-service restaurant** self *m*; **self-taught** autodidacte

sell [sel] **1** *v/t* vendre **2** *v/i of products* se vendre; **sell-by date** date *f* limite de vente; **seller** vendeur(-euse) *m*(*f*); **selling** COM vente *f*; **selling point** COM point *m* fort

Sellotape® ['seləteɪp] *Br* scotch *m*

semester [sɪ'mestər] semestre *m*

semi ['semɪ] *truck* semi-remorque *f*; **semicircle** demi-cercle *m*; **semiconductor** ELEC semi-conducteur *m*; **semifinal** demi-finale *f*; **semifinalist** demi-finaliste *m/f*

seminar ['semɪnɑːr] séminaire *m*

semi'skilled *worker* spécialisé

senate ['senət] Sénat *m*; **senator** sénateur(-trice) *m(f)*

send [send] envoyer (***to*** a)

◆ **send back** renvoyer

◆ **send for** *doctor* faire venir; *help* envoyer chercher

sender ['sendər] *of letter* expéditeur(-trice) *m(f)*

senile ['siːnaɪl] sénile; **senility** sénilité *f*

senior ['siːnjər] (*older*) plus âgé; *in rank* supérieur; **senior citizen** personne *f* âgée; **seniority** *in job* ancienneté *f*

sensation [sen'seɪʃn] sensation *f*; **sensational** sensationnel

sense [sens] **1** *n* sens *m*; (*common* ~) bon sens *m*; (*feeling*) sentiment *m*; ***come to one's ~s*** revenir à la raison; ***it doesn't make ~*** cela n'a pas de sens **2** *v/t* sentir; **senseless** (*pointless*) stupide

sensible ['sensəbl] sensé; *clothes, shoes* pratique; **sensibly** raisonnablement

sensitive ['sensətɪv] sensible; **sensitivity** sensibilité *f*

sensor ['sensər] détecteur *m*

sensual ['senʃʊəl] sensuel; **sensuality** sensualité *f*

sensuous ['senʃʊəs] voluptueux

sentence ['sentəns] **1** *n* GRAM phrase *f*; LAW peine *f* **2** *v/t* LAW condamner

sentiment ['sentɪmənt] (*sentimentality*) sentimentalité *f*; (*opinion*) sentiment *m*; **sentimental** sentimental; **sentimentality** sentimentalité *f*

sentry ['sentrɪ] sentinelle *f*

separate **1** ['sepərət] *adj* séparé **2** ['sepəreɪt] *v/t* séparer (***from*** de) **3** *v/i of couple* se séparer; **separated** *couple* séparé; **separately** séparément; **separation** séparation *f*

September [sep'tembər] septembre *m*

septic ['septɪk] septique

sequel ['siːkwəl] suite *f*

sequence ['siːkwəns] ordre *m*

serene [sɪ'riːn] serein

sergeant ['sɑːrdʒənt] sergent *m*

serial ['sɪrɪəl] feuilleton *m*; **serialize** *novel on TV* adapter en feuilleton; **serial number** *of product* numéro *m* de série

series ['sɪriːz] série *f*

serious ['sɪrɪəs] *person, company* sérieux; *illness, situation, damage* grave; **seriously** *injured* gravement; *under-*

staffed sérieusement; ***take s.o. ~*** prendre qn au sérieux; **seriousness** *of person, situation, illness etc* gravité *f*

sermon ['sɜːrmən] sermon *m*

servant ['sɜːrvənt] domestique *m/f*

serve [sɜːrv] **1** *n in tennis* service *m* **2** *v/t & v/i* servir; **server** *in tennis* serveur(-euse) *m(f)*; COMPUT serveur *m*; **service 1** *n also in tennis* service *m*; *for vehicle, machine* entretien *m*; ***~s*** services *mpl* **2** *v/t vehicle, machine* entretenir; **service charge** service *m*; **serviceman** MIL militaire *m*; **service station** station-service *f*; **serving** *of food* portion *f*

session ['seʃn] session *f*; *meeting, talk* discussion *f*

set [set] **1** *n* (*collection*) série *f*; (*group of people*) groupe *m*; MATH ensemble *m*; THEA (*scenery*) décor *m*; *for movie* plateau *m*; *in tennis* set *m* **2** *v/t* (*place*) poser; *movie, novel etc* situer; *date, time, limit* fixer; *alarm* mettre; *broken limb* remettre en place; *jewel* sertir; ***~ the table*** mettre la table **3** *v/i of sun* se coucher; *of glue* durcir **4** *adj ideas* arrêté; (*ready*) prêt

◆ **set off 1** *v/i on journey* partir **2** *v/t alarm etc* déclencher

◆ **set out 1** *v/i on journey* partir **2** *v/t ideas, goods* exposer

◆ **set up 1** *v/t company, equipment, machine* monter; *market stall* installer; *meeting* arranger; F (*frame*) faire un coup à **2** *v/i in business* s'établir

'setback revers *m*

settee [se'tiː] *Br* (*couch, sofa*) canapé *m*

setting ['setɪŋ] *of novel, play, house* cadre *m*

settle ['setl] **1** *v/i of bird* se poser; *of dust* se déposer; *of building* se tasser; *to live* s'installer **2** *v/t dispute, issue, debts* régler; *nerves, stomach* calmer; ***that ~s it!*** ça règle la question!

◆ **settle down** (*stop being noisy*) se calmer; (*stop wild living*) se ranger; *in an area* s'installer

◆ **settle for** (*accept*) accepter

settled ['setld] *weather* stable; **settlement** *of claim, debt, dispute*, (*payment*) règlement *m*; *of building* tassement *m*; **settler** *in new country* colon *m*

'set-up (*structure*) organisation *f*; (*relationship*) relation *f*; F (*frame-up*) coup *m* monté

seven ['sevn] sept; **seventeen** dix-sept; **seventeenth** dix-septième; **seventh** septième; **seventieth** soixante-dixième; **seventy** soixante-dix

sever ['sevər] sectionner; *relations* rompre

several ['sevrl] plusieurs
severe [sɪ'vɪr] *illness* grave; *penalty* lourd; *winter, weather* rigoureux; *teacher* sévère; **severely** *punish, speak* sévèrement; *injured* grièvement; *disrupted* fortement; **severity** *of illness* gravité *f*; *of penalty* lourdeur *f*; *of winter* rigueur *f*; *of teacher* sévérité *f*
sew [soʊ] coudre
sewage ['suːɪdʒ] eaux *fpl* d'égouts; **sewer** égout *m*
sewing ['soʊɪŋ] *skill* couture *f*; (*that being sewn*) ouvrage *m*
sex [seks] sexe *m*; ***have ~ with*** coucher avec; **sexist 1** *adj* sexiste **2** *n* sexiste *m/f*; **sexual** sexuel; **sexuality** sexualité *f*; **sexually** sexuellement; **sexy** sexy *inv*
shabbily ['ʃæbɪlɪ] *dressed* pauvrement; *treat* mesquinement; **shabby** *coat etc* usé; *treatment* mesquin
shack [ʃæk] cabane *f*
shade [ʃeɪd] **1** *n for lamp* abat-jour *m*; *of color* nuance *f*; *on window* store *m*; ***in the ~*** à l'ombre **2** *v/t from sun* protéger du soleil; *from light* protéger de la lumière
shadow ['ʃædoʊ] ombre *f*
shady ['ʃeɪdɪ] *spot* ombragé; *character* louche
shaft [ʃæft] *of axle* arbre *m*; *of mine* puits *m*
shake [ʃeɪk] **1** *n*: ***give sth a good ~*** bien agiter qch **2** *v/t bottle* agiter; *emotionally* bouleverser; ***~ one's head*** *in refusal* dire non de la tête; ***~ hands with s.o.*** serrer la main à qn **3** *v/i of hands, voice, building* trembler; **shaken** *emotionally* bouleversé; **shake-up** remaniement *m*; **shaky** *table etc* branlant; *after illness, shock* faible; *voice, hand* tremblant; *grasp of sth, grammar etc* incertain
shall [ʃæl] ◇ *future*: ***I ~ do my best*** je ferai de mon mieux ◇ *suggesting*: ***~ we go now?*** si nous y allions maintenant?
shallow ['ʃæloʊ] *water* peu profond; *person* superficiel
shame [ʃeɪm] **1** *n* honte *f*; ***what a ~!*** quel dommage! **2** *v/t* faire honte à; **shameful** honteux; **shameless** effronté
shampoo [ʃæm'puː] shampo(o)ing *m*
shape [ʃeɪp] **1** *n* forme *f* **2** *v/t clay, character* façonner; *the future* influencer; **shapeless** *dress etc* informe; **shapely** *figure* bien fait
share [ʃer] **1** *n* part *f*; FIN action *f* **2** *v/t & v/i* partager; **shareholder** actionnaire *m/f*
shark [ʃɑːrk] requin *m*
sharp [ʃɑːrp] **1** *adj knife* tranchant; *mind, pain* vif; *taste* piquant **2** *adv* MUS trop haut; ***at 3 o'clock ~*** à 3 heures pile;
sharpen *knife, skills* aiguiser

shatter ['ʃætər] **1** *v/t glass, illusions* briser **2** *v/i of glass* se briser; **shattered** ['ʃætərd] F (*exhausted*) crevé F; F (*very upset*) bouleversé; **shattering** *news* bouleversant

shave [ʃeɪv] **1** *v/t* raser **2** *v/i* se raser **3** *n*: ***have a ~*** se raser; **shaven** *head* rasé; **shaver** rasoir *m* électrique

shawl [ʃɒːl] châle *m*

she [ʃiː] elle; ***there ~ is*** la voilà

sheath [ʃiːθ] *for knife* étui *m*; *contraceptive* préservatif *m*

shed[1] [ʃed] *v/t blood, tears* verser; *leaves* perdre

shed[2] [ʃed] *n* abri *m*

sheep [ʃiːp] mouton *m*; **sheepdog** chien *m* de berger; **sheepish** penaud

sheer [ʃɪr] pur; *cliffs* abrupt

sheet [ʃiːt] drap *m*; *of paper, metal, glass* feuille *f*

shelf [ʃelf] étagère *f*; ***shelves*** *set of shelves* étagère(s) *f*(pl)

shell [ʃel] **1** *n of mussel, egg* coquille *f*; *of tortoise* carapace *f*; MIL obus *m* **2** *v/t peas* écosser; MIL bombarder; **shellfire** bombardements *mpl*; **shellfish** fruits *mpl* de mer

shelter ['ʃeltər] **1** *n* abri *m* **2** *v/i* s'abriter (***from*** de) **3** *v/t* (*protect*) protéger; **sheltered** *place* protégé; ***lead a ~ life*** mener une vie protégée

shelve [ʃelv] *fig* mettre en suspens

shepherd ['ʃepərd] berger (-ère) *m*(*f*)

sheriff ['ʃerɪf] shérif *m*

shield [ʃiːld] **1** *n* MIL bouclier *m*; *sports trophy* plaque *f*; *badge*: *of policeman* plaque *f* **2** *v/t* (*protect*) protéger

shift [ʃɪft] **1** *n* (*change*) changement *m*; (*move, switchover*) passage *m* (***to*** à); *at work* poste *m*; *people* équipe *f* **2** *v/t* (*move*) déplacer; *production, employee* transférer; *stains etc* faire partir **3** *v/i* (*move*) se déplacer; *in attitude* virer; **shifty** *pej*: *person* louche; *eyes* fuyant

shin [ʃɪn] tibia *m*

shine [ʃaɪn] **1** *v/i* briller; *fig*: *of student etc* être brillant (***at, in*** en) **2** *n on shoes etc* brillant *m*; **shiny** brillant

ship [ʃɪp] **1** *n* bateau *m*, navire *m* **2** *v/t* (*send*) expédier **3** *v/i of new product* être lancé (sur le marché); **shipment** envoi *m*; **shipowner** armateur *m*; **shipping** (*sea traffic*) navigation *f*; (*sending*) expédition *f*; **shipwreck** naufrage *m*; **shipyard** chantier *m* naval

shirt [ʃɜːrt] chemise *f*

shit [ʃɪt] **1** *n* P merde *f* P **2** *v/i* P chier P **3** *int* P merde P; **shitty** F dégueulasse F

shiver ['ʃɪvər] trembler

shock [ʃɑːk] **1** *n* choc *m*; ELEC décharge *f*; ***be in ~*** MED être en état de choc **2** *v/t* choquer;

shock absorber MOT amortisseur *m*; **shocking** choquant; F (*very bad*) épouvantable
shoddy ['ʃɑːdɪ] *goods* de mauvaise qualité; *behavior* mesquin
shoe [ʃuː] chaussure *f*, soulier *m*; **shoelace** lacet *m*; **shoemaker** cordonnier(-ière) *m(f)*; **shoe mender** cordonnier(-ière) *m(f)*; **shoestore** magasin *m* de chaussures
shoot [ʃuːt] **1** *n* BOT pousse *f* **2** *v/t* tirer sur; *and kill* tuer d'un coup de feu; *movie* tourner **3** *v/i* tirer
◆ **shoot down** *airplane* abattre; *fig: suggestion* descendre
◆ **shoot up** *of prices* monter en flèche; *of children, new buildings etc* pousser
shooting star ['ʃuːtɪŋ] étoile *f* filante
shop [ʃɑːp] **1** *n* magasin *m* **2** *v/i* faire ses courses; ***go ~ping*** faire les courses; **shopkeeper** commerçant *m*,-ante *f*; **shoplifter** voleur(-euse) *m(f)* à l'étalage; **shoplifting** vol *m* à l'étalage
shopping *items* courses *fpl*; ***go ~*** faire des courses; **shopping bag** sac *m* à provisions; **shopping list** liste *f* de commissions; **shopping mall** centre *m* commercial
shore [ʃɔːr] rivage *m*; ***on ~*** *not at sea* à terre
short [ʃɔːrt] **1** *adj* court; *in height* petit; ***be ~ of*** manquer de **2** *adv*: ***cut ~*** abréger; ***go ~ of*** se priver de; ***in ~*** bref; **shortage** manque *m*; **shortcoming** défaut *m*; **shortcut** raccourci *m*; **shorten** raccourcir; **shortfall** déficit *m*; **short-lived** de courte durée; **shortly** (*soon*) bientôt; ***~ before/after that*** peu avant/après; **shortness** *of visit* brièveté *f*; *in height* petite taille *f*; **shorts** short *m*; *underwear* caleçon *m*; **shortsighted** myope; *fig* peu perspicace; **short-sleeved** à manches courtes; **short-tempered** *by nature* d'un caractère emporté; *at a particular time* de mauvaise humeur; **short-term** à court terme
shot [ʃɑːt] *from gun* coup *m* de feu; (*photograph*) photo *f*; (*injection*) piqûre *f*; **shotgun** fusil *m* de chasse
should [ʃʊd]: ***what ~ I do?*** que dois-je faire?; ***you ~n't do that*** tu ne devrais pas faire ça; ***you ~ have heard him*** tu aurais dû l'entendre
shoulder ['ʃoʊldər] épaule *f*
shout [ʃaʊt] **1** *n* cri *m* **2** *v/t & v/i* crier; **shouting** cris *mpl*
shove [ʃʌv] **1** *n*: ***give s.o. a ~*** pousser qn **2** *v/t & v/i* pousser
shovel ['ʃʌvl] pelle *f*
show [ʃoʊ] **1** *n* THEA, TV spectacle *m*; (*display*) démonstration *f* **2** *v/t* montrer; *at exhibition* présenter; *movie* pro-

jeter **3** *v/i* (*be visible*) se voir; *of movie* passer

◆ **show in** faire entrer

◆ **show off 1** *v/t skills* faire étalage de **2** *v/i pej* crâner

◆ **show up 1** *v/t shortcomings etc* faire ressortir **2** *v/i* F (*arrive, turn up*) se pointer F; (*be visible*) se voir

'show business monde *m* du spectacle; **showcase** *also fig* vitrine *f*; **showdown** confrontation *f*

shower ['ʃauər] **1** *n of rain* averse *f*; *to wash* douche *f*; *party: petite fête avant un mariage ou un accouchement à laquelle tout le monde apporte un cadeau*; ***take a ~*** prendre une douche **2** *v/i* prendre une douche

'show-off *pej* prétentieux (-euse) *m*(*f*); **showroom** salle *f* d'exposition; **showy** voyant

shred [ʃred] **1** *n of paper etc* lambeau *m*; *of meat etc* morceau *m* **2** *v/t documents* déchiqueter; *in cooking* râper; **shredder** *for documents* déchiqueteuse *f*

shrewd [ʃruːd] perspicace; **shrewdness** perspicacité *f*

shriek [ʃriːk] **1** *n* cri *m* aigu **2** *v/i* pousser un cri aigu

shrill [ʃrɪl] perçant

shrimp [ʃrɪmp] crevette *f*

shrine [ʃraɪn] lieu *m* saint

shrink[1] [ʃrɪŋk] *v/i of material* rétrécir; *of support* diminuer

shrink[2] [ʃrɪŋk] *n* F (*psychiatrist*) psy *m* F

shrivel ['ʃrɪvl] se flétrir

shrub [ʃrʌb] arbuste *m*; **shrubbery** massif *m* d'arbustes

shrug [ʃrʌg]: ***~ (one's shoulders)*** hausser les épaules

shudder ['ʃʌdər] **1** *n of fear, disgust* frisson *m*; *of earth* vibration *f* **2** *v/i with fear, disgust* frissonner; *of earth* vibrer

shuffle ['ʃʌfl] *v/t cards* battre

shun [ʃʌn] fuir

shut [ʃʌt] **1** *v/t* fermer **2** *v/i of door, box* se fermer; *of store* fermer

◆ **shut down 1** *v/t business* fermer; *computer* éteindre **2** *v/i of business* fermer ses portes; *of computer* s'éteindre

◆ **shut up** F (*be quiet*) se taire; ***shut up!*** tais-toi!

shutter ['ʃʌtər] *on window* volet *m*; PHOT obturateur *m*

shuttle bus ['ʃʌtl] *at airport* navette *f*

shy [ʃaɪ] timide; **shyness** timidité *f*

sick [sɪk] malade; *sense of humor* noir; ***be ~*** *Br* (*vomit*) vomir; **sicken 1** *v/t* (*disgust*) écœurer; (*make ill*) rendre malade **2** *v/i*: ***be ~ing for*** couver; **sickening** écœurant; **sick leave** congé *m* de maladie; **sickness** maladie *f*; (*vomiting*) vomissements *mpl*

side [saɪd] côté *m*; SP équipe *f*; ***take ~s*** (*favor one ~*) prendre parti; ***~ by ~*** côte à côte; **side effect** effet *m* secondaire; **sidestep** éviter; *fig also* contourner; **side street** rue *f* transversale; **sidewalk** trottoir *m*; **sideways** de côté

siege [siːdʒ] siège *m*

sieve [sɪv] *for flour* tamis *m*

sift [sɪft] tamiser; *data* passer en revue

sigh [saɪ] **1** *n* soupir *m* **2** *v/i* soupirer

sight [saɪt] spectacle *m*; (*power of seeing*) vue *f*; ***~s*** *of city* monuments *mpl*; ***know by ~*** connaître de vue; **sightseeing**: ***go ~*** faire du tourisme; **sightseer** touriste *m/f*

sign [saɪn] **1** *n* signe *m*; (*road~*) panneau *m*; *outside shop* enseigne *f* **2** *v/t & v/i* signer

signal ['sɪgnl] **1** *n* signal *m* **2** *v/i of driver* mettre son clignotant

signatory ['sɪgnətɔːrɪ] signataire *m/f*

signature ['sɪgnətʃər] signature *f*

significance [sɪg'nɪfɪkəns] importance *f*; **significant** *event, sum of money, improvement etc* important; **significantly** *larger, more expensive* nettement

signify ['sɪgnɪfaɪ] signifier

'sign language langage *m* des signes; **signpost** poteau *m* indicateur

silence ['saɪləns] **1** *n* silence *m* **2** *v/t* faire taire; **silent** silencieux

silhouette [sɪluː'et] silhouette *f*

silicon ['sɪlɪkən] silicium *m*

silk [sɪlk] **1** *adj shirt etc* en soie **2** *n* soie *f*; **silky** soyeux

silliness ['sɪlɪnɪs] stupidité *f*; **silly** bête

silo ['saɪloʊ] silo *m*

silver ['sɪlvər] **1** *adj ring* en argent; *hair* argenté **2** *n* argent *m*; **silverware** argenterie *f*

similar ['sɪmɪlər] semblable (***to*** à); **similarity** ressemblance *f*; **similarly** de la même façon

simple ['sɪmpl] simple; **simple-minded** *pej* simple, simplet; **simplicity** simplicité *f*; **simplify** simplifier; **simplistic** simpliste; **simply** (*absolutely*) absolument; (*in a simple way*) simplement

simultaneous [saɪməl'teɪnɪəs] simultané; **simultaneously** simultanément

sin [sɪn] **1** *n* péché *m* **2** *v/i* pécher

since [sɪns] **1** *prep & adv* depuis; ***I've been here ~ last week*** je suis là depuis la semaine dernière **2** *conj in expressions of time* depuis que; (*seeing that*) puisque

sincere [sɪn'sɪr] sincère; **sincerely** sincèrement; ***Sincerely yours*** Je vous prie d'agréer, Madame/Monsieur, l'expression de mes sentiments les meilleurs; **sincerity** sincérité *f*
sinful ['sɪnfʊl] *deeds* honteux; ~ ***person*** pécheur *m*, pécheresse *f*
sing [sɪŋ] chanter
singe [sɪndʒ] brûler légèrement
singer ['sɪŋər] chanteur(-euse) *m(f)*
single ['sɪŋgl] **1** *adj* (*sole*) seul; (*not double*) simple; *bed* à une place; (*not married*) célibataire **2** *n* MUS single *m*; (~ *room*) chambre *f* à un lit; *person* personne *f* seule; **~s** *in tennis* simple *m*; **single-handed** tout seul; **single-minded** résolu; **single parent** mère/père qui élève ses enfants tout seul; **single parent family** famille *f* monoparentale; **single room** chambre *f* à un lit
singular ['sɪŋgjʊlər] GRAM **1** *adj* au singulier **2** *n* singulier *m*
sinister ['sɪnɪstər] sinistre
sink [sɪŋk] **1** *n* évier *m* **2** *v/i of ship, object* couler; *of sun* descendre; *of interest rates etc* baisser **3** *v/t ship* couler; *money* investir
sinner ['sɪnər] pécheur *m*, pécheresse *f*
sip [sɪp] **1** *n* petite gorgée *f* **2** *v/t* boire à petites gorgées
sir [sɜːr] monsieur *m*
siren ['saɪrən] sirène *f*
sirloin ['sɜːrlɔɪn] aloyau *m*
sister ['sɪstər] sœur *f*; **sister-in-law** belle-sœur *f*
sit [sɪt] (~ *down*) s'asseoir; ***she was sitting*** elle était assise
◆ **sit down** s'asseoir
sitcom ['sɪtkɑːm] sitcom *m*
site [saɪt] **1** *n* emplacement *m*; *of battle* site *m* **2** *v/t new offices etc* situer
sitting ['sɪtɪŋ] *of committee, court, for artist* séance *f*; *for meals* service *m*; **sitting room** salon *m*
situated ['sɪtʊeɪtɪd] situé; **situation** situation *f*; *of building etc* emplacement *m*
six [sɪks] six; **sixteen** seize; **sixteenth** seizième; **sixth** sixième; **sixtieth** soixantième; **sixty** soixante
size [saɪz] *of room, jacket* taille *f*; *of project* envergure *f*; *of loan* montant *m*; *of shoes* pointure *f*; **sizeable** *meal, house* assez grand; *order, amount* assez important
skate [skeɪt] **1** *n* patin *m* **2** *v/i* patiner; **skateboard** skateboard *m*; **skateboarding** skateboard *m*; **skater** patineur(-euse) *m(f)*; **skating** patinage *f*; **skating rink** patinoire *f*
skeleton ['skelɪtn] squelette

m

skeptic ['skeptɪk] sceptique *m/f*; **skeptical** sceptique; **skepticism** scepticisme *m*

sketch [sketʃ] **1** *n* croquis *m*; THEA sketch *m* **2** *v/t* esquisser; **sketchy** *knowledge etc* sommaire

ski [skiː] **1** *n* ski *m* **2** *v/i* faire du ski

skid [skɪd] **1** *n* dérapage *m* **2** *v/i* déraper

skier ['skiːər] skieur(-euse) *m(f)*; **skiing** ski *m*

skilful *etc Br* → ***skillful***

skill [skɪl] technique *f*; **~s** compétences *fpl*; **skilled** habile; **skillful** habile; **skillfully** habilement

skim [skɪm] *surface* effleurer

skimpy ['skɪmpɪ] *account etc* sommaire; *dress* étriqué

skin [skɪn] **1** *n* peau *f* **2** *v/t animal* écorcher; *tomato* peler; **skin diving** plongée *f* sous-marine autonome; **skinny** maigre; **skin-tight** moulant

skip [skɪp] **1** *n* (*little jump*) saut *m* **2** *v/i* sautiller **3** *v/t* (*omit*) sauter; **skipper** capitaine *m/f*

skirt [skɜːrt] jupe *f*

skull [skʌl] crâne *m*

skunk [skʌŋk] mouffette *f*

sky [skaɪ] ciel *m*; **skylight** lucarne *f*; **skyline** silhouette *f*; **skyscraper** gratte-ciel *m inv*

slab [slæb] *of stone, butter* plaque *f*; *of cake* grosse tranche *f*

slack [slæk] *rope* mal tendu; *work* négligé; *period* creux; **slacken** *rope* détendre; *pace* ralentir; **slacks** pantalon *m*

slam [slæm] claquer

slander ['slændər] **1** *n* calomnie *f* **2** *v/t* calomnier; **slanderous** calomnieux

slang [slæŋ] *also of a specific group* argot *m*

slant [slænt] **1** *v/i* pencher **2** *n* inclinaison *f*; *given to a story* perspective *f*; **slanting** *roof* en pente; *eyes* bridé

slap [slæp] **1** *n* (*blow*) claque *f* **2** *v/t* donner une claque à

slash [slæʃ] **1** *n cut* entaille *f*; *in punctuation* barre *f* oblique **2** *v/t painting, skin* entailler; *prices* réduire radicalement

slaughter ['slɒːtər] **1** *n of animals* abattage *m*; *of people, troops* massacre *m* **2** *v/t animals* abattre; *people, troops* massacrer; **slaughterhouse** abattoir *m*

slave [sleɪv] esclave *m/f*

slay [sleɪ] tuer; **slaying** (*murder*) meurtre *m*

sleaze [sliːz] POL corruption *f*; **sleazy** *bar, character* louche

sleep [sliːp] **1** *n* sommeil *m*; ***go to ~*** s'endormir **2** *v/i* dormir

◆ **sleep with** (*have sex with*) coucher avec

'**sleeping bag** sac *m* de couchage; **sleeping car** RAIL wagon-lit *m*; **sleeping pill** som-

nifère *m*; **sleepwalker** somnambule *m/f*; **sleepwalking** somnambulisme *m*; **sleepy** *person* qui a envie de dormir; *yawn*, *town* endormi; ***I'm* ~** j'ai sommeil
sleet [sli:t] neige *f* fondue
sleeve [sli:v] *of jacket etc* manche *f*; **sleeveless** sans manches
slender ['slendər] mince; *chance*, *margin* faible
slice [slaɪs] **1** *n of bread*, *pie* tranche *f*; *fig*: *of profits* part *f* **2** *v/t loaf etc* couper en tranches
slick [slɪk] **1** *adj performance* habile; *pej* (*cunning*) rusé **2** *n of oil* marée *f* noire
slide [slaɪd] **1** *n for kids* toboggan *m*; PHOT diapositive *f* **2** *v/i* glisser; *of exchange rate etc* baisser **3** *v/t item of furniture* faire glisser
slight [slaɪt] *person*, *figure* frêle; (*small*) léger; ***no, not in the* ~*est*** non, pas le moins du monde; **slightly** légèrement
slim [slɪm] *person* mince; *chance* faible
slime [slaɪm] (*mud*) vase *f*; *of slug etc* bave *f*; **slimy** *liquid etc* vaseux
sling [slɪŋ] **1** *n for arm* écharpe *f* **2** *v/t* F (*throw*) lancer
slip [slɪp] **1** *n* (*mistake*) erreur *f* **2** *v/i* glisser; *in quality*, *quantity* baisser
◆ **slip up** (*make a mistake*) faire une gaffe
slipped 'disc [slɪpt] hernie *f* discale
slipper ['slɪpər] chausson *m*
slippery ['slɪpərɪ] glissant
'slip-up (*mistake*) gaffe *f*
slit [slɪt] **1** *n* (*tear*) déchirure *f*; (*hole*), *in skirt* fente *f* **2** *v/t* ouvrir, fendre
sliver ['slɪvər] petit morceau *m*; *of wood*, *glass* éclat *m*
slob [slɑ:b] *pej* rustaud(e) *m*(*f*)
slog [slɑ:g] *long walk* trajet *m* pénible; *hard work* corvée *f*
slogan ['slougən] slogan *m*
slop [slɑ:p] (*spill*) renverser
slope [sloup] **1** *n* inclinaison *f*; *of mountain* côté *m* **2** *v/i* être incliné
sloppy ['slɑ:pɪ] F *work*, *in dress* négligé; (*too sentimental*) gnangnan F
slot [slɑ:t] fente *f*; *in schedule* créneau *m*; **slot machine** *for vending* distributeur *m* (automatique); *for gambling* machine *f* à sous
slovenly ['slʌvnlɪ] négligé
slow [slou] lent; ***be* ~** *of clock* retarder
◆ **slow down 1** *v/t* ralentir **2** *v/i* ralentir; *in life* faire moins de choses
'slowdown *in production* ralentissement *m*; **slowly** lentement; **slowness** lenteur *f*
sluggish ['slʌgɪʃ] lent; *river* à cours lent
slum [slʌm] *area* quartier *m*

pauvre; *house* taudis *m*
slump [slʌmp] **1** *n in trade* effondrement *m* **2** *v/i of economy* s'effondrer; *of person* s'affaisser
slur [slɜːr] **1** *n on character* tache *f* **2** *v/t words* mal articuler
slush [slʌʃ] neige *f* fondue; *pej (sentimental stuff)* sensiblerie *f*; **slush fund** caisse *f* noire
slut [slʌt] *pej* pute *f* F
sly [slaɪ] (*furtive*) sournois; (*crafty*) rusé
small [smɒːl] petit
smart[1] [smɑːrt] *adj* élégant; (*intelligent*) intelligent; *pace* vif
smart[2] [smɑːrt] *v/i* (*hurt*) brûler
'smart card carte *f* à puce; **smartly** *dressed* avec élégance
smash [smæʃ] **1** *n noise* fracas *m*; (*car crash*) accident *m*; *in tennis* smash *m* **2** *v/t break* fracasser; (*hit hard*) frapper **3** *v/i break* se fracasser
smattering ['smætərɪŋ]: ***have a ~ of Chinese*** savoir un peu de chinois
smear [smɪr] **1** *n of ink etc* tache *f*; *Br* MED frottis *m*; *on character* diffamation *f* **2** *v/t character* entacher
smell [smel] **1** *n* odeur *f*; ***sense of ~*** sens *m* de l'odorat **2** *v/t* sentir **3** *v/i unpleasantly* sentir mauvais; (*sniff*) renifler; **smelly** qui sent mauvais
smile [smaɪl] **1** *n* sourire *m* **2** *v/i* sourire
smirk [smɜːrk] petit sourire *m* narquois
smoke [smoʊk] **1** *n* fumée *f* **2** *v/t also food* fumer **3** *v/i of person* fumer; **smoker** fumeur(-euse) *m(f)*; **smoke-free** non-fumeur *inv*; **smoking**: ***no ~*** défense de fumer; **smoky** enfumé
smolder ['smoʊldər] *of fire* couver
smooth [smuːð] **1** *adj surface, skin, sea* lisse; *ride, flight, crossing* bon; *pej: person* mielleux **2** *v/t hair* lisser; **smoothly** *without any problems* sans problème
smother ['smʌðər] *person, flames* étouffer
smoulder *Br* → ***smolder***
smudge [smʌdʒ] **1** *n* tache *f* **2** *v/t paint* faire des traces sur; *ink, mascara* étaler
smug [smʌg] suffisant
smuggle ['smʌgl] passer en contrebande; **smuggler** contrebandier(-ière) *m(f)*; **smuggling** contrebande *f*
smutty ['smʌtɪ] *joke* grossier
snack [snæk] en-cas *m*
snag [snæg] (*problem*) hic *m* F
snake [sneɪk] serpent *m*
snap [snæp] **1** *n sound* bruit *m* sec; PHOT instantané *m* **2** *v/t break* casser **3** *v/i break* se casser net **4** *adj decision, judgement* rapide, subit;

snappy *person*, *mood* cassant; *decision* prompt; ***be a ~ dresser*** s'habiller chic; **snapshot** photo *f*
snarl [snɑːrl] **1** *n of dog* grondement **2** *v/i of dog* gronder en montrant les dents
snatch [snætʃ] (*grab*) saisir; F (*steal*) voler; F (*kidnap*) enlever
snazzy ['snæzɪ] F *necktie etc* qui tape F
sneakers ['sniːkərz] tennis *mpl*
sneaky ['sniːkɪ] F (*underhanded*) sournois
sneer [sniːr] **1** *n* ricanement *m* **2** *v/i* ricaner
sneeze [sniːz] **1** *n* éternuement *m* **2** *v/i* éternuer
snicker ['snɪkər] pouffer de rire
sniff [snɪf] renifler
sniper ['snaɪpər] tireur *m* embusqué
snitch [snɪtʃ] **1** *n* (*telltale*) mouchard(e) *m*(*f*) F **2** *v/i* (*tell tales*) vendre la mèche
snivel ['snɪvl] pleurnicher
snob [snɑːb] snob *m/f*; **snobbery** snobisme *m*; **snobbish** snob *inv*
◆ **snoop around** [snuːp] fourrer le nez partout
snooty ['snuːtɪ] arrogant
snooze [snuːz] **1** *n* petit somme *m* **2** *v/i* roupiller F
snore [snɔːr] ronfler; **snoring** ronflement *m*
snorkel ['snɔːrkl] tuba *m*
snort [snɔːrt] *of bull*, *horse* s'ébrouer; *of person* grogner
snow [snoʊ] **1** *n* neige *f* **2** *v/i* neiger; **snowball** boule *f* de neige; **snowdrift** amoncellement *m* de neige; **snowman** bonhomme *m* de neige; **snowplow** chasse-neige *m inv*; **snowstorm** tempête *f* de neige; **snowy** *weather* neigeux; *roads*, *hills* enneigé
snub [snʌb] **1** *n* rebuffade *f* **2** *v/t* snober; **snub-nosed** au nez retroussé
snug [snʌg] bien au chaud; (*tight-fitting*) bien ajusté
so [soʊ] **1** *adv* si, tellement; ***~ kind*** tellement gentil; ***not ~ much for me*** pas autant pour moi; ***~ much easier*** tellement plus facile; ***drink ~ much*** tellement boire; ***~ many people*** tellement de gens; ***I miss you ~*** tu me manques tellement; ***~ am/do I*** moi aussi; ***~ is/does she*** elle aussi; ***and ~ on*** et ainsi de suite **2** *pron*: ***I hope ~*** je l'espère bien; ***I think ~*** je pense que oui; ***50 or ~*** une cinquantaine, à peu près cinquante **3** *conj* (*for that reason*) donc; (*in order that*) pour que (+*subj*); ***~ (that) I could come too*** pour que je puisse moi aussi venir; ***~ what?*** F et alors?
soak [soʊk] (*steep*) faire tremper; *of water* tremper; **soaked** trempé

soap [soʊp] *for washing* savon *m*; **soap (opera)** feuilleton *m*; **soapy** savonneux
soar [sɔːr] *of rocket, prices etc* monter en flèche
sob [sɑːb] **1** *n* sanglot *m* **2** *v/i* sangloter
sober ['soʊbər] en état de sobriété; (*serious*) sérieux
so-'called (*referred to as*) comme on le/la/les appelle; (*incorrectly referred to as*) soi-disant *inv*
soccer ['sɑːkər] football *m*
sociable ['soʊʃəbl] sociable
social ['soʊʃl] social; (*recreational*) mondain; **social democrat** social-démocrate *m/f*; **socialism** socialisme *m*; **socialist 1** *adj* socialiste **2** *n* socialiste *m/f*; **socialize** fréquenter des gens; **social worker** assistant sociale *m*, assistante sociale *f*
society [sə'saɪətɪ] société *f*
sociologist [soʊsɪ'ɑːlədʒɪst] sociologue *m/f*; **sociology** sociologie *f*
sock[1] [sɑːk] *n for wearing* chaussette *f*
sock[2] [sɑːk] *v/t* (*punch*) donner un coup de poing à
socket ['sɑːkɪt] ELEC *for light bulb* douille *f*; *Br* (*wall* ~) prise *f* de courant; *of eye* orbite *f*
soda ['soʊdə] (~ *water*) eau *f* gazeuse; (*soft drink*) soda *m*; (*ice-cream* ~) soda *m* à la crème glacée
sofa ['soʊfə] canapé *m*
soft [sɑːft] doux; (*lenient*) gentil; **soften** *position* assouplir; *impact, blow* adoucir; **softly** doucement; **software** logiciel *m*
soggy ['sɑːgɪ] *soil* détrempé; *pastry* pâteux
soil [sɔɪl] **1** *n* (*earth*) terre *f* **2** *v/t* salir
solar energy ['soʊlər] énergie *f* solaire
soldier ['soʊldʒər] soldat *m*
sole[1] [soʊl] *n of foot* plante *f*; *of shoe* semelle *f*
sole[2] [soʊl] *adj* seul; *responsibility* exclusif
solely ['soʊlɪ] exclusivement
solemn ['sɑːləm] solennel; **solemnity** solennité *f*; **solemnly** solennellement
solicit [sə'lɪsɪt] *of prostitute* racoler
solid ['sɑːlɪd] (*hard*) dur; (*without holes*) compact; *gold, silver etc, support* massif; **solidarity** solidarité *f*; **solidify** se solidifier; **solidly** *built* solidement; *in favor of* massivement
solitaire [sɑːlɪ'ter] *card game* réussite *f*
solitary ['sɑːlɪterɪ] *life, activity* solitaire; (*single*) isolé; **solitude** solitude *f*
solo ['soʊloʊ] **1** *adj* en solo **2** *n* MUS solo *m*; **soloist** soliste *m/f*
soluble ['sɑːljʊbl] *substance, problem* soluble; **solution**

also mixture solution *f*
solve [sɑːlv] résoudre; **solvent** *financially* solvable
somber, *Br* sombre ['sɒmbər] sombre
some [sʌm] **1** *adj*: ***~ cream/chocolate/cookies*** de la crème/du chocolat/des biscuits; ***~ people say that …*** certains disent que … **2** *pron*: ***~ of the money*** une partie de l'argent; ***~ of the group*** certaines personnes du groupe, certains du groupe; ***would you like ~?*** est-ce que vous en voulez?; ***give me ~*** donnez-m'en **3** *adv* (*a bit*) un peu; **somebody** quelqu'un; **someday** un jour; **somehow** (*by one means or another*) d'une manière ou d'une autre; (*for some unknown reason*) sans savoir pourquoi; **someone** → ***somebody***; **someplace** → ***somewhere***
somersault ['sʌmərsɒːlt] **1** *n* roulade *f*; *by vehicle* tonneau *m* **2** *v/i of vehicle* faire un tonneau
'something quelque chose; **sometime** un de ces jours; ***~ last year*** dans le courant de l'année dernière; **sometimes** parfois; **somewhat** quelque peu; **somewhere 1** *adv* quelque part **2** *pron*: ***let's go ~ quiet*** allons dans un endroit calme; ***~ to park*** un endroit où se garer
son [sʌn] fils *m*
song [sɑːŋ] chanson *f*
'son-in-law beau-fils *m*; **son of a bitch** V fils *m* de pute V
soon [suːn] (*in a short while*) bientôt; (*quickly*) vite; (*early*) tôt; ***how ~?*** dans combien de temps?; ***as ~ as*** dès que; ***as ~ as possible*** le plus tôt possible; ***~er or later*** tôt ou tard; ***the ~er the better*** le plus tôt sera le mieux
soothe [suːð] calmer
sophisticated [sə'fɪstɪkeɪtɪd] sophistiqué; **sophistication** sophistication *f*
sophomore ['sɑːfəmɔːr] étudiant(e) *m*(*f*) de deuxième année
soprano [sə'prɑːnoʊ] soprano *m*/*f*
sordid ['sɔːrdɪd] sordide
sore [sɔːr] **1** *adj* F (*angry*) fâché; (*painful*): ***is it ~?*** ça vous fait mal? **2** *n* plaie *f*
sorrow ['sɑːroʊ] chagrin *m*
sorry ['sɑːrɪ] *day* triste; *sight* misérable; ***(I'm) ~!*** (*apologizing*) pardon!; ***be ~*** être désolé
sort [sɔːrt] **1** *n* sorte *f*; ***~ of …*** F plutôt **2** *v/t also* COMPUT trier
SOS [esoʊ'es] S.O.S. *m*; *fig*: *plea for help* appel *m* à l'aide
so-'so F comme ci comme ça F
soul [soʊl] *also fig* âme *f*
sound[1] [saʊnd] **1** *adj* (*sensible*) judicieux; *judgment* solide; (*healthy*) en bonne santé; *sleep* profond **2** *adv*: ***be ~***

asleep être profondément endormi
sound[2] [saʊnd] **1** *n* son *m*; (*noise*) bruit *m* **2** *v/i*: ***that ~s interesting*** ça a l'air intéressant
soundly ['saʊndlɪ] *sleep* profondément; *beaten* à plates coutures; **soundproof** insonorisé; **soundtrack** bande *f* sonore
soup [suːp] soupe *f*
sour ['saʊər] *apple, milk* aigre; *comment* désobligeant
source [sɔːrs] *of river, information etc* source *f*
south [saʊθ] **1** *n* sud *m*; ***the South of France*** le Midi **2** *adj* sud *inv*; *wind* du sud **3** *adv travel* vers le sud; **South Africa** Afrique *f* du sud; **South African 1** *adj* sud-africain **2** *n* Sud-Africain *m*, Sud-Africaine *f*; **South America** Amérique *f* du sud; **South American 1** *adj* sud-américain **2** *n* Sud-Américain(e) *m(f)*; **southeast 1** *n* sud-est *m* **2** *adj* sud-est *inv* **3** *adv travel* vers le sud-est; **southeastern** sud-est *inv*; **southerly** *wind* du sud; *direction* vers le sud; **southern** du Sud; **southerner** habitant(e) *m(f)* du Sud; **southernmost** le plus au sud; **South Pole** pôle *m* Sud; **southward** vers le sud; **southwest 1** *n* sud-ouest *m* **2** *adj* sud-ouest *inv* **3** *adv* vers le sud-ouest; **southwestern** sud-ouest *inv*
souvenir [suːvə'nɪr] souvenir *m*
sovereign ['sɑːvrɪn] *state* souverain
sow[1] [saʊ] *n* (*female pig*) truie *f*
sow[2] [soʊ] *v/t seeds* semer
space [speɪs] espace *m*; (*room*) place *f*; **space shuttle** navette *f* spatiale; **space station** station *f* spatiale; **spacious** spacieux
spade [speɪd] *for digging* bêche *f*; ***~s*** *in card game* pique *m*
spaghetti [spə'getɪ] spaghetti *mpl*
Spain [speɪn] Espagne *f*
spam (mail) [spæm] spam *m*
span [spæn] (*cover*) recouvrir; *of bridge* traverser
Spaniard ['spænjərd] Espagnol *m*, Espagnole *f*; **Spanish 1** *adj* espagnol **2** *n language* espagnol *m*; ***the ~*** les Espagnols
spanner ['spænər] *Br* clef *f*
spare [sper] **1** *v/t time* accorder; (*lend*: *money*) prêter; (*do without*) se passer de; ***can you ~ the time?*** est-ce que vous pouvez trouver un moment? **2** *adj* (*extra*) *cash* en trop; *pair of glasses, clothes* de rechange **3** *n* pièce *f* de rechange; **spare part** pièce *f* de rechange; **spare ribs** côtelette *f* de porc dans

l'échine; **spare room** chambre *f* d'ami; **spare time** temps *m* libre; **spare wheel** roue *f* de secours; **sparing**: ***be ~ with*** économiser; **sparingly** en petite quantité

spark [spɑːrk] étincelle *f*

sparkle ['spɑːrkl] étinceler; **sparkling wine** vin *m* mousseux

'spark plug bougie *f*

sparse [spɑːrs] *vegetation* épars

spartan ['spɑːrtn] *room* spartiate

spasmodic [spæz'mɑːdɪk] intermittent; *conversation* saccadé

spate [speɪt] *fig* série *f*, avalanche *f*

spatial ['speɪʃl] spatial

speak [spiːk] **1** *v/i* parler (***to, with*** à); ***~ing*** TELEC lui-même, elle-même **2** *v/t foreign language* parler; **speaker** *at conference* intervenant(e) *m(f)*; (*orator*) orateur(-trice) *m(f)*; *of sound system* haut-parleur *m*; ***French/Spanish ~*** francophone *m/f* / hispanophone *m/f*

special ['speʃl] spécial; *effort, day etc* exceptionnel; **specialist** spécialiste *m/f*; **specialize** se spécialiser (***in*** en, dans); **specially** → ***especially***; **specialty** spécialité *f*

species ['spiːʃiːz] espèce *f*

specific [spə'sɪfɪk] spécifique; **specifically** spécifiquement; **specifications** *of machine etc* spécifications *fpl*; **specify** préciser

specimen ['spesɪmən] *of work* spécimen *m*; *of blood, urine* prélèvement *m*

spectacular [spek'tækjʊlər] spectaculaire

spectator [spek'teɪtər] spectateur(-trice) *m(f)*

spectrum ['spektrəm] *fig* éventail *m*

speculate ['spekjʊleɪt] *also* FIN spéculer; **speculation** spéculations *fpl*; FIN spéculation *f*; **speculator** FIN spéculateur(-trice) *m(f)*

speech [spiːtʃ] discours *m*; (*ability to speak*) parole *f*; (*way of speaking*) élocution *f*; **speechless** *with shock, surprise* sans voix

speed [spiːd] **1** *n* vitesse *f* **2** *v/i* (*go quickly*) se précipiter; *of vehicle* foncer; *drive too quickly* faire de la vitesse; **speedboat** vedette *f*; *with outboard motor* hors-bord *m inv*; **speed bump** dos d'âne *m*, ralentisseur *m*; **speed-dial button** bouton *m* de numérotation abrégée; **speedily** rapidement; **speeding** *when driving* excès *m* de vitesse; **speed limit** limitation *f* de vitesse; **speedometer** compteur *m* de vitesse; **speedy** rapide

spell[1] [spel] **1** *v/t word* écrire, épeler; ***how do you ~ it?***

comment ça s'écrit? **2** *v/i*: ***he can/can't ~*** il a une bonne/mauvaise orthographe
spell[2] *n of time* période *f*
spelling ['spelɪŋ] orthographe *f*
spend [spend] *money* dépenser; *time* passer; **spendthrift** *pej* dépensier(-ière) *m*(*f*)
sperm [spɜːrm] spermatozoïde *m*; (*semen*) sperme *m*
sphere [sfɪr] *also fig* sphère *f*
spice [spaɪs] (*seasoning*) épice *f*; **spicy** *food* épicé
spider ['spaɪdər] araignée *f*; **spiderweb** toile *f* d'araignée
spike [spaɪk] pointe *f*; *on plant, animal* piquant *m*
spill [spɪl] **1** *v/t* renverser **2** *v/i* se répandre **3** *n of oil* déversement *m* accidentel
spin[1] [spɪn] **1** *n* (*turn*) tour *m* **2** *v/t* faire tourner **3** *v/i of wheel* tourner
spin[2] *v/t wool etc* filer; *web* tisser
spinach ['spɪnɪdz] épinards *mpl*
spinal ['spaɪnl] de vertèbres; **spinal column** colonne *f* vertébrale; **spinal cord** moelle *f* épinière; **spine** colonne *f* vertébrale; *of book* dos *m*; *on plant, hedgehog* épine *f*; **spineless** (*cowardly*) lâche
'spin-off retombée *f*
spiny ['spaɪnɪ] épineux
spiral ['spaɪrəl] **1** *n* spirale *f* **2** *v/i rise quickly* monter en spirale
spire ['spaɪr] *of church* flèche *f*
spirit ['spɪrɪt] esprit *m*; (*courage*) courage *m*; **spirited** (*energetic*) énergique; **spirits** (*alcohol*) spiritueux *mpl*; (*morale*) moral *m*; ***be in good/poor ~*** avoir/ne pas avoir le moral; **spiritual** spirituel
spit [spɪt] *of person* cracher
spite [spaɪt] malveillance *f*; ***in ~ of*** en dépit de; **spiteful** malveillant; **spitefully** avec malveillance
splash [splæʃ] **1** *n noise* plouf *m*; *small amount of liquid* goutte *f*; *of color* tache *f* **2** *v/t person* éclabousser; *water, mud* asperger **3** *v/i of person* patauger; ***~ against sth*** *of waves* s'écraser contre qch; **splashdown** amerrissage *m*
splendid ['splendɪd] magnifique; **splendor**, *Br* **splendour** splendeur *f*
splint [splɪnt] MED attelle *f*
splinter ['splɪntər] **1** *n of wood, glass* éclat *m*; *in finger* écharde *f* **2** *v/i* se briser
split [splɪt] **1** *n damage* fente *f*; (*disagreement*) division *f*; (*of profits etc*) partage *m*; (*share*) part *f* **2** *v/t wood* fendre; *log* fendre en deux; (*cause disagreement in, divide*) diviser **3** *v/i of wood etc* se fendre; (*disagree*) se diviser

◆ **split up** *of couple* se séparer

spoil [spɔɪl] *child* gâter; *surprise, party* gâcher; **spoilsport** F rabat-joie *m/f*; **spoilt** *child* gâté

spoke [spoʊk] *of wheel* rayon *m*

spokesperson ['spoʊkspɜːrsən] porte-parole *m/f*

sponge [spʌndʒ] éponge *f*; **sponger** F parasite *m/f*

sponsor ['spɑːnsər] **1** *n for club membership* parrain *m*, marraine *f*; RAD, TV, SP sponsor *m/f* **2** *v/t for club membership* parrainer; RAD, TV, SP sponsoriser; **sponsorship** RAD, TV, SP sponsorisation *f*

spontaneous [spɑːn'teɪnɪəs] spontané; **spontaneously** spontanément

spool [spuːl] bobine *f*

spoon [spuːn] cuillère *f*; **spoonful** cuillerée *f*

sporadic [spə'rædɪk] intermittent

sport [spɔːrt] sport *m*; **sporting** *event*; sportif; (*fair, generous*) chic *inv*; **sports car** voiture *f* de sport; **sportsman** sportif *m*; **sportswoman** sportive *f*; **sporty** *person* sportif

spot¹ [spɑːt] *n on skin* bouton *m*; *in pattern* pois *m*

spot² *n* (*place*) endroit *m*

spot³ *v/t* (*notice, identify*) repérer

'spot check contrôle *m* au hasard; **spotless** impeccable; **spotlight** *beam* feu *m* de projecteur; *device* projecteur *m*; **spotty** *with pimples* boutonneux

spouse [spaʊs] *fml* époux *m*, épouse *f*

spout [spaʊt] **1** *n* bec *m* **2** *v/i of liquid* jaillir **3** *v/t* F débiter

sprain [spreɪn] **1** *n* foulure *f*; *serious* entorse *f* **2** *v/t ankle, wrist* se fouler; *seriously* se faire une entorse à

sprawl [sprɒːl] s'affaler; *of city* s'étendre; **sprawling** tentaculaire

spray [spreɪ] **1** *n of sea water* embruns *mpl*; *from fountain* gouttes *fpl* d'eau; *for hair* laque *f*; *container* atomiseur *m* **2** *v/t perfume, lacquer* vaporiser; *paint, weed-killer etc* pulvériser; ~ ***graffiti on sth*** peindre des graffitis à la bombe sur qch; **spraygun** pulvérisateur *m*

spread [spred] **1** *n of disease, religion etc* propagation *f*; F (*big meal*) festin *m* **2** *v/t* (*lay*), *butter* étaler; *news, rumor, disease* répandre; *arms, legs* étendre **3** *v/i* se répandre; **spreadsheet** COMPUT feuille *f* de calcul; *program* tableur *m*

sprightly ['spraɪtlɪ] alerte

spring¹ [sprɪŋ] *n season* printemps *m*

spring² [sprɪŋ] *n device* ressort *m*
spring³ [sprɪŋ] **1** *n* (*jump*) bond *m*; (*stream*) source *f* **2** *v/i* bondir
'springboard tremplin *m*; **springtime** printemps *m*
sprinkle ['sprɪŋkl] saupoudrer; **sprinkler** *for garden* arroseur *m*; *in ceiling* extincteur *m*
sprint [sprɪnt] **1** *n* sprint *m* **2** *v/i* SP sprinter; *fig* piquer un sprint F; **sprinter** SP sprinteur(-euse) *m*(*f*)
spy [spaɪ] **1** *n* espion(ne) *m*(*f*) **2** *v/i* faire de l'espionnage **3** *v/t* (*see*) apercevoir
◆ **spy on** espionner
squabble ['skwɑːbl] **1** *n* querelle *f* **2** *v/i* se quereller
squalid ['skwɒːlɪd] sordide; **squalor** misère *f*
squander ['skwɒːndər] gaspiller
square [skwer] **1** *adj in shape* carré; ~ ***mile*** mile carré **2** *n shape*, MATH carré *m*; *in town* place *f*; *in board game* case *f*
squash¹ [skwɑːʃ] *n vegetable* courge *f*
squash² [skwɑːʃ] *n game* squash *m*
squash³ [skwɑːʃ] *v/t* (*crush*) écraser
squat [skwɑːt] **1** *adj in shape* ramassé **2** *v/i sit* s'accroupir; *illegally* squatter
squeak [skwiːk] **1** *n of mouse* couinement *m*; *of hinge* grincement *m* **2** *v/i of mouse* couiner; *of hinge* grincer
squeal [skwiːl] **1** *n* cri *m* aigu; *of brakes* grincement *m* **2** *v/i* pousser des cris aigus; *of brakes* grincer
squeamish ['skwiːmɪʃ] trop sensible
squeeze [skwiːz] *hand* serrer; *shoulder*, (*remove juice from*) presser; *fruit*, *parcel* palper
squid [skwɪd] calmar *m*
squirm [skwɜːrm] se tortiller
St (= ***saint***) St(e) (= saint(e)); (= ***street***) rue
stab [stæb] poignarder
stability [stə'bɪlətɪ] stabilité *f*; **stabilize 1** *v/t* stabiliser **2** *v/i* se stabiliser; **stable 1** *adj* stable **2** *n for horses* écurie *f*
stack [stæk] **1** *n* (*pile*) pile *f* **2** *v/t* empiler
stadium ['steɪdɪəm] stade *m*
staff [stæf] (*employees*) personnel *m*; (*teachers*) personnel *m* enseignant
stage¹ [steɪdʒ] *n in project etc* étape *f*
stage² [steɪdʒ] **1** *n* THEA scène *f* **2** *v/t play* mettre en scène; *demonstration* organiser
stagger ['stægər] **1** *v/i* tituber **2** *v/t* (*amaze*) ébahir; *coffee breaks etc* échelonner; **staggering** stupéfiant
stagnant ['stægnənt] *water*, *economy* stagnant; **stagnate** *fig* stagner
'stag party enterrement *m* de

vie de garçon

stain [steɪn] **1** *n* (*dirty mark*) tache *f*; *for wood* teinture *f* **2** *v/t* (*dirty*) tacher; *wood* teindre; **stained-glass window** vitrail *m*; **stainless steel** acier *m* inoxydable

stair [ster] marche *f*; ***the ~s*** l'escalier *m*; **staircase** escalier *m*

stake [steɪk] **1** *n of wood* pieu *m*; *when gambling* enjeu *m*; (*investment*) investissements *mpl*; ***be at ~*** être en jeu **2** *v/t tree* soutenir avec un pieu; *money* jouer; *person* financer

stale [steɪl] *bread* rassis; *air* empesté; *fig*: *news* plus très frais

stalk[1] [stɔːk] *n of fruit, plant* tige *f*

stalk[2] [stɔːk] *v/t animal, person* traquer

stall[1] [stɒːl] *n at market* étalage *m*; *for cow, horse* stalle *f*

stall[2] [stɒːl] **1** *v/i of vehicle, engine* caler; (*play for time*) chercher à gagner du temps **2** *v/t engine* caler; *person* faire attendre

stalls [stɒːlz] THEA orchestre *m*

stalwart ['stɒːlwərt] *supporter* fidèle

stamina ['stæmɪnə] endurance *f*

stammer ['stæmər] **1** *n* bégaiement *m* **2** *v/i* bégayer

stamp[1] [stæmp] **1** *n for letter* timbre *m*; *device, mark* tampon *m* **2** *v/t letter* timbrer; *passport* tamponner

stamp[2] [stæmp] *v/t*: ***~ one's foot*** taper du pied

stance [stæns] position *f*

stand [stænd] **1** *n at exhibition* stand *m*; (*witness ~*) barre *f* des témoins; (*support, base*) support *m*; ***take the ~*** LAW venir à la barre **2** *v/i* (*be situated*) se trouver; *as opposed to sit* rester debout; (*rise*) se lever **3** *v/t* (*tolerate*) supporter; (*put*) mettre

◆ **stand by** **1** *v/i* (*not take action*) rester là sans rien faire; (*be ready*) se tenir prêt **2** *v/t person* soutenir; *decision* s'en tenir à

◆ **stand down** (*withdraw*) se retirer

◆ **stand for** (*tolerate*) supporter; (*represent*) représenter

◆ **stand out** *be visible* ressortir

◆ **stand up** **1** *v/i* se lever **2** *v/t* F poser un lapin à

◆ **stand up for** défendre

◆ **stand up to** (*face*) tenir tête à

standard ['stændərd] **1** *adj procedure etc* normal; ***~ practice*** pratique *f* courante **2** *n* (*level*) niveau *m*; *moral* critère *m*; TECH norme *f*; **standardize** normaliser; **standard of living** niveau *m* de vie

'standby *fly* en stand-by;

standing *in society* position *f* sociale; (*repute*) réputation *f*; **standoffish** distant; **standpoint** point *m* de vue; **standstill**: ***be at a ~*** être paralysé; ***bring to a ~*** paralyser

staple[1] ['steɪpl] *n foodstuff* aliment *m* de base

staple[2] ['steɪpl] **1** *n fastener* agrafe *f* **2** *v/t* agrafer

stapler ['steɪplər] agrafeuse *f*

star [stɑːr] **1** *n in sky* étoile *f*; *fig also* vedette *f* **2** *v/t of movie* avoir comme vedette(s); **starboard** de tribord

stare [ster]: ***~ into space*** regarder dans le vide; ***it's rude to ~*** ce n'est pas poli de fixer les gens

stark [stɑːrk] **1** *adj landscape, color* austère; *reminder, contrast etc* brutal **2** *adv*: ***~ naked*** complètement nu

starry ['stɑːrɪ] *night* étoilé; **Stars and Stripes** bannière *f* étoilée

start [stɑːrt] **1** *n* début *m* **2** *v/i* commencer; *of engine, car* démarrer; ***~ing from tomorrow*** à partir de demain **3** *v/t* commencer; *engine, car* mettre en marche; *business* monter; **starter** *of meal* entrée *f*; *of car* démarreur *m*

startle ['stɑːrtl] effrayer; **startling** surprenant

starvation [stɑːr'veɪʃn] inanition *f*; **starve** souffrir de la faim; ***I'm starving*** F je meurs de faim F

state[1] [steɪt] **1** *n* (*condition, country, part of country*) état *m*; ***the States*** les États-Unis *mpl* **2** *adj capital, police etc* d'état; *banquet, occasion etc* officiel

state[2] [steɪt] *v/t* déclarer; *name and address* décliner

'State Department Département *m* d'État (américain); **statement** *to police* déclaration *f*; (*announcement*) communiqué *m*; (*bank ~*) relevé *m* de compte; **state of emergency** état *m* d'urgence; **state-of-the-art** de pointe; **statesman** homme *m* d'État

static (electricity) ['stætɪk] électricité *f* statique

station ['steɪʃn] **1** *n* RAIL gare *f*; *of subway*, RAD station *f*; TV chaîne *f* **2** *v/t guard etc* placer; **stationary** immobile

stationery ['steɪʃənərɪ] papeterie *f*

'station wagon break *m*

statistical [stə'tɪstɪkl] statistique; **statistically** statistiquement; **statistician** statisticien(ne) *m(f)*; **statistics** *science* statistique *f figures* statistiques *fpl*

statue ['stætʃuː] statue *f*; **Statue of Liberty** Statue *f* de la Liberté

status ['steɪtəs] statut *m*; (*prestige*) prestige *m*; **status symbol** signe *m* extérieur de richesse

statute ['stætʃuːt] loi *f*

staunch [stɒːntʃ] *supporter* fervent
stay [steɪ] **1** *n* séjour *m* **2** *v/i* rester; ~ ***in a hotel*** descendre dans un hôtel; ~ ***right there!*** tenez-vous là!
◆ **stay behind** rester; *in school* rester après la classe
◆ **stay up** (*not go to bed*) rester debout
steadily ['stedɪlɪ] *improve etc* de façon régulière; **steady 1** *adj hand* ferme; *voice* posé; (*regular*) régulier; (*continuous*) continu **2** *adv*: ***be going*** ~ *of couple* sortir ensemble **3** *v/t person* soutenir; *voice* raffermir
steak [steɪk] bifteck *m*
steal [stiːl] **1** *v/t* voler **2** *v/i* (*be a thief*) voler; ~ ***in/out*** entrer/sortir à pas feutrés
stealthy ['stelθɪ] furtif
steam [stiːm] **1** *n* vapeur *f* **2** *v/t food* cuire à la vapeur; **steamed up** F fou de rage; **steamer** *for cooking* cuiseur *m* à vapeur
steel [stiːl] **1** *adj* (*made of* ~) en acier **2** *n* acier *m*; **steelworker** ouvrier(-ière) *m*(*f*) de l'industrie sidérurgique
steep¹ [stiːp] *adj hill etc* raide; F *prices* excessif
steep² [stiːp] *v/t* (*soak*) faire tremper
steer¹ [stɪr] *n animal* bœuf *m*
steer² [stɪr] *v/t* diriger
steering ['stɪrɪŋ] MOT direction *f*; **steering wheel** volant *m*
stem¹ [stem] *n of plant* tige *f*; *of glass* pied *m*; *of word* racine *f*
stem² [stem] *v/t* (*block*) enrayer
stench [stentʃ] odeur *f* nauséabonde
stencil ['stensɪl] **1** *n* pochoir *m*; *pattern* peinture *f* au pochoir **2** *v/t pattern* peindre au pochoir
step [step] **1** *n* (*pace*) pas *m*; (*stair*) marche *f*; (*measure*) mesure *f* **2** *v/i*: ~ ***forward/back*** faire un pas en avant/en arrière
◆ **step down** *from post etc* se retirer
◆ **step up** (*increase*) augmenter
'**stepbrother** demi-frère *m*; **stepdaughter** belle-fille *f*; **stepfather** beau-père *m*; **stepladder** escabeau *m*; **stepmother** belle-mère *f*; **stepsister** demi-sœur *f*; **stepson** beau-fils *m*
stereo ['sterɪoʊ] (*sound system*) chaîne *f* stéréo; **stereotype** stéréotype *m*
sterile ['sterəl] stérile; **sterilize** stériliser
sterling ['stɜːrlɪŋ] FIN sterling *m*
stern¹ [stɜːrn] *adj* sévère
stern² [stɜːrn] *n* NAUT arrière *m*
sternly ['stɜːrnlɪ] sévèrement
steroids ['sterɔɪdz] stéroïdes

mpl

stew [stuː] ragoût *m*

steward ['stuːərd] *on plane, ship* steward *m*; *at demonstration, meeting* membre *m* du service d'ordre; **stewardess** *on plane, ship* hôtesse *f*

stick[1] [stɪk] *n* morceau *m* de bois; *of policeman* bâton *m*; (*walking* ~) canne *f*

stick[2] [stɪk] **1** *v/t with adhesive* coller (***to*** à); F (*put*) mettre **2** *v/i* (*jam*) se coincer; (*adhere*) adhérer

◆ **stick by** F ne pas abandonner

◆ **stick to** (*adhere to*) coller à; F (*keep to*) s'en tenir à; F (*follow*) suivre

◆ **stick up for** F défendre

sticker ['stɪkər] autocollant *m*; **stick-in-the-mud** F encroûté(e) *m(f)*; **sticky** gluant; *label* collant

stiff [stɪf] *brush, cardboard, mixture etc* dur; *muscle, body* raide; *in manner* guindé; *drink* bien tassé; *competition* acharné; *fine* sévère; **stiffness** *of muscles* raideur *f*; *in manner* aspect *m* guindé

stifle ['staɪfl] étouffer; **stifling** étouffant

stigma ['stɪgmə] honte *f*

still[1] [stɪl] **1** *adj* calme **2** *adv*: ***keep ~!*** reste tranquille!; ***stand ~!*** ne bouge pas!

still[2] [stɪl] *adv* (*yet*) encore, toujours; (*nevertheless*) quand même

'**stillborn**: ***be ~*** être mort à sa naissance; **still life** nature *f* morte

stilted ['stɪltɪd] guindé

stimulant ['stɪmjʊlənt] stimulant *m*; **stimulate** stimuler; **stimulating** stimulant; **stimulation** stimulation *f*; **stimulus** (*incentive*) stimulation *f*

sting [stɪŋ] **1** *n from bee, jellyfish* piqûre *f* **2** *v/t & v/i* piquer; **stinging** *criticism* blessant

stink [stɪŋk] **1** *n* (*bad smell*) puanteur *f*; F (*fuss*) grabuge *m* F **2** *v/i* (*smell bad*) puer; F (*be very bad*) être nul

stipulate ['stɪpjʊleɪt] stipuler; **stipulation** condition *f*; *of will, contract* stipulation *f*

stir [stɜːr] **1** *v/t* remuer **2** *v/i of sleeping person* bouger; **stirring** *music, speech* émouvant

stitch [stɪtʃ] **1** *n* point *m*; ***~es*** MED points *mpl* de suture **2** *v/t* (*sew*) coudre; **stitching** (*stitches*) couture *f*

stock [stɑːk] **1** *n* (*reserve*) réserves *fpl*; COM *of store* stock *m*; *animals* bétail *m*; FIN actions *fpl*; *for soup etc* bouillon *m*; ***be in/out of ~*** être en stock/épuisé **2** *v/t* COM avoir (en stock)

'**stockbreeder** éleveur *m*; **stockbroker** agent *m* de change; **stock exchange** bourse *f*; **stockholder** actionnaire *m/f*; **stockist** revendeur *m*; **stock market**

marché *m* boursier; **stockpile 1** *n of food, weapons* stocks *mpl* de réserve **2** *v/t* faire des stocks de
stocky ['stɑːkɪ] trapu
stodgy ['stɑːdʒɪ] *food* bourratif
stoical ['stoʊɪkl] stoïque; **stoicism** stoïcisme *m*
stomach ['stʌmək] **1** *n* (*insides*) estomac *m*; (*abdomen*) ventre *m* **2** *v/t* (*tolerate*) supporter
stone [stoʊn] pierre *f*; (*pebble*) caillou *m*; **stoned** F *on drugs* défoncé F
stool [stuːl] *seat* tabouret *m*
stoop[1] [stuːp] *v/i* (*bend down*) se pencher
stoop[2] [stuːp] *n* (*porch*) perron *m*
stop [stɑːp] **1** *n for train, bus* arrêt *m* **2** *v/t* arrêter; (*prevent*) empêcher; *check* faire opposition à; **~ *doing sth*** arrêter de faire qch **3** *v/i* s'arrêter
◆ **stop over** faire escale
'stopgap bouche-trou *m*; **stoplight** (*traffic light*) feu *m* rouge; (*brake light*) stop *m*; **stopover** étape *f*; **stopper** *for bottle* bouchon *m*; **stop sign** stop *m*; **stopwatch** chronomètre *m*
storage ['stɔːrɪdʒ] COM emmagasinage *m*; *in house* rangement *m*; **store 1** *n* magasin *m*; (*stock*) provision *f*; (**~*house***) entrepôt *m* **2** *v/t* entreposer; COMPUT stocker; **storefront** devanture *f* de magasin; **storekeeper** commerçant(e) *m*(*f*)
storey *Br* → ***story***[2]
storm [stɔːrm] *with rain, wind* tempête *f*; (*thunder~*) orage *m*; **stormy** orageux
story[1] ['stɔːrɪ] (*tale, account*, F: *lie*) histoire *f*; (*newspaper article*) article *m*
story[2] ['stɔːrɪ] *of building* étage *m*
stout [staʊt] *person* corpulent, costaud
stove [stoʊv] *for cooking* cuisinière *f*; *for heating* poêle *m*
stow [stoʊ] ranger
◆ **stow away** s'embarquer clandestinement
'stowaway passager clandestin *m*, passagère clandestine *f*
straight [streɪt] **1** *adj line, back, knees* droit; *hair* raide; (*honest, direct*) franc; (*not criminal*) honnête; *whiskey etc* sec; (*tidy*) en ordre; (*conservative*) sérieux; (*not homosexual*) hétéro F **2** *adv* (*in a straight line*) droit; (*directly, immediately*) directement; ***go ~*** F *of criminal* revenir dans le droit chemin; **~ *ahead*** tout droit; **~ *away*, ~ *off*** tout de suite; **~ *out*** très clairement; **~ *up*** *without ice* sans glace; **straighten** redresser; **straightforward** (*honest, direct*) direct; (*sim-

ple) simple
strain[1] [streɪn] **1** *n on rope, engine* tension *f*; *on heart* pression *f*; ***suffer from ~*** souffrir de tension nerveuse **2** *v/t back* se fouler; *eyes* s'abîmer; *finances* grever
strain[2] [streɪn] *v/t vegetables* faire égoutter; *oil, fat etc* filtrer
strained [streɪnd] *relations* tendu; **strainer** *for vegetables etc* passoire *f*
strait [streɪt] détroit *m*; **strait-laced** collet monté *inv*
strange [streɪndʒ] (*odd, curious*) étrange, bizarre; (*unknown, foreign*) inconnu; **strangely** (*oddly*) bizarrement; ***~ enough, …*** c'est bizarre, mais …; **stranger** étranger(-ère) *m* (*f*); ***he's a complete ~*** je ne le connais pas du tout; ***I'm a ~ here myself*** moi non plus je ne suis pas d'ici
strangle ['stræŋgl] étrangler
strap [stræp] *of purse, shoe* lanière *f*; *of brassiere, dress* bretelle *f*; *of watch* bracelet *m*; **strapless** sans bretelles
strategic [strə'tiːdʒɪk] stratégique; **strategy** stratégie *f*
straw [strɒː] *material, for drink* paille *f*; **strawberry** fraise *f*
stray [streɪ] **1** *adj animal, bullet* perdu **2** *n* animal *m* errant **3** *v/i of animal* vagabonder; *of child* s'égarer; *fig*: *of eyes, thoughts* errer (***to*** vers)
streak [striːk] **1** *n of dirt, paint* traînée *f*; *in hair* mèche *f*; *fig*: *of nastiness etc* pointe *f* **2** *v/i move quickly* filer
stream [striːm] ruisseau *m*; *fig*: *of people* flot *m*; **streamline** *fig* rationaliser; **streamlined** *car, plane* caréné; *organization* rationalisé
street [striːt] rue *f*; **streetcar** tramway *m*; **streetlight** réverbère *m*; **street people** sans-abri *mpl*; **street value** *of drugs* prix *m* à la revente;
strength [streŋθ] force *f*; (*strong point*) point *m* fort; **strengthen 1** *v/t body* fortifier; *bridge, currency, bonds etc* consolider **2** *v/i* se consolider
strenuous ['strenjʊəs] fatigant; **strenuously** *deny* vigoureusement
stress [stres] **1** *n* (*emphasis*) accent *m*; (*tension*) stress *m* **2** *v/t syllable* accentuer; *importance etc* souligner; **stressed out** F stressé F; **stressful** stressant
stretch [stretʃ] **1** *n of land, water* étendue *f*; *of road* partie *f* **2** *adj fabric* extensible **3** *v/t material* tendre; *small income* tirer le maximum de; F *rules* assouplir **4** *v/i to relax muscles, to reach sth* s'étirer; (*spread*) s'étendre; **stretcher** brancard *m*
strict [strɪkt] strict; **strictly**

strictement; ***it is ~ forbidden*** c'est strictement défendu
stride [straɪd] **1** *n* (grand) pas *m* **2** *v/i* marcher à grandes enjambées
strident ['straɪdnt] strident; *demands* véhément
strike [straɪk] **1** *n of workers* grève *f*; *in baseball* balle *f* manquée; *of oil* découverte *f*; **be on ~** être en grève **2** *v/i of workers* faire grève; (*attack: of wild animal*) attaquer; *of killer* frapper; *of disaster* arriver; *of clock* sonner **3** *v/t also fig* frapper; *match* allumer; *oil* découvrir
◆ **strike out** *delete* rayer
strikebreaker ['straɪkbreɪkər] briseur(-euse) *m*(*f*) de grève; **striker** (*person on strike*) gréviste *m*/*f*; *in soccer* buteur *m*; **striking** (*marked, eye-catching*) frappant
string [strɪŋ] ficelle *f*; *of violin, tennis racket* corde *f*; **stringed instrument** instrument *m* à cordes
stringent ['strɪndʒnt] rigoureux
strip [strɪp] **1** *n* bande *f*; (*comic ~*) bande *f* dessinée **2** *v/t* (*remove*) enlever; (*undress*) déshabiller **3** *v/i* (*undress*) se déshabiller; *of stripper* faire du strip-tease; **strip club** boîte *f* de strip-tease
stripe [straɪp] rayure *f*; MIL galon *m*; **striped** rayé
stripper ['strɪpər] strip-teaseuse *f*; ***male ~*** strip-teaseur *m*; **striptease** strip-tease *m*
stroke [strouk] **1** *n* MED attaque *f*; *when painting* coup *m* de pinceau; *style of swimming* nage *f* **2** *v/t* caresser
stroll [stroul] **1** *n* balade *f* **2** *v/i* flâner; **stroller** *for baby* poussette *f*
strong [strɑːŋ] fort; *structure* solide; *candidate* sérieux; *support, supporter* vigoureux; **strongly** fortement; **strong-minded**: ***be ~*** avoir de la volonté; **strong point** point *m* fort; **strongroom** chambre *f* forte; **strong-willed** qui sait ce qu'il/elle veut
structural ['strʌktʃərl] *damage* de structure; *fault, problems* de construction; **structure** **1** *n* (*something built*) construction *f*; *of novel, poem etc* structure *f* **2** *v/t* structurer
struggle ['strʌgl] **1** *n* lutte *f* **2** *v/i with a person* se battre; ***~ to do sth*** avoir du mal à faire qch
strut [strʌt] se pavaner
stub [stʌb] *of cigarette* mégot *m*; *of check, ticket* souche *f*
stubborn ['stʌbərn] *person, refusal etc* entêté; *defense* farouche
stubby ['stʌbɪ] boudiné
stuck [stʌk] F: ***be ~ on s.o.*** être fou de qn

student ['stu:dnt] *at high school* élève *m/f*; *at college, university* étudiant(e) *m(f)*
studio ['stu:dɪoʊ] studio *m*; *of artist* atelier *m*
studious ['stu:dɪəs] studieux;
study 1 *n room* bureau *m*; (*learning*) études *fpl*; (*investigation*) étude *f* **2** *v/t & v/i* étudier
stuff [stʌf] **1** *n* (*things*) trucs *mpl*; *substance, powder etc* truc *m*; (*belongings*) affaires *fpl* **2** *v/t turkey* farcir; ***~ sth into sth*** fourrer qch dans qch; **stuffing** *for turkey* farce *f*; *in chair, toy* rembourrage *m*; **stuffy** *room* mal aéré; *person* vieux jeu *inv*
stumble ['stʌmbl] trébucher; **stumbling block** pierre *f* d'achoppement
stump [stʌmp] **1** *n of tree* souche *f* **2** *v/t*: ***I'm ~ed*** je colle F
stun [stʌn] étourdir; *animal* assommer; *fig* (*shock*) abasourdir; **stunning** (*amazing*) stupéfiant; (*very beautiful*) épatant
stunt [stʌnt] *for publicity* coup *m* de publicité; *in movie* cascade *f*; **stuntman** *in movie* cascadeur *m*
stupefy ['stu:pɪfaɪ] stupéfier
stupendous [stu:'pendəs] prodigieux
stupid ['stu:pɪd] stupide; **stupidity** stupidité *f*
sturdy ['stɜ:rdɪ] robuste
stutter ['stʌtər] bégayer
style [staɪl] (*method, manner*) style *m*; (*fashion*) mode *f*; (*fashionable elegance*) classe *f*; **stylish** qui a de la classe; **stylist** (*hair ~*) styliste *m/f*
subcommittee ['sʌbkəmɪtɪ] sous-comité *m*
subconscious [sʌb'kɑ:nʃəs] subconscient; **subconsciously** subconsciemment
subcontract [sʌbkən'trakt] sous-traiter; **subcontractor** sous-traitant *m*
subdivide [sʌbdɪ'vaɪd] sous-diviser
subdue [səb'du:] contenir
subheading ['sʌbhedɪŋ] sous-titre *m*
subhuman [sʌb'hju:mən] sous-humain
subject 1 ['sʌbdʒɪkt] *n of country*, GRAM, (*topic*) sujet *m*; (*branch of learning*) matière *f* **2** ['sʌbdʒɪkt] *adj*: ***be ~ to*** être sujet à **3** [səb'dʒekt] *v/t* soumettre (***to*** à); **subjective** subjectif
sublet ['sʌblet] sous-louer
submachine gun [sʌbmə'ʃi:ngʌn] mitraillette *f*
submarine ['sʌbməri:n] sous-marin *m*
submission [səb'mɪʃn] (*surrender*), *to committee etc* soumission *f*; **submissive** soumis; **submit 1** *v/t plan* soumettre **2** *v/i* se soumettre
subordinate [sə'bɔ:rdɪnət] **1** *adj position* subalterne **2** *n* subordonné(e) *m(f)*

subpoena [sə'piːnə] LAW **1** *n* assignation *f* **2** *v/t person* assigner à comparaître

◆ **subscribe to** [səb'skraɪb] *magazine etc* s'abonner à; *theory* souscrire à

subscriber [səb'skraɪbər] *to magazine* abonné(e) *m*(*f*); **subscription** abonnement *m*

subsequent ['sʌbsɪkwənt] ultérieur

subside [səb'saɪd] *of waters* baisser; *of winds* se calmer; *of building* s'affaisser; *of fears* s'apaiser

subsidiary [səb'sɪdɪrɪ] filiale *f*

subsidize ['sʌbsɪdaɪz] subventionner; **subsidy** subvention *f*

substance ['sʌbstəns] substance *f*

substandard [sʌb'stændərd] de qualité inférieure

substantial [səb'stænʃl] considérable; *meal* consistant; **substantially** (*considerably*) considérablement; (*in essence*) de manière générale

substantive [səb'stæntɪv] réel

substitute ['sʌbstɪtuːt] **1** *n* substitut *m* (***for*** de); SP remplaçant(e) *m*(*f*) (***for*** de) **2** *v/t* remplacer; ***~ X for Y*** remplacer Y par X; **substitution** remplacement *m*

subtitle ['sʌbtaɪtl] sous-titre *m*

subtle ['sʌtl] subtil

subtract [səb'trækt] soustraire

suburb ['sʌbɜːrb] banlieue *f*; ***the ~s*** la banlieue; **suburban** typique de la banlieue; *attitudes etc* de banlieusards

subversive [səb'vɜːrsɪv] **1** *adj* subversif **2** *n* personne *f* subversive

subway ['sʌbweɪ] métro *m*

succeed [sək'siːd] **1** *v/i* réussir; *to throne* succéder à; ***~ in doing sth*** réussir à faire qch **2** *v/t* (*come after*) succéder à;

success réussite *f*; ***be a ~*** avoir du succès; **successful** *person* qui a réussi; *talks, operation* réussi; ***be ~ in doing sth*** réussir à faire qch; **successfully** avec succès; **successive** successif; ***on three ~ days*** trois jours de suite; **successor** successeur *m*

succinct [sək'sɪŋkt] succinct

succumb [sə'kʌm] (*give in*) succomber

such [sʌtʃ] **1** *adj*: ***~ a*** (*so much of a*) un tel, une telle; ***it was ~ a surprise*** c'était une telle surprise; (*of that kind*): ***~ as*** tel/telle que; ***there is no ~ word as …*** le mot … n'existe pas **2** *adv* tellement; ***~ an easy question*** une question tellement facile

suck [sʌk] **1** *v/t candy etc* sucer **2** *v/i* P: ***it ~s*** c'est merdique P; **sucker** F *person* niais(e) *m*(*f*); F (*lollipop*) su-

cette *f*; **suction** succion *f*
sudden ['sʌdn] soudain; **suddenly** tout à coup, soudain
sue [suː] poursuivre en justice
suede [sweɪd] daim *m*
suffer ['sʌfər] **1** *v/i* souffrir **2** *v/t experience* subir; **suffering** souffrance *f*
sufficient [sə'fɪʃnt] suffisant; ***not ~ funds*** pas assez d'argent; **sufficiently** suffisamment
suffocate ['sʌfəkeɪt] **1** *v/i* s'étouffer **2** *v/t* étouffer; **suffocation** étouffement *m*
sugar ['ʃʊgər] **1** *n* sucre *m* **2** *v/t* sucrer
suggest [sə'dʒest] suggérer; **suggestion** suggestion *f*
suicide ['suːɪsaɪd] suicide *m*
suit [suːt] **1** *n for man* costume *m*; *for woman* tailleur *m*; *in cards* couleur *f* **2** *v/t of clothes, color* aller à; **suitable** approprié, convenable; **suitably** convenablement; **suitcase** valise *f*
suite [swiːt] *of rooms* suite *f*; *furniture* salon *m* trois pièces; MUS suite *m*
sulk [sʌlk] bouder; **sulky** boudeur
sullen ['sʌlən] maussade
sultry ['sʌltrɪ] *climate* lourd; *sexually* sulfureux
sum [sʌm] (*total, amount*) somme *f*; *in arithmetic* calcul *m*
◆ **sum up 1** *v/t* (*summarize*) résumer; (*assess*) se faire une idée de **2** *v/i* LAW résumer les débats
summarize ['sʌməraɪz] résumer; **summary** résumé *m*
summer ['sʌmər] été *f*
summit ['sʌmɪt] *also* POL sommet *m*
summon ['sʌmən] *staff, meeting* convoquer; **summons** LAW assignation *f* (à comparaître)
sun [sʌn] soleil *m*; **sunbathe** prendre un bain de soleil; **sunbed** lit *m* à ultraviolets; **sunblock** écran *m* solaire; **sunburn** coup *m* de soleil; **sunburnt**: ***be ~*** avoir des coups de soleil; **Sunday** dimanche *m*; **sunglasses** lunettes *fpl* de soleil; **sunny** *day* ensoleillé; *disposition* gai; ***it's ~*** il y a du soleil; **sunrise** lever *m* du soleil; **sunset** coucher *m* du soleil; **sunshade** *handheld* ombrelle *f*; *over table* parasol *m*; **sunshine** soleil *m*; **sunstroke** insolation *f*; **suntan** bronzage *m*; ***get a ~*** bronzer
super ['suːpər] **1** *adj* F super *inv* F **2** *n* (*janitor*) concierge *m/f*
superb [sʊ'pɜːrb] excellent
superficial [suːpər'fɪʃl] superficiel
superfluous [sʊ'pɜːrfluəs] superflu
superintendent [suːpərɪn'tendənt] *of apartment block* concierge *m/f*

superior [suː'pɪrɪər] **1** *adj* supérieur **2** *n in organization* supérieur *m*
superlative [suː'pɜːrlətɪv] **1** *adj* (*superb*) excellent **2** *n* GRAM superlatif *m*
'supermarket supermarché *m*
'superpower POL superpuissance *f*
supersonic [suːpər'sɑːnɪk] supersonique
superstition [suːpər'stɪʃn] superstition *f*; **superstitious** superstitieux
supervise ['suːpərvaɪz] *children activities etc* surveiller; *workers* superviser; **supervisor** *at work* superviseur *m*
supper ['sʌpər] dîner *m*
supplement ['sʌplɪmənt] (*extra payment*) supplément *m*
supplier [sə'plaɪr] COM fournisseur(-euse) *m(f)*; **supply** **1** *n of electricity, water etc* alimentation *f* (*of* en); ***~ and demand*** l'offre et la demande; ***supplies*** *of food* provisions *fpl* **2** *v/t goods* fournir
support [sə'pɔːrt] **1** *n for structure* support *m*; (*backing*) soutien *m* **2** *v/t structure* supporter; *financially* entretenir; (*back*) soutenir; **supporter** *of politician, football etc team* supporteur(-trice) *m(f)*; *of theory* partisan(e) *m(f)*; **supportive** *attitude* de soutien; ***be very ~ of s.o.*** beaucoup soutenir qn
suppose [sə'poʊz] (*imagine*) supposer; ***be ~d to do sth*** (*be meant to, said to*) être censé faire qch; ***supposing*** ... (et) si ...; **supposedly** apparemment
suppress [sə'pres] réprimer; **suppression** répression *f*
supremacy [suː'preməsɪ] suprématie *f*; **supreme** suprême; **Supreme Court** Cour *f* suprême
surcharge ['sɜːrtʃɑːrdʒ] surcharge *f*
sure [ʃʊr] **1** *adj* sûr; ***make ~ that ...*** s'assurer que ... **2** *adv*: ***~ enough*** en effet; ***it ~ is hot today*** F il fait vraiment chaud aujourd'hui; ***~!*** F mais oui, bien sûr!; **surety** *for loan* garant(e) *m(f)*
surf [sɜːrf] **1** *n on sea* écume *f* **2** *v/t the Net* surfer sur
surface ['sɜːrfɪs] **1** *n* surface *f* **2** *v/i from water* faire surface; (*appear*) refaire surface; **surface mail** courrier *m* par voie terrestre ou maritime
'surfboard planche *f* de surf; **surfer** surfeur(-euse) *m(f)*; **surfing** surf *m*; ***go ~*** aller faire du surf
surge [sɜːrdʒ] *in electric current* surtension *f*; *in demand etc* poussée *f*
surgeon ['sɜːrdʒən] chirurgien *m(f)*; **surgery** chirurgie *f*; **surgical** chirurgical; **surgically** *remove* par opération chirurgicale
surly ['sɜːrlɪ] revêche

surmount [sər'maʊnt] *difficulties* surmonter
surname ['sɜːrneɪm] nom *m* de famille
surpass [sər'pæs] dépasser
surplus ['sɜːrpləs] **1** *n* surplus *m* **2** *adj* en surplus
surprise [sər'praɪz] **1** *n* surprise *f* **2** *v/t* étonner; ***be/look ~d*** être/avoir l'air surpris; **surprising** étonnant; **surprisingly** étonnamment
surrender [sə'rendər] **1** *v/i of army* se rendre **2** *v/t weapons etc* rendre **3** *n* capitulation *f*; (*handing in*) reddition *f*
surrogate mother ['sʌrəgət] mère *f* porteuse
surround [sə'raʊnd] **1** *v/t* entourer **2** *n of picture etc* bordure *f*; **surrounding** environnant; **surroundings** environs *mpl*; *setting* cadre *m*
survey 1 ['sɜːrveɪ] *n of modern literature etc* étude *f*; *Br of building* inspection *f*; (*poll*) sondage *m* **2** [sər'veɪ] *v/t* (*look at*) contempler; *Br building* inspecter; **surveyor** *Br* expert *m*
survival [sər'vaɪvl] survie *f*; **survive 1** *v/i* survivre **2** *v/t accident*, (*outlive*) survivre à; **survivor** survivant(e) *m*(*f*)
suspect 1 ['sʌspekt] *n* suspect(e) *m*(*f*) **2** [sə'spekt] *v/t person* soupçonner; (*suppose*) croire; **suspected** *murderer* soupçonné; *cause, heart attack etc* présumé
suspend [sə'spend] (*hang*), *from office* suspendre; **suspenders** *for pants* bretelles *fpl*; *Br* porte-jarretelles *m*
suspense [sə'spens] suspense *m*; **suspension** *in vehicle, from duty* suspension *f*
suspicion [sə'spɪʃn] soupçon *m*; **suspicious** (*causing suspicion*) suspect; (*feeling suspicion*) méfiant; ***be ~ of s.o.*** se méfier de qn; **suspiciously** *behave* de manière suspecte; *ask* avec méfiance
sustain [sə'steɪn] soutenir; **sustainable** durable
SUV [esjuː'viː] (= ***sports utility vehicle***) véhicule *m* utilitaire sport
swab [swɑːb] tampon *m*
swallow[1] ['swɑːloʊ] *v/t & v/i* avaler
swallow[2] ['swɑːloʊ] *n bird* hirondelle *f*
swamp [swɑːmp] **1** *n* marécage *m* **2** *v/t*: ***be ~ed with*** être submergé de; **swampy** marécageux
swap [swɑːp] échanger (***for*** contre)
swarm [swɔːrm] **1** *n of bees* essaim *m* **2** *v/i*: ***the town was ~ing with ...*** la ville grouillait de ...
swarthy ['swɔːrðɪ] basané
swat [swɑːt] *insect* écraser
sway [sweɪ] **1** *n* (*influence, power*) emprise *f* **2** *v/i in wind* se balancer; *because drunk, ill* tituber

swear [swer] **1** *v/i* (*use swearword*) jurer; *~ **at s.o.*** injurier qn **2** *v/t* LAW, (*promise*) jurer ◆ **swear in** *witnesses etc* faire prêter serment à
'swearword juron *m*
sweat [swet] **1** *n* sueur *f* **2** *v/i* transpirer, suer; **sweat band** bandeau *m* en éponge; **sweater** pull *m*; **sweatshirt** sweat(-shirt) *m*; **sweaty** plein de sueur
sweep [swi:p] **1** *v/t floor, leaves* balayer **2** *n* (*long curve*) courbe *f*; **sweeping** *statement* hâtif; *changes* radical
sweet [swi:t] *taste, tea* sucré; F (*kind*) gentil; F (*cute*) mignon; **sweetcorn** maïs *m*; **sweeten** sucrer; **sweetheart** amoureux(-euse) *m(f)*
swell [swel] **1** *v/i of wound, limb* enfler **2** *adj* F (*good*) super F *inv* **3** *n of the sea* houle *f*; **swelling** MED enflure *f*
swerve [swɜ:rv] *of driver, car* s'écarter brusquement
swift [swɪft] rapide
swim [swɪm] **1** *v/i* nager **2** *n* baignade *f*; ***go for a ~*** aller se baigner; **swimmer** nageur(-euse) *m(f)*; **swimming** natation *f*; **swimming pool** piscine *f*; **swimsuit** maillot *m* de bain
swindle ['swɪndl] **1** *n* escroquerie *f* **2** *v/t* escroquer; ***~ s.o. out of sth*** escroquer qch à qn
swing [swɪŋ] **1** *n* oscillation *f*; *for child* balançoire *f*; ***~ to the Democrats*** revirement *m* d'opinion en faveur des démocrates **2** *v/t object in hand, hips* balancer **3** *v/i* se balancer; (*turn*) tourner; *of public opinion etc* virer
Swiss [swɪs] **1** *adj* suisse **2** *n person* Suisse *m/f*; ***the ~*** les Suisses *mpl*
switch [swɪʧ] **1** *n for light* bouton *m*; (*change*) changement *m* **2** *v/t* (*change*) changer de **3** *v/i* (*change*) passer ◆ **switch off** *lights, engine, PC* éteindre; *engine* arrêter ◆ **switch on** *lights, engine, PC* allumer; *engine* démarrer
Switzerland ['swɪtsərlənd] Suisse *f*
swivel ['swɪvl] pivoter
swollen ['swoulən] *stomach* ballonné; *ankles, face* enflé
syllabus ['sɪləbəs] programme *m*
symbol ['sɪmbəl] symbole *m*; **symbolic** symbolique; **symbolism** symbolisme *m*; **symbolist** symboliste *m/f*; **symbolize** symboliser
symmetrical [sɪ'metrɪkl] symétrique; **symmetry** symétrie
sympathetic [sɪmpə'θetɪk] (*showing pity*) compatissant; (*understanding*) compréhensif
◆ **sympathize with** ['sɪmpə-

θaɪz] *person* compatir avec; *views* avoir des sympathies pour
sympathizer ['sɪmpəθaɪzər] POL sympathisant(e) *m(f)*; **sympathy** (*pity*) compassion *f*; (*understanding*) compréhension (***for*** de)
symphony ['sɪmfənɪ] symphonie *f*
symptom ['sɪmptəm] MED, *fig* symptôme *m*
synchronize ['sɪŋkrənaɪz] synchroniser
synonym ['sɪnənɪm] synonyme *m*; **synonymous** synonyme
synthesizer ['sɪnθəsaɪzər] MUS synthétiseur *m*; **synthetic** synthétique
syphilis ['sɪfɪlɪs] syphilis *f*
Syria ['sɪrɪə] Syrie *f*; **Syrian 1** *adj* syrien **2** *n* Syrien(ne) *m(f)*
syringe [sɪ'rɪndʒ] seringue *f*
syrup ['sɪrəp] sirop *m*
system ['sɪstəm] système *m*; (*orderliness*) ordre *m*; (*computer*) ordinateur *m*; **systematic** systématique; **systematically** systématiquement
systems analyst COMPUT analyste-programmeur(-euse) *m(f)*

T

table ['teɪbl] table *f*; *of figures* tableau *m*; **tablecloth** nappe *f*; **table lamp** petite lampe *f*; **table of contents** table *f* des matières; **tablespoon** cuillère *f* à soupe
tablet ['tæblɪt] MED comprimé *m*
tabloid ['tæblɔɪd] *newspaper* journal *m* à sensation
taboo [tə'buː] tabou *inv in feminine*
tacit ['tæsɪt] tacite
tack [tæk] **1** *n nail* clou *m* **2** *v/t in sewing* bâtir **3** *v/i of yacht* louvoyer
tackle ['tækl] **1** *n* (*equipment*) attirail *m*; SP tacle *m*; *in rugby* plaquage *m* **2** *v/t* SP tacler; *in rugby* plaquer; *problem* s'attaquer à; (*confront*) confronter; *physically* s'opposer à
tacky ['tækɪ] *paint*, *glue* collant; F (*cheap*, *poor quality*) minable F
tact [tækt] tact *m*; **tactful** diplomate; **tactfully** avec tact
tactical ['tæktɪkl] tactique; **tactics** tactique *f*
tactless ['tæktlɪs] qui manque de tact, peu délicat
tag [tæg] (*label*) étiquette *f*
tail [teɪl] queue *f*; **tail light** feu *m* arrière
tailor ['teɪlər] tailleur *m*; **tai-**

lor-made *also fig* fait sur mesure

'tail pipe *of car* tuyau *m* d'échappement

take [teɪk] prendre; (*transport, accompany*) amener; *subject at school, photograph, photocopy, stroll* faire; *exam* passer; (*endure*) supporter; (*require: courage etc*) demander; ***how long will it ~ you to ...?*** combien de temps est-ce que tu vas mettre pour ...?

◆ **take after** ressembler à

◆ **take away** *object* enlever; *pain* faire disparaître; MATH soustraire (***from*** de)

◆ **take back** *object* rapporter; *person to a place* ramener; ***she wouldn't take him back*** *husband* elle ne voulait pas qu'il revienne

◆ **take down** *from shelf* enlever; *scaffolding* démonter; *pants* baisser; (*write down*) noter

◆ **take in** (*take indoors*) rentrer; (*give accommodation to*) héberger; (*make narrower*) reprendre; (*deceive*) duper; (*include*) inclure

◆ **take off 1** *v/t clothes, hat* enlever; *10% etc* faire une réduction de; (*mimic*) imiter **2** *v/i of airplane* décoller; (*become popular*) réussir

◆ **take on** *job* accepter; *staff* embaucher

◆ **take out** *from bag, pocket* sortir (***from*** de); *tooth, word from text* enlever; *money from bank* retirer; *to dinner, theater etc* emmener; *insurance policy* souscrire à

◆ **take over 1** *v/t company etc* reprendre **2** *v/i* POL arriver au pouvoir; *of new director* prendre ses fonctions; (*do sth in s.o.'s place*) prendre la relève

◆ **take up** *carpet etc* enlever; (*carry up*) monter; *dress etc* raccourcir; *judo, Spanish etc* se mettre à; *new job* commencer; *space, time* prendre; *offer* accepter

'takeoff *of airplane* décollage *m*; (*impersonation*) imitation *f*; **takeover** COM rachat *m*; **takeover bid** offre *f* publique d'achat, OPA *f*; **takings** recette *f*

tale [teɪl] histoire *f*

talent ['tælənt] talent *m*; **talented** doué; **talent scout** dénicheur(-euse) *m(f)* de talents

talk [tɒːk] **1** *v/t & v/i* parler; ***~ business*** parler affaires **2** *n* (*conversation*) conversation *f*; (*lecture*) exposé *m*; ***~s*** pourparlers *mpl*

◆ **talk back** répondre

talkative ['tɒːkətɪv] bavard; **talk show** talk-show *m*

tall [tɒːl] grand

tally ['tælɪ] **1** *n* compte *m* **2** *v/i* correspondre; *of stories* concorder

tame [teɪm] apprivoisé; *not wild* pas sauvage; *joke etc* fade

◆ **tamper with** ['tæmpər] toucher à

tampon ['tæmpɑːn] tampon *m*

tan [tæn] **1** *n from sun* bronzage; *color* marron *m* clair **2** *v/i in sun* bronzer **3** *v/t leather* tanner

tangent ['tændʒənt] MATH tangente *f*

tangible ['tændʒɪbl] tangible

tangle ['tæŋgl] enchevêtrement *m*

tango ['tæŋgoʊ] tango *m*

tank [tæŋk] MOT, *for water* réservoir *m*; *for fish* aquarium *m*; MIL char *m*; *for skin diver* bonbonne *f* d'oxygène; **tanker** (*oil* ~) pétrolier *m*; *truck* camion-citerne *m*

tanned [tænd] bronzé

tantalizing ['tæntəlaɪzɪŋ] alléchant

tantrum ['tæntrəm] caprice *m*

tap [tæp] **1** *n Br* (*faucet*) robinet *m* **2** *v/t* (*knock*) taper; *phone* mettre sur écoute

tape [teɪp] **1** *n for recording* bande *f*; *recording* cassette *f*; *sticky* ruban *m* adhésif **2** *v/t conversation etc* enregistrer; *with sticky tape* scotcher; **tape deck** platine *f* cassettes; **tape drive** COMPUT lecteur *m* de bandes; **tape measure** mètre *m* ruban

taper ['teɪpər] *of stick* s'effiler; *of column, pant legs* se rétrécir

'tape recorder magnétophone *m*; **tape recording** enregistrement *m*

tar [tɑːr] goudron *m*

tardy ['tɑːrdɪ] tardif

target ['tɑːrgɪt] **1** *n in shooting* cible *f*; *fig* objectif *m* **2** *v/t market* cibler

'target audience public *m* cible; **target date** date *f* visée; **target market** marché *m* cible

tariff ['tærɪf] (*customs* ~) taxe *f*; (*prices*) tarif *m*

tarmac ['tɑːrmæk] *at airport* tarmac *m*

tarnish ['tɑːrnɪʃ] ternir

tarpaulin [tɑːr'pɒːlɪn] bâche *f*

tart [tɑːrt] tarte *f*

task [tæsk] tâche *f*; **task force** commission *f*; MIL corps *m* expéditionnaire

taste [teɪst] **1** *n* goût *m* **2** *v/t* goûter; (*perceive taste of*) sentir; *try, fig* goûter à **3** *v/i*: ***it ~s like …*** ça a (un) goût de …; **tasteful** de bon goût; **tastefully** avec goût; **tasteless** *food* fade; *remark, décor* de mauvais goût; **tasting** *of wine* dégustation *f*; **tasty** délicieux

tattered ['tætərd] en lambeaux

tattoo [tə'tuː] tatouage *m*

taunt [tɒːnt] **1** *n* raillerie *f* **2** *v/t* se moquer de

taut [tɒːt] tendu

tax [tæks] **1** *n on income* impôt *m*; *on goods, services* taxe *f* **2** *v/t income* imposer; *goods, services* taxer; **taxable income** revenu *m* imposable; **taxation** *act* imposition *f*; (*taxes*) charges *fpl* fiscales; **tax bracket** fourchette *f* d'impôts; **tax-deductible** déductible des impôts; **tax evasion** fraude *f* fiscale; **tax-free** hors taxe; **tax haven** paradis *m* fiscal
taxi ['tæksɪ] taxi *m*; **taxi driver** chauffeur *m* de taxi
taxing ['tæksɪŋ] exténuant
'taxi stand, *Br* **'taxi rank** station *f* de taxis
'taxpayer contribuable *m/f*; **tax return** déclaration *f* d'impôts; **tax year** année *f* fiscale
TB [tiː'biː] (= ***tuberculosis***) tuberculose *f*
tea [tiː] *drink* thé *m*; **teabag** sachet *m* de thé
teach [tiːʧ] enseigner; *person* enseigner à; **teacher** professeur *m/f*; *in elementary school* instituteur(-trice) *m(f)*; **teaching** *profession* enseignement *m*
'teacup tasse *f* à thé
teak [tiːk] tek *m*
team [tiːm] équipe *f*; **team spirit** esprit *m* d'équipe; **teamster** camionneur(-euse) *m(f)*; **teamwork** travail *m* d'équipe
teapot ['tiːpɑːt] théière *f*
tear¹ [ter] **1** *n in cloth etc* déchirure *f* **2** *v/t paper, cloth* déchirer **3** *v/i* (*run fast, drive fast*): ***she tore down the street*** elle a descendu la rue en trombe
◆ **tear down** *poster* arracher; *building* démolir
◆ **tear out** *page* arracher
◆ **tear up** déchirer; *contract etc* annuler
tear² [tɪr] *n in eye* larme *f*; ***be in ~s*** être en larmes; **tearful** *look* plein de larmes; **tear gas** gaz *m* lacrymogène
tease [tiːz] taquiner
'teaspoon cuillère *f* à café
technical ['teknɪkl] technique; **technically** (*strictly speaking*) en théorie; **technician** technicien(ne) *m(f)*; **technique** technique *f*
technological [teknə'lɑːdʒɪkl] technologique; **technology** technologie *f*; **technophobia** technophobie *f*
teddy bear ['tedɪber] ours *m* en peluche
tedious ['tiːdɪəs] ennuyeux
tee [tiː] *in golf* tee *m*
teenage ['tiːneɪdʒ] *fashion* pour adolescents; **teenager** adolescent(e) *m(f)*
teens [tiːnz] adolescence *f*
teeny ['tiːnɪ] F tout petit
teeth [tiːθ] *pl* → ***tooth***
teethe [tiːð] faire ses dents
telecommunications [telɪkəmjuːnɪ'keɪʃnz] télécommunications *fpl*
telegraph pole ['telɪgræf-

poul] *Br* poteau *m* télégraphique
telepathic [telɪ'pæθɪk] télépathique; **telepathy** télépathie *f*
telephone ['telɪfoun] **1** *n* téléphone *m* **2** *v/t person* téléphoner à **3** *v/i* téléphoner; **telephone book** annuaire *m*; **telephone booth** cabine *f* téléphonique; **telephone call** appel *m* téléphonique; **telephone conversation** conversation *f* téléphonique; **telephone directory** annuaire *m*; **telephone number** numéro *m* de téléphone
telephoto lens [telɪ'foutoulenz] téléobjectif *m*
telesales ['telɪseɪlz] télévente *f*
telescope ['telɪskoup] téléscope *m*
televise ['telɪvaɪz] téléviser
television ['telɪvɪʒn] *also set* télévision *f*; ***on ~*** à la télévision; **television program**, *Br* **television programme** émission *f* télévisée; **television studio** studio *m* de télévision
tell [tel] **1** *v/t story* raconter; *lie* dire; ***I can't ~ the difference*** je n'arrive pas à faire la différence; ***~ s.o. sth*** dire qch à qn; ***~ s.o. to do sth*** dire à qn de faire qch **2** *v/i* (*have effect*) se faire sentir; **teller** *in bank* guichetier(-ière) *m*(*f*); **telling off**: ***get a ~*** se faire remonter les bretelles F; **telltale 1** *adj signs* révélateur **2** *n* rapporteur(-euse) *m*(*f*)
temp [temp] **1** *n employee* intérimaire *m*/*f* **2** *v/i* faire de l'intérim
temper ['tempər] (*bad ~*) mauvaise humeur *f*; ***lose one's ~*** se mettre en colère
temperament ['temprəmənt] tempérament *m*; **temperamental** (*moody*) capricieux
temperate ['tempərət] tempéré
temperature ['temprətʃər] température *f*
temple[1] ['templ] REL temple *m*
temple[2] ['templ] ANAT tempe *f*
tempo ['tempou] MUS tempo *m*
temporarily [tempə'rerɪlɪ] temporairement; **temporary** temporaire
tempt [tempt] tenter; **temptation** tentation *f*; **tempting** tentant
ten [ten] dix
tenacious [tɪ'neɪʃəs] tenace; **tenacity** ténacité *f*
tenant ['tenənt] locataire *m*/*f*
tend[1] [tend] *v/t lawn* entretenir; *sheep* garder; *the sick* soigner
tend[2] [tend] *v/i*: ***~ to do sth*** avoir tendance à faire qch
tendency ['tendənsɪ] tendance *f*
tender[1] ['tendər] *adj* (*sore*) sensible; (*affectionate*), *steak*

tendre
tender[2] ['tendər] *n* COM offre *f*
tenderness ['tendənɪs] *of kiss etc* tendresse *f*; *of steak* tendreté *f*
tendon ['tendən] tendon *m*
tennis ['tenɪs] tennis *m*; **tennis ball** balle *f* de tennis; **tennis court** court *m* de tennis; **tennis player** joueur(-euse) *m(f)* de tennis
tenor ['tenər] MUS ténor *m*
tense[1] [tens] *n* GRAM temps *m*
tense[2] [tens] *adj* tendu
tension ['tenʃn] tension *f*
tent [tent] tente *f*
tentative ['tentətɪv] *smile, steps* hésitant; *conclusion, offer* provisoire
tenth [tenθ] dixième
tepid ['tepɪd] *also fig* tiède
term [tɜːrm] (*period, word*) terme *m*; *Br* EDU trimestre *m*; (*condition*) condition *f*; ***be on good/bad ~s with s.o.*** être en bons/mauvais termes avec qn; ***in the long/short ~*** à long/court terme
terminal ['tɜːrmɪnl] **1** *n at airport* aérogare *m*; *for buses* terminus *m*; *for containers*, COMPUT terminal *m*; ELEC borne *f* **2** *adj illness* incurable; **terminally**: ***~ ill*** en phase terminale; **terminate 1** *v/t* mettre fin à; *pregnancy* interrompre **2** *v/i* se terminer; **termination** *of contract* résiliation *f*; *in pregnancy* interruption *f* volontaire de grossesse
terminus ['tɜːrmɪnəs] terminus *m*
terrace ['terəs] terrasse *f*
terrain [te'reɪn] terrain *m*
terrible ['terəbl] horrible, affreux; **terribly** (*very*) très
terrific [tə'rɪfɪk] génial; **terrifically** (*very*) extrêmement, vachement F
terrify ['terɪfaɪ] terrifier; **terrifying** terrifiant
territorial [terə'toːrɪəl] territorial; **territory** territoire *m*; *fig* domaine *m*
terror ['terər] terreur *f*; **terrorism** terrorisme *m*; **terrorist** terroriste *m/f*; **terrorist attack** attentat *m* terroriste; **terrorize** terroriser
terse [tɜːrs] laconique
test [test] **1** *n scientific, technical* test *m*; *academic, for driving* examen *m* **2** *v/t* tester, mettre à l'épreuve; **test-drive** *car* essayer
testicle ['testɪkl] testicule *m*
testify ['testɪfaɪ] LAW témoigner
testimony ['testɪmənɪ] LAW témoignage *m*
testy ['testɪ] irritable
tetanus ['tetənəs] tétanos *m*
text [tekst] **1** *n* texte *m*; *message* texto *m* **2** *v/t* envoyer un texto à; **textbook** manuel *m*; **text-message** texto *m*, SMS *m*
textile ['tekstaɪl] textile *m*
texture ['tekstʃər] texture *f*

than [ðæn] que; *with numbers* de; ***faster ~ me*** plus rapide que moi

thank [θæŋk] remercier; ***~ you*** merci; ***no ~ you*** (non) merci; **thankful** reconnaissant; **thankfully** (*luckily*) heureusement; **thankless** *task* ingrat; **thanks** remerciements *mpl*; ***~!*** merci!; ***~ to*** grâce à; **Thanksgiving (Day)** jour *m* de l'action de grâces, Thanksgiving *m*

that [ðæt] **1** *adj* ce, cette; *masculine before vowel* cet; ***~ one*** celui-là, celle-là **2** *pron* cela, ça; ***give me ~*** donne-moi ça; ***~'s tea*** c'est du thé; ***what is ~?*** qu'est-ce que c'est que ça?; ***who is ~?*** qui est-ce? **3** *rel pron* que; ***the car ~ you see*** la voiture que vous voyez **4** *adv* (*so*) aussi; ***~ expensive*** aussi cher **5** *conj* que; ***I think ~ …*** je pense que …

thaw [θɒː] *of snow* fondre; *of frozen food* se décongeler

the [ðə] le, la; *pl* les; ***to the station/theater*** à la gare/au théâtre; ***~ more I try*** plus j'essaie

theater, *Br* **theatre** ['θɪətər] théâtre *m*; **theatrical** *also fig* théâtral

theft [θeft] vol *m*

their [ðer] leur; *pl* leurs; (*his or her*) son, sa; *pl* ses; **theirs** le leur, les leurs; ***it's ~*** c'est à eux/elles

them [ðem] *object* les; *indirect object* leur; *with prep* eux, elles; ***I know ~*** je les connais; ***I gave ~ a dollar*** je leur ai donné un dollar; ***this is for ~*** c'est pour eux/elles; ***who? – ~*** qui? – eux/elles

theme [θiːm] thème *m*; **theme park** parc *m* à thème

themselves [ðem'selvz] eux-mêmes, elles-mêmes; *reflexive* se; *after prep* eux, elles; ***they gave ~ a holiday*** ils se sont offerts des vacances

then [ðen] (*at that time*) à l'époque; (*after that*) ensuite; *deducing* alors; ***by ~*** alors

theoretical [θɪə'retɪkl] théorique; **theoretically** en théorie; **theory** théorie *f*

therapeutic [θerə'pjuːtɪk] thérapeutique; **therapist** thérapeute *m/f*; **therapy** thérapie *f*

there [ðer] là; ***over ~/down ~*** là-bas; ***~ is/are …*** il y a …; ***is/are ~ …?*** est-ce qu'il y a…?, y a-t-il …?; ***~ is/are not …*** il n'y a pas …; ***~ you are*** voilà; ***~ and back*** aller et retour; ***~ he is!*** le voilà!; ***~, ~!*** allons, allons; ***we went ~ yesterday*** nous y sommes allés hier; **thereabouts**: ***$500 or ~*** environ 500 $; **therefore** donc

thermometer [θər'mɑːmɪtər] thermomètre *m*

thermos flask ['θɜːrməsflæsk] thermos *m*

these [ðiːz] **1** *adj* ces **2** *pron* ceux-ci, celles-ci
thesis ['θiːsɪs] thèse *f*
they [ðeɪ] ils, elles; (*he or she*) il; ***there ~ are*** les voilà; ***~ say that …*** on dit que …
thick [θɪk] épais; F (*stupid*) lourd; ***it's 3 cm ~*** ça fait 3 cm d'épaisseur; **thicken** *sauce* épaissir; **thick-skinned** *fig* qui a la peau dure
thief [θiːf] voleur(-euse) *m(f)*
thigh [θaɪ] cuisse *f*
thin [θɪn] *material* léger, fin; *layer* mince; *person* maigre; *line* fin; *soup* liquide
thing [θɪŋ] chose *f*; ***~s*** (*belongings*) affaires *fpl*
think [θɪŋk] penser; ***I ~ so*** je pense que oui; ***I don't ~ so*** je ne pense pas; ***I'll ~ about it*** *offer* je vais y réfléchir
◆ **think over** réfléchir à
◆ **think through** bien examiner
◆ **think up** *plan* concevoir
'think tank comité *m* d'experts
thin-skinned ['θɪnskɪnd] *fig* susceptible
third [θɜːrd] **1** *adj* troisième **2** *n* troisième *m/f*; **thirdly** troisièmement; **third-party** tiers *m*; **third-party insurance** *Br* assurance *f* au tiers; **Third World** Tiers-Monde *m*
thirst [θɜːrst] soif *f*; **thirsty** assoiffé; ***be ~*** avoir soif
thirteen [θɜːr'tiːn] treize; **thirteenth** treizième; **thirtieth** trentième; **thirty** trente
this [ðɪs] **1** *adj* ce, cette; *masculine before vowel* cet; ***~ one*** celui-ci, celle-ci **2** *pron* cela, ça; ***~ is good*** c'est bien; ***~ is …*** c'est …; *introducing s.o.* je vous présente … **3** *adv*: ***~ high*** haut comme ça
thorn [θɔːrn] épine *f*; **thorny** *also fig* épineux
thorough ['θɜːroʊ] *search, knowledge* approfondi; *person* méticuleux; **thoroughbred** *horse* pur-sang *m*; **thoroughly** complètement; *clean, search for, know* à fond
those [ðoʊz] **1** *adj* ces **2** *pron* ceux-là, celles-là
though [ðoʊ] **1** *conj* (*although*) bien que (*+subj*), quoique (*+subj*); ***as ~*** comme si **2** *adv* pourtant
thought [θɒːt] pensée *f*; **thoughtful** pensif; *book* profond; (*considerate*) attentionné; **thoughtless** inconsidéré
thousand ['θaʊznd] mille *m*; ***~s of*** des milliers *mpl* de; **thousandth** **1** *adj* millième **2** *n* millième *m/f*
thrash [θræʃ] rouer de coups; SP battre à plates coutures
◆ **thrash out** *solution* parvenir à
thrashing volée *f* de coups; ***get a ~*** SP se faire battre à plates coutures

thread [θred] **1** *n* fil *m*; *of screw* filetage *m* **2** *v/t needle, beads* enfiler; **threadbare** usé jusqu'à la corde
threat [θret] menace *f*; **threaten** menacer; **threatening** menaçant
three [θriː] trois; **three-quarters** les trois-quarts *mpl*
threshold ['θreʃhould] *of house, new era* seuil *m*
thrifty ['θrɪftɪ] économe
thrill [θrɪl] **1** *n* frisson *m* **2** *v/t*: ***be ~ed*** être ravi; **thriller** thriller *m*; **thrilling** palpitant
thrive [θraɪv] *of plants* bien pousser; *of business* prospérer
throat [θrout] gorge *f*; **throat lozenge** pastille *f* pour la gorge
throb [θrɑːb] **1** *n of heart* pulsation *f*; *of music* vibration *f* **2** *v/i of heart* battre fort; *of music* vibrer
throne [θroun] trône *m*
throttle ['θrɑːtl] **1** *n on motorbike, boat* papillon *m* des gaz **2** *v/t* (*strangle*) étrangler
through [θruː] **1** *prep* ◇ (*across*) à travers; ***go ~ the city*** traverser la ville ◇ (*during*) pendant; ***all ~ the night*** toute la nuit; ***Monday ~ Friday*** du lundi au vendredi (inclus) ◇ (*by means of*) par **2** *adv*: ***wet ~*** mouillé jusqu'aux os **3** *adj*: ***be ~*** (*have arrived*: *of news etc*) être parvenu; ***we're ~ of couple*** c'est fini entre nous; ***be ~ with s.o./sth*** en avoir fini avec qn/qch; **throughout** **1** *prep* tout au long de, pendant tout(e) **2** *adv* (*in all parts*) partout
throw [θrou] **1** *v/t* jeter, lancer; *of horse* désarçonner; (*disconcert*) déconcerter; *party* organiser **2** *n* jet *m*; ***it's your ~*** c'est à toi de lancer
◆ **throw away** jeter
◆ **throw out** *old things* jeter; *from bar, home* jeter dehors, mettre à la porte; *from country* expulser; *plan* rejeter
◆ **throw up** **1** *v/t ball* jeter en l'air **2** *v/i* (*vomit*) vomir
throw-away ['θrouəweɪ] (*disposable*) jetable; *remark* en l'air; **throw-in** SP remise *f* en jeu
thru [θruː] → ***through***
thrust [θrʌst] (*push hard*) enfoncer
thud [θʌd] bruit *m* sourd
thug [θʌg] brute *f*
thumb [θʌm] **1** *n* pouce *m* **2** *v/t*: ***~ a ride*** faire de l'auto-stop; **thumbtack** punaise *f*
thunder ['θʌndər] tonnerre *m*; **thunderous** *applause* tonitruant; **thunderstorm** orage *m*; **thunderstruck** abasourdi; **thundery** *weather* orageux
Thursday ['θɜːrzdeɪ] jeudi *m*
thus [ðʌs] ainsi
thwart [θwɔːrt] contrarier
tick [tɪk] **1** *n of clock* tic-tac *m*;

Br (*checkmark*) coche *f* **2** *v/i* faire tic-tac
ticket ['tɪkɪt] *for bus, museum* ticket *m*; *for train, airplane, theater, concert, lottery* billet *m*; *for speeding, illegal parking* P.V. *m*; **ticket machine** distributeur *m* de billets; **ticket office** billetterie *f*
ticking ['tɪkɪŋ] *noise* tic-tac *m*
tickle ['tɪkl] chatouiller
tidal wave ['taɪdlweɪv] raz-de-marée *m*
tide [taɪd] marée *f*
tidiness ['taɪdɪnɪs] ordre *m*; **tidy** *person, habits* ordonné; *room, house, desk* en ordre
◆ **tidy up 1** *v/t room, shelves* ranger; ***tidy o.s. up*** remettre de l'ordre dans sa tenue **2** *v/i* ranger
tie [taɪ] **1** *n* (*necktie*) cravate *f*; SP (*even result*) match *m* à égalité; ***he doesn't have any ~s*** il n'a aucune attache **2** *v/t laces* nouer; *knot* faire; *hands* lier **3** *v/i* SP *of teams* faire match nul; *of runner* finir ex æquo
◆ **tie down** attacher; *fig* (*restrict*) restreindre
◆ **tie up** *hair* attacher; *person* ligoter; *boat* amarrer
tier [tɪr] *of hierarchy* niveau *m*; *of seats* gradin *m*
tight [taɪt] **1** *adj clothes, knot, screw* serré; *shoes* trop petit; (*properly shut*) bien fermé; *not leaving much time* juste; *security* strict; F (*drunk*) bourré F **2** *adv hold* fort; *shut* bien; **tighten** *control, security* renforcer; *screw* serrer; (*make tighter*) resserrer; **tight-fisted** radin; **tightly** *adv* → ***tight*** *adv*; **tightrope** corde *f* raide; **tights** *Br* collant *m*
tile [taɪl] *on floor, wall* carreau *m*; *on roof* tuile *f*
till[1] [tɪl] → ***until***
till[2] [tɪl] (*cash register*) caisse *f*
tilt [tɪlt] pencher
timber ['tɪmbər] bois *m*
time [taɪm] **1** *n* temps *m*; (*occasion*) fois *f*; ***have a good ~*** bien s'amuser; ***what's the ~?*** quelle heure est-il?; ***the first ~*** la première fois; ***all the ~*** pendant tout ce temps; ***at the same ~*** *speak, reply etc*, (*however*) en même temps; ***in ~*** à temps; ***on ~*** à l'heure **2** *v/t* chronométrer; **time bomb** bombe *f* à retardement; **time difference** décalage *m* horaire; **time-lag** laps *m* de temps; **time limit** limite *f* dans le temps; **timely** opportun; **time out** SP temps *m* mort; **timer** *device* minuteur *m*; **timesaving** économie *f* de temps; **timescale** *of project* durée *f*; **time switch** minuterie *f*; **time zone** fuseau *m* horaire
timid ['tɪmɪd] timide
tin [tɪn] *metal* étain *m*; **tinfoil** papier *m* aluminium
tinge [tɪndʒ] soupçon *m*

tingle ['tɪŋgl] picoter
tinkle ['tɪŋkl] *of bell* tintement *m*
tinsel ['tɪnsl] guirlandes *fpl* de Noël
tint [tɪnt] **1** *n of color* teinte *f*; *for hair* couleur *f* **2** *v/t*: **~ one's hair** se faire une coloration; **tinted** *glasses* teinté; *paper* de couleur pastel
tiny ['taɪnɪ] minuscule
tip[1] [tɪp] *n* (*end*) bout *m*
tip[2] [tɪp] **1** *n advice* conseil *m*; *money* pourboire *m* **2** *v/t waiter etc* donner un pourboire à
◆ **tip off** informer
'tip-off renseignement *m*, tuyau *m* F
tipped [tɪpt] *cigarettes* à bout filtre
tippy-toe ['tɪpɪtoʊ]: **on ~** sur la pointe des pieds
tipsy ['tɪpsɪ] éméché
tire[1] ['taɪr] *n* pneu *m*
tire[2] ['taɪr] **1** *v/t* fatiguer **2** *v/i* se fatiguer
tired ['taɪrd] fatigué; **tiredness** fatigue *f*; **tireless** *efforts* infatigable; **tiresome** (*annoying*) fatigant; **tiring** fatigant
tissue ['tɪʃuː] ANAT tissu *m*; *handkerchief* mouchoir *m* en papier; **tissue paper** papier *m* de soie
title ['taɪtl] *of novel, person etc* titre *m*; LAW titre *m* de propriét é (**to** de); **titleholder** SP tenant(e) *m*(*f*) du titre
to [tuː] **1** *prep* à; **~ Japan** au Japon; **~ Chicago** à Chicago; **~ my place** chez moi; **~ the north of** au nord de; **give sth ~ s.o.** donner qch à qn **2** *with verbs*: **~ speak, ~ shout** parler, crier; **learn ~ drive** apprendre à conduire; **too heavy ~ carry** trop lourd à porter **3** *adv*: **~ and fro** *walk, pace* de long en large
toast [toʊst] **1** *n for eating* pain *m* grillé; *when drinking* toast *m*; **propose a ~ to s.o.** porter un toast à qn **2** *v/t when drinking* porter un toast à
toaster grille-pain *m inv*
tobacco [tə'bækoʊ] tabac *m*
today [tə'deɪ] aujourd'hui
toddler ['tɑːdlər] jeune enfant *m*
to-do [tə'duː] F remue-ménage *m*
toe [toʊ] orteil *m*; *of sock, shoe* bout *m*; **toenail** ongle *m* de pied
together [tə'geðər] ensemble; (*at the same time*) en même temps
toilet ['tɔɪlɪt] toilettes *fpl*; **toilet paper** papier *m* hygiénique; **toiletries** articles *mpl* de toilette
token ['toʊkən] *sign* témoignage *m*; *Br* (*gift* **~**) bon *m* d'achat; *instead of coin* jeton *m*
tolerable ['tɑːlərəbl] *pain etc* tolérable; (*quite good*) ac-

ceptable; **tolerance** tolérance *f*; **tolerant** tolérant; **tolerate** tolérer
toll[1] [toʊl] *v/i of bell* sonner
toll[2] [toʊl] *n* (*deaths*) bilan *m*
toll[3] [toʊl] *n for bridge, road* péage *m*
'toll booth poste *m* de péage; **toll-free** TELEC gratuit; **~ *number*** numéro *m* vert
tomato [tə'meɪtoʊ] tomate *f*; **tomato ketchup** ketchup *m*
tomb [tu:m] tombe *f*; **tombstone** pierre *f* tombale
tomcat ['tɑ:mkæt] matou *m*
tomorrow [tə'mɔ:roʊ] demain; ***the day after ~*** après-demain; **~ *morning*** demain matin
ton [tʌn] tonne *f* courte (*=907 kg*)
tone [toʊn] *of color, conversation* ton *m*; *of musical instrument* timbre *m*; *of neighborhood* classe *f*; **~ *of voice*** ton *m*; **toner** toner *m*
tongue [tʌŋ] langue *f*
tonic ['tɑ:nɪk] MED fortifiant *m*; **tonic (water)** Schweppes® *m*, tonic *m*
tonight [tə'naɪt] ce soir; *sleep* cette nuit
too [tu:] (*also*) aussi; (*excessively*) trop; ***me ~*** moi aussi; **~ *much rice*** trop de riz
tool [tu:l] outil *m*
tooth [tu:θ] dent *f*; **toothache** mal *m* de dents; **toothbrush** brosse *f* à dents; **toothpaste** dentifrice *m*; **toothpick** cure-dents *m*
top [tɑ:p] **1** *n also clothing* haut *m*; (*lid: of bottle etc*) bouchon *m*; *of pen* capuchon *m*; *of the class, league* premier(-ère) *m(f)*; MOT: *gear* quatrième *f*/cinquième *f*; ***on ~ of*** sur; ***be at the ~ of*** être en haut de; ***be at the ~ of*** *league* être premier de; ***get to the ~*** *of company, mountain etc* arriver au sommet **2** *adj branches* du haut; *floor* dernier; *player etc* meilleur; *speed* maximum; *note* le plus élevé; **~ *official*** haut fonctionnaire *m*
topic ['tɑ:pɪk] sujet *m*; **topical** d'actualité
topless ['tɑ:plɪs] aux seins nus; **topmost** *branch* le plus haut; *floor* dernier; **topping** *on pizza* garniture *f*
topple ['tɑ:pl] **1** *v/i* s'écrouler **2** *v/t government* renverser
top 'secret top secret *inv*
topsy-turvy [tɑ:psɪ'tɜ:rvɪ] sens dessus dessous
torment 1 ['tɔ:rment] *n* tourment *m* **2** [tɔ:r'ment] *v/t person, animal* harceler
tornado [tɔ:r'neɪdoʊ] tornade *f*
torpedo [tɔ:r'pi:doʊ] **1** *n* torpille *f* **2** *v/t also fig* torpiller
torrent ['tɑ:rənt] *also fig* torrent *m*
torture ['tɔ:rtʃər] **1** *n* torture *f* **2** *v/t* torturer
toss [tɑ:s] **1** *v/t ball* lancer;

rider désarçonner; *salad* remuer

total ['toʊtl] **1** *adj* total; *disaster* complet; *idiot* fini; ***he's a ~ stranger*** c'est un parfait inconnu **2** *n* total *m*; **totalitarian** totalitaire; **totally** totalement

totter ['tɑːtər] tituber

touch [tʌtʃ] **1** *n sense* toucher *m*; ***lose ~ with s.o.*** perdre contact avec qn; ***in ~*** SP en touche **2** *v/t also emotionally* toucher; *exhibits etc* toucher à **3** *v/i of two things* se toucher

◆ **touch down** *of airplane* atterrir; SP faire un touché-en-but

'**touchdown** *of airplane* atterrissage *m*; SP touché-en-but; **touching** touchant; **touchline** SP ligne *f* de touche; **touch screen** écran *m* tactile; **touchy** *person* susceptible

tough [tʌf] *person, material* résistant; *meat, question, exam, punishment* dur

tour [tʊr] **1** *n* visite *f*; *as part of package* circuit *m* (**of** dans); *of band etc* tournée *f* **2** *v/t area* visiter **3** *v/i of tourist* faire du tourisme; *of band* être en tournée; **tour guide** accompagnateur(-trice) *m(f)*; **tourism** tourisme; **tourist** touriste *m/f*; **tourist industry** industrie *f* touristique; **tourist information office** office *m* de tourisme

tournament ['tʊrnəmənt] tournoi *m*

'**tour operator** tour-opérateur *m*, voyagiste *m*

tow [toʊ] remorquer

◆ **tow away** *car* emmener à la fourrière

toward [tɔːrd] vers; *with attitude, feelings etc* envers

towel ['taʊəl] serviette *f*

tower ['taʊər] tour *f*

town [taʊn] ville *f*; **town center**, *Br* **town centre** centre-ville *m*; **town council** conseil *m* municipal; **town hall** hôtel *m* de ville

toxic ['tɑːksɪk] toxique; **toxin** toxine *f*

toy [tɔɪ] jouet *m*

trace [treɪs] **1** *n of substance* trace *f* **2** *v/t (find)* retrouver; *draw* tracer

track [træk] *path, (racecourse)* piste *f*; *motor racing* circuit *m*; *on record, CD* morceau *m*; RAIL voie *f* (ferrée); ***~ 10*** RAIL voie 10; ***keep ~ of sth*** suivre qch

◆ **track down** *person* retrouver; *criminal* dépister; *object* dénicher

tracksuit *Br* survêtement *m*

tractor ['træktər] tracteur *m*

trade [treɪd] **1** *n* commerce *m*; *(profession, craft)* métier *m* **2** *v/i (do business)* faire du commerce **3** *v/t (exchange)* échanger (***for*** contre); **trade fair** foire *f* commerciale;

trademark marque *f* de commerce; **trade mission** mission *f* commerciale; **trader** commerçant(e) *m(f)*
tradition [trə'dɪʃn] tradition *f*; **traditional** traditionnel; **traditionally** traditionnellement
traffic ['træfɪk] circulation *f*; *at airport, in drugs* trafic *m*
◆ **traffic in** *drugs* faire du trafic de
'**traffic circle** rond-point *m*; **traffic cop** F agent *m* de la circulation; **traffic jam** embouteillage *m*; **traffic light** feux *mpl* de signalisation; **traffic sign** panneau *m* de signalisation
tragedy ['trædʒədɪ] tragédie *f*; **tragic** tragique
trail [treɪl] **1** *n* (*path*) sentier *m*; *of blood* traînée *f* **2** *v/t* (*follow*) suivre à la trace; (*tow*) remorquer **3** *v/i* (*lag behind*) traîner; **trailer** *pulled by vehicle* remorque *f*; (*mobile home*) caravane *f*; *of movie* bande-annonce *f*
train[1] [treɪn] *n* train *m*
train[2] [treɪn] **1** *v/t* entraîner; *dog* dresser; *employee* former **2** *v/i of team, athlete* s'entraîner; *of teacher etc* faire sa formation
trainee stagiaire *m/f*; **trainer** SP entraîneur(-euse) *m(f)*; *of dog* dresseur(-euse) *m(f)*; **~s** *Br*: *shoes* tennis *mpl*; **training** *of new staff* formation *f*; SP entraînement *m*
'**train station** gare *f*
traitor ['treɪtər] traître *m*, traîtresse *f*
◆ **trample on** piétiner
trampoline ['træmpəliːn] trampoline *m*
tranquil ['træŋkwɪl] tranquille; **tranquility**, *Br* **tranquillity** tranquillité *f*; **tranquilizer**, *Br* **tranquillizer** tranquillisant *m*
transaction [træn'zækʃn] *of business* conduite *f*; *piece of business* transaction *f*
transatlantic [trænzət'læntɪk] transatlantique
transcript ['trænskrɪpt] transcription *f*
transfer 1 [træns'fɜːr] *v/t* transférer **2** [træns'fɜːr] *v/i when traveling* changer; *in job* être muté (*to* à) **3** ['trænsfɜːr] *n* transfert *m*; **transferable** *ticket* transférable; **transfer fee** *for sportsman* prix *m* de transfert
transform [træns'fɔːrm] transformer; **transformation** transformation *f*; **transformer** ELEC transformateur *m*
transfusion [træns'fjuːʒn] transfusion *f*
transit ['trænzɪt]: *in* **~** en transit; **transition** transition *f*; **transitional** de transition; **transit lounge** *at airport* salle *f* de transit; **transit pas-**

senger passager(-ère) *m(f)* en transit
translate [træns'leɪt] traduire; **translation** traduction *f*; **translator** traducteur(-trice) *m(f)*
transmission [trænz'mɪʃn] TV, AUT transmission *f*; **transmit** *news, program* diffuser; *disease* transmettre; **transmitter** RAD, TV émetteur *m*
transparency [træns'pærənsɪ] PHOT diapositive *f*; **transparent** transparent; (*obvious*) évident
transplant MED **1** ['trænsplænt] transplantation *n f*; *organ transplanted* transplant *m* **2** [træns'plænt] *v/t* transplanter
transport 1 ['trænspɔːrt] *n* transport *m* **2** [træn'spɔːrt] *v/t* transporter; **transportation** *of goods, people* transport *m*
transvestite [træns'vestaɪt] travesti *m*
trap [træp] **1** *n also fig* piège *m* **2** *v/t also fig* piéger; **trappings** *of power* signes extérieurs *mpl*
trash [træʃ] (*garbage*) ordures *fpl*; F *goods etc* camelote *f* F; *fig*: *person* vermine *f*; **trash can** poubelle *f*; **trashy** *goods* de pacotille; *novel* de bas étage
traumatic [traʊ'mætɪk] traumatisant; **traumatize** traumatiser
travel ['trævl] **1** *n* voyages *mpl* **2** *v/i* voyager **3** *v/t miles* parcourir; **travel agency** agence *f* de voyages; **travel agent** agent *m* de voyages; **traveler**, *Br* **traveller** voyageur(-euse) *m(f)*; **traveler's check**, *Br* **traveller's cheque** chèque-voyage *m*; **travel expenses** frais *mpl* de déplacement; **travel insurance** assurance-voyage *f*
trawler ['trɔːlər] chalutier *m*
tray [treɪ] *for food, photocopier* plateau *m*; *to go in oven* plaque *f*
treacherous ['tretʃərəs] traître; **treachery** traîtrise *f*
tread [tred] **1** *n* pas *m*; *of staircase* dessus *m* des marches; *of tire* bande *f* de roulement **2** *v/i* marcher
treason ['triːzn] trahison *f*
treasure ['treʒər] **1** *n* trésor *m* **2** *v/t gift etc* chérir; **treasurer** trésorier(-ière) *m(f)*; **Treasury Department** ministère *m* des Finances
treat [triːt] **1** *n* plaisir *m*; ***it's my ~*** (*I'm paying*) c'est moi qui paie **2** *v/t* traiter; ***~ s.o. to sth*** offrir qch à qn; **treatment** traitement *m*
treaty ['triːtɪ] traité *m*
treble ['trebl] **1** *adv*: ***~ the price*** le triple du prix **2** *v/i* tripler
tree [triː] arbre *m*
tremble ['trembl] trembler
tremendous [trɪ'mendəs]

(*very good*) formidable; (*enormous*) énorme; **tremendously** (*very*) extrêmement; (*a lot*) énormément
tremor ['tremər] *of earth* secousse *f* (sismique)
trench [trentʃ] tranchée *f*
trend [trend] tendance *f*; (*fashion*) mode *f*; **trendy** branché
trespass ['trespæs] entrer sans autorisation; ***no ~ing*** défense d'entrer; **trespasser** *personne qui viole la propriété d'une autre*
trial ['traɪəl] LAW procès *m*; *of equipment* essai *m*; ***be on ~*** LAW passer en justice
triangle ['traɪæŋgl] triangle *m*; **triangular** triangulaire
tribe [traɪb] tribu *f*
tribunal [traɪ'bju:nl] tribunal *m*
tributary ['trɪbjəterɪ] *of river* affluent *m*
trick [trɪk] **1** *n to deceive* tour *m*; (*knack*) truc *m* **2** *v/t* rouler; **trickery** tromperie *f*
trickle ['trɪkl] **1** *n* filet *m*; *fig* tout petit peu *m* **2** *v/i* couler goutte à goutte
tricky ['trɪkɪ] (*difficult*) délicat
trifling ['traɪflɪŋ] insignifiant
trigger ['trɪgər] *on gun* détente *f*
◆ **trigger off** déclencher
trim [trɪm] **1** *adj* (*neat*) bien entretenu; *figure* svelte **2** *v/t hair* couper un peu; *hedge* tailler; *costs* réduire; (*decorate: dress*) garnir **3** *n cut* taille *f*
trinket ['trɪŋkɪt] babiole *f*
trip [trɪp] **1** *n* (*journey*) voyage *m*; (*outing*) excursion *f* **2** *v/i* (*stumble*) trébucher **3** *v/t* (*make fall*) faire un croche-pied à
◆ **trip up 1** *v/t* (*make fall*) faire un croche-pied à; (*cause to go wrong*) faire trébucher **2** *v/i* (*stumble*) trébucher; (*make a mistake*) faire une erreur
triple ['trɪpl] → ***treble***
trite [traɪt] banal
triumph ['traɪʌmf] triomphe *m*
trivial ['trɪvɪəl] insignifiant; **triviality** banalité *f*
trolley ['trɑ:lɪ] (*streetcar*) tramway *m*
troops [tru:ps] troupes *fpl*
trophy ['troʊfɪ] trophée *m*
tropic ['trɑ:pɪk] GEOG tropique *m*; **tropical** tropical; **tropics** tropiques *mpl*
trot [trɑ:t] trotter
trouble ['trʌbl] **1** *n* (*difficulties*) problèmes *mpl*; (*inconvenience*) dérangement *m*; (*disturbance*) affrontements *mpl*; ***get into ~*** s'attirer des ennuis **2** *v/t* (*worry*) inquiéter; (*bother, disturb*) déranger; *of back, liver etc* faire souffrir; **troublemaker** fauteur(-trice) *m*(*f*) de troubles; **troubleshooting** dépannage *m*; **troublesome** pénible

trousers ['traʊzərz] *Br* pantalon *m*
trout [traʊt] truite *f*
truant ['tru:ənt]: ***play ~*** faire l'école buissonnière
truce [tru:s] trêve *f*
truck [trʌk] camion *m*; **truck driver** camionneur(-euse) *m(f)*; **truck stop** routier *m*
trudge [trʌdʒ] **1** *v/i* se traîner **2** *n* marche *f* pénible
true [tru:] vrai; *friend, American* véritable; ***come ~*** *of hopes, dream* se réaliser; **truly** vraiment; ***Yours ~*** je vous prie d'agréer mes sentiments distingués
trumpet ['trʌmpɪt] trompette *f*
trunk [trʌŋk] *of tree, body* tronc *m*; *of elephant* trompe *f*; (*large suitcase*) malle *f*; *of car* coffre *m*
trust [trʌst] **1** *n* confiance *f*; FIN fidéicommis *m* **2** *v/t* faire confiance à; **trusted** éprouvé; **trustee** fidéicommissaire *m/f*; **trustful, trusting** confiant; **trustworthy** fiable
truth [tru:θ] vérité *f*; **truthful** honnête
try [traɪ] **1** *v/t & v/i* essayer; LAW juger; ***~ to do sth*** essayer de faire qch; ***you must ~ harder*** tu dois faire plus d'efforts **2** *n rugby* essai *m*; **trying** (*annoying*) éprouvant
T-shirt ['ti:ʃɜ:rt] tee-shirt *m*
tub [tʌb] (*bath*) baignoire *f for liquid* bac *m*; *for yoghurt* pot *m*; **tubby** boulot
tube [tu:b] (*pipe*) tuyau *m*; *of toothpaste* tube *m*; **tubeless** *tire* sans chambre à air
Tuesday ['tu:zdeɪ] mardi *m*
tuft [tʌft] touffe *f*
tug [tʌg] **1** *n* NAUT remorqueur *m* **2** *v/t* tirer
tuition [tu:'ɪʃn] cours *mpl*
tumble ['tʌmbl] tomber; **tumbledown** qui tombe en ruines; **tumbler** *for drink* verre *m*; *in circus* acrobate *m/f*
tummy ['tʌmɪ] F ventre *m*; **tummy ache** mal *m* de ventre
tumor, *Br* **tumour** tumeur *f*
tumult ['tu:mʌlt] tumulte *m*; **tumultuous** tumultueux
tuna ['tu:nə] thon *m*
tune [tu:n] **1** *n* air *m* **2** *v/t instrument* accorder
◆ **tune up 1** *v/i of orchestra* s'accorder **2** *v/t engine* régler
tuneful ['tu:nfl] harmonieux; **tune-up** *of engine* règlement *m*
tunnel ['tʌnl] tunnel *m*
turbine ['tɜ:rbaɪn] turbine *f*
turbulence ['tɜ:rbjələns] *in air travel* turbulences *fpl*; **turbulent** agité
turf [tɜ:rf] gazon *m*; *piece* motte *f* de gazon
turkey ['tɜ:rkɪ] dinde *f*
turmoil ['tɜ:rmɔɪl] confusion *f*
turn [tɜ:rn] **1** *n* (*rotation*) tour *m*; *in road* virage *m*; *in vaudeville* numéro *m*; ***take ~s doing sth*** faire qch à tour

de rôle; ***it's my~*** c'est à moi **2** *v/t wheel* tourner; **~ *the corner*** tourner au coin de la rue **3** *v/i of driver, car, wheel* tourner; *of person* se retourner; ***it has ~ed cold*** le temps s'est refroidi

◆ **turn around 1** *v/t object* tourner; *company* remettre sur pied; COM *order* traiter **2** *v/i* se retourner; *with a car* faire demi-tour

◆ **turn away 1** *v/t* (*send away*) renvoyer **2** *v/i* (*walk away*) s'en aller; (*look away*) détourner le regard

◆ **turn back 1** *v/t edges, sheets* replier **2** *v/i of walkers, in course of action* faire demi-tour

◆ **turn down** *offer* rejeter; *volume, heating* baisser; *edge* replier

◆ **turn off 1** *v/t TV, heater* éteindre; *faucet* fermer; *engine* arrêter **2** *v/i of car, driver* tourner; *of machine* s'éteindre

◆ **turn on 1** *v/t TV, heater* allumer; *faucet* ouvrir; *engine* mettre en marche; F *sexually* exciter **2** *v/i of machine* s'allumer

◆ **turn over 1** *v/i in bed* se retourner; *of vehicle* se renverser **2** *v/t* (*put upside down*) renverser; *page* tourner; FIN avoir un chiffre d'affaires de

◆ **turn up 1** *v/t collar* remonter; *volume* augmenter; *heating* monter **2** *v/i* (*arrive*) arriver, se pointer F

turning ['tɜːrnɪŋ] *in road* virage; **turning point** tournant *m*; **turnout** *at game etc* nombre *m* de spectateurs; **turnover** FIN chiffre *m* d'affaires; **turnpike** autoroute *f* payante; **turn signal** MOT clignotant *m*

turquoise ['tɜːrkwɔɪz] turquoise

turtle ['tɜːrtl] tortue *f* de mer; **turtleneck sweater** pull *m* à col cheminée

tusk [tʌsk] défense *f*

tutor ['tuːtər] *Br*: *at university* professeur *m/f*; (***private***) **~** professeur *m* particulier

tuxedo [tʌk'siːdou] smoking *m*

TV [tiː'viː] télé *f*; ***on ~*** à la télé; **TV dinner** plateau-repas *m*; **TV guide** guide *m* de télé; **TV program**, *Br* **TV programme** programme *m* télé

twang [twæŋ] **1** *n in voice* accent *m* nasillard **2** *v/t guitar string* pincer

tweezers ['twiːzərz] pince *f* à épiler

twelfth [twelfθ] douzième; **twelve** douze

twentieth ['twentɪɪθ] vingtième; **twenty** vingt

twice [twaɪs] deux fois; **~ *as much*** deux fois plus

twig [twɪg] brindille *f*

twilight ['twaɪlaɪt] crépuscule *m*

twin [twɪn] jumeau *m*, jumelle *f*; **twin beds** lits *mpl* jumeaux
twinge [twɪndʒ] *of pain* élancement *m*
twinkle ['twɪŋkl] scintiller
'twin room chambre *f* à lits jumeaux
twirl [twɜːrl] **1** *v/t* faire tourbillonner; *mustache* tortiller **2** *n of cream etc* spirale *f*
twist [twɪst] **1** *v/t* tordre; **~ *one's ankle*** se tordre la cheville **2** *v/i of road* faire des méandres; *of river* faire des lacets **3** *n in rope* entortillement *m*; *in road* lacet *m*; *in plot* dénouement *m* inattendu; **twisty** *road* qui fait des lacets
twitch [twɪtʃ] *nervous* tic *m*
twitter ['twɪtər] *of birds* gazouiller
two [tuː] deux; ***the ~ of them*** les deux
tycoon [taɪ'kuːn] magnat *m*
type [taɪp] **1** *n* (*sort*) type *m* **2** *v/i* (*use a keyboard*) taper **3** *v/t with a typewriter* taper à la machine
typhoon [taɪ'fuːn] typhon *m*
typhus ['taɪfəs] typhus *m*
typical ['tɪpɪkl] typique; ***that's ~ of you!*** c'est bien de vous!; **typically** typiquement
typist ['taɪpɪst] dactylo *m/f*
tyrannical [tɪ'rænɪkl] tyrannique; **tyrannize** tyranniser; **tyranny** tyrannie *f*; **tyrant** tyran *m*
tyre *Br* → ***tire***[1]

U

ugly ['ʌglɪ] laid
UK [juː'keɪ] (= ***United Kingdom***) R.-U. *m* (= Royaume-Uni)
ulcer ['ʌlsər] ulcère *m*
ultimate ['ʌltɪmət] (*best, definitive*) meilleur possible; (*final*) final; (*fundamental*) fondamental; **ultimately** (*in the end*) en fin de compte
ultimatum [ʌltɪ'meɪtəm] ultimatum *m*
ultrasound ['ʌltrəsaund] MED ultrason *m*
ultraviolet [ʌltrə'vaɪələt] ultraviolet
umbrella [ʌm'brelə] parapluie *m*
umpire ['ʌmpaɪr] arbitre *m/f*
UN [juː'en] (= ***United Nations***) O.N.U. *f* (= Organisation des Nations unies)
unable [ʌn'eɪbl]: ***be ~ to do sth*** *not know how to* ne pas savoir faire qch; *not be in a position to* ne pas pouvoir faire qch
unacceptable [ʌnək'septəbl] inacceptable
unaccountable [ʌnə-

'kaʊntəbl] inexplicable
un-American [ʌnə'merɪkən] (*not fitting*) antiaméricain
unanimous [juː'nænɪməs] *verdict* unanime; **unanimously** à l'unanimité
unapproachable [ʌnə'proʊʧəbl] *person* d'un abord difficile
unarmed [ʌn'ɑːrmd] *person* non armé
unassuming [ʌnə'suːmɪŋ] modeste
unattached [ʌnə'tæʧt] *without a partner* sans attaches
unattended [ʌnə'tendɪd] laissé sans surveillance
unauthorized [ʌn'ɒːθəraɪzd] non autorisé
unavoidable [ʌnə'vɔɪdəbl] inévitable
unbalanced [ʌn'bælənst] *also* PSYCH déséquilibré
unbearable [ʌn'berəbl] insupportable
unbeatable [ʌn'biːtəbl] imbattable
unbeaten [ʌn'biːtn] *team* invaincu
unbelievable [ʌnbɪ'liːvəbl] *also* F incroyable
unbias(s)ed [ʌn'baɪəst] impartial
unblock [ʌn'blɑːk] *pipe* déboucher
unbreakable [ʌn'breɪkəbl] incassable
unbutton [ʌn'bʌtn] déboutonner
uncanny [ʌn'kænɪ] étrange, mystérieux
unceasing [ʌn'siːsɪŋ] incessant
uncertain [ʌn'sɜːrtn] incertain; **uncertainty** *of the future* caractère *m* incertain; ***there is still ~ about*** des incertitudes demeurent quant à …
uncle ['ʌŋkl] oncle *m*
uncomfortable [ʌn'kʌmftəbl] inconfortable
uncommon [ʌn'kɑːmən] inhabituel
uncompromising [ʌn'kɑːmprəmaɪzɪŋ] intransigeant
unconditional [ʌnkən'dɪʃnl] sans conditions
unconscious [ʌn'kɑːnʃəs] MED, PSYCH inconscient
uncontrollable [ʌnkən'troʊləbl] incontrôlable
unconventional [ʌnkən'venʃnl] non conventionnel
uncooperative [ʌnkoʊ'ɑːpərətɪv] peu coopératif
uncover [ʌn'kʌvər] découvrir
undamaged [ʌn'dæmɪdʒd] intact
undecided [ʌndɪ'saɪdɪd] *question* laissé en suspens; ***be ~ about*** être indécis à propos de
undeniable [ʌndɪ'naɪəbl] indéniable
under ['ʌndər] sous; (*less than*) moins de; ***it is ~ investigation*** cela fait l'objet d'une enquête

'undercarriage train *m* d'atterrissage
'undercover clandestin; **~ agent** agent *m* secret
under'cut COM: **~ *the competition*** vendre moins cher que la concurrence
under'done *meat* pas trop cuit; *pej* pas assez cuit
under'estimate sous-estimer
under'fed mal nourri
under'go subir
under'graduate *Br* étudiant(e) (de D.E.U.G. ou de licence)
'underground 1 *adj* souterrain; POL clandestin **2** *adv work* sous terre
under'hand (*devious*) sournois
under'line *text* souligner
under'lying sous-jacent
under'mine saper
underneath [ʌndər'ni:θ] **1** *prep* sous **2** *adv* dessous
'underpants slip *m*
'underpass *for pedestrians* passage *m* souterrain
underprivileged [ʌndər'prɪvɪlɪdʒd] défavorisé
under'rate sous-estimer
understaffed [ʌndər'stæft] en manque de personnel
under'stand comprendre; **understandable** compréhensible; **understandably** naturellement; **understanding 1** *adj person* compréhensif **2** *n* compréhension *f*; (*agreement*) accord *m*
under'take *task* entreprendre; **~ *to do sth*** (*agree to*) s'engager à faire qch; **undertaking** (*enterprise*) entreprise *f*; (*promise*) engagement *m*
under'value sous-estimer
'underwear sous-vêtements *mpl*
'underworld *criminal* monde *m* du crime organisé
under'write FIN souscrire
undeserved [ʌndɪ'zɜ:rvd] non mérité
undesirable [ʌndɪ'zaɪrəbl] indésirable
undisputed [ʌndɪ'spju:tɪd] *champion* incontestable
undo [ʌn'du:] défaire
undoubtedly [ʌn'dautɪdlɪ] à n'en pas douter
undress [ʌn'dres] **1** *v/t* déshabiller; ***get ~ed*** se déshabiller **2** *v/i* se déshabiller
undue [ʌn'du:] excessif; **unduly** (*excessively*) excessivement
unearth [ʌn'ɜ:rθ] *also fig* déterrer
uneasy [ʌn'i:zɪ] *relationship, peace* incertain vouloir signer cela
uneatable [ʌn'i:təbl] immangeable
uneconomic [ʌni:kə'nɑ:mɪk] pas rentable
uneducated [ʌn'edʒəkeɪtɪd] sans instruction
unemployed [ʌnɪm'plɔɪd] **1** *adj* au chômage **2** *npl*: ***the***

~ les chômeurs(-euses); **unemployment** chômage *m*
unequal [ʌn'iːkwəl] inégal
unerring [ʌn'ɜːrɪŋ] *judgment, instinct* infaillible
uneven [ʌn'iːvn] *surface, ground* irrégulier
uneventful [ʌnɪ'ventfl] *day, journey* sans événement
unexpected [ʌnɪk'spektɪd] inattendu; **unexpectedly** inopinément
unfair [ʌn'fer] injuste
unfaithful [ʌn'feɪθfl] *husband, wife* infidèle; ***be ~ to s.o.*** tromper qn
unfamiliar [ʌnfə'mɪljər] peu familier
unfasten [ʌn'fæsn] *belt* défaire
unfavorable [ʌn'feɪvərəbl] défavorable
unfinished [ʌn'fɪnɪʃt] inachevé
unfold [ʌn'foʊld] **1** *v/t letter* déplier; *arms* ouvrir **2** *v/i of story etc* se dérouler; *of view* se déployer
unforeseen [ʌnfɔːr'siːn] imprévu
unforgettable [ʌnfər'getəbl] inoubliable
unforgivable [ʌnfər'gɪvəbl] impardonnable
unfortunate [ʌn'fɔːrtʃənət] malheureux; **unfortunately** malheureusement
unfounded [ʌn'faʊndɪd] non fondé
unfriendly [ʌn'frendlɪ] *person, welcome, hotel* froid
ungrateful [ʌn'greɪtfl] ingrat
unhappiness [ʌn'hæpɪnɪs] chagrin *m*; **unhappy** malheureux; *customers etc* mécontent (***with*** de)
unharmed [ʌn'hɑːrmd] indemne
unhealthy [ʌn'helθɪ] *person* en mauvaise santé; *food, atmosphere* malsain; *economy* qui se porte mal
unheard-of [ʌn'hɜːrdəv]: ***be ~*** ne s'être jamais vu
unhygienic [ʌnhaɪ'dʒiːnɪk] insalubre
unification [juːnɪfɪ'keɪʃn] unification *f*
uniform ['juːnɪfɔːrm] **1** *n* uniforme *m* **2** *adj* uniforme
unify ['juːnɪfaɪ] unifier
unilateral [juːnɪ'lætərəl] unilatéral
unimaginable [ʌnɪ'mædʒɪnəbl] inimaginable
unimaginative [ʌnɪ'mædʒɪnətɪv] qui manque d'imagination
unimportant [ʌnɪm'pɔːrtənt] sans importance
uninhabitable [ʌnɪn'hæbɪtəbl] inhabitable; **uninhabited** inhabitée
unintentional [ʌnɪn'tenʃnl] non intentionnel; **unintentionally** sans le vouloir
uninteresting [ʌn'ɪntrəstɪŋ] inintéressant
uninterrupted [ʌnɪntə'rʌptɪd] ininterrompu

union ['juːnjən] POL union *f*; (*labor* ~) syndicat *m*
unique [juː'niːk] unique
unit ['juːnɪt] unité *f*
unite [juː'naɪt] **1** *v/t* unir **2** *v/i* s'unir; **united** uni; *efforts* conjoint; **United Kingdom** Royaume-Uni *m*; **United Nations** Nations *fpl* Unies
United States (of A'merica) États-Unis *mpl* (d'Amérique)
unity ['juːnətɪ] unité *f*
universal [juːnɪ'vɜːrsl] universel; **universe** univers *m*
university [juːnɪ'vɜːrsətɪ] université *f*
unjust [ʌn'dʒʌst] injuste
unkind [ʌn'kaɪnd] méchant, désagréable
unknown [ʌn'noʊn] inconnu
unleaded [ʌn'ledɪd] *gas* sans plomb
unless [ən'les] à moins que (+*subj*)
unlikely [ʌn'laɪklɪ] improbable
unlimited [ʌn'lɪmɪtɪd] illimité
unload [ʌn'loʊd] décharger
unlock [ʌn'lɑːk] ouvrir
unluckily [ʌn'lʌkɪlɪ] malheureusement; **unlucky** *day* de malchance; *choice* malheureux; *person* malchanceux; ***that was so ~ for you!*** tu n'as vraiment pas eu de chance!
unmanned [ʌn'mænd] *spacecraft* sans équipage
unmarried [ʌn'mærɪd] non marié
unmistakable [ʌnmɪ'steɪkəbl] reconnaissable entre mille
unnatural [ʌn'nætʃrəl] contre-nature
unnecessary [ʌn'nesəserɪ] non nécessaire
unnerving [ʌn'nɜːrvɪŋ] déstabilisant
unobtainable [ʌnəb'teɪnəbl] *goods* qu'on ne peut se procurer; TELEC hors service
unobtrusive [ʌnəb'truːsɪv] discret
unoccupied [ʌn'ɑːkjʊpaɪd] (*empty*) vide; *position* vacant; *person* désœuvré
unofficial [ʌnə'fɪʃl] non officiel; **unofficially** non officiellement
unorthodox [ʌn'ɔːrθədɑːks] peu orthodoxe
unpack [ʌn'pæk] **1** *v/t case* défaire **2** *v/i* défaire sa valise
unpaid [ʌn'peɪd] *work* non rémunéré
unpleasant [ʌn'pleznt] désagréable
unplug [ʌn'plʌg] *TV, computer* débrancher
unpopular [ʌn'pɑːpjələr] impopulaire
unprecedented [ʌn'presɪdentɪd] sans précédent
unpredictable [ʌnprɪ'dɪktəbl] imprévisible
unpretentious [ʌnprɪ'tenʃəs] modeste
unproductive [ʌnprə'dʌktɪv]

meeting, discussion, land improductif
unprofessional [ʌnprəˈfeʃnl] non professionnel; *workmanship* peu professionnel
unprofitable [ʌnˈprɑːfɪtəbl] non profitable
unprovoked [ʌnprəˈvoʊkt] *attack* non provoqué
unqualified [ʌnˈkwɑːlɪfaɪd] non qualifié
unquestionably [ʌnˈkwesʧnəblɪ] sans aucun doute; **unquestioning** *attitude* aveugle
unreadable [ʌnˈriːdəbl] *book* illisible
unrealistic [ʌnrɪəˈlɪstɪk] irréaliste
unreasonable [ʌnˈriːznəbl] déraisonnable
unrelated [ʌnrɪˈleɪtɪd] sans relation (***to*** avec)
unrelenting [ʌnrɪˈlentɪŋ] incessant
unreliable [ʌnrɪˈlaɪəbl] pas fiable
unrest [ʌnˈrest] agitation *f*
unrestrained [ʌnrɪˈstreɪnd] *emotions* non contenu
unroll [ʌnˈroʊl] *carpet* dérouler
unruly [ʌnˈruːlɪ] indiscipliné
unsanitary [ʌnˈsænɪterɪ] *conditions, drains* insalubre
unsatisfactory [ʌnsætɪsˈfæktərɪ] insatisfaisant; (*unacceptable*) inacceptable
unscathed [ʌnˈskeɪðd] (*not injured*) indemne; (*not damaged*) intact
unscrew [ʌnˈskruː] *sth screwed on* dévisser; *top* décapsuler
unscrupulous [ʌnˈskruːpjələs] peu scrupuleux
unselfish [ʌnˈselfɪʃ] désintéressé
unsettled [ʌnˈsetld] incertain; *lifestyle* instable; *bills* non réglé; *issue* non décidé
unshaven [ʌnˈʃeɪvn] mal rasé
unskilled [ʌnˈskɪld] *worker* non qualifié
unsophisticated [ʌnsəˈfɪstɪkeɪtɪd] peu sophistiqué
unstable [ʌnˈsteɪbl] instable
unsteady [ʌnˈstedɪ] *on feet* chancelant; *ladder* branlant
unsuccessful [ʌnsəkˈsesfl] *attempt* infructueux; *writer* qui n'a pas de succès; *candidate, marriage* malheureux; **unsuccessfully** sans succès
unsuitable [ʌnˈsuːtəbl] inapproprié
unswerving [ʌnˈswɜːrvɪŋ] *loyalty* inébranlable
unthinkable [ʌnˈθɪŋkəbl] impensable
untidy [ʌnˈtaɪdɪ] en désordre
untie [ʌnˈtaɪ] *knot* défaire; *prisoner, hands* détacher
until [ənˈtɪl] **1** *prep* jusqu'à; ***from Monday ~ Friday*** de lundi à vendredi; ***not ~ Friday*** pas avant vendredi **2** *conj* jusqu'à ce que; ***can you wait ~ I'm ready?*** est-ce que vous pouvez attendre

que je sois prêt?
untiring [ʌn'taɪrɪŋ] *efforts* infatigable
untold [ʌn'tould] *riches, suffering* inouï; *story* inédit
untrue [ʌn'truː] faux
unused [ʌn'juːzd] *goods* non utilisé
unusual [ʌn'juːʒl] inhabituel; (*strange*) bizarre; **unusually** anormalement, exceptionnellement
unveil [ʌn'veɪl] *statue etc* dévoiler
unwell [ʌn'wel] malade
unwilling [ʌn'wɪlɪŋ]: ***be ~ to do*** refuser de faire; **unwillingly** à contre-cœur
unwind [ʌn'waɪnd] **1** *v/t tape* dérouler **2** *v/i of tape, story* se dérouler; (*relax*) se détendre
unwise [ʌn'waɪz] malavisé
unwrap [ʌn'ræp] déballer
unzip [ʌn'zɪp] *dress etc* descendre la fermeture-éclair de; COMPUT décompresser
up [ʌp] **1** *adv*: ***~ in the sky/on the roof*** dans le ciel/sur le toit; ***~ here*** ici; ***~ there*** là-haut; ***be ~*** (*out of bed*) être debout; *of sun* être levé; *of temperature* avoir augmenté; (*have expired*) être expiré; ***what's ~?*** F qu'est-ce qu'il y a?; ***~ to 1989*** jusqu'à 1989; ***he came ~ to me*** il s'est approché de moi; ***what are you ~ to these days?*** qu'est-ce que tu fais en ce moment?; ***be ~ to something*** (***bad***) être sur un mauvais coup; ***I don't feel ~ to it*** je ne m'en sens pas le courage; ***it's ~ to you*** c'est toi qui décides; ***it's ~ to them to solve it*** c'est à eux de le résoudre **2** *prep*: ***further ~ the mountain*** un peu plus haut sur la montagne; ***they ran ~ the street*** ils ont remonté la rue en courant; ***we traveled ~ to Paris*** nous sommes montés à Paris **3** *n*: ***~s and downs*** hauts *mpl* et bas
'upbringing éducation *f*
up'date *file* mettre à jour
up'grade moderniser; *ticket* surclasser
upheaval [ʌp'hiːvl] bouleversement *m*
up'hold *rights* maintenir
'upkeep maintien *m*
'upload COMPUT transférer
up'market *Br restaurant, hotel* chic; *product* haut de gamme
upon [ə'pɑːn] → ***on***
upper ['ʌpər] supérieur
'upright 1 *adj citizen* droit **2** *adv sit* (bien) droit; **upright piano** piano *f* droit
'uprising soulèvement *m*
'uproar vacarme *m*; *fig* protestations *fpl*
up'set 1 *v/t* renverser; *emotionally* contrarier **2** *adj emotionally* contrarié, vexé; **upsetting** contrariant
upside 'down à l'envers; *car* renversé

up'stairs 1 *adv* en haut; **~** ***from us*** au-dessus de chez nous **2** *adj room* d'en haut
up'stream en remontant le courant
up'tight F (*nervous*) tendu; (*inhibited*) coincé
up-to-'date à jour
'upturn *in economy* reprise *f*
upward ['ʌpwərd]: ***move sth ~*** élever qch; **~** ***of 100*** au-delà de 100
uranium [jʊ'reɪnɪəm] uranium *m*
urban ['ɜːrbən] urbain
urge [ɜːrdʒ] **1** *n* (forte) envie *f* **2** *v/t*: **~** ***s.o. to do sth*** encourager qn à faire qch; **urgency** urgence *f*; **urgent** urgent
urinate ['jʊrəneɪt] uriner; **urine** urine *f*
US [juː'es] (= ***United States***) USA *mpl*
us [ʌs] nous
USA [juːes'eɪ] (= ***United States of America***) USA *mpl*
usage ['juːzɪdʒ] usage *m*
use 1 [juːz] *v/t also pej: person* utiliser **2** [juːs] *n* utilisation *f*; ***it's no ~ waiting*** ce n'est pas la peine d'attendre
◆ **use up** épuiser
used[1] [juːzd] *car etc* d'occasion
used[2] [juːst]: ***be ~ to*** être habitué à; ***get ~ to*** s'habituer à
used[3] [juːst]: ***I ~ to work there*** je travaillais là-bas avant; ***I ~ to know him well*** je l'ai bien connu autrefois
useful ['juːsfʊl] utile; **usefulness** utilité *f*; **useless** inutile; F (*no good*) nul F; **user** *of product* utilisateur(-trice) *m(f)*; **user-friendly** facile à utiliser; COMPUT convivial
usual ['juːʒl] habituel; ***as ~*** comme d'habitude; **usually** d'habitude
utensil [juː'tensl] ustensile *m*
utilize ['juːtɪlaɪz] utiliser
utter ['ʌtər] **1** *adj* total **2** *v/t sound* prononcer; **utterly** totalement

V

vacant ['veɪkənt] *building* inoccupé; *look* vide, absent; *Br: position* vacant; **vacantly** *stare* d'un air absent; **vacate** *room* libérer
vacation [veɪ'keɪʃn] vacances *fpl*; ***be on ~*** être en vacances
vaccinate ['væksɪneɪt] vacciner; **vaccination** vaccination *f*; **vaccine** vaccin *m*
vacuum ['vækjʊəm] **1** *n* vide *m* **2** *v/t floors* passer l'aspirateur sur
vagrant ['veɪgrənt] vagabond *m*
vague [veɪg] vague; **vaguely**

vaguement
vain [veɪn] **1** *adj person* vaniteux; *hope* vain **2** *n*: ***in ~*** en vain
valiant ['væljənt] vaillant
valid ['vælɪd] valable; **validate** *with official stamp* valider; *theory* confirmer; **validity** validité *f*; *of argument* justesse *f*; *of claim* bien-fondé *m*
valley ['vælɪ] vallée *f*
valuable ['væljʊbl] **1** *adj* de valeur; *colleague, help, advice* précieux **2** *npl*: ***~s*** objets *mpl* de valeur; **valuation** estimation *f*, expertise *f*; **value** **1** *n* valeur *f* **2** *v/t* tenir à, attacher un grand prix à
valve [vælv] soupape *f*, valve *f*; *in heart* valvule *f*
van [væn] *small* camionnette *f*; *large* fourgon *m*
vandal ['vændl] vandale *m*; **vandalism** vandalisme *m*; **vandalize** vandaliser
vanilla [və'nɪlə] **1** *n* vanille *f* **2** *adj* à la vanille
vanish ['vænɪʃ] disparaître; *of clouds, sadness* se dissiper
vanity ['vænətɪ] *of person* vanité *f*
vapor ['veɪpər] vapeur *f*; **vaporize** *of atomic bomb, explosion* pulvériser; **vapour** *Br* → ***vapor***
variable ['verɪəbl] **1** *adj* variable; *moods* changeant **2** *n* MATH, COMPUT variable *f*; **variant** variante *f*; **variation** variation *f*; **varied** varié; **variety** variété *f*; **various** (*several*) divers, plusieurs; (*different*) divers, différent
varnish ['vɑːrnɪʃ] **1** *n* vernis *m* **2** *v/t* vernir
vary ['verɪ] varier; ***it varies*** ça dépend
vase [veɪz] vase *m*
vast [væst] vaste; *improvement* considérable; **vastly** *improve etc* considérablement; *different* complètement
Vatican ['vætɪkən]: ***the ~*** le Vatican
vault[1] [vɒːlt] *n in roof* voûte *f*; ***~s*** *of bank* salle *f* des coffres
vault[2] [vɒːlt] **1** *n* SP saut *m* **2** *v/t beam etc* sauter
VCR [viːsiː'ɑːr] (= ***video cassette recorder***) magnétoscope *m*
veal [viːl] veau *m*
veer [vɪr] virer; *of wind* tourner
vegetable ['vedʒtəbl] légume *m*; **vegetarian** **1** *n* végétarien(ne) *m(f)* **2** *adj* végétarien; **vegetation** végétation *f*
vehement ['viːəmənt] véhément
vehicle ['viːɪkl] véhicule *m*
veil [veɪl] voile *m*
vein [veɪn] ANAT veine *f*
velocity [vɪ'lɑːsətɪ] vélocité *f*
velvet ['velvɪt] velours *m*
vendetta [ven'detə] vendetta *f*
vending machine ['vendɪŋ]

distributeur *m* automatique; **vendor** LAW vendeur(-euse) *m(f)*
veneer [və'nɪr] placage *m*; *of politeness* vernis *m*
venerable ['venərəbl] vénérable; **veneration** vénération *f*
venereal disease [və'nɪrɪəl] M.S.T. *f*, maladie *f* sexuellement transmissible
venetian blind [və'niːʃn] store *m* vénitien
venom ['venəm] venin *m*
ventilate ['ventɪleɪt] ventiler; **ventilation** ventilation *f*; **ventilator** ventilateur *m*; MED respirateur *m*
venture ['ventʃər] **1** *n* (*undertaking*) entreprise *f*; COM tentative *f* **2** *v/i* s'aventurer
venue ['venjuː] *for meeting, concert etc* lieu *m*; *hall also* salle *f*
veranda [və'rændə] véranda *f*
verb [vɜːrb] verbe *m*; **verbal** (*spoken*) oral, verbal; **verbally** oralement, verbalement
verdict ['vɜːrdɪkt] LAW verdict *m*; (*opinion, judgment*) avis *m*, jugement *m*
verge [vɜːrdʒ] *of road* accotement *m*, bas-côté *m*; ***be on the ~ of …*** être au bord de…
verification [verɪfɪ'keɪʃn] (*check*) vérification *f*; **verify** (*check*) vérifier, contrôler; (*confirm*) confirmer
vermin ['vɜːrmɪn] (*insects*) vermine *f*, parasites *mpl*; (*rats etc*) animaux *mpl* nuisibles
vermouth [vər'muːθ] vermouth *m*
versatile ['vɜːrsətəl] *person* plein de ressources, polyvalent; *piece of equipment* multiusages; **versatility** *of person* adaptabilité *f*, polyvalence *f*; *of piece of equipment* souplesse *f* d'emploi
verse [vɜːrs] (*poetry*) vers *mpl*, poésie *f*; *of poem* strophe *f*; *of song* couplet *m*
version ['vɜːrʃn] version *f*
versus ['vɜːrsəs] contre
vertical ['vɜːrtɪkl] vertical
vertigo ['vɜːrtɪgou] vertige *m*
very ['verɪ] **1** *adv* très; ***was it cold? – not ~*** faisait-il froid? – non, pas tellement; ***the ~ best*** le meilleur **2** *adj* même; ***at that ~ moment*** à cet instant même, à ce moment précis; ***that's the ~ thing I need*** c'est exactement ce dont j'ai besoin
vessel ['vesl] NAUT bateau *m*, navire *m*
vest [vest] gilet *m* *Br*: *undershirt* maillot *m* (de corps)
vestige ['vestɪdʒ] vestige *m*; *fig* once *f*
vet[1] [vet] *n* (*veterinarian*) vétérinaire *m/f*, véto *m/f* F
vet[2] [vet] *v/t applicants etc* examiner
vet[3] [vet] *n* MIL F ancien combattant *m*
veteran ['vetərən] **1** *n* vétéran *m* **2** *adj* (*old*) antique; (*old*

and experienced) aguerri, chevronné
veterinarian [vetərə'nerɪən] vétérinaire *m/f*
veto ['vi:toʊ] **1** *n* veto *m inv* **2** *v/t* opposer son veto à
via ['vaɪə] par
viable ['vaɪəbl] viable
vibrate [vaɪ'breɪt] vibrer; **vibration** vibration *f*
vice[1] [vaɪs] *n* vice *m*
vice[2] [vaɪs] *Br* → ***vise***
vice 'president vice-président *m*
vice versa [vaɪs'vɜ:rsə] vice versa
vicious ['vɪʃəs] vicieux; *dog* méchant; *person*, *temper* cruel; *attack* brutal; **viciously** brutalement
victim ['vɪktɪm] victime *f*; **victimize** persécuter
victorious [vɪk'tɔ:rɪəs] victorieux; **victory** victoire *f*
video ['vɪdɪoʊ] **1** *n* vidéo *f*; *actual object* cassette *f* vidéo **2** *v/t* filmer; *tape off TV* enregistrer; **video camera** caméra *f* vidéo; **video cassette** cassette *f* vidéo; **video recorder** magnétoscope *m*; **videotape** bande *f* vidéo
vie [vaɪ] rivaliser
Vietnam [vɪet'næm] Vietnam *m*; **Vietnamese 1** *adj* vietnamien **2** *n* Vietnamien(ne) *m(f)*; *language* vietnamien *m*
view [vju:] **1** *n* vue *f*; (*assessment, opinion*) opinion *f*, avis *m*; ***in ~ of*** compte tenu de, étant donné **2** *v/t* considérer, envisager **3** *v/i* (*watch TV*) regarder la télévision; **viewer** TV téléspectateur(-trice) *m(f)*; **viewpoint** point *m* de vue
vigor ['vɪgər] vigueur *f*; **vigorous** vigoureux; **vigorously** vigoureusement; **vigour** *Br* → ***vigor***
village ['vɪlɪdʒ] village *m*; **villager** villageois(e) *m(f)*
villain ['vɪlən] escroc *m*; *in drama* méchant *m*
vindicate ['vɪndɪkeɪt] (*prove correct*) confirmer, justifier; (*prove innocent*) innocenter
vindictive [vɪn'dɪktɪv] vindicatif
vine [vaɪn] vigne *f*
vinegar ['vɪnɪgər] vinaigre *m*
vineyard ['vɪnjɑ:rd] vignoble *m*
vintage ['vɪntɪdʒ] **1** *n of wine* millésime *m* **2** *adj* (*classic*) classique
violate ['vaɪəleɪt] violer; **violation** violation *f*; (*traffic ~*) infraction *f* au code de la route
violence ['vaɪələns] violence *f*; **violent** violent
violin [vaɪə'lɪn] violon *m*; **violinist** violoniste *m/f*
VIP [vi:aɪ'pi:] (= ***very important person***) V.I.P. *m*
viral ['vaɪrəl] viral
virgin ['vɜ:rdʒɪn] vierge *f*;

male puceau *m* F; **virginity** virginité *f*
virile ['vɪrəl] viril; **virility** virilité *f*
virtual ['vɜːrtʃʊəl] quasi-; **virtually** (*almost*) pratiquement, presque
virtue ['vɜːrtʃuː] vertu *f*; **virtuous** vertueux
virus ['vaɪrəs] virus *m*
visa ['viːzə] visa *m*
vise [vaɪz] étau *m*
visibility [vɪzə'bɪlətɪ] visibilité *f*; **visible** visible
vision ['vɪʒn] (*eyesight*) vue *f*; REL vision *f*
visit ['vɪzɪt] **1** *n* visite *f*; (*stay*) séjour *m* **2** *v/t* rendre visite à; *doctor, dentist* aller voir; *city, country* aller à/en; *castle, museum* visiter; *website* consulter; **visitor** (*guest*) invité *m*; (*tourist*) visiteur *m*
visor ['vaɪzər] visière *f*
visual ['vɪʒʊəl] visuel; **visualize** (*imagine*) (s')imaginer; (*foresee*) envisager, prévoir; **visually** visuellement
vital ['vaɪtl] (*essential*) vital, essentiel; **vitality** vitalité *f*; **vitally**: ~ ***important*** d'une importance capitale
vitamin ['vaɪtəmɪn] vitamine *f*; **vitamin pill** comprimé *m* de vitamines
vivacious [vɪ'veɪʃəs] plein de vivacité, vif; **vivacity** vivacité *f*
vivid ['vɪvɪd] vif; *description* vivant; **vividly** vivement; *remember* clairement; *describe* de façon vivante
V-neck ['viːnek] col *m* en V
vocabulary [voʊ'kæbjʊlərɪ] vocabulaire *m*; (*list of words*) glossaire *m*
vocal ['voʊkl] vocal; **vocalist** MUS chanteur(-euse) *m(f)*
vocation [və'keɪʃn] vocation *f*; **vocational** *guidance* professionnel
vodka ['vɑːdkə] vodka *f*
vogue [voʊg] vogue *f*; ***be in*** ~ être en vogue
voice [vɔɪs] **1** *n* voix *f* **2** *v/t opinions* exprimer; **voicemail** messagerie *f* vocale
volcano [vɑːl'keɪnoʊ] volcan *m*
volley ['vɑːlɪ] volée *f*
volt [voult] volt *m*; **voltage** tension *f*
volume ['vɑːljəm] volume *m*
voluntarily [vɑːlən'terɪlɪ] de son plein gré, volontairement; **voluntary** volontaire; *work* bénévole; **volunteer 1** *n* volontaire *m/f*; (*unpaid worker*) bénévole *m/f* **2** *v/i* se porter volontaire
vomit ['vɑːmət] **1** *n* vomi *m*, vomissure *f* **2** *v/i* vomir
voracious [və'reɪʃəs] vorace; *reader* avide
vote [voʊt] **1** *n* vote *m* **2** *v/i* POL voter (***for*** pour; ***against*** contre); **voter** POL électeur *m*; **voting** POL vote *m*
◆ **vouch for** [vaʊtʃ] *truth, person* se porter garant de

vow [vaʊ] **1** *n* vœu *m*, serment *m* **2** *v/t*: **~ *to do*** jurer de faire
vowel [vaʊl] voyelle *f*
voyage ['vɔɪɪdʒ] voyage *m*
vulgar ['vʌlgər] vulgaire
vulnerable ['vʌlnərəbl] vulnérable
vulture ['vʌltʃər] vautour *m*

W

waddle ['wɑːdl] se dandiner
wade [weɪd] patauger
wafer ['weɪfər] *cookie* gaufrette *f*; REL hostie *f*
waffle ['wɑːfl] *to eat* gaufre *f*
wag [wæg] remuer
wages [weɪdʒɪz] salaire *m*
waggle ['wægl] remuer
wail [weɪl] hurler
waist [weɪst] taille *f*
wait [weɪt] **1** *n* attente *f* **2** *v/i* attendre
◆ **wait for** attendre
◆ **wait on** (*serve*) servir
◆ **wait up**: ***don't wait up*** (***for me***) ne m'attends pas pour aller te coucher
waiter ['weɪtər] serveur *m*; ***~!*** garçon!; **waiting list** liste *f* d'attente; **waiting room** salle *f* d'attente; **waitress** serveuse *f*
waive [weɪv] renoncer à
wake [weɪk] **1** *v/i*: **~** (***up***) se réveiller **2** *v/t person* réveiller
walk [wɒːk] **1** *n* marche *f*; (*path*) allée *f*; ***go for a ~*** aller se promener **2** *v/i* marcher; *as opposed to driving* aller à pied; (*hike*) faire de la marche **3** *v/t dog* promener
◆ **walk out** *of spouse* prendre la porte; *from theater etc* partir; (*go on strike*) se mettre en grève
walker ['wɒːkər] (*hiker*) randonneur(-euse) *m*(*f*); *for baby* trotte-bébé *m*; *for old person* déambulateur *m*; **walking** (*hiking*) randonnée *f*; **walkout** (*strike*) grève *f*; **walkover** (*easy win*) victoire *f* facile
wall [wɒːl] mur *m*
wallet ['wɑːlɪt] (*billfold*) portefeuille *m*
'wallpaper **1** *n also* COMPUT papier *m* peint **2** *v/t* tapisser; **wall-to-wall carpet** moquette *f*
waltz [wɒːlts] valse *f*
wan [wɑːn] *face* pâlot
wander ['wɑːndər] (*roam*) errer; (*stray*) s'égarer
wangle ['wæŋgl] F réussir à obtenir (par une combine)
want [wɑːnt] **1** *n*: ***for ~ of*** par manque de, faute de **2** *v/t* vouloir; (*need*) avoir besoin de; **~ *to do sth*** vouloir faire qch; ***I ~ to stay here*** je veux rester ici; ***she ~s you to go back*** elle veut que tu reviennes (*subj*) **3** *v/i*: **~ *for nothing***

ne manquer de rien; **wanted** *by police* recherché
war [wɔːr] guerre *f*; *fig* lutte *f*
ward [wɔːrd] *Br*: *in hospital* salle *f*; *child* pupille *m/f*
◆ **ward off** éviter
warden ['wɔːrdn] *of prison* gardien (ne) *m(f)*; *Br*: *of hostel* directeur (-trice) *m (f)*
'**wardrobe** *for clothes* armoire *f*; (*clothes*) garde-robe *f*
warehouse ['werhaʊs] entrepôt *m*
'**warfare** guerre *f*; **warhead** ogive *f*
warily ['werılı] avec méfiance
warm [wɔːrm] chaud; *welcome*, *smile* chaleureux
◆ **warm up 1** *v/t* réchauffer **2** *v/i* se réchauffer; *of athlete etc* s'échauffer
warmly ['wɔːrmlı] chaudement; *welcome*, *smile* chaleureusement; **warmth** *also fig* chaleur *f*; **warm-up** SP échauffement *m*
warn [wɔːrn] prévenir; **warning** avertissement *m*
warp [wɔːrp] *of wood* gauchir; **warped** *fig* tordu
warrant ['wɔːrənt] **1** *n* mandat *m* **2** *v/t* justifier; **warranty** garantie *f*
warrior ['wɔːrıər] guerrier (-ière) *m(f)*
wart [wɔːrt] verrue *f*
wary ['werı] méfiant; ***be ~ of*** se méfier de
wash [wɑːʃ] **1** *n*: ***have a ~*** se laver **2** *v/t clothes*, *dishes* laver **3** *v/i* se laver
◆ **wash up** (*wash one's hands and face*) se débarbouiller
washable ['wɑːʃəbl] lavable; **washbasin, washbowl** lavabo *m*; **washcloth** gant *m* de toilette; **washed out** (*tired*) usé; **washer** *for faucet etc* rondelle *f*; **washing** lessive *f*; ***do the ~*** faire la lessive; **washing machine** machine *f* à laver; **washroom** toilettes *fpl*
wasp [wɑːsp] guêpe *f*
waste [weıst] **1** *n* gaspillage *m*; *from industrial process* déchets *mpl*; ***it's a ~ of time/money*** c'est une perte de temps/d'argent **2** *adj* non utilisé **3** *v/t* gaspiller; **waste basket** corbeille *f* à papier; **waste disposal (unit)** broyeur *m* d'ordures; **wasteful** gaspilleur; **wasteland** désert *m*; **wastpaper** papier(s) *m(pl)* (*jeté(s) à la poubelle*)
watch [wɑːtʃ] **1** *n timepiece* montre *f*; ***keep ~*** monter la garde **2** *v/t* regarder; (*look after*) surveiller **3** *v/i* regarder; **watchful** vigilant
water ['wɒːtər] **1** *n* eau *f* **2** *v/t plant* arroser **3** *v/i*: ***my mouth is ~ing*** j'ai l'eau à la bouche; **watercolor**, *Br* **watercolour** aquarelle *f*; **watered down** *fig* atténué; **waterfall** chute *f* d'eau; **waterline** ligne *f* de flottaison; **waterlogged** dé-

trempé; *boat* plein d'eau; **watermelon** pastèque *f*; **waterproof** imperméable; **waterside** bord *m* de l'eau; **waterskiing** ski *m* nautique; **watertight** *compartment* étanche; *fig*: *alibi* parfait; **waterway** voie *f* d'eau; **watery** *soup* trop clair; *coffee* trop léger

watt [wɑːt] watt *m*

wave[1] [weɪv] *n in sea* vague *f*

wave[2] [weɪv] **1** *n of hand* signe *m* **2** *v/i with hand* saluer; *of flag* flotter **3** *v/t flag etc* agiter

'wavelength RAD longueur *f* d'onde; ***be on the same ~*** *fig* être sur la même longueur d'onde

waver ['weɪvər] hésiter

wavy ['weɪvɪ] ondulé

wax [wæks] cire *f*

way [weɪ] (*method, manner*) façon *f*; (*route*) chemin *m* (***to*** de); ***this ~*** (*like this*) comme ça; (*in this direction*) par ici; ***by the ~*** (*incidentally*) au fait; ***in a ~*** (*in certain respects*) d'une certaine façon; ***lose one's ~*** se perdre; ***be in the ~*** (*be an obstruction*) gêner le passage; *disturb*) gêner; ***no ~!*** pas question!; **way in** entrée *f*; **way of life** mode *m* de vie; **way out** sortie *f*; *fig* issue *f*

we [wiː] nous

weak [wiːk] faible; *tea, coffee* léger; **weaken 1** *v/t* affaiblir **2** *v/i* s'affaiblir; *in negotiation etc* faiblir; **weakness** faiblesse *f*

wealth [welθ] richesse *f*; **wealthy** riche

weapon ['wepən] arme *f*

wear [wer] **1** *n*: ~ (***and tear***) usure *f* **2** *v/t* (*have on*) porter; (*damage*) user **3** *v/i* (*wear out*) s'user; ***~ well*** (*last*) faire bon usage

◆ **wear down** user

◆ **wear off** *of effect* se dissiper

◆ **wear out 1** *v/t* (*tire*) épuiser; *shoes, carpet* user **2** *v/i of shoes, carpet* s'user

wearily ['wɪrɪlɪ] avec lassitude; **weary** las

weather ['weðər] **1** *n* temps *m* **2** *v/t crisis* survivre à; **weather-beaten** hâlé; **weather forecast** prévisions météorologiques *fpl*, météo *f*; **weatherman** présentateur *m* météo

weave [wiːv] **1** *v/t cloth* tisser **2** *v/i of cyclist* se faufiler

web [web] *of spider* toile *f*: ***the ~*** COMPUT le Web; **web page** page *f* de Web; **web site** site *m* Web

wedding ['wedɪŋ] mariage *m*; **wedding anniversary** anniversaire *m* de mariage; **wedding day** jour *m* de mariage; **wedding dress** robe *f* de mariée; **wedding ring** alliance *f*

wedge [wedʒ] *to hold sth in*

place cale *f*; *of cheese etc* morceau *m*
Wednesday ['wenzdeɪ] mercredi *m*
weed [wi:d] **1** *n* mauvaise herbe *f* **2** *v/t* désherber; **weedkiller** herbicide *f*; **weedy** F chétif
week [wi:k] semaine *f*; ***a ~ tomorrow*** demain en huit; **weekday** jour *m* de la semaine; **weekend** week-end *m*; ***on the ~*** *this one* ce week-end; *every one* le week-end; **weekly 1** *adj* hebdomadaire **2** *n magazine* hebdomadaire *m* **3** *adv be published* toutes les semaines; *be paid* à la semaine
weep [wi:p] pleurer
wee-wee ['wi:wi:] F pipi *m* F; ***do a ~*** faire pipi
weigh [weɪ] peser
◆ **weigh up** (*assess*) juger
weight [weɪt] poids *m*; **weightlessness** apesanteur *f*; **weightlifter** haltérophile *m/f*; **weightlifting** haltérophilie *f*; **weighty** *fig* (*important*) sérieux
weir [wɪr] barrage *m*
weird [wɪrd] bizarre; **weirdo** F cinglé(e) *m(f)* F
welcome ['welkəm] **1** *adj* bienvenu; ***you're ~!*** je vous en prie! **2** *n* accueil *m* **3** *v/t* accueillir; *fig*: *news, announcement* se réjouir de; *opportunity* saisir
weld [weld] souder
welfare ['welfer] bien-être *m*; *financial assistance* sécurité *f* sociale; ***be on ~*** toucher les allocations; **welfare check** chèque *m* d'allocations; **welfare state** État *m* providence; **welfare worker** assistant social *m*, assistante sociale *f*
well[1] [wel] *n for water, oil* puits *m*
well[2] [wel] **1** *adv* bien; ***~ done!*** bien!; ***as ~*** (*too*) aussi; ***as ~ as*** (*in addition to*) en plus de; ***very ~*** *acknowledging order* entendu; *reluctantly agreeing* très bien; ***~, ~!*** *surprise* tiens, tiens!; ***~ …*** *uncertainty, thinking* eh bien … **2** *adj*: ***be ~*** aller bien; **well-balanced** équilibré; **well-behaved** bien élevé; **well-being** bien-être *m*; **well-done** *meat* bien cuit; **well-dressed** bien habillé; **well-earned** bien mérité; **well-heeled** F cossu; **well-informed** bien informé; **well-known** connu; **well-meaning** plein de bonnes intentions; **well-off** riche; **well-timed** bien calculé; **well-wisher** personne *f* apportant son soutien
west [west] **1** *n* ouest *m* **2** *adj* ouest *inv*; *wind* d'ouest **3** *adv travel* vers l'ouest; **westerly** *wind* d'ouest; *direction* vers l'ouest; **western 1** *adj* de l'Ouest **2** *n movie* western *m*; **Westerner** occidental(e); **westernized** occidentalisé;

West Indian 1 *adj* antillais **2** *n* Antillais(e) *m(f)*; **West Indies**: ***the ~*** les Antilles *fpl*; **westward** vers l'ouest

wet [wet] mouillé; (*rainy*) humide; **wet suit** *for diving* combinaison *f* de plongée

whack [wæk] F (*blow*) coup *m*

whale [weɪl] baleine *f*

what [wɑːt] **1** *pron* ◇: ***~?*** quoi?; ***~ for?*** (*why?*) pourquoi?; ***so ~?*** et alors?
◇ *as object*: ***~ did he say?*** qu'est-ce qu'il a dit?, qu'a-t-il dit?; ***~ is that?*** qu'est-ce que c'est?; ***~ is it?*** (*what do you want?*) qu'est-ce qu'il y a?
◇ *as subject* qu'est-ce qui; ***~ just fell off?*** qu'est-ce qui vient de tomber?
◇ *relative as object* ce que; ***I did ~ I could*** j'ai fait ce que j'ai pu
◇ *relative as subject* ce qui; ***I didn't see ~ happened*** je n'ai pas vu ce qui s'est passé
◇ *suggestions*: ***~ about heading home?*** et si nous rentrions? **2** *adj* quel, quelle; *pl* quels, quelles; ***~ color is the car?*** de quelle couleur est la voiture?

whatever [wɑːt'evər]: ***~ the season*** quelle que soit la saison; ***~ you do*** quoi que tu fasses; ***ok, ~*** F ok, si vous le dites

wheat [wiːt] blé *m*

wheel [wiːl] roue *f*; (*steering ~*) volant *m*; **wheelchair** fauteuil *m* roulant; **wheel clamp** *Br* sabot *m* de Denver

wheeze [wiːz] respirer péniblement

when [wen] quand; ***on the day ~*** le jour où; **whenever** *each time* chaque fois que; *regardless of when* n'importe quand

where [wer] où; ***~ from?*** d'où?; ***~ to?*** où?; ***this is ~ I used to live*** c'est là que j'habitais; **whereas** tandis que; **wherever 1** *conj* partout où; ***sit ~ you like*** assieds-toi où tu veux **2** *adv* où (donc); ***~ can it be?*** où peut-il bien être?

whet [wet] *appetite* aiguiser

whether ['weðər] (*if*) si; ***~ you approve or not*** que tu sois (*subj*) d'accord ou pas

which [wɪʧ] **1** *adj* quel, quelle; *pl* quels, quelles **2** *pron* ◇ *interrogative* lequel, laquelle; *pl* lesquels, lesquelles; ***~ are your favorites?*** lesquels préférez-vous?
◇ *relative*: *subject* qui; *object* que; *after prep* lequel, laquelle; *pl* lesquels, lesquelles

whiff [wɪf]: ***catch a ~ of*** sentir

while [waɪl] **1** *conj* pendant que; (*although*) bien que (+*subj*) **2** *n*: ***a long ~*** longtemps; ***for a ~*** pendant un moment

whim [wɪm] caprice *m*

whimper ['wɪmpər] pleurnicher; *of animal* geindre

whine [waɪn] *of dog etc* gémir; F (*complain*) pleurnicher
whip [wɪp] **1** *n* fouet *m* **2** *v/t* (*beat*) fouetter; *cream* battre; F (*defeat*) battre à plates coutures
whirlpool ['wɜːrlpuːl] *in river* tourbillon *m*; *for relaxation* bain *m* à remous
whisk [wɪsk] **1** *n* fouet *m* **2** *v/t eggs* battre
whiskey ['wɪskɪ] whisky *m*
whisper ['wɪspər] chuchoter
whistle ['wɪsl] **1** *n sound* sifflement *m*; *device* sifflet *m* **2** *v/t & v/i* siffler
white [waɪt] **1** *n color, of egg* blanc *m*; *person* Blanc *m*, Blanche *f* **2** *adj* blanc; **white-collar worker** col *m* blanc; **White House** Maison *f* Blanche; **white lie** pieux mensonge *m*; **whitewash 1** *n* blanc *m* de chaux; *fig* maquillage *m* de la vérité **2** *v/t* blanchir à la chaux; **white wine** vin *m* blanc
whittle ['wɪtl] *wood* tailler au couteau
◆ **whittle down** réduire
whizzkid ['wɪzkɪd] F prodige *m*
who [huː] *interrogative* qui; *relative*: *subject* qui; *object* que; ***the woman ~ you saw*** la femme que tu as vue; **whoever** qui que ce soit; ***~ gets the right answer*** celui/celle qui trouve la bonne réponse
whole [hoʊl] **1** *adj* entier; ***the ~ town*** toute la ville **2** *n* tout *m*, ensemble *m*; ***on the ~*** dans l'ensemble; **whole-hearted** inconditionnel; **wholesale** de gros; *fig* en masse; **wholesaler** grossiste *m/f*; **wholesome** sain; **wholly** totalement
whom [huːm] *fml* qui
whore [hɔːr] putain *f*
whose [huːz] *interrogative* à qui; *relative* dont; ***~ is this?*** à qui c'est?; ***a country ~ economy is boomimg*** un pays dont l'économie prospère
why [waɪ] pourquoi
wicked ['wɪkɪd] méchant
wicker ['wɪkər] osier *m*
wicket ['wɪkɪt] *in station, bank etc* guichet *m*
wide [waɪd] *street, field* large; *experience* vaste; ***be 12 foot~*** faire 3 mètres et demi de large; **widely** largement; ***~ known*** très connu; **widen 1** *v/t* élargir **2** *v/i* s'élargir; **wide-open** grand ouvert; **wide-ranging** de vaste portée; **widespread** répandu
widow ['wɪdoʊ] veuve *f*; **widower** veuf *m*
width [wɪdθ] largeur *f*
wield [wiːld] *weapon* manier; *power* exercer
wife [waɪf] femme *f*
wig [wɪg] perruque *f*
wiggle ['wɪgl] *tooth etc* remuer; *hips* tortiller

wild [waɪld] **1** *adj animal, flowers* sauvage; *teenager* rebelle; *party* fou; *scheme* délirant; *applause* frénétique
wilderness ['wɪldərnɪs] désert *m*
'**wildlife** faune *f* et flore *f*
wilful *Br* → ***willful***
will¹ [wɪl] *n* LAW testament *m*
will² [wɪl] *n* (*willpower*) volonté *f*
will³ [wɪl] *v/aux*: ***I ~ let you know tomorrow*** je vous le dirai demain; ***the car won't start*** la voiture ne veut pas démarrer; ***~ you tell her that ...?*** est-ce que tu pourrais lui dire que ...?; ***~ you stop that!*** veux-tu arrêter!
willful ['wɪlfl] *person, refusal* volontaire; **willing** *helper* de bonne volonté; ***be ~ to do sth*** être prêt à faire qch; **willingly** (*with pleasure*) volontiers; **willingness** empressement *m*; **willpower** volonté *f*
willy-nilly [wɪlɪ'nɪlɪ] (*at random*) au petit bonheur la chance
wilt [wɪlt] *of plant* se faner
wily ['waɪlɪ] rusé
wimp [wɪmp] F poule *f* mouillée
win [wɪn] **1** *n* victoire *f* **2** *v/t & v/i* gagner; *prize* remporter
wince [wɪns] tressaillir
wind¹ [wɪnd] *n* vent *m*; (*flatulence*) gaz *m*
wind² [waɪnd] **1** *v/i of path, river* serpenter **2** *v/t* enrouler
◆ **wind up 1** *v/t clock, car window* remonter; *speech* terminer; *affairs* conclure; *company* liquider **2** *v/i* (*finish*) finir
'**wind-bag** F moulin *m* à paroles F; **windfall** *fig* aubaine *f*
winding ['waɪndɪŋ] *path* qui serpente
window ['wɪndoʊ] *also* COMPUT fenêtre *f*; *of airplane, boat* hublot *m*; *of store* vitrine *f*; ***in the ~*** *of store* dans la vitrine; **window seat** *on train* place *f* côté fenêtre; *on airplane* place côté hublot; **window-shop**: ***go ~ping*** faire du lèche-vitrines; **windowsill** rebord *m* de fenêtre; **windshield**, *Br* **windscreen** pare-brise *m*; **windshield wiper** essuie-glace *m*; **windsurfer** véliplanchiste *m/f*; **windsurfing** planche *f* à voile; **windy** venteux; ***it's so ~*** il y a tellement de vent
wine [waɪn] vin *m*; **wine cellar** cave *f* (à vin); **wine list** carte *f* des vins; **winery** établissement *m* viticole
wing [wɪŋ] *of bird, airplane*, SP aile *f*; **wingspan** envergure *f*
wink [wɪŋk] *of person* cligner des yeux
winner ['wɪnər] gagnant(e) *m(f)*; **winning** gagnant; **winning post** poteau *m* d'arrivée; **winnings** gains *mpl*
winter ['wɪntər] hiver *m*; **win-**

ter sports sports *mpl* d'hiver; **wintry** d'hiver
wipe [waɪp] essuyer; *tape* effacer; **wiper** ['waɪpər] → ***windshield wiper***
wire ['waɪr] fil *m* de fer; *electrical* fil *m* électrique; **wireless phone** téléphone *m* sans fil; **wiring** ELEC installation *f* électrique; **wiry** *person* nerveux
wisdom ['wɪzdəm] sagesse *f*
wise [waɪz] sage; **wisecrack** F vanne *f* F; **wisely** *act* sagement
wish [wɪʃ] **1** *n* vœu *m*; ***best ~es*** cordialement; *for birthday, Christmas* meilleurs vœux **2** *v/t* souhaiter
◆ **wish for** vouloir
wisp [wɪsp] *of hair* mèche *m*; *of smoke* traînée *f*
wistful ['wɪstfl] nostalgique; **wistfully** avec nostalgie
wit [wɪt] (*humor*) esprit *m*; *person* homme *m*/femme *f* d'esprit
witch [wɪʧ] sorcière *f*; **witchhunt** *fig* chasse *f* aux sorcières
with [wɪð] avec; ***~ no money*** sans argent; ***tired ~ waiting*** fatigué d'attendre; ***the woman ~ blue eyes*** la femme aux yeux bleus; ***I live ~ my aunt*** je vis chez ma tante; ***are you ~ me?*** (*do you understand?*) est-ce que vous me suivez?
withdraw [wɪð'drɒː] **1** *v/t* retirer **2** *v/i* se retire; **withdrawal** retrait *m*; **withdrawal symptoms** (symptômes *mpl* de) manque *m*; **withdrawn** *person* renfermé
wither ['wɪðər] se faner
with'hold *information, name, payment* retenir; *consent* refuser
with'in (*inside*) dans; *in expressions of time* en moins de; *in expressions of distance* à moins de
with'out sans
with'stand résister à
witness ['wɪtnɪs] **1** *n* témoin *m* **2** *v/t* être témoin de
witticism ['wɪtɪsɪzm] mot *m* d'esprit; **witty** plein d'esprit
wobble ['wɑːbl] osciller; **wobbly** bancal
wolf [wʊlf] **1** *n* loup *m* **2** *v/t*: **~** (***down***) engloutir
woman ['wʊmən] femme *f*; **womanizer** coureur *m* de femmes; **womanly** féminin
womb [wuːm] utérus *m*
women ['wɪmɪn] *pl* → ***woman***; **women's lib** libération *f* des femmes
wonder ['wʌndər] **1** *n* (*amazement*) émerveillement *m*; ***no ~!*** pas étonnant! **2** *v/i* se poser des questions; ***I ~ if you could help*** je me demandais si vous pouviez m'aider; **wonderful** merveilleux; **wonderfully** (*extremely*) merveilleusement
won't [woʊnt] → ***will not***

wood [wʊd] bois *m*; **wooded** boisé; **wooden** (*made of wood*) en bois; **woodpecker** pic *m*; **woodwork** *parts made of wood* charpente *f*; *activity* menuiserie *f*

wool [wʊl] laine *f*; **woolen**, *Br* **woollen 1** *adj* en laine **2** *n* lainage *m*

word [wɜːrd] **1** *n* mot *m*; *of song*, (*promise*) parole *f* **2** *v/t article*, *letter* formuler; **word processor** traitement *m* de texte

work [wɜːrk] **1** *n* travail *m*; ***out of ~*** au chômage **2** *v/i of person* travailler; *of machine*, (*succeed*) marcher

◆ **work out 1** *v/t solution*, (*find out*) trouver; *problem* résoudre **2** *v/i at gym* s'entraîner; *of relationship etc* bien marcher

workable ['wɜːrkəbl] *solution* possible; **workaholic** F bourreau *m* de travail; **workday** (*hours of work*) journée *f* de travail; (*not weekend*) jour *m* de travail; **worker** travailleur(-euse) *m*(*f*); **workforce** main-d'œuvre; **work hours** heures *fpl* de travail; **working class** classe *f* ouvrière; **working-class** ouvrier; **working hours** → ***work hours***; **workload** quantité *f* de travail; **workman** ouvrier *m*; **workmanlike** de professionnel; **workmanship** fabrication *f*; **work of art** œuvre *f* d'art; **workout** séance *f* d'entraînement; **work permit** permis *m* de travail; **workshop** *also seminar* atelier *m*

world [wɜːrld] monde *m*; **world-class** de niveau mondial; **World Cup** *in soccer* Coupe *f* du monde; **world-famous** mondialement connu; **worldly** du monde; *person* qui a l'expérience du monde; **world record** record *m* mondial; **world war** guerre *f* mondiale; **worldwide 1** *adj* mondial **2** *adv* dans le monde entier

worn-'out *shoes*, *carpet* trop usé; *person* éreinté

worried ['wʌrɪd] inquiet; **worry 1** *n* souci *m* **2** *v/t* inquiéter **3** *v/i* s'inquiéter; **worrying** inquiétant

worse [wɜːrs] **1** *adj* pire **2** *adv play*, *perform*, *feel* plus mal; **worsen** empirer

worship ['wɜːrʃɪp] **1** *n* culte *m* **2** *v/t God* honorer; *fig*: *person*, *money* vénérer

worst [wɜːrst] **1** *adj* pire **2** *adv*: ***the areas ~ affected*** les régions les plus (gravement) touchées

worth [wɜːrθ]: ***be ~ …*** valoir; ***be ~ it*** valoir la peine; **worthwhile**: ***it's not ~ waiting*** cela ne vaut pas la peine d'attendre

worthy ['wɜːrðɪ] *person*, *cause* digne

would [wʊd]: ***I ~ help if I could*** je vous aiderais si je pouvais; ***~ you like to go to the movies?*** est-ce que tu voudrais aller au cinéma?; ***~ you tell her ...?*** pourriez-vous lui dire que ...?
wound [wuːnd] **1** *n* blessure *f* **2** *v/t with weapon, words* blesser
wow [waʊ] *int* oh là là!
wrap [ræp] *gift* envelopper; *scarf etc* enrouler; **wrapping** emballage *m*; **wrapping paper** papier *m* d'emballage
wrath [ræθ] colère *f*
wreath [riːθ] couronne *f*
wreck [rek] **1** *n of ship* navire *m* naufragé; *of car* épave *f* **2** *v/t* détruire; **wreckage** *of ship* épave *m*; *of airplane* débris *mpl*; *of marriage, career* restes *mpl*; **wrecker** *truck* dépanneuse *f*
wrench [rentʃ] **1** *n tool* clef *f* **2** *v/t (pull)* arracher
wrestle ['resl] lutter; **wrestler** lutteur(-euse) *m(f)*; **wrestling** lutte *f*
wriggle ['rɪgl] *(squirm)* se tortiller
wrinkle ['rɪŋkl] *in skin* ride *f*; *in clothes* pli *m*
wrist [rɪst] poignet *m*; **wristwatch** montre *f*
write [raɪt] écrire; *check* faire
◆ **write off** *debt* amortir; *car* bousiller F
writer ['raɪtər] *of letter, book, song* auteur *m/f*; *of book* écrivain *m/f*; **write-up** critique *f*
writhe [raɪð] se tordre
writing ['raɪtɪŋ] *(handwriting, script)* écriture *f*; *(words)* inscription *f*; ***in ~*** par écrit; **writing paper** papier *m* à lettres
wrong [rɒːŋ] **1** *adj information, decision, side, number* mauvais; *answer also* faux; ***be ~*** *of person* avoir tort; *of answer* être mauvais; *morally* être mal; ***get the ~ train*** se tromper de train; ***what's ~?*** qu'est-ce qu'il y a? **2** *adv* mal; ***go ~*** *of person* se tromper; *of marriage, plan etc* mal tourner **3** *n* mal *m*; *injustice* injustice *f*; **wrongful** injuste; **wrongly** à tort
wry [raɪ] ironique

X, Y

xenophobia [zenoʊ'foʊbɪə] xénophobie *f*
X-ray ['eksreɪ] **1** *n* radio *f* **2** *v/t* radiographier
yacht [jɑːt] yacht *m*; **yachting** voile *f*
Yank [jæŋk] F Ricain(e) *m(f)* F
yank [jæŋk] *v/t* tirer violemment

yard[1] [ɑːrd] *of prison etc* cour *f*; *behind house* jardin *m*; *for storage* dépôt *m*
yard[2] [ɑːrd] *measurement* yard *m*
'yardstick point *m* de référence
yarn [jɑːrn] (*thread*) fil *m*; F (*story*) (longue) histoire *f*
yawn [jɒːn] **1** *n* bâillement *m* **2** *v/i* bâiller
year [jɪr] année; ***be six ~s old*** avoir six ans; **yearly 1** *adj* annuel **2** *adv* tous les ans
yeast [jiːst] levure *f*
yell [jel] **1** *n* hurlement *m* **2** *v/t & v/i* hurler
yellow ['jeloʊ] jaune
yelp [jelp] **1** *n of animal* jappement *m*; *of person* glapissement *m* **2** *v/i of animal* japper; *of person* glapir
yes [jes] oui; *after negative question* si; **yes man** *pej* béni-oui-oui *m* F
yesterday ['jestərdeɪ] hier; ***the day before ~*** avant-hier
yet [jet] **1** *adv*: ***the best ~*** le meilleur jusqu'ici; ***as ~*** pour le moment; ***have you finished ~?*** as-tu (déjà) fini?; ***he hasn't arrived ~*** il n'est pas encore arrivé; ***~ bigger*** encore plus grand **2** *conj* (*however*) néanmoins
yield [jiːld] **1** *n from crops, investment etc* rendement *m* **2** *v/t fruit, good harvest* produire; *interest* rapporter **3** *v/i* (*give way*) céder; AUT céder la priorité
yoga ['joʊgə] yoga *m*
yoghurt ['joʊgərt] yaourt *m*
yolk [joʊk] jaune *m* (d'œuf)
you [juː] ◇ *familiar singular*: *subject* tu; *object* te; *before vowel* t'; *after prep* toi; ***he knows ~*** il te connaît; ***for ~*** pour toi
◇ *polite singular, familiar plural and polite plural, all uses* vous
◇ *indefinite* on; ***~ never know*** on ne sait jamais
young [jʌŋ] jeune; **youngster** jeune *m/f*; *child* petit(e) *m(f)*
your [jʊr] *familiar* ton, ta; *pl* tes; *polite* votre; *pl familiar and polite* vos
yours [jʊrz] *familiar* le tien, la tienne; *pl* les tiens, les tiennes; *polite* le/la vôtre; *pl* les vôtres; ***a friend of ~*** un(e) de tes ami(e)s; un(e) de vos ami(e)s; *~ at end of letter* bien amicalement
your'self *familiar* toi-même; *polite* vous-même; *reflexive* te; *polite* se; *after prep* toi; *polite* vous; ***did you hurt ~?*** est-ce que tu t'es fait mal/ est-ce que vous vous êtes fait mal?
your'selves vous-mêmes; *reflexive* vous; *after prep* vous; ***did you hurt ~?*** est-ce que vous vous êtes fait mal?
youth [juːθ] jeunesse *f*; (*young man*) jeune homme *m*; (*young people*) jeunes

mpl; **youth club** centre *m* pour les jeunes; **youthful** juvénile

yuppie ['jʌpɪ] F yuppie *m/f*

Z

zap [zæp] F COMPUT (*delete*) effacer; (*kill*) éliminer; (*hit*) donner un coup à; (*send*) envoyer vite fait

zeal [ziːl] zèle *m*

zero ['zɪroʊ] zéro *m*

zest [zest] *enjoyment* enthousiasme *m*

zigzag ['zɪgzæg] **1** *n* zigzag *m* **2** *v/i* zigzaguer

zilch [zɪltʃ] F que dalle F

zip ['zɪp] *Br* fermeture *f* éclair

◆ **zip up** *dress, jacket* remonter la fermeture éclair de; COMPUT compresser

'zip code code *m* postal; **zipper** fermeture *f* éclair

zit [zɪt] F *on face* bouton *m*

zone [zoʊn] zone *f*

zonked [zɑːŋkt] P (*exhausted*) crevé F

zoo [zuː] jardin *m* zoologique

zoology [zuː'ɑːlədʒɪ] zoologie *f*

'zoom lens zoom *m*

zucchini [zuː'kiːnɪ] courgette *f*

Numbers / Les nombres

Cardinal Numbers / Les nombres cardinaux

0 zero, *Br aussi* nought *zéro*
1 one *un*
2 two *deux*
3 three *trois*
4 four *quatre*
5 five *cinq*
6 six *six*
7 seven *sept*
8 eight *huit*
9 nine *neuf*
10 ten *dix*
11 eleven *onze*
12 twelve *douze*
13 thirteen *treize*
14 fourteen *quatorze*
15 fifteen *quinze*
16 sixteen *seize*
17 seventeen *dix-sept*
18 eighteen *dix-huit*
19 nineteen *dix-neuf*
20 twenty *vingt*
21 twenty-one *vingt et un*
22 twenty-two *vingt-deux*
30 thirty *trente*
31 thirty-one *trente et un*
40 forty *quarante*
50 fifty *cinquante*
60 sixty *soixante*
70 seventy *soixante-dix*

71 seventy-one *soixante et onze*
72 seventy-two *soixante-douze*
79 seventy-nine *soixante-dix-neuf*
80 eighty *quatre-vingts*
81 eighty-one *quatre-vingt-un*
90 ninety *quatre-vingt-dix*
91 ninety-one *quatre-vingt-onze*
100 a hundred, one hundred *cent*
101 a hundred and one *cent un*
200 two hundred *deux cents*
300 three hundred *trois cents*
324 three hundred and twenty-four *trois cent vingt-quatre*
1000 a thousand, one thousand *mille*
2000 two thousand *deux mille*

Verbes irréguliers anglais

Vous trouverez ci-après les trois formes principales de chaque verbe : l'infinitif, le prétérit et le participe passé.

arise - arose - arisen
awake - awoke - awoken, awaked
be (am, is, are) - was (were) - been
bear - bore - borne
beat - beat - beaten
become - became - become
begin - began - begun
bend - bent - bent
bet - bet, betted - bet, betted
bid - bid - bid
bind - bound - bound
bite - bit - bitten
bleed - bled - bled
blow - blew - blown
break - broke - broken
breed - bred - bred
bring - brought - brought
broadcast - broadcast - broadcast
build - built - built
burn - burnt, burned - burnt, burned
burst - burst - burst
buy - bought - bought
cast - cast - cast
catch - caught - caught
choose - chose - chosen
cling - clung - clung
come - came - come
cost (*v/i*) - cost - cost
creep - crept - crept
cut - cut - cut
deal - dealt - dealt
dig - dug - dug
dive - dived, dove [douv] (1) - dived
do - did - done
draw - drew - drawn
dream - dreamt, dreamed - dreamt, dreamed
drink - drank - drunk
drive - drove - driven
eat - ate - eaten
fall - fell - fallen
feed - fed - fed
feel - felt - felt
fight - fought - fought
find - found - found
flee - fled - fled
fling - flung - flung
fly - flew - flown
forbid - forbad(e) - forbidden
forecast - forecast(ed) - forecast(ed)
forget - forgot - forgotten
forgive - forgave - forgiven
freeze - froze - frozen
get - got - got, gotten (2)
give - gave - given

go - went - gone
grind - ground - ground
grow - grew - grown
hang - hung, hanged - hung, hanged (3)
have - had - had
hear - heard - heard
hide - hid - hidden
hit - hit - hit
hold - held - held
hurt - hurt - hurt
keep - kept - kept
kneel - knelt, kneeled - knelt, kneeled
know - knew - known
lay - laid - laid
lead - led - led
lean - leaned, leant - leaned, leant (4)
leap - leaped, leapt - leaped, leapt (4)
learn - learned, learnt - learned, learnt (4)
leave - left - left
lend - lent - lent
let - let - let
lie - lay - lain
light - lighted, lit - lighted, lit
lose - lost - lost
make - made - made
mean - meant - meant
meet - met - met
mow - mowed - mowed, mown
pay - paid - paid
plead - pleaded, pled - pleaded, pled (5)
prove - proved - proved, proven
put - put - put
quit - quit(ted) - quit(ted)
read - read [red] - read [red]
ride - rode - ridden
ring - rang - rung
rise - rose - risen
run - ran - run
saw - sawed - sawn, sawed
say - said - said
see - saw - seen
seek - sought - sought
sell - sold - sold
send - sent - sent
set - set - set
sew - sewed - sewed, sewn
shake - shook - shaken
shed - shed - shed
shine - shone - shone
shit - shit(ted), shat - shit(ted), shat
shoot - shot - shot
show - showed - shown
shrink - shrank - shrunk
shut - shut - shut
sing - sang - sung
sink - sank - sunk
sit - sat - sat
slay - slew - slain
sleep - slept - slept
slide - slid - slid

sling - slung - slung
slit - slit - slit
smell - smelt, smelled - smelt, smelled
sow - sowed - sown, sowed
speak - spoke - spoken
speed - sped, speeded - sped, speeded
spell - spelt, spelled - spelt, spelled (4)
spend - spent - spent
spill - spilt, spilled - spilt, spilled
spin - spun - spun
spit - spat - spat
split - split - split
spoil - spoiled, spoilt - spoiled, spoilt
spread - spread - spread
spring - sprang, sprung - sprung
stand - stood - stood
steal - stole - stolen
stick - stuck - stuck
sting - stung - stung
stink - stunk, stank - stunk
stride - strode - stridden
strike - struck - struck
swear - swore - sworn
sweep - swept - swept
swell - swelled - swollen
swim - swam - swum
swing - swung - swung
take - took - taken
teach - taught - taught
tear - tore - torn
tell - told - told
think - thought - thought
thrive - throve - thriven, thrived (6)
throw - threw - thrown
thrust - thrust - thrust
tread - trod - trodden
wake - woke, waked - woken, waked
wear - wore - worn
weave - wove - woven (7)
weep - wept - wept
win - won - won
wind - wound - wound
write - wrote - written

(1) **dove** n'est pas utilisé en anglais britannique
(2) **gotten** n'est pas utilisé en anglais britannique
(3) **hung** pour les tableaux mais **hanged** pour les meurtriers
(4) l'anglais américain n'emploie normalement que la forme en **-ed**
(5) **pled** s'emploie en anglais américain ou écossais
(6) la forme **thrived** est plus courante
(7) mais **weaved** au sens de *se faufiler*